# THE BRITISH GENERAL ELECTION OF 1992

*Other books in this series*

# The British General Election of 1992

David Butler
*Fellow of Nuffield College, Oxford*

Dennis Kavanagh
*Professor of Politics, University of Nottingham*

# M
### St. Martin's Press

First published 1992 by
THE MACMILLAN PRESS LTD
Houndmills, Basingstoke, Hampshire RG21 2XS
and London
Companies and representatives
throughout the world

ISBN 0–333–56812–5 hardcover
ISBN 0–333–56903–2 paperback

A catalogue record for this book is available
from the British Library.

Copy-edited and typeset by Grahame & Grahame Editorial, Brighton

Printed in Great Britain by
Mackays of Chatham PLC
Chatham, Kent


First published in the United States of America 1992 by
Scholarly and Reference Division,
ST. MARTIN'S PRESS INC.,
175 Fifth Avenue,
New York, N.Y. 10010

ISBN 0–312–08666–0

Library of Congress Cataloging-in-Publication Data
Butler, David, 1924–
The British General Election of 1992 / David Butler, Dennis
Kavanagh.
p.    cm.
Includes bibliographical references and index.
ISBN 0–312–08666–0
1. Great Britain. Parliament—Elections, 1992. 2. Elections—
Great Britain. 3. Great Britain—Politics and government—1979–
I. Kavanagh, Dennis. II. Title.
JN956.B868   1992
324.941′0859—dc20                                   92–27877
                                                           CIP

# Contents

# List of Tables

# List of Illustrations

# List of Plates

# Preface

This is the fourteenth Nuffield College study of a British General Election and is the sixth study written jointly by the present authors. It necessarily follows in the mould of its predecessors, since the series is designed to make possible comparison of one election with another. However, the 1992 election was unique in many ways, raising new and difficult problems about long-term trends in party support and about the impact of modern electioneering and opinion polls, both before and during the final three weeks. British parties have increasingly come to believe that it is 'the long campaign' in the months preceding the dissolution of Parliament that actually decides the outcome. We have therefore covered in more detail than ever before the pre-campaign preparations of the two main parties. The long campaign is now an established part of British elections and parties are sure to learn the lessons of 1992.

Opinion polls coloured the coverage and the conduct of the 1992 Campaign to an exceptional degree and their failure to foreshadow the Conservative lead recorded on April 9 has left an enduring mark on the political scene. The breakdown of a measuring instrument that seemed to work so well in previous contests leaves a challenge both to pollsters and to commentators that will not be quickly met.

In our efforts to describe and explain the election, we have once again been greatly helped by intellectual and practical support from our colleagues in Nuffield College and Nottingham University and by financial support from the Economic and Social Research Council.

We owe a great deal to the politicians, party officials and advisers who have so generously given of their time in some hundreds of interviews during the last few years and to the many candidates who replied to our post-election questionnaire. Any authority that these pages may have is due in large measure to the access and the insights the participants have allowed us. We are deeply grateful to them.

We have made inordinate demands on the research skills of Roger Mortimore and the secretarial skills of Audrey Skeats and April Pidgeon. We must also thank, among the readers of our manuscript, Lewis Baston, Vernon Bogdanor, Simon Henig and Peter Morris, and we must pay due tribute to our long-suffering wives and families.

DAVID BUTLER
DENNIS KAVANAGH

*10 July 1992*

.

# 1 A Changed Scene: 1987–1992

The 1992 election saw the Conservative government being re-elected with an adequate parliamentary majority. The election could be dismissed as just another milestone in the long Conservative hegemony. But it was in fact one of the most interesting and unexpected of post-war elections. Its outcome was not inevitable. It presents as great a challenge to its chroniclers as any of the fourteen elections covered in the Nuffield series. The first of these studies was undertaken by Ronald McCallum in 1945 with the avowed aim of preventing myths growing up about the 1945 election comparable to those surrounding 1918 and 1931. Nineteen ninety-two may have a greater potential for myth-making than any of its predecessors.

There was one essential difference between 1992 and the three earlier Conservative victories. Mrs Thatcher, who had led the party for fifteen years, was absent. At the time of her reluctant departure from office she had established her right to be considered among the most outstanding Prime Ministers of the twentieth century. She, uniquely, had given her name to an -ism, a style and a set of policies, and she had proved the most successful election-winner in her party's history.

The first post-Thatcher general election has to be seen in the context of the Thatcher years. The privatisation of many state undertakings, the consequent reduction in the size of the public sector, and the extension of popular capitalism through share ownership, deregulation, and wider home ownership were intended achievements of the Thatcher governments. So was the curtailment of union power. On the negative side, unemployment, which soared to record levels in the early 1980s, again moved up towards the three million mark ten years later. Mrs Thatcher's administration began and ended with the economy in severe recession; on both occasions government policies bore much of the blame.

For the political parties the 1980s were the most turbulent years of the post-war era. The Conservatives dominated a one-sided parliament because of opposition disarray. The Labour Party split; the Social Democratic Party came into being and the Alliance rose as a formidable third force, before disintegrating and then emerging as another new party, the Liberal Democrats.

1

*Table 1.1     Economic and political indicators, 1987–92*

|      |   | (1)<br>Real<br>personal<br>disposable<br>income<br>(1985=100) | (2)<br>Weekly<br>earnings<br>(1988=100) | (3)<br>Retail<br>prices<br>(1985=100) | (4)<br>Year on<br>Year in-<br>flation<br>(%) | (5)<br>Unem-<br>ployment<br>(UK) (%) | (6)<br>Days lost<br>in strikes<br>(000s) | (7)<br>Gross<br>domestic<br>product<br>(1985=100) | (8)<br>Balance<br>of<br>payments<br>(£m) |
|------|---|------|------|------|------|------|------|------|------|
| 1987 | 3 | 108.1 | 92.6  | 107.9 | 4.4  | 10.0 | 313  | 109.5 | −1215 |
|      | 4 | 110.7 | 95.8  | 109.1 | 4.1  | 9.3  | 263  | 110.2 | −2423 |
| 1988 | 1 | 110.9 | 96.8  | 109.6 | 3.5  | 9.1  | 1020 | 111.3 | −3257 |
|      | 2 | 114.3 | 98.6  | 112.3 | 4.3  | 8.3  | 512  | 112.2 | −3099 |
|      | 3 | 115.4 | 100.9 | 113.8 | 5.5  | 7.9  | 1895 | 113.4 | −3331 |
|      | 4 | 117.4 | 103.7 | 116.2 | 6.5  | 7.0  | 274  | 114.1 | −5833 |
| 1989 | 1 | 117.6 | 105.8 | 118.1 | 7.7  | 7.0  | 186  | 114.7 | −4778 |
|      | 2 | 121.4 | 107.8 | 121.5 | 8.2  | 6.5  | 449  | 114.7 | −4989 |
|      | 3 | 121.2 | 110.0 | 122.6 | 7.7  | 6.2  | 2594 | 115.5 | −6065 |
|      | 4 | 121.9 | 112.8 | 125.0 | 7.6  | 5.9  | 199  | 115.9 | −4572 |
| 1990 | 1 | 123.5 | 115.5 | 127.3 | 7.8  | 5.7  | 1194 | 116.8 | −5349 |
|      | 2 | 123.6 | 118.7 | 133.2 | 9.6  | 5.7  | 393  | 117.4 | −5217 |
|      | 3 | 124.6 | 121.2 | 135.4 | 10.4 | 5.7  | 157  | 116.1 | −2619 |
|      | 4 | 125.3 | 123.5 | 137.5 | 10.0 | 6.0  | 159  | 115.1 | −2261 |
| 1991 | 1 | 123.3 | 126.0 | 138.3 | 8.7  | 6.7  | 135  | 114.3 | −2303 |
|      | 2 | 124.7 | 128.1 | 141.2 | 6.0  | 7.6  | 263  | 113.3 | −208  |
|      | 3 | 123.6 | 130.8 | 141.9 | 5.3  | 8.3  | 199  | 113.5 | −1240 |
|      | 4 | 123.0 | 132.4 | 143.2 | 4.2  | 8.7  | 164  | 113.2 | −642  |
| 1992 | 1 | 124.2 | 135.7 | 144.0 | 4.1  | 9.2  | 105  | 112.5 | −1964 |

Sources: 1–5, 7, 8, 12, 13 *Economic Trends*; 9–11 *Financial Statistics*; 6 *Employment Gazette*; 14, 15 MORI

In contrast to the usual post-war situation in which Labour and Conservative shares of the popular vote were closely matched, the two-party system was hardly competitive; the Conservative leads over Labour in the elections of the 1980s were post-war records: from 1950 to 1979 the gap between the leading parties was never more than 7 percent; it was 11 percent in 1987 and 14 percent in 1983.

There were significant social changes in the 1980s; some would have happened in any event but many were assisted by the Thatcher governments. They included greater prosperity for the majority in work, an impressive growth in private home ownership and self-employment, and a steady shift of jobs from manufacturing to services. Population continued to move from the cities to the suburbs and from the North to the South of England. In the 1890s Sir William Harcourt said 'We are all socialists now' but in the 1980s Britain was more bourgeois than ever. Two statistics make the point. In 1950 there was 29 percent home ownership; in 1990 the figure was 67 percent. In 1950 manual workers made up 68 percent of the labour force; at the end of the 1980s the figure

| (9) FTSE 100 Share Index (1 Jan 1984 = 1000) | (10) US$ to £ | (11) Sterling Exchange Rate Index (1985 = 100) | (12) Interest Rates % | (13) House Prices (1985 = 100) | (14) MORI 'State of the Economy Poll': Net Optimists | (15) MORI Polls (Voting Intention) Con | Lab | LD |
|---|---|---|---|---|---|---|---|---|
| 2303 | 1.61 | 90.5 | 9.5 | 135 | +10 | 48 | 35 | 15 |
| 1806 | 1.75 | 92.7 | 9.0 | 143 | +7 | 47 | 37 | 14 |
| 1774 | 1.79 | 93.5 | 8.8 | 149 | +9 | 46 | 38 | 14 |
| 1806 | 1.83 | 96.6 | 8.2 | 158 | +10 | 46 | 41 | 11 |
| 1820 | 1.69 | 95.2 | 11.1 | 179 | −11 | 46 | 39 | 12 |
| 1810 | 1.78 | 96.7 | 12.4 | 190 | −22 | 44 | 39 | 14 |
| 2004 | 1.75 | 97.1 | 13.0 | 194 | −15 | 43 | 39 | 14 |
| 2117 | 1.63 | 93.6 | 13.4 | 201 | −26 | 39 | 44 | 11 |
| 2326 | 1.59 | 91.7 | 14.0 | 208 | −18 | 38 | 45 | 9 |
| 2256 | 1.58 | 88.1 | 15.0 | 204 | −28 | 40 | 48 | 6 |
| 2308 | 1.65 | 88.1 | 15.0 | 201 | −37 | 34 | 51 | 9 |
| 2266 | 1.67 | 88.6 | 15.0 | 198 | −31 | 34 | 51 | 8 |
| 2213 | 1.85 | 94.2 | 15.0 | 201 | −36 | 36 | 48 | 10 |
| 2116 | 1.94 | 94.1 | 14.1 | 198 | −22 | 39 | 45 | 11 |
| 2278 | 1.91 | 93.8 | 13.5 | 196 | −19 | 42 | 41 | 13 |
| 2501 | 1.71 | 91.4 | 11.9 | 195 | −2 | 39 | 41 | 15 |
| 2584 | 1.68 | 90.7 | 10.9 | 198 | +4 | 40 | 41 | 15 |
| 2499 | 1.77 | 90.9 | 10.5 | 198 | −3 | 40 | 43 | 13 |
| 2521 | 1.77 | 90.6 | 10.5 | 192 | +1 | 40 | 40 | 17 |

was 48 percent. The working class was a new minority. Between 1979 and 1990 trade union membership fell from 50 percent to 36 percent of the workforce and among manual employees more were homeowners than were council tenants. These social trends meant that the predominantly Conservative-voting groups were increasing while the Labour-voting ones were in decline. But, of course, voting behaviour is not always socially determined. The experience of Australia, Sweden and France showed that parties of the centre-left could poll well in affluent societies.

In some respects the 1980s might be viewed as a reaction to the 1970s. Mrs Thatcher's ability to dictate the political agenda was facilitated in large part by public disillusion with what had gone before. The 1970s were associated with weak government and the spectre of ungovernability – the Heath and Callaghan administrations had been largely paralysed by industrial disruption and the revolt against their incomes policies. The 1970s had seen the speeding up of the country's relative economic decline, with soaring inflation and only a limited improvement in living standards. The decade was also characterised by corporatist bargains over incomes policy between the government and the major interests. The 1980s heard no advocacy of a social contract or of a prices and incomes policy, and no serious talk of ungovernability, of devolution for Scotland, or of Britain's withdrawal from the European Community. The curbing of trade union power, the privatisation of public utilities, the attack on inflation, the criticism of welfare 'dependency' and the restoration of the authority of central government could all be regarded as attempts to exorcise the ghosts of the 1970s.

The 1980s belonged so clearly to the Conservative Party that some commentators claimed that Britain had one-party government. A middle-aged Labour MP could see the best years of his career going to waste in opposition. Of those who had served in the last Labour Cabinet, only John Smith, Roy Hattersley and John Morris were likely to be in another one. The speed with which Mr Kinnock moved on to the new ground of politics in the later 1980s underlined the Conservatives' achievement. Labour came to terms with markets, back-pedalled on public ownership, and accepted lower income-tax rates, as well as the sale of council houses to tenants; it also endorsed Britain's continued membership of the European Community and some of the new trade union legislation. There was to be no going back to 1979.

Yet the Conservative position was not as dominant as it appeared. The large majorities in the House of Commons in 1983 and 1987 were a product of a majoritarian electoral system and a split opposition. First-past-the-post voting and three-party politics produced a parliamentary landslide, with some 60 percent of the seats being won with 42 percent of the vote. The Conservatives' success was also due to the perceived unelectability of Labour – a consequence of its adoption of unilateralism and other self-defeating policies as well as of its divisions and Michael Foot's leadership in 1983. In 1987 some of the support for the Conservatives was plainly conditional, gained from voters who associated the party with good economic times. That support began to melt away late in 1989 under the impact of high inflation, high interest rates and high mortgage rates.

Yet surveys about values showed that the Conservative Party had failed to win the hearts and minds of most voters. Polls suggested that on the whole the British wanted a society in which the state provided welfare rather than leaving individuals to look after themselves; they preferred a managed economy rather than a free market one. Most people appeared to be relatively happy about their personal circumstances but unhappy about the state of the nation, particularly in the public services. By large majorities they said they would prefer more state spending on public services, even if it involved higher rates of tax. Thatcherism was, in the words of Ivor Crewe, 'a crusade that failed'. This was disappointing for Mrs Thatcher who had wanted to make people more self-reliant, more enterprising and less dependent upon state provision. After a full decade in office with a clear parliamentary majority (something granted to no other political leader this century) the opinion polls suggested she had failed to wean the electorate away from the old consensus.

From the middle of 1990 onwards the longest recession since the war hit every industrial nation but Britain was particularly blighted as Table 1.1 shows. Unemployment, which had dropped in three years from 3m. to 1.6m., rose inexorably. The Gross Domestic Product (GDP), which was growing by 5 percent in 1987, was falling in 1991. Inflation shot up from 3 percent at the beginning of 1988 to 10 percent three years later. In the same period the annual rate of growth slumped from 5 percent to zero. A false panic induced by the stock market collapse on 19 October 1987 was the prelude to an excessive zeal for keeping a stable exchange rate.

But the boom mood continued for some time. In his 1988 budget Nigel Lawson cut the top rate of income tax from 60 percent to 40 percent and the standard rate from 27 percent to 25 percent. In May 1988 interest rates were reduced to 8.5 percent, their lowest level for 10 years. It soon became clear, however, that the tax cuts were irrelevant in the face of a surge in credit, rising inflation and a widening trade deficit. At this stage Mr Lawson preferred to curb inflation through management of exchange rates and interest rates, rather than through control of the money supply. Since 1985 the Chancellor had favoured British entry to the ERM but Mrs Thatcher, supported by Sir Alan Walters, would not hear of it. He therefore shadowed the D mark and reduced interest rates to restrain the rise in the value of the pound. He pursued this policy without Mrs Thatcher's knowledge and, when she found out, it was the cause of tension between them. She wanted the pound to find its own level in the exchange markets.

At the same time, as we show in Chapter 3, the Labour Party managed to reform its policies and its internal structure to a notable degree; on Europe, on nuclear weapons and on the market economy its stance in 1992 was radically different from that in 1987. The centre parties also underwent a total reconstruction and rebirth; David Owen's wing of Social Democracy, after a lively struggle, faded away while the rest of the Alliance, in its new Liberal Democratic guise, behaved in some ways as a party of practicality rather than of gestures, more like the SDP than the old Liberals.

The Conservatives, after a buoyant start, became enmeshed in their self-inflicted problems with the poll-tax (or Community Charge), with the approach to Europe and with the handling of the recession. In a sudden spasm at the very end of the decade, they threw out the architect of their dominance throughout the 1980s, Margaret Thatcher. Of the 23 Cabinet members at the 1987 dissolution only six were still in office at the 1992 dissolution. The loss of Willie Whitelaw, through ill-health, in January 1988 removed the only senior minister in the Cabinet who could have restrained Mrs Thatcher while her relations with Nigel Lawson and Geoffrey Howe were deteriorating.

## CHRONOLOGY OF EVENTS, 1987–92

### 1987

| | |
|---|---|
| 11 Jun. | General Election returns Con government with 102 majority |
| 13 Jun. | Reshuffle: Havers succeeds Hailsham |
| 14 Jun. | Rift between D. Steel and D. Owen over Lib/SDP merger |
| 1 July | Single European Act comes into force |
| 29 Aug. | R. Maclennan becomes leader of SDP |
| 31 Aug. | SDP council approves merger talks in principle |
| 17 Sep. | Liberal Assembly votes for merger |
| 1 Oct. | Labour Party Conference votes for revised selection procedures |
| 6 Oct. | Con Conference votes for immediate implementation of poll-tax |
| 16 Oct. | Great storm in South of England |
| 19 Oct. | Big stock exchange slump |
| 26 Oct. | Mackay becomes Lord Chancellor |
| 8 Nov. | IRA bomb Remembrance Day parade at Enniskillen, Co Fermanagh |
| 18 Nov. | King's Cross fire, 31 die |
| 19 Dec. | Second Reading of poll-tax bill |

### 1988

| | |
|---|---|
| 10 Jan. | Whitelaw resigns from Cabinet |
| 13 Jan. | *Voices and Choices for All* (joint Liberal-SDP policy document) issued and withdrawn |
| 23 Jan. | Liberal Special Assembly votes 2099 to 385 for ballot |
| 25 Jan. | *Labour Listens* launched |
| 27 Jan. | Labour NEC suspends Southwark & Bermondsey constituency party |
| 28 Jan. | Court of Appeal rejects appeal by Birmingham Six |
| 31 Jan. | SDP Council votes 273 to 28 (49 abstentions) for merger |
| 4 Feb. | ILEA to be abolished on March 30, 1990 |
| 9 Feb. | Commons votes 318 to 264 to be televised |
| 25 Feb. | Electricity privatisation plans announced |
| 2 Mar. | Libs vote 87.9% for merger. SDP vote 65.3% (SLD launched Mar. 3) |
| 6 Mar. | Three IRA members shot dead by SAS in Gibraltar |
| 8 Mar. | D. Owen launches continuing SDP |

| 15 Mar. | N. Lawson tax-cutting budget |
|---------|------------------------------|
| 29 Mar. | Agreement on BAe takeover of Rover |
| 8 Apr. | Base rate down to 8% |
| 18 Apr. | Con revolt reduces government majority to 25 on poll-tax |
| 28 Apr. | *Death on the Rock* programme |
| 5 May | Local Elections. Lab gains |
| 17 May | Base rate 7 ½ % |
| 2 Jun. | Spycatcher case finally rejected in Australia |
| 5 Jun. | Kinnock on Trident 'something for something' |
| 14 Jun. | D. Davies resigns as Labour defence spokesman |
| 6 Jul. | Piper Alpha oil-rig disaster |
| 8 Jul. | EETPU suspended by TUC (expelled Sept. 5) |
| 14 Jul. | Kensington by-election. Cons hold seat |
| 22 Jul. | L. Brittan to be EEC Commissioner |
| 25 Jul. | DHSS split into DSS and Dept. of Health |
| 28 Jul. | P. Ashdown defeats A. Beith 41,401 to 16,202 |
| 29 Jul. | B. Millan to be EEC Commissioner |
| 8 Aug. | Bank rate up to 12% |
| 20 Sep. | Mrs Thatcher's Bruges speech |
| 26 Sep. | SLD agree to call themselves Democrats |
| 2 Oct. | Kinnock defeats T. Benn 89% to 11% for Lab leadership |
| 3 Oct. | R. Cook elected to Labour NEC, M. Meacher defeated |
| 6 Oct. | Lab Conference confirms unilateralism |
| 12 Oct. | Cons promise privatisation of coal |
| 19 Oct. | D. Hurd's N. Ireland broadcasting ban |
| 1 Nov. | Autumn statement: Lawson predicts £10bn surplus |
| 9 Nov. | Student loans announced |
| 10 Nov. | SNP win Glasgow Govan by-election |
| 23 Nov. | British Steel privatisation offer |
| 25 Nov. | Base Rate up from 12% to 13% |
| 2 Dec. | Charter 88 launched |
| 12 Dec. | Clapham rail crash |
| 15 Dec. | Epping Forest by-election |
| 16 Dec. | Edwina Currie resigns over salmonella in eggs |
| 21 Dec. | Pan Am bomb at Lockerbie kills 270 |

**1989**

| 8 Jan. | M1 air crash, 47 killed |
|--------|-------------------------|
| 25 Jan. | Green Papers on reform of legal profession |
| 31 Jan. | White Paper *Working for Patients* outlines major changes to NHS |
| 14 Feb. | Ayatollah's *fatwa* against Salman Rushdie |
| 23 Feb. | Richmond by-election: Tories win on split vote despite 20% fall in support |
| 1 Apr. | Introduction of poll-tax in Scotland |
| 15 Apr. | Hillsborough football crowd disaster |

| 4 May | Tenth anniversary of Thatcher's premiership |
| 13 May | D. Owen indicates SDP can no longer flourish as a national party |
| 18 May | Labour publishes policy review *Meet the Challenge, Make the Change* |
| 15 Jun. | Euro-elections. Lab 45 MEPs, Con 32 (13 Lab gains). Greens get 15% of vote |
| 26 Jun. | Madrid summit. Britain agrees to enter ERM when three conditions are met |
| 24 Jul. | Sir G. Howe becomes Leader of House; J. Major Foreign Secretary |
| 2 Oct. | Lab Conference endorses multilateral disarmament |
| 16 Oct. | SLD ballot changes name to Liberal Democrat |
| 19 Oct. | Court of Appeal frees 'Guildford Four' |
| 26 Oct. | N. Lawson resigns. J. Major to Exchequer, D. Hurd to FCO |
| 15 Nov. | Autumn economic statement foreshadows fall in growth |
| 21 Nov. | Televising Commons begins |
| 5 Dec. | Mrs Thatcher defeats Sir A. Meyer 314 to 24 (31 abstentions) |

**1990**

| 3 Jan. | M. Howard replaces N. Fowler at Dept of Employment |
| 20 Mar. | Major's budget (first televised budget): introduction of TESSAs |
| 22 Mar. | Lab wins Mid-Staffordshire by-election on 21% swing |
| 31 Mar. | Poll-tax riots |
| 1 Apr. | Poll-tax starts in England |
| 1 Apr. | Strangeways prison riot begins (last prisoners surrender Apr. 25) |
| 19 Apr. | 44 Con MPs rebel against Hong Kong Citizenship Bill |
| 3 May | Lab gains 300 local council seats but Cons gain in Wandsworth and Westminster |
| 4 May | D. Hunt succeeds P. Walker as Secretary of State for Wales |
| 24 May | Lab publishes *Looking to the Future* |
| 3 Jun. | SDP votes 17 to 5 to suspend its activities |
| 14 Jul. | N. Ridley resigns after *Spectator* interview. P. Lilley succeeds to Trade |
| 25 Jul. | NEC suspends Liverpool Labour Party |
| 30 Jul. | I. Gow killed by bomb |
| 2 Aug. | Iraq seizes Kuwait |
| 27 Aug. | 3 of 4 defendants in Guinness trial found guilty |
| 7 Sep. | Lord Sanderson replaces M. Forsyth as Scottish Conservative chairman |
| 9 Sep. | Mrs Thatcher on TV expects to stay PM at least until 1995 |
| 22 Sep. | Salmond succeeds Wilson as leader of SNP |
| 8 Oct. | UK joins ERM |
| 18 Oct. | Liberal Democrats win Eastbourne by-election |
| 1 Nov. | Sir G. Howe resigns (speaks in Commons Nov. 13) |
| 20 Nov. | M. Thatcher 204, M. Heseltine 152 (Nov. 22 Thatcher gives up) |

| 27 Nov. | J. Major 185, M. Heseltine 131, D. Hurd 56 |
| 28 Nov. | Major becomes PM, N. Lamont to Exchequer, C. Patten Con Party chairman, M. Heseltine to Environment |

**1991**

| 6 Jan. | Mrs Thatcher accepts Presidency of Bruges Group |
| 15 Jan. | 53 Labour MPs defy party over Gulf War |
| 16 Jan. | Active hostilities start in Gulf |
| 7 Feb. | IRA mortar attack on Downing Street |
| 10 Feb. | J. Taylor confirmed as Conservative candidate for Cheltenham |
| 24 Feb. | Land hostilities start in Gulf (victory by Feb. 28) |
| 26 Feb. | Liberals publish *Shaping Tomorrow Starting Today* |
| 7 Mar. | Liberals win Ribble Valley by-election on 25% swing |
| 19 Mar. | Budget raises VAT to reduce poll-tax |
| 21 Mar. | Heseltine announces replacement of poll-tax by Council Tax |
| 16 Apr. | Labour publishes *Labour's Better Way for the 1990s* |
| 2 May | Cons lose 900 seats in local elections. Lab and Lib Dems each gain 500 |
| 9 May | Government uses Parliament Act to secure passing of War Crimes Bill |
| 16 May | Labour win Monmouth by-election on 13% swing |
| 18 Jun. | Mrs Thatcher makes US speeches critical of European Community |
| 4 Jul. | Labour holds Liverpool Walton, Militant Labour gets only 7% |
| 5 Jul. | BCCI assets frozen by Bank of England |
| 22 Jul. | Major launches Citizen's Charter |
| 19 Aug. | Abortive coup in Soviet Union |
| 1 Oct. | Government confirms no election until 1992 |
| 15 Oct. | Fourteen Con MPs rebel over defence cuts |
| 16 Oct. | ITC announces new ITV franchise winners |
| 28 Oct. | *Opportunity 2000* launched to get more women into top jobs |
| 5 Nov. | Death of Robert Maxwell reveals huge frauds |
| 7 Nov. | Liberal Democrats win Kincardine & Deeside, Labour win Langbaurgh, both on lower swings than for three years |
| 25 Nov. | Appeal Court quashes conviction of Tottenham Three |
| 5–7 Dec. | Lab NEC expels two militant MPs, Fields and Nellist |
| 10 Dec. | Maastricht summit allows British opt-outs on EMU and Social Charter |
| 25 Dec. | Gorbachev resigns as Soviet Union disintegrates |

**1992**

| 6 Jan. | Cons launch 'Labour's Tax Bombshell' campaign |
| 8 Jan. | Lab launch of 'Made in Britain' campaign |
| 8 Jan. | Ravenscraig closure announced |
| 14 Jan. | Lab dinner at Luigi's: confusion over plans for NICs |
| 5 Feb. | Ashdown admits affair |

10 Mar.    Budget
11 Mar.    Election announced

The government's attempts to apply market principles ever more widely met with mixed success. The privatisation of water in late 1989 and of electricity a year later excited more criticism than the earlier disposal of gas, steel and telecommunications (though the shares were eagerly taken up). The disposal of the ailing Rover Group to British Aerospace in August 1988 failed to halt the decline of the motor industry. But the sale of nationalised assets yielded £22bn. for the Exchequer in the course of the parliament.

The commitment to a poll-tax, in place of the domestic rates as a source of local government finance, was begun in 1985 and confirmed in the 1987 manifesto. It might not have proved so disastrous but for the unexpected vote at the October 1987 party conference to implement the tax at one fell swoop rather than phase it in over four years. This timing meant that its most painful effects would be felt late in the parliament. Alarmed Conservative MPs, led by Michael Mates (but with the backing of the out-of-office Michael Heseltine), gave the successive Environment Secretaries, Nicholas Ridley and Chris Patten, as much difficulty as the vociferous Labour opposition. The launch of the tax a year earlier in Scotland than elsewhere provoked a great outburst and the beginning of a Scottish Nationalist upsurge, most notably manifest in their triumph in the November 1988 Govan by-election. On 31 March 1990 a demonstration against the poll-tax produced more violent scenes than had occurred in London for many years. The Conservative handling of the issue represented perhaps the most spectacular reversal of a flagship policy ever seen in Britain.

The tax was not the only headache for Environment Secretaries. Local government expenditure, not only by 'loony left' councils, seemed out of control and increasingly stringent rate-capping devices were instituted to enforce restraints on spending. Councils were also compelled to put the provision of some services out to competitive tender. On the credit side, some Conservative councils which had been most ruthless in applying business methods managed to reduce rates and then poll-tax to negligible levels. The Conservatives' worst-ever local government results in May 1990 were masked by the party's triumph in their star-performing London boroughs, Westminster and Wandsworth.

The poll-tax stole most of the domestic headlines. But the government was busy on other controversial reforms. Under Kenneth Clarke and William Waldegrave the Department of Health provided for NHS hospitals to secure partial autonomy under trust status and for some family doctors

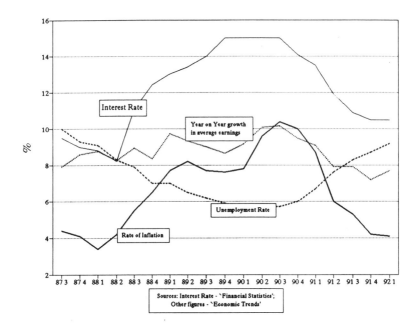

*Figure 1.1    Economic indicators, 1987–92*

to be allocated 'budgets'; a kind of internal market was established in the Health Service. Robin Cook, Labour's spokesman, denounced these 'opt-outs' and 'market principles' as destructive of the whole ethos of the service. Although some doctors were won round to the changes, polls showed that the public was deeply suspicious. When the Conservatives denounced 'Labour lies' on the subject, they only heightened the salience of the issue. Fears of privatisation of the NHS were seen as a major factor in the Conservatives' May 1991 defeat in the Monmouth by-election.

When Mr Clarke moved office from Health to Education he did not escape controversy, for he inherited Kenneth Baker's far-reaching and controversial Education Reform Act (1988). He implemented the schemes for general testing of children at the age of seven, for student loans and for schools to opt out of local authority control, and he tried to overhaul the schools inspectorate.

Another area where the government faced trouble was over law and order. Not only did crime statistics continue to soar but a series of proven miscarriages of justice cast a cloud over the police and the judicial system. The Guildford Four, the Maguire family, and the Birmingham Six (as well as some of the Broadwater Farm rioters) all had murder or conspiracy convictions quashed because of police misconduct or because of prosecution and Appeal Court errors. Lord Mackay, a reforming Lord Chancellor, met with resistance from the Bar but he did at least get John Major's government to set up a Royal Commission under Lord Runciman to look into the administration of justice.

Less publicity was attracted by far-reaching changes in the civil service as, following *The Next Steps* (a Cabinet Office document published in February 1988), many executive functions were hived off into independent agencies. In April 1991 the number of Department of Social Security employees dropped from 80,000 to 2,600 as the Benefits Agency and other quangos took over all its functions except policy-making.

The televising of the House of Commons which began in November 1990 had a substantial impact on the public image of politics.[1] Mr Speaker Weatherill became a household pet, not only in Britain but also in America, thanks to satellite and cable TV. The duels between Mr Major and Mr Kinnock and the increasingly yah-boo quality of House of Commons debate did nothing for the prestige of parliament.

The environment rose much higher on the national agenda. The most effective protest votes ever cast in Britain may have been those given in the 1989 European election. Almost 15 percent of those who went to the polls supported the Greens, and the Liberal Democrats fell to fourth place in every constituency but one. The Green vote soon subsided but all the parties took energetic steps to establish their environmental credentials. Mrs Thatcher could indeed point to her September 1988 speech to the Royal Society which preceded the Green breakthrough.

There were some memorable events of the period which fall into no pattern and which excited no particular party conflict or electoral response, yet which formed the backdrop to the political life of the period. In December 1988 Edwina Currie, the much publicised junior Agriculture Minister, had to resign for her outspoken remarks about salmonella poisoning in eggs. I⁻ July 1990 Nicholas Ridley was forced from the Cabinet because he had expressed his anti-German feelings too strongly in an interview with the *Spectator*.

Among the seemingly insoluble problems of the post-1945 world the Cold War, incomparably the most important of them, seemed to dissolve. There was also light in South Africa where President de Klerk released Nelson Mandela, ended apartheid, and embarked on a shaky path towards a non-racial government. The intolerable impasse in the Middle East continued but, despite the Gulf War, James Baker, the American Secretary of

State, did at least launch his 'peace process' in 1990 and induced countries which had not spoken formally for forty years to meet over the conference table. Even in Indo-China there was some relaxation of tension, with a UN-inspired reconciliation in Cambodia and the development of links with Vietnam. In Africa pacification proceeded in the trouble spots of Angola and Mozambique. The Ethiopian dictatorship fell. Multi-party elections were restored in several states, most notably in Zambia. But famine, civil war and tyranny were still much in evidence, especially in Zaire and Somalia.

In June 1989 the ruthlessness of the Chinese in putting down a student demonstration in Tiananmen Square evoked world-wide protests and a sustained cold-shouldering of everything Chinese. In February 1989 the dying Ayatollah Khomeini sentenced Salman Rushdie to death for his *Satanic Verses*, enjoining any follower to carry out the *fatwa*. This led to a diplomatic breach with Iran and sustained expressions of solidarity with Mr Rushdie who had to go into permanent hiding under British police protection. A further strain on relations with Iran lay in the fate of four British hostages held in the Lebanon by the pro-Iranian Hezbollah. They provided a constant source of headlines until their release, repeatedly foreshadowed, was finally achieved late in 1991.

Disaster and scandal left their mark on the period. The explosion of the Piper Alpha North Sea drilling rig in July 1988 had, in addition to its horror, a significant effect on the balance of payments and consequently on the exchange rate over the next two years. A football crowd disaster at Hillsborough attracted much attention in April 1989. The terrorist bomb that blew up a Pan Am 727 over Lockerbie in December 1988 compounded British and American troubles in the Middle East. There was a protracted scandal over share price manipulation in the Guinness takeover of Distillers, with prosecutions lasting throughout the parliament. The successive downfalls of the Polly Peck empire, of the Bank of Credit and Commerce International, and of Robert Maxwell's ramifying companies, together with the problems of Lloyd's, led to much adverse comment on the judgement of bankers and the ethics of the City of London.

The sad story of violence in Northern Ireland continued. Atrocities by the IRA and revenge attacks by Protestant paramilitaries regularly made headlines. Occasionally the violence crossed the Irish Sea and in July 1990 the IRA murdered Ian Gow, the MP who had resigned from the government in protest at the Anglo-Irish agreement. Peter Brooke, who took over the Northern Ireland office in July 1989, sought a new initiative and in April 1991 and again in March 1992 succeeded in convening all-party talks: but they did not get very far. The bi-partisan approach in the House of

*Figure 1.2    Opinion poll trends, 1987–92*

Commons was largely maintained, but Labour ceased to support the annual renewal of the Prevention of Terrorism Act and protested strongly about the ban which Douglas Hurd imposed in October 1988 on broadcasts by IRA or Sinn Fein supporters. This excited civil libertarian protests from the Labour and Liberal Democratic parties as well as from all the broadcasting organisations.

When Saddam Hussein seized Kuwait in August 1990 Mrs Thatcher placed Britain firmly behind the United Nations and the United States in demanding a withdrawal and in contributing to the forces necessary to enforce it. Gerald Kaufman and Neil Kinnock came out resolutely in support and, although Tony Benn and two dozen other Labour MPs protested against military action, no one could accuse the leadership, or the party as a whole, of disloyalty to the war effort. The ex-marine Paddy Ashdown gave his support and his comments on the war did much to raise his national status. Mrs Thatcher had resigned before the brief and triumphant military action began in February 1991; it was commented in some quarters that national unity was much easier to sustain with John

Major at No 10. The sad sequels of the war for the Kurds and the Shi'ites, as well as the pre-eminent role of the American forces, meant that victory in the Gulf had far less impact on British politics than victory in the Falklands had had nine years earlier.

Electorally, the Conservatives fared poorly. They had a good start, while the opposition parties picked themselves up from the debacle of 1987, but the opinion polls turned against them by late 1988. They fared badly in the May 1989 Euro-elections and they lost each of the last seven seats they had to defend in by-elections. Mid-Staffordshire went to Labour on a swing of 21 per cent in March 1989 and in October 1990 they lost Eastbourne (where they had a 27 percent majority) to the Liberal Democrats. At the time of Mrs Thatcher's downfall in November the Conservatives had been well behind in the polls for 18 months. John Major's election restored them briefly to the lead but after the Gulf War ended in February, Labour stayed ahead or level for most of the time, and in March Ribble Valley, the Conservatives' 13th safest seat, fell to the Liberal Democrats. The opinion polls never provided the evidence to justify an early dissolution.

From 1987 to 1989 the Alliance parties had a miserable time separating and forming into re-labelled units. Paddy Ashdown took over as leader of a fairly shattered Social and Liberal Democratic Party in July 1988 and for a while he had to fend off the challenge of the residual Social Democrats until David Owen finally threw in the towel in the summer of 1990. The Liberal Democrats languished below 10 percent in the opinion polls until their October 1990 breakthrough in the Eastbourne by-election. But in 1991 they fared astonishingly well in the May local elections and showed sustained national support at around 15 percent. They had recovered the position as a serious third party which a year or two earlier they seemed to have forfeited completely.

Europe was never far from the headlines. Mrs Thatcher made increasingly plain her unease at developments in the Community and in particular at the initiatives of Jacques Delors (who started his second term as President of the Community in 1989). She saw proposals for a Social Charter and a monetary union involving a single currency as unacceptable threats to the sovereignty of the United Kingdom.

On 20 September 1988 Mrs Thatcher delivered a speech at Bruges which established her as the leader of the Eurosceptics.

'To try to suppress nationhood at the centre of a European conglomerate would be highly damaging . . . We have not rolled back the frontiers of the state in Britain to see them reimposed at a European level with a European superstate exercising a new dominance from Brussels.'

But the Single European Act of 1986, with its extension of majority voting in the Council of Ministers, was in place and the preparations for a frontier-free internal market by 1992 moved forward; from 1989 onwards there was the prospect of inter-governmental conferences that would recommend further measures of monetary and political union. The Bruges speech excited deep anxiety in the many Conservative MPs with a deep commitment to Europe. In May 1989 the triumphalism with which the tenth anniversary of Mrs Thatcher's premiership was celebrated was counter-productive. Was it a peak from which there could only follow a decline?

At the Madrid Summit in June 1989, after a subsequently-leaked private confrontation with the Chancellor of the Exchequer and the Foreign Secretary, Mrs Thatcher reluctantly agreed that Britain should enter the Exchange Rate Mechanism of the European Monetary System if specific conditions were met. The unhappiness of Mr Lawson at her hostility was public knowledge, but it was still a shock when on 31 October 1989 he abruptly resigned, ostensibly because Mrs Thatcher would not detach herself from her economic adviser, Sir Alan Walters, but in fact because of sustained sniping from No 10. During 1990 the Foreign Secretary, Douglas Hurd and John Major, who had taken over at the Treasury, persuaded the Prime Minister to take a slightly more pragmatic approach to the European Community and eventually induced her on 8 October 1990 to authorise British entry to the Exchange Rate Mechanism. Her ability to deny the Chancellor his way had been weakened since she had lost Nigel Lawson on the issue; moreover the rise in inflation to 10.6 percent in August made membership more attractive in terms of sustaining market confidence.

At the Rome meeting of the European Council on October 27 and 28, Britain and Mrs Thatcher were isolated yet again, this time over the content and timing of stages two and three of the European Monetary Union. She declared that she would veto any future EMU treaty and accused the foreign heads of government of 'living in cloud-cuckoo land'.

However, Sir Geoffrey Howe, who, after being brutally removed from the Foreign Office in July 1990, had soldiered on as Leader of the House, was provoked beyond endurance by Mrs Thatcher's performance in Rome and her subsequent (30 October 1990) outburst in the House:

'I do not want the Commission to increase its powers at the expense of the House . . . . Mr Delors said . . . that he wanted the European Parliament to be the democratic body of the Community, he wanted the Commission to be the Executive and he wanted the Council of Ministers to be the Senate. No. No. No.'

Sir Geoffrey resigned. When Mrs Thatcher let it be known that she regarded his departure as over style not substance, Sir Geoffrey was goaded into a devastating resignation speech:

> 'People throughout Europe see our Prime Minister finger-wagging, hear her passionate "No. No. No." much more than the content of carefully worded formal texts. The task has become futile . . . of trying to pretend there was a common policy when every step forward risked being subverted by some casual comment or impulsive answer . . . . That is why I have resigned.'

This was enough to make it certain that Mrs Thatcher would again be challenged in the annual leadership election due one week later and Michael Heseltine had no option but to enter the race. The story of the next two weeks has been well told and need not be rehearsed in detail here.[2]

On the first ballot, Mrs Thatcher led Mr Heseltine by 204 votes to 152, two short of the required 15 percent majority. She said she would fight on but on the next day, November 21, after consulting her cabinet one by one, she decided to withdraw. Mr Hurd and Mr Major then joined in the contest and, during a hectic weekend of lobbying, all three candidates promised to review the poll-tax. The result was declared on Tuesday, November 27 – Major 185, Heseltine 131, Hurd 56. Everyone immediately rallied round John Major; and on November 28 he was sworn in as Prime Minister. He was plainly Mrs Thatcher's preference as successor but from the start his style was very different. The polls soon showed that his appeals for a caring, classless society and his conciliatory approach were appreciated.

At the time, Mrs Thatcher's ousting as party leader and Prime Minister in November 1990 appeared the turning-point of the parliament. A huge Conservative deficit in the opinion polls was transformed into a clear lead once John Major replaced her. Her election to the leadership of the party in 1975 had largely been the product of back-bench resentment at Mr Heath's style; she in her turn was ousted because her followers decided that she was no longer a winner.

Like most of her predecessors she went unwillingly, at a low point in her fortunes: the government was trailing in the polls, she herself was unpopular, and the economy was in recession. When the opportunity came in November 1990, a sufficiently large minority of MPs withheld their support to weaken her fatally. Many felt the party was simply unelectable under her – and her poll-tax – and were aware that surveys showed that

Cummings, *Daily Express*, 24 March 1991

there would be a dramatic upsurge in Tory voting support with a new leader.

The change of mood was to some degree exemplified in the personality of the new Prime Minister. It was as though there had been a change of government without a general election. John Major, like most twentieth-century premiers, first assumed office in mid-parliament. He was a low-key, listening Prime Minister. In contrast to Mrs Thatcher; he believed in the importance of consultation and winning consent, and went out of his way to demonstrate this. It was not just a matter of giving Cabinet ministers more scope for suggesting policies, consulting with interest groups, appointing a Royal Commission on the legal system, and receiving Sir Ian McKellen in Downing Street to hear the grievances of homosexuals. He believed that, although conviction politics as practised by Mrs Thatcher had worked in the 1980s, they would be counter-productive in the changed mood in the 1990s. Colleagues welcomed Mr Major's early call for 'a country at ease with itself' and compared him with Stanley Baldwin and that leader's efforts to restore harmony between the classes after the 1926 General Strike. Mrs Thatcher, for one, was not too happy with the comparison. As some historians regretted the wasted opportunities in foreign and economic policy in the inter-war years after the fall of Lloyd George, so it was rumoured that Mrs Thatcher doubted that her inheritance was safe in her successor's hands.

The change of leadership provided both an opportunity and a challenge for Mr Major. He was very different from his predecessor. But too much discontinuity, particularly on the poll-tax and on Europe, might alienate Mrs Thatcher's supporters. Mr Major shifted ground but, by careful Cabinet and party management, he kept the Conservatives largely united on these two issues. Therefore, while seeking to build on the achievements of the Thatcher years, he also tried to map out a new agenda to deal with dissatisfaction over public services and make his own mark on the 1990s.

Mr Lamont's first Budget in March 1991 trimmed back mortgage tax relief, uprated the value of child benefit and provided money to offset the poll-tax, all measures which signalled a break with Thatcherism. Clearly some policies would not be reversed, notably the privatisation programme, the union reforms, the lower marginal rates of income tax and the quest for greater value for money in the public sector. But there was cross-party agreement on the need to improve the quality of life in Britain, particularly through the public services of health and education, by giving greater rights to the consumers of these services as well as providing more funds. On 22 July 1991 John Major launched the Citizen's Charter. This aimed to improve public services in the 1990s by providing consumers with more choice, information and opportunities to lodge complaints. The idea was accepted across the main parties, though all put their own glosses on it.

There remained, however, some important differences between the parties. Apart from reorganising local government finance and the civil service, the Conservatives showed little interest in reform of government or constitutional matters. That agenda had traditionally been left to the Liberals. But Labour, for so long out of power, also had plans to curb the executive via the introduction of a charter of rights, decentralisation of power from Whitehall to the regions, and the creation of an elected second chamber; the party also demonstrated an open mind by establishing a working party on electoral reform.

The vast changes in Soviet Russia and Eastern Europe, which so fundamentally revolutionised the world situation, overshadowed the whole parliament. The super-power confrontation that had dominated international politics for more than forty years withered away. US-Soviet negotiations on arms reduction were already cutting down on international tension and defence spending when in 1989 the Soviet Army pulled out of Afghanistan. The subsequent two years saw the ending of Soviet authority in the states of Eastern Europe and then in the USSR itself. Talk about the 'peace dividend' that would follow the curtailment of arms expenditure was matched by anxious calls from MPs with factories and defence installations in their constituencies and from people attached to particular regiments in danger of merger or extinction.

The defence scene also changed with the removal of American Cruise missiles from Greenham Common in March 1991 and with the advance of the Trident submarine construction beyond the point of no return (as well as its acceptance by the Labour Party). The success of Anglo-American co-operation in the Gulf War did not prevent a certain decline in the transatlantic link after George Bush succeeded Ronald Reagan, and as the American economy slumped and the Uruguay round of GATT tariff negotiations became bogged down.

A sequel to the withdrawal of the Soviet Union from Eastern Europe was the reunification of Germany, sponsored by Chancellor Kohl after the Berlin Wall fell in December 1989 and implemented within a year. Suddenly the population of the richest of the four large nations in the European Community grew by one quarter. For a while the poverty and dislocation of Eastern Germany would be a drag on West Germany, but every country on the Continent realised the far-reaching implications for the balance of power. Germany, the enemy, defeated in two world wars, was on the way to becoming the dominant power in Europe.

A recognition of this lay behind some of the complex manoeuvrings before the Maastricht summit in December 1991. The twelve countries of the Community had to agree on the modifications to the Treaty of Rome implied by the inter-governmental conferences on economic and political union. Britain stood out as the most committed defender of national sovereignty. Many of the twelve were happy to sacrifice unanimous voting and to join in monetary union because they saw these changes as a means of keeping Germany in check. (Indeed the Germans seemed to express most doubts about a European Central Bank on the Bundesbank model, lest they be dragged down by the rest.) Commentators suggested that British reluctance reflected Mr Major's fear that a commitment to a common European currency would provoke Mrs Thatcher to split the Conservative Party. Yet Britain also resisted an endorsement of the Social Charter which could have far-reaching repercussions for British industrial practices. It does seem to have been touch-and-go whether British intransigence would lead to the failure of the Maastricht summit or to the exclusion of Britain from the counsels of the other eleven. But at the very end a compromise was reached: Britain could decide at a later date whether to join in a common currency or to accept the points of the Social Charter. Mr Major was able to claim Maastricht as a success; Mrs

Thatcher stayed silent and Europe, seen by many as a rock on which the Conservatives would founder, ceased to be a political hazard – at least for the time being. What was remarkable during this period was that the Labour Party, which had fought the 1983 election on getting out of the Community, had now moved full circle, unequivocally criticising Mr Major's reservations and promising to implement the Social Charter and to join in European Monetary Union at the earliest opportunity.

Each general election is a unique combination of personalities, events and issues. But there were striking analogies between the election of 1992 and that of 1964, when Labour under Harold Wilson won by just five seats. The Conservatives had won the 1951, 1955 and 1959 general elections with increasing majorities. These victories, combined with the decline of the Labour vote and of the manual working class, triggered much doubt about the future of the Labour Party; it was argued that the Conservatives were now clearly the normal party of government. Mrs Thatcher in 1987 had repeated the sequence and her 100-seat majority was almost identical to Mr Macmillan's in 1959. After both elections demographic and sociological trends seemed to be working against Labour, and its image was of a divided and backward-looking party. Yet in the succeeding 1959 and 1987 parliaments the Conservative government lost its way. The economy was mismanaged; the Cabinet was divided on key policies. There were spectacular resignations and dismissals – Mr Macmillan sacked a third of his Cabinet in 1962 – followed by an unexpected and divisive change of Prime Minister. There was a similarity in the attention given to the country's relative economic decline and the quality of public services, as well as to the emergence of a 'new' Labour Party.

It is worth recording that in 1964 the voter's verdict was something of a negative one. The narrowness of Labour's victory (its share of the vote rose by only 0.3 percent over 1959), the fall in turnout, and the Liberal resurgence suggested that:

> Many voters were torn between their desire, on the one hand, to bring an end to the period of Conservative government which had brought with it economic recession . . . and, on the other hand, their doubts about the Labour Party's past disunity, its financial competence and its administrative capacity.[3]

Nineteen ninety-two seemed to indicate a similar scenario.

Regardless of the outcome of the 1992 general election, political records would be broken. A fourth consecutive election success for the Conservatives would be unprecedented. Labour was desperate to avoid an unprecedented fourth consecutive defeat – but a Labour victory required an 8 percent swing of votes, far larger than any in the post-war period. There was also speculation about whether the outcome would confirm the trends of recent elections, notably the decline of class voting, the growing division between a Labour-dominated northern Britain and a Conservative-dominated south, the weakening of party loyalty and the growth of multi-party politics.

NOTES

1.  Other broadcasting developments that impinged upon the election were the arrival of satellite television and the reassignment of the terrestrial ITV franchises. The reallocation of franchises under the 1990 Broadcasting Act was announced in October 1991. It represented one of the last paradoxes of Mrs Thatcher's market economics: the commercial television channels were allocated sometimes to the highest bidder and sometimes to the lowest. Mrs Thatcher's favourite TV-am lost its franchise because it bid too low. But Television South-West (TSW) was put out of business because its bid was deemed so high that it could not survive without sacrificing programme quality. Granada TV continued on a low bid because of its quality – but then parted with the key figure who had been deemed responsible for that quality.

    However, the new franchise holders would not take over until January 1993; by contrast, satellite TV had already established itself by the time of the election. The Murdoch-owned Sky channel began broadcasting in February 1989 and quickly absorbed its rival British Satellite Broadcasting (BSB). Though the audience was slow in growing, Sky provided a continuous news service which covered parliament and some other political events more exhaustively than the terrestrial outlets.

2.  See B. Anderson, *John Major: the making of the Prime Minister* (London: Fourth Estate, 1991); A. Watkins, *A Conservative Coup: the fall of Margaret Thatcher* (London: Duckworth, 1991); R. Shepherd, *The Power Brokers: the Tory Party and its Leaders* (London: Hutchinson, 1991).

3.  *The British General Election of 1964*, p. 300.

# 2 Conservatives: Thatcher to Major

Conservative Party morale and confidence were high after the decisive 1987 election victory. The mood was triumphalist as Mrs Thatcher made clear to the new parliament that her administration would continue with radical measures and not consolidate. While the government embarked on a programme of reforms, Labour and the Alliance parties were preoccupied with the aftermath of defeat. Commentators suggested that Labour had to make up so much electoral ground that the Conservatives could confidently anticipate a long hold on office. More cautious voices wondered, however, how long two of the factors that had been crucial to the success of the government would continue: the division of non-Conservative electoral support between the Alliance and Labour, and the continuance of economic growth and improvement in living standards.

The government enjoyed a commanding lead in the opinion polls for the first eighteen months of the parliament – a record for a government in the post-war period (see Fig. 1.2 on p. 14). But the political tide turned abruptly in the spring of 1989 and the party found itself trailing Labour by as much as 20 per cent in early 1990. Safe Conservative seats were lost in by-elections, morale on the back benches slumped, and by the end of 1990 Mrs Thatcher herself had been forced to resign.

Conservative confidence took a battering in the mid-term of the parliament, not least because tensions within the Cabinet contributed much to the collapse of Conservative confidence. Further troubles followed the demotion in July 1989 of Sir Geoffrey Howe from the Foreign Office to the Leadership of the House of Commons, as well as Nigel Lawson's sensational resignation from the Treasury in October 1989, and the reluctant resignation in July 1990 of Nicholas Ridley (after his expression of anti-German and anti-EC views in a *Spectator* interview). The final straw was Sir Geoffrey's decision on 1 November 1990 to leave the government, which precipitated the exit of Mrs Thatcher herself three weeks later. The ministerial departures owed much to disagreement over policy, particularly over the European Community, and in the case of Mr Ridley to the widespread assumption that his views were not dissimilar to hers. Senior ministers were divided on whether Britain should join the

Exchange Rate Mechanism (ERM) of the European Monetary System, and on how far the Community should move towards greater integration. But there were other problems. Rising inflation in 1990 was tackled by tough interest rate policies which hurt home-owners, cost jobs, bankrupted businesses and eroded Conservative support. Anxieties over Europe and the economy damaged the standing of the party and Mrs Thatcher, and, when voters in England and Wales received their first poll-tax bills in early 1990, the government was thrown even more onto the defensive.

Indeed, the poll-tax was an increasing source of worry, even though few defended household rates as a major source of local government revenue. The 1987 election manifesto had announced a scheme 'to abolish the unfair domestic rating system and replace rates with a fairer Community Charge', a fixed charge for local services to be paid by all adults, with a few exceptions and rebates. The scheme was introduced in Scotland in 1989 and in England and Wales a year later. In many constituencies, particularly in the north, there were strong protests at the size of the bills; MPs were embarrassed and party activists demoralised by the bitter reaction of voters. The new charge was expensive to collect and widely regarded as unfair; many people simply refused to pay. The evidence of opinion polls and local elections, as well as the Mid-Staffordshire by-election reverse in March 1990, convinced many Tory MPs in marginal constituencies that, unless there was a major change to the tax, they would lose their seats. Few cabinet ministers spoke out in defence of the tax but Mrs Thatcher's total commitment to it made it appear permanent.

Mrs Thatcher's governments had suffered mid-term slumps before. She herself had lost parliamentary support in 1981 and 1986 but she had never faced a direct challenge to her leadership of the party. In November 1989, however, Sir Anthony Meyer stood against her in the first contest since the rules were changed in 1975 to allow an annual leadership election. The candidacy of Sir Anthony, an elderly back-bencher, was hardly a serious one and was easily defeated. The election showed, however, that up to 60 MPs were dissatisfied enough to vote for him or to abstain in the ballot and a large number more told the whips of their unease; the whips in turn warned Mrs Thatcher that many MPs were unhappy about her tone on Europe and that a stronger challenger would attract more support. Their warning fell on deaf ears.

There was continuing speculation about the leadership ambitions of Michael Heseltine, a back-bencher since his abrupt resignation from the Cabinet in January 1986. Some ministers expressed resentment at the evident skill and relish with which he exploited his freedom from ministerial office. In public he never expressed criticism of Mrs Thatcher personally or even of the broad thrust of government policy; he made a point of stating that he could not envisage any circumstances in which he would directly challenge her for the leadership. But he clearly represented a different form of Conservatism – his support for more positive government involvement with industry and his desire to link Britain's future more actively with the European Community were in many respects a throwback to the policies of the discredited Heath government. And privately he made no secret of his leadership ambitions.

Central Office had not won much praise during the 1987 election, although it shared in the victory celebrations. The party chairmanship had not been a happy post under Mrs Thatcher. Only Cecil Parkinson (1981–83) had clearly been a success. Her first appointment, Lord Thorneycroft, had left under a cloud in 1981; John Selwyn Gummer (1983–85) made little impact; and her relations with Norman Tebbit deteriorated during his chairmanship (1985–87). Detailed accounts of the confrontations between Mrs Thatcher and Norman Tebbit in the final week of the 1987 election campaign continued to reverberate for many months into the new Parliament.[1]

In spite of Mr Tebbit's well-known opposition, the post of chairman seemed to be available to Lord Young. Many objections were raised to the idea – he was not a member of the House of Commons and so could not mingle freely with MPs around the Chamber; he had never fought an election; his position as Secretary of State at the Department of Trade and Industry would open him to a potential conflict of interest if he had to make judgements about take-over bids involving companies which made contributions to party funds. Lord Young, for one, also felt that there was an anti-semitic tinge in the opposition to his appointment. But he wanted the chairmanship, he was close to Mrs Thatcher, and she wanted him to take the post. In the end Mrs Thatcher offered him a choice between continuing in his present position, or combining the DTI, although without responsibility for mergers, with the party chairmanship. He decided to stay as he was.

There was some surprise when Mrs Thatcher then appointed Peter Brooke, a junior minister at the Treasury, to take charge in Smith Square. Brooke had managerial skills but was neither a political heavyweight nor a skilled communicator. Early in a parliament the position of chairman may be seen as a stopgap post, and Mr Brooke's influence was limited because his was not seen as a full-term appointment. In his brief spell he managed to reorganise the Central Office into three sections, dealing with communications, research, and organisation; he also appointed a Director of Communications, and tightened budget control. But the Euro-election campaign in June 1989 (see p. 14) turned out disastrously, Labour's clear victory being its first in a national election since October 1974.

The Cabinet reshuffle in July 1989 provided an opportunity for Mrs Thatcher to appoint a new chairman, one who was expected to be in the post for the next general election. There was some lobbying for the Defence Secretary, Tom King, and for the Employment Secretary, Norman Fowler, but in the end she turned to Kenneth Baker, a senior minister who was skilled in public relations. As chairman he was frequently in Central Office, making it clear that he did not want to be as tied up with cabinet committees as Norman Tebbit had been. He liked to describe himself as the party's first full-time chairman, claiming that the demands of the post had grown so much that any successor would also have to be full-time.

Mr Baker took seriously the chairman's role as a communicator and made himself available (some said, too available) around the clock for media interviews. He was also determined to work closely with Mrs Thatcher. Divisions or misunderstandings between Number 10 and Central Office, such as had occurred under Mr Tebbit, would be fatal for both. Victory at the next general election would be good for his own eventual leadership prospects as well as for Mrs Thatcher. He believed that the outcome of the next election would be determined by the state of the economy, the standing of Mrs Thatcher, and the electorate's perceptions of the quality of life. When he took over, high inflation and interest rates were hurting the pockets of many Conservative voters and the party was well behind Labour in the opinion polls.

The local elections in May 1990 were held at a bad time for the Conservatives, following the gloomy budget and the arrival of the first poll-tax bills. Mr Baker claimed that the elections would be a referendum on the tax and then skilfully singled out the successes in the Tory flagship councils of Westminster and Wandsworth as vindications of the poll-tax. He talked of clawing back Labour's lead in the opinion polls to single figures by the end of 1990, and privately claimed that, with the return to two-party politics, a 46 percent share of the vote would be required to win the next election.

In June 1990 John Wakeham, Secretary of State for Energy, was given the role of co-ordinating government information activities. In fact this had less to do with direct contact with the media than with the co-ordination of policies within government; it was an attempt to resurrect the old liaison committee of staff from No 10 and Central Office which had operated under

Lord Whitelaw. After the promotion of John Major to the leadership, this committee developed into the No 12 Committee (see below p. 38).

The Conservative Research Department (CRD) inevitably lost influence during the 1980s as the party continued in office. This was assisted by Mrs Thatcher's distrust of the Heathite line pursued by the CRD under Chris Patten (up to 1979) and by her preference for the independent Centre for Policy Studies (CPS). Ministers relied on their civil servants, but the Prime Minister had her Policy Unit, open to ideas from the free market think-tanks like the Institute of Economic Affairs ( IEA ), and the Adam Smith Institute. Mr Baker regarded the policy work of the Research Department less as an academic exercise and more as a marketing or communication tool; this development was unwelcome to its head, Robin Harris, who left at the end of 1989, moving to the Policy Unit in Downing Street. He was succeeded in February 1990 by Andrew Lansley, a former civil servant ( he had been principal private secretary to Norman Tebbit at the DTI and more recently Policy Director with the Association of British Chambers of Commerce).

The party had lacked a Director of Communications since the departure of Sir Gordon Reece in 1985. Shortly before the 1987 election Mr Tebbit had submitted various names to Mrs Thatcher but none had been acceptable. After 'screening' by Bernard Ingham, Sir Gordon Reece and Tim Bell, Mrs Thatcher agreed in February 1989 to the appointment of Brendan Bruce, a director and account executive of D'Arcy Masius Benton & Bowles. It was his initiative that led the party to adopt a new logo; the existing flame was replaced by a torch, associated with freedom. But his first campaign venture – the European elections in June 1989 – was not auspicious. The Conservatives lost decisively, and the anti-European flavour of the campaign and the slogan, 'Diet of Brussels', were criticised by many in the party. Brendan Bruce thought that the Conservatives had to regain the skilled workers who had defected since the 1987 election and that the party should shift to the right. He cultivated the editors and political correspondents of the Thatcherite tabloids.

As long as Mrs Thatcher was leader, the public relations man, Tim Bell, was also influential. He had handled the party's campaign on behalf of Saatchi in 1979 and 1983, before leaving the agency amid some acrimony in 1984. Now that Saatchi were no longer working for the party, Bell was expected to play a major role. In mid-Parliament, Mr Baker and Mr Bruce sought to shape the agenda in the run-up to the next general election. They wanted to prevent Labour campaigning on its favourable issues of schools, health, and fairness and instead to put it on the defensive about inflation, Europe, defence, taxes and trade unions.

Finance was a continuing source of concern. Lord McAlpine left his post as a Treasurer in June 1990 and responsibility for raising funds fell to Lord Beaverbrook and Sir Hector Laing. The expected deficit from the 1987 election was compounded by the extra expenses of the Euro-elections, the modernisation of Central Office, and the installation of a new computer system (at a combined cost of some £4 million), as well as by the cutback in contributions from firms suffering the effects of the recession and the slump in the stock market in 1990. In the year ending March 1991 the accumulated deficit was some £12 million and in that financial year total income of £13 million was £5 million short of expenditure. It fell to Mr Baker's successor as Chairman, Chris Patten, to handle the revelations that large sums had been paid by foreign benefactors, notably John Latsis, a Greek shipping millionaire, and Sir Yue-Kong Pao, a leading Hong Kong businessman. The party experimented with new ways of raising funds through direct mail and through arranging lunches for potential contributors to meet senior ministers.[2]

Elsewhere in Central Office the two posts of Director of Campaigns and of Organisation were merged following the retirement of Sir Anthony Garner from the organisation post; John Lacy was promoted from his post of responsibility for special seats to the new post. By-election disasters made Mr Lacy's tenure uncomfortable.

Another key figure in Central Office during the Baker tenure was the Vice-Chairman and MP for Hazel Grove, Tom Arnold. He had responsibility for parliamentary candidates, for campaign preparation and for the Central Office budget, and he oversaw the party's major opinion polling exercise.

The poll-tax was the most damaging of issues. It alienated the public, demoralised MPs and demotivated party workers as they faced the resentment of voters whose bills had increased sharply. Central Office urgings in early 1990 for some offset to the impact of the bills were rejected as too costly and unrealistic. In the event, much larger sums were subsequently spent in reducing poll-tax demands.

Central Office nonetheless pursued a fighting defence during 1990. The May 1990 local government elections, although showing substantial net losses, were presented as a success by Kenneth Baker (see p. 10). He followed up with the 'Summer Heat on Labour' campaign between May and September 1990, which, as the shock effect of the poll-tax receded, may have helped to reduce the opinion poll deficit to single figures. The gap widened again during the autumn, however, and the party conference was driven on to the defensive slogan, 'The Strength to Succeed'. The media and party workers were left unsure as to the themes on which the party would fight for a fourth term.

One of John Major's first decisions was to transfer Kenneth Baker from Central Office to the Home Office, and to appoint Chris Patten to the chairmanship of the party. Fifteen months earlier the chairmanship had seemed to be a launching pad for Mr Baker to succeed Mrs Thatcher. It proved to be a graveyard and his name was never mentioned in the leadership election. The unpopularity of the poll-tax, by-election disasters, the challenges to Mrs Thatcher's leadership, and the Lawson and Howe resignations made his spell in Central Office an unhappy one. His frequent appearances on television came to be associated with further government setbacks. The range of problems continually distracted him from effective planning for the election. Number 10 Downing Street, too, was distracted by short-term issues and never engaged in thinking about strategy. History should have warned Mr Baker that the chairmanship of Central Office has not been a route to the leadership: of the 27 previous party chairmen, only Neville Chamberlain (chairman 1930–31) had eventually succeeded to the party leadership.

Conservative preparations for the election were transformed after the replacement of Margaret Thatcher by John Major in November 1990. Virtually all the strategic and tactical thinking had been based on the assumption of a Thatcher campaign. Associates who claimed to know her mind concluded that she was anticipating a June 1991 election, repeating the four-year cycle of success of 1983 and 1987. She – the superstar – would have dominated the campaign, and Labour would have been attacked not only as incompetent and untrustworthy but also as making only cosmetic policy changes to disguise their continuing socialism. Others thought that, had she survived, she would have dissolved Parliament after the Gulf War. But she was never in a position to make the choice and very little work had been done on campaign strategy or policy. For Baker and Bruce crisis management and then the leadership election had taken precedence over election preparations. 'At the beginning of 1991 we found that the bloody cupboard was bare', said one of the new senior appointments to Central Office.

John Major was Mrs Thatcher's choice to succeed her. She regarded him as the best man to carry on with her work. But Major was a very different personality and, in terms of party management and electoral appeal, it paid dividends to emphasise the difference. The election of a new leader demanded a new game plan. His declared ambitions to make Britain 'a country at ease with itself' and to keep Britain 'at the very heart of Europe' struck a different note from his predecessor. His differences from Mrs Thatcher may have been more symbolic than substantive but voters distinguished him from her. Mrs Thatcher once told a speechwriter that she did not know what 'One Nation' meant. John Major did. If 'Time for a Change' was required, many of his colleagues saw his advent as being the change the electorate wanted. Kenneth Clarke, in a typically direct assessment, dubbed it 'Thatcherism with a Human Face'.

Colleagues and, according to surveys, voters were impressed by John Major's 'niceness'. Colleagues also paid tribute to his willingness to listen and to consider different points of view. He made a point of not being in the hands of public relations advisers and not being packaged – a comment on Mrs Thatcher as well as on Neil Kinnock. In response to complaints that he lacked vision and was 'grey', he said 'What you see is what you get'. He continued to live at his Huntingdon home and the media portrayed him favourably as a young family man with a mortgage, who liked football and cricket, used the NHS and had experienced unemployment. Yet, by the time he addressed his first party conference as leader in October 1991, Mr Patten had persuaded him to make use of the speechwriting talents of Sir Ronald Millar and he was also advised informally by Sir Gordon Reece. Millar and Reece had been close associates of Mrs Thatcher.

John Major made a series of keynote speeches, not to express Majorism – a term he and his staff derided – but to express his vision. In Bonn on 11 March 1991 he spoke of his determination to place Britain at 'the heart of Europe'. The concept of a Citizen's Charter was floated at the time. In July he gave a lecture at the Centre for Policy Studies in which he set out the principles of his policies on education – 'the top of my personal agenda'. These included: less coursework in the GCSE; the expansion of grant-maintained schools; better pay for good teachers; more information and opportunities for involvement by parents, and more straightforward tests of pupils. Finally, in his speech to the party conference in October he declared his belief in 'the power to own and the right to choose', themes which were developed in the near-term campaign (see Chapter 5).

If at first the main source of John Major's public appeal was that he was not Mrs Thatcher, this soon gave way to support for his own personal qualities. Surveys suggested that while Mrs Thatcher dominated the image of the Conservative party, with her strengths and weaknesses defining those of the party, voters drew a distinction between Mr Major and the Conservative party. His approval ratings ran far above those of the party and he was credited with many compassionate qualities not attributed to his predecessor. 'We can sweep the country on his personality', said one insider. Conservative strategists thought long and hard about how they could use the appeal of John Major to add to the popularity of the Conservative Party. By the middle of 1991 it had been decided that the famous director, John Schlesinger, would make a film about

*Table 2.1  Satisfaction and dissatisfaction with Government
and party leaders*

| | (*Average of monthly findings*) | | | | | |
| | Government | | Thatcher | | Kinnock | |
| | Sat | Dissat | Sat | Dissat | Sat | Dissat |
|---|---|---|---|---|---|---|
| | % | % | % | % | % | % |
| 1988 | 39 | 52 | 43 | 51 | 29 | 49 |
| 1989 | 33 | 59 | 40 | 54 | 38 | 48 |
| 1990 | 23 | 71 | 26 | 70 | 40 | 46 |
| | | | Major | | | |
| 1991 | 26 | 74 | 49 | 36 | 40 | 48 |

*Source*: MORI

Major's progress from Brixton to Downing Street. In addition, following Mr Major's informal talks to British troops in the Gulf, plans were laid for him, sitting on a stool, to conduct 'Ask John Major' question and answer sessions with Conservative-inclined voters (later they were renamed 'Meet John Major'). But John Major was not happy about being packaged. 'The crucial thing is that the Prime Minister should be comfortable with what he is doing' was the refrain in Central Office.

There was some irony in the transfer of Chris Patten from the Environment Department to the chairmanship. He had been personal assistant to Lord Carrington, whose chairmanship of the party between 1972 and 1974 culminated in Mr Heath's disastrous 'Who Governs?' election in February 1974. The young Patten had a ringside view of those events and was not impressed with the footwork of his masters. In April 1974 he had been appointed by Edward Heath to be Director of the Conservative Research Department. Although, as party leader, Mrs Thatcher managed to insert a number of her sympathisers into Central Office, Patten's One Nation Toryism remained largely immune to Thatcherism. It was a source of wonder that he survived in his post until his election as MP for Bath in 1979. His 'wet' views and his advocacy of a major role for the government in the economy and social services would have made his appointment as Director unthinkable as long as Mrs Thatcher was in Downing Street.

Mr Patten's earlier experience in the party headquarters and his continued interest in election campaigning and political communications gave him certain advantages. His expertise as a writer of manifestos was widely recognised. More than most party chairmen he propounded 'new' Tory themes. He talked and wrote much of the need for the party to be identified with caring capitalism and to have a 'social market' message, like the Christian Democrats in West Germany. The market should be used for generating and allocating wealth, but the government should direct its resources to promote social welfare. In a much quoted interview with the magazine *Marxism Today* he signalled his break with the rhetoric of Thatcherism ('There is no such thing as society') by claiming that the Conservative party should locate itself more in a Christian Democratic tradition, being 'explicit about the social responsibilities that should go along with successful individualism'. He took the view that there was no point in refighting the battles of the 1970s; that was 'as relevant as talking about the battle of Bosworth Field'.[3] As chairman, Mr Patten bore the brunt of the right-wing's criticism that the Major government was betraying Thatcherism and was not attacking Labour vigorously enough. More dangerously, his policy pronouncements were interpreted as positioning him as John Major's intellectual guru – a status he had not sought and one which, as he recognised, could raise resentment.

We have seen that Mr Patten's inheritance at Central Office was not enviable. Three-and-a-half years into the parliament, the party still had no election strategy and no advertising agency; it had hardly started policy preparation and was heavily in debt. He had grave reservations about the effectiveness of Central Office as a campaigning body, but serious reform could not be undertaken before the election, which it was his task to win. He made his presence felt in a number of areas. Compared to Mr Baker he spent less time in Central Office and more in Downing Street, maintaining close contact with Mr Major and the Policy Unit. He was also more interested in drafting papers and in the detail of government policy, where Mr Baker had been more interested in presentation. The appointment of John Cope as a Deputy Chairman relieved Chris Patten of some of the day-to-day administration in Smith Square. Mr Cope assumed duties covering community affairs, finance and organisation, and acted in effect as the chief executive of Central Office. But he did not wholly master the byzantine bureaucracy of Central Office and Michael Stern, the MP for Bristol North-West, was added as Vice-Chairman. Gillian Shephard, MP, was later appointed as another Deputy Chairman.

Mr Patten liked to remember that he had been the last Director of the Conservative Research Department under whom 'the University of Old Queen Street' had flourished. He thought that the formulation of new ideas had been left for too long to the right-wing think tanks and toyed with the idea of dividing the Research Department into two, a secretarial body for everyday affairs and a think-tank which could deal with themes for the long term. But his immediate preoccupation in the first half of 1991 was to prepare election plans, including a draft manifesto and a communications strategy.

Shortly before her resignation Mrs Thatcher had established a number of policy groups to prepare the ground for the manifesto. Most of the groups contained about a dozen members drawn from MPs and experts who supported the party. Each policy group was chaired by the Cabinet minister with the relevant responsibilities and each was encouraged to evaluate present policies as well as to suggest new ones; most reports ran to five thousand words or so. Mr Patten asked the policy groups to submit reports by April 1991, so that he and Sarah Hogg, the head of John Major's Policy Unit, could prepare a manifesto in case of a summer dissolution. In fact, this election option was not taken seriously in No 10 and little work was done.

But John Major and his Policy Unit were determined to make their own mark on the policy-making process. In late March the Prime Minister, Chris Patten, Richard Ryder and other No 10 aides considered ideas to be developed over the summer. At the heart of John Major's thinking lay the Citizen's Charter. This brought together many of his concerns about the public sector – privatisation, deregulation, contracting out, performance pay, independent inspections, quality management, and greater information. A small unit was set up in the Cabinet Office to develop ideas and Francis Maude, a Treasury minister, chaired a series of bilateral meetings with ministers to secure agreement on policy. In July *The Citizen's Charter* White Paper (Cm 1599) was published. It contained many proposals from departments for improving public services and a number were inserted into the final manifesto (see p. 92). The Prime Minister was prepared to consider radical policies but he wanted them also to be practical, affordable and capable of being explained to the ordinary voter. One poll-tax was more than enough.

Speculation continued on how to solve the problem of communications. The party had studied presentations from many advertising agencies during 1989 and 1990, and in September 1990 Brendan Bruce wrote a paper for the chairman on advertising strategy. The recommendation, supported by Tom Arnold, was that Tim Bell should be put in overall control. Rather than employ a single agency to deal with all aspects of communications. Mr Bell would commission different groups to deal with broadcasts, advertising and other parts of the communications campaign. Mr Baker, however, wanted to get the October party conference out of the way, and after that the Bruce proposal was quickly overtaken by Sir Geoffrey Howe's resignation and the leadership campaign. By the end of the year there was a new Prime Minister and a new party chairman.

Mr Patten considered the paper in December and turned down the key recommendations. He preferred to have a single agency to cope with the demands of a hectic election campaign, and he rejected a role for Tim Bell whom he regarded as 'too much old guard' as well as being liable to attract an undue amount of personal publicity.

It was hardly a surprise therefore when Brendan Bruce was replaced as the party's Communications Director in January 1991. His successor was the 32-year-old Shaun Woodward, a television editor from the popular programme *That's Life*, and before that a parliamentary lobbyist for the National Consumer Council and a producer on the current affairs programmes, *Newsnight* and *Panorama*. Mr Woodward was already on the Conservative candidates' list and was married to the daughter of a government minister. He had been invited to see Mr Patten in December 1990 to give his opinion on the party's political broadcasts and the two men soon found that they shared similar views. Mr Woodward thought that many young voters, who were less interested in materialistic values and unconvinced by Thatcherism, found the party's portrayal of Labour as extremist incredible. His preferred communications strategy would emphasise the public's doubts about Labour's competence. Like Mr Patten he regarded the arrival of John Major as an opportunity to present a new image for the party. Mr Woodward echoed his predecessor, however, in claiming that the impact of good communication was slight compared with that of political issues, personalities and circumstances.

Shaun Woodward's appointment acknowledged the importance of television in the coming election. As a television producer he was familiar with the attempts of the parties to 'manage' the media, and the opportunities which they had missed. He would be a gamekeeper turned poacher. He thought that the Conservative media performance in 1987 had left a lot to be desired. Stephen Robin, the party's broadcasting officer, had submitted a devastating report on the failures in 1987. The weaknesses included the failure to inform senior Conservatives about the party's theme for the day, or to co-ordinate Mrs Thatcher's activities with the chosen theme. At times Mr Woodward gave the impression of wanting to achieve for the party what Peter Mandelson had allegedly done for Labour in 1987.

The replacement of Bruce by Woodward was the beginning of a reshaping of the Central Office communications personnel. The Director of Presentations, Harvey Thomas, left in April 1991, following disagreements with Mr Patten about his own position and about the best way to present Mr Major; essentially he wanted to continue with the 'star' treatment which had been accorded to Mrs Thatcher. He was replaced by Russ Pipe from ITN. Over the summer, Mary Bartholomew, from the public relations firm, Shandwick, conducted an audit of the party's communications operation. As a result of her recommendations, communication officers were appointed in most of the twelve regions in England and Wales; their job was to liaise with the regional press and broadcasting media. In November the party's press officer Christine Wall departed and was replaced by Ms Bartholomew, who was given leave from Shandwick. The high-level bending of editorial ears was largely left to Mr Patten and Mr Woodward. The changes of personnel reflected Mr Patten's determination not to fight a Thatcher-style campaign; although Mr Major would be a key figure there would be no heroics. Central Office would have to learn new tricks to cope with a new leader.

In January 1991, Woodward had asked Shandwick to invite samples of work from over thirty advertising agencies, suitable for a large (but un-named) corporate client planning a massive campaign. Three agencies – WCRS, D'Arcy Masius Benton & Bowles, and JWT – were seriously considered and the second was actually the party's preferred choice until it withdrew. The decision to choose Saatchi was made by Patten and Woodward, with Sir Gordon Reece and Peter Gummer from Shandwick providing crucial advice. The announcement in late March that Saatchi would have the account was held up until the party was reassured that the agency's finances were stable. Although Saatchi had handled the party's account in the previous three general elections, the appointment came as a surprise. In the closing week of the 1987 campaign, Mrs Thatcher had lost confidence in the agency and the contract was terminated in 1988; that had appeared to be the end of the relationship. In choosing Saatchi, Mr Patten wanted to rebuild the creative atmosphere of 1978 and 1979, when the agency had first acted for the party. The agency was to be involved in all aspects of the party's communication strategy – broadcasts, press conferences, posters and advertisements.

The agency selected a team of a dozen who worked in some secrecy on the top floor of its palatial Berkeley Square office. The team was led by the agency chairman, Bill Muirhead, and Jeremy Sinclair, the Creative Director of Saatchi & Saatchi Worldwide. Except for Sinclair, none of the team had worked on the 1987 Tory campaign. Later, Maurice Saatchi became closely involved. A good part of Woodward's time was spent with the advertising team; there were meetings early each Monday morning to plan the work for the week ahead, a four hour strategy session each Thursday, and then a session on Fridays.

The agency rapidly decided that the party needed to rethink its position on the 'caring' social issues. The party was associated with lack of caring – at a time when caring had become fashionable. Under Mrs Thatcher notions of 'fairness', 'social justice' and 'public service' had been dealt with by the market. Under the 'caring' Mr Major the party now faced two dangers. By appearing to accept Labour's criticisms about the limits of markets it was fighting on Labour's ground; by introducing market forces into education and health it confused and worried the voters. The agency argued that the party should return to its traditional strength – in economic management – and link this with improving public services.

In July 1991, Saatchi and Central Office experimented with the concentrated fire of a party broadcast, some poster advertising and a high-profile press launch, based on David Mellor's costings of Labour's spending plans at £35 billion. The 1,000 posters of 'Labour's Going for Broke' were produced at a cost of £250,000. Subsequent research showed the effectiveness of this theme, but the timing proved flawed; there was no scope for a follow-through because Parliament went into recess the next week.

The party also embarked on an ambitious polling exercise. After the 1987 election, it had been decided to expand the private research and make more use of qualitative work. The key figure in this was the American, Dick Wirthlin, a consultant to Ronald Reagan's Presidential campaigns. In December 1989 he was appointed a part-time (two days per month) adviser on polling and opinion research. Conservative contacts with Republican campaigners in the United States had increased in the 1970s and became closer still during the Reagan presidency. Wirthlin had already made presentations of his work to a group of Conservative ministers and officials in 1984 and 1986. He claimed that, although voters' preferences on personalities and policies fluctuated, values were more stable; if the party could understand and, to some extent, shape these values, then it would be much better placed to develop an effective communications strategy. The research required time-consuming and expensive in-depth interviews in which voters spoke about their major concerns. This work was carried out in large-scale surveys by the party's long established pollster, Harris. The research suggested that the most important values which the electorate sought in parties were in order: 1. Hope; 2. Security; 3. Peace of mind.

The purpose of the research was to develop a general campaign strategy and suggest phrases and themes for party communications. Tom Arnold made presentations to individual cabinet ministers and to strategy weekends at Hever Castle, Kent, in January 1990 and January 1991.

Yet the work was never properly integrated into a communications strategy (Saatchi made little use of it); few ministers were consulted and some of those who were had reservations, and (contrary to Wirthlin's insistence) the links between values and political issues were rarely made. Mrs Thatcher and Kenneth Baker were supportive and, had they remained in post, the party's election campaign might have been shaped by this approach. Mrs Thatcher attended presentations of the data in September 1989 and twice in January 1990. However, she had too many preoccupations, the research never seriously engaged her or Mr Baker's attention and it was never integrated into an overall communications package.

At Hever Castle in January 1990, the party's strategy was based upon seven 'Strategic Imperatives'. These were to:

- Reinforce the perception of Hope tied to the Future, upheld by Peace of Mind and Opportunity;
- Further reinforce the strong leadership of the Prime Minister;
- Use fully the advantage of incumbency, particularly the timing of the campaign;
- Maximise the political advantage of our organisational and financial resources;
- Neutralise voters' negative attitudes to our handling of the NHS and community charge;
- Develop the 'off-set' issues of the environment and education/training and blunt Labour's attack that we are 'unfair, do not care, and are building a selfish society';
- Highlight Labour's vulnerabilities.

A meeting was convened at St Ermin's Hotel in London in June to plan ways of implementing the strategy. But Mr Baker showed little interest in it and the meeting was unproductive. Once Mrs Thatcher and Mr Baker had left their posts, the Wirthlin research lacked influential support. Critics also considered that suggestions such as the Conservatives' need to make voters feel more 'positive', were 'fine but how do you do it in the middle of a recession?'. Another sceptic brutally dismissed it as 'an expensive way of learning nothing'. Chris Patten was not impressed, certainly in relation to the costs (some £500,000 in 1990) and, desperate for savings, he terminated the Wirthlin contract with effect from 31 March 1991.

On the other hand, supporters of the exercise wondered if the party had missed an opportunity. They believed that the research indicated how issues and presentation could be combined to make an impact on values and therefore gain votes. Wirthlin continued to give advice on strategy, and Tom Arnold and Keith Britto, Central Office's expert on polling since 1974, made suggestions for new research to the Chairman.

As in the previous parliament, the party continued with its omnibus surveys and other occasional polls conducted by Gallup, and with surveys by Harris into marginal seats, and other research. In 1990 these showed that much of the old Alliance support had gone to Labour and that defection from the Conservatives was disproportionately among C2s. These lost voters were instrumental in outlook and sought good reasons for returning to the Conservative fold. Like Labour's private polls, the surveys showed that, in spite of the deteriorating economy, the party was still seen as ahead of Labour on economic competence. A study of marginal seats in August 1991 was particularly encouraging – so much so that Mr Patten doubted its accuracy. In addition, some advice was informally offered to Tom Arnold and Shaun Woodward by Gordon Heald of Gallup and by Robert Worcester, Chairman of MORI, who had polled privately for Labour since 1969. After 1987 Labour dispensed with Worcester's services and turned elsewhere for its polling (see p. 92). Mr Wirthlin had employed Worcester as a consultant, and he saw some but not all of the data.

Election planning required co-operation between the government and Central Office. At the end of January 1991 a general election Planning Committee began its regular weekly sessions, which continued to the dissolution of the parliament. It consisted of key figures in Central Office and among John Major's advisers, and was chaired by Chris Patten. The first version of the party's 'war book' for the election was drawn up for a June 6 election, and revised in late September for an election on November 7 or 14. In February 1991, on the initiative of Richard Ryder, the Chief Whip, a No 12 committee (it met at 12 Downing St, the Chief Whip's residence) was established to co-ordinate party and government activity on a day to day basis. It consisted of Ryder, Patten, John MacGregor (Leader of the House of Commons), John Wakeham and Lord Waddington (Leader of the House of Lords). In addition, Judith Chaplin, the Prime Minister's political secretary and Sarah Hogg or somebody from the Policy Unit was present, as well as Andrew Lansley and Shaun Woodward from Central Office. The group met daily at 8.15 a.m., planned tactics, and agreed themes for each day or week. It continued to meet throughout the summer recess, and became even more significant in planning the party's near term campaign (see pp. 79– 85).

Any government drawing up an election programme has to strike a balance between continuity and change. In 1991 an equilibrium had to be found between defending the Thatcher governments' record over the previous 11 years and emphasising the new approach of John Major. One key participant said, 'We are trying to achieve incremental change to fit the change of Prime Minister. In supermarket terms we want to sell an updated product, not a new brand.' Ministers were careful to say that they were building on Thatcherism, not ditching it. Much of the work of the first two terms of government was accepted – privatisation, union reforms, value for money in the public sector and lower marginal rates of income tax. But the differences in tone could not be denied. Many of the former Cabinet ministers most closely associated with Mrs Thatcher – Norman Tebbit, Nicholas Ridley and Cecil Parkinson – announced their intention to stand down at the next general election. This gave some of them added freedom to voice their disappointment over John Major's ending of the poll-tax and to warn against any more sympathetic attitude towards the European Community. Removed from Number 10, Mrs Thatcher accepted the presidency of the 'Bruges Group' and the 'Conservative Way Forward' group, which joined the 'No Turning Back' MPs in defence of Thatcherite policies. In a March 1991 American television interview Mrs Thatcher said, 'I see a tendency to try to undermine what I have achieved and to go back to giving more power to government.' The sense of discontinuity was even more marked when Mr Lamont presented his first Budget on March 19. This restored the annual uprating of child benefit, ended mortgage tax relief at higher rates, and cut poll-tax bills dramatically by increasing grants to local authorities on the basis of a two and a half percent increase in VAT.

Apart from replacing the poll-tax Mr Major could be credited with other initiatives, though they were largely of tone and style. He and Douglas Hurd broke with Mrs Thatcher's confrontational style with other EC leaders, an approach which they regarded as counter-productive. The party was largely pro-European but it contained a minority, including Mrs Thatcher, which was deeply sceptical of further integration. Mr Major's wish to see Britain 'at the very heart of Europe' was balanced by his dismissal of federalism. But as the Maastricht summit approached, Mr Major was careful to stress domestic concerns. In July 1991 he launched the Citizen's Charter, which contained a series of performance targets for the public services and greater rights for consumers of the services.

The reality of election timing is that, after due allowance is made for holidays and other special factors, Prime Ministers are effectively have very few dates to choose from. The most important limits are those set by the government's political standing which depends largely upon the performance of the economy. As the various options are passed up so the party war books are updated. Mrs Thatcher's tentative plan for a June 1991 election was contingent on the economy and then public opinion turning around some months before, as in 1982 and 1986. At the time when her leadership came under challenge in November 1990, neither the opinion polls nor the economic statistics were reassuring.

The change of leader produced a sudden resurgence for the Conservatives in the opinion polls, which provoked speculation about an early general election. Dates mentioned included February 1991, when the new register would come into effect, or March, in the afterglow of the Gulf war and a tax-cutting budget. There were rumours that John Major wanted an early election (by June 1991 at the latest) to gain a personal mandate. But he was aware of the difficulties in going early – the need to defuse the poll-tax (which would cost money and take time), the fragile state of the economy, the (by now ritualistic) charges that he was 'cutting and running' and the problem often put by Mr Patten, 'What do we say?'. The Treasury always appeared to be thinking in terms of an election in 1992 when, it claimed, there would be signs of economic recovery. Mr Patten advised Mr Major to go either very early or very late and, once the May–June option had passed, he thought that that effectively meant 1992. But John Major still considered autumn a realistic option. In private, Mr Patten also warned that the Conservative lead after the Gulf war would probably disappear and that Labour would be 10 percent ahead by April 1991. The heavy by-election defeats at Ribble Valley in March and Monmouth in May, the Conservative decline in the opinion polls, and the absence of any economic upturn seemed to rule out the option of an autumn dissolution. Media speculation about an election in early summer and again in the autumn but no dissolution, did not convey the impression of a confident government.

Over the summer Mr Major made the headlines with his trips to the Unites States and the USSR. Though unemployment rose, inflation came down month by month and base rates were reduced by stages to 10.5 percent. Conservative strategists had effectively ruled out a 1991 poll but a sudden upturn in the opinion polls in late September raised the prospect of a November election. In the *Independent* (September 17), Peter Jenkins wrote under the headline HOW CAN HE RESIST THE TEMPTATIONS OF NOVEMBER?:

> Now my money is on November. A bandwagon is rolling that will take a deal of stopping . . . . That Mr. Kinnock will lose is fast becoming the conventional wisdom. It has taken its grip upon the media, where it is shared even by journalists sympathetic to the Labour leader. This,

too, will help to shape the atmosphere and create an irresistible surge towards November. Such fashionable consensus is often wrong, as it proved in 1970. That is the gamble the Prime Minister will have to take. Yet I shall be surprised, if not dumbfounded, if he does not take it.

A mini-campaign was launched, attacking Labour's links with the unions, and adherence to the minimum wage and European Social Charter. The fact that both MORI and Gallup gave narrow Tory leads in the polls led some correspondents, encouraged by a government briefing, to predict a November election. But Mr Patten was not persuaded by the party's private polls showing that Tory support was strong in the marginals, and over the weekend of September 22 polls showed a clear Labour lead. The decision to announce that there would not be an election was not handled adroitly. On Sunday, September 29 when John Major and Chris Patten met at Downing Street to inspect the posters prepared by Saatchi, they decided to scotch the election story and to prevent the build-up of media expectation that had occurred in the summer. But because most political reporters were at the Labour Party Conference in Brighton, it could not be done via Gus O'Donnell, the No 10 press secretary. The task was therefore left to John Wakeham, who phoned the news to favoured political editors on September 30, the day before Neil Kinnock's major speech to the Labour Party Conference. The announcement failed to upstage Mr Kinnock's speech and gave rise to the charge that the government was ducking the verdict of the electorate. Conservative election strategists were determined to take advantage of the autumn to prepare a long campaign in the build-up to a dissolution. There was to be no alternative to going to the end of the road.

NOTES

1. See *The British General Election of 1987*, pp. 109–22.
2. The scale of central party activity is not easy to measure. Much may be done in the offices of ministers, shadow ministers and MPs. For what it is worth the number employed in the party headquarters in London in 1991, before the extra recruitment for the election, seems to have been:

| | |
|---|---|
| Conservative Central Office (32 Smith Square) | 200 |
| Labour Party Headquarters (150 Walworth Road) | 152 |
| Liberal Democrat Headquarters | 17 |

The reported annual income and expenditure of the parties was:

|                         | *Income* | *Expenditure* |
|-------------------------|----------|---------------|
| Conservatives (1990–1)  | £13.0m   | £18.1m        |
| Labour                  | £ 7.9m   | £ 6.8m        |
| Liberal Democrats       | £ 1.6m   | £ 1.3m        |

The areas covered by this expenditure would certainly vary between the parties.

*Source*: M. Pinto-Duschinsky, 'Political Parties' in P. Catterall, *Contemporary Britain 1991* (Oxford: Basil Blackwell, 1992).

3. See Philip Stephens' interview with Chris Patten, *Financial Times*, 31 December 1990.

# 3 Labour: Seeking Electability

The 1980s were disastrous for the Labour Party. Although the party moved back into an opinion poll lead over the Conservatives soon after its 1979 election defeat, that had only lasted until late in 1981. At the end of 1989 the party was in a commanding lead again (see Figure 1.2, p. 14). But the years in between were a catalogue of defeats, divisions and disappointments. The general elections of 1983 and 1987 marked the worst outcomes since 1931. The split in 1981 and the creation of the Social Democratic Party weakened Labour and created a rival home for non- or anti-Conservative voters.

Optimists could comfort themselves that Labour had been in bad situations before. Commentators had argued in 1959, after the party had lost three successive general elections, that the reduction in the size of the working class and the growth of affluence would lead to continued decline – but Labour then managed to win four of the next five general elections. However, in many respects the position after 1987 was worse than in 1959. Labour had then been 6 percent of the vote behind the Conservatives and the Liberals had gained only 6 percent; in 1987 Labour was 12 percent behind the Conservatives and the Alliance had 23 percent of the vote. The only consolation – and it was a small one – was that in 1987 Labour had clearly beaten the Alliance for second place.

In the 1983 and 1987 general elections the continued existence of a substantial centre party seemed to impose a ceiling on Labour's electoral support and indeed to act as a constant reminder of the party's past, and perhaps future, extremism. After 1987 doubts about Labour's ability to achieve the 8 percent swing necessary to gain a majority prompted a new interest among centre-left politicians and commentators in proportional representation and in organised anti-Tory tactical voting. After 1987 few Labour front-benchers thought that Labour could get a clear majority, though it might recover sufficiently to deny the Conservatives an outright victory. The party hardly existed as an electoral force in much of the south; many skilled workers had shifted to the Tories, a number of middle-class professional supporters had deserted to the Alliance, and Alliance support was not going to wither away completely. Other demographic changes –

the decline in numbers of the working-class, of council house tenants and of trade union members, together with the growth of the middle-class, of house ownership and of non-unionised employment – worked against the party.[1] Britain appeared to have secure one-party government, albeit based on only 42 percent of the vote. Such interpretations gained strength once the breakup of the Alliance in 1988 failed to lead to a Labour recovery.

Yet from such an unpromising position Labour entered the 1992 election with transformed policies, a more attractive image, a substantially changed organisation, and a good chance of victory. Much survey evidence about the values of the electorate showed that the Conservatives, in spite of landslide election victories, had not won the hearts and minds of voters. The government had, of course, gained immensely from the split opposition and the electoral system; a 42 percent share of the vote produced a landslide in seats. A crucial part of Conservative support in 1987 also depended upon the feeling that the economy was doing well; a significant number had voted for instrumental or conditional reasons. Predictably, much of this pocket-book support fell away in 1990 under the impact of high inflation and rising interest and mortgage rates. Mr Kinnock, however, was aware that recession was a two-edged sword; it could make people even more fearful of switching to an untried Labour government. Finally, the government depended on the perceived 'unelectability' of Labour with its divisions, its ties to unpopular trade unions, its weakness on defence and its 'loony left'. It was Mr Kinnock's achievement to remove many of these 'negatives'.

At the 1987 general election the Labour Party had already distanced itself from the 1983 manifesto. It accepted the sale of council houses to tenants, as well as Britain's membership of the European Community; it agreed with lower rates of direct taxation, and no longer wanted any return to old style public ownership. Mr Kinnock faced the problem: how much further could the party move without a damaging split? And, in particular, what should be done about the commitment to unilateralism – a policy with which he had been so closely identified? Although most party activists, including those in the trade unions, believed in the unilateral renunciation of nuclear weapons, a growing number of front-benchers were convinced that the policy was an electoral millstone – and that the cost of unilateralism could be continuance in opposition and the denial of any opportunity to implement the party's other policies. Leaders had been chastened to find in 1986 that the more the party explained its defence policy the more votes it lost. It appeared, however, that there was simply nothing to be done about unilateralism as long as Neil Kinnock was Labour leader.

At first Mr Kinnock gave contradictory signals on his thinking about a full-scale review of policy. Soon after the 1987 election, at a meeting of the NEC on July 6 he dismissed a proposal from Geoff Bish, the party's long-serving Director of Policy Development, for a general review. Mr Kinnock's public line was that the recent election manifesto had been excellent. But Mr Kinnock had been thinking of a review even before the election; 'there are many teeth to be drawn', he said to a colleague. After the election Tom Sawyer, the chairman of the Home Policy committee of the NEC, privately suggested the idea of a policy review to the leader and was not rebuffed. Mr Kinnock continued to keep his cards close to his chest; he was keen to prepare the ground, and he did not want a review to be centred in Walworth Road, the party's headquarters, which he did not consider up to the job. Yet the euphoria inspired by a well-crafted election campaign was soon overtaken by realisation of how bad the result had been. Awareness of how much electoral ground Labour had to make up, as well as the sullen resignation among much of the left and the grassroot activists, strengthened the hand of reformers. The widespread recognition that something radical had to be done led to acceptance of a far-reaching review of party policy.

Close colleagues of Mr Kinnock were determined to use the election defeat as an opportunity to modernise the party. Replacing the red flag with a red rose as the party symbol and adopting modern techniques of communication might help to a degree. But could skilful presentation be effective without major changes in policy? The high marks observers accorded to the presentation of the 1987 election campaign only drew attention to the problem of the product being sold – the party's policies. Privately funded research after the election showed that, for all the moderation of the leadership and of the manifesto, the Labour Party in 1987 was still widely perceived as committed to high taxation, untrustworthy on defence, unreliable on inflation, and beholden to the trade unions. To become electable the party had to detach itself from the misperceptions of its policies and if necessary from the actual policies. According to one shadow minister in February 1989:

'I'm a moderniser and would go even further than we have so far. I want to get rid of old junk Labour, which is essentially conservative. The old left is the most conservative part of the party.'

Reformers therefore pressed for a full-scale review of policy, one which would take account of how much society had changed over the previous decade. A phrase often used by them and by Mr Kinnock was that the party had to 'remove the barriers to voting Labour' – old fashioned nationalisation, high taxation and unilateralism.

Mr Kinnock's slowness to show his hand meant that many of the early initiatives actually came from Patricia Hewitt and Charles Clarke in his private office. Ms Hewitt, Mr Kinnock's press officer, was impressed by how the Conservatives had managed in the 1980s to capture a few themes, like freedom and strong leadership, and to become identified with popular policies such as the sale of council houses, increased parental choice in education, and curbing of the trade unions. Labour's new ground, strategists argued, should be better public services, fairness, and quality of life.

Reformers were relying on the party's Shadow Communications Agency to educate the party about the public mood and the need to look forward. This body had been the idea of Peter Mandelson, the party's Director of Campaign and Communications (1985–90). It was largely a volunteer team of advertisers, headed by Philip Gould and Chris Powell, and was essentially an addendum to the Director, to whom it reported.[2] Soon after the 1987 election defeat, Mandelson wrote a memo to the NEC urging that the review should shift from being based on the traditional policy-committee process to one based on communications. The agency's presentations to the NEC and to the shadow cabinet, *Labour and Britain in the 1990s*, drew on sample surveys and qualitative research. The evidence they presented about the party's electoral weaknesses and its poor image was devastating. Between 1964 and 1987 Labour's share of the vote had fallen from 44 percent to 31 percent. Some part of Labour's electoral decline could be explained in terms of adverse social change – above all, the reduction in the size of the unionised working class. But perhaps half could be explained by its poor image, weak leadership and unpopular policies – and something could be done about these. The popularity of party policies was often not translated into votes, largely because of doubts about the party's competence. Labour's image was still damaged by memories of the last Labour government with the 'winter of discontent' of 1979 and the IMF rescue package of 1976, as well as high taxes, and trade union exploitation of power. The Conservatives were associated with increasing freedom, opportunity and popular choice. The survey material also reported that most Labour voters in 1987 had voted out of habit and that defence, the 'loony left' and union domination were major negatives for the rest of the electorate.

What was both reassuring and challenging in the material was the limited extent to which a decade of Conservative government had helped Thatcherite values to take hold among the public. By large majorities, voters said that they preferred a society in which there was state provision of welfare rather than individuals looking after themselves and a managed economy rather than a free market one. A significant majority also supported greater public spending for social services rather than tax cuts, and government action rather than reliance on the market to provide jobs and equality.[3] A MORI survey for the *Sunday Times* in summer 1988 suggested that 54 percent of people supported a society based on 'socialist values' compared to 39 percent which backed the 'Thatcherite values'.

Centre-left parties were doing well in Australasia and in much of Western Europe. The left's share of the vote had hardly declined over two decades in Austria, Scandinavia, Italy and West Germany and had increased substantially in France and Spain. Wider home ownership and affluence did not therefore necessarily doom a party of the centre-left. Only in Britain had the left suffered such a spectacular erosion. The research also suggested that social and value changes presented opportunities for the party – new patterns of work, changing roles for women, concern over the environment and education, and demands for greater rights for consumers and for better education and training.

The decision to set up the policy review was passed without much debate at the 1987 party conference. The conference was largely indifferent and the left, fearing a sell-out but not wanting to rock the boat, held its fire. Tom Sawyer played a major role in gaining union support and Mr Kinnock was pleased to have him involved because he hoped that this would guarantee NUPE support for the review. (Sawyer eventually broke with his NUPE leader Rodney Bickerstaffe, and voted with the majority on the union's executive to abandon the union's traditional unilateralist position.) Each group had two joint convenors, one from the shadow cabinet and one from the NEC; the members of each were drawn from the two bodies, with outside advisers. Among those on the NEC only Tony Benn and Dennis Skinner refused to serve on any policy group. The seven Policy Review Groups were organised on thematic rather than on departmental lines and covered:

| | |
|---|---|
| People at Work | Physical and Social Environment |
| A Productive and Competitive Economy | Economic Equality |
| Consumers and the Community | Britain in the World |
| Democracy and the Individual | |

Since 1985 the party leadership had been attempting to write a statement on contemporary aims and values of socialism. The intention was in part to update the earlier statement, which went back to the 1918 programme,

*Labour and the New Social Order*, without suffering the fate in 1959 of Hugh Gaitskell's failure to revise Clause IV; in part to combat the misrepresentation of Labour values; and in part to exclude anti-party groups like Militant. Various politicians and academic sympathisers drafted versions but none was satisfactory to Mr Kinnock. Eventually he and Roy Hattersley decided to try their hand. Much of the final 'Aims and Values' statement was written by Hattersley and drew heavily on his recently published *Choose Freedom*. Although the draft version bore the signatures of the leader and deputy leader, some members of the shadow cabinet, notably Robin Cook and David Blunkett, found it too sympathetic to the market and forced some revisions.

But calls by commentators for Labour to develop a so-called big idea – something akin to Thatcherism for the Conservatives – were not met by the statement or the policy review. Subsequently, education and training, 'fairness', supply side socialism and constitutional reform were regarded as candidates. In truth neither Mr Kinnock nor most of his senior colleagues took seriously the call for a big idea.

There were complaints from the left at what was happening in the policy review. Successive versions were dismissed by Tony Benn as 'T-shirt socialism' and by Eric Heffer as making the party an 'SDP Mark II'. There was, however, little support for the view of Mr Benn and Mr Heffer that the party should fight harder for socialist policies. Ken Livingstone was an irritant to the leadership, but Mr Benn was increasingly seen as a spent force; his challenge for the leadership in 1988 (when he secured only 11 percent to Neil Kinnock's 89 percent) showed the impotence of the left. The union leaders kept their distance and, apart from a passionate defence of unilateralism by the Transport and General Workers' Ron Todd at the 1988 party conference, gave the party leader a free hand. They accepted the end of the closed shop, they welcomed co-operation with the EC, and they were particularly enthusiastic about the Social Charter. Indeed, the speech of Jacques Delors to the TUC Conference in September 1988 gave a boost to those who wanted to turn Labour into a West European social democratic party.

In retrospect, it can be seen that the policy review served different purposes. It was a means of preparing a programme for a Labour government. It could clarify and thus resolve disagreements – during the 1983 and 1987 campaigns leading Labour politicians had been manifestly muddled about party policies on defence and tax. The policy review provided revisionists with an opportunity to press for changes, including the abandonment of unilateralism. It was a way of buying time while Mr Kinnock and the leaders made up their minds and educated the party, particularly on defence and markets. It was also linked to a campaign to shake up local parties and make them into more effective campaign teams. Reformers felt that too many local parties were inward-looking and out of touch with the concerns of ordinary people. However, a programme of public meetings in 1988, called *Labour Listens*, which enabled front-bench politicians to meet invited audiences of 'target' groups of voters and organisations, was not a success.

There were three phases to the policy review. In 1988 most of the groups submitted preliminary reports on values and themes to the annual Conference; the exceptions were the groups dealing with the sensitive issues of industrial relations and defence. The work of the groups moved slowly: Labour's standing in the opinion polls remained poor and any proposals seemed to have little chance of being translated into a government programme. Mr Kinnock chose not to involve himself in the details but took an interest in the delicate subjects of defence, social ownership and the economy and at the outset he had closely involved himself in drawing up terms of reference and membership of groups. The second phase was the consolidation of the groups' recommendations into a programme, *Meet the Challenge, Make the Change* in May 1989, and this was approved at the party conference in October. The third phase, in early 1990, dealt with outstanding policy matters, notably defence. On 24 May 1990 the final programme *Looking to the Future* was issued. Essentially, this was a revised version of *Meet the Challenge*.

Bryan Gould, the shadow spokesman on Trade and Industry, chaired the Productive Economy group, and its report accepted a modest state role in regulating the utilities, with the state's main activity lying in the support of training, investment and research – in a word, supply side socialism. There would be no return to old style Morrisonian nationalisation for the privatised telecommunications industry or for water and electricity, not least because of the heavy costs of compensating shareholders. Instead the state would take powers to regulate these industries and to promote competition.

John Smith, the Shadow Chancellor, chaired the group on Economic Equality. Its report abandoned the 1983 and 1987 manifesto promises of targets for reducing unemployment and made the reduction of inflation a priority. Public spending commitments were limited, in line with the goal of stabilising public spending as a share of GDP. Only the increases in pensions and child benefit were priorities; other spending commitments would wait on economic growth. The tax and benefits package outlined in the report remained essentially in place until the 1992 election. Labour's anti-inflation policy was provided by membership of the exchange rate mechanism of the European Monetary System, and the constraints on borrowing that this involved. Mr Smith's view was that the mechanism would remove about 60 percent of the government's ability to shape its macro-economic policy. On taxation, there would be a bottom rate of 20 percent and a top rate of 50 percent (or 59 percent with the inclusion of higher national insurance contributions on those earning more than £21,000). Gordon Brown, then Shadow Chief Secretary to the Treasury, and Margaret Beckett carried out a public spending check on all the review proposals. As far as possible, proposals which the Conservatives could cost were removed and the remaining promises were qualified with the statement that they could only be carried out when economic circumstances allowed. Mr Kinnock and Mr Smith also had talks with public sector union leaders about a form of incomes policy but this made no progress.

The context in which Labour's spending plans were drawn up in 1988 and 1989, was more favourable than the one prevailing in 1991 and 1992. As the recession took hold there were mutterings about the wisdom of sticking to the promised pensions and child benefit increases and plans for higher taxes on the better-off, but no serious discussion about cutting them back took place. Up to the calling of the 1992 election any such proposal would have caused a major row.

There was some overlap in the work of the policy groups chaired by Bryan Gould and John Smith; Mr Smith felt that the Mr Gould's work on industrial policy too often strayed into economic policy and contradicted the market friendly message he was trying to convey. Compared to Smith, Gould favoured a more interventionist role for government in the economy and in the City and he was more sceptical about the European Community. The reshuffle of posts in November 1989 in which Bryan Gould moved to Environment and Gordon Brown to Trade and Industry made for a more harmonious team and the economic policy review continued under a single body chaired by John Smith.

Another big change concerned Europe. In the 1983 general election Labour had called for British withdrawal. Soon after he assumed the leadership in 1983 Neil Kinnock was conceding in private that the passage of time meant that Britain's future was now locked into the European Community. A number of left-wingers and union leaders were increasingly impressed with how EC countries pursued more 'progressive' social and economic policies. The visit of Jacques Delors, President of the European Commission, to the TUC Conference was crucial in converting union leaders, particularly Ron Todd. Delors argued that many of Labour's social and workplace policies could actually be delivered through the Social Charter, which was fiercely opposed by the Conservative Party.

A decade of Labour impotence at Westminster pushed others towards a greater interest in the Community. As one sceptic said, 'Perhaps we can bring in Brussels to overcome our defeats in Westminster'. On a more personal note, Neil Kinnock appreciated the way in which he was treated as a serious politician by other Socialists on the Continent, eager for a more positive stance from Labour.

Labour supporters of British membership were encouraged by the party's success in the 1989 Euro-elections and by the unenthusiastic attitude of Mrs Thatcher, speaking for a Conservative Party divided on Europe. A number of commentators were quick to point to Mrs Thatcher's negativism as a factor in the poor showing of the Conservatives. For Labour, Europe was above all about the Social Charter, with its proposals for greater employment rights.

Labour's qualitative research suggested that voters viewed Europe favourably once it was seen as helping Britain to 'catch up' with European working standards. Within the Shadow Cabinet the leading sceptic about Europe was Bryan Gould. He was increasingly by-passed, however, as the economic co-ordinating role fell to John Smith. In late 1988 the party came out in favour of Britain joining the Exchange Rate Mechanism, a year ahead of the government, and in September 1991 the party's economic sub-committee recommended acceptance of economic monetary union. Mr Kinnock played a major role in both decisions.

The industrial relations package led to some difficulties between Neil Kinnock and Michael Meacher. Although there was general agreement in the shadow cabinet that Conservative legislation had moved the balance too far in favour of employers, there was little support for the reinstatement of all the pre-1979 privileges of the unions. A code for picketing would be introduced, but pre-strike ballots would be retained and limited secondary action would be overseen by a new industrial relations court. The replacement of Mr Meacher by Tony Blair in 1989 produced further changes. Mr Blair argued with union leaders that there could be no return to 1979 and that labour law in Britain should be brought into line with that on the Continent. It was on his initiative that the party abandoned its commitment to the closed shop. He took the view that if the TUC was serious about the Social Charter, then the closed shop would have to go.

Some were disappointed that the proposals from Roy Hattersley's Constitutional/Home affairs group were not more radical. It advocated an elected Senate to replace the House of Lords, a charter of rights, a freedom of information act, and regional government, but offered no programme for implementing these ideas and no priority between measures. It ruled out electoral reform as well as the incorporation of the European Convention

on Human Rights into British law. Robin Cook was a tireless campaigner
for proportional representation but Mr Hattersley and most front-benchers
were opposed – despite the growing pressure from Scotland for a change.
Some insiders suspected that Mr Kinnock was shifting on the question, but
he did not publicly reveal his willingness to entertain change until early
1992 (see p. 90). He certainly wanted to encourage debate and his office
hit upon the idea of a committee of enquiry led by somebody who was not
on the NEC or in the Shadow Cabinet. A committee headed by Raymond
Plant, Professor of Politics at Southampton University, was established to
review the electoral system for electing a new second chamber and regional
assemblies. In 1990 the party conference, in a defeat for the platform,
insisted that it should also consider elections to the House of Commons.
Over the succeeding months the Labour leader worked closely with the
Plant commission on the timing and substance of the reports. Electoral
reform, hitherto 'undiscussable' in the Labour Party, was at last on the
agenda.

Though Mr Kinnock and Mr Hattersley took care to avoid controversy
on the issue, their views differed. Mr Hattersley was dismissive of the
new pressure group for constitutional change, Charter 88, and thought
that proportional representation was a whim. Mr Kinnock, on the other
hand, considered that the subject had not been properly discussed in
Britain. Conservatives were not interested in it and Liberals promoted it
for party advantage. Labour, he felt, had the chance to shape the debate. If
proportional representation was to come, he wanted to retain the member's
link with the constituency and to impose a threshold, perhaps 5 percent of
the vote, to discourage a proliferation of small parties. Debate was essential
if widespread support was to be built for change. A large majority for a
new system would increase the likelihood that reform would be lasting.
Defenders said that he knew that he would not only have to educate his
own party but also reach out to other parties to build a coalition for change.
But critics complained that his nudge and wink approach was confusing.

On the delicate issue of defence Mr Kaufman, the new Shadow Foreign
Secretary, took advantage of a general mood of 'leave it to Gerald'. In the
1987 election the party's defence position was, according to Mr Kaufman,
impossible; it voted to remain in NATO but to kill off Polaris and Trident
and remove American bases in Britain. Mr Kaufman consulted widely
in the party, and visited Washington, Bonn, Brussels and Moscow for
talks. Although he kept Mr Kinnock informed about his thinking, the
rest of the party was in the dark. Rumours persisted throughout 1988 that
unilateralism or a bilateral deal with the USSR were to be ditched in favour
of a policy of negotiating away Britain's nuclear weapons; this provoked

threats of a major revolt from prominent left-wingers. Particularly crucial for Mr Kaufman was a visit to Moscow in January 1989 when the Soviet leaders signalled their lack of interest in unilateral or bilateral moves by Britain.

In late March 1989 Mr Kaufman typed up the final report in his office, delivered it to Mr Kinnock and left for a two-week visit to the United States and New Zealand. The report rejected a time-table for a non-nuclear policy and proposed a multilateral package, which would place Britain's nuclear capability on the table in disarmament negotiations. Mr Kaufman regarded his proposals as coherent – they would stand or fall as one – and feared that the Labour leader might insist on the removal of Trident and the American bases. But in the end only a few drafting changes were made. It was now up to the leader to get the policy through the NEC and the party conference.

Mr Kinnock's contradictory signals in media interviews about his defence thinking did little to build up confidence in his leadership, but he was helped by events in Eastern Europe and the erosion of the Soviet military threat. He made a passionate defence of the policy switch to the NEC in May 1989. He told colleagues that he had visited the capitals of the world preaching the unilateralist case and found that no-one believed him. Other West European socialist leaders wanted Labour to retain nuclear weapons for use in arms negotiations. So far as he was concerned, circumstances had changed and he was changing with them. On the NEC Mr Kinnock had to spend some time reassuring Robin Cook and David Blunkett but the new policy sailed through the 1989 conference. As so often the left accepted policy shifts to the right from Neil Kinnock that it would not have done from anybody else. The overwhelming desire to win the next election overcame thirty years of bitter division on defence within the Labour Party.

The work of the groups was formally co-ordinated by the campaign management team. This body was chaired by Tom Sawyer and included senior officers from Walworth Road and Mr Kinnock's office, with a major role being played by Charles Clarke, Peter Mandelson and Patricia Hewitt. Drawing on published opinion polls and private qualitative research the Shadow Communications Agency provided information on attitudes about policy for most groups and made suggestions about presentation. There were specific recommendations about language, including, for example, a preference for 'fairness' rather than 'equality', a term seen to be associated with levelling down. Most of the survey findings were an encouragement to reformers and a warning to sceptics. Some of the media reports on all these developments and particularly the book *Labour Rebuilt*, by two sympathetic journalists, overstate the influence of the communications agency on the details of the policy review.[4] Heavyweight politicians – John Smith, Roy Hattersley and Gerald Kaufman – knew what they wanted in their working parties, and largely achieved it; Jack Cunningham and Bryan Gould had long favoured decentralisation and greater power for the regions. The final statement on economic policy was the product of consultations between the party's senior figures. Above all, once Mr Kinnock was prepared to move on Europe and defence, the bulk of the relatively uncommitted moved with him. It is far-fetched to see these policies as the product of survey research.

Mr Kinnock's introduction to the updated programme, *Looking to the Future* (May 1990) emphasised fiscal prudence: 'We will not spend, nor can we afford to spend, more than Britain can afford', and 'Making comes before taking'. Labour wanted to live down its reputation as a high tax party; its programmes would be realistic and carefully costed. The document also made sympathetic noises about the market and the need for partnership between government and industry, particularly in training and investment. The new policy stance was reflected in the choice of language. Policy proposals now referred to 'consumers' or 'citizens', not 'workers'. Socialism was no longer defined in terms of public ownership of the commanding heights of the economy but in terms of diffusing power, encouraging participation, and 'giving people more control over their lives'. Press reactions to *Looking to the Future*, though luke-warm, could certainly have been worse. *The Times* thought that, like Gorbachev in the USSR, Kinnock had tried but still not delivered on modernisation and the *Independent* found it a 'respectable document', but added 'it still lacks intellectual vitality'. However, it was clear that the policy development was helping to change perceptions of the party and improve its electability.

The policy review was initiated from the top of the party. It was not a response to demands from the grass-roots, or even from MPs, and some shadow ministers showed little engagement or commitment. Mr Kinnock succeeded in removing many of Labour's negatives – the reasons which people gave for not voting for the party. But he felt that the review was less successful in looking towards the 1990s, in getting the party to respond to the kind of society Britain was becoming. So much political energy had been spent into squaring party groups threatened by change that little remained for articulating positive themes. The policy review was clearer about what Labour and Neil Kinnock had given up than what they stood for.

In the 1980s there had been greater evidence of fresh thinking among the Conservative inclined think-tanks like the Centre for Policy Studies, the Institute of Economic Affairs and the Adam Smith Institute. Labour lacked such an infrastructure of policy support and new ideas were largely a prerogative of the right. The Fabians were no longer the force they had once been and centre-left groups like *Samizdat* and *Charter 88* were more interested in issues of civil liberties and constitutional reform than in preparing an agenda for a Labour government. Indeed, because both groups advocated proportional representation and, by extension, coalition government, Mr Kinnock would have nothing to do with them. Labour and trade union leaders were impressed by the usefulness of the West German Social Democratic Party's think-tank, the Friedrich Ebert Stiftung. Shadow ministers mixed frequently with West European socialists at seminars and conferences, and went on fact-finding tours on the Continent.

The Labour leader took great interest in the establishment in 1989 of the centre-left Institute of Public Policy Research. Clive Hollick, the head of the financial and media group MAI, had suggested the idea to Neil Kinnock in 1985 and was helpful in raising money, and John Eatwell, a Cambridge economics don and Mr Kinnock's economic adviser since 1986, suggested themes and recruits. Its director was James Cornford and Patricia Hewitt left Neil Kinnock's office at the end of 1988 to become its deputy director. She was trusted by Mr Kinnock and her writing skills and creativity made her influential in all discussions about campaign strategy. The Institute took advantage of its arms-length relationship with Labour to float new ideas; it explored ways in which egalitarian and non-market concepts could be translated into policies and it established links with Labour-supporting intellectuals. In some respects it was replacing the party's Research Department. The early papers from the IPPR were sympathetic to such market mechanisms as road pricing and 'green' taxes to protect the environment; they also proposed child-care vouchers and a new, written constitution. A number of ideas promoted or developed by the IPPR found their way into the policy review; among these were British entry into the ERM, an independent housing bank, a British baccalaureate to replace existing 18-year-old qualifications, flexible working arrangements and flexible retirement.

The Shadow Communications Agency continued to make major strategy presentations to the Shadow Cabinet and the campaign management team. These presentations were based on surveys by NOP, qualitative research and secondary analysis of NOP surveys. In February 1989 the agency noted that Labour had now trailed the Conservatives in the opinion polls for 28 months; if Labour could not close the gap it might be seen as an inevitable loser. The promise of Neil Kinnock's 'New Model Party' had faded, and the party had made no improvement in its standing on the key 'trust' issues of leadership, economic competence, unity and extremism. Labour had to gain seats in the European elections and narrow the deficit in the opinion polls. In a nutshell, building trust in Labour required:

- A LEADERSHIP THAT HAS DELIVERED A NEW LABOUR PARTY
- POLICIES THAT YOU CAN RELATE TO AND TRUST, AND THAT WILL WORK
- AN ECONOMIC TEAM THAT IS SENSIBLE AND COMPETENT

In late July 1990 a presentation was held against the background of a Labour lead of 12 percent in the opinion polls, effectively the party's high point in the parliament. The Prime Minister was unpopular and the poll-tax dominated the news and was damaging for the government. The presentations regularly covered the public mood and the strengths and weaknesses of Labour and Conservatives; they recommended Labour themes, and made suggestions for the communication of policies and for negative and positive campaigning.

Between 1987 and 1990 Labour had improved its image in many respects. As had long been the case, Labour led on the 'caring issues' – unemployment, health and education – and the Conservatives enjoyed a lead on the 'strength' issues – leadership, defence and law and order. There was nothing new about the Conservative deficit on what the agency termed 'compassionate and caring values', but the worsening economy meant that it had now also lost its reputation for economic competence. However, whereas the Conservatives could still win an election by restoring that reputation, Labour would not get back on its social agenda alone. It had first of all to overcome the fact that it was not accepted as credible economically.

What was striking, among so much good news in the shadow agency presentation, was the lack of trust in Labour's ability to provide good government and the widespread doubts about how it would pay for its programme. In spite of the large lead in the polls, the NOP research showed a deep scepticism whether Labour could make things better. It showed that under a Labour government, more people expected:

- price rises to go up faster, not slower
- the standard of living to be be lower, not higher
- the economy to be weaker, not stronger
- taxes for the great majority to be increased, not decreased.

Electors were concerned about the quality of life, which meant not just about public services and their need for more resources, but also about their own sense of personal financial well-being. In turn, this was reflected in worry over high prices, poll-tax bills, and interest and mortgage rates. Two crucial groups of Labour target voters were defined by the agency as 'The Money Centre' and 'The Concerned Centre'. The former involved 'soft' Labour and floating voters and amounted to a fifth of the electorate, predominantly working class and based in the north and midlands. The second group also amounted to a fifth of the electorate and were middle class, based in the south and concerned over education and the environment. Importantly, both groups were worried about Labour's tax policies and economic competence.

The next major agency presentation to the party leadership was in March 1991, after the change from Thatcher to Major and the successful war in the Gulf. It showed that Labour still lagged on economic competence and leadership. The agency recommended a strong Neil Kinnock crusade in which he would make a series of speeches, spelling out his vision for Britain. It also recommended a higher profile for John Smith and the economic team. The theme of the summer campaign should be that Labour was 'Ready for Government' and a strong economic campaign that should help the party to become seen as economically competent before the election. In fact the news over the summer was dominated by the coup against Gorbachev and John Major's trips abroad. The opposition drew very little coverage. On September 15, Harris and ICM reported 5 percent and 4 percent leads for the Conservatives. Labour research at the time revealed that a majority of voters expected the Conservatives to privatise health and education. As a result, Labour then launched a 'Secret Agenda' campaign and this may have regained some ground. At least, the polls turned in Labour's favour.

The late 1980s marked the retreat of the left in local government, in the trade unions and in the PLP.[5] The defeat of Arthur Scargill in the miners' strike in 1985 was the final throw of political strike action. The new realism in the unions was represented by Bill Jordan and Gavin Laird in the newly merged Engineering and Electricians Union and by John Edmonds of the General and Municipal Workers Union; but Ron Todd continued to lead a left-wing executive on the Transport and General Workers. In local government the major figures of the left like David Blunkett and Ken Livingstone were elected to the Commons in 1987 and Derek Hatton of Liverpool moved away into public relations. The left's attempt to organise a local government campaign against rate-capping in 1985, by refusing to set a rate, collapsed. Successive rate cappings and financial penalties, together with the abolition of the Labour metropolitan authorities and the steady reduction of local government responsibilities limited the opportunities for Labour's left in local government. The leadership condemned the anti-poll-tax federation as a body dominated by Militant, suspended 16 Labour councillors in Liverpool for voting against setting a poll-tax, and refused to support the campaign for not paying of the poll-tax (although this was backed by more than a score of hard left Labour MPs). Within the PLP the membership of the hard-left Campaign Group dropped to 25.

Plans were announced to loosen the party's trade union connection. In June 1990 the NEC agreed to reduce the unions' total voting strength at the conference from 90 percent to 70 percent after the next general election. This was a risk; for much of the party's history the trade unions had supported the parliamentary leaders against the left wing constituency parties. But the union block vote had few supporters and giving the constituencies greater weight might encourage more people to join as individual members. It was decided that, for every 30,000 extra members recruited, the vote of the local parties at the conference would increase by one percent and that of the unions be reduced by one percent.

Few parliamentary leaders were prepared to defend Labour's traditional way of making policy through the submission of resolutions by the NEC which could then be composited and pushed through the conference by union block votes. Too often party policies had been ignored by Labour governments to the disillusion of the activists. The party, like many of its West European counterparts, was moving towards the adoption of a rolling programme with a standing commission which would report in alternate years. It was hoped that a more limited role for the conference would produce policy recommendations which would be taken more seriously by a Labour government. In April 1990 the NEC accepted in principle the idea of setting up after the next general election a 190-member Policy Forum, which would be divided into seven commissions. In the same year the party conference also accepted a proposal for 'one member, one vote' in the selection of parliamentary candidates but rejected another proposal to end the mandatory reselection of MPs. It also supported a phased programme over the next three general elections, or ten years, to ensure that at least half the members of the PLP would be women, and it advocated minimum quotas for women on the NEC and as constituency party officers.

Throughout the parliament the leadership moved steadily to weed out supporters of the Militant Tendency. Local parties in Lambeth, Birkenhead and Liverpool were all purged without too much fanfare. As part of its policy of exercising greater control over by-election candidates the NEC imposed its own nominee, Peter Kilfoyle, in Liverpool Walton in the July 1991 by-election. He was challenged in the contest by a left-wing candidate who attracted a derisory number of votes. There was relief when Frank Field fought off a left challenge and held on to the nomination in Birkenhead in 1991. Until the establishment in 1988 of local commissions to examine constituency parties, all this had taken an enormous amount of the NEC's – and Neil Kinnock's – time. By April 1992 the party had expelled over a hundred members. In 1991 the party conference voted to uphold the exclusion of two MPs, Terry Fields and Dave Nellist, from the conference by 9–1 majorities. Both MPs were subsequently expelled from the PLP.

The adoption of the 'one member, one vote' in the constituency parties produced some interesting results in the annual election to the constituency party section of the NEC. In 1989 Ken Livingstone was voted off the NEC and in 1991 Gerald Kaufman was elected. Surveys of party members in 1990 showed that the activists were drawn heavily from the public sector and that most were on the left on key issues on defence, public ownership and more spending on social issues.[6]

As so often there was a continuing financial crisis. By 1988 the party was already over £2 million in debt and this had worsened by the end of the parliament. A quarter of the Walworth Road staff were made redundant and *Labour Weekly*, the party's newspaper, was closed. In the Spring of 1988 Price Waterhouse, the party's auditors, suggested further economies and tighter financial controls. But early in 1991, the party took on extra workers in anticipation of a June general election, and these costs further exacerbated the financial problem.

Labour had ceased to be a mass party. Individual membership was at a record low of 267,000 in 1988 and in January 1989, Neil Kinnock launched a campaign to enrol a million members. A large membership might make local parties more representative of Labour voters and prevent left-wing cliques taking over moribund local parties in inner cities. But the campaign failed; the nominal party membership in 1991 was only 320,000, a figure that greatly exaggerated the actual number of paid-up members.

Peter Mandelson had been Director of Campaigns and Communications since 1985. He was widely praised for converting the party machine to the use of modern communications methods and for improving the party's image as well as for his guidance of Mr Kinnock. But in 1990 Mr Mandelson won nomination for the safe Labour seat of Hartlepool and resigned his post. By the time of his departure he had attracted his share of critics in shadow cabinet and in Walworth Road – not only for his high profile but for the way it was felt that he had used his position to promote certain front-benchers and downgrade others. He was effective in promoting the work of the agency, partly because of his strong personality and partly because he enjoyed the support of Mr. Kinnock. His departure left a major gap in the Shadow Communications Agency, particularly in sending a positive message after the completion of the policy review, and getting senior politicians to respond more favourably to the agency's suggestions.

John Underwood, a television producer, was appointed to the post in June 1990. He worked in parallel with Mr Mandelson for four months and took over immediately after the annual party conference in 1990. Mr Kinnock and Mr Mandelson had favoured the latter's deputy, Colin Byrne, for the post. But the NEC was looking for a person who would be a 'team' player, who did not have ambitions to become a Labour MP and who would not, by implication, be too identified with Mr Kinnock. The perception of Mr Mandelson's close relations with Mr Kinnock and the prominent role given to him in the Monmouth by-election undermined Mr Underwood's position. Mr Underwood also felt that his deputy Colin Byrne was not carrying out instructions and insisted, with the support of the party's General Secretary, Larry Whitty, on his removal. When Mr Kinnock refused to accept the ultimatum, Mr Underwood resigned on 5 June 1991. Critics of Mr Underwood complained that he was not forceful enough in handling the press or in handling the Shadow Communications Agency. He was then replaced by David Hill, Mr Hattersley's long-serving special adviser, and a person skilled in dealing with the Westminster lobby.

Since the 1970 general election private polling for Labour had been carried out by MORI. In the build up to the 1987 election the Shadow Communications Agency had drawn heavily on its own qualitative research and made little use of the MORI work. Its post-election opinion study, *Britain in the 1990s*, was prepared largely by volunteers (see p. 46) and the relationship with MORI was ended. During 1990 NOP conducted a series of studies of the values of British voters and these were incorporated into the shadow agency's strategic thinking. In contrast to MORI, NOP worked more directly to the agency (see p. 150).

Jack Cunningham replaced Frank Dobson as the party's campaign co-ordinator in October 1989 and became chairman of the general election planning group. This group consisted of the Walworth Road directors and members of Neil Kinnock's office, and met monthly on Thursdays at 10.30 a.m. when Parliament was sitting. Its remit was to deal with the nuts and bolts of election planning. One of its early decisions was to select key seats which the party had to win to form a majority; for these it appointed temporary organisers. At the weekly shadow cabinet, there was a regular slot for Jack Cunningham to talk about campaign planning. From autumn 1991 Mr Cunningham also chaired a Monday morning meeting to plan media strategy and House of Commons business for the week ahead. This was established following an initiative in August 1991 from Roy Hattersley and other front-benchers at a time when the government was dominating the news agenda. The group consisted of five front-benchers (Hattersley, Kaufman, Brown, Cook and Gould), as well as David Hill and representatives from the leader's office. The Thursday sessions were felt by some to have been sidetracked into issues of party management – e.g. candidate selection, and conference planning – and to have lost sight of campaign strategy. In early 1990, it was decided to remedy this by convening an earlier, smaller and unofficial meeting at 9 a.m. (consisting of Cunningham, Whitty, Hill and Clive Hollick). This body prepared and co-ordinated campaign strategy. Mr Cunningham also instigated a series of shadow cabinet seminars at which campaign strategy was reviewed and to which the agency made presentations.

By 1990 Labour increasingly resembled a social democratic party on Swedish or German lines. The leadership maintained regular contacts with European Community officials in Brussels and with other West European socialist parties. There was much talk of Labour's policy review being the equivalent of the German Social Democrats' conversion at Bad Godesberg in 1959. But it had been done gradually – particularly the major shifts on defence and Europe. The party had become more sympathetic to the market as a means of creating wealth, to labour laws that gave rights to workers rather than unions, and to measures to protect the environment. Labour was confident about its main agenda – jobs and economic recovery, education, health, training and transport – and campaigners lost no opportunity to reiterate these themes.

Labour was now perhaps divided less on traditional left-right lines than between old Labour and new Labour. Old Labour was identified with the values and interests of the past, with high taxes, public ownership, trade unions, council housing, heavy industry and the north. New Labour sought to identify the party with skills training, new ways of working, improved public services, greater rights for women and families, and protection of the environment. In keeping with the fresh image of the party much of the leadership presented an image of being youthful, articulate, clean cut and well dressed. On the economy and taxation John Smith and Gordon Brown gained a sympathetic hearing at City lunches for the party's policies, and Tony Blair, as shadow spokesman on employment from 1989, reshaped the party's stand on industrial relations.

Commentators discussed what the changes in the Labour Party and its policies might mean for British politics. Was the public mood moving back towards Labour's traditional collectivist and redistributive ideas? Or had Labour betrayed its principles, accepted much of the Thatcherite agenda, and simply promised to administer the new order more fairly and efficiently? Was this the final victory of Anthony Crosland and revisionism? For the first time since Labour emerged as a national party in 1918 there was no public ownership option for the voters. Peter Kellner, noting that state socialism in the sense of state ownership had become a 'wasm', wrote:

> This is an historic moment in the evolution of British politics; yet one that is in danger of passing unremarked.[7]

Mr Kinnock would deny that he had killed off socialism, although the term rarely found its way into party publications or his speeches. Circumstances, particularly the reduced effectiveness of the nation state in macro-economic management, had done it. The 'Kinnock project' that his close friends spoke about was to change Labour into being electable. Neil Kinnock knew that the process of killing so many sacred cows was watched with resignation rather than enthusiasm by party activists.

In his speeches to the party conference Mr Kinnock praised the role of markets and promised that a Labour government, with its policies of investment, training, and co-operation with employers and unions would make them work more efficiently. 'New' Labour took on board many of the lessons of the 1980s both from Britain and abroad. These included the need for more economic incentives and competition; for partnership between government and business; for job retraining; for putting industrial relations into a legal framework that would achieve a 'balance' between the two sides; for a more positive British role in the European Community; for government to be an 'enabler' rather than as a universal problem-solver; for constitutional reform, including fixed-term parliaments and, above all, for creating wealth before spending it. As early as 1983, shortly after he became leader, Neil Kinnock expressed his awareness of the political implications of social change. Labour had to win support

> 'from the homeowners as well as the homeless, the stable family as well as the single parent, the confidently employed, as well as the unemployed, the majority as well as the minorities.'

Ironically, the biggest changes had been on the defence and European policies which had led many to break with Labour in 1981 to form the Social Democratic Party. By 1989 Labour was more than ever the party the Social Democrats had sought to become. One shadow minister closely associated with policy-making in the party looked back:

'It has been a major cleansing process. Politicians can only live with policies that they think are intellectually credible. For years leaders knew they were talking rubbish about public ownership, taxes and the unions. Even if they were convinced themselves, they knew they could never persuade voters – as on defence. Now they can speak out clearly about profits, incentives and competition.'

Mr Kinnock's standing with colleagues rose during the parliament. He went through a bad period in late 1988, seeming depressed; he was portrayed on a *New Statesman* cover with the headline 'NOT WAVING, BUT DROWNING'. Although the leadership challenge of Mr Benn was easily defeated, it seemed to inhibit Mr Kinnock. Some colleagues mourned the absence of a series of flagship speeches which would spell out his vision and define the message of the new Labour Party. Neil Kinnock's performance in the House of Commons, particularly at question time, also left room for dissatisfaction. The merits of John Smith and even Roy Hattersley stood out in comparison. Neil Kinnock's media interviews on defence – moving away from unilateralism and then backtracking – mystified people on both sides of the debate. By January 1989 Labour was still ten points behind the Conservatives and Mr Kinnock's standing in the polls was poor. He was seen by some colleagues as the inevitable leader of the party but as one who could not lead it to victory.

Yet in the last years of the parliament Mr Kinnock appeared unassailable, in total control of the party and with a commanding majority on the National Executive. He relied heavily on his private office, Charles Clarke his long-serving adviser, together with Neil Stewart, and Julie Hall, his Press Secretary. All were loyal, discreet and, in spite of personality and policy differences between them, dedicated to achieving the changes in the party which he wanted. The reason for his dominance of the NEC was in part the presence on it of shadow ministers – Robin Cook, John Prescott, Bryan Gould, David Blunkett and later Gerald Kaufman – who helped to get policies through, but even more, of the trade union members who were overwhelmingly supportive. At Prime Minister's Question Time Mr Kinnock's performances improved and he was more relaxed when faced by John Major. He became increasingly confident in handling colleagues and they in turn gave him most of the credit for the party's recovery as an electoral force. There were complaints, notably from the left, about Mr Kinnock's authoritarianism and the leader had few enthusiastic defenders in the PLP. But he gained high marks for his courage and persistence in making the party respectable and he exploited the party's desperate eagerness to win in the next general election. By March 1990 opinion polls at last reported that a majority of voters expected Labour to win the next general election and he was no longer at such a disadvantage against Mrs Thatcher. But Labour's campaign team were aware that he did not add to Labour's electoral appeal and had little appeal to female voters.

Mr Kinnock had some difficulty keeping his shadow cabinet united in support of British involvement in the Gulf when Iraq invaded Kuwait. Five junior front-benchers resigned on the issue and 36 Labour MPs voted against the party line to support a motion expressing support for British troops. But he gave a clear lead and was determined not to allow Labour to be wrong-footed as it had been over the Falklands. His key position was support for the United Nations policy. And on the Maastricht settlement, when many in the Shadow Cabinet wanted to accept the opt-out clause on monetary union negotiated by John Major and Douglas Hurd, Mr Kinnock insisted that it was a sham, and sought to identify Labour as the party of Europe.

Mr Kinnock made a stand on many points but he had to take account of the views of senior colleagues. He regarded himself as an Attlee, a leader of a team, not a Mrs Thatcher. He genuinely wanted shadow ministers to develop new policies. He had moved gradually, even tortuously, on defence and was sensitive to the unilateralist views of close colleagues. He was coming round to the case for proportional representation and appreciated that Labour could seize the issue of constitutional reform. A well-publicised 'State of the Nation' survey, sponsored by the Joseph Rowntree Reform Trust[8] in March 1991, showed public support for constitutional change and for proportional representation.[9] Private research, presented to him later that month, suggested that if Labour summoned a convention, on the Scottish model, to consider electoral reform, this could be worth an extra 3 or 4 percent of the vote for Labour. But, sensitive to Roy Hattersley's doubts, Mr Kinnock made no overt move. His concern over the party's tax plans, also had to be weighed against the unwillingness of John Smith to reveal his plans until he had seen the Treasury books. Some members of the campaign management team were arguing in September that Labour's spending and tax plans had been drawn up before the recession and should now be modified. Gordon Brown was sympathetic to the case for a review but Mr Smith was not prepared to change. Mr Kinnock also knew that if Labour lost the next election, John Smith had promised his supporters that he would stand for the leadership. Mr Kinnock sometimes noted that, despite the good press which some of his colleagues gained, it was he who, almost singlehandedly, had fought the battles to modernise the party.

Labour's agency proposed a strategy for the party to gain the initiative over the 1991 summer recess. It argued that Labour's battleground was Europe, the environment (although neither of these proved to be salient), a modern constitution (although, on the key issue of electoral reform, the party was divided), economic recovery and social welfare. Mr Kinnock, it proposed, should make a series of speeches outlining his vision of Britain and there should be posters and speaking campaigns on Labour's themes. But, after the by-election success in Monmouth in May 1991, Labour failed to advance. John Major and foreign affairs dominated the news and the party was unable to increase its lead over the Tories on the social issues or to narrow the deficit on leadership and economic competence.

Labour faced a huge challenge as the general election approached. To get a clear majority it had to win over 90 seats and achieve an 8 percent swing, a post-war record. In many Southern and Midlands constituencies that it had once held, it now had to rise from third place if it was to win. Although after 1989 Labour was regularly in the lead in the opinion polls and won four by-elections, it was remembered that in 1981 and 1985–86 the Conservative government had gone through very bad periods, trailing in the opinion polls and losing by-elections by large margins. However, the 1990 trough was even deeper. Perhaps the Conservatives could be beaten.

In 1990 and 1991 there was a sense among politicians and commentators that the tide of opinion had turned from Thatcherite ideas – from exalting the individual to exalting the community, from promoting economic efficiency to promoting social welfare – and that the Labour lead represented something more significant than the usual mid-term recovery for an opposition party. In looking back on the parliament, three factors seemed dominant in Labour's recovery. The first was the collapse of the Alliance after 1987. Although this was not due to Labour, Labour's carefully cultivated moderation helped to remove many of the barriers which had switched voters to the Alliance, and helped the party back towards occupying the centre ground; it was now clearly the only effective challenger to the government. Second, the Conservative government was losing votes through its own mistakes – rising inflation and interest rates, the poll-tax (much associated with Mrs Thatcher) and the National Health Service reforms. Third, the Conservative Party was increasingly seen as divided or extreme and it had forfeited much of its reputation for economic competence. But Labour's lead in the opinion polls was not deep-rooted; it had been abruptly overturned when John Major replaced Mrs Thatcher and again during the Gulf War. Some Labour leaders had come to regard

Mrs Thatcher as a major electoral asset to Labour and regretted that their fox had been shot. Although by May 1991 the party regained a lead in the opinion polls it was no longer by the large margins that had prevailed in Mrs Thatcher's last eighteen months.

According to the old adage, oppositions do not win elections, governments lose them. Labour, however, by its own policy review and its own conduct, had been able to take advantage of the opportunities which the government had presented. But for all Labour's successes – and the scale of the recovery since 1987 was remarkable – there were still doubts, not least among front-benchers. If the party had abandoned so many vote-losing policies, if so many of its policies were popular with voters, if it could win by-election and European elections, and if the Conservatives were so vulnerable on so many fronts, then why had Labour failed to achieve a decisive lead in the opinion polls? Did enough voters think that Labour had sufficiently changed? Would enough of them vote for a Labour government?

NOTES

1.  For discussion of the effects of demographic changes on Labour's support, see A. Heath *et al.*, *Understanding Political Change* (Oxford: Pergamon, 1991) and R. Rose and I. McAllister, *The Loyalties of Voters* (London: Sage, 1990).
2.  See *The British General Election of 1987*, pp. 59–73.
3.  On values, see I. Crewe, 'Values: The Crusade that Failed' in D. Kavanagh and A. Seldon (eds), *The Thatcher Effect* (Oxford: Clarendon Press, 1989) and J. Rentoul and J. Ratford *Me and Mine* (London: Unwin Hyman, 1989).
4.  See C. Hughes and P. Wintour, *Labour Rebuilt* (London: Fourth Estate, 1990) and I. Crewe, 'The Policy Agenda', *Contemporary Record*, February 1990.
5.  P. Seyd, *The Rise and Fall of the Labour Left* (Basingstoke: Macmillan, 1987).
6.  See P. Seyd and P. Whiteley, *Labour's Grass-Roots* (Oxford: Clarendon Press, 1992).
7.  *Independent*, August 8, 1991.
8.  See 'Citizenship and the British Constitution', *Parliamentary Affairs*, October 1991.
9.  See P. Dunleavy and S. Weir, *Independent*, 25 April 1991 and P. Kellner, *Independent*, 24 May 1991. See also J. Curtice, *New Statesman*, 9 September 1991 and V. Bogdanor, *New Statesman*, 2 November 1991.

# 4 Liberal Democrats and Peripheral Politics

Since the 1920s the battle to win seats in the House of Commons and to form a government has been fought between Conservative and Labour. But in the 1970s other groupings gained a lot more votes and a few more seats. In 1983 and 1987 the third parties elected over 40 MPs and secured 25 percent of the popular vote. Only the disproportional effects of the electoral system prevented the fragmentation of the vote in the country being reflected accurately in the House of Commons. In general elections in the 1950s Conservative and Labour provided the top two candidates in over 95 percent of seats. In the 1980s they provided them in less than half. But this third force was extremely heterogeneous, encompassing Liberals, Social Democrats, Welsh and Scottish nationalists and five different parties in Northern Ireland.

During the 1987 parliament the leaders of the main political parties could each claim to have played a significant part in the recovery of their parties. Mr Kinnock continued with his project of making Labour electable after its humiliating defeat, and John Major, taking over from Mrs Thatcher in November 1990 transformed the the Conservatives' electoral chances. It fell to Paddy Ashdown to build the new Liberal Democrat Party on the ruins of the Alliance of Social Democrats and Liberals. The Alliance had preached the need for co-operation between parties but had failed to practice it at leadership level. The two leaders, David Owen and David Steel, had never shared an agreed strategy and the bickering after the 1987 election alienated many supporters. Much criticism was directed to the structure of the Alliance, with two parties and two leaders. As differences of tone and emphasis had emerged between David Owen and David Steel during the 1987 campaign so the media had played the game of 'hunt the split'. John Pardoe, who had chaired the election campaign committee, complained that David Owen and David Steel persistently defied agreed decisions: 'The campaign was the greatest disappointment of my life.'[1]

Alliance leaders found little consolation in gaining the support of 22 percent of the electorate in the 1987 general election. Although that was the second largest share of the vote by a third party since the 1920s, Labour had clearly won the battle for second place and the Alliance had failed to break the two-party mould of British politics.

If the election campaign had been a bad experience, the breakup of the Alliance was even more dispiriting. On June 12, the day after the vote, David Owen made clear that he would oppose a merger of the two parties, and he could expect to be backed by the SDP National Committee which was meeting the following Monday, June 15. But prominent Liberals, including Paddy Ashdown and Alan Beith, were already calling for outright amalgamation. Caught between the two forces, David Steel on Sunday June 14 called for discussions on a merger. David Owen regarded this as a pre-emptive move and rejected it. In the face of deadlock the SDP decided to hold a ballot of members on merger. David Owen resigned the leadership of the SDP in August 1987 once the ballot showed support for a merger.

Soon after the annual party conferences merger negotiations began, and the merger was approved by a Special Liberal Assembly in January 1988 and by the SDP Council. In the ensuing ballot of members 65 percent of Social Democrats and 85 percent of the Liberals supported merger. David Owen then led a rump, called the continuing SDP, and two of his MPs, John Cartwright and Rosie Barnes, supported him; the other two, Robert Maclennan and Charles Kennedy, went with the merger. A handful of Liberals under Michael Meadowcroft held out against the merger but were quickly marginalised.

By-elections in Epping Forest in December 1988, and at Richmond (Yorks) in February 1989 showed that strong support still existed for a third force. But grassroots membership and activity fell off rapidly. At one point in June and July 1988 resignations were arriving at party headquarters and the House of Commons at a disturbing rate.

In a leadership election for the new party in July 1988 Paddy Ashdown beat Alan Beith by 41,000 votes to 16,000. The new party, however, had an identity problem. The draft constitution had offered the name 'New Liberal and Social Democratic Party' keeping 'Alliance' as a short title. The title actually adopted at the merger was 'Social and Liberal Democratic Party' (SLDP or SLD), with the official short title for everyday use of 'Democrats' approved by its first Assembly in September 1988. But this new name, which received short shrift from some former Liberals, failed to catch on and the party became the 'Liberal Democrats' after a postal ballot of the membership in October 1989.

Paddy Ashdown came into a daunting inheritance. On the day he moved into party headquarters as leader, officers from the Inland Revenue were threatening to close down the building because the party was technically bankrupt. His first task was to deal with the organisation. He replaced

Andy Ellis as General Secretary with Graham Elson, a businessman and former Oxfordshire Liberal councillor. The deficit of over £600,000 forced the dismissal of staff, and over the next three years the deficit was gradually reduced to £70,000.

The party was more coherent than the old Liberal machine. The new party had a high ratio of members who were active; the fact that a significant proportion were serving councillors meant that many actually had exercised political power at the local level. Indeed, the party had over 3,700 councillors, often serving in places where the party had a share of control. Conferences were less controversial than the old Liberal assemblies and the delegates were more willing to trust the platform and defer to the leader. In managing the party Mr Ashdown relied heavily on Clive Lindley, Peter Lee and Tim Clement Jones. He also kept in close touch with the Association of Liberal Democrat Councillors. On matters of strategy his key advisers were Tom McNally and Des Wilson, whilst on policy matters Alan Beith and Robert Maclennan were key advisers.

Mr Ashdown chaired the Policy Committee and he shifted the party away from supporting an incomes policy and a quasi-corporatist management of the economy. He welcomed the free market and greater competition and, not a little to his own surprise, easily carried the Liberal Democrats with him. As ever, political and constitutional reform was at the heart of the party's programme – electoral reform, decentralisation and devolution for the regions, a Freedom of Information Act and greater power sharing with the EC. The 1991 party conference also supported the imposition of an extra penny on the standard rate of income tax to provide extra funds for education.

The party learnt how far it had to go when the Euro-elections came in May 1989. The Liberal Democrat vote (6 percent) was less than half that won by the Greens (15 percent). As one leading Liberal Democrat said, 'We are no longer the cop-out vote'. The party then fell to 4 percent in the opinion polls. But in the next year, the opinion polls turned upwards and the party did well in the 1990 local elections. The capture of the safe Tory seat of Eastbourne at a by-election in October 1990 was a turning-point and was followed by increasing support in 1991. The small number of Liberal Democrat MPs meant that the party had little impact in Parliament. Nevertheless Paddy Ashdown was helped by the clear line of support for the government which he took during the Gulf War and the enhanced media coverage which he then gained.

Mr Ashdown was impressed by the extent of electoral volatility; the party loyalty of many voters was fragile. He claimed to be more interested in attracting the support of a hard core of 10 to 15 percent on which he could build, rather than an ephemeral 30–40 percent; he was courting what he called 'inner-directed voters'. He soon abandoned his improbable goal of displacing Labour as the prime alternative to the Conservatives but, at a time of growing convergence in policy between the two major parties, he wished to stake out what he called the new radical ground. He was not impressed by divisions of the voters into traditional social class or left-right ideological categories and classified the electorate more in terms of their values. He wanted to mark out an agenda for the 1990s, one which he thought would be dealing with constitutional reform, as well as with greater rights and protection for women and the family, with protecting the environment and improving public services. His task as leader was to change the culture of the party, to make it more serious and government-oriented, and to project himself as a major political figure.

In contrast to Dr Owen, Mr Ashdown was not willing to campaign for a hung or balanced parliament. His colleagues and aides debated how to handle the inevitable question of what Liberal Democrats should do in a hung parliament. He would refuse to indicate a preference between the other parties but would be willing to co-operate with any party that would promise proportional representation and a four- or five-year term of office. Looking to the long term the best result for his party would be a clear Labour defeat at the next general election, one that would force Labour to adopt proportional representation or be part of a realignment of the centre-left. He took the view that Labour on its own could not win a general election and he did not want Labour to declare its support for PR in advance of the election, fearing that it would remove one of the Democrat's distinct policies. A *Guardian* ICM poll (2 February 1992) reported that more than half, both of Labour and of Conservative voters, favoured a deal with the Liberal Democrats – even at the cost of PR – if this was necessary for their party to have a share of government. Mr Major was clear in his repudiation of PR – but Mr Kinnock seemed during 1991 to have an open mind.

When John Major replaced Mrs Thatcher, Paddy Ashdown found it easier to be more even-handed between the two main parties. But for all his refusal to indicate a preference for working with Labour or Conservative he faced a dilemma. On key policies – an elected Scottish Assembly, support for education, electoral reform – Labour was more sympathetic; moreover, Mr Kinnock had distanced his party from unilateralism and public ownership. Any hung parliament would have been a consequence of the Conservative's loss of at least 50 seats. In other words, on policy and electoral grounds, the Liberal Democrats were more likely to come to a post-election arrangement with Labour than Conservative.

By 1991 Mr Ashdown looked a considerable leader and his popularity rivalled John Major's and exceeded Mr Kinnock's. For all his seriousness about policy, however, surveys regularly showed that it was the party's image, not its policy, that attracted electoral support; the Liberal Democrats, like the old Alliance parties, were neither Labour nor Conservative. And although surveys showed that many more voters were prepared to vote Liberal Democrat, they also showed that many supporters were prepared to defect.

Des Wilson was appointed as Campaign Director in February 1990. He had been a member of the Alliance campaign team in 1987 but it had exercised little influence over the two party leaders, particularly David Owen. This time Mr Wilson insisted on being unpaid and on having full authority. It was agreed that during the election he would have complete control over expenditure, allocation of manpower and campaign management and that the Election Planning Group, which he chaired, would run the campaign once the election was announced. The party's election priorities were to hold on to its existing seats, to enhance Mr Ashdown's reputation and to run a professional campaign. Resources would overwhelmingly be concentrated in the key seats – the 20 held by Liberal Democrats and another 30 – and would go mainly into computers and newsletters. At the national level the focus would be on rallies, press conferences and broadcasts.

The Owenite Social Democratic Party soon ceased to be viable and withdrew as a national party. Its achievement at Richmond (Yorks) in February 1989, when it came within 2,600 votes of winning and pushed the Liberal Democrats into third place, proved to be a false dawn. A humiliating performance in the May 1989 local elections precipitated the announcement that the SDP was no longer a national party expecting to fight all seats. In June 1990 (soon after the Bootle by-election, when its candidate drew just 155 votes, less even than the Monster Raving Loony Party) the party's constitution was suspended by its national committee, its three MPs thereafter sitting as independents. David Owen met with senior Conservatives, including John Major, in early 1991 and appeared willing to offer his endorsement for the government if the Conservatives would refrain from fielding candidates against Rosie Barnes and John Cartwright, the other two SDP MPs. Chris Patten, the Conservative Chairman, made clear that he could not deliver any constituency to another party. In August Dr Owen announced his retirement at the next general election and his refusal to support the Liberal Democrats. In February 1992 a number of young SDP activists declared their backing for the Conservatives. Other SDP members felt a clear call towards Labour, and 'Social Democrats for a Labour Victory' campaigned in a number of West London marginals at the election.

On the other side of the Alliance Michael Meadowcroft, the ex-Liberal MP, led a small group of opponents of the merger. But this continuing 'Liberal' party proved a trifling irritant.

The Liberal Democrats were badly squeezed in terms of media coverage in the first few weeks of 1992. The Conservatives and, to a lesser extent, Labour launched ambitious campaigns to dominate the agenda and open up a decisive lead in voting intentions (see Chapter 5). Des Wilson demanded in vain that the informal election rules, under which the Liberal Democrats would get some four-fifths of the broadcasting coverage for each of the main parties, should apply also to the pre-campaign politics. But the main publicity that the Liberal Democrats achieved in this period came through the revelation in February of Paddy Ashdown's affair with a secretary some years earlier. He seemed to be the victim of a dirty tricks campaign. (It also became known that Conservative Central Office had a dossier on Ashdown, which it had handed to *Panorama*, the BBC's current affairs programme.) His frank admission of the affair had the apparent effect of increasing both his personal standing and support for his party.

In spite of the troubled birth of the new party and the strong recovery of Labour, it was clear as the election approached that the constituency of the old Alliance was almost as strong as ever. It commanded a steady 15 percent of the vote in the opinion polls and could look forward to gaining from the enhanced coverage it would get in the general election. Notwithstanding earlier refusals to talk of hung parliaments, in early March Mr Ashdown laid down his terms for a post-election coalition – 'proportional representation is the absolute bottom line'. In 1983 and 1987 the Alliance leaders had indulged in heady talk of 'breaking the mould' of party politics and overtaking Labour in popular votes. This time the ambitions were more modest – to add a few to their twenty-two seats and to fight a good campaign.

In recent elections Scotland had grown apart from England.[2] Labour domination in Scottish politics increased and in 1987 the party held 50 of the 72 seats, in sharp contrast to its fate in England. The Conservatives had declined in Scotland to only 10 seats and less than a quarter of the vote, in a period when it was becoming increasingly dominant south of the Border. The decision of the Scottish Nationalists to contest every seat meant that in effect Scotland had a four-party system. It was only in the 1974 elections that the party returned more than 3 MPs, although 14 of Scotland's 72 seats have at some time seen an SNP victory,

After the disappointments in the 1987 election the Conservatives reformed the party organisation in Scotland. In 1989 Michael Forsyth was made chairman of the Scottish Conservative party. He took the view that Scotland needed a dose of more Thatcherite policies and that, compared with England, the Scots were over-governed, over-taxed, and over-dependent on employment in the public sector and 'yesterday's industries'; they also had too many council-houses. He proved to be an uncomfortable colleague for the Secretary of State for Scotland Malcolm Rifkind and John Major moved him from the chairmanship in late 1990. But in Scottish public opinion the Conservatives made no progress. In the European elections in 1989 they won only 21 percent of the vote, finishing below the nationalists (25 percent) and losing their two seats. The Conservatives were also hurt politically by the poll-tax, not least by its introduction in April 1989, a year ahead of England and Wales.

Scottish politics were, of course, different because of the constitutional question. Opinion polls indicated that around one-third of the electorate favoured some form of independence (either inside or outside the European Community) and that over 40 percent wanted a devolved assembly with some taxation and spending power. Support for the *status quo* rarely exceeded 20 percent. In the run-up to the 1992 election opinion polls recorded an increase in desire for constitutional change, with a significant move towards the option offered by the SNP of 'independence in Europe'. One remarkable poll for the *Scotsman* and ITN in January showed 50 percent favouring independence. The polls also showed increased backing for the SNP and a decline for Labour and Conservatives. Psephologists estimated that the Nationalists might increase their share of seats from three to nine or ten and that the Conservatives could be reduced to a mere three or four seats.

Scots were complaining about being subject to policies determined at Westminster which they had not voted for and which were inappropriate. This was often coupled with a challenge to the Conservative government's mandate to govern in Scotland. During the 1980s the pressure for constitutional change was connected with the unpopularity of Margaret Thatcher's style and personality, the reduction of influence in local government, the introduction of the poll-tax a year earlier than in England and Wales and the refusal by Westminster to offer any devolution that would reflect the different voting patterns in Scotland. This mood was also exacerbated by the suspension of the Scottish Affairs Select Committee, because there were not enough Conservative back-benchers to sit on it. There was much talk about a 'doomsday scenario', a situation where Scotland swung even further against the Conservatives, while the electorate south of the border elected another Conservative government.

The opposition parties formed a Campaign for a Scottish Assembly (CSA) and in July 1988 published a report 'A Claim of Right for Scotland'. This recommended the establishment of a constitutional convention to draw up plans for a Scottish parliament. Soon afterwards the SNP indicated its reservations and subsequently withdrew from the process. The Conservative Party in Scotland had already made clear that it did not intend to participate in the Convention.

The first meeting of the Convention was held in March 1989. It was attended by the Labour, Liberal Democrat, Green and Communist parties, as well as by representatives of trade unions, churches, local authorities, women's groups and other interests. The Convention unanimously adopted a Declaration asserting the sovereign right of the Scottish people to determine its own form of government. Three years later, at its final pre-election meeting in February 1992, it agreed procedures for a future Scottish parliament and endorsed a system of electoral reform. It also endorsed a statutory obligation on parties to select an equal number of men and women candidates and suggested the use of an Additional Member System to achieve greater equality between the sexes if this was not achieved by the constituency elections.

The Conservative Party in Scotland was the only party that defended the Union in its existing form. It dismissed the Convention as an irrelevance, a body formed by those who had lost in United Kingdom elections and used as a voice by vested interests. Critics noted that there was no proposal from the Convention to reduce the number of Scottish MPs at Westminster. It was significant that the Convention refused to entertain the radical option which would have had the Scottish parliament collect all taxes raised in Scotland and pay a share to Westminster for common services. Instead it proposed that virtually all of the programme of the Scottish parliament should be financed by a block grant from Westminster, although this would risk regular and acrimonious negotiations over the size of the grant.

This debate proceeded without the participation of the SNP, which suspected that the Convention would be dominated by the Labour Party and its scheme for self-government within the Union. The SNP developed its own policy of 'independence in Europe', which involved severing all direct ties with London. It envisaged a future Scotland that would resemble other smaller European Community countries such as Denmark. The high point for the Nationalists had been Jim Sillars' victory in the Govan by-election, won from Labour in November 1988. At the time, Labour was trailing the

Conservatives in the opinion polls and it appeared that the largely working class electorate of Govan were giving up on a Labour Party which had no prospect of unseating the Conservatives at Westminster. Although this nationalist surge was not maintained in subsequent by-elections, opinion polls showed support for the SNP at around 20 percent. Given the greater visibility it would have in a general election, the party could hope to increase its vote and build on the three seats which it had won in 1987.

The coming election held out the possibility of a significant role for the 'other' parties. Most of the opinion polls pointed to a hung parliament and the possibility of negotiations between Labour or Conservative with the minor parties. In Scotland the January poll in the *Scotsman* helped to make the coming election campaign be seen as all about independence. In fact most Scots, like people south of the border, were primarily concerned with bread-and-butter issues. The Scottish edition of the *Sun* came out for the nationalists; but the larger selling *Daily Record*, which was firmly Labour, kept the idea of a Scottish Assembly to the fore. In the weeks leading up to the dissolution the Scottish media and the visiting English journalists focussed on constitutional issues and forecast a Tory debacle, although any Nationalist upsurge was primarily eating into the Labour vote.

There was supposed to be an alliance between the SNP and Plaid Cymru. But Welsh nationalism with its linguistic base is very different from Scottish nationalism and Plaid Cymru knew that its prospects were confined to consolidating its position in the five predominantly Welsh-speaking constituencies (out of the 38 seats in Wales).

As dramatic as the fall and recovery of Liberal Democrat support during the 1987–92 parliament was the sudden rise and fall of the Green Party, which temporarily threatened to fill the vacuum left by the Alliance's demise. The Green vote in the 1987 election had been insignificant. However, a rising tide of interest in environmental affairs helped them to burst into sudden prominence by taking 15 percent of the vote at the European elections – moving into third place nationally – and, on the same day, saving a parliamentary deposit for the first time in the Vauxhall by-election. From this point onwards the party had to be taken seriously: the opinion polls began to report Green support separately, and in the 1990 local elections they averaged 8 percent of the vote in the wards they contested in England. However, a decline then set in, prompted partly by the concerted attempts of the established parties to take on board environmental concerns, but also by the ridicule surrounding the party's most prominent spokesman, the former TV football commentator David

Icke, after he publicly claimed to be the son of God. By the end of the year the Greens had dropped once more below the notice of the opinion polls. At its 1991 conference the party approved modernisation of its structure, its panel of 32 speakers being replaced by an executive committee of 9, with Jonathon Porritt and Sara Parkin its effective joint leaders. In January 1992 it elected two principal speakers, Richard Lawson and Jean Lambert, to front its campaign in the election. The Greens were plainly going to make little impact on the election but the Scottish Nationalists and the Liberal Democrats had strong and expanding bases. At the beginning of 1992 the coming election looked very far from being a two-horse race.

NOTE

1. I. Crewe and M. Harrop (eds), *Political Communications: the General Election Campaign of 1987* (Cambridge: Cambridge University Press, 1989), p. 55.
2. We are indebted to Alice Brown of the Edinburgh University Unit for the Study of Government for her help in supplying material on Scottish politics.

# 5 The Near Term Campaign: Winter 1991–92

Opposition leaders invariably proclaim their eagerness for an election battle and campaign managers regard it as their duty to have 'the machine' and 'the troops' ready for the fray. Participants and commentators invoke analogies with sport or military battle. Each party regularly updates its war book, a bulky file (the Conservatives needed two large volumes) containing daily programmes for press conferences, photo-opportunities, rallies, broadcasts, schedules of main speakers, advertisements, posters and other 'events'. Each war book also contains material on the party's strengths and weaknesses, suggestions for deflecting the attack of the opposition, and proposals for promoting favoured issues and themes. It includes advice on how to cope with known future events, such as the routine publication of official economic statistics, or the incidence of international conferences.

More than ever, election campaigns are managed and orchestrated. Each party attempts to shape the agenda so that the media reflects its views on its favourite issues. Public opinion is monitored via opinion polls. An election campaign is increasingly seen by those in charge as an exercise in marketing and many of the skills of selling goods and services to customers are now applied to the electorate. These developments have given greater scope to experts in opinion polling, advertising and public relations, and sometimes led to tensions with the politicians and party officers. This campaign management reached a new peak for the Conservatives in 1979 and for Labour in 1987. By 1992 all parties were in the business of orchestration; 'thinking strategically' was a buzz phrase in every camp. Without this there could be no co-ordinated communications activity, nor could front-bench spokesmen identify priorities or timetable initiatives.

Two pieces of wisdom were current in the party headquarters prior to the 1992 campaign. One, voiced by both Conservative and Labour, was that campaigns shifted only a few votes. They pointed to the 1987 general election when the gap between Labour and Tories hardly moved during the campaign. In five of the previous six general elections the final performance of the Labour and Conservative parties was remarkably close to the average of the opinion polls in the three months before dissolution. Of course, underneath the apparent stability of the electorate there was a good deal of what pollsters called 'churning', as voters switched their preferences between parties or plunged into indecision. Surveys showed that something like a quarter of voters were in this uncertain state; however, by polling day many of these changes had been self-cancelling so that in the end there was little net movement. The period of the campaign was likened to trench warfare: therefore the parties were in danger of being bogged down; therefore they had to make advances in the more open manoeuvring of the pre-campaign period. Having trailed in the opinion polls for much of the 1979 and 1983 parliaments, the Conservative government had made a decisive breakthrough in the last months before the campaigns began and then held onto a large part of that recovered lead. In April 1982 the upsurge in Conservative support followed the recapture of the Falklands. In late 1986 the Conservative lead developed after the party's successful conference, helped by a generous autumn public spending round, a tax-cutting Budget and mistakes by Labour.

In 1991–92 the Conservatives were determined to mount a powerful communications assault well before the official campaign began. In their planning both Labour and Conservative campaigners drew on an academic study of the *long campaign*, the activities of the parties in the months preceding the 1987 election campaign.[1] This reported the findings of a panel study of voters which showed that working-class readers of the right-wing tabloids shifted in large numbers to the Conservatives some six months before polling day. The switchers were particularly attracted by Conservative economic 'successes', as presented in the tabloids.

The other piece of wisdom, expressed more frequently in the Labour and Liberal Democrat camps, was that the government of the day rarely saw its position improve during the election campaign. If Labour could enter the campaign ahead of or even close to the Conservatives then, on past form, it could snatch victory or at the least, deny John Major success. The same line of thinking made Conservatives determined to open a clear lead over Labour. While Liberal Democrats and Nationalists looked to improve their standing during the election because of the greater publicity they would gain, the Conservative and Labour parties thought of the pre-campaign period as crucial for opening a decisive lead. The electorate had to be won over before the dissolution of parliament. Once again, British voters were to be exposed to a long campaign.

Anyone reading through the Labour and Conservative campaign documents and position papers from this period must be impressed by the accuracy with which the parties were able to anticipate the campaigning themes of the other side. The Conservatives, for example, foresaw that Labour would fight on the themes of 'Time for a Change', that Labour was now different, and that the Conservatives had a secret agenda for privatising the social services. They were also expecting Labour to concentrate on health and education and to provide human interest stories which would damage the government. As far back as 18 December 1990, shortly after John Major became Prime Minister, Philip Gould wrote in a Labour strategy paper that the Conservatives' central message would be:

You can't trust Labour. You can trust Major.

He added that the Conservative core themes would be choice, ownership, low taxes and decent public services. Conservatives would exploit popular fears of Labour but, following the Bush campaign in 1988, would try to keep Mr Major above the fray. These parts of the Labour strategy document read like the Conservative war book.

If Labour was seeking to narrow its deficit on leadership, tax and economic management, then Saatchi & Saatchi were urging the Conservatives to increase their lead on these issues. The Shadow Communications Agency expected Conservatives to produce secret documents and dossiers about Labour plans and Labour leaders, while Saatchi anticipated that Labour would produce a 'tragic' health story. In both parties the documents were of a high quality, based on research; they provided a realistic assessment of each party's strengths and weaknesses, and they contained constructive suggestions for gaining votes.

A stimulus to the idea of a Conservative pre-election campaign was the visit of Shaun Woodward, Bill Muirhead of Saatchi and Tom Arnold to the USA in late September 1991 to meet Dick Wirthlin and Roger Ailes, Bush's 1988 campaign adviser. They were interested in what lessons could be learned from the successful 1984 Reagan campaign, because that had occurred against the background of an economic recession and Wirthlin had been Reagan's campaign consultant. They were impressed at how President Reagan had used the last few months before the campaign to dictate the agenda, through the co-ordination of speeches and press conferences, proposals to Congress and well-publicised tours. On their return Arnold and Woodward floated the idea to Chris Patten of imposing greater co-ordination on the party's communications.

The decisive move in creating a near term campaign was an initiative by Richard Ryder, the Chief Whip, on 14 October 1991, shortly after the Conservative Party Conference. He proposed that the No 12 committee should launch a campaign to test the party's machinery and prepare the ground for the general election. The campaign would run until John Major's visit to the party's annual Central Council meeting at Torquay on 13–14 March 1992, and would assume April 9 as the election date. Chris Patten then asked Andrew Lansley, Director of the party's Research Department, to write a strategy paper for the No 12 committee. Saatchi were also convinced of the need for ministers to pursue targeted communications objectives in the run-up to the election campaign. The document went through several drafts and incorporated a strategy paper from the agency on the salience and rating of political issues (based on Gallup data), and a communications brief from the Research Department, which drew on discussions with political advisers to ministers. This paper was first discussed on October 16 by the five members of the committee, Ryder, MacGregor, Patten, Wakeham and Lord Waddington. It was then rewritten by Sarah Hogg and Jonathan Hill, of the Policy Unit, and the themes of 'Power to Choose and Right to Own' (raised in John Major's speech at the party conference) added. The paper was discussed by the No 12 group on October 30, together with the Prime Minister, Lamont, Hurd, Clarke and (significantly) Heseltine. Effectively, this was to be the Prime Minister's core group of ministerial advisers on the election. A number of ideas which were to form part of the election strategy were discussed at this early stage. Recommendations for the party included:

- fighting on the promise of a fourth term, a new leader and new ideas, rather than on its 13-year record.
- reducing the importance of health as an election issue
- emphasising that the Conservatives were the party of low inflation and that Labour had no such commitment
- emphasising the themes of the power to choose and the right to own.

The Cabinet approved the paper on November 7 and ministers were asked to submit ideas for presentations.

By mid-November, the working paper on the communications strategy ran to 50 pages and was now entitled *The Near Term Campaign*. What was emerging was a serious attempt to mesh together the short-term work of government and the day-to-day communications output of Central Office and Saatchi. It contained a draft timetable of events, policy initiatives and announcements, broadcasts, posters, ministerial speeches and visits, all of which would be co-ordinated in an attempt to set the agenda and place Labour on the defensive. The government was urged to seize the opportunity to dominate the news, exploiting ministerial statements, parliamentary questions, control of parliamentary time and, ultimately, the Budget. Incumbency was a crucial basis for winning the near term campaign. The party's target voters were two distinctive groups – former Conservatives and voters who liked John Major but did not support the party (to a disproportionate extent Liberal Democrats and middle-class women), and middle-aged C2 men. The paper was approved by the 'political' Cabinet on November 19.

Shaun Woodward, Andrew Lansley and somebody from the agency (either Jeremy Sinclair or Maurice Saatchi) visited each Cabinet minister in charge of a government department between November 29 and December 16. (At first, Chris Patten had opposed these visits on the grounds that ministers were too busy.) In discussions, usually lasting some 90 minutes, the team offered polling evidence about the public mood, particularly about the salience of issues and about how the public rated the parties' trust and competence on them. Issues were divided into four categories. First, on matters like taxation which were highly salient to the public and favourable to the Conservatives the party was to be aggressive. Sixty percent of voters, for example, believed that Labour would increase direct taxation, and the party should exploit this by developing the income tax implications of the £35bn. price tag which David Mellor had attached to Labour's spending plans in June. Second, on issues low in salience but favourable to the party – like defence or law and order – it should try to promote public awareness and be aggressive. In these two categories of issues Conservatives should seek to highlight the policy differences with Labour. Third, on issues which were low in salience and on which the Conservatives were rated poorly, – like social security or environment – the party should remain quiet. Fourth, on an issue like health (highly salient, but on which the party scored poorly), it was recommended that spokesmen should try to reassure the public through announcements such as the Patient's Charter and the reduced waiting times for operations. But the party was warned against trying to increase public interest in the subject.

Above all, Conservative communications should seek to dent Labour's credibility on its strong issues. What, for instance, was Labour's answer to alleged NHS under-funding? What were the consequences of its defence policies for jobs? What would happen to taxes if its spending plans went ahead? Throughout the near term campaign the party's communications should be co-ordinated, spokesmen should reiterate the agreed message, and policy differences with Labour should be made clear. The substance of these discussions was to agree the timetable for political events and initiatives, based on the objective of concentrating activity or issues together into 'weeks', in which the government and party would seek to set and dominate the agenda.

To keep the election at the forefront of ministerial minds the Prime Minister introduced a political session at the end of each weekly Cabinet meeting, without civil servants present. Ministers were expected to accept and even solicit interviews with the media, and all ministers were formally required to consider whether they needed to 'update their television presentational skills'. On December 19 the Cabinet endorsed a final draft of the near term campaign. The programme would run for 11 weeks, with a separate theme for each week. It would start with leadership in the week beginning 30 December 1991, move to taxation the following week and then on to other themes. Each weekly plan would be submitted to the 'political Cabinet' for approval the preceding week, while the No 12 committee would exercise day to day control of activity and the special advisers would meet every Wednesday to prepare plans for the Cabinet.

The Conservatives were planning an innovation in British campaigning. In his paper to Cabinet on December 19 Chris Patten warned:

> It is a half-way house between customary activity and election conditions. It requires us to place political priorities above rigid Departmental considerations and for Departmental heads to be prepared to insist upon adherence to the timetable where Departmental officials may regard this as extraneous to the announcement itself. It means suspending rigid demarcations of who speaks about what or when, and adopting the election campaign imperative that each of us participates to the full in getting the Party's message across, while recognising whose task it is to take the lead.

Conservative strategists regarded this as opening the election campaign and one made the comment:

> 'We want a long campaign, not only to expose Labour's policies but also to exhaust Labour. It is like the 1914–18 war. We have more resources and can outlast and outspend them.'

Apart from a deliberate disclosure of the existence of these plans by Woodward to Patrick Wintour for an article in the *Guardian* on January 23, and a reference to it in a report by Elinor Goodman on Channel 4, the near term campaign as such was not reported by the media. The information was made available to the *Guardian* as the best means of warning Labour voters and strategists of the efficiency of the Conservative machine.

In addition, the Conservatives had their two-volume war book, drawn up by Colin Hook, an expert in strategic planning. He had joined Central Office in November 1989, on the invitation of Kenneth Baker and Sir Tom Arnold, to undertake general election planning. The book was perhaps the most elaborate and detailed set of preparations which any British party has ever undertaken. Much of it dealt with the minutiae of the programmes for the Prime Minister, the party chairman, and other key figures. It stressed the central focus of the campaign: 'It must be emphasised that the most important target group is the media.' It added that the focus on John Major would make the election campaign 'more Presidential in its style and manner than hitherto experienced'. Cabinet ministers were urged to be disciplined, co-ordinated, to refrain from providing distracting copy at the press conferences and always to follow the daily press conference for the theme of the day. It was also recommended that a health minister be available daily in London 'to defuse rather than magnify the story' on health.

Shaun Woodward was determined to emulate not only the co-ordination shown by the Reagan campaign in 1984 but also that allegedly achieved by Labour's Shadow Communications Agency in 1987. In a strategy paper written in November 1991 he tried to anticipate what he called 'Labour's Election Surprise', and suggested that, to turn the last stages of the campaign in its favour, Labour would support PR. He referred to a MORI poll, conducted in May 1991, which showed that if Labour supported proportional representation this would be worth an extra two or three points, largely from friendly Liberal Democrats. The Conservative Party should prepare its response. In the event, John Major's party conference speech in October had already ruled out post-election deals with the Liberals or change to the electoral system. Other voices dismissed the usefulness of such 'If only' survey questions.

The Saatchi & Saatchi agency was more intimately involved in the preparation of strategy than in 1983 and 1987. It was being employed earlier in the parliamentary cycle and the removal of many of the old Thatcher guard gave it an advantage in experience. Maurice Saatchi and Jeremy Sinclair took the view that there was not much mileage for the Conservatives in talking about a social market or caring capitalism. In fact John Major was careful not to use such terms; he did not like them and did not want to suggest that he was breaking too sharply with the policies of his predecessor. Although the personality of John Major had softened the party's image compared to the one it had under Mrs Thatcher, the overall result was that, for many voters, the party had lost its sense of direction. Saatchi wanted the party to emphasise its traditional sources of strength. There was much to do, as one of its memos noted:

- Most of our *strong* issues have *low* salience
- Most of our *weak* issues have *high* salience.

The earlier Treasury costing of Labour's spending plans at £35 billion had not been connected to their tax implications and Saatchi only brought those in late in the year. But now that John Smith had virtually ruled out higher borrowing to finance Labour's spending plans the agency looked at the £35 billion in terms of what it would mean for taxes. This led in late 1991 to the key strategic decision that Labour would cost '£1,000 more tax a year for the average taxpayer' and the 'Tax Bombshell' poster in January.

Not all Saatchi ideas were accepted, notably the suggested scale of expenditure. Mr Patten was not prepared to splash money about, particularly on press advertisements and this was a continuing source of tension between Patten and the agency. In October the agency submitted two communications budgets, one which would cost £9.3 million (with £7 million for press advertising) or a more modest one of £6.5 million (with £4.1 million for press advertising). In January Chris Patten approved a budget of £5 million to cover both the near term and the election campaign.

By the end of 1991 neither the economy nor the political mood were favourable for the government. There was no sign of economic recovery and the Chancellor's earlier optimistic statements were now held up to ridicule. The trade deficit reached a record £20 billion while headlines were made by the rising number of mortgage repossessions, by growing unemployment, and by poor retail sales, particularly in the Tory heartland of the south-east. A MORI poll on December 29 reported a Labour lead of 6 percent and a spectacular decline in economic optimism. Economic recovery hardly seemed destined to arrive before the second half of 1992. The government's image was more unfavourable than at the same stage before the 1983 and 1987 elections. Gallup found that on such questions as which party 'keeps its promises', 'understands Britain's problems' and 'looks after people like me', Conservative support had declined by some 10 percent from the levels of late 1986. The original strategy of delaying the election until 1992, on the ground that the economy would be stronger and voters more optimistic, seemed to be a gamble that had gone wrong. Writing in the *Guardian* on 23 December 1991, David McKie observed that John Major had 'bungled the timing of the general election, as politicians contemplate polls pointing to a hung parliament and economic portents which do not look good for the Government'.

The Conservative Party therefore needed some good news and the near term campaign certainly provided some. In the first week of 1992, for example, there was a lengthy profile of Michael Heseltine in the *Sunday Times*, one of Douglas Hurd on BBC television's *Newsnight*, an interview with Norman Lamont in the *Financial Times* and extended coverage of Chris Patten and John Major. The second week began with a sharp attack by Chris Patten on Labour's tax and spending plans on January 6 and the launch on 1,000 sites of a 'bombshell' poster, charging that "You'd pay £1,000 more tax a year under Labour" (see pp. 103–5). The following day the *Daily Mail* carried an article by the Treasury minister David Mellor on Labour's tax plans. On January 9 there was a party political broadcast on the theme, 'Worse off under Labour', and on January 12 there was a lengthy interview with John Major in the *Sunday Times*. Conservatives were heartened by the increasing public interest in taxation and were gratified at the upsurge in party support in the opinion polls. Gallup reported an increase in the Conservative lead over Labour as the party best able to deal with taxes from 4 percent to 18 percent between November 1991 and January 1992. In the following weeks, Conservative spokesmen launched the weekly initiatives on defence, education, foreign affairs, law and order and so forth – largely in accordance with plans. In the final two weeks of the near term campaign the government returned to the economy and, at the beginning of March in the week of the Budget, to taxation again.

Meanwhile, the work of government continued. There was a relatively generous public spending round in the autumn, with notable increases for health and education. (Labour's financial team noted that the increased borrowing requirement took the country near to the 3 percent limit of GDP agreed by EC members.) John Major and Douglas Hurd gained praise for keeping Cabinet and party largely united over the close-run negotiations at Maastricht on December 9–10. The effective public relations work associated with this helped to convince ministers that they could dominate news management by effective co-ordination. The government continued to release proposals to improve the rights of consumers of public services under the Citizen's Charter. Over a three-week period in February and early March, the government announced new schemes and extra funding to the value of nearly £4 billion. Pay rises above inflation were provided for teachers, the armed forces and the medical professions, while funds for defence contracts and road improvements were announced together with help for Manchester in its bid to host the Olympic Games in the year 2000. In reply to Labour accusations that the government was bribing the voters with their own money, ministers retorted that the funds were part of planned spending or drawn from the contingency reserve. In February John Major visited Scotland and spoke in Glasgow of his determination to preserve the Union.

To a remarkable degree the Conservative campaign was to be the reverse of their successful effort in 1987: in 1992, 10 Downing Street was to be intimately linked with operations in Central Office and there would be close relations between the Prime Minister and the party chairman; there would be a coherent communications strategy to which all party spokesmen would be expected to adhere; there would be no battle between rival advertising agencies, for advertising was exclusively in the hands of Saatchi & Saatchi; there would be a major effort to co-ordinate the content and timing of ministers' speeches, press conferences, election broadcasts, tours and photo-opportunities; and key ministers would accord priority to appearing on regional television.

The Labour party had spent a good part of the parliament in campaigning. By the time of the October 1991 party conference, it had already launched three major statements of the policy review and the campaign team had proven itself in local elections, by-elections and the Euro-elections. Labour campaigners knew that the more successful the party was electorally, the longer John Major would delay calling an election. They claimed to have 'won' the battle of the party conferences and to have made John Major appear indecisive, by forcing him to delay the election. But a long pre-campaign period would severely stretch their stock of ideas for keeping the party in the news.

The preparation of themes for the election was in the hands of the Shadow Communications Agency. Its core membership comprised David Hill, Patricia Hewitt, Roger Jowell (a public opinion researcher), Richard Glendenning (from NOP), Gez Sagar (the party press officer), Julie Hall (Mr Kinnock's Press Secretary) and Deborah Mattinson (from the qualitative research group, GMA) together with Chris Powell and colleagues from the BNP advertising agency. The co-ordinator of the team was Philip Gould, filling the role played by Peter Mandelson in 1987. The agency had responsibility for producing an overall communications package that would cover surveys, broadcasts, press relations and policy launches. This group met on most Friday mornings at 8.30 for an hour or so in Covent Garden, where NOP had its offices.

In September a key strategy presentation was made first to Mr Kinnock, then to John Smith and his economic team, and finally to the shadow cabinet. The paper reflected Labour's clear sense of its battleground – the social agenda, on which it had a huge advantage over the government. But the document was also frank about the party's weaknesses, particularly on taxation and leadership. In 1987 the party had led the Conservatives on the main social issues but, trailing on economic competence, had not been able to translate this into votes. Since 1987 it had removed many of the negatives (though taxation and leadership remained) and made itself more electable. The problem for any Labour pre-election campaign was to narrow the gap on economic management and taxation sufficiently to gain votes from the party's advantage on social issues. This challenge was not a new one. Towards the end of the thirteen-year spell of Tory government (1951–64) the party had enjoyed a big lead in the opinion polls during 1963 and 1964, in spite of having only a modest advantage over the Tories on economic competence. But as the 1964 election approached its rating on economic competence fell and its lead on voting intentions evaporated. Would the same happen again? It was too much to expect Labour to overtake the Conservatives on economic competence but it must narrow the deficit. The party should do this by emphasising its economic vision, and its policy of modernisation not privatisation; this was to be reflected in the new year in the 'Made in Britain' campaign.

Private polling showed continuing doubts about the party's economic competence and fears that inflation would rise faster and taxes would increase more under a Labour government than under a Conservative government. Even the less well-off saw themselves as suffering from Labour's tax plans, perhaps because they too aspired to higher incomes. Of those giving reasons which would deter them from voting Labour, 75 percent mentioned tax. Campaigners were urged to broaden the argument on taxation from income tax and to emphasise that the money left in one's pocket was also reduced by interest rates, poll-tax, inflation and VAT. They should turn the tables on the tax issue and make plain that whereas a Conservative increase in VAT would hurt everybody, an increase in the higher rate of income tax would affect only a minority. The document stated 'Debate in the narrow area of income tax will always favour the Conservatives'. Some advisers were more pointed in their advice: if Labour did not revise its tax plans and, therefore, its spending commitments, prepared before the recession, it would have great difficulty in winning the election. In a recession, Labour should avoid any increase in taxes. If Mr Kinnock was persuaded by these warnings, he took no decisive action to shift Mr Smith's position.

The agency suggested that the party should deal with Mr Kinnock's image problem by giving a higher profile to attractive and able frontbenchers. He should be protected from hazards, particularly from contact with the tabloids, and should appear in as many statesman-like settings as possible. But they were hopeful that his personal ratings would improve during the campaign.

Labour also had problems with its target voters. The party was urged to concentrate on the undecideds (who were particularly bothered about the economy) and the non-voters, (who were most concerned about the NHS). Labour should pin the privatisation label on the Conservatives (three-quarters of voters believed the allegations that the Conservatives would privatise the health service) and contrast it with Labour's interest in modernisation. But many of the converts to Labour were weak supporters and vulnerable to economic and tax arguments. The agency concluded: 'Realistically, these are always likely to go Tory when the chips are down', and 'Reliance on economic pessimism will not win power'.

The agency planned a near term campaign for Labour, although the phrase was not used. The party's message should be, 'It's Time for Labour'. This would be advanced by three positive themes; 'Made In Britain', publicising the party's plans for industrial modernisation; 'Modernisation not Privatisation', promoting proposals to improve the public services; and 'Opportunity Britain', advocating a fairer system of taxes. These positive themes should be backed up with attacking press conferences which would report, *inter alia*, that waiting lists had doubled over the lifetime of the government, that 900 bankruptcies were occurring each week, and that 3,000 jobs were lost daily. People should be warned that a vote for the Conservative party was a vote for privatising the health service, 3.5 million unemployed and 22 percent VAT. This was Labour's guerrilla warfare.

Like the Conservatives, the party planned a timetable of weekly issue events up to the week beginning March 9 when, it was anticipated, the election would be announced for April 9. It would start with 'Made in Britain': a launch that evoked echoes of Harold Wilson's campaign in 1964 in its emphasis on modernisation through investment, training and partnership between government and industry. On January 27 the theme of the week was 'You're Better Off With Labour' which was backed by the VATMAN poster. On February 3 the weekly theme was 'modernisation not privatisation', backed by a poster. The next two weeks were given over to health and health poster campaigns. Labour's pre-election efforts were to end with John Smith's 'Shadow Budget'.

At the end of 1991 Labour enjoyed a lead in the opinion polls. But in January this lead was reversed as the Conservative's tax campaign took hold. Labour's campaigns – 'Made in Britain' and the 'You'll be better off with Labour' (on taxes and benefits) – were linked to party political broadcasts; they represented Labour's attempt to reduce its deficit on economic competence. But this was not effective in face of the Conservative tax onslaught and Mr Kinnock was frustrated that his economic team were not taking steps to blunt the Conservative tax campaign. Only in February, when it was clear that the economy was still in recession, did Labour recover its lead in the opinion polls. A good day for Labour was February 13, when the government announced increases in prescription charges and the headlines were made by the record number of mortgage repossessions, by a further rise in unemployment figures, and by depressing company results. These reports underpinned Labour's health and economy attacks. This was a reminder that effective communications include 'real' world events, as well as party-initiated messages, and the effectiveness of the latter are enhanced when they are supported by the former.

If this economic news was bad for the government, then Labour regretted that health did not develop as an issue. There was no peg for a hospital privatisation row, as at the Monmouth by-election, and no reports of underfunding in hospitals or of tragedies which could be traced to the government's policies. 'We needed to fight a guerrilla war on health, but the tabloids were not on our side' said one member of the agency. There was also some frustration that Robin Cook, the party's health spokesman, retreated at this time into what he called 'purdah' to prepare a more positive message on the issue. Labour's senior campaigners regarded January as 'a disaster'.

Some advisers, notably Patricia Hewitt and Clive Hollick, argued that the Labour Party should support electoral reform. They anticipated that if Labour looked like winning the election, then Conservatives and their supporters in the press would try and frighten the electorate. Proportional representation might provide reassurance that the party sought consensus and would not give in to the unions or the left wing. They wanted the topic to be broached well in advance of the election: to leave it until the run-up to the election would look like a 'fix'. Although Jack Cunningham and Robin Cook, some trade union leaders and some back-benchers also supported electoral reform, they were aware of the intense political resistance in other quarters. Mr Kinnock's silence was a sign that he had not closed the door on the subject and Charles Clarke and Ms Hewitt argued that he had nothing to lose by at least proposing a constitutional convention on the Scottish model (see p. 74) to consider the subject.

Scotland, which presented a headache for the government and an opportunity for Labour, was the key which helped unlock the door on electoral reform. The party had already promised that it would create an elected Scottish Assembly with tax-raising powers in the first session of Parliament. In January 1992 the NEC approved a recommendation from the Plant committee (see p. 52) for the Assembly to be elected either by the alternative vote or the additional member system. But could PR be confined just to Scotland and an elected second chamber? In a BBC Radio interview on *Weekend World* on January 5, Mr Kinnock indicated that he had an open mind on the issue and would welcome further discussion. He added, 'Then we can come to the conclusion of that debate, and resolve that decision about the direction in which the system should go.' However tortuous the wording, it was clear that Mr Kinnock was sympathetic to proportional representation, and the manifesto would make a move in this direction. Roy Hattersley went along with the idea of discussion but was still opposed to PR.

Neil Kinnock caused the party some embarrassment when, prompted by his staff, he entertained journalists to a private dinner at *Luigi's* restaurant in the West End on January 14. This dinner soon acquired its own mythology. It was one of a series designed to improve relations between the leader and the press. In discussing the Conservative taxation attacks, Mr Kinnock drew attention to an earlier policy document which stated that the party retained the option of phasing in the higher national income contributions over the lifetime of parliament. Mr Smith's team were that day studying the financial implications of a gradual lifting of the ceiling on NICs and Mr Kinnock and Mr Smith had discussed the matter the previous night – but no decision had been taken. Phasing would ease the burden of those faced with higher taxes and insurance contributions. But the idea of phasing had been dropped in recent statements which simply stated that Labour would abolish the 'ceiling' on NICs. John Smith reacted frostily when news of the dinner conversation leaked. He suspected that he was being 'bounced' into phasing, because Mr Kinnock was reacting to an adverse opinion poll, and he and his team resisted. In the end, the two men agreed a common line that no options, including phasing, were excluded.

The *Luigi's* incident was a symptom of the difficulties at the top of the party about taxation and spending and, specifically, between Mr Kinnock and Mr Smith. The tax issue was to be an important item in

Labour's election post-mortem. Mr Kinnock and Mr Smith had agreed over a year earlier that Labour would have a shadow budget in order to counter speculation about Labour's tax plans and to answer questions about how Labour would finance its spending. The leader had his doubts about the electoral wisdom of the tax package but, since it was decided, he wanted it to be more actively projected before the election. Mr Kinnock's aides and other key campaigners urged Mr Smith in December and again in January to publicise Labour's tax plans – largely in order to pre-empt the Conservatives' attack. But Mr Smith argued that the plans could only be framed responsibly and retain the element of surprise if they followed a government Budget and financial statement (see below pp. 103–5). *Luigi's* settled nothing, but advertised Labour's disarray on tax for all to see.

Labour front-benchers were ready to admit the problems which they had in selling Mr Kinnock to the electorate. Even when Labour led the Conservative Party handsomely in the opinion polls Neil Kinnock still ran well behind John Major (particularly among women), and up to a third of Labour voters did not think he was doing a good job as opposition leader. In reply he would point out that it was usual for opposition leaders to be behind the Prime Minister of the day in the opinion polls; although Mrs Thatcher trailed Mr Callaghan in 1979 and Ted Heath trailed Harold Wilson in 1970, this had not prevented their parties from winning the general election. Mr Kinnock's answer to queries about his lack of ministerial experience was to point to what he had achieved as leader of the Labour Party.

In January 1992 the campaign strategy committee was replaced by the leader's committee, a body which in the past had formally directed the campaign once the election was called. Hitherto, however, until 1987, this had only been set up on the eve of an election. The committee consisted of heavyweight representatives from the trade unions (notably Ron Todd, John Edmonds, Tom Sawyer and Eddie Haigh), from the shadow cabinet (Smith and Cunningham) and from the NEC (Prescott and Jo Richardson) as well as members of both bodies (Kinnock, Hattersley and Bryan Gould). The weekly Monday meetings (dealing with media) and the monthly Campaign Strategy Committee on Thursdays chaired by Jack Cunningham continued. There were some complaints that the meetings were too large (the first had an attendance of 20 and the second about 12) and that the business of campaign preparations lacked the wholehearted engagement of senior politicians (although Roy Hattersley and Gerald Kaufman were assiduous attenders at the Monday meeting). The key meeting continued to be with the private Campaign Advisory Team which Jack Cunningham assembled on Thursdays; the Team included Whitty and Hill from Walworth Road, Clarke, Stewart and Hall from Neil Kinnock's office, and Lord Hollick, Philip Gould and later Hewitt. But the secrecy increased the difficulty of getting decisions implemented, not least by party headquarters.

As in 1987, the preparation of Labour's war book was in the hands of Sue Nye, who worked under the direction of Charles Clarke. She drew up a schedule of where and when front-bench spokesmen would be appearing, together with a comprehensive list of press conferences, rallies and interviews. It was kept secret until the very last moment to stop lobbying from front-benchers. There was some consternation when it emerged that the original draft did not schedule John Smith to address a major gathering. However he was then included in the mass rally proposed by Neil Kinnock's office for Sheffield, the only venue available in the middle of the campaign. The idea was inspired by a rally which President Mitterrand had held in his Presidential campaign. It should be a dignified but exciting occasion, designed to to give heart to Labour activists and show that the party could attract thousands to such an event.

An election requires a manifesto. It was understood that the Conservative document would be written in the Downing Street Policy Unit. The near term strategy paper had recommended that the party adopt radical ideas, based on the themes of ownership and choice, and should argue 'Much work remains to be done', not 'Steady as she goes'. Ministers had been asked to submit drafts for a manifesto, but the response had been patchy because the election option was not taken seriously. The shape of the manifesto was most influenced by a strategy meeting at Chequers on November 17 and 18. It was attended by John Major, Chris Patten, Richard Ryder, Judith Chaplin and some people from the Policy Unit. The Policy Unit drew together existing proposals and made other suggestions around the themes of the Right to Own and the Power to Choose. It made presentations on what were to be the core themes of the manifesto – choice, ownership, responsibility and greater opportunity. Among the policies for further consideration were: liberalisation of transport; expansion of GP fundholding; policing; further reform in education, training and housing; and better support for poorer pensioners. In January John Major again invited Cabinet ministers to suggest ideas for inclusion in the manifesto. Those suggestions were considered at a series of meetings which the Prime Minister had with Michael Heseltine, Douglas Hurd, Chris Patten, Kenneth Clarke and Norman Lamont; Sarah Hogg, who would be in charge of writing the manifesto, was also in attendance. The sessions were useful for John Major, providing him with an opportunity to familiarise himself with new policy areas.

Ministers whose proposals involved extra funds or new lines of policy appeared before the 'A' team. In late January Norman Lamont became aware of the large public sector borrowing requirement which would influence his Budget and insisted on the exclusion or modification of a number of spending commitments. If the government was to be credible in its attack on Labour's spending plans, it had to demonstrate prudence itself. Among the proposals which disappeared were the extension of tax relief to women for childcare, the abolition of inheritance tax, and modifications of pledges to reduce waiting time for operations, and to cut income tax in the future.

Chris Patten wanted the gradual release of the more attractive proposals during the near term campaign, arguing that this would gain favourable publicity and demonstrate that the government still had radical ideas. This was turned down in 10 Downing Street, on the ground that each initiative would require clearance from senior ministers and take up too much government time. During February the Policy Unit worked through various drafts, largely on the lines agreed at Chequers in November, although the idea of having the manifesto on the four themes was not pursued. The contents of the manifesto were finally agreed by the 'A' team on March 5 and by the Cabinet on March 12, when the contents of the Budget were known. John Major wrote the foreword and Chris Patten the conclusion. The body of the manifesto was largely drafted or edited by Sarah Hogg, on the basis of drafts submitted by ministers and work by members of the Policy Unit.

Labour's policy proposals had already been launched a number of times in the course of the parliament, most recently in the 1991 document *Opportunity Britain*, which was effectively a draft manifesto. The key role in writing the manifesto was played by Patricia Hewitt, on unpaid leave for the election from her post with the Institute of Public Policy and Research. In February her draft was delivered by Charles Clarke to Gerald Kaufman and Roy Hattersley (both members of the National Union of Journalists), and they made substantial revisions. Clarke also discussed relevant sections with most shadow ministers. At the manifesto meeting on March 16, between the shadow cabinet and National Executive Committee, passages were added and deleted, as shadow ministers objected to the drafts for their portfolios. The amendments were conveyed to Ms Hewitt and Geoff Bish in an adjoining room, and the manifesto was re-written.

There was the expected opposition to specific items from Tony Benn and Dennis Skinner, who insisted on their objections being put to a vote; they were usually in a minority of two. They wanted a pledge to repeal the Conservative government's industrial relations laws and opposed Britain's membership of the ERM. (Tony Benn compared its effect to that of the gold standard on Britain's economy in the 1920s.) But the general mood of the meeting was to give Neil Kinnock a manifesto on which he thought he could win. A key phrase in *Opportunity Britain* and most other policy documents, that public spending commitments would depend on economic growth was omitted ('We will not spend, nor will we promise to spend, more than Britain can afford') and this became a matter for some post-election criticism. The final draft was sent for clearance to John Smith and Margaret Beckett but they and the economic team were preoccupied with preparing the shadow budget.

Although the party leaders' offices in both cases played the key parts, there was a clear difference of approach between Labour and the Conservatives over the preparation of the manifesto. Conservative senior ministers were more closely and continuously involved than their Labour counterparts; and the Conservatives' final drafting session was more concerned with presentation and editing, compared to the substantive discussion which dominated Labour's manifesto meeting.

Mr Lamont's March 10 Budget was eagerly anticipated by Conservatives and, in conjunction with Labour's shadow budget, helped to shape the election campaign. He received much advice to the effect that he should use the Budget as an opportunity to emphasise the divide with Labour over taxation. By cutting, say, 2p off the standard rate of income tax he could dramatise the issue and force Labour to enter the election with a commitment to increase taxes; Labour had already promised that it would repeal any income tax reduction. But the Chancellor's options were effectively limited by the worsening state of public finances. Although the government had earlier scorned the idea of creating a third band of tax, in addition to those of 25p and 40p, Mr Lamont announced the creation of a 20p band for the first £2,000 of taxable income, a measure targeted to help the low paid. Its attraction was that the possibility of extending this bottom band opened the door towards the gradual implementation of the party's stated goal – a basic rate of 20p. Labour and Liberal Democrats immediately denounced the tax cut for the low paid as irresponsible and voted against it.

But in the short-term, Labour had to come up with an alternative package showing that it would not tax the low paid more heavily than the Conservatives. One member of Labour's economic team regarded the Budget as 'tactically brilliant' for the way in which it had reduced John Smith's options. The team had been working on a package which would protect those earning up to £25,000, and the expected tax-cutting Budget (involving, probably, 1p off the standard rate) would have left them some scope for doing so. Mr Smith's surprise was to cut NICs for all wage-earners by 1p. But now he was caught between Labour's spending plans ('set in concrete', said a resigned adviser), Mr Kinnock's refusal to allow an increase of £1 billion on the borrowing requirement, and the necessity to treat the low paid at least as favourably as Mr Lamont had done. Faced with the choice between concentrating help on the low-paid or on those earning between £20,000 and £25,000, Mr Kinnock immediately chose the former. The final shape of the shadow budget was the product of agreement between Mr Kinnock and Mr Smith and both were aware of the risks they were taking. The 1p cut in NICs was abandoned.

Mr Lamont's Budget was followed on March 11 by the announcement of the election date and at the weekend by the Conservative's Central Council meeting at Torquay, a useful launching pad for the government. It marked the end of the near term campaign and of the No 12 committee. By the weekend of March 15 the opinion polls suggested that the Budget had had little positive impact. NOP actually put Labour ahead by 5 percent and an average of the major polls showed the parties neck and neck. The Budget did not look like an election winner.

The Conservatives before 1964 and Labour in mid-1974 had both planned their government activities with a view to a coming general election. But never has a party in office been so systematic in its adoption of a near term election strategy as the Conservatives were in 1992. How successful was the campaign in setting the scene for the coming general election? Ministers claimed one great achievement – they had established their central message that Labour was the party of high taxes. Having openly admitted that the economy had not yet recovered, they could now argue that Labour would only makes things worse. The campaign would be largely negative – attacking Labour.

But, on the evidence of the opinion polls, the near term campaign achieved little. The Conservatives asked Gallup to track the progress of the campaign by monitoring the public mood on issues. As Table 5.1 shows, there was little movement between the first (January 4–8) and the last surveys (February 27 / March 3). Indeed, whereas at the start 80 percent expected taxes to go up under a Labour government, only 75 percent did so at the end. On these figures it is difficult to say that the campaign was

*Table 5.1     Expectations of Labour Government led by Neil Kinnock*

|                                    | 4/9 Jan. | 27 Feb./3 March |
|------------------------------------|----------|-----------------|
| *Taxes would go up*                |          |                 |
| Would                              | 80       | 75              |
| Would Not                          | 12       | 17              |
| Don't Know                         | 8        | 8               |
| *There would be more strikes*      |          |                 |
| Would                              | 45       | 45              |
| Would Not                          | 41       | 42              |
| Don't Know                         | 13       | 13              |
| *Unemployment would rise*          |          |                 |
| Would                              | 37       | 35              |
| Would Not                          | 47       | 49              |
| Don't Know                         | 16       | 16              |
| *The cost of living would go up*   |          |                 |
| Would                              | 66       | 43*             |
| Would Not                          | 23       | 43              |
| Don't Know                         | 16       | 14              |
| *Britain's defences would be cut*  |          |                 |
| Would                              | 60       | 59              |
| Would Not                          | 24       | 26              |
| Don't Know                         | 16       | 14              |

* Prices would go up faster

*Source*: Gallup for the Conservative Party

successful. But defenders of the campaign could point out that the previous November Gallup found that only 61 percent expected tax rises. And the surveys did not measure changes in the salience of the tax issue or how influential it might be on voting. Other surveys also showed that the tax attack had given many voters a specific idea of how much extra Labour would cost them in tax. More worrying for Conservative leaders, however, was health: when asked about their expectations from a future Conservative government two thirds of all voters (including 43 percent of Conservatives) mentioned the privatisation of the NHS.

Conservatives acknowledged that the campaign faltered badly after the tax success in January and that Labour had regained the initiative in February. The campaign was hardly as positive as had been planned, because, some claimed, no manifesto items were released. After late January the campaign was less successful in planting articles in the press, or getting spokespeople on the air. Yet most Conservative strategists welcomed the effect of the campaign. Bad economic news had been offset by aggressive campaigning, particularly on tax, key communication images had been established (e.g. the tax 'bombshell' and the so-called 'Double Whammy' which, Mr Patten explained, meant that taxes and prices would rise under Labour), and senior ministers had been re-politicised, ready for an election campaign expected to be the hardest-fought for a generation.

In January Labour had clearly been outgunned in terms of documents, statements and other initiatives. The party lacked resources but it also suffered from not being in office and therefore from an inability to make news. In contrast to the Conservatives Labour's senior political figures did not appear to be as closely or continuously linked to their party's campaign preparations. Whereas John Major was personally involved in key meetings and decisions, it is striking that Mr Kinnock left so much to Charles Clarke and Neil Stewart, from his office, to represent his views on key campaign committees. Mr Kinnock was kept informed of developments and committees were made aware of his views but it was his choice to keep his distance from campaign committees. Some members were frustrated at their lack of access to him but he seemed preoccupied with other matters – managing the party and shadow cabinet and preparing for speeches and Prime Minister's Questions. Some of his advisers considered that he should realise that the next election was his last chance ('he wins or he's out') and that he should grasp the nettles of electoral reform and tax. But Mr Kinnock had always proceeded gradually, building assured majorities for each change. He was gambling that his 'wait and see' strategy would not be damaging.

There was also some regret in Neil Kinnock's office that John Smith and Margaret Beckett had not been more involved in campaign planning and more positive in responding to suggestions for neutralising the Conservative tax attack, particularly for a pre-emptive tax campaign. And the party headquarters had a much smaller role than Central Office had in the near term campaign. The old weaknesses – leadership and taxation – were still there. Although many things that were planned did not happen – notably background documents from the Research Department and major speeches from the party leader and others – Table 5.1 reports Conservative tracking polls which show that Labour's poll rating did not suffer. Labour's pre-election effort appeared not only to have survived the Conservative onslaught but its own final pre-election polls (Table 5.2) found that the party had achieved its best all round position in the parliament.

Mr Major had few options over the election date. When, in late September, a November 1991 election was ruled out, he effectively boxed himself in. There was never a run of opinion polls which gave a good margin to the government. Given the uncertainties and the trend in

*Table 5.2   Comparative expectations of the parties in Government*

|  | Con | Lab |
|---|---|---|
| *The Parties in government – Best at* | | |
| Getting the economy out of recession | 24% | 29% |
| Improving the NHS | 20% | 57% |
| Improving Education | 26% | 48% |
| Reducing Unemployment | 11% | 37% |
| Helping Manufacturing Industry | 21% | 49% |
| *Which party will . . .* | | |
| Make you better off | 33% | 33% |
| Run the economy well | 45% | 45% |
| *Fourth-term fears of Tory Government* | | |
| Will privatise the NHS | 62% | |
| Will increase VAT to 22% | 58% | |
| Unemployment will rise to 3.5 million | 65% | |

*Source*: NOP polls for Labour Party, February 1992

recent general elections for governments to lose rather than gain ground in a campaign, caution was understandable. Conservatives were also aware of how sudden upturns in government popularity in the opinion polls in 1970 and 1974 had faded by polling day.

The much-vaunted power of the Prime Minister to dissolve at a time favourable to his government assumes (a) that he has plenty of time, (b) that his party has a substantial lead in the polls and (c) that the economic conditions are good. After November none of these conditions applied. From October most people – the No 12 committee, the commentators and the Labour campaigners – seem to have regarded April 9 as polling day and to have planned accordingly. Because this likelihood was never authoritatively denied, it became something of a challenge for John Major. Would he delay again, until May 7 or even till June, as Mr Lamont appeared to want? Not to call an election in April might once again suggest uncertainty and a fear of meeting the verdict of the electorate. Debates in the Commons became increasingly rowdy, and there were reports that investors were holding off until a new government was elected. On March 8, Douglas Hurd called publicly for an election to restore economic confidence.

But Mr Major's position was not an enviable one. One reason for not dissolving in 1991 – the promise of an economic recovery in 1992 – had not been delivered. Indeed, in February, official figures revealed a fall in GNP of 2.4 percent, the largest for 60 years. By early January 1992 Mr Major accepted that the earlier Treasury forecasts had been too optimistic; there would be no visible signs of economic recovery until the second half of the year, when it would be too late to hold an election. Government spokesmen would have to content themselves with arguing that the conditions for recovery were now in place rather than pointing to evidence that recovery was under way. Conservative ministers and strategists still expected to win – just. Few at the centre of the Labour campaign expected an outright victory. But they could reasonably expect to deny the Conservatives a majority; if there was a hung parliament, John Major had apparently cut the Conservatives off from most of the minor parties. Because he had made clear that he would not tinker with the Union, or bring in proportional representation. Labour seemed to have a better chance of making the post-election deals needed in a hung parliament.

Few governments willingly continue into the fifth year of a parliament. The 1945 government did, but since then only the parliaments of 1959 and October 1974 have entered a fifth year. In both cases the governments appeared to be hanging on, hoping that the tide would turn in their favour. John Major was now in a poor position. Like Mr Callaghan in 1979, he was calling an election when the opinion polls and the economic indicators were pointing the wrong way and were indeed worse than for the election dates that he had turned down earlier. When Mrs Thatcher asked for a dissolution in May 1987 unemployment was falling, living standards had been improving steadily, inflation was low and, of course, her party was enjoying a high lead in the opinion polls. Rarely had a government appeared to so mistime the political-economic cycle.

NOTES

1.    W. Miller *et al.*, *How Voters Change* (Oxford: Clarendon Press, 1990).

# 6 The Deceptive Battle: March–April 1992

The election had been long awaited. By the end of February the parliament had lasted longer than any in peacetime since the quinquennial Act of 1911, except for the full five-year term of 1959– 64. Until the end of February the media speculated on a May 7 or June 11 contest but then stories began to leak out about Conservative booking of poster sites. The election date was an open secret well before it was announced.

On Budget day, March 10, a statement was published that the Prime Minister was to see the Queen at 7.30 p.m. on Wednesday, March 11. However at the last moment it was revealed that the time had been advanced to noon. The Cabinet met briefly at 11 a.m., and at 12.30, on his return from Buckingham Palace to Downing Street, John Major told the date, April 9, to the waiting cameramen:

'There is a lot that I want to do in this country. There is a lot that we can do to make this country an even better place to live in . . . . We have a stack of new ideas to take government closer to the people and make sure that people have more choice, more opportunity. Those are the themes we will be putting forward to the people.'

Then, in a folksy way, he went over to chat with a party of school children saying that, although it was not his real home, Downing Street was a very nice place to live in. The announcement gave April 27 for the meeting of Parliament and May 6 for the Queen's Speech. It was noted that this allowed two weeks longer pause than usual after the voting, largely because of the Easter break but possibly, some suggested, to allow for the possible complications of a hung parliament.

The decision to hold the election on April 9 had long been taken. But when was it to be announced? There was no question of surprising the Opposition, but the visit to the Queen and the official statement had to be delayed for two reasons. The Budget was due on March 10. The broadcasting organisations would switch to their election rules for allocating time as soon as the announcement was made. The civil service too would move towards its election stance; ministers remain ministers but by convention civil servants present them only with essential business; new announcements of policy are not normally made through the government machine once the date for dissolution is known. Perhaps because, in contrast to 1983 and 1987, the outcome was so much in doubt, some civil servants were said this time to have been exceptionally scrupulous in distancing themselves from their ministers as soon as polling day was declared. At the top level they became occupied with preparing papers for whatever government the election might produce and it was commented that they were putting more effort into their task than in 1983 or 1987.

Parliament met for three days after the announcement, hurriedly clearing such business as could be agreed non-controversially. The only major casualty of the dissolution was the Asylum Bill; Labour would not allow it to pass because the government would not concede sufficient safeguards over appeal procedures. But the controversial Education (Schools) Bill and an Army Bill were rushed through their final stages in a truncated form; and £100 million extra of public spending commitments, on top of those made in the Budget, were hastily announced on March 11.

In the House of Commons on March 12 Mr Kinnock challenged Mr Major to a television debate.

'Why will he not debate [his] record? Is it because he is ashamed of it, or because he is afraid of it? . . . . Why does he not join me and the Leader of the Liberals and say to the broadcasting organisations "We have nothing to fear from the British people. Let's fix a date. Let's get on with it".'

Mr Major laughed off the proposal as the time-honoured trick of 'every party politician that expects to lose' and, quoting *Love's Labour Lost*, suggested that Mr Kinnock 'draweth out the thread of his verbosity' in such a way that neither he nor Mr Ashdown would get a word in edgeways. Mr Patten argued that 'we are not operating a presidential system' but Mr Major would be available for questions.

Mr Kinnock was able to launch Labour's assault at a March 12 press conference in London and then in Edinburgh on March 13 where the Scottish Labour Party was meeting. In a rousing speech he denounced the Conservatives' 'recession election' and Mr Lamont's 'incompetent 20p bribe'. He promised to 'invest, invest, invest' and he attacked the fear engendered by past Conservative policies. 'We will make a fresh start. It is time for a change. It is time for Labour.'

The Conservative campaign effectively began at Torquay where the party's Central Council was holding its routine spring gathering on March

13 and 14. Each of the leading ministers rallied the faithful with well-honed attacks on Labour. Mr Heseltine put in a star turn on the first day, mocking Mr Kinnock, as always wrong 'not on the little things but on the big things of our time, defence and Europe'.

Mr Major provided the climax. There was the standard attack on Labour. He suggested that PR stood for Paddy's Roundabout: 'We won't be joining him for the ride' (thus setting the scene for his onslaught three weeks later, linking any hung parliament to a Lib-Lab pact). But he offered a more uplifting finale.

'I want to bring into being a different kind of country, to bury for ever old divisions in Britain between north and south, blue-collar and white-collar, polytechnic and university. They're old-style, old hat.'

In a *Frost on Sunday* TV interview on March 15 Neil Kinnock claimed that he had changed his mind on Europe before the 1983 election and boasted of the significant alterations in party policy since he became Leader. However he argued that if Labour had won in 1983 the country would have become significantly better off. Chris Patten described Mr Kinnock's remarks as 'a staggering blunder . . . . you certainly can't trust him when he says he really has abandoned all the cranky notions that Labour argued so passionately for in their 1983 programme'.

On March 15 John Major gave the first of four informal *Meet John Major* meetings where, sitting on a bar-stool, he took unscripted questions from an invited audience in front of the television cameras within a large transportable stage set. Central Office saw it as 'a high-wire venture' – it would show off his relaxed competence but it could easily meet with accidents. The first gathering in his own Huntingdon was with sympathetic constituents and it was criticised as too stage-managed and pat-ball. A more headline-grabbing gimmick was used by Paddy Ashdown when on Sunday, March 29, he went by high-speed catamaran to address a meeting in Boulogne and to emphasise his party's European credentials.

The parties quickly set in train their election routines. For the Liberal Democrats on every weekday there was a 6.55 a.m. meeting before the daily press conference held at the National Liberal Club at 7.15. At 8 o'clock the Strategy Group[1] met at the party headquarters in Cowley Street, and at 8.30 Paddy Ashdown went off on his campaigning. The Management team met at 10 a.m. and the Media team at 11. At 5 p.m. the Strategy Group reassembled and at 5.30 the Management team made its final decisions on nuts and bolts. At 10 p.m. there was a hand over to an overnight team which would analyse newspapers. At about 11 p.m.

Paddy Ashdown and Des Wilson would foregather to settle any outstanding problems.

The Labour Party gave its first press conference at Walworth Road on March 12 but by March 16 it had moved many of its activities to an elaborate suite constructed on the second floor at 4 Millbank, a refurbished office block 100 yards from Parliament, which also houses many operations by the BBC and other broadcasting organisations. Briefings on the press and the polls were prepared for a 6.45 a.m. meeting under Jack Cunningham. At 7.15 a.m. there was a meeting to plan the press conference. The press conference at 7.45 a.m. was sometimes delayed or disturbed by the arrival of the journalists being bussed from the Liberal Democrat gathering. It was also disturbed by the departure less than half-an-hour later of the journalists seeking to make their way through the security arrangements at 32 Smith Square for the Conservative conference. Neil Kinnock would stay around chatting and making arrangements for half-an-hour before launching on his day's journeying. At 9.45 a.m. the Campaign Management Team[2] met briefly with Jack Cunningham back in Walworth Road. It gathered again for its main discussion at 7.30 p.m.

The Conservatives started with an internal 7 a.m. meeting to review the press and opinion polls, in preparation for a 7.30 meeting to brief the Prime Minister and the other participants at the press conference. After the 8.30 press conference a smaller group assembled in the Prime Minister's room to settle any big strategic issues, as well as to confirm the programme for future press conferences. The Prime Minister then set forth on his travels and later that morning, after a larger co-ordination meeting, Chris Patten helicoptered to his Bath constituency for most of the day. At 4 p.m. there was a 'Spin' meeting, a small group engaged in tactical thinking. At 6 p.m. another meeting agreed the details of the next day's handouts and cleared the decks for a meeting at 7.30 or later with the Prime Minister in Downing Street. But exhaustion seems to have led to the abandonment of a routine late-night meeting. The Conservative campaign was to receive a lot of advice, solicited and unsolicited. Former campaign consultants and tabloid newspaper editors eagerly proffered suggestions about how the adverse message of the opinion polls could be reversed. John Wakeham sometimes acted as a lightning conductor. He had a daily lunch with Sir Tim Bell, Sir Gordon Reece and others at Lord McAlpine's house, round the corner from Central Office. Editors and leading businessmen were among the guests and could go away feeling that they had been informed and that they had been heard.

In a bold move to recover ground lost during the near term campaign, John Smith produced a full-scale alternative budget on March 16 with much fanfare (which stole coverage that the Liberal Democrats were expecting for their manifesto). It confirmed the party's plans to raise the top rate of tax from 40 percent to 50 percent and to remove the exemption of top incomes from the 9 percent National Insurance Contribution. By taxing the rich considerably more and the poor a very little less, Mr Smith could boast that eight taxpayers out of ten, including everyone earning less than

*Table 6.1   Main daily campaign themes*

| Date | | Conservative | Labour | Liberal Democrats |
|---|---|---|---|---|
| **March** | | | | |
| W | 11 | | Attack budget | |
| | | | NHS (Georgina Norris ad) | |
| Th | 2 | | Launch *Time for Change* | Education – 1p tax rise |
| | | | Industry | |
| F | 13 | (Tax) | Investment/Economy | Tax/Economy |
| | | (Attack Georgina Norris ad) | Poll Tax | Attack Georgina Norris ad |
| Sa | 14 | Torquay launch – no deals | Budget | |
| Su | 15 | Major 'talkabout': Kinnock | Tory 'hidden manifesto' | London rally. PR |
| | | No deals, no PR, | | |
| | | no devolution | | |
| M | 16 | Pensions | Shadow Budget launch | Manifesto launch |
| Tu | 17 | Education – '39 Steps' | Education | Tax |
| | | PPB: 'Major, the Journey' | | |
| W | 18 | Manifesto launch | Manifesto launch | Economic recovery/ |
| | | | | investment |
| Th | 19 | Tax | Economic Recovery | |
| F | 20 | Cost of Labour | Poll Tax/Fair Rates | Inflation |
| | | Labour 'mob rule' | | Housing |
| Sa | 21 | Lab tax/spending plans | Minimum wage | Education |
| Su | 22 | Thatcher at rally | Policies for business | Education |
| | | Record defended | (business brunch) | C-UU deal 'sinister' |
| M | 23 | Mortgages/Housing | Jobs | Education |
| | | Union power | VAT | C-UU deal |
| Tu | 24 | Europe/Foreign Affairs | Health | Education |
| | | | Training/Manufacturing | |
| | | | PPB: Jennifer | |
| W | 25 | Labour PPB/Kinnock | Health Budget launched | Health-attack negative |
| | | PPB: ball and chain | | campaigns |
| Th | 26 | (Unions) | NHS: dossier of new cases | 'Green issues' |
| | | Jennifer – mole hunting | Jennifer – mole-hunting, | PPB: education |
| | | | Julie Hall | |
| F | 27 | 'People power'– vision | NHS – can't trust Tories | Recession |
| | | for Britain | (Jennifer) | Leeds rally |
| | | | Glasgow rally | |
| Sa | 28 | | | (Europe) |
| Su | 29 | Leicester rally: socialists | Women's issues | Ashdown in Boulogne: |
| | | and socialism | (Mother's Day) | Europe PR |
| M | 30 | Tax | Tax – 80% better off | PR |
| | | 'Nightmare on Kinnock | PPB: Kinnock & team | |
| | | Street' | | |
| Tu | 31 | Tax | Business failures | Attacks 'wasted vote' |
| | | Pay (*Daily Mail* story) | Education Plan launch | argument |
| **April** | | | | |
| W | 1 | Defence | NHS | PPB: winnable seats |
| | | LD trojan horse | Sheffield rally | |

| Date | Conservative | Labour | Lib Dems |
|------|-------------|--------|----------|
| **April** | | | |
| Th 2 | Government record Crime/Law & Order | Consensus government, PR Poll Tax PPB? | Constitution, PR |
| F 3 | Economy PPB: Winter of Discontent (Labour phone number) | Outline Labour Queen's Speech Training | Economy |
| Sa 4 | Attack on PR Business | Poll Tax | |
| Su 5 | Wembley Rally: 'Wake up, Britain' | Millbank Centre gathering PR, constitutional change, consensus government | Prefers coalition to pact (Leak to Monday papers on 4 cabinet posts demand) |
| M 6 | Constitution: the Union, PR, Hung parliaments | Recession Housing/mortgages PPB | Education Terms for deal |
| Tu 7 | Wembley Rally Economy, Immigration '10 reasons to vote Tory' PPB | NHS Blackburn rally | St Austell rally: Tory bullying squeeze LD vote |
| W 11 | Predict win | Predict win | Taunton rally – negative campaign |

£21,000 a year, would be better off (though, of course, the Conservatives disputed this).

In a debate on TV that evening, Mr Lamont was outclassed by Mr Smith and the alternative budget was sympathetically received. The Conservatives later reproached themselves with being slow to respond with a detailed statistical refutation of Mr Smith's figures – this did not come for four days, by which time the campaign had moved on to other themes.

Labour felt that Mr Smith had contained the inevitable challenge 'where's the money coming from?' and that their 'carefully costed' programme should not frighten the voters. But both parties knew from their private polls that tax could well prove the key issue of the campaign. The Conservatives were to revert to it at almost every press conference. On March 20 Norman Lamont published his response to John Smith's 'Budget' but this failed to offer any knock-out counter. More promising was the costing of Labour's manifesto which followed on March 22; 'The Price of Labour – £1250 a year for Every Family' was produced to reinforce the ubiquitous poster 'Labour's Double Whammy – "More Taxes, Higher Prices".'

However, Mr Major's avowed goal of lowering income tax to 20p came under some criticism. On March 23 the *Guardian* argued that the budget deficit in the coming year would be £32bn. (or even more on some calculations) not the Treasury's forecast £28bn. If the *Guardian*'s revelation was designed to help the Labour Party some observers commented that it might have the opposite effect. Any suggestion of financial crisis was more likely to frighten the voters into voting Conservative, even if the Conservatives were to blame.

The *Financial Times* reacted interestingly to the *Guardian*'s figures:

> It is the economy, not the government's finances, that is currently in a sorry state. The UK has suffered the deepest recession of any European country; but it also has one of the lowest outstanding stocks of government debt as a percentage of gross domestic product. Moreover both parties are committed to seemingly prudent restrictions on public borrowing.

In private Conservatives were quite frank about their problems in discussing the economy. They were dogged by the recession but they wanted to dent the credibility of Labour's tax and spending proposals. Unfortunately John Smith consistently outscored Norman Lamont in debate. Since the party's main economic spokesman lacked plausibility the message had to be carried by John Major and Michael Heseltine with support from David Mellor and John Maples. Norman Lamont was unhappy about accusations that he was being sheltered from the media and threatened to undertake media interviews without reference to Central Office.

By March 30 when the Conservatives felt forced to allow Mr Lamont into the limelight again, the Chancellor admitted that it might be a long time before further tax reductions were possible and he also seemed to cast doubt on the early achievement of Mr Major's firmly declared goal of zero inflation.

Parties are eager to launch their manifestos as soon as they can so that candidates can quote from them in the constituencies. But, however fully drafted in advance, they have to wait until after the election announcement for final repolishing and approval.

The Liberal Democrats issued their manifesto, *Changing Britain for Good*, on Monday, March 16. They boasted of their realistic 'hairshirt policies' for national recovery. As expected the document promised wide-ranging constitutional reform. It also promised a more positive role in the European Community. It pledged to add one penny on the basic rate of tax to fund improvements in education. It promised also to repeal a number of the government's education and health reforms, notably to end the City Technology Colleges, general practitioners' fund-holding scheme and the hospital trusts. Des Wilson withdrew Paddy Ashdown from a Channel 4 news interview with Jon Snow when the programme decided not to lead with the Liberal manifesto.

The Conservative Party delayed their manifesto by a day lest it be over-shadowed by Labour's alternative budget expected on March 17; Labour in fact had advanced its budget to March 16, fearing that it would be over-shadowed by the Conservative manifesto. Thus the Conservative manifesto emerged simultaneously with Labour's on March 18. It was a 30,000-word document, entitled *The Best Future for Britain*. Most commentators saw it as worthy but dull, finding that, in essence, it invited the electorate to vote for more of the same; it was considered short of large themes. It had nothing on constitutional or electoral matters and its policies for education, health and housing were essentially a continuation of current policies. Its lack of zip was seen, at the time, as a symbol of the Conservative campaign. The *Financial Times* took the view that it was twice as long and expensive as the Labour manifesto but not twice as good. John Major replied to questions at the press conference that the manifesto was very much his own work, 'It's all me'. The manifesto proposed to sell off British Coal and some services of British Rail. It would establish an Urban Regeneration Agency for the cities and introduce a rents-to-mortgages scheme for council tenants. On health it promised to reduce waiting times for certain operations and to boost resources; it gave assurances that there would be no privatisation and no further structural changes to the service. It also proposed a Millennium Fund to raise money for the arts and heritage.

The Labour manifesto, too, *It's Time to Get Britain Working Again*, had no surprises. It underlined the party's support for the European Community and for membership of the Exchange Rate Mechanism. It emphasised the party's commitment to investing in education and training and it promised a package to foster industrial recovery as well as a Bill of Rights and a Freedom of Information Act. It also said that in the first session a Scottish parliament would be established with tax-raising powers. The party confirmed that it had abandoned unilateralism and that it would keep nuclear weapons 'as long as others have them'. The party promised a £1.6 billion investment in the National Health Service. It would also retain ballots before strikes and for the election of union officials (there will be no return to the trade union legislation of the 1970s). There would be no renationalisation of the corporations and firms which had been privatised by Conservative governments, but they would be subject to more regulation and competition. The role of government was 'not to replace the market, but to ensure the market works properly'. Labour would set up a national investment bank and regional development agencies. It would also introduce a minimum wage and end compulsory competitive tendering.

The *Guardian* commented:

> How on earth do you judge a manifesto? As a good read, like a book?
> By those lights – now that all three booklets are to hand – the Liberal
> Democrat essay far out-distances its competitors with a fizz of ideas and
> an absence of fudge. There are plenty of good little things in the Labour
> window. But the Labour and Tory divide also remains distinct. A Tory
> record of economic management, there to be judged: a blankness of
> detail on policies, like BR privatisation, that are bound to be politically
> dangerous; a jovial sense of continuing energy, but attached to little you
> could call conviction.

Rarely have manifestos made less impact. Almost all the significant
policy points in each document had been leaked or splashed in advance.
Those who had slaved over the texts commented ruefully on the negligible
reaction to their words. But at least there were no significant gaffes to be
exploited. The key election points of the Conservatives' 'You can't trust
Labour'; 'You can't trust Mr Kinnock'; and 'Labour's Tax Bombshell'
were already well launched. Labour too had made plain its themes,
'Save the National Health Service'; 'Increase pensions and child benefit';
'Remember the recession and the poll-tax'; 'Modernise not Privatise';
'Time for a Change'. The Liberal Democrats were more innovative with
their insistence on an extra 1p on the income tax to pay for educational
improvements, but, as always, the party's other proposals were not taken
very seriously by the press. 'The Liberals get away with murder,' said one
senior journalist. 'I can't treat Paddy like I treat Kinnock or Major, as
someone who might be Prime Minister with a working majority. I can't,
with a straight face, press home serious "What would you do?" questions.'
Roy Hattersley put it more cruelly on March 12: since Mr Ashdown was
'never going to have a foot in the door of No 10 he can say whatever he
likes, whatever is most convenient'.

Each party chose a theme for its carefully staged morning press conference. Chris Patten, Jack Cunningham and Des Wilson always took the chair
for their parties (except at weekends when the Prime Minister took over
from Chris Patten and Bryan Gould took over from Jack Cunningham).
The routine was for two or three spokesmen to make statements usually
lasting two or three minutes each (and handed out as press releases) and
then to answer questions. Chris Patten was partially successful in insisting
that the early questions should focus on the statements but inevitably the
national headlines provided the staple fare of questions; these came on
the whole from the most senior press and television correspondents. The

press conferences were good-humoured and well-attended occasions and no spokesman was seriously caught out, partly because of the way the conferences were managed. Robin Oakley of *The Times* commented after the election.

> Both Mr Patten and, even more ruthlessly, Dr Cunningham, suppressed supplementaries. It was particularly irritating at the Labour press conferences, which opened with up to five statements read out by front-bench spokesmen, sharply limiting the question period and allowing Dr Cunningham the excuse that it was 'selfish' for any journalist to seek to come back on an unanswered question in the limited time.
>
> The one time John Major faced any difficulty was when the *Independent*, the BBC and *The Times* all pursued the same question on the overall tax burden during one press conference and repeated a question which was not fully answered. Organised 'gang bangs' are not an attractive proposition. But if all continue to pursue our own separate agendas on these occasions, constantly switching subjects, the politicians will continue to have an easy ride.[3]

Labour and the Liberal Democrats kept almost completely to their original plans for the press conferences. The Conservatives were much more flexible and half of their press conferences were rescheduled – often to the great annoyance of the ministers involved. No fewer than eight of the nineteen morning conferences made Labour's tax plans or economic recovery the central theme. Bored journalists groaned audibly when the Conservatives reverted insistently to tax and when Labour harped yet again on the health service. But Mr Heseltine was unapologetic at the March 28 press conference:

> 'It's all right for the Conservatives to talk about tax in week one, to talk about tax in week two and to talk about tax in week three because otherwise if a Labour government won the whole country would talk about nothing except tax for the next five years.'

Labour, in deference to the poll findings, put John Smith together with Neil Kinnock on the platform whenever possible. Chris Patten arranged, when he could, for the Prime Minister to be accompanied by Douglas Hurd, Michael Heseltine or Kenneth Clarke.

Mr Major appeared at 17 out of the 19 Conservative morning conferences, Mr Kinnock at 16 out of 21 for Labour and Mr Ashdown at 16 out of 21 for the Liberal Democrats. Each Leader gave a well-heralded press conference in Scotland.

The campaign was relatively free from external distractions. But for several days from March 23 the break-up of the Duke of York's marriage drove the election from the front pages of the tabloids while the death on March 29 and the funeral on April 1 of Earl Spencer, father of the Princess of Wales, provided another sustained Royal distraction. In the wider world the struggles in Yugoslavia, the referendum in South Africa, and the American presidential primaries drew some attention in the media – but nothing occurred to provide a major text for partisan comment in the campaign. Perhaps the main rival to the election was England's struggle to the final ( March 25) of the World Cup cricket competition: it was indeed suggested that, had England won, it would have redounded to the advantage of the cricket-loving John Major (some drew parallels with the World Cup defeat in soccer on the eve of the 1970 poll).

Before the 1987 election the White House had intervened in the election, with President Reagan conspicuously snubbing Mr Kinnock and lavishing praise on Mrs Thatcher. Less was heard in 1992, although on the day the election was announced George Bush did say:

'It is not for the U.S. President to try to intervene in elections in any other country, but the respect I have for the Prime Minister knows no bounds. John Major is a superb leader.'

John Major in his speeches and Neil Kinnock, who gave three formal lectures among his campaign efforts, covered a wide range of issues in some detail. But their words attracted little attention. The public usually heard only the one-liners on the themes (mainly negative ones) that the media or the spin doctors had decided were central to the contest.

There were many subjects which played little or no part in the campaign. Party differences over whether the fourth Trident submarine should be built were little publicised and a Tory attack on Labour's CND connections did not catch media attention. Indeed it was, for the first time since 1979, a defence-free and foreign policy-free contest. 'That was a triumph for us,' said one senior Labour front-bencher, 'they were issues from which we could not possibly profit.' Gerald Kaufman was offered a press conference but turned it down, saying that Labour shouldn't draw attention to foreign affairs. Europe (which a few months earlier, in the days of Mrs Thatcher and of Maastricht, had seemed so important) attracted little notice. Despite the Greens, the environment was not argued about

'D'you think Labour has come clean or is it the Tory dirty tricks department?'

Jak: *Mail on Sunday*, 5 April 1992

at the national level. Even the poll-tax excited far less comment than might have been expected. The unions were very quiet and, despite an attack from Michael Howard on March 19, their role excited little discussion.

A dirty campaign had been predicted but very few personal smears were made public although there were allegations of deliberate rumour-mongering and of destabilising hate mail to prominent figures or their wives. There were repeated suggestions that one or other of the tabloids was going to launch a sex scandal and the names of leading figures in each of the parties were suggested as targets. The fact that no stories reached publication may have been due to implicit non-aggression pacts or to fear of the libel laws. On April 4 the *Independent*, citing a hint in the previous day's *Sun* about a highplaced 'Romeo MP', anticipated the publication of new revelations, perhaps in a German magazine. It was later suggested that there was some leaning on the press from Conservative sources who feared that such stories might have a counter-productive impact.[4] Paddy Ashdown, after all, had seemed to have been more helped than harmed when an outdated private affair had been dragged up at the beginning of February (see p. 92).

There were several reports about the campaign in Cheltenham where the black barrister, John Taylor, was defending a marginal seat but immigration and race hardly came into the election at the national level, although Kenneth Baker on March 26 did talk about the need to check the abuse of asylum seekers and on April 3 Lord Whitelaw refused to speak on behalf of Sir Nicholas Fairbairn in Perth after the latter had exploded:

# 5 YEARS HARD LABOUR.

**TAXES UP**

**MORTGAGES UP**

**PRICES UP**

CONSERVATIVE ☒

# LABOUR'S DOUBLE WHAMMY

**1. MORE TAXES**

**2. HIGHER PRICES**

CONSERVATIVE

## VOTE FOR RECOVERY.

## NOT THE START OF A NEW RECESSION.

Just as recovery is under way, Labour would start a new recession. A Conservative win will end uncertainty, raise confidence and speed Britain ahead. Labour would put taxes up, mortgages up, inflation up and strikes up. That's why 90% of business leaders say that Britain needs the Conservatives to keep Britain moving forward.

**VOTE CONSERVATIVE ☒**

# WHAT DOES THE CONSERVATIVE PARTY OFFER A WORKING CLASS KID FROM BRIXTON?

**THEY MADE HIM PRIME MINISTER.**

No wonder John Major believes everyone should have an equal opportunity.

**CONSERVATIVE ☒**

# Sorry, but we're going to have to let you go.

Since Mr. Major got his job, 850,000 have lost theirs.

Labour

# Tory Defence Policy. "It's not our recession."

Labour

## Tory Health Policy. More Plastic Surgeons.

Labour want a health service that can afford to treat its patients, not one that treats patients that can afford to pay.
Labour will stop the privatisation of the NHS and create a truly national health service.

Labour

## Vote today to rebuild the economy.

Labour will end the recession this year with a £1 billion Economic Recovery Package.

Labour

'Under a Labour government this country would be swamped with immigrants of every colour and race and on any excuse of asylum or bogus marriage or just plain deception.'

Conservative Central Office made available details of the left-wing past of particular Labour candidates. But compared to past elections, little was done to terrify the voters with demon figures. Tony Benn, Ken Livingstone and Arthur Scargill attracted negligible national publicity. The eloquent Mr Benn made only two speeches outside his Chesterfield constituency. Trade union leaders were silent at Labour's request.

It was not a rowdy campaign although one of the Prime Minister's staff commented later, 'It felt pretty rowdy at the time'. Mr Major was hit by an egg on two occasions and Mrs Thatcher by a bunch of daffodils on one. ('I am very sorry for the daffodils,' she commented.) The roughest scenes were in Bolton on March 19 where protesters jostled Mr and Mrs Major in the market square and fired the Prime Minister into an attack on 'the ugly face of Labour which I hate', and in Luton on March 28 when, shouted down by militants, John Major cried 'Look at them. They want to take the country back to socialism. Don't let the people who take to the streets take your country.'

There were a couple of reports of Conservative candidates being physically attacked. Sir Tom Arnold, the Conservative vice-chairman was badly bruised in Hazel Grove. But despite talk of burglary and bugging the extent of vandalism at local headquarters seems to have been even smaller than in previous contests. A Conservative legal adviser noted that there was less 'rushing to lawyers' over alleged libels or breaches of electoral law.

The secondary spokesmen embarrassed their parties with fewer blunders or contradictions than in some past campaigns. Mr Prescott admitted in an *Election Call* phone-in on March 30 that Labour's minimum wage proposals would result in some job losses. Mr Hattersley spoke on March 18 of re-nationalising water. Both were promptly repudiated by party headquarters and the media did little to follow up the *Daily Mail*'s exploitation of these lapses.

Mr Baker slipped temporarily from the Conservative line of refusing to contemplate anything but outright victory, admitting at a press conference on April 2 that 1992 was more important than 1983 or 1987 'because there is the possibility of a change of government'.

Simon Hughes on *Election Call* on March 25 deviated from the party line on defence cuts and nuclear weapons but meekly accepted Paddy Ashdown's amiable rebuke at the next day's press conference.

The clumsiness of Norman Lamont in his media appearances after the

Budget and of William Waldegrave during the Jennifer's ear affair led to their being removed from prominence for much of the election. But at the same time Labour ensured a low profile for Mr Kaufman, Mr Prescott and Mr Meacher.

The election was not one for great oratory. Few speeches were quoted at length, which may not have been surprising when even the best one-liners at press conferences failed to be reported. Mr Major was at his most eloquent in Manchester on March 19 when, warning his audience against a Labour victory, he parodied a 1983 speech of Neil Kinnock:

'I warn you not to be qualified. I warn you not to be successful. I warn you not to buy shares. I warn you not to be self-employed. I warn you not to accept promotion. I warn you not to save. I warn you not to buy a pension. I warn you not to own a home.'

He also provided a memorable phrase on March 30 when he spoke of a 'nightmare on Kinnock Street' (an allusion to the cult horror film 'Nightmare on Elm Street', which was to receive its British TV premiere the following night); the phrase was quickly adopted by the *Sun* as the title of its April 8 apocalyptic feature on life under Labour.

Mr Kinnock at Sheffield spoke to his rally audience rather than to the wider electorate. But he moved his enthusiastic followers with:

'All over the country people are coming to Labour because they know we have the policies, we have the team, we have the determination to get Britain working again. People are saying we can't go on with a Government that caused recession, continued the recession and doesn't have a clue how to get out of recession. We can't go on with a Government that has allowed important parts of the National Health Service to become dependent on fund-raising by charities. We can't go on with a Prime Minister who in one breath promises tax cuts, and a Chancellor who, in the next breath, says there is no room for manoeuvre.'

Mr Ashdown was an effective speaker at rallies, trying always to sound positive. At Bath, on April 4, he said:

'These are the issues which this election should have been about. About the opportunity for education, and our responsibility to fund it adequately. About the needs for new skills, to deal with the new technologies and the new, competitive world. About individual rights, and equality of opportunity. About the threat of pollution, and the measures we can take to deal with it now. About our future in Europe, which must not be pushed to one side. And about the quality of our democracy, and how we raise its standards. That is what this election should have been about. Not about the bickering and the insults, but about the future, and what it means. And when we cast our vote next Thursday, that is what our vote should be about.'

A new feature of 1992 was the widespread use of large posters, paid for centrally and put up without reference to the constituency parties. Provided that the posters were distributed nationally and not targeted on marginal seats, and provided that there was no reference to local candidates or issues, these advertisements were believed to fall outside the law limiting constituency expenditure. The Conservatives put up 4,500 posters: they had booked the sites (in the name of major commercial products) three weeks in advance of the election announcement. Labour's effort was half that size and the Liberal Democrats one tenth.

|                  | 48 sheet sites | Cost   |
|------------------|----------------|--------|
| Conservative     | 4500           | £1.5m  |
| Labour           | 2200           | £0.5m  |
| Liberal Democrats | 500           | £0.17m |

The Natural Law Party used smaller sites (32, 16, or 4 sheet) but more of them. It was estimated that they had 6,500 sites at a cost of £0.25m.

Advertisements can be a challenge to graffiti artists. Two were arrested for changing YOU CAN'T TRUST LABOUR into YOU CAN TRUST LABOUR. Another widespread variant was to add to the suggestion of industrial unrest of LABOUR IN – EVERYBODY OUT, the additional word CELEBRATING.

Rival advertisers were quick to jump on the bandwagon, the Conservative's 'Double Whammy' reappearing to advertise furniture with the slogan '1. Radical Products, 2. Conservative Prices', while the *Guardian* put up posters which parodied those of both the parties.

Newspaper advertising was less extensive than in previous elections. The Liberal Democrats selectively placed six full-page advertisements in the *Guardian*, the *Independent*, the *Observer* and *The Times* but only used one paper for each advertisement in the course of the campaign. Labour placed 83 full-page advertisements, as well as a number of smaller ones in the *Guardian* appealing for funds. Apart from one burst on March 19 the Conservatives almost eschewed press advertising until the last week when, under pressure from editors and at favourable rates (and financed by anxious last-minute donors), they bought full-pages in all the nationals, bringing their total for the campaign to 54. In 1987 they had splurged on eleven full-pages in each of the main nationals in the last four days before the vote. They boasted that this time they spent less than Labour. In 1987 it was calculated that the Conservatives were responsible for over 75 percent of the media spend on election advertising. In 1992 the percentage was under 40 percent.

The Natural Law campaign launched itself cryptically on March 16 with double-page advertisements in some newspapers claiming to prove by equation that Vedic Science offered 'The Source of All Order and Harmony'; four days later the Natural Law Party came into the open as an election campaigner, taking double-page spreads to set out its entire unworldly manifesto opposite pictures of 119 of its candidates.

Interest groups entered into the campaign with quite extensive press advertising. Some people thought that the NALGO campaign of 76 full-page displays was counterproductive;[5] like one from the Inland Revenue Staff Federation it may have served mainly to link Labour with the unions. But there were also advertising campaigns from doctors and from the anti-hunting lobby which could hardly have helped the Conservatives. On the other side the Institute of Directors put full page anti-Labour advertisements in the quality press.

There were also well-publicised surveys which showed the disillusion with government policies among the professions – notably doctors and nurses as well as teachers at every level – and fear of Labour among the business community.

When nominations closed on March 17, 2948 candidates had been nominated – a record number. Except for the Nationalists in Scotland, fourth and fifth parties made little impact on the campaign, although 841 were nominated in Great Britain and 89 in Northern Ireland. The Greens fielded 256 candidates but, in contrast to their role in the 1989 European election, they attracted little attention except for their one television broadcast (see p. 174). The same could be said of Michael Meadowcroft's 73 true believing Liberals who, despite targetting Liberal Democrats, failed to cost them any seats. More splash was created by the Maharishi's Natural Law Party campaign which put up 309 candidates; but despite its expensive poster and press advertising campaign, and its endorsement by the Beatle, George Harrison, it only drew the attention appropriate to an effort which was to win an average of 0.4 percent of the vote, less even than the achievement of the 30 candidates with Monster Raving Loony labels.

The most serious challenge to the established parties arose from the six deselected MPs. David Nellist, one of two expelled Militant members, came a close third in Coventry South-East, Terry Fields in Liverpool Broadgreen, Ron Brown in Leith, and Syd Bidwell in Southall all retained about 10 percent of the vote. The only other outsider to get into double figures was Tommy Sheridan, a Scottish Militant protester who fought Glasgow Pollok from the cell where he was serving a six-month sentence over resistance to the poll-tax; he came second, winning 19 percent of the vote. John Browne, the one deselected Conservative, forfeited his deposit in Winchester. (See pp. 339–43 for minor party performance.) The last surviving MPs from the SDP, John Cartwright and Rosie Barnes, fought Woolwich and Greenwich gallantly (aided by being given a clear run by the Liberal Democrats) but each lost narrowly to Labour.

The campaign in Northern Ireland was, as ever, remarkably detached from everywhere else. Most of the seventeen seats were utterly safe; the interest lay in how the Unionist vote would be shared between the Official and Democratic factions in the three seats where they clashed and in how the vote would split between SDLP and Sinn Fein in the thirteen seats where they battled for Catholic support. The most exciting contest was in the one seat that changed hands, West Belfast, where enough Unionists and others voted tactically for the SDLP's Dr Hendron to oust Sinn Fein's Gerry Adams (who for the duration of the campaign was exempted from the 1988 ban on direct broadcast appearances). The Official Unionists fought a deliberately low profile campaign designed to deprive the Paisleyites and Sinn Fein of the excitement that always benefited them; they felt vindicated by the results.

The United Kingdom campaign intruded in Northern Ireland in two ways. The Conservative Party contested seats for the first time in many years. Most of their 11 candidates fared derisorily but Laurence Kennedy presented a serious and well-reported challenge to the Popular Unionist, James Kilfedder, in North Down. There was local disappointment that John Major never explicitly endorsed the Conservative challenge in Northern Ireland.

However it was the position of the Ulster Unionists in a hung parliament that excited most comment on the British side of the Irish Sea. Both Mr Molyneaux's Official Unionists and Mr Paisley's Democratic Unionists made plain that they would not enter into any coalition and that they would at least abstain to allow whichever party was largest to form a government. Mr Molyneaux said on election eve:

'We would not recklessly say that, unless we get our way on all things, we will bring the government down . . . . We are not demanding anything – the two parties are very well aware of our position. If they don't want to aggravate us and entice us into the opposition lobby, they will know how to avoid those.'

He was plainly referring to the extension of the Anglo-Irish agreement; but he also referred to Labour's promises of devolution for Scotland and made plain that in a hung parliament Northern Ireland would expect comparable treatment.

The betting odds which had started at 4–7 on a Tory clear victory dropped by April 1 to 2–1 against the Tories winning most seats and to 3–1 against on April 8 before ending on April 9 at 4–5 on. The IG futures Index moved downwards as the election advanced.

*Table 6.2    IG Futures Index*

|          | Con | Lab | LB |
|----------|-----|-----|----|
| Mar. 11  | 311 | 306 | 25 |
| Mar. 18  | 302 | 306 | 25 |
| Mar. 25  | 301 | 303 | 24 |
| Apr.  1  | 301 | 303 | 25 |
| Apr.  8  | 291 | 309 | 26 |
| Apr.  9  | 302 | 301 | 23 |

The Stock Exchange fluttered less than might have been expected. The FTSE-100 Index started at 2522 on March 11. It had dipped to 2456 by March 20 but was still at 2440 on March 31. The polls on 'Red Wednesday' pushed it by Friday April 3 to its lowest, 2382. It recovered during polling day to 2436 and, when the results were known on April 10, it jumped to 2572.

Ever since the trade statistics scuppered the Labour Party in the last days of the 1970 campaign, parties have been wary about the routine announcements that come out each month. In 1992 these did not favour the Conservatives, but at least polling day was timed so that they were got out of the way in the first week of the campaign. On March 17 figures showed a 0.7 percent fall in industrial output. On March 19 it transpired that there was a 40,000 rise in unemployment in February, the twenty-second successive month to show an increase. The next day an unchanged inflation figure for February was announced – not the hoped-for continuation of decline.

Ministers put the standard gloss on the statistics but they inevitably fuelled Labour's assault on 'the Conservative-made recession' – or as John Smith put it the Tories' three Rs – 'recession, redundancy, repossession'. The hopeful suggestions of an interest rate cut before April 9 faded as the campaign advanced.

The parties carried further than before their pursuit of star endorsements. The candidatures of Sebastian Coe for the Conservatives and Glenda Jackson for Labour were well publicised. But many other names were invoked: Andrew Lloyd Webber, Richard Branson, the *Coronation Street* actor William Roache, the footballer John Barnes, the rugby player Rob Andrew, the rock star Bill Wyman and the astronomer Patrick Moore gave public support to the Conservatives. The athlete Steve Cram, the disc-jockey Paul Gambaccini, the astrophysicist Stephen Hawking, the violinist Nigel Kennedy and numerous pop and rock stars came out for Labour. But Ian Botham threatened to sue when the *Sun* named him as a Conservative supporter in a front-page exclusive.

David Owen, retiring from Parliament, had a final political fling, repeatedly hinting at what he might do. Before, on April 5, in a *Mail on Sunday* article, he advised people to vote Conservative (although he, in Bow and Poplar, would vote Liberal Democrat to keep Labour out). His main reason was that the Conservatives would better defend the country from the uncountenanced demands of Brussels. But he got scarcely more general publicity than a former spoiler, Enoch Powell, who likened John Major to an inglorious Roman Emperor:

> 'If you vote for the Conservative candidate [in Huntingdon], you betray your country . . . . When the Praetorian soldiers who had murdered Caligula dragged Claudius out of the blanket in which he was hiding to succeed Caligula, he knew better than to disobey them.'

Other figures refrained from rocking the boat. Little was heard from the five living ex-Prime Ministers. The discretion shown in Mrs Thatcher's excursions at the beginning of the campaign as well as in her address to Conservative candidates were greeted with undisguised relief at Central Office.

One argument against an April election had been that it would coincide with the arrival of poll-tax bills. On March 13 figures for the poll-tax in each local authority were released and ten days later the bills began to arrive. The impact seems to have been less than expected; it was, after all, the last year of the poll-tax and the bills were lower than many had feared. Where they were high it may have been the local council, usually

Riddell, *Independent*, 29 March 1992

Labour-controlled, that was blamed rather than the government. Sometimes the Conservatives had to sidestep efforts to get them to apologise for having inflicted the poll-tax on the nation. Labour spokesmen regularly referred to the poll-tax in their litany about Conservative incompetence and heartlessness and suggested that the government's substitute council tax would prove almost as unworkable. The Liberal Democrats joined in the assault but argued that Labour's 'Fair Rates' alternative was about as bad; their own panacea, a local income-tax, was advocated, largely uncriticized – but largely unnoticed.

The Conservatives got a poor press at the end of the first week of the campaign. The *Sunday Times* observed on March 22:

> If the royal separation had not deflected the attention of the nation Labour might now enjoy an unassailable lead.

The *Daily Telegraph* ( March 21) complained, 'The Tory campaign lacks an electric charge' and Mrs Thatcher remarked in Finchley that it was 'bogged down in detail'.

It is hard to tell the story of the election in a narrative way. It lacked pattern or sequence. Some themes were reiterated day after day but not in an exchange of argument or with any development of ideas. The parties reiterated their messages and tried to make occasional points of their opponents stumbles. But the only real confrontation of the campaign was on a very peripheral matter – the war of Jennifer's ear.

On Tuesday, March 24, Labour's election broadcast was designed to launch their strongest theme, the preservation of the National Health Service. Robin Cook, as Labour's shadow health spokesman, was eloquent on the subject and the experience of two small girls, miserable with blocked ear canals, was used to illustrate his case. Child actresses showed one girl getting immediate treatment using private medicine while the other had her NHS operation repeatedly delayed. Labour made plain that the broadcast was based on actual examples and, in an unguarded moment at a preview for journalists, Julie Hall, Mr Kinnock's press secretary, revealed that the unfortunate child was called Jennifer (and on March 26 Miss Hall defended her action in an impulsive intervention at Mr Kinnock's Nottingham press conference). The *Independent* and the *Daily Express* got on to the girl's real name even before the broadcast and pursued her and her parents. The consultant in the case (after trying to phone the Labour Party) made contact with Conservative Central Office who put him in touch with the *Daily Express*. In fact the girl's mother was a Conservative and her grandfather, hearing about the filming, had faxed the Conservative Area Office with a warning some days earlier. From Wednesday to Friday, the press conferences were filled with revelations and arguments about who leaked the name of the family to the media and about the propriety of using such cases. For a moment Peter Hitchens, the key *Daily Express* reporter, became a central campaign figure. Mr Heseltine called

Labour's conduct outrageous and scandalous. Mr Waldegrave likened Labour's behaviour to that of the Nazi propaganda machine. There was also confusion over whether the delay in Jennifer's operation had been due to administrative bungling or to a weekend shortage of specialist nurses. Labour compounded its difficulties by releasing a list of ten other cases, several of which were erroneous or issued without the permission of those involved. The Conservatives, too, compounded their difficulties, first when it emerged that a party official had put the consultant in touch with the press and, later, when William Waldegrave, the Health Secretary, appearing at a prearranged press conference with a team of doctors, revealed this fact and admitted that the Conservatives had, before the film was shown, received that fax from the child's grandfather.

The original film had made an arguable political point in a very powerful way. It did not need the assertion that it was an actual case. Once Mr Kinnock and Miss Hall had revealed that it did refer to a specific case the sequel was inevitable. The argument over who leaked the names and over journalistic ethics, ruthlessly exploited by the Conservative tabloids, masked the essence of the argument and made it extraordinarily difficult for Labour to exploit the NHS issue. The following Sunday, the papers were full of a story that Labour had scrapped a further election broadcast that was to have dealt with health – even though the party had in fact never planned more than one health broadcast. Certainly Labour at first welcomed the row since it highlighted the health issue, propelling it to the top of the issues agenda for the rest of the campaign, and keeping the tax question out of the headlines; later some strategists came to regret what they had done and opinion polls suggested that voters had an adverse reaction to the bickering and slanging. At the same time others regretted that they did not continue to attack the handling of the broadcast by Conservative Central Office and felt that they failed to take advantage of the higher salience of the health issue. What is undeniable is that the broadcast preceded the opinion polls' report of a large Labour lead. Nevertheless the Liberal Democrats, who had ostentatiously refrained from comment on Jennifer's case, felt that they had benefited from standing clear of this petty and irrelevant row.

In the short run the affair jolted the Conservatives. On Saturday, March 28, Cecil Parkinson, Sir Marcus Fox and others in the party publicly criticised the management of the campaign. Mrs Thatcher was reported in the *Sunday Times* to be saying privately that the Tory efforts 'did not have enough oomph, enough whizz, enough steam'. Some Sunday headlines suggested disarray. The first is from the *Observer*:

TOP TORIES GET JITTERS AS CAMPAIGN 'WOBBLES'

TORY ROW OVER CAMPAIGN GROWS (*Sunday Times*)

However other papers had a counter:

TORIES NARROW THE POLL GAP (*Sunday Telegraph*)

LABOUR HALTS NEW HEALTH BROADCAST (*Independent on Sunday*)

MAJOR LEADS POLL REVIVAL (*Sunday Express*)

Michael Heseltine was quick to deny that the Conservative campaign was 'wobbling'. 'What troubles?' he said, 'We have been doing extremely well', and he denounced 'the armchair generals' who were complaining. In fact the suggestion that there were sudden changes in personnel or functions to cope with a lagging campaign had little substance – although there was some Downing Street irritation about some aspects of Central Office efficiency.

It may be worth recording one mid-campaign verdict by the *Economist* on the efforts of Mr Major – and of others.

> Standing on his soapbox, jabbing his finger at hecklers and warning of mob rule, he has seemed a forlorn figure, acting outrage rather than feeling it. When his speech at Birmingham included an attack on Mr Kinnock's temperament, he seemed positively embarrassed by it. Mr Heseltine, by contrast, has been behaving in a way that would have made Mr Major hide under the duvet for a fortnight. He ruthlessly exploits the 'Kinnock factor', portraying the Labour leader as a vacuous airhead; accuses John Smith, the shadow chancellor, of behaving like a pickpocket; terrifies the middle classes about the socialists' plans for their taxes and mortgages. Mr Heseltine and Mr Smith have been the star turns in the two campaigns, out-performing their leaders. But the television election has been centred on the leader, so the two stars have not been seen all that much.

Opinion polls played a major role throughout the campaign. Their record is traced in Chapter 7. At times the wide divergence in individual findings made headlines but throughout the campaign every poll of polls showed a narrow lead for Labour. Some Conservatives later asserted that they never believed these findings while Labour campaigners said that they knew they

APRIL 1ST

Nicholas Garland, *Daily Telegraph*, 1 April 1992

were not doing as well as the polls suggested. The Liberal Democrats, however, certainly accepted their reported rise from 15 percent to 20 percent and there is no doubt that, when the polls due to be published on Wednesday, April 1, leaked out on Tuesday night with Labour leads over the Conservatives of 7 percent, 6 percent and 4 percent (see p. 139), party morale was affected. There was no panic reaction in Central Office but much gloom; Labour began to contemplate the possibility of outright victory. The following night at Sheffield the party held its triumphal rally in Sheffield, assembling the full Shadow Cabinet and glitzy show business personalities.

It was to be the biggest political assembly since the war. It was partly modelled on President Mitterand's campaign rallies. All those who were there were fired by the atmosphere and the stage-management. The speakers gave the impression that Labour had already won the election. Indeed, Roy Hattersley was so overcome that on three occasions in his speech he said 'Labour has won the election'. But Neil Kinnock in a triumphal entry shouted to the crowd, like a pop-star 'You're all ri', you're all ri'.' The shot of this moment was shown repeatedly on television and was adjudged by friend and foe to be disastrous. 'The vision of a Labour Camelot gave way to the atmosphere of a Welsh rugby club.' 'The Welsh boyo suddenly took over from the national statesman.' In fact Mr Kinnock went on to make one of his best speeches.

'In nine days' time Britain is going to have a Labour government. One of the main reasons for that is people know we will govern as we have campaigned – strongly, positively, looking to the future. What's at issue in this election is not the soap boxes that people stand on, but the cardboard boxes that people live in. The decent British people are revolted by a government that has broken the consensus of 40 years – a government that has created poverty as a matter of policy, just as it has used unemployment as an instrument of economic management.'

The speech was little reported but those in the hall found the atmosphere wonderful. It was praised by the BBC's John Cole and by the Conservatives' former rally director, Harvey Thomas.

But outsiders had a different impression. Matthew Parris in *The Times* commented prophetically the following day (even though he had left Sheffield before the climax of the rally):

Image throttled intellect and a quiet voice in every reporter present whispered that there was something disgusting about the occasion. These voices will grow.

William Waldegrave likened the Sheffield gathering to a Nuremberg rally and there was widespread criticism of Mr Kinnock's populist heartiness. Labour's private polls suggested that the public did not much notice it – and it was far down in the 9 o'clock news. But it was to acquire a mythic status as one of the key mistakes in the campaign. Many Labour candidates replying to our post-election questionnaire commented on the counter-productive impact of its razzmatazz and its triumphalism.

Education was to have been a key theme in the election. The polls showed it following the health service as the main domestic issue in the public mind. The Liberal Democrats hijacked it as their issue on March 16 with their manifesto pledge to earmark a one percent tax increase to meet the crying need for improvements in school funding and in training facilities. The next day the Conservatives filled in with their launch of '39 steps to better education' while the Labour Party waited until March 31 for Mr Kinnock to set out, in Salford, Labour's proposals. The Liberal Democrats did secure some headlines with a repetition of their theme that, after proportional representation, education would be their top priority in any negotiations in a hung parliament. But it certainly was not a high priority in the media coverage of the campaign.

The possibility of a hung parliament lay heavily over the election. John Major with his 'stone-cold certainty' of a clear majority refused

Cummings, *Daily Express, 5 April 1992*

to consider how the Conservatives would behave if no party secured 326 seats. At the beginning Neil Kinnock followed a similar line. It was left to Paddy Ashdown to fuel the discussion that the poll findings inevitably provoked. From the start he said that he believed the country needed stable government and that he would co-operate with any party that would offer a deal for the life of the parliament provided that the enactment of proportional representation was part of that deal. But he stressed that he would be willing to vote down the Queen's Speech and force a second election if he could not get proportional representation. He admitted to Brian Walden that such a strategy might prove 'a risk within my own party' and Sir David Steel and Charles Kennedy in BBC's *On the Record* on March 29 seemed to repudiate his line; there were sharp words before Mr Ashdown enforced his authority.

The Liberal Democrats tried throughout the campaign to make plain that they were equidistant both from Conservative and Labour, although on March 19 Paddy Ashdown admitted in a Robin Day interview that an arrangement with the Conservatives might be harder to achieve, and to sell to his party, than an arrangement with Labour. There were mentions as the campaign advanced of various issues besides PR and education that would come high in the Liberal Democrats' priority list in a negotiation.

However on April 1 Mr Major turned at last to a serious attack on the Liberal Democrats. He spoke of 'Mr Kinnock's Trojan Horse with yellow posters', and of Paddy Ashdown as the doorkeeper to a Labour Britain: 'PR has nothing to do with fair play. It's all about power play.'

On April 6 it was suggested in *The Times* that Paddy Ashdown would demand four seats in a coalition cabinet; the story came from a good source and was designed to steal headlines. But it backfired making the party seem 'somewhat above itself'. Paddy Ashdown had to deny the story.

They were however dismayed when, at the press conference on April 2 (which the constitutional pressure group, Charter 88, had designated Democracy Day), Neil Kinnock went much further than before in seeming to endorse PR. Both the Leader's Committee and the Management Team had agreed a press conference for the afternoon of April 2, at which Roy Hattersley would address constitutional issues, including electoral reform. But at the morning conference Neil Kinnock was asked an anticipated question about PR and he gave a reply that had been drafted by his staff two nights earlier. It restated the passage from the manifesto but added an invitation to Liberal Democrats to join the working party. The original draft had contained a reference to the Scottish constitutional convention as a model, but this was omitted when Mr Hattersley objected. The final statement was agreed with Mr Kinnock, Jack Cunningham and David Hill

Nicholas Garland, *Daily Telegraph*, 4 April 1992

shortly before the press conference began. Mr Kinnock's invitation to the Liberal Democrats to join the Plant working party left some of the centre uncomfortable. Nevertheless on the *Granada 500* programme on April 6 he dodged a question on whether he was in favour of PR, saying that he was waiting for the Labour Party's Working Party under Professor Plant to report. The next day at the Conservative press conference Chris Patten and Michael Heseltine offered a vulgar but effective parody of 'the greatest living Welshman's' evasiveness. On April 6 Kenneth Baker at Stroud launched a powerful attack on PR. Citing elections the previous day in Italy and in two German *länder*, he said:

> 'Proportional representation has helped the fascists to march again in Europe. It is a terrible warning to us about what could happen if we threw away our system of first-past-the-post elections. That is what Mr Ashdown wants to do. It is what Mr Kinnock is prepared to do as the price for power. If PR turned out to have the same results it could be a pact with the devil.'

Mr Kinnock's flirtation with PR and his subsequent emphasis on a broad-based co-operative approach to government was designed to soften Labour's image and allay fears about a Labour government. It deeply worried the Liberal Democrats who realised that anti-Labour voters, seeing

Labour and the Liberal Democrats getting closer together, might recoil into the arms of the Conservatives. Paddy Ashdown moved swiftly to distance his party from Labour saying that the Liberal Democrats could not support a Labour government if it was going to tax middle management at 59 percent. But the damage was probably done. Fear both of a Labour government and a hung parliament drove voters from both the opposition parties in the last few days.

Mr Major, whose campaigning style had attracted considerable criticism, got into his stride as the campaign advanced. He abandoned the *Meet John Major* chats and, against security advice, he travelled with a much publicised soap-box – a genuflexion towards the campaigning style of yore – onto which he jumped in crowded shopping centres to drive home his repeated message about taxation. He developed an effective style of speaking at rallies and an extra one, ticket only, was added. At the end of the campaign he gave heavy emphasis to a theme which he had ventilated earlier without attracting much notice, the need to maintain the unity of the United Kingdom. Some expressed scepticism about taking up a subject which was seen as a vote-loser north of the border and of little interest elsewhere. But there seems to be little doubt that he touched a patriotic chord as he spoke with clarity and conviction on constitutional issues about which Neil Kinnock seemed to equivocate.

> 'If I could summon up all the authority of this office, I would put it into this single warning – the United Kingdom is in danger. Wake up, my fellow countrymen! Wake up now before it is too late!'

Many candidates testified to the effectiveness of this theme in winning or holding votes both in England and in Scotland.

The Conservative strategy had been to focus on tax in each of the first three weeks of the campaign and on leadership in the last week. But how was the point about leadership to be made? Neil Kinnock helped with his Sheffield lapse, and his changes of policy were featured in an election broadcast, but John Major, with his firm manner as he highlighted his personally chosen themes, about the preservation of the United Kingdom and of the electoral system, managed to end the campaign on a rising note. His final broadcast of April 7 was judged the best of the election and his rally speech at Wembley that night epitomised his style:

> 'I have lived life in many stations. I believe I understand what makes the heart of Britain best . . . . I want a Britain that offers dignity and security to older people. I want a Britain where there is a helping hand

for those who need it. Where people can get a hand up, not just a hand out. A country that is fair and free from prejudice, a classless society at ease with itself.'

As the campaign ended there was a general expectation of a hung parliament. The Prime Minister, despite a glancing reference to the subject on April 6, continued to express absolute confidence and he may have been encouraged by the polling day headlines, many of which noted a rally to the Conservatives. The poll of polls still put Labour ahead but when Central Office had collated its constituency reports on April 7, it enabled Chris Patten to tell the Prime Minister that the Conservatives would be the largest party with not less than 305 seats – and that he might get a clear majority with up to 335 seats.

Morale had stayed high in the Conservative camp and among the Downing Street team, although few shared the Prime Minister's 'stone cold certainty' of a clear majority. There was some late queasiness in Walworth Road but the Labour Party still expected the Conservatives to fall well short of the numbers needed to continue in government. On April 7 John Eatwell for Mr Kinnock had a long talk with Sir Terry Burns, the Permanent Secretary at the Treasury, on what would have to be done at once if Labour took office, and there were other contacts between senior Labour figures and Sir Robin Butler, the Secretary of the Cabinet. Some Cabinet ministers were alleged to have cleared their desks. As the polling booths opened, a change of government was seen as a probability by most people in the Westminster world – and as a possibility by almost all.

Election night was startling. Both the BBC and ITN had invested much money and effort in exit polls. At 10 p.m. these indicated 305 seats as the likeliest Conservative figure – an outcome that would almost certainly yield a Labour minority government. But from the first result at 11.07 (when Sunderland South reported only a 2.2 percent swing to Labour), no constituency moved far enough towards the opposition to point to a Labour victory. At 11.23 in the third result, the key marginal of Basildon stayed firmly in Conservative hands and it was plain that the unexpected was happening. The broadcasters, enmeshed in their exit polls, were slow to acknowledge that the Conservatives were heading for a clear victory, especially after Labour gained Pendle and Hyndburn on 4 percent swings, and the Liberal Democrats won Cheltenham, and then in the most outstanding result of the night, Bath, where Chris Patten paid the price for his Tory chairmanship and for the local impact of the poll-tax.[6]

# THE INDEPENDENT

No 1,709    THURSDAY 9 APRIL 1992    Published in London    40p

Kinnock and Major both confident as polls put Labour and Tories neck and neck

# It's too close to call

### Dealers gamble on City rumours

---

# The Daily Telegraph

ESTABLISHED 1855   NO. 42,547    **THURSDAY, APRIL 9, 1992**    LONDON AND MANCHESTER    45p

# Polls put parties neck and neck

---

# THE TIMES

No 64,302    THURSDAY APRIL 9 1992    45p

**APPOINTMENTS**
Pages 7-17
Life & Times section

### Late surge by Tories closes gap on Labour in final hours of campaign

# Polls put parties neck and neck

## Role of power-broker beckons for Ashdown
By ROBIN OAKLEY, POLITICAL EDITOR

**ELECTION 92 WITH THE TIMES**

**THE NATION'S VIEW**

At 10pm the polls close and within two hours the first results will show the likely swing. Today *The Times* gives you the electoral map, an hour-by-hour guide to the declarations, a look back at

---

# FINANCIAL TIMES

NEWSPAPER
*of* THE YEAR

Thursday April 9 1992    EUROPE'S BUSINESS NEWSPAPER    60p

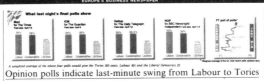

*A weighted average of the above four polls would give the Tories 303 seats, Labour 301 and the Liberal Democrats 22*

### Opinion polls indicate last-minute swing from Labour to Tories

# Election poised on knife-edge

---

40p
Thursday
April 9
1992
Published in London
and Manchester

# *The* Guardian

**Final polls put parties neck and neck   Labour strategists look to tactical voting in marginals   Lib Dems fear 'drift' in South**

# Tory hopes rise after late surge

However, by 1 a.m. the outcome was clear for all to see. Although 607 of the 651 seats counted on the night, the Conservatives had to wait till soon after noon on Friday for the 326th victory that gave them a clear majority. They ended with 336 seats to Labour's 271. The biggest surprise was in Scotland where the Conservatives firmly defied the expected trend and gained marginally in seats and votes while the SNP's added votes brought them no bonus. The results and their implications are analysed in detail in Chapter 13 and the Appendices. Perhaps a chapter on the campaign should end with the shock of the headlines in the final editions on Friday, April 10.[7]

# Major set for victory in tight fight

# Tory surge wins fourth term

# Tories set to be largest party

# Tories head for victory

# THE MAN WHO GOT IT RIGHT

# THE GREAT ESCAPE

# MAJOR WINS 4th TRIUMPH

# NICE GUYS DO FINISH FIRST

NOTES

1.  Paddy Ashdown, Des Wilson, Lord Holme, Alec McGivan, Ollie Grender, Chris Rennard, Tim Clement Jones.
2.  The campaign management team consisted of Jack Cunningham, four Walworth Road directors (Hill, Joyce Gould, Bish and Mike Watts), Julie Hall, Charles Clarke and Neil Stewart from Neil Kinnock's office, the two heads of the Key Units (Sally Morgan and Robert Hill), the chief press officer Gez Sagar as well as Philip Gould, Patricia Hewitt and Clive Hollick.

    The General Secretary's post-election report admitted that during the campaign, owing to the need for speed, the key decisions were made by a small group of people, usually including Jack Cunningham, Patricia Hewitt, David Hill, Philip Gould and somebody from Neil Kinnock's office.
3.  Quoted in the International Press Institute Report, *Potholes on the Campaign Trail*, a collection of editors' reflections on the problems they faced during the election.
4.  In a broadcast interview on 19 July 1992, the editor of the *Sun*, Kelvin Mackenzie, made allegations – which he subsequently amplified in print – that, during the election, 'a prominent member of the Cabinet' had given him the names and telephone numbers of several women who had had affairs with Paddy Ashdown. (He stressed that the minister's claims had been investigated and had proved to be untrue.) Sir Norman Fowler, the new Chairman of the Party, hastened to report that every member of the Cabinet had explicitly denied any such conduct.
5.  NALGO is not affiliated to the Labour Party. Since it does not have to pay affiliation fees its political fund is the richest of any union and it could well afford the £2m it must have spent on press advertising during the campaign. Michael Howard, the Employment Secretary, complained to the Advertising Standards Authority about a NALGO advertisement that described government training schemes as half-baked. He said it breached the 'honest, decent, legal and truthful' rules in the code. The Authority rejected the complaint because the advertisement was about a matter of public controversy; it did not offend against taste or decency, nor was it an unwarrantable appeal to fear.
6.  The press had regularly satirised the Jekyll and Hyde contrast between the rough 'Mr Nasty', the Conservative Chairman in Smith Square, helicoptering into the sweet, reasonable Mr Nice, the constituency candidate in Bath.
7.  The headlines are, in the order presented, from: *The Times, Guardian, Daily Telegraph, Independent, Evening Standard, Today, Daily Express,* and *Daily Mail*.

# 7   The Waterloo of the Polls

The 1992 election in Britain will long be remembered, like the 1948 presidential election in America, for the opinion polls' disastrous error in predicting the results. In 1948 the Gallup Poll forecast that Dewey would beat Truman. Gallup (which actually fared better than the two other nationwide polls) was wrong, being out by 8.5 percent on the percentage lead. In Britain, forty-four years later, a final poll of polls, based on the four polls actually published on polling day, suggested a 0.9 percent Labour lead; the Conservatives won by 7.6 percent – an 8.5 percent error, the largest ever. *IS THIS WORSE THAN 2015?*

Before this debacle, the polls had played an important part in the campaign. As we report elsewhere ( p. 168) they made more front-page news stories than almost any other topic in the campaign. On one calculation, polls absorbed ten percent of all election coverage. It was the first election since 1974 when the outcome seemed in doubt and the polls' forecast of a close outcome undoubtedly contributed to the excitement. The polls had proved misleading in 1951, in 1970 and again in 1974, but at least the findings gave one consistent message; throughout the campaign it was always the same party that was shown to be in the lead. But in 1992, of the fifty reputable nationwide polls published during the campaign, ten put the Conservatives ahead, thirty-eight put Labour ahead, and two were level. In the final week only one poll, by Gallup, had the Conservatives ahead ( but only by 0.5 percent). Every poll of polls based on the previous five or six surveys showed a Labour lead – but it never exceeded half a percent and for most of the time it was between 1 percent and 2 percent ( Fig 7.1). Since a uniform projection from the 1987 results suggested that Conservative and Labour alike needed at least a 4 percent lead in votes to win a clear victory, a hung parliament always seemed overwhelmingly likely. It was an assumption that coloured all the conduct and, even more, the coverage of the campaign.

Even before the election the polls had contributed to the policy making and campaign strategy of the Conservative and Labour parties (see pp. 36–8 and 55–6). They were also considered when John Major discussed the timing of the election: 'In settling the date, on a scale of one to ten, I'd put polls at eleven', said one Conservative adviser. But in August 1991 some encouraging polls in the marginals by Harris failed to persuade Chris Patten to advise the Prime Minister to call a November

*The British General Election of 1992*

Table 7.1    Opinion polls on voting intentions, March 13–April 9

| OPINION POLLS | Date Pub | Samp Size | Field Dates | Con (%) | Lab (%) | Lib Dem (%) | Con lead over Lab |
|---|---|---|---|---|---|---|---|
| NOP/Mail on Sund. | 15.3 | 1054 | 11.3 | 41 | 40 | 15 | 1 |
| MORI/Times | 13.3 | 1054 | 11/12.3 | 38 | 41 | 16 | –3 |
| Harris/LWT | 15.3 | 2186 | 11/12.3 | 37 | 41 | 17 | –4 |
| Harris/Observer | 15.3 | 1054 | 11/12.3 | 40 | 43 | 12 | –3 |
| MORI/Sunday Times | 15.3 | 1544 | 11/12.3 | 40 | 39 | 18 | 1 |
| Harris/Express | 14.3 | 1086 | 11/13.3 | 39 | 40 | 16 | –1 |
| NOP/S.Independent | 15.3 | 2153 | 12/13.3 | 40 | 41 | 14 | –1 |
| ICM/S.Express | 15.3 | 1086 | 13.3 | 39 | 40 | 16 | –1 |
| Harris/Express | 17.3 | 1081 | 15/16.3 | 41 | 38 | 17 | 3 |
| MORI/Times | 18.3 | 1099 | 16.3 | 38 | 43 | 16 | –5 |
| ICM/Guardian | 18.3 | 1100 | 17.3 | 38 | 43 | 16 | –5 |
| Gallup/Telegraph | 19.3 | 984 | 17/18.3 | 40.5 | 38.5 | 18 | 2 |
| NOP/Independent | 19.3 | 1262 | 17/18.3 | 38 | 42 | 17 | –4 |
| MORI/Sunday Times | 22.3 | 1257 | 18/20.3 | 38 | 41 | 19 | –3 |
| Harris/Observer | 22.3 | 1096 | 19/20.3 | 40 | 39 | 17 | 1 |
| ICM/S.Express | 22.3 | 1115 | 20.3 | 37 | 42 | 16 | –5 |
| NOP/S.Independent | 22.3 | 1004 | 19/21.3 | 38 | 40 | 16 | –2 |
| NOP/Mail on Sund. | 22.3 | 1085 | 20/21.3 | 39 | 41 | 15 | –2 |
| Harris/Express | 24.3 | 1077 | 21/23.3 | 43 | 38 | 15 | 5 |
| Harris/ITN | 24.3 | 2158 | 22/23.3 | 38 | 42 | 16 | –4 |
| MORI/Times | 25.3 | 1109 | 23.3 | 38 | 41 | 17 | –3 |
| ICM/Guardian | 25.3 | 1096 | 24.3 | 39 | 40 | 17 | –1 |
| NOP/Independent | 26.3 | 1326 | 24/25.3 | 39 | 42 | 14 | –3 |
| Gallup/Telegraph | 26.3 | 1092 | 24/25.3 | 40 | 40.5 | 16.5 | –0.5 |
| NMR/European | 26.3 | 1105 | 24/25.3 | 38 | 39 | 19 | –1 |
| MORI/Sunday Times | 29.3 | 1292 | 25/27.3 | 38 | 40 | 20 | –2 |
| Harris/Observer | 29.3 | 1057 | 26/27.3 | 40 | 38 | 17 | –2 |
| ICM/S.Express | 29.3 | 1136 | 27.3 | 36 | 38 | 20 | –2 |
| NOP/S.Independent | 29.3 | 1000 | 26/28.3 | 39 | 40 | 16 | –1 |
| NOP/Mail on Sund. | 29.3 | 1099 | 27/28.3 | 37 | 41 | 18 | –4 |
| Harris/Express | 30.3 | 1108 | 28/30.3 | 40 | 39 | 17 | 1 |
| MORI/Times | 1.4 | 1126 | 30.3 | 35 | 42 | 19 | –7 |
| Harris/ITN | 31.3 | 2152 | 28/31.3 | 35 | 41 | 19 | –6 |
| ICM/Guardian | 1.4 | 1080 | 31.3 | 37 | 41 | 18 | –4 |
| Gallup/Telegraph | 2.4 | 1095 | 31.3/1.4 | 38 | 37.5 | 20.5 | 0.5 |
| NOP/Independent | 2.4 | 1302 | 31.3/1.4 | 37 | 39 | 19 | –2 |
| Gallup/S.Teleg | 4.4 | 1043 | 2/3.4 | 37.5 | 37.5 | 22 | 0 |
| MORI/Sunday Times | 4.4 | 1265 | 1/3.4 | 37 | 39 | 21 | –2 |
| Harris/Observer | 4.4 | 1090 | 2/3.4 | 38 | 40 | 17 | –2 |
| ICM/S.Express | 4.4 | 1139 | 3.4 | 37 | 39 | 19 | –2 |
| NOP/S.Independent | 4.4 | 1006 | 2/4.4 | 38 | 41 | 17 | –3 |
| NOP/Mail on Sund. | 4.4 | 1104 | 3/4.4 | 35 | 41 | 20 | –6 |
| ICM/Press Association | 6.4 | 10460 | 31.3/3.4 | 36 | 39 | 20 | –3 |
| Harris/Express | 7.4 | 1093 | 4/6.4 | 37 | 38 | 21 | –1 |
| Harris/ITN | 7.4 | 2210 | 4/7.4 | 38 | 40 | 18 | –2 |
| MORI/First Tuesday | 7.4 | 1065 | 6/7.4 | 37 | 40 | 20 | –3 |
| Gallup/Telegraph | 9.4 | 2478 | 7/8.4 | 38.5 | 38 | 20 | 0.5 |
| MORI/Times | 9.4 | 1731 | 7/8.4 | 38 | 39 | 20 | –1 |
| NOP/Independent | 9.4 | 1746 | 7/8.4 | 39 | 42 | 17 | –3 |
| ICM/Guardian | 9.4 | 2186 | 8.4 | 38 | 38 | 20 | 0 |

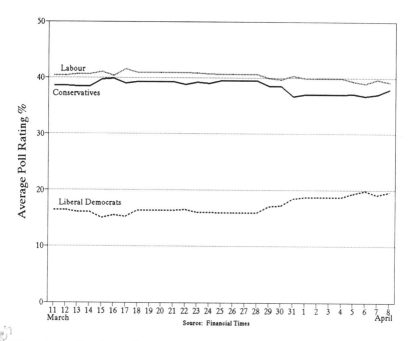

*Figure 7.1    Opinion poll trends during the campaign*

election. Mr Patten felt vindicated when, shortly afterwards, national polls reported a Labour lead. The marginal polls were studied again in February and showed that the Conservative Party's position had worsened in London and the north-west.

The polling industry continued to be in the hands of the big five companies which made up the Association of Professional Opinion Poll Organisations, listed here with the key figures in their political work.

| | |
|---|---|
| Gallup | Robert Wybrow |
| MORI ( Market & Opinion Research International) | Robert Worcester |
| Harris | Robert Waller |
| NOP ( National Opinion Polls) | Nick Moon |
| ICM ( International Communications & Marketing) | Nick Sparrow |

These companies provided the overwhelming bulk of the regularly published nationwide surveys and they all subscribed to the code of conduct, agreed in 1970, about making available details of their methods as well as all their findings. In 1989 NOP had taken over private polling for Labour from MORI but Harris remained the main pollster for the Conservatives, who also commissioned some work from Gallup. NOP provided exit polls for the BBC; Harris did so for the ITN and ICM did so for Murdoch's *Sky Television* and *the Sun* and *Today* newspapers. Panel polls were conducted weekly throughout the election by MORI for the *Sunday Times* and by NOP for the *Independent on Sunday*.

Table 7.1 sets out the voting intention findings of the national polls during the campaign period. On the whole, the picture is a stable one, although John Major misleadingly claimed at times that the polls 'are all over the place'. Broadly, the Conservatives drifted down from 40 percent to 38 percent as the weeks progressed and Labour from 41 percent to 39 percent; the Liberal Democrats rose from 15 percent to 19 percent. The gap between the two main parties was virtually the same at the end as it had been at the beginning. Very few findings were more than an acceptable 2 percent from the trendline.[1] Harris, however, was embarrassed on March 24 when it simultaneously reported a 5 percent Conservative lead for the *Daily Express* but a 4 percent Labour lead for ITN, and again on April 1 when it reported a 1 percent Conservative lead for the *Daily Express* just before telling ITN of a 6 percent Labour lead. The difference was attributed to different fieldwork dates and to the chances of sampling. It was, however, strange that Harris advised commentators not to compare the two polls, because the interviews for the *Daily Express* had been conducted on Sunday. That paper still claimed: 'It is likely to be a more accurate reflection of opinion than surveys conducted during week days, in the street when many are at work.'

The greatest oddity in the polling – and the greatest shock to the contestants – came late on the evening of April 1 when three findings were released, each showing the largest Labour lead of the campaign: 4 percent (ICM, for the *Guardian*), 6 percent (Harris, for ITN) and 7 percent (MORI, for *The Times*). Some of the pollsters found these leads extraordinary and tried to reassure Conservative leaders by expressing scepticism about their own findings. Granted the past record of accuracy of the polls, these figures seemed to put a Conservative win out of the question. But commentators and partisans were brought down to earth twenty-four hours later; NOP, in the *Independent*, showed Labour only 2 percent ahead while Gallup reported a 0.5 percent Conservative lead in the *Daily Telegraph*. Some commentators saw in that spectacular blip to

*Table 7.2    Scottish polls*

|        | MORI<br>April 2 | PA<br>April 7 | System 3<br>April 7 | ICM<br>April 8 | Actual Result<br>April 9 |
|--------|-----------------|---------------|---------------------|----------------|--------------------------|
|        | %               | %             | %                   | %              | %                        |
| Con    | 21              | 21            | 21                  | 22             | 25.7                     |
| Lab    | 44              | 40            | 41                  | 41             | 39.0                     |
| Lib Dem| 12              | 12            | 13                  | 11             | 13.1                     |
| SNP    | 23              | 25            | 24                  | 25             | 21.5                     |

Labour the seeds of the party's downfall. It encouraged the triumphalism of the Sheffield rally (see p. 125) and it helped to waken the public to the real possibility of a Labour victory.

There were a number of constituency polls, some conducted by students but some by experienced companies. This was a marked reduction on 1987 and their record was patchy. Most were of course taken early in the campaign. In six out of 40 or so a Conservative defeat was wrongly indicated, and in others the percentage margin was wildly out. There were also polls in London marginals, in Greater London as a whole, in Yorkshire marginals, in the West Midlands, in Welsh marginals and in the North of Scotland. The number of marginal polls was also down on 1987. Each of these significantly underestimated the final support for the Conservatives. In Scotland more serious polls were reported by System 3 for the *Herald*, ICM for the *Scotsman* and by MORI for the *Sunday Times Scotland*. They under-estimated the final Conservative vote (Table 7.2), but by a smaller margin than occurred south of the border.

During the campaign the polls reported a decline in support for Scottish independence. At the end, MORI found 28 percent wanting full autonomy, 45 per cent a Scottish Assembly within the UK, and 23 percent the *status quo*. But only 33 percent saw the government of Scotland as among the most important issues which would decide their vote. In most respects the priorities and attitudes of Scottish voters differed little from those of party supporters south of the border.

There were also polls among specialist groups. A Gallup survey among top businessmen (commissioned by Conservative Central Office but generally released) found, not surprisingly, that by 80 percent to 4 percent they thought that the economy would prosper more under the Conservatives than under Labour. A MORI poll for the *Financial Times* (on March 16) gave details of businessmen's pessimistic forecasts about the economic

*Table 7.3     Final polls*

|  | Con | Lab | Lib Dem | Other | Con lead | Error on lead |
|---|---|---|---|---|---|---|
| MORI | 38 | 39 | 20 | 2 | −1 | 8.6 |
| NOP | 39 | 42 | 17 | 2 | −3 | 10.6 |
| Gallup | 38.5 | 38 | 20 | 3.5 | 0.5 | 7.1 |
| ICM | 38 | 38 | 20 | 4 | 0 | 7.6 |
| Result (GB) | 42.8 | 35.2 | 18.3 | 3.7 | 7.6 | − |

See Table 7.1 for fuller detail.

consequences of a Labour win or a hung parliament. Polls among teachers and to a lesser extent among doctors showed a significant move towards Labour since 1987.[2]

The Catholic *Universe* published a breakdown of Gallup findings which suggested a 6 percent lead for the Conservatives among Anglicans and a 13 per cent lead for Labour among Catholics. An *Irish Times*/MORI poll found only a 4 percent Labour lead among the Irish in Britain.

The unanimity of the polls in indicating a hung parliament meant that they shared almost equally in the recrimination when the Conservatives emerged from the election with a 7.6 percent advantage in votes (Table 7.3). Some pollsters detected an increase (of 1 percent on average) for the Conservatives in their late polling and the press headlines on polling day duly forecast a close outcome (see p. 131).

What went wrong with the forecasts? They were using the same methods as in previous elections and they were interviewing on late Tuesday and during Wednesday. Methods that produced a good record of prediction in 1979, 1983 and 1987 led to disaster in 1992. And the failure of the pre-election polls to spot the outcome was compounded when predictions based on the exit polls on radio and television at 10 p.m. on April 9 (although close to the final share of the votes) suggested that the Conservatives would win only 305 seats.

It is not possible to give a definitive explanation for the failure of the polls. They were honourably conducted by experienced professionals who had every interest in getting the answer right. They had claimed credit for successes in previous elections and Robert Worcester before polling day declared in his MORI newsletter, 'Surely the best test of any poll is "Did they get it right on the night?"' They were using techniques that had served them well in the past – and five competitive firms all failed by much the same extent.

There were no obvious changes in the structure of society or the psychology of the citizen which suggest why the vote on April 9 was so unexpected. It seems probable that a number of disparate factors lie behind the pollsters' disaster. These may be summarised under six heads.

## 1. The sampling frame

Sample size was not the problem. All the pollsters used samples of over 1,000 and the PA/ICM poll which actually involved over 10,000 was in line with all the rest. Some critics suggested that pollsters drew on the outdated 1981 census. But in fact they relied on registration data and other information collected by the Office of Population Censuses and Surveys (OPCS) and the National Readership Survey (which is based on a list of postal addresses and is independent of the census) as well as other market research sources. Peter Kellner, in the *Independent*, suggested that, because the exit polls contained markedly more up-market respondents than were found in polls conducted during the campaign, society had become more middle-class than pollsters realised: to some extent[3] this may have been a consequence of higher turnout in Tory-held seats. But there remains the possibility that the quota controls designed by pollsters and applied by their interviewers were not adequate, although little had changed from 1987 when they seemed to work well.[4]

The Market Research Society (MRS) report[5] controversially claimed that the pro-Labour bias was long-standing; opinion polls had on average overestimated Labour's share of the vote by 1.4 percent in elections since 1959. The pollsters objected to the inclusion of 1992 in the calculation and to counting elections before 1970. On an average of the final forecasts from 1970 to 1987, the bias virtually disappeared.

## 2. The electoral register

The MRS report suggested that the polls may have been good at assembling representative samples of Britain's adults but not so good at constructing samples of electors. Some of those interviewed by the pollsters may not have been able to vote because they are not on the register. It is impracticable for the interviewer to check authoritatively whether the respondent has actually got a vote. Some pollsters did ask a question and filtered out those who said they were not registered. But pollsters could not measure exactly how many non-electors fell into their sample. If people left off the register, through removal or administrative error or a desire to avoid the poll-tax, expressed voting intentions they could distort the findings.

The register in 1991 contained almost two million fewer names than the OPCS estimate for the resident adult population compared to a shortfall of just over one million in 1987. But even if the extra 900,000 missing names were wholly due to poll-tax evaders dodging registration, the MRS calculates that this could at most account for 1.2 percent of the pollsters' 8.5 percent error in the gap between the parties – and probably much less. The shortfall in the numbers on the register was certainly due in part to an increase in efficiency by registration officers in clearing 'dead' names off their lists (see pp. 230–1).

## 3.   Differential refusals

*[handwritten annotation: IN 2015, POLLSTERS CONNECTION WITH THE ELDERY ELECTORATE DIDN'T FULLY ENGAGE. THE ONLINE QUESTIONAIRE WAS NOT FULLY CONNECTED WITH ELDERS]*

Pollsters find that the elderly are more likely to refuse to be interviewed, and if interviewed, to refuse to reveal their voting intention; if the substitutes, within the age group, are younger and less Conservative, this will create a bias; moreover, if Labour voters are more forthcoming than Conservatives any substitution for refusals may compound the bias. Post-election recall surveys found that the non-respondents (covering the 'refusals', 'undecided' and 'don't knows') in the end voted heavily Conservative. This could have been a source of late swing or some could have intended to vote Conservative all along. The fact that all the exit polls, which were free from the problem of differential turnout and quota sampling, underestimated the Conservative lead gives further credence to differential refusal as a source of error. The MRS report concludes that refusals could explain some 2 percent of the 8.5 percent error in the party lead.[6] There is however, no obvious reasons why this tendency should suddenly have developed between 1987 and 1992.

## 4.   Lying

It was widely suggested after the election that there was systematic deception by a number of Tory-inclined interviewees, either from simple perversity or because they thought it unfashionable to vote for 'selfish' reasons. This is another hypothesis rejected by interviewers and polling organisations, as well as by the MRS report.

## 5.  Differential turnout

Pollsters always have to allow for the fact that some of the people interviewed may fail to vote. If those who said they were going to support the Conservatives were more zealous than the rest in recording their votes, this could explain some of the pollsters' error. Turnout rose most strongly in Conservative areas and least in strong Labour areas (see pp. 345–7). The differences were not great but the MRS study was willing to attribute 0.6 per cent of the 8.5 percent error to the greater willingness of Conservatives to turn out.

## 6.  Late swing

People may have switched their allegiance in the twenty-four hours or so between being interviewed and voting. A massive late swing to the Conservatives would be much the simplest – and to the pollsters the most convenient – explanation. Labour's private polls recorded a slippage of support in the final days (see pp. 150–1). Various academic and journalist reinterview polls make clear that a significant number of people voted differently on April 9 from the way they had indicated in interviews conducted between April 6–8. But the net change was not great and at best seems to account for 2 percent of the 8.5 percent error on the lead. Indeed preliminary analysis from the British Election Survey study suggests an even lower figure. It is impossible to be certain whether any late movements should be ascribed to specific arguments and events in the final days or just to the sudden reality of the polling station when, faced with a ballot paper, wavering voters had to decide whether they wanted to risk a hung parliament or a Labour government. What is clear is that more people, and in particular more Conservative voters, claimed to have decided at the last moment. As Table 7.4 shows the Harris/ITN exit poll found a contrast with 1987.

These Conservative percentages can be translated into actual votes:

|      | On day | Last week | In campaign | Earlier |
|------|--------|-----------|-------------|---------|
| 1987 | 688,000 | 826,000 | 3,165,000 | 9,082,000 |
| 1992 | 1,264,000 | 1,405,000 | 3,512,000 | 7,586,000 |

This would suggest that well over a million more people decided to vote Conservative in the final days of this campaign than in 1987, and pollsters can claim that this offers the simplest explanation for part of their error.

*Table 7.4    Time of decision by Conservative and Labour voters (%)*

|      | On polling day | | Last week | | During Campaign | | Earlier | |
|------|-----|-----|-----|-----|-----|-----|-----|-----|
|      | Con | Lab | Con | Lab | Con | Lab | Con | Lab |
| 1987 | 5   | 8   | 6   | 8   | 23  | 18  | 66  | 64  |
| 1992 | 9   | 8   | 10  | 8   | 25  | 22  | 54  | 60  |

*Source*: Harris/ITN exit poll

But an explanation based primarily on late swing does not satisfy many critics. The MRS report discounted it as the overwhelming source of error. On the basis of 'recall' panel surveys and other fresh post-election polls it concluded that the Conservatives might have gained one percent from last minute switches, drawn equally from Labour and Liberal Democrat. If the polls were correct in their reports of voting intentions on the Wednesday, the swing would have had to be enormous on the Thursday. The final pre-election polls contained no hint of why there should be a last minute swing of this magnitude and no election day commentary reported any shift in the agenda which could account for it. In 1970 and in February 1974 there were gradual shifts in the salience of issues which could explain the change in voting behaviour. In 1992, however, according to the polls, Labour enjoyed a huge lead on the social issues and these were dominant for voters. Ivor Crewe, in *The Times* on April 9, claimed that tax had been a damp squib for the Conservatives (because advantages from income tax cuts were partly lost due to value-added tax rises and the poll-tax), and that the party had not made the economy into a central issue. He continued: ' . . . Labour captured the high ground of the agenda. The sharpest changes of opinion were about the issues that counted'.

A guess at the possible contribution of these six explanations can be offered, drawing largely but not exclusively on the MRS report.

These guesses still are not enough to explain an 8.5 percent shortfall. But it is worth drawing attention to the element that distinguished the 1992 election from its predecessors – the overwhelming and repeated indications that it was going to be a close-run thing. The reactions of a significant number of electors must have been conditioned by the repeated headlines about neck-and-neck polls. Both their responses to interviewers and their behaviour in the voting-booth may have been distorted in a way that did not occur in 1983 or 1987.

*Table 7.5   Possible components of poll error*

| | |
|---|---|
| Sampling frame | 1.0 |
| Electoral register | 1.0 |
| Differential refusals | 1.5 |
| Systematic lying | – |
| Differential turnout | 0.5 |
| Late swing | 1.5 |
| Total | 5.5 |

However, this book can certainly offer no final verdict on the misleading message of the pre-election polls. Much work is being done within the market research industry and by those involved in academic surveys to identify what went wrong. What is clear is that there is no single explanation for this massive failure in what had become a trusted instrument in election analysis.

The failure of the exit polls is different from that of the earlier surveys. The exit polls conducted on April 9 were on a random not a quota basis and there could be no question of late swing, since the voters were interviewed after they had voted. In one way the exit polls lend some support to the late swing theory. The nationwide surveys conducted separately both for the BBC and ITN each suggested a 4 percent lead for the Conservatives – 3.6 percent below the actual figure but within an acceptable margin of error and very different from the 0.9 percent Labour lead suggested by the final pre-election polls.

But on the night BBC and ITN ignored these nationwide surveys (which, to be fair, were not conducted for prediction purposes) and relied on the findings of their separate polls in marginal seats, which indicated a much closer race. Table 7.6 shows the forecasts broadcast when the polls closed on April 9 with some warnings of sampling error ('plus or minus 15 seats' said the BBC.)

The error of both the BBC and ITN predictions was in some part due to erroneous prior estimates which had been made for special seats; these included the eight seats that had changed hands in by-elections (because the sample size would be too small to pick up their inevitably differential behaviour) together with places where a party rebel was standing and a number of Scottish constituencies. The misleading story offered by the broadcasters was also due to the fact that the exit polls correctly found that Labour was faring better in marginals. Those who had to interpret the exit polls say that their judgement was affected by the general expectation of a hung parliament. It was unfortunate that both the BBC and ITN

*Table 7.6   Exit poll predictions of seats*

|            |            | Con | Lab | Lib | Other |
|------------|------------|-----|-----|-----|-------|
| BBC/NOP    | 10.00 p.m. | 301 | 298 | 24  | 29    |
| (BBC/NOP   | 10.55 p.m. | 305 | 296 | 22  | 28)   |
| ITN/Harris | 10.00 p.m. | 305 | 294 | 25  | 27    |
| SKY/ICM    | 10.00 p.m. | 302 | 307 | 18  | 24    |

The BBC/NOP 10.55 p.m. poll included some data not available at 10 p.m.

compounded their misfortune by being slow to jettison their marginals' exit poll in favour of the actual results which pointed to a clear Conservative victory an hour or more before the broadcasters admitted it. The percentage error of the exit polls (under 2 percent for each the Conservative and the Labour vote) suggests that there was some late swing – but the fact that the all the exit polls, which were free from the problem of differential turnout and quota sampling, still underestimated the Conservative lead gives further credence to differential refusal as a significant cause of error.

Did the erroneous polls matter? Investors certainly thought so when on April 1, £6 billion was wiped off the values of shares, following the announcement of the Labour blip in the polls. And, if Conservative support was understated throughout the campaign and Labour was in fact not in the lead, it is arguable that the polls affected voting behaviour. Some observers have suggested that the prospect of a Labour government helped to drive some Liberal Democrats back to the Conservatives and stiffened the resolve of a number of lukewarm Conservatives.[5] The polls certainly contributed to the impression that Labour was winning the campaign and may have reinforced among Labour strategists and the media commentators a false view of the strength of Labour's vote. It is worth quoting at length the view of a central figure in Labour's campaign:

'Labour's campaign, the pollsters, the broadcast media and the press all submerged the Tory vote. Submerged it because people were guilty and because a kind of social dynamic had been established that made Labour more acceptable than the Conservatives. This led people to be publicly embarrassed and uncertain about expressing support for the Conservatives. But it was also submerged in the sense that many people hid from themselves their real intentions, feelings and view of where their self-interest lay. The strength of Labour's campaign was reflected into a majority shifting from thinking the Conservatives would win into a majority thinking that Labour would win.'

The attention of the media was on polls about voting intentions. But the polls covered many other topics. Quickie polls suggested that the March 10 Budget did not win votes and John Smith was regularly preferred to Norman Lamont as Chancellor. The Conservative lead as the best party to manage the economy remained undented, however, and the party's tax arguments were more accepted than those of Labour. Labour's advantage on the health issue was sustained; the importance given to the issue increased, although public and private polls showed that its lead as the best party to handle the NHS was cut back by the rumpus following the party's controversial broadcast. The voters (80 percent of them) gave a public-spirited answer in approving the Liberal Democrat proposal of an extra penny on income tax to pay for education; by huge margins they also said they were willing to pay more income tax to improve public services.

But were people serious in their answers to these or other 'iffy' questions? After the election, people were more willing to admit the economic reasons for their vote. The Harris ITN exit poll found that only 30 percent said that they would be better off under Labour tax and benefits proposals, compared to 49 percent who said they would be worse off. The wording of the question was important. NOP polls for Labour found that some 75 percent of voters said that they would pay more tax to fund better public services like the NHS. But when they were asked whether they preferred Labour's proposals for tax increases or Conservative proposals for tax cuts, the split was almost 50–50; and when they were asked who they trusted or preferred to manage the economy the Conservatives clearly won. For several elections now questions on taxation versus public spending have been only weakly correlated with voting choice. Some Labour leaders may have attached too much importance to this single question.

Much publicity was given to questions about the leaders. The palm for the best campaign seemed to go to Paddy Ashdown, with Mr Kinnock second. The *Sunday Times* panel reported that John Major's lead of 18 percent over Mr Kinnock on who would make the best Prime Minister narrowed to 9 percent between week one and week four. When it asked the panel members whether they were satisfied with the job each party leader was doing, Mr Major fared even worse. In week one his satisfaction rating was +14 while Mr Kinnock's was –12. By week four, both were at +2.

Tactical voting was investigated with questions about second preference and 12 percent told MORI that they were voting not for their favourite party but for the one most likely to keep another party out. Evidence about voter uncertainty was fully reported. Undecideds in the first week were, according to MORI, 14 percent (compared to 11 percent in 1987), although MORI's claim that as many as 11 million changed their voting intention was comparable to that for 1987. In the first week Harris reported that 48 percent expected a Conservative win and 24 percent a Labour win. But as the campaign advanced, more and more expected a hung parliament. After the event commentators expressed the view that indecisive voters switched disproportionately to the Conservative Party because they feared a hung parliament or a Labour government. Philip Gould observed that such voters 'might well have preferred a hung parliament to a Labour government'.

The Conservatives had made full use of survey research by various organisations in the run-up to the election, although the ambitious exercise created by Dick Wirthlin had been wound down (see pp. 36–7). Before the election the party had used its poll findings to make news stories. A question added to a System Three survey in Scotland showed little support for regional government and in November 1989 a Gallup survey found that Labour MPs were divided over Mr Kinnock's stance towards the EC. A later commissioned poll among businessmen showing their fear of Labour was also released.

During the campaign the party relied on their traditional pollster, Harris. A variety of polls were conducted – some full-scale surveys and some qualitative studies with groups. In 1979 the party had abandoned daily polling, finding that the amount of survey material generated was too large to be absorbed. In 1983 and 1987 it had used 'fast feedback' a panel of opinion leaders, but this was not repeated in 1992. The most important intelligence came from four weekly strategy surveys, reporting on March 15, 22 and 29 and April 4, in time for the Sunday strategy meetings with John Major. There were also two 'quickie' surveys on March 20 and 27, surveys in a few seats where Liberal Democrats posed a threat and a one-off, 800-sample survey in ten West Midlands marginals late in March. There were four qualitative studies directed mainly at the election broadcasts and three qualitative studies with floaters. Reactions to the party's broadcasts were mixed. The research suggested that blatantly negative messages were not appreciated, but more subtle ones, 'that *implied* a point (and) encouraged the respondents to think about the message', were more successful. The attack on Mr Kinnock was judged successful. A qualitative study early on in the campaign measuring the impact of the party

. Chris Patten and David Mellor, 21 January 1992 (*Tony Andrews, Financial Times*)

2. (*left*) John Major 'Meet the People' in his constituency, 15 March 1992 (*Ashley Ashwood, Financial Times*)

3. (*below*) John Major, Chris Patten, Michael Heseltine, Douglas Hurd, Norman Lamont: Manifesto launch, 18 March 1992 (*Tony Andrews, Financial Times*)

4. (*left*) Chris Patten and Michael Heseltine: Press Conference, 23 March 1992 (*Financial Times*)

5. (*right*) John Major, Chris Patten, Margaret Thatcher, Candidates' Meeting, 22 March 1992 (*Independent*)

6. (*below*) John Major at Luton, 28 March 1992 (*Independent*)

7.  (*above*) Gerald Kaufman, John Smith, Jack Straw, Neil Kinnock, Margaret Beckett, John Cunningham: Labour Press Conference (*Financial Times*)

.   (*above*) Neil Kinnock at the Sheffield Rally (*David Kampfner*)

.   (*right*) Roy Hattersley: 'Labour has won the Election', Sheffield Rally, 1 April 1992 (*David Kampfner*)

10. Norman Lamont as Vatman, John Smith, Margaret Beckett, John Cunningham, 28 January 1992

11. (*left*) Neil Kinnock at Southampton, 3 April 1992 (*Sean Smith, Guardian*)

12. (*right*) Launching 'Made in Britain', Gordon Brown and John Smith, 8 January 1992 (*Martin Argles, Guardian*)

13. Des Wilson, Paddy Ashdown, Graham Elson, outside the Liberal Democrat Headquarters, 11 March 1992

14. (*left*) Des Wilson and Paddy Ashdown, Press Conference, 24 March 1992 (*Financial Times*)

15. (*below*) 'Vote Tactical', Oxford, March 1992 (*Peter Hamilton*)

16. (*above*) Charles Kennedy in Dingwall Town Hall, 25 March 1992 (*Don McPhee*)

17. (*right*) Dave Nellist in Coventry, 23 March 1992 (*John Snowdon, Guardian*)

18. The Scottish National Party, 1 April 1992 (*Scotsman Publications*)

19.  (*above*)
     Smith Square:
     Chris Patten,
     Norma Major,
     John Major,
     Sir John Lacy,
     Douglas Hurd,
     Election Night,
     1992: Conservative

20.  (*left*)
     Walworth Road:
     Neil Kinnock,
     Glenys Kinnock,
     Bryan Gould:
     Election Night,
     1992: Labour

21.  (*bottom left*)
     Declaration of
     Austin Mitchell's
     election at Great
     Grimsby

22.  Peter Snow, BBC at the Swingometer, Election Night, 1992

23.  Julia Sommerville, Alastair Stewart, Jon Snow, ITN Election Night, 9/10 April 1992 (*John Curtis*)

posters, found that 'You Can't Trust Labour' was the best remembered poster, followed by the 'Double Whammy' (see p. 112).

One of the more interesting quickie questions found that 48 percent saw the contest as John Major's first election against 41 percent who saw it as the Conservative government's fourth election. Another comforting quickie result was that by 52 percent to 31 percent people believed that there would be a general £24-a-week tax increase under Labour. (Labour's private polls found that this precise claim was not widely believed, although most accepted that there would be a significant increase in tax under Labour.) Studies among floating voters showed in the second week a huge reaction against slanging and negative campaigning. All the polls – public and private – and the qualitative research found this, largely as a reaction to Labour's health broadcast.

The final strategy survey recorded a depressing fall during the campaign in belief in a Conservative win – from 41 percent at the beginning of the campaign to 29 percent; it reported voting intentions at Con 37 percent, Lab 37 percent, Lib Dem 22 percent. It also showed support from C2s, the target of so much Conservative attention, as 13 percent down on 1987. To add to this discouragement, the survey in West Midlands' marginals showed that Liberal Democrats, if squeezed, would divide 2-to-1 for Labour.

Very little in the findings of these highly confidential surveys can have conflicted with what was generally available from the public polls, which were duly analysed and reported by Keith Britto to a small group of strategists in Central Office. Chris Patten insisted on personally presenting poll findings to John Major and Sarah Hogg. Reading through the Conservative private poll reports it is hard to believe that they contributed much to the party's strategic thinking. They revealed no sharp or unreported movements of opinion. Perhaps their main achievement was to give assurance of the absence of subterranean movements. They confirmed that John Major and the tax issue continued to be advantageous for the Conservatives, and that, when the party added the threat of higher mortgages to the tax and prices 'double whammy' of a Labour government, this did have an impact. A question asking voters, irrespective of the party they supported, who they *trusted* most to handle issues (as opposed to which party would best handle them) found a marked increase in preference for the Conservatives. As a result, trust was emphasised more in the party's communications. But on the whole they revealed no new target areas or propaganda successes.

During the election Labour relied on NOP to run daily surveys, except on the first two Sundays, yielding 28 polls in all, plus one on the Friday after the election. The 600 or so interviews were conducted by telephone between 4.30 and 8 p.m. every day and the results were phoned through to Deborah Mattinson by 9 p.m. On the basis of the faxed replies, together with some 15 pages of verbatim comments, she wrote her notes which were then conveyed to Patricia Hewitt for the media monitoring group which met at 6.30 a.m. the next day. In the evening at 7.30, a full presentation was made by Philip Gould to the campaign management team. One of the regular questions was to ask people what had impressed them favourably or unfavourably about each party's campaign. This gave them a number of positive and negative responses for each party. NOP regularly pre-tested election broadcasts with small groups. But the Jennifer's ear broadcast was tested only the night before, too late to take any remedial action if any had been needed. For most of the time, Labour's campaign attracted more positive responses and fewer negative ones than the Conservatives. There was, however, a striking rise in the number of negatives for Labour in the week following the broadcast, which helped to frighten Labour off from pursuing the health theme. NOP also interviewed a panel of Labour-inclined floaters each weekend. Starting with a sample of 700 at the first weekend the number gradually fell to 400 at the final weekend. In addition, surveys were conducted in six marginals, where it was found that Labour was doing slightly better than it was nationally.

The private polls clearly reflected the weakening of Labour's support in the last three days. The voting returns were based on a 'rolling' aggregate of three days' results and updated in the light of the final day's figures. On Monday it reported a Labour lead of 3 percent; on Wednesday it reported that the parties were virtually level, and in a post-election survey, conducted the day after polling day, it found a Conservative lead of 5 percent. Although Labour's private polls, like the public ones, confirmed the party's strength on the social issues, they contained more warnings of the weaknesses of its position on economic management and tax. Three-quarters of voters expected taxes and prices to rise for most people under Labour and 61 percent expected higher mortgages. Conservative polls produced similar findings and Tory strategists expressed scepticism about Labour's chances, given the voters' doubts about its economic competence. On the regular questions there was slippage in the final three days – on 'competence' (–11 points), 'best future' (–4 points), 'likelihood to be better off' (–9 points). The party's post-election qualitative research strongly confirmed the failure of Labour to present itself as a party which would fulfil the aspirations of many ordinary people.

Qualitative research had earlier been used to refine the language for questionnaires as well as to deepen understanding of what lay behind the survey responses. For several months before the election the agency had employed six groups to test pre-election broadcasts, policy packages and even the shadow budget. The discussions had also shown that a focus on how health service cut-backs lengthened waiting times for operations was a powerful attacking theme. The thinking and morale of the Shadow Communications Agency were also shaped by some 50 group discussions held among floating voters in marginal seats. Throughout the campaign these failed to provide encouragement, even when the opinion polls reported a Labour lead. The discussions were used to complement the surveys and provide a battery of verbatim quotes, which Mr Kinnock made a point of reading. People close to the leader claimed that he was aware throughout of the fragility of a crucial part of Labour's support, and that he could not have been surprised at the slippage at the end. On TV-am on June 28 he told David Frost that he had known he was losing.

One agency member reported that the qualitative research in key groups revealed that even on subjects where the survey findings were positive, did not translate into votes for the party. 'They might agree with your themes and policies but, when you discussed the matter with them, it was clear they would not be voting Labour'. Another said: 'Underneath the figures, there was no enthusiasm for Labour. I think that they were never going to vote Labour, even when they said they were.' The qualitative research conducted immediately after the election was particularly depressing, showing a deep hostility to Labour as old-fashioned and opposed to the ordinary aspirations of an increasingly prosperous electorate.

The Liberal Democrats had too little money to indulge in much polling. But they knew that their fortunes turned on tactical voting in a very limited number of seats. In February they commissioned small-scale telephone surveys in seventeen target constituencies. They asked questions about candidate recognition and local issues with a view to shaping the style of their local appeals. But they also asked about voting intentions and although their sample sizes, 400 or so, were unacceptably small by professional pollsters' standards, they did in some favourable cases publicise the findings locally in order to show Labour voters and waverers that only the Liberal Democrats had a chance of ousting the Conservatives.

The costs of private polling for the parties are relatively modest, certainly when compared to some other activities. During the campaign the Conservatives spent about £250,000, Labour about £200,000 and the small Liberal operation cost £40,000. After the election both Labour and Conservative parties being heavily in debt decided to re-think their future

polling programmes. Conservatives argued that if the design of questionnaires and analysis of responses were done in-house, the costs of polling
could be halved. A number of Labour strategists drew a lot from qualitative
research and were likely to expand this in future. In presentations in June
1992 to the NEC inquest into the election defeat the agency relied heavily
on this material rather than opinion surveys. These depth interviews made
clear that the party faced huge cultural barriers if it was to recapture the
necessary electoral support.

Discussion of the performance of the polls continued long after polling
day. Some participants complained that the polls had been wrong throughout in reporting a Labour lead. Conservatives stated that the public polls
in no way corresponded with the mood that they were encountering in the
constituencies and Labour's confidence was largely induced by its reported
poll lead. Labour leaders believed that, even if their vote would not be
sufficient to guarantee a Labour majority in seats, it would at least deny
victory to the Conservatives. After the event Labour strategists also felt that
the poll forecasts of a hung parliament or a Labour win drove away 'soft'
supporters as they came to the day of decision. The influence of polls on the
reporting of the campaign was considerable, and some commentators were
rueful about the way in which they had allowed themselves to be misled.
In the last days of the campaign the media became more convinced that
there would be no clear majority and spent much time on the political and
constitutional implications.

Some part of the media critique of the Conservative campaign was driven
by the negative poll findings and the peoplemeter reactions to the party's
broadcasts (see p. 170). In turn this effected a sharp reversal in public
perceptions of the likely winner of the election (see p. 148), and also
triggered grass roots complaints about the Conservative campaign. The
poll findings inspired critical questions at Conservative press conferences
– 'If things are so good, why are you behind in the opinion polls?'. In a
speech on May 21 Shaun Woodward complained about the journalists who
slavishly accepted the polling figures, and said:

'The opinion polls truly took over, determining much of the television
news agenda in this campaign – not only the style of how the campaign was reported but also acting as judge and jury on the parties
themselves.'

The polls were regarded not as snapshots taken at one point in the campaign
but, wrongly, as predictions of what would happen on polling day. After the
1992 experience the media and politicians might be more sceptical readers

of opinion polls. A number of editors promptly declared their reluctance to lead with opinion polls at a future general election. Hugo Young in the *Guardian* (April 11) declared that:

> The opinion poll business has proved to rest on fantasy . . . They simply did not find out what sort of nation this really is.

It is clear that opinion polls had been used to some extent to shape Labour's policy review. Mr Kinnock was persuaded by opinion poll findings that Labour could gain electoral advantage if it assumed a more sympathetic stance on proportional representation (see p. 64). But John Major, when confronted by survey evidence that proportional representation or self-determination for Scotland were popular, argued that the party must fight harder to persuade people otherwise. He assumed correctly that many people had only weak views on electoral reform and Scottish devolution and a clear stand would help to gain support.

In 1948 the pollsters' debacle did no lasting damage to the polling industry. Polls may get public opinion wrong – but no one has found a more reliable substitute. Politicians and journalists want to know what people think. Except when people go *en masse* to vote in referendums or elections, there is no accurate way of knowing how opinions divide. A sensitive reporter, an observant taxi-driver, an experienced canvasser may develop a wonderful feel for the public mood. But solid estimates of numbers can only come from asking a systematically selected cross-section of the population what they think. Polls are here to stay. But pollsters can make mistakes and what happened in 1992 will induce a healthy scepticism in politicians and public alike.

NOTES

1. A comparison of the five main pollsters' findings during the campaign shows some differences. Their average Labour leads ranged from 1.1 percent (Gallup) to 3.0 percent (MORI) and their average Liberal vote from 16.6 per cent (NOP) to 18.7 percent (Gallup).
2. See *Times Educational Supplement*, March 27 and *Independent*, April 2.
3. See Peter Kellner, *Independent*, 30 April 1992 and 1 May 1992.
4. Pollsters admitted that in drawing their nationwide sample of constituencies they had not introduced a weighting for constituency size. Since the electorates in Conservative seats were, on average, 9,000 greater than in Labour seats, this could have produced a bias of almost one percent in

favour of Labour. (See Table A2.1 for the difference between the overall and the mean swing which offers one measure of the differential impact of constituency size.)

5.   Soon after the election the MRS announced a committee of enquiry into why the polls had got it wrong and what follows is much influenced by their findings released on June 12.

6.   ICM announced (*Guardian*, 24 August 1992) that its post-election studies showed that there was a special degree of reluctance among Conservative voters about voicing their choice. In future surveys, ICM planned to use a ballot-box for respondents to fill in their voting intentions secretly.

# 8 Politics on the Air

## Martin Harrison

The 1992 campaign will surely be remembered as The Long Election. As early as the first week in January a presenter on Radio 4's *Today* programme was wondering on air whether the pace could be sustained until polling day. For weeks no political interview was complete without its ritual, fruitless questions about the election date. Scarcely an evening passed without at least one story heralding the coming campaign. The Conservatives' bid to brand Labour as the high-tax party was picked up by television and radio as early as January 6; before the month was out the press was reporting that the party had seized the election agenda. Similarly, each fresh batch of economic indicators was offering a chance to pin responsibility for the recession on the Conservatives and the Liberal Democrats benefited from the enhanced attention third parties tend to receive when an election is imminent. Yet political coverage still reflected 'peacetime' news values rather than the dictates of the stop watch and the BBC could hand the Prime Minister a public relations coup as the 'castaway' in the fiftieth anniversary edition of *Desert Island Discs* in January without a storm about political balance. The chief current affairs programmes were free to cover some of the principal issues in a slightly more relaxed atmosphere; *Panorama's* debate on the constitutional future of Scotland was not subsequently matched in network prime time when the election finally arrived.[1]

Nevertheless, the broadcasters were aware of being under constant scrutiny. Kenneth Baker's warning in February that 'the BBC has got to be very careful over the next eight to ten weeks' was unusual for its naked lack of subtlety but was symptomatic of the lobbying and bullying all parties engaged in during the run-up. Des Wilson made objections about insufficient coverage of the Liberal Democrats as early as January, while Labour's campaign director acknowledged that 'it's a rare day when we don't complain about radio or TV' and Labour MPs tabled a Commons motion protesting that BBC2's *Newsnight* 'followed the *Daily Mail* line like a flock of sheep'.

Oddly, there was less pressure once the election was under way, partly because so much of the coverage was indisputably balanced, bland (or

155

both) and partly because party officials had other distractions. They surfaced again in the closing stages. Michael Heseltine complained on *Today* (April 6) that the Corporation was failing to be 'independent' and the *Sunday Times* (April 5) reported 'intense and colossal bitterness' among 'senior Tories', who were 'considering a fundamental review of the BBC's charter to avenge what they regard as unfair election coverage'. (Noting that Central Office had itself been under attack, the paper added that 'the anguish at Smith Square looks like an alibi to come'.) Even with victory behind it Central Office continued rehearsing its grievances, hinting darkly about the future of the licence fee until calmer voices counselling magnanimity prevailed. Labour and the Liberal Democrats were less paranoid but no less active.

As always, the broadcasters claimed to be unaffected; 'It's a bad day when the phone stops ringing', as one television journalist put it. But the stock disclaimers were not totally convincing. Why otherwise were editors so slow to stop covering 'poster campaigns' that in fact amounted to a single site being hired for the duration of a photo-call? Why cover a poster campaign at all? Was it pure coincidence when, more than once, the handling of stories changed from one bulletin to the next following a party protest? And why, otherwise, was so much of the news coverage so passive and defensive? Why, above all, did the BBC drop 'Sliding Into Slump', prepared by its Economics Editor, Peter Jay, for the first election edition of *Panorama*? Described as essentially an account of the circumstances leading up to the recession, the item was vetoed by Samir Shah, editor of weekly programmes, on the ground that it was inappropriately backward-looking. Critics described the decision to pull the item (which received a late evening screening after polling day) as a 'pre-emptive cringe'; the Corporation and the Conservatives flatly denied that there had been pressure. Be that as it may, the manner in which the incident was handled gave exactly the wrong signals to BBC staff at a critical juncture. The real problem about the broadcasters' response to the campaign was not that it was biased or adversarial but that it was so often collusive, just as in 1987 – as a timely but unheeded *Dispatches* on Channel 4 demonstrated at the start of the campaign.

One of the problems the broadcasters faced was that, although this prom-ised to be the closest contest in years, the long run-up had already given much of their audience its fill of politics. Nevertheless, all made a major commitment of resources to their coverage. The volume of programming on the terrestrial networks, about 200 hours, was only slightly up on 1987. Even so, from early morning, with *Good Morning Britain*, *BBC Breakfast News* and *Channel Four Daily*, through daytime news on the hour, together with the extended Radio 4 *Campaign Reports* morning, afternoon and evening, and through the prestige offerings in prime time to the close of *Midnight Special* at around 2.00 a.m., the election was never far away. Viewers with access to *Sky News* who were so minded could follow the campaign right around the clock. While disruption of the schedules by election programmes irritated many people, anyone who was wholly antipathetic to campaigning could escape it completely by energetic channel-hopping. The 2.4 million homes with satellite or cable – ironically an exceptionally rich catchment of C2 voters, of whom so much was heard during the campaign – had even less difficulty in turning themselves into election-free zones. However, they could not do that while keeping up with what else was happening in the world. There were no election-free news programmes. Indeed, from John Major's announcement of the date through to polling day every one of the 300 or so main news bulletins on radio and terrestrial television carried election news. They did so even when there was no election news beyond a rehash of the previous evening's items and previews of the party leaders' engagement. Editors seemed incapable of letting the story drop. One yearned at times for that distant evening when the announcer stated firmly, 'There is no news tonight'. It did not come. BBC1's *Nine o'Clock News* was the only news programme to be systematically extended, going from 25 to 45 minutes on weekdays immediately the election was declared, but *Channel Four News* added weekend bulletins and Radio 4 ran longer current affairs sequences and weekend bulletins. (One casualty was *Feedback*, thus eliminating the one radio programme discussing listeners' criticism of radio output until after polling day.)

Neither the BBC nor ITN was on top form for this campaign. The BBC was wrestling with changes forced on it by a new Broadcasting Act, looking ahead to the exceptionally uncertain outcome of negotiations on its new charter and coping with a particularly difficult transition between directors-general. Its news and current affairs operation was still not entirely reconciled to the changes in managerial ethos and in approach to news handling imposed by the incoming director-general, John Birt. ITN was also facing an uncertain future after a particularly difficult period, managerially and financially, entailing many premature departures, including Sir Alastair Burnet. Controversial though Sir Alastair was, his sureness of judgment was at times sorely missed. The newcomer, *Sky News*, on the Astra satellite, had only a fraction of the resources of its established rivals and only a 1.7 percent share of viewing in satellite homes, though its reach was enhanced in the mornings by providing the news service for TV-am. Inevitably a marginal player in its first election,

*Sky News* nevertheless reached all the party headquarters and major media outlets. And, with its more flexible scheduling and its ability to carry news conferences and speeches live and at length, it opened fresh dimensions to the electoral role of television.

As always, the election swamped almost everything else for the entire month, absorbing 65 percent of the main bulletins on BBC1 and 59 percent on ITV (against 60 percent and 52 percent respectively in 1987) and 80 percent on Channel 4 (72.5 percent). At 43 percent Radio 4 also ran ahead of 1987 (37 percent), while still managing to carry many stories television missed or skimped. Television's month-long retreat into parochialism caused frustration among overseas reporters, some of them filing stories in discomfort and even danger, only to find London's attention elsewhere. *Channel Four News* was particularly prone to lump all non-election stories into a hurried round-up section. BBC1 led its main evening news with the election on all but three evenings, demoting it only for two royal stories and a helicopter crash. ITV cut away more readily, leading three times on the royals, twice on a helicopter crash and once each on an earthquake in Turkey and a pop idol's libel action.

ITN's greater readiness to break away from the election was even more evident in its daytime bulletins and in its tenacious coverage of the saga of Brightness, 'the fifteen-foot whale that captured the nation's heart'. Brightness had escaped from captivity in the Crimea to Turkey, where he was endangered by rising temperatures until, as ecologists pondered a 'mercy mission' to airlift him back to polar regions amid speculation that he might have been trained for special missions by the KGB, his Russian masters arrived to reclaim him, ITN's intrepid reporter accompanying him home to the Crimea, making the most of his exclusive to the last. Brightness had not only provided the light relief ITN traditionally looks for to round off its bulletins but had won greater attention than Britain's future relationship with Europe, foreign affairs and law and order combined.

If *Sky News* was offering what might in some ways be the shape of electoral news to come, the principal means by which the election reached the vast majority of voters remained the news on the senior networks. While these might be the dying years of their ascendancy, BBC1's two evening bulletins were still reaching some 14.6 million viewers on an average weeknight and ITV's around 12.3 million. Audiences for both dipped perceptibly over the course of the campaign.[2] In terms of time these bulletins were only a fraction of the output; there were other bulletins over the course of the day, *Channel Four News* and *Newsnight* on BBC2 with their more extended analysis and scrutiny of the issues, BBC1's *On The Hustings*, with its long extracts from speeches around midnight, paralleled by *The World Tonight* and *Election Platform* on Radio 4, Channel 4's *Midnight Special* and indeed the quite extraordinarily rich and varied range of programmes reporting and discussing the election. But although the politicians kept a particularly vigilant eye on *Today, The World at One* and *Newsnight*, programmes which they themselves followed and knew to be monitored by everyone else who counted in the campaign, their principal efforts were reserved for the flagship programmes, knowing that for many people what was shown there, for most intents and purposes, *was* the election campaign. The agenda of these programmes had become the place where party wills and wiles clashed most fiercely, each bidding to impose its hierarchy of issues and to secure the most favourable images. (One of the most furious Conservative complaints about BBC coverage was not that it had failed to cover John Major's speeches but that it had omitted to carry the clips they thought showed him to best advantage.) With all parties having learned the lessons of 1983 and 1987 the only real difference in the 1992 campaign was that party managers were more determined than ever to control and manage the process. If reporters were naive enough to see the leaders' tours as an opportunity for news gathering, Paddy Ashdown, for one, was quick to disillusion them. He told ITN's Libby Weiner (*Lunchtime News*, March 17),

'You know perfectly well that we intend to make sure you get the messages that we want to portray. Of course you're going to be trying to get the messages that you want across, but I'm determined that we should make sure the messages we want to portray are the ones that come across. And that's the way it will be with our party as with the other two.'

This preoccupation with the agenda was not confined to the parties. The BBC's Director of News and Current Affairs saw the *Today* programme as 'helping to set the day's agenda' – though other journalists adamantly rejected such a role. Network and regional news repeatedly presented headlines like 'Employment figures dominate the election' or 'The election battle moves to the health service' – both of them encapsulations of the day's events that raised as many questions as they answered. In this struggle for the agenda the criteria of victory were not entirely clear, and by a mixture of accident and design the broadcasters frequently muddied the waters. Sometimes their opening, midway and closing headlines ran in varied order; sometimes the first headline and first story differed, and sometimes the story given the biggest play came well into the programme. (In an interesting variant of this technique, The *Nine o'Clock News*

*Table 8.1    Election leads in main evening news programmes*

| | BBC | ITN |
|---|---|---|
| **March** | | |
| 12 | Major rejects calls for TV debate | Major rejects debates on TV |
| 13 | Parties stake out their position on tax as the debate gets under way | Kinnock promises Britain under Labour free of fear |
| 14 | PM promises reforming partnership with people | (2) Major: the Battle of Britain has begun |
| 15 | (2) Major says Labour has fetish for taxes | (3) Labour to pledge that half million will be free from tax |
| 16 | Lab 'budget': everyone earning up to £22,000 a year would be better off | Smith spells out Labour tax plan |
| 17 | Fall in factory production fuels debate over recession | Recession may have deepened: parties debate who can do better |
| 18 | Con and Lab roll out their manifestoes | Con and Lab manifestoes |
| 19 | (2) Unemployment's up again | (2) Another sharp rise in unemployment |
| 20 | Inflation stays unchanged | Major: Lab hasn't really changed |
| 21 | Con attack Lab spending plans | (2) Major dismisses polls as Lab nudges up its lead |
| 22 | Thatcher: task is not finished | Thatcher: task is not finished |
| 23 | Britain's trade gap narrows slightly | Major says Labour are cracking |
| 24 | Election battle has moved to health service | Skilled manual workers swing to Labour in election poll |
| 25 | Lab broadcast on health creates uproar: JM says Lab has blackened NHS, unfit to govern | The real family in Labour's peb on health service |
| 26 | The election campaign turns into a whodunnit | Con and Lab say they didn't leak the name of the child portrayed in Lab's election broadcast |
| 27 | K and M renew their battle on the NHS | Kinnock: only Labour can stop rot in NHS |
| 28 | Major rejects criticism of Con campaign | Major's megaphone message |
| 29 | (2) Going to the wall: the business failure rate | (2) Why the election went on a day trip to Boulogne |
| 30 | PM warns of a 'nightmare on Kinnock Street' | Major warns voters: beware of nightmare on Kinnock Street |
| 31 | M and K dismiss suggestions taxes must rise | Lab well clear of the Tories in 3 new polls |
| **April** | | |
| 1 | Major accuses Ashdown of being doorkeeper for a Labour Britain | Major: don't let Ashdown be doorman to a Labour Britain |

*Table 8.1   Election leads in main evening news programmes (continued)*

| BBC | ITN |
|---|---|
| **April** | |
| 2  Neil Kinnock has made a new offer on PR | Mr Ashdown said tonight his party will insist on electoral reform |
| 3  Ashdown warns other parties not to go it alone with a minority govt. | (2) Labour complain after Tory broadcast urges phone-in protest |
| 4  LDs accuse other parties of 'gazing in the gutter' | Labour's still ahead in the polls but Tories say we'll still win |
| 5  JM warns voters not to sleep-walk into a Lab govt. | Major says Scots devolution would divorce two great countries |
| 6  Lab and Con say no deals with LibDems | Kinnock: no deal as polls put him ahead in hung parliament |
| 7  Party leaders have been making their final push | Major says its Kinnock or me but Tories stay behind in polls |
| 8  The parties have made their final appeals for votes | Major: we *will* win as polls show parties neck and neck |

*The election was the lead in all cases except where indicated in brackets.

managed to 'flag' significant changes in the polls without breaching John Birt's contentious instruction not to lead on a poll.) *Channel Four News'* preference for exceptionally convoluted headlines also served as a useful defence mechanism. Both networks found it useful to lead on 'objective' occurrences like the publication of the monthly economic indicators or, for ITN only, a new poll. (Ironically, ITN on four occasions made a poll favouring Labour its first headline, yet it was the BBC – which never once headlined polls – that attracted Conservative ire.) BBC TV's headlines were slightly more likely to be low key or neutral than ITN's ('The party leaders have been making their final push' compared with 'Major says its Kinnock or me – but Tories stay behind in polls'). Nevertheless, both networks had a weakness for the striking phrase which the Conservatives exploited considerably more successfully than their rivals. John Major's 'nightmare on Kinnock Street' was a phrase few editors would resist; Paddy Ashdown's description of the old parties as 'gazing in the gutter' ran a close second. Such carefully crafted shafts could be even more telling than the soundbites, of which so much was heard in popular discussion of the campaign. Noting this, the parties will doubtless be calling on their phrasesmiths for an even greater contribution to 'democratic dialogue' in future campaigns.

Despite the difficulty at times in discerning exactly what 'the agenda' was, there seems little doubt that the Conservatives had the edge. Table 8.1 indicates (sometimes in compressed form) the top headline on each evening of the campaign. Bearing in mind that a 'Conservative' opener would normally be followed by a 'Labour' qualifier or second lead, and vice versa, if primacy carries any sort of premium there seems little doubt that the Conservatives had the edge. Making some admittedly arbitrary judgments, BBC1 arguably tended towards them on ten occasions to Labour's five and the Liberal Democrats' two, with nine evenings moot or neutral. Their advantage was narrower on ITN: twelve Conservative to Labour's eleven and the Liberal Democrats' two with five neutral or uncertain. (Explicitly Conservative leads quite clearly outnumbered Labour's on both channels, with the advantage being reduced if poor economic results are credited to Labour.) The Conservative edge was emphasised by a tendency for neutrally-headlined stories to be structured in the hierarchical order of Major, Kinnock, Ashdown.

Few of these headlines were positive; those 'warning', 'accusing', 'attacking' or 'rejecting' comfortably outstrip those 'promising' or 'offering'. They set the tone for much that followed. A Loughborough University team that analysed lead stories on television for the *Guardian* (11 April) found that all three parties were more often reported attacking opponents than presenting or defending their own policies.[3] The Liberal Democrats were the most negative; over forty percent of their statements attacked opponents, mostly variations on 'a plague on both your houses'. Under twenty percent of lead items contained a positive statement of the Liberal Democrat case. The Conservative ratio of forty percent negative statements to just over twenty percent positive was slightly narrower. Labour's was the nearest to balance, in proportions of roughly 38 percent to 34 percent. What the survey could not show was whether this strongly negative balance was a true reflection of the campaign or whether newsmen's traditional preference for negative stories was asserting itself. In either case, the prevalence of negative news may well explain the adverse reaction of many viewers to what they saw. As Hugo Young wrote a little earlier, 'We are all immersed, stewed, marinated in scepticism'.

Looking beyond the headlines, there was much less doubt about what the election was 'about', as reported by radio and television news. As Table 8.2 shows, the most prominent issue on all channels was the economy, above all its current condition and proposals and prospects for recovery. Other issues came and went at particular points of the campaign, but the economy kept recurring from the start of the campaign in the wake of the Budget, sustained by Labour's shadow budget (which was reported almost as extensively as the real thing – taking the first nineteen minutes

*Table 8.2    Relative prominence of issues in news coverage*

| | BBC1 | ITV | C4 | R4 | All 1992 | All 1987 |
|---|---|---|---|---|---|---|
| Economic policy | 1 | 1 | 1 | 1 | 1 | 5= |
| Taxation | 2 | 2 | 2 | 2 | 2 | 7 |
| Constitutional | 4 | 3 | 5= | 8 | 3 | na |
| NHS | 3 | 5= | 4 | 3 | 4 | 3= |
| 'Jennifer's ear' | 7 | 4 | 3 | 5 | 5 | – |
| Education | 6 | 5= | 7 | 4 | 6 | 3= |
| PR | 8 | 8 | 5= | 6 | 7 | na |
| Hung Parliament | 5 | 7 | 9 | 7 | 8 | 8 |
| Employment | 9 | 9 | 8 | 9 | 9 | 2 |
| Public Expenditure | 10 | .. | .. | 11 | 10 | .. |
| Northern Ireland | 11 | .. | .. | 10 | 11 | na |
| Environment | 12 | 10 | .. | 12 | 12 | .. |

.. = under 1%

of the *Nine o'Clock News*), and carried through to the closing surge of Conservative warnings against Labour's profligacy. Despite Labour's attempts to pin blame for the recession on the Tories and to present John Smith as a reassuringly safe pair of hands at the Treasury, this was not natural Labour campaigning territory. Nor was taxation, despite Labour's claim that its proposals would benefit eight in ten voters. However, by the close of the campaign, tax had almost run its course, taking under five percent of coverage in the final week – just when Labour most needed to reinforce its message in the face of attack by the tabloids. Overall, the economy and taxation accounted for a little under sixteen percent of news time. There was slightly less consensus between channels on the rest of the agenda. For the first time in many years it was not the exclusive preserve of the big parties; the fact that constitutional questions and electoral reform featured so prominently reflected news perceptions of the importance of the campaign in Scotland and, to a lesser degree, in Wales, subsequently fanned by the possibility of a hung parliament. Before the election the NHS had seemed Labour's strongest suit. However, the momentum the party had built up by the middle of the campaign was never regained after the Jennifer Bennett affair broke on March 25.

The way in which the war of Jennifer's ear captured the agenda was the most extraordinary episode in the campaign on the air, explicable only in terms of the mounting frustration among journalists at a boring campaign and the intensity of news management by the parties. Frustrations boiled over, news management collapsed, the ratpack roared off out of control, scenting a 'real story' at last, and both parties and broadcasters lurched off course. Like the parties, the broadcasters did not take the lead; their early bulletins on the morning after Labour's broadcast, confined themselves to reporting fairly low-key Conservative and Liberal Democrat criticism. By the evening, though, the affair had more or less taken over, with 10 minutes 45 seconds on the *Nine o'Clock News*, compared with 3 minutes 31 seconds for Labour's presentation on the NHS. Even programmes like *Newsnight* and *Channel Four News*, which normally distance themselves from the merely sensational or trivial, joined the turmoil. Quite what the story was about depended on who was telling it; by turns it was about waiting lists, sloppy teamwork by Labour headquarters, Neil Kinnock's fitness to be prime minister, dirty tricks by Central Office or journalistic ethics. It *was* a good story: it contained a sick child, a divided family, a whodunnit, a minister made to look foolish and journalists squabbling among themselves. Julie Hall's emotional denial of responsibility for the leak of Jennifer's name and the disorderly Labour and Conservative news conferences, which came across much more vividly on television than in the press, offered the most compelling and unpredictable images of the campaign.

Nevertheless, when pursuit of the story eclipsed all else, including the Liberal Democrats who ostentatiously refused to join in the furore, it had clearly got out of hand. Eventually this produced the remarkable spectacle of Michael Heseltine pleading with the media, 'on behalf of all political parties',

'to give us the chance to get on to the issues . . . .    We depend on you. There is no other way we can get over what we want to say'. (*The World This Weekend*, March 28)

As the affair petered out the political correspondents voiced their distaste at what Michael Brunson described as 'a pretty demeaning spectacle'. Senior television journalists looked back with embarrassment. One recalled that, although at the start of the campaign they had resolved not to fall in behind the tabloids, they had done just that. He blamed what he considered a lapse in standards on an absence of firm editorial control. Whatever the verdict on the broadcasters' handling of the episode, one consequence was to obscure the thrust of Labour's campaign on health. Jennifer Bennett and her glue ear received more coverage than housing, transport, pensions, law and order, defence, foreign affairs and Europe – indeed, than several of these put together. Some of these featured briefly as an 'issue-of-the-day'; others attracted no more than fleeting attention. Looking forward to the campaign, the BBC's Head of News and Current Affairs had recognised a duty

> to report the campaign as it unfolds. That means looking at what the parties are saying, but our second job is to ensure that all the other issues we think important are covered. (*Guardian*, February 17)

In the event, only a narrow range of issues featured substantially in the news – though some others received considerably more attention in current affairs programmes. The issues listed in Table 8.2 were the only ones receiving more than one percent of election news time on the main radio and television bulletins.

In 1987 the most controversial issue of the ensuing parliament, the poll-tax, was barely touched on in the election news. In 1992, Europe was as striking an absentee. Yet the unresolved questions about Britain's relationship with the Community and the Community's own uncertain course overhung almost all else; whichever party won would have to undertake ratification of the Maastricht Treaty. Yet, neither party wanted to address these questions and, apart from a scattering of references by the SNP to an independent Scotland within the Community, the European dimension went virtually unreported, except for a few briefing features – though several minority and regional programmes did tackle it several times. Only a few weeks into the new parliament the government would reject a referendum on the Maastricht Treaty on the ground that its approach to Europe had just been confirmed by the electorate.

Europe was not the only lost issue. Defence, which topped the bill in 1987, had almost vanished. The Citizen's Charter, so close to John Major's heart, rated only occasional passing mentions. So, too, with local government reform. When ITN's *Lunchtime News* opened a slot during which politicians answered questions submitted by viewers, it was noticeable how matters like child care allowances and nursery education were raised, of which otherwise very little was heard. This may not have been entirely unconnected with the Loughborough survey's finding that out of 1,031 appearances by politicians only 33 were by women. Party news conferences featuring 'women's issues' received little coverage. On other occasions, though, news programmes did pick up comments from the day's exchanges and presented briefing reports on questions that were otherwise being neglected. John Birt's controversial 'mission to explain' laid a particular mark on the *Nine o'Clock News*, which mustered a range of specialist correspondents to set out and compare the parties' stance on particular issues. A similar technique was deployed to deal with the conflicting assessments of Labour's budget proposals and the various economic indicators. Useful though such features were in helping voters through the welter of claim and counter-claim they were not at all popular with the politicians, especially when the broadcasters called on nominally independent commentators to assess their proposals. The King's Fund and the Institute for Fiscal Studies were among the most frequently cited. Labour had reason to be apprehensive at the predominance of experts drawn from the City on economic matters – though in the event their predominantly downbeat assessments can scarcely be said to have favoured the government. Both big parties were irked by the prominence the BBC gave to a report by Coopers & Lybrand, Deloitte concluding they would have far less room for manoeuvre on taxation and expenditure than either was suggesting. Even so, if the broadcasters erred it was in the direction of failing to see that matters of substance were aired rather than in promoting their own agenda.

The requirements of balance prevented any party winning outright victory in the battle for the agenda. Nevertheless, the tables suggest that the Conservatives had a clear edge not only in headlines but in the ground on which the campaign was fought and in air time. Reversing the position in 1987, they received more attention on all four networks and, according to the Loughborough findings, in both *Today* and *Newsnight* – the two programmes the Conservatives most love to hate. Quite why this was so is by no means clear, though it could be that the Conservatives' more attacking style was considered more newsworthy. By contrast, the drop in the Liberal Democrats' share of coverage compared with 1987 was expected, once the broadcasters had decided that they should have fewer party broadcasts. In the event they did better than might have been expected, despite their lack of recognised national figures. Although Des Wilson complained at inadequate coverage early in the campaign, and though they were almost eclipsed by the Jennifer Bennett affair, they came back strongly towards the end, when it seemed that they might be arbiters in a hung parliament. For similar reasons the minor parties received more attention than for many years.

The battle for coverage is of course not wholly, perhaps not even mainly, about issues. Increasingly it is about personalities and images, with the pictures counting far more in the minds of campaign managers than the words. Television crews unfailingly followed each of the party leaders as he criss-crossed the country from one photo-opportunity to the next. Practically every BBC1 and ITN bulletin contained its sequence of three packages on the leaders' day, much of which – and it amounted to at least fifteen percent of total coverage – contained no explicit issue content.

It was, however, implicitly but noncommittally eloquent of the party's concern for health or education or the leader's qualities of statesmanship. Labour was particularly lavish in its deployment of black limousines to promote its image of a government-in-waiting. Labour's photo-opportunities seemed slightly better organised than the Conservatives, but on all sides much of the material generated by these frenetic expeditions was worthless. Just why was the prime minister wandering round that DIY warehouse, that garden centre or that freight yard full of fertiliser? Not only viewers wondered. On at least one occasion John Major himself was reported to have rung his Policy Unit at No 10 to complain that he had no idea what he was supposed to be doing at some particularly futile photo-opportunity. The only times when this singularly bloodless form of politicking came to life was when the camera caught the unplanned spontaneous reaction with 'real people' rather than a reception line. Ironically enough, it was a sprinkling of left-wingers in Bolton that drove the point home. John Major stood up to their barracking and subsequently resorted to his soap box (in truth a Central Office packing case, but why spoil a good myth?) when the occasion allowed. In complaining that he did not look a prime minister Edwina Currie uttered what others in his party privately feared, yet these occasions in fact stood in contrast to the defensive smothering of Neil Kinnock, whose personal qualities rarely had a chance to come across.

Mostly, these nightly packages was not only repetitive, boring and uninformative, they were unacceptably complaisant. Travelling day-by-day with the candidates and their minders, only the more experienced and strong-minded could maintain both their distance from the reporting pack and from the party spin doctors. It was singularly difficult for anyone to do a proper professional job, and some reporters came uncomfortably close to simply relaying what the party they were following wanted conveyed at any given moment. Their carefully phrased reservations were often delivered across the accompanying pictures and drowned by them. The incident at the end of the campaign when Paddy Ashdown walked into Libby Weiner's live piece for ITN's *Lunchtime News* and engaged in badinage, patting her around the shoulders all the while, was symptomatic of a more general cosiness on which journalists looked back uneasily in their post-election inquests. Editors, as always, justified the leader packages on the ground of a responsibility to report what the parties were doing. (They could have added their need to get a substantial return for the substantial costs involved.) But since the parties claimed that they were only responding to television's hunger for pictures, the argument was not entirely persuasive. The obligation to report what the parties were doing did not extend to persisting with coverage of John Major's question and answer sessions. These were sampled, dismissed as boring, given short shrift in the coverage – and quickly dropped. Radio and *Channel Four News*, meanwhile, reported the campaign competently enough while paying only minimal attention to the leaders' comings and goings.

The commitment of such large resources to the leaders confirmed the tendency of the broadcast media over a succession of elections to presidentialise their presentation – even when a party might prefer, as Labour said it did in this campaign, to emphasise the team rather than a leader who was widely felt not to be up to the job. So Table 8.3 presents a familiar pattern, with three individuals quoted more often than all others and taking a high proportion of all the time given to their party.

In some respects the omissions are more interesting than the inclusions. It goes without saying that anyone with vaguely unorthodox views was kept well under wraps, but there were also figures of some ranking, such as Gerald Kaufman and Michael Meacher on the Labour side, who were scarcely seen in the national news, either because they were thought accident-prone or insufficiently *sympathique*. Similarly, for the government, Norman Lamont, an uneasy performer, was put on view as little as possible and, following his handling of a news conference during the Jennifer's ear affair William Waldegrave vanished so comprehensively from the screen that Robin Cook impishly promised that the new Labour government would dispatch a search party for him. But it was striking how many people who would be prominent in the new government featured very modestly during the campaign.

Next to policies and personalities the most frequent theme in the news was the horse-race. This took up more time than anything except the economy and the taxation issue. *News at Ten* had poll news in its opening 'bong' on six evenings – an emphasis it may subsequently have rued. BBC bulletins were barred from following suit but the *Nine o'Clock News* nevertheless gave the polls more airtime than its rival due to Peter Snow's virtuoso deployment of computer graphics and protracted exegeses of the BBC's 'Poll of Polls' – a grandiose tag for a moving average of other people's polls. Much of this erudition was devoted to analysing day-by-day variations within sampling error. As John Cole so wisely put it, 'If you interpret it within the strict rules the polls don't show anything at all'. The implications of this eminently sensible observation were too heretical to be heeded.

The increasing professionalisation of electioneering led news pro-grammes to devote more attention than ever to laying bare the techniques

Table 8.3  Politicians quoted in radio and television news (number of times)

| | BBC1 | ITV | C4 | R4 | Total | | BBC1 | ITV | C4 | R4 | Total |
|---|---|---|---|---|---|---|---|---|---|---|---|
| *Conservative* | | | | | | *Labour* | | | | | |
| Major | 159 | 138 | 47 | 125 | 469 | Kinnock | 162 | 128 | 42 | 120 | 452 |
| Patten | 39 | 18 | 9 | 29 | 95 | Smith | 37 | 22 | 9 | 23 | 91 |
| Heseltine | 31 | 15 | 13 | 16 | 75 | Gould | 19 | 11 | 9 | 18 | 57 |
| Lamont | 25 | 8 | 3 | 16 | 52 | Cook | 20 | 8 | 8 | 13 | 49 |
| Thatcher | 15 | 11 | 6 | 11 | 43 | Cunningham | 15 | 5 | 4 | 14 | 38 |
| Waldegrave | 13 | 9 | 5 | 12 | 39 | Brown | 20 | 5 | 2 | 9 | 36 |
| Clarke | 14 | 3 | 4 | 11 | 32 | Hattersley | 13 | 6 | 5 | 12 | 36 |
| Lang | 12 | 4 | 3 | 4 | 23 | Dewar | 17 | 3 | 3 | 2 | 25 |
| Hurd | 11 | 3 | 2 | 6 | 22 | Straw | 9 | 3 | 2 | 5 | 19 |
| Mellor | 5 | 8 | 2 | 7 | 22 | Blair | 6 | 1 | 0 | 8 | 15 |
| Baker | 6 | 2 | 3 | 8 | 19 | 30 Others | 23 | 12 | 9 | 8 | 52 |
| Fairbairn | 3 | 6 | 1 | 7 | 17 | | | | | | |
| Rifkind | 7 | 5 | 2 | 0 | 14 | | | | | | |
| Whitelaw | 3 | 3 | 1 | 3 | 10 | | | | | | |
| Lilley | 5 | 0 | 1 | 4 | 10 | | | | | | |
| 37 Others | 25 | 20 | 11 | 27 | 83 | | | | | | |
| *Other Parties* | | | | | | *Lib Dem* | | | | | |
| Salmond (SNP) | 14 | 13 | 4 | 12 | 43 | Ashdown | 144 | 122 | 33 | 120 | 419 |
| Sillars (SNP) | 12 | 2 | 1 | 6 | 21 | Wilson | 20 | 10 | 8 | 17 | 55 |
| Wigley (PC) | 9 | 4 | 1 | 6 | 20 | Steel | 11 | 3 | 4 | 4 | 22 |
| Adams (Sinn Fein) | 6 | 3 | 1 | 5 | 15 | Kennedy | 7 | 5 | 1 | 7 | 20 |
| Molyneaux (UU) | 6 | 4 | 1 | 3 | 14 | Beith | 7 | 5 | 1 | 7 | 20 |
| Hume (SDLP) | 5 | 2 | 4 | 0 | 11 | Bruce | 6 | 3 | 3 | 2 | 14 |
| Owen (–) | 4 | 2 | 4 | 0 | 10 | Carlile | 6 | 3 | 2 | 3 | 14 |
| Lambert (Green) | 5 | 2 | 0 | 3 | 10 | 27 Others | 27 | 9 | 9 | 8 | 53 |
| 20 Others | 15 | 11 | 7 | 13 | 46 | | | | | | |

of manipulation to which viewers were being subjected. The most notable innovation was *Channel Four News'* weekly feature with 'Peoplemetering' – a process by which panels of uncommitted voters viewed party broadcasts and pressed buttons to record their moment by moment reactions, the sum of which was translated to a computer plot. For those unfamiliar with the technique, long used to test commercials, the way in which viewers' moods shifted with the variations in the message was strikingly illustrated. The limitation of this exercise was that, although the panels invariably reacted adversely to a hostile approach, the professionals believed that these negative messages lingered longer in the memory than positive ones. The same programme also enlisted three professional campaigners to analyse campaign developments over the previous week. Although their world-weary approach may have seemed a touch cynical for some, for others it was a useful demystification of the attempts to woo them. Certainly these critics were less inhibited than the political correspondents presenting their nightly assessments of the state of play. These had to be impeccably balanced while managing to convey to viewers with finely-tuned political antennae what they really thought – all without giving offence. Those who succeeded, in this difficult genre, like John Cole for the BBC, compelled admiration, but the rituals of balance required the expenditure of a large commitment of time for modest illumination. However, balance also ensured that, even when things looked blackest for the Conservatives, their defeat was never allowed to seem inevitable.

The mixture of constraint, inhibition and passivity in so much of the coverage made it an easy target. Far too much of it was politics on the politicians' terms, filling the time but scarcely meriting attention. Even the most substantial and serious coverage was inclined to be restless and highly fragmented. A typical election package on *The Nine o'Clock News* could include over one hundred changes of speaker or subject, without counting repeated changes of shot. The average length of soundbite for the party leaders was down to about eighteen seconds, still somewhat ahead of the 9.8 seconds recorded in the United States in 1988 but closing fast. The *Nine o'Clock News* gave Labour's shadow budget an impressive nineteen minutes, but only 77 seconds was John Smith speaking. Such presentations were marvels of videotape editing but did nothing for respect or comprehension of policies or politicians. Yet many individual items or initiatives shone through. The most notable, if not the most exciting, were the briefing items dispassionately setting the differing party positions side by side. One clip that lingers in the memory is Labour's Sheffield rally, described by John Cole, almost overwhelmed by the din and the glitz, as 'the most astonishing political meeting' he had seen since John Kennedy

Table 8.4    *Party shares of news coverage*[1]

|      | Con (%) | Lab (%) | Lib Dem (%) | Others (%) | Total (%) |
|------|---------|---------|-------------|------------|-----------|
| BBC1 | 35.3    | 30.6    | 25.4        | 7.8        | 100.0     |
| ITV  | 38.1    | 30.7    | 25.6        | 5.6        | 100.0     |
| C4   | 40.0    | 30.7    | 26.8        | 3.5        | 100.0     |
| R4   | 35.7    | 31.4    | 23.2        | 9.7        | 100.0     |
| All  | 36.8    | 30.8    | 25.2        | 7.2        | 100.0     |

1.  National bulletins on BBC1, ITV and Channel 4, Radio 4 at 8 a.m.,
    1 p.m., 6 p.m. and midnight, 12 May–8 April 1992.

in New York. The report superbly caught an exuberance teetering over into triumphalism – but (no fault of Cole's) carried only 68 seconds of Neil Kinnock in three separate soundbites. There was also a superb little piece by Michael Nicholson for *News at Ten* on canvassing in Hartlepool, recalled simply for the way in which it showed how real professionalism can make something of the most routine of assignments even within the constraints of an election. Finally, there were the opportunities to hear what the politicians themselves were saying, without having them served up salami-style, which Sky and the *Hustings* programmes offered.

While network news received much the greatest attention from the parties, it by no means carried the whole reporting burden. Because they are not seen in London BBC and ITV regional programmes are subject to considerably less scrutiny from the party managers, even though some have larger audiences than some of the networked public affairs programmes and cumulatively their reach is substantial. HTV-Cymru, STV, Grampian and their BBC counterparts had a particularly important role in covering the issues relating to independence, home rule or maintenance of the Union with a thoroughness and intensity that could not be envisaged in national programming. (There were few truly regional issues within England, but many issues could be fleshed out and given a human dimension within the regional framework.) While London had its rush of blood over the Jennifer Bennett affair practically every regional programme followed the underlying story through with a comparable local example. So it was with education, employment and the argument over whether the economy was emerging from recession. Regional news felt bound to report on VIP visits to their area but, standing apart from the London-based travelling circus, they were markedly more inclined to draw attention to the manipulative, artificial nature of the activities they were showing.

Albeit gently, the regions were more likely than the nationals to find a quirky, humorous or even an ever-so-slightly disrespectful turn of phrase. They also focused at times on problems that failed to make the national bulletins, such as the difficulties facing dairy farmers or rural homelessness. And they offered a rather different set of faces and voices from the repetitive range that occupied so much of the national coverage.

The extended interview with party leaders is now part of election tradition; all duly appeared on *Panorama, This Week, Walden, Frost On Sunday, Newsnight* and *On The Record*. However, all three leaders were by now so well rehearsed and so skilled at parrying unwelcome questions that none of the interviews produced either great illumination for earnest enquirers or the gaffes or the novelty on which waiting reporters could pounce. Both these full dress occasions and many of the shorter interviews were often too undemanding and too predictable. 'Did people actually learn anything from them? Did they tell us anything new?', the editor of *Today* wondered. It was time, he thought, to look again at the political interview, and to consider whether it had a future (*Ariel*, May 25). Happily the same conventions did not apply when ordinary voters were questioning politicians – as the encounter between Margaret Thatcher and Diana Gould over the sinking of the *General Belgrano* in the Falklands war classically demonstrated in 1983. Of several programmes carrying on the tradition *Election Call* on BBC1 and Radio 4 was again the point at which the politicians were at greatest risk. Almost every morning brought a potentially dangerous encounter between a party spokesman and a voter displaying great tenacity or one able to speak more knowledgeably and personally than the politician. Neil Kinnock encountered a trade unionist who was convinced from her experience of the introduction of equal pay that a statutory minimum wage would cause job losses. Tony Blair was also wrong-footed over the minimum wage by the proprietor of a day nursery. Charles Kennedy had to admit that the Liberal Democrats' pledge to raise petrol prices could be inflationary. Michael Heseltine met a lady trenchantly demanding how the public could be expected to trust a cabinet whose members had stabbed Mrs Thatcher in the back. And John Major caused subsequent embarrassment by appearing, momentarily, to accept that the election might produce a hung parliament (his questioner was a Liberal Democrat professional who appeared to have slipped under the producers' guard). He also had a sticky moment in *The Granada 500*, where the leaders appeared before an audience transported from marginal Bolton to the Grosvenor House Hotel, when he was asked directly, 'Do you seriously expect us to forgive and forget the inhumanity of the poll-tax?'

(Loud applause). In the same programme Neil Kinnock was pressed on his views about PR. He had already refused to answer in a number of formal interviews, extricating himself with only minimal damage. When he tried to do the same in the closing moments of this session he met vocal and visible derision.

There were many more such occasions in the regions, with programmes like ITV's *Central Choice* mounting encounters between politicians and voters, which at best had a vitality that the more formal set-pieces lacked, if at times verging on providing a bear garden. Granada's *On the Knocker*, which followed the campaign in Hyndburn, and Yorkshire's fly-on-the-wall reportage on Attercliffe, were particularly enterprising presentations of a very different election from the one most people were following nightly. Here was a world of obscure candidates, constituency agents and enthusiasts, participating for love or precious little money, operating from inadequate premises, addressing envelopes, organising canvassing, having to watch every penny, doing their best to rate a paragraph in the local rag. These programmes showed a different electoral reality, far removed from the world of photo-opportunities and spin doctoring, a world where traditional rituals that one might have imagined had vanished or become irrelevant were still being played out – even if they were now assisted by a personal computer and a portable telephone.

Among a rich range of supporting programmes two were of note for very different reasons. *Star Chamber*, on Channel 4, seated leading politicians in a futuristic set, where a speaking computer fed them a mix of pertinent and impertinent questions on such matters as telling lies, their first sexual experience – and their politics. Among those subjecting themselves to this bizarre set-up was Tony Benn. Apart from eliciting the fact that he had once had a crush on Rita Hayworth his session produced probably the most radical set of policy statements aired during the entire campaign.

For the dedicated or insomniac minority *Midnight Special* on Channel 4, chaired with relaxed bonhomie by Vincent Hanna, tackled topics that were largely ignored elsewhere, achieving an elucidatory rather than a competitive atmosphere even on highly contentious issues. It was also marked by a note of humour and a whiff of heterodoxy that peak-time programmes conspicuously lacked. For example, Edwina Currie was asked, during a discussion of political morality following a Conservative broadcast, whether she had ever told a white lie. She promptly replied, 'Well, I think that was the most wonderful party political broadcast I have ever seen'.

## PARTY ELECTION BROADCASTS

The long-drawn decline of the party broadcasts continued, finding reflection here in the omission of the summary table found in earlier volumes. Once they *were* the election. Now, on radio, most of the party programmes were slightly reworked soundtracks of the television broadcasts. This seemed a somewhat casual approach to audiences which, even now, were often comfortably into seven figures. Only the Green Party really seized its opportunity, and showed that attention to the particular qualities of radio need not be unduly onerous: a single voice reading a gently satirical commentary on the state of the planet and the condition of British politics composed and delivered in the style of *Listen With Mother*. It caught the attention and brought a smile; of how many party broadcasts could that be said?

Among the minor parties, the nationalists (in their home countries), the Natural Law Party, the Liberals and the Greens qualified for broadcasts. (True to principle the Greens recycled part of their broadcast from the European election campaign.) The Liberal Democrats protested at being granted only four television broadcasts to the bigger parties' five, not least because of the implications for the amount of coverage they could expect in other programmes. ITV's decision to screen the major party broadcasts at 6.55 p.m. was seen as a 'demotion' from the prestige slot before *News at Ten* but actually brought a large early-evening audience preparing to watch the soap operas, and perhaps not so weary of politics. BBC1's switch from a slot immediately before its main news to one at the end, by contrast, placed the broadcasts after an extended chunk of electioneering.

In 1987, the most striking single event of the campaign on television was Labour's brilliant presentation of Neil Kinnock by Hugh (*Chariots of Fire*) Hudson. That memory and the greater attention now being paid to the parties' techniques of manipulation meant that, even before the Jennifer Bennett affair, the broadcasts received an exceptional degree of attention. Snippets appeared in news programmes or were analysed in *Channel Four News* or BBC1's *The Vote Race*. Whole broadcasts were screened and discussed in *After Midnight*, something that would once have caused grave offence but now barely produced a ripple. Several broadcasts had at least part of their message substantially amplified in this way.

Some became events in their own right. When the Conservatives met the challenge from Hugh Hudson by enlisting their own star director, John (*Midnight Cowboy*) Schlesinger, his first programme was presented at the British Academy of Film and Television Arts with the pizzazz of a commercial launch. Chris Patten fielded questions on its cost, artistic style and political rationale as if he were at Cannes rather than in Piccadilly; previews and reviews appeared in the broadsheets. This was probably the first party broadcast to have its own title. *The Journey* was about John Major's odyssey from boyhood in Coldharbour Lane to Downing Street. Inspired by a passage in his speech to the 1991 Conservative conference, it used his story to present and illustrate his vision of the Conservative Party as the party of opportunity. His trip back to childhood haunts took him to Brixton market, where he revisited the market stall where he once bought kippers, past the area where, in a reminiscence that had its full significance later, he first campaigned on his soapbox, and to his teenage home in Burton Road. 'Now, is it still there?', he asked. 'It is! It is! It's still there! It's hardly changed!' Conservative assurances that this was a genuine revelation were subsequently marred by the current occupier, an unemployed man 'for whom the Conservative years have done no favours', as the *Daily Telegraph* (19 March) put it with impeccable disloyalty. He reported seeing the prime minister trampling over his lawn a few months earlier. This part of the broadcast produced an instant dip on the Peoplemeter; the kipper buying was not well received either. The programme seemed only to catch a favourable response when it moved from Mr Major's personal odyssey to speak about opportunity and individualism. It also featured the Conservative election theme, Purcell's Rondeau from Abdelazer, rearranged in a modern idiom by Andrew Lloyd Webber to underline Mr Major's 'honesty, integrity and accessibility'. (In fact, the programme strayed from reality to myth more than once.) Unfortunately for lovers of the piece as an organ voluntary, a number of clergy felt impelled to banish it from the repertoire for the duration of the campaign in the interests of political neutrality. (Many tastes would have found it a shade strident for Lent in any case.)

The second Conservative broadcast began as starkly and incomprehensibly as an early AIDS commercial. A blacksmith in his smithy hammered at what, it eventually became clear, were shackles tying voters to three iron balls, 'Taxes Up', 'Prices Up' and 'Mortgages Up'. The anonymous voice-of-doom commentator (the actor Robert Powell) recited the horrors of taxation and inflation a Labour government would bring, including the extra £1,250 tax required of 'the average taxpayer'. Pseudo voxpops gave appalled reactions to propositions like, 'How would you feel about another £40 a month on your mortgage bill?' A young mother wistfully replaced a pack of Jaffa Cakes on the supermarket shelves, unable to afford them due to higher taxes. But all this need not happen; the programme had its upbeat ending with a Conservative victory striking away the shackles and the Jaffa Cakes replaced in the shopping basket. No politician featured in this extended commercial, directed by Bob Maloney, better known for his work for Guinness and Martini. Had it been a commercial it would of course have had no chance of passing the industry's vetting procedures.

This powerful video nasty was followed by a further onslaught over defence, again featuring no politician. It began with two young children getting up to play with their home computer after being tucked away to bed. The stylised violence of the computer war-game was intercut with shots of conflict from around the world. The message was that, despite the ending of the Cold War, we live in 'an increasingly dangerous, unstable world'. Labour, led by a man who had belonged to CND for over thirty years, and which was prepared to cut defence expenditure, was not to be trusted. The Conservatives, led by a man who worked for disarmament but had also led the country through the Gulf War, could be.

The next broadcast created a minor storm. It featured a happy land blessed by fewer strikes, low inflation, a rising share of world trade and ever-increasing public services, whose superior economic performance was attested by a clutch of continental 'vox pops'. Slipped into the tape after the press preview was an invitation to anyone recognising this country to ring a number – that of Labour headquarters. Labour learned about this merry prank before transmission time and protested (triggering replays on the news), but to no avail. The remainder of the programme attacked Neil Kinnock as a man desperate for power who would change any policy to get elected. But had Labour really changed? Returning yet again to the theme of taxes under Labour, John Major urged that there was only one choice: 'forward with me or backwards with Neil Kinnock'. The last broadcast opened with an apotheosis of John Major, admiring colleagues celebrating his qualities, and library clips alternating between Major on the world stage and a warm, outgoing Major, equally charming with the sick, the old and assorted multi-ethnic tots. His closing talk to camera was at last almost wholly positive. Couched in bland generalities ('I want to build a country that is at ease with itself.'), and with little hint of difficult choices to come, it was as quietly effective a performance as he is likely to give: a *nice* man, and *so* reassuring.

While the Conservatives were keeping their ministers away from the screen, Labour emphasised its team, not least to counter anxieties about Neil Kinnock. Produced by Hugh Hudson, the first programme opened and closed on Kinnock but also featured six shadow ministers within its five minutes. This was Labour's unfailingly upbeat vision of the new age, with not a negative image to be seen. It was stunningly shot, with the camera swooping from snowy mountains over picturesque villages, schools, King's College Cambridge and the City, underpinned with the throbbing chords of Labour's campaign theme by Michael (*Robin Hood: Prince of Thieves*) Kamen. Sometimes it was so visually compelling that the politicians' voiceovers were lost. And at times film-making took over from politics to produce a Beautiful Britain calendar. As a Labour official remarked, 'it makes the country look so bloody marvellous, you'd think: why change the government?'

There could be no misunderstanding Labour's next programme, although that, too, was almost too perfectly shot. In under five minutes, it told the story of two little girls, both suffering from 'glue ear'. One had parents who could afford a private operation, the other had not, and had to endure an agonizing wait. Directed by Mike Newell, the story was told without words, using child actors, accompanied by a piano version of the B. B. King song, 'Someone Really Loves You'. At the end of that sequence Neil Kinnock spoke for one minute, contrasting privatisation, which supposedly lay ahead under the Conservatives, with Labour's proposals for the NHS. (Viewers north of the Border missed all this, and were instead treated to Donald Dewar's celebration of Scottish resurgence and devolution.) Although some distaste was voiced at the element of emotional exploitation in Labour's broadcast, even opponents acknowledged that it was superbly done; members of the panel on which it was tested before transmission were said to have been moved to tears. Labour's mistake lay in exploiting a single case on the basis of inadequate staff work. Instead of consolidating one of the party's strongest points the broadcast blew up in its face.

Unsurprisingly Labour's third shot was more conventional. Produced by John McGrath, its opening scenes of industrial dereliction were far removed from Hudson's Beautiful Britain. Neil Kinnock and his ministers-in-waiting followed, returning noticeably more soberly to the themes of climbing out of recession, regenerating industry and Labour's social programme. The fourth broadcast was still more minimalist, with vox pops and shadow ministers alternating, all against plain backgrounds, the only additional effects being the theme music rising and receding. Negative remarks were left to the vox pops, leaving no fewer than ten shadow ministers, three of them women (the Conservative series had contained none in principal roles), reiterating a fragment of Labour's economic and social proposals. The final programme targeted floaters and waverers. Hugh Hudson's film was a succession of talking heads, some well known like Professor Stephen Hawking, Nigel Kennedy and Steve Cram, the others a politically correct mix of ordinary people, identified by name and occupation to illustrate the breadth of Labour's appeal, personifying a sense of community said to have been lost during the Thatcher decade. Gradually the endorsements switched from Labour as a party to Neil Kinnock, with clips displaying his personal warmth. There were also snatches of a 1991 chart topper by a Liverpool group, The Farm, titled appropriately enough, 'All Together Now'.

The Liberal Democrats' broadcast were low-budget affairs, drawing heavily on 'real people' to voice concerns that were picked up by spokespersons. Several of these 'real people', from what seemed to be a job lot of vox pops, appeared in more than one programme. All four broadcasts returned repeatedly to the failures of the old parties and the old system, but there were also more positive themes, notably Europe, which had merited no more than passing mentions in the other parties' broadcasts. Part of the second broadcast was reshot at a late stage to emphasise more powerfully the party's commitment to higher taxes to finance better education and training. The third programme met the 'wasted vote' argument head on with captions listing all the 250-odd seats where the party claimed to be the principal challenger, contending audaciously that the only really wasted votes were those cast for parties that had had their chance and failed. The final broadcast seemed less certain of itself, with a commentary by Paddy Ashdown over reprises of his campaign and photo-opportunities, as if viewers had not seen enough of all that already, and reminders of his days as Capt. Ashdown R.M. and on the dole. He ended with a call for the other parties to forswear the insecurity of running a minority government, but to join with the Liberal Democrats in achieving the firm smack of coalition rule. An audacious gesture again – but one that looked so cruelly irrelevant a few days later.

Ashdown was of course not alone in misreading the signs. April 9 brought with it that culminating ritual of a modern election: the results programmes. Here, above anywhere else in an election, is where the BBC and ITV battle it out, toe-to-toe, to see who has the faster results, brightest pundits and glitziest sets. The benefits these electronic dinosaurs bring to their viewers is not always so evident. Individual results were delivered with impressive speed, but the analysis was slow to reorient itself from the false steer given by a pair of unfortunate exit polls; many viewers went to bed expecting to wake up with a hung parliament. Radio recovered more rapidly, perhaps because it was less a captive of its own logistics than television.

Since there was of course not a hung parliament, the broadcasters were given years in which to think through the next campaign – and the parties to ponder the future and the ethics of their broadcasts. There was recognition on both sides of a need for fresh thinking.[4] Whether the resolve to rethink will be sufficiently searching, or whether routine and caution will prevail, remains to be seen in 1996 – in a very different audiovisual landscape.

NOTES

1. The assistance of the following is gratefully acknowledged: Jennifer Doyle (research assistant), R. A. Franklin, D. Harrison, C. Harrison, B. Tutt, M. Harrop, D. Hutchison and those BBC and Independent Television journalists who gave their views on a non-attributable basis.

2. In an ITC-sponsored survey 87 percent of respondents claiming to have viewed TV news at least once a day before the election, dropping to 83 percent during the election. By comparison, 66 percent said they read news pages before the campaign and 63 percent during it. (J. M. Wober, 'Televising the Election: A Preliminary Report on Knowledge, News Use and Attitudes in Three Parts of the United Kingdom', *ITC Research Paper*, May 1992, p. 8.)

3. See M. Billig *et al.*, 'The Election Campaign: Two Shows for the Price of One', *British Journalism Review*, 3:2 Summer 1992.

4. In the ITC survey, 88 percent thought TV covered the election 'very' or 'fairly' well, 8 percent said 'not very well' or 'not at all well', with 4 percent don't knows. For the press the results were, respectively, 62 percent and 22 percent with 16 percent of don't knows. With 65 percent 'don't knows', responses for radio were not comparable; 78 percent thought that the BBC and ITV could be relied on to give unbiased and truthful coverage, compared with 23 percent for newspapers. Where unfairness was alleged, it was more frequently attributed to BBC1 than to ITV, particularly with respect to the Labour campaign and, in Scotland, the SNP.

While 29 percent thought there was 'much too much' TV coverage and 36 percent that there was 'too much', 34 percent said 'about right' and only 2 percent that there was too little. Sizeable majorities thought there was not enough coverage of minor parties and that some subjects were not dealt with adequately. Viewers felt there had been too much coverage of the polls, politicians' personalities, analysis by political correspondents, press conferences and walkabouts but that formats allowing popular participation had been under-used.

The sample thought the Liberal Democrats 'came over' best in the televised campaign, followed by Labour and the Conservatives. However, although even at the end of the campaign there were striking shortcomings in viewers' knowledge, Conservative policies and leaders were more widely known than those of their opponents.

The BBC (*Reactions to 1992 General Election Coverage*, SP 92/33/230, July 1992) reports broadly similar findings. Accusations of unfairness seemed to be less than in 1987 and were equally spread between the main parties. Viewers' perceived knowledge of party policies remained virtually unchanged between the beginning and end of the campaign. In the minority expressing concern about TV coverage, most mentioning a specific issue (23 percent) were about Jennifer's ear, 22 percent about the amount of coverage and 10 percent about the 'slanging match between politicians and parties'.

# 9 A Tabloid War

## Martin Harrop and Margaret Scammell

IT'S THE *SUN* WOT WON IT the *Sun* proclaimed in the days following the election. The headline was a typical piece of *Sun* self-aggrandizement but there can be no doubt that the Conservative tabloids generally, and the *Sun* in particular, did a good propaganda job for the party in the last crucial week of the campaign.

Going into the election, the circumstances seemed less favourable for the Conservative press than in the campaigns of the 1980s. John Major was not Margaret Thatcher, the Gulf was not the Falklands, and the 1990s recession was certainly not the 1980s boom. The tabloids had thrived on the colourful personalities of the 1980s but now they had to learn to paint the subtler shades of politics in the 1990s.

Besides, the newspaper industry had problems of its own.[1] Circulation, especially of the tabloids, was down (Table 9.1) and advertising revenues, always sensitive to the economic cycle, even more so. The Press Complaints Commission, a self-regulating body set up in 1991 as one of the recommendations of the Calcutt Committee on *Privacy and Related Matters* (Cm. 1102), contributed to a more hostile environment for the tabloids. Among the general public, reaction against the *Sun*'s critical coverage of the behaviour of soccer fans during the Hillsborough disaster in 1989 had a similar effect. By 1991, according to Gallup, journalists had fallen to bottom place in a list of the esteem of various occupations.

These problems notwithstanding, the newspaper industry had developed since 1987. The industry as a whole had completed its move out of Fleet Street and many titles had introduced colour printing and Saturday supplements. The *Guardian* was redesigned, *The Times* changed its typeface and, most radical of all, the *Dundee Courier and Advertiser* finally decided to put news on its front page.

Some established titles, such as the *Daily Telegraph*, were now restored to profitability. For newcomers, however, the road to profitability remained hard. Indeed, *News on Sunday*, the *Sunday Correspondent*, the *Post* and the *Sunday Scot* had all folded, the last three not living long enough to fight a general election. Robert Maxwell's weekly newspaper, *The European*, founded in 1990, was losing money but it continued to publish during the

Table 9.1    Partisanship and circulation of national daily newspapers

| Name of paper Ownership group (Chairman) Editor Preferred result | Circulation[1] (1987 in brackets) ('000) | Readership[2] (1987 in brackets) ('000) | % of readers in social class[3] (1987 in brackets) | | | |
|---|---|---|---|---|---|---|
| | | | AB | C1 | C2 | DE |
| Daily Mirror[4] – – Ed. R. Stott Lab victory | 2 903 (3 123) | 8 035 (9 012) | 6 (6) | 18 (19) | 36 (37) | 40 (38) |
| Daily Express United Newspapers (Lord Stevens) Ed. N. Lloyd Con victory | 1 525 (1 697) | 3 643 (4 405) | 20 (20) | 34 (30) | 26 (28) | 20 (22) |
| Sun News International PLC (R. Murdoch) K. MacKenzie Con victory | 3 571 (3 993) | 9 857 (11 316) | 5 (6) | 17 (18) | 35 (35) | 43 (41) |
| Daily Mail Associated Newspapers (H. C. Hardy) Ed. D. English Con victory | 1 675 (1 759) | 4 303 (4 525) | 24 (26) | 32 (31) | 25 (25) | 19 (18) |
| Daily Star United Newspapers (Lord Stevens) Ed. B. Hitchen No endorsement[5] | 806 (1 289) | 2 628 (4 027) | 4 (4) | 14 (15) | 38 (37) | 44 (44) |
| Today News International PLC (R. Murdoch) Ed. M. Dunn Con victory | 533 (307) | 1 408 (1 008) | 12 (16) | 26 (28) | 37 (31) | 25 (25) |
| Daily Telegraph Hollinger, Inc. (C. Black) Ed. M. Hastings Con victory | 1 038 (1 147) | 2 492 (2 775) | 49 (53) | 32 (28) | 11 (12) | 7 (7) |
| Guardian Scott Trust (H. Young) Ed. P. Preston Lab victory, more Lib Dems | 429 (494) | 1 214 (1 458) | 52 (51) | 27 (29) | 11 (10) | 11 (10) |

| Name of paper Ownership group (Chairman) Editor Preferred result | Circulation[1] 1987 in brackets) ('000) | Readership[2] (1987 in brackets) ('000) | % of readers in social class[3] (1987 in brackets) | | | |
|---|---|---|---|---|---|---|
| | | | AB | C1 | C2 | DE |
| *The Times* News International PLC (R. Murdoch) Ed. S. Jenkins Con victory | 386 (442) | 1 035 (1 216) | 61 (55) | 26 (28) | 8 (8) | 6 (8) |
| *Independent* Newspaper Publishing PLC (R. Dahrendorf) Ed. A. Whittam-Smith No endorsement | 390 (293) | 1 083 (816) | 52 (48) | 29 (32) | 11 (12) | 7 (8) |
| *Financial Times* Pearson (Lord Blakenham) Ed. R. Lambert Not a Con majority | 290 (280) | 668 (743) | 57 (53) | 30 (30) | 8 (11) | 5 (6) |

*Notes*
1. ABC figures for April 1992 (1987: January–June). *Daily Sport* (no endorsement) excluded.
2. Joint Industry Committee for National Readership Surveys (JICNAR), Jan. 1991–Dec. 1991 average.
3. JICNAR's definition classifies the population aged 15 or over as follows: AB (professional, administrative, managerial) – 18%; C1 (other non-manual) – 24%; C2 (skilled manual) – 27%; and DE (semi-skilled or unskilled, residual) – 31%.
4. Ownership group and chairman uncertain pending legal procedures.
5. But during campaign was mostly pro-Conservative and strongly anti-Labour.

campaign. The only new newspapers which survived were 'seventh-day adjuncts' of daily parents: the *Independent on Sunday*, linked to the *Independent*, and *Scotland on Sunday*, launched by the *Scotsman* in 1988.

## How individual newspapers covered the campaign

The best-selling *Sun* paid less attention to the election than any other national daily except the *Star* (Table 9.2). Yet after a muted start its coverage became the most memorable of any paper. It lost no opportunity to pour scorn on Kinnock's credibility and it waged a sustained campaign contrasting 'untrustworthy' Kinnock to 'honest' John Major. It suggested some Kinnock-flee zones if Labour won: the Aussie outback, the Arctic

Table 9.2  Profile of press content

| | Daily Mirror | Daily Express | Sun | Daily Mail | Daily Star | Today | Daily Telegraph | Guardian | The Times | Independent | Financial Times |
|---|---|---|---|---|---|---|---|---|---|---|---|
| *Mean number of pages* | | | | | | | | | | | |
| Monday to Friday | 39 | 52 | 44 | 55 | 37 | 44 | 41 | 44 | 47 | 37 | 44 |
| Saturday | 45 | 63 | 65 | 80 | 44 | 61 | 211 | 114 | 101 | 115 | 46 |
| (May/June 1987, all weekdays) | (33) | (41) | (32) | (41) | (30) | (44) | (37) | (33) | (43) | (30) | (50) |
| *Front-page lead stories on election* | | | | | | | | | | | |
| Number (25 days) | 13 | 19 | 9 | 18 | 5 | 13 | 24 | 23 | 25 | 22 | 20 |
| (May/June 1987, 22 days) | (9) | (18) | (11) | (15) | (3) | (13) | (16) | (18) | (16) | (19) | (10) |
| *Editorials on election* | | | | | | | | | | | |
| Number/out of | 22/22 | 28/29 | 37/63 | 34/43 | 19/56 | 27/59 | 34/50 | 38/53 | 35/68 | 24/46 | 28/51 |
| Per cent | 100 | 97 | 59 | 79 | 34 | 46 | 68 | 72 | 51 | 52 | 55 |
| (May/June 1987, per cent) | (64) | (87) | (50) | (74) | (33) | (72) | (56) | (56) | (40) | (62) | (39) |

*Note*: All tables in this chapter cover the period 12 March – 9 April.

circle and the Space Shuttle. It claimed that a Kinnock win would lead to a 'campaign of strikes, demos and wrecking that will make the winter of discontent look like a Teddy Bear's picnic'. It worked up to a crescendo in the final week of the campaign, with a front-page editorial devoted to Major's qualities: A MAN FOR ALL REASONS. On the eve of poll, the banner NIGHTMARE ON KINNOCK STREET topped eight consecutive pages, describing graphically the dire consequences of a Labour victory – including a warning that loft conversions would need the approval of lesbian and gay groups on left-wing councils. The *Sun* psychic, following on from her conversations with Stalin in 1987, revealed 'exclusively' that Mao and Trotsky vote Labour from the grave, Queen Victoria and Elvis Presley vote Conservative, Hitler votes Loony and Genghis Khan doesn't know.

The *Sun* saved its most brazen deed until polling day. The front page pictured Kinnock's head inside a light bulb and ran this headline on a blue background: IF KINNOCK WINS TODAY WILL THE LAST PERSON IN BRITAIN PLEASE TURN OUT THE LIGHTS. 'We do not want to influence your choice of Prime Minister,' ran the copyline, 'but if it's a bald bloke with wispy red hair and two K's in his surname, we'll see you at the airport'. The *Sun*'s outrageousness, sometimes reaching self-caricature, possibly reduced its impact but certainly rendered it the most entertaining and audacious of the tabloids.

The *Daily Mirror*, by contrast, waged a more serious and traditional campaign. It followed Labour's agenda closely, savaging the government's record on education, crime, employment, tax, homelessness and the NHS. It pursued these issues not just on the front page but with a series of double-page spreads under the banner, 'the state of the nation', which used individual 'heartbreak' stories to highlight government failure. Where the *Sun* had found a miner with three cars who couldn't 'afford to vote Labour', the *Mirror* discovered homeless youths wandering the streets of the capital, with only a puppy for company.

The *Mirror* struggled almost single-handedly against Fleet Street's overwhelming assault on Labour's tax plans. It chipped away with a number of inside-page stories on the Conservatives' hidden tax costs but led on the subject only once. On April 6, it accused Major of tax fraud, increasing the overall tax burden while donning the mantle of tax-cutter. 'Never has a Prime Minister been guilty of so much deception,' said its leader column. Other attacks on the Prime Minister were unpleasantly personal: 'Spot the fish face', 'silly Moo', 'a cardboard cut out'.

The paper's final exhortations employed Labour's campaign slogan, IT'S TIME FOR A CHANGE, and echoed its 'vote for them' formula of 1987 (and 1945). On the eve of poll, a solid nine pages urged readers to 'remember our people': the homeless, the jobless, the pensioners, the servicemen, the children and the sick. On polling day itself, the *Mirror* gave over its front page to the Red Rose logo, a picture of Kinnock and the headline: THE TIME IS NOW – VOTE LABOUR.

The *Mirror* painted a negative picture of Britain in penury, much as it had done in 1987, and presented a Labour vote as a caring concern for needy others. There was little positive reflection of the progressive, dynamic, upwardly mobile image Labour leaders were trying to create. The lasting impression was of a worthy but old-fashioned campaign. The *Mirror* fought a good battle but it was fighting on the wrong terrain.

The *Daily Express* waged the most committed political campaign of all the populars, carrying election stories as front-page leads more frequently than any other tabloid (Table 9.2). It operated as, in effect, a daily propaganda agency for Conservative Central Office, taking its cue from the party and aggressively pursuing the party's agenda of tax and leadership. It brought back its Moscow correspondent, Peter Hitchens, to hound the Kinnock campaign, a task he performed with gusto, as he battled to ask Labour's leader the 'key' question – 'Why are you a liar?' However the *Express* shared the mid-campaign frustration of the Conservative press at Major's apparently faltering performance: 'if the trumpet give an uncertain sound, who shall prepare himself for battle . . . .  The Tories are drinking in the Last Chance Saloon.'

In the final week, when the *Express's* own Harris poll suggested a Labour victory, the paper switched its main thrust to scaring 'floaters' from the Liberal Democrats. Ironically, this was the first time in the campaign that the Liberal Democrats forced their way to the top of the tabloid agenda. The *Express*, *Mail* and *Star* all rallied around the theme that a vote for 'nice' Paddy Ashdown would let in 'nasty' Neil Kinnock, leader of what the *Express* described as 'a socialist shower dominated by student politicos and polytechnic lecturers'. DON'T THROW IT ALL AWAY was the *Express's* eve-of-poll headline over its front-page editorial, illustrated by a cartoon of Ashdown's Trojan horse. On polling day itself, the *Express* led on the news of a late Conservative surge but it did not abandon its attack on Paddy Ashdown, warning once more that a vote for the Liberal Democrats would benefit Labour.

Despite its unabashed bias, the *Express* ran a genuinely wide-ranging spread of opinions in weekly campaign commentaries. It also carried the Little Englander views of Bernard Ingham: 'Cry England, Harry and St. George when you enter the polling booth – and vote Conservative to preserve the UK.' Early on, Ingham had predicted a Conservative victory by 20 seats and, thus, might have saved the *Express* the expense of troubling the pollsters.

The *Daily Mail* was noticeably more restrained in its praise for John Major, more critical of the Conservative campaign and more willing to concede Neil Kinnock's achievements in re-fashioning Labour. It acknowledged that Labour's leader was a 'class act' in set speeches and that the recession had undermined the Conservatives' reputation for economic management. All this left a suspicion that the *Mail*'s editor, Sir David English, may have been among those Conservatives who had still not quite forgiven the party for overthrowing Margaret Thatcher. Indeed, the *Mail* began its coverage with a backwards glance at 'the Iron Lady who bestrode the political, yes and the world, stage'.

However, there was no doubt about the *Mail's* desire for a Conservative victory. Two days before polling, it devoted its front page to a leader under the headline, WARNING, which argued that 'Mr Smith's budget would at a stroke turn recession to slump'. IF YOU MAKE IT, THEY'LL TAKE IT, said the *Mail*. Another full-page editorial the following day warned that the voters' choice was to 'put the clock back with Kinnock' or to go forward with Major. This issue contained 13 pages, including advertisements, in which the lead story was pro-Conservative. On polling day, readers were confronted with pictures of Kinnock and Major over the front-page comment, WHICH MAN DO YOU TRUST?

Technically the *Star* was non-partisan during the campaign, the only tabloid to remain so. In its final editorials it set great store by its independence: 'unlike the *Sun* we have not trotted out every Tory tirade', nor, unlike the *Mirror*, peddled 'every Labour scare'. It restricted its guidance to a plea not to waste votes on Paddy Ashdown: 'it's Conservative or Labour. That's a vote. Not a wave of a lettuce leaf.' IT'S UP TO YOU was the headline over a front-page editorial on April 8.

However the tone of the *Star*'s coverage was consistently hostile to Labour. As with the other Conservative tabloids, the paper's limited election coverage was built round attacks on the Labour Party (Table 9.3). Under a Labour government, strikes would return, millions would be barred from using their credit cards and the cost of going to the football would go up to £24. Neil Kinnock was compared to Dracula rising from his tomb, baring his fangs as he sniffs the heady scent of power. The Liberal Democrats, however, could claim equally contemptuous treatment. As the campaign progressed and the prospect of a hung parliament grew, so the *Star* turned its attention to proportional representation. 'PR stands for Prat's Rule', an editorial informed its readers. The *Star*'s election coverage was

## Daily Express

WEDNESDAY, APRIL 8, 1992    WEATHER SHOWERS    30p

### You, the British people, have achieved great things for yourselves and for your country

# DON'T THROW IT ALL AWAY

BRITAIN has changed over the last 13 years, and changed radically — FOR THE BETTER.

---

## Daily Mail

WEDNESDAY, APRIL 8, 1992    30p

NATIONAL NEWSPAPER OF THE YEAR

### We can still win, say the Tories

# MAJOR SET FOR LAST LAP SPRINT

By GORDON GREIG, Political Editor

JOHN MAJOR spearheaded a supreme effort by the Tories in the closing stages of the election campaign last night.

Senior party figures are convinced there is evidence that he can still win.

Confident: Mr Major yesterday

### Italians want to dump PR and go British

THE Tories then stand against proportional representation and the support of disillusioned Italians last night.

---

## THE Sun

WEDNESDAY, APRIL 8, 1992    25p    Today's TV: Pages 22 and 33

**PAGE ONE OPINION**
### WHO WILL BEST RUN BRITAIN?

# A QUESTION OF TRUST

KINNOCK: We can have no confidence in his judgment    MAJOR: He's solid and dependable with a cool head

**NIGHTMARE ON KINNOCK STREET: Pages 2, 3, 4, 5, 6, 7, 8, 9 & 34**

---

## DAILY Mirror

FORWARD WITH THE PEOPLE    25p

### ELECTION '92

# IT'S TIME FOR CHANGE

## 13 Tory years.. NOW look at Britain's misery

**REMEMBER US TOMORROW**
TURN TO PAGE 2

Table 9.3   Coverage of major political parties in front-page lead stories and in editorials about the election

| | Daily Mirror | Daily Express | Sun | Daily Mail | Daily Star | Today | Daily Telegraph | Guardian | The Times | Inde-pendent | Financial Times | Total |
|---|---|---|---|---|---|---|---|---|---|---|---|---|
| *Front-page lead stories* | | | | | | | | | | | | |
| Conservative | 9 | 10 | 3 | 3 | – | 5 | 6 | 12 | 4 | 7 | 4 | 63 |
| Labour | 3 | 6 | 6 | 14 | 2 | 3 | 7 | 1 | 6 | 2 | 6 | 56 |
| Liberal Democrat | – | 1 | – | 1 | 1 | – | – | – | 3 | 1 | – | 7 |
| More than one party | – | 2 | – | – | 2 | 4 | 11 | 10 | 12 | 12 | 10 | 63 |
| Total | 12 | 19 | 9 | 18 | 5 | 12 | 24 | 23 | 25 | 22 | 20 | 189 |
| *Editorials* | | | | | | | | | | | | |
| Conservative | 18 | 7 | 10 | 8 | 3 | 9 | 13 | 13 | 14 | 5 | 8 | 108 |
| Labour | 4 | 19 | 19 | 20 | 6 | 3 | 14 | 6 | 9 | 4 | 8 | 112 |
| Liberal Democrat | – | 2 | 3 | 3 | 3 | 3 | 2 | 4 | 2 | 3 | 1 | 26 |
| More than one party | – | – | 1 | 2 | 2 | 6 | 1 | 12 | 5 | 9 | 9 | 47 |
| Total | 22 | 28 | 33 | 33 | 14 | 21 | 30 | 35 | 30 | 21 | 26 | 293 |

the most tasteless on offer, completely unrelieved by the humour and energy of the *Sun*. Mercifully it was also the slightest.

By marked contrast, *Today*, the only other tabloid whose loyalties were in doubt, offered the least slanted election news in the popular press. *Today* had opened the campaign running the slogan, PROPER NEWS NOT PROPAGANDA alongside its mast-head. True to its promise it maintained an admirable balance for most of the campaign. It listed its Cabinet of all the talents, featuring John Smith as PM, Michael Heseltine as Chancellor and Neil Kinnock as Home Secretary. It criticised 'Patten's Puppies' in Conservative Central Office, condemned racism in Cheltenham's Conservative Party and said Labour was 'far ahead in tactics and skill'.

*Today* also displayed some sympathy for the Liberal Democrats, praising Paddy Ashdown for his campaign style. However, as the election entered its final week, the paper began to show some of the tell-tale signs of a traditional Conservative tabloid. On the day that the *Mail* and *Express* first warned of the dangers of a Liberal Democrat vote, *Today's* leader urged readers to cast a real vote, 'not a protest'. The sober, reasoned tone of all its coverage hitherto was suddenly dropped for an editorial three days before polling, which suggested that an egg flung at John Major was evidence that a 'group of loony, left-wing anarchists' was still at large. However its final verdict in favour of the Conservatives was based on the belief that Major's leadership was more trustworthy than Kinnock's. *Today's* decision meant that all Murdoch's five papers, with their combined circulation of some 10 million, supported the Conservatives.

Except for *Today*, tabloid coverage was based on knocking copy. The Conservative papers featured Labour more than their own party in front-page leads and editorials; the *Mirror*, by contrast, focused on Conservative weakness rather than Labour strength (Table 9.3). The same pattern holds for party advertising. The recession, it seemed, intensified the natural tendency towards negative propaganda.

The political balance among the quality dailies was somewhat more even, largely due to the *Financial Times'* surprising last-minute declaration of support for Labour, albeit only as the largest party in a hung parliament. With the *Guardian* also supporting Labour, and the *Independent* remaining independent, the Conservative cause among the daily broadsheets was defended by the *Daily Telegraph* and *The Times*.

In tone of reporting and choice of headlines, the *Telegraph* played with a straight bat; its commitment to a Conservative victory was released only in editorials and commentaries. Although the *Telegraph* was by some distance the most ardent of the Conservative broadsheets, it too seemed less sure

Table 9.4   *Party supported by daily newspaper readers*
*(1987 in brackets)*

| Newspaper | | Party supported by readers | | |
|---|---|---|---|---|
| | | Con % | Lab % | Lib Dem % |
| Daily Telegraph | 1992 | 72 | 11 | 16 |
| | (1987) | (80) | (5) | (10) |
| Daily Express | 1992 | 67 | 15 | 14 |
| | (1987) | (70) | (9) | (18) |
| Daily Mail | 1992 | 65 | 15 | 18 |
| | (1987) | (60) | (13) | (19) |
| Financial Times | 1992 | 65 | 17 | 16 |
| | (1987) | (48) | (17) | (29) |
| The Times | 1992 | 64 | 16 | 19 |
| | (1987) | (56) | (12) | (27) |
| Sun | 1992 | 45 | 36 | 14 |
| | (1987) | (41) | (31) | (19) |
| Today | 1992 | 43 | 32 | 23 |
| | (1987) | (43) | (17) | (40) |
| Daily Star | 1992 | 31 | 54 | 12 |
| | (1987) | (28) | (46) | (18) |
| Independent | 1992 | 25 | 37 | 34 |
| | (1987) | (34) | (34) | (27) |
| Daily Mirror | 1992 | 20 | 64 | 14 |
| | (1987) | (20) | (55) | (21) |
| Guardian | 1992 | 15 | 55 | 24 |
| | (1987) | (22) | (54) | (19) |

Source: MORI.

of itself than in the glory years of the 1980s. Like all the Conservative press, the *Telegraph* found it easier to attack Neil Kinnock ('He has little to say and says it at inordinate length') than to defend its own man ('John Major is impressively competent'). The paper also acknowledged that Conservative economic policy had deepened the present recession, even if Labour's protectionist instincts would worsen the next one. Its final editorial conceded that the 'glittering promises' of the Thatcher years had crumbled: 'But we are in no doubt that if the electorate fails to pardon the Conservatives at the polls today, it will pay a price at the hands of a Labour government, perhaps sustained by the Liberal Democrats, which will set back this country a generation.'

*Table 9.5    Photographs of leading party politicians in national daily newspapers (1987 in brackets)*

| Politician | Number of photos | | % of all photos | |
|---|---|---|---|---|
| *Conservative* | 1144 | (509) | 49 | (39) |
| John Major | 334 | | | |
| Margaret Thatcher | 98 | (196) | | |
| Norma Major | 82 | | | |
| Chris Patten | 57 | | | |
| Michael Heseltine | 50 | (18) | | |
| Norman Lamont | 46 | | | |
| Kenneth Clarke | 20 | | | |
| Norman Tebbit | 18 | (38) | | |
| Kenneth Baker | 17 | (20) | | |
| Sebastian Coe | 13 | | | |
| *Labour* | 917 | (525) | 39 | (40) |
| Neil Kinnock | 277 | (175) | | |
| Glenys Kinnock | 77 | (38) | | |
| John Smith | 63 | | | |
| Robin Cook | 29 | | | |
| Glenda Jackson | 26 | | | |
| Margaret Beckett | 23 | | | |
| Roy Hattersley | 23 | (31) | | |
| Denis Healey | 21 | (37) | | |
| Jack Cunningham | 20 | | | |
| Gerald Kaufman | 18 | | | |
| *Liberal Democrat* | 293 | (245) | 12 | (19) |
| Paddy Ashdown | 158 | | | |
| Des Wilson | 14 | | | |
| Jane Ashdown | 12 | | | |
| David Steel | 10 | (78) | | |
| Cyril Smith | 10 | | | |
| Roy Jenkins | 9 | (6) | | |

*Notes*:
1. 1987 figures are only shown where there was a significant number of photographs for that politician.
2. 1322 photographs of Natural Law candidates not included in total. Most of these were in advertisements. 53 photos of politicians from other parties (mainly SDP) also excluded.

Table 9.6   Partisanship and circulation of national Sunday newspapers

| | Preferred result | Readership (Jan.–Dec. 91) ('000) | Average Circulation (April 1992) ('000) |
|---|---|---|---|
| News of the World | Con victory | 12 807 | 4 768 |
| Sunday Mirror | Lab victory | 9 120 | 2 774 |
| The People | Lab victory | 6 581 | 2 165 |
| The Mail on Sunday | Con victory | 5 677 | 1 941 |
| Sunday Express | Con victory | 4 580 | 1 666 |
| The Sunday Times | Con victory | 3 568 | 1 167 |
| The Observer | Lab victory | 1 839 | 541 |
| The Sunday Telegraph | Con victory | 1 734 | 558 |
| Independent on Sunday | Not a Con win | 1 332 | 402 |

*Sources*: circulation – ABC. Readership – JICNARS.

*The Times'* front-page news stories and headlines also betrayed little bias. In Peter Riddell and Matthew Parris, *The Times* also had two of the most perceptive and, especially in the case of Parris, entertaining columnists in Fleet Street. *The Times* was cooler towards the Conservatives and warmer towards Labour than in past elections. It became an outspoken critic of the Conservative campaign and John Major's 'nervous' performance. But, to paraphrase one editorial, it was fantasy to think that Labour would make a better job of running the country; and at the end it argued that decent, honest, likeable John Major 'deserves to be given a first vote of confidence'.

Probably more than any other broadsheet, the *Guardian* allowed a little partisan gloss to colour its news pages. Perhaps this was unsurprising, since the *Guardian* now has a smaller proportion of Conservative readers than any other national daily (Table 9.4). The *Guardian's* pro-Labour stance emerged more strongly from its front-page headlines than from its rambling and under-edited editorials. It formally declared itself in the Labour camp on April 7: 'It *is* time for a change.' The following day, it expressed its many concerns about Labour, which beneath its surface gloss had said little of substance. Hugo Young's column on polling day captured the ambivalence of its leader-writers. This was an election for sceptics, wrote Young; voters were fed up with the Conservatives but could find no enthusiasm for Labour.

The *Independent* claimed that it was 'the only paper that will bring you unbiased reporting'. In many ways the *Independent* provided the most imaginative and individual coverage of the election. It commissioned research on the parties' spending plans, and gave space to a series of nonpolitical celebrities (such as soccer broadcaster Jimmy Greaves) to say who they were voting for and why. In the last week it ran a series of three leader columns putting the case for each of the three major parties.

The quality dailies offered wide-ranging and substantial coverage of the campaign. Their front pages were rarely diverted from the election, certainly less often than in 1987 (Table 9.2). They all ran daily special sections on the campaign, which both highlighted and compartmentalized election coverage. Business sections, and to a greater extent than previously, colour magazines, also contributed election material. A conscientious reader of any one of the broadsheets would have emerged from the campaign generally well-informed – and aware in particular that neither of the major party's public spending plans would be sustainable in the real, post-election, world.

Whether press coverage was excessive is a matter for newspaper readers. In a MORI sample, some 56 percent felt that the press paid too much attention to the election; that compares with 52 percent in 1987 and 36 percent in 1983. These figures reflect the high profile nature of the campaign in the newspapers. Every daily bar the *Sun* featured the election as its front-page lead more often than in 1987 (Table 9.2).

In terms of photographs of politicians appearing in the national dailies, the Conservatives held a clear lead this time (Table 9.5). This can largely be explained by the continued appeal of Margaret Thatcher to the snappers. Her photograph appeared more often than any other Conservative politician's except John Major's. Mrs Thatcher beat Norma Major into third place in the Conservative charts. But overall, leaders' spouses continued to gain ground, with Glenys Kinnock now established in second place on Labour's list, and only John Smith for competition. Paddy Ashdown accounted for 48 percent of the Liberal Democrat photographs, a high proportion which must have contributed to the impression of a one-man band.

With only four issues published between the announcement and polling day, the Sunday papers are less central to election campaigns than the dailies. Five Sundays (with a combined circulation of 10.1m) supported the Conservatives, while three (circulation 5.5m) favoured Labour (Table 9.6). Like its sister paper, the new *Independent on Sunday* remained formally uncommitted although its editor, Ian Jack, published a signed editorial explaining why he would not be voting Conservative. The only Sunday paper to change its allegiance from 1987 was the *Observer*, which

Table 9.7 Front-page lead stories about the general election campaign, 12 March–9 April, 1992

| Date | Daily Mirror | Daily Express | Sun | Daily Mail | Daily Star | Today | Daily Telegraph | Guardian | The Times | Independent | Financial Times |
|---|---|---|---|---|---|---|---|---|---|---|---|
| **Mar** | | | | | | | | | | | |
| 12 | They're Off | Major:I'm a Winner | Ian Botham Backs Major | Health Ad: Labour's 1st Dirty Trick | (McGuigan Libel) | The Dead Heat is On | Major and Kinnock Confident | Major Gambles on Election | City Nervous as Major Calls Election | Tax Battle for No. 10 | Parties Draw Battle Lines |
| 13 | UK Schools: Bottom of the Class | Labour No to 20p Tax | (40p bet wins £556,000) | Labour Votes to Tax Poor | Lib Dem Candidate says He's Homosexual | Major Refuses TV Debate | Tory Gamble Unnerves City | PM Spurns TV Debate | Labour Starts with Lead | (Aid for Russia) | Labour Clings to Narrow Lead |
| 14 | (Star and Suicide) | Big Yes for Tory Tax Cuts | (Biggest Baby) | Heseltine Condemns Labour | (Mister Magic) | (Baby Murder) | Tories Attack Kinnock's Inexperience | (South Africa) | Kinnock Pledges to Banish Fear | Kinnock and Major Opening Shots | Kinnock Sets Out Election Message |
| 16 | Tories Waste Millions on Dole Uniforms | Kinnock Backs '83 Manifesto | Kinnock Admits He was Wrong in Past | Kinnock Backs '83 Manifesto | (Rig Disaster) | (Rig Disaster) | Business Goes Against Lab | PM Seeks Interest Rate Cut | Labour: Top Tax Rate at £40,000 | Labour Shows Tax Plans | Business Chiefs Want Tory Win |
| 17 | Goodbye to All This | Tories Race to 3% Lead | (Steph Quits Job) | Labour's Tax Plans Criticised | (Ticket Tout) | Effect of Labour's Tax | Labour seeks To Up Tax on Better Off | Tories Gun for Smith Budget | Labour Loads Taxes on Rich | Labour Gamble on Taxation | Lab Budget May Help 8/10 |
| 18 | (York Split) | (York Split) | (York Split) | (York Split) | (York Split) | (York Split) | Polls Predict Labour Win | Labour Takes 5 Point Lead | Labour Takes 5 Point Lead | PM Promises Education 'Revolution' | (Bank Takeover) |
| 19 | (York Split) | (York Split) | (York Split) | (York Split) | (York Split) | (York Split) | Gallup Puts Tories 2 Points Ahead | (SA Referendum) | Leaders Trade Insults | Polls Split on Lab Lead | (SA referendum) |
| 20 | (York Split) | (York Split) | (York Split) | (York Split) | (York Split) | (York Split) | (York Split) | Jobless at Centre Stage | Major Comes Out Fighting on Tax | Parties Row Over Jobless High | Tories Attack Lab on Tax as Jobless Rises |
| 21 | (York Split) | (York Split) | (York Split) | (York Split) | (York Split) | (York Split) | Voters Face Stark Choice Says Major | Rattled Tories Switch Tack | Labour Drops Independent School Threat | Major Takes Off Gloves | (Docklands Debts) |
| 23 | (Queen) | Labour Tax Lies Exposed | (Di's Dad) | John Smith Would Bring Inflation | (Di's Dad) | Rousing Thatcher Speech | Thatcher and Major Rally Tories | Britain's Economy in the Red | Thatcher Lifts Tories | (French Local Elections) | Tories Enlist Thatcher Aid |
| 24 | Woman Hits Thatcher with Flowers | Poll Shows 5% Tory Lead | Labour Threatens Mortgages | Labour to Ration Mortgages | Strikes Will Return Under Labour | A Long Way to Go for Kinnock | Poll Bolsters Tories | Storm Over Public Borrowing | Tax Deadlock as Major on Defensive | Tories at Odds on Tax | Tax Admission Forces Tory Shake Up |
| 25 | (Cricketers Aussie Walk-out) | Labour's Broadcast on NHS Panned | (Cricketers Aussie Walk-out) | (Cricketers Aussie Walk-out) | (Cricketers Aussie Walk-out) | Emotive Lab Broadcast on NHS | Kinnock Tries to Make NHS Key Issue | Mellor Warns of New Austerity | 2 Point Cut in Lab Lead | Labour Plays NHS Card | Labour Lead in Polls |

| Date | | | | | | | | | | | |
|---|---|---|---|---|---|---|---|---|---|---|---|
| 26 | Tories Guilty on NHS | Labour Lied in NHS Broadcast | Will Kinnock Ever Tell the Truth? | Labour's Broadcast Exploits Little Girl | Lab Uses Girl as Pawn in Broadcast | Lab MP's Wife has Job in Private Health | Row Over Labour's Broadcast on NHS | Tories Come Unstuck Over Lie on Lab's Broadcast | Row Over Lab NHS Broadcast | Fury Over Lab NHS Claims | Row Over Health Grows |
| 27 | Tory Dirty Trick Over NHS | Lab Wrong on NHS Again | (Fergie) | Lab In New NHS Mess | (Tyson Sentenced) | (Whale War) | Mole Hunt in NHS Row | Huge Row Over Lab's Broadcast | NHS Leak Hides Issues | Broadcast Row Continues | Health Sparks Attack |
| 28 | (Fergie) | (Society Swindler) | (Society Swindler) | (Society Swindler) | (Society Swindler) | (Roy Castle Cancer) | Major Changes Tactics | Crisis in Con Campaign | Tories Change Tack for Key Weekend | Tories Switch Tactics | Charges Fly in NHS Leak Row |
| 30 | (Di's Grief) | (Di's Grief) | (Di's Grief) | (Di's Grief) | (Di's Grief) | (Di's Grief) | Major Leads Tax Attack on Labour | Tories Shake Up Campaign Team | Tories Pin Hopes on Don't Knows | Tories Defy Opinion Polls | Tory Assault on Kinnock Pay Pledge |
| 31 | (Di's Grief) | Major Will Cut Tax Every Year | Benn: We'll Turn Red in No. 10 | Labour Plans to Pay Unions More | NHS Issue a Problem for Major | (Plane Near Disaster) | Major Warns of Nightmare Under Labour | Major Tax Pledge Disproved | Leaders Swing Back to Tax | Parties' Tax Gaps Exposed | Major Pledges Annual Tax Cut |
| Apr 1 | The Truth About the NHS | Labour Has Poll Lead | Lab MP has 3 Houses | Labour Will not Deny Pay Plan | Tories Attack Kinnock | (Libya Hostages) | Labour Poll Break-through | Polls Show Tory Defeat | Lab 7 Point Poll Lead | Lab Extends Lead in Polls | Labour Claims Breakthrough |
| 2 | (Spencer Funeral) | Major Says Libs Will Let Lab In | (Spencer Funeral) | Beware the Lib Dems | Opinion Polls Volatile | (Spencer Funeral) | Major Warns Libs Would Let Lab in | Lab and Con Target Lib Dems | Major Changes Aim as Polls Boost Libs | PM Warns: Beware Ashdown | (Aid to Russia) |
| 3 | (Howerd Heart Attack) | Tory Campaign Takes Off | Major Will Be the Best PM | Labour Try to Seduce Ashdown | (Crazy Killers) | (Cruel Farmer) | Privatisation Dilemma for Labour | Kinnock Opens PR Poker Game | Kinnock Hint on PR | Kinnock Shift on PR | Labour Hints at PR Deal |
| 4 | (Donovan Libel) | David Owen Backs Major | (Donovan Libel) | Car Chief's Dread Cost of Kinnock | (Donovan Libel) | (Whale Rescue) | Tories Focus on Kinnock's Credibility | Pound Becomes an Issue | Ashdown Would Veto Lab Tax | (UN Demands to Libya) | Parties Fight for Middle Ground |
| 6 | Major's Tax Fraud | Britain in Danger of Lab Govt | (Whale Rescue) | Major: We'll Bring Down Mortgages | (Souness) | (Souness Heart Op) | Major: Break-up Facing UK | Parties Face Autumn Poll | Ashdown Wants 4 in Cabinet | Major Plays Down Tax Cuts | Major Warns of UK Break-up |
| 7 | Crippled Hero Waits for New Hip | Baker Warns of Mass Immigration | (Souness) | Immigration Warning | (Souness) | (Souness Heart Op) | Baker: PR Pact with Devil | Scramble for Floating Voters | Major Gamble: Attacks Hung Parliaments | Labour Surge in Marginals | Polls Confirm Labour Lead |
| 8 | It's Time for Change | Don't Throw Away Con Achievement | Choose the Leader You Trust | Major Set for Last Sprint | It's Up to You About Future | Elections Must be Labour Lead | Photo-Finish as Polls Trim Stance | Major Softens PR | Parties Court Floating Voters | Major Playing with Fire | Business Election Fears Grow |
| 9 | The Time is Now: Vote Labour | Tory Surge | Quit Britain if Kinnock Wins | Tories Closing in Last Polls | Major Gets Poll Perk | Vote for Your Future | Poll: Parties Neck and Neck | Tories Late Surge | Parties Neck and Neck | It's Too Close to Call | Election on Knife Edge. |

*Note:* based on early editions. Some headlines reworded for succinctness.

this time managed a lukewarm endorsement of Labour: 'worth taking a chance on.'

Despite his paper's support for the Conservatives, it is doubtful that Andrew Neil, the radical Conservative editor of the *Sunday Times*, cemented many friendships with Central Office. He became one of the most outspoken critics of the Conservative campaign. The *Sunday Times* had been one of only two Conservative papers to back Michael Heseltine against Mrs Thatcher in the party leadership contest; and Neil's signed editorials made clear his admiration for Heseltine while criticising Major's lacklustre performance. FIT TO BE HUNG was the headline over Neil's final campaign leader.

Nor did the *Sunday Telegraph* find much zest in supporting Majorism. Its final leader said 'it would not be a catastrophe if Labour won'. In signed articles Peregrine Worsthorne argued that elections in the UK and the USA had become contests between 'political pygmies'. Since none of these 'creepy classless cyphers' could convert will into action, it didn't matter who won. Eventually, however, Worsthorne did reject Labour – on the intriguing grounds that its opposition to fox-hunting revealed its anti-English character.

The *Sunday Express* was one of the few Sundays to essay some vigorous Conservative propaganda. 'Lest we forget' was a regular feature reminding its many older readers of the true horrors of Labour rule: 'Do you remember struggling past rotting rubbish bags just to get out of your front door, and eating your dinner by torchlight? If so, write to Readers Remember, *Sunday Express*.' Its final leader argued that life was better under the Conservatives: 'Look around your home this morning. Look at the video recorder, and the car in the garage outside. Look at the clothes your children wear and the range of food in the fridge . . . . For the vast majority of our people life has never been better.'

'Fed up with the Tories, not sure of Labour' – the line is from *New Statesman* but something similar could be plucked from the other main political weeklies, the *Economist* and the *Spectator*. The *New Statesman's* main thrust was less pro-Labour than anti-Tory. It advised tactical voting as the best bet to get rid of the Conservatives and move towards proportional representation. The previously-Thatcherite *Economist* found little to cheer in either Major's or Kinnock's programme. 'May the worse lot lose' grumbled its cover on April 4. Only the Liberal Democrats, with their commitment to proportional representation and an independent central bank, won the *Economist's* admiration. The *Spectator* took the opposite line. The Liberal Democrats, it argued, were little different from Labour except that they had fewer principles. The *Spectator* urged a Conservative vote, mainly on the issue of proportional representation. For all its recent errors of judgement, the Conservative Party was the one party pledged to maintain a political system 'which is – still – the envy of the world'.

## Scotland

In Scotland, as in England, the *Sun* (Scottish circulation 289,700) led the way. The *Scottish Sun* campaigned for Scottish independence. 'Rise now and be a nation again', an editorial had pronounced on 23 January 1992. But the *Scottish Sun's* endorsement of the SNP was not unconditional: 'The *Scottish Sun's* stand today DOES NOT mean we are throwing our weight behind everything the SNP stand for. Our election manifesto would differ somewhat from theirs.' Indeed, the socialism of the SNP was an obvious stumbling block, and the paper continued to campaign strongly against Labour, using material from London. On election day, the front page was nearly the same as the London edition, with the addition of a box at the top of the page, saying 'Nats say freedom is ours'. Inside, the editorial was headed, THE SCOTTISH SUN SPEAKS ITS MIND. ENOUGH SAID. VOTE SNP.

The political affiliations of the other papers were more predictable. Among the dailies, the *Daily Record* (circulation 760,003), the Daily *Mirror*'s stable mate, remained firmly Labour. The *Dundee Courier and Advertiser* (circulation 116,600) remained Conservative: NOT THE TIME FOR CHANGE, it announced on April 9, followed a week later by the jaundiced comment, SO MUCH FOR DEVOLUTION. The *Aberdeen Press and Journal* (circulation 105,800) remained non-committal but feared that a devolved assembly would be dominated by a 'potentially horrendous combination of Glasgow councillors and Edinburgh lawyers'.

The Scottish press, particularly the broadsheets, offered extensive coverage of the constitutional issue. Both of Scotland's quality 'nationals' supported the Liberal Democrats. The *Scotsman* (circulation 85,520) wrote that NOW IS THE MOMENT TO CHANGE THE SHAPE OF SCOTTISH GOVERNMENT, but said that where the Liberal Democrats are not strong 'the Labour Party offers the best guarantee of a Scottish Parliament within the next few years. It is what we want too.' The *Herald* (circulation 118,836) said that 'In the various ways open to it Scotland should vote for constitutional change within the union.' But there was a tiredness about the constitutional debate in the campaign itself. The issue had received such a thorough airing in the six months building up to the election that there was, as one Scottish journalist pointed out, 'nothing new to be said'.

**The campaign in progress**

John Major's declaration of the April 9 polling date, universally foretold by the press, was one of the few near-certainties of this election. It was 'a little like announcing that Christmas Day would fall on December 25,' wrote Robert Hardman in the *Daily Telegraph*. The predictability of the date enabled the qualities to publish special election supplements within days of the announcement. For all their information, these supplements probably offered more employment to psephologists than enlightenment to readers.

Leader columns, especially in the qualities, found few great divides in outlook or ideology between the post-Thatcher Conservatives and Neil Kinnock's pragmatic Labour Party. As the *Financial Times* noted, there was little to choose between them apart from personalities. This posed a major problem for the Conservative press, spoilt by the excitements of the 1980s. It needed, and got, a close contest to awaken it from its slumbers.

The lack of clear-cut choice was not to the taste of the qualities either. In an unusually robust editorial, the *Guardian* found little to generate enthusiasm: the Conservatives 'are most acidly reviled'; as for Labour, 'for a party of change and idealism, they are pathetic'. The paper warned that whichever party won, it would inherit a nation of cynics at odds with its rulers.

Tax and the personal contest between Major and Kinnock dominated the early Conservative tabloid leaders. 'It's a straight choice between Honest John and Crafty Kinnock', said the *Sun*. For the *Daily Mail*, the differences between the parties were fewer than in Mrs Thatcher's day, but were still profound; it was a fight between tax cutters in the blue corner and tax addicts in the red. The *Mirror*, calling itself the only anti-Conservative paper in the daily market, signalled Labour's 'time for a change' appeal: 'This Government is tired out, bereft of all ideas short of bribery. It is time for the Tories to go.'

John Smith's alternative budget (March 16) thrust tax to the top of the press agenda, eclipsing the Liberal Democrat's manifesto launch on the same day. The *Mail* ran five pages on the alternative budget, compared to just one on the Liberal Democrat manifesto. The *Mail* also had the million-aire composer, Andrew Lloyd Webber, popping up to say, 'the trouble with the Labour Party is that it has this absurd notion that high earners are rich'. John Smith's budget, always a high risk affair, was virtually friendless in Fleet Street, save for the faithful *Mirror* and the ambivalent *Guardian*. In the *Sunday Telegraph*, Frank Johnson reckoned that 'Mr Smith means the end of civilisation'. The *Independent* described the proposed tax increases

*Table 9.8   Editorials about the general election in daily newspapers, by topic*

| Topic | Number of editorials |
|---|---|
| Taxation/public spending | 33 |
| Exhortation to vote | 19 |
| Party strategies & prospects | 17 |
| Manifestos | 16 |
| Health | 16 |
| Constitutional/electoral reform, devolution | 14 |
| Recession | 12 |
| Party election broadcasts | 12 |
| Education | 11 |
| Budget/shadow budget | 11 |
| Challenge of Liberal Democrats | 7 |
| Fitness to govern | 7 |
| Mass media/television | 7 |
| Trade unions | 6 |
| European Community | 6 |
| Hung Parliament | 5 |
| Public disorder during Major's electioneering | 5 |
| Other | 122 |
| Total | 326 |

*Note*: 'Jennifer Bennett' stories coded under party election broadcasts.

as 'savage' and issued a warning which, with hindsight, looks prophetic: 'If Labour fails to oust this unpopular government, it will be largely because yesterday Mr Smith refused to think again.'

Under the headline THE PIPS SQUEAK, *The Times* editorial declared that the election was now about a real issue, tax. The Conservative tabloids relished the chance to perform their historic mission of explaining to the poor why the rich need lots of money: 'millions of hard-working Britons . . . . will be clobbered' (*Sun*); Labour was waging 'class war' upon the middle class (*Express*); 'If you make it – they'll take it' (*Mail*). All three, and the *Telegraph*, carried tables and/or real-life cases purporting to show how much more ordinary people would pay under Labour, techniques that were to be repeated throughout the campaign. Some of these tables were closely based on Conservative Central Office propaganda and did not even indicate whether the amount by which Labour would clobber you was per week, month or year. Still, the tables *looked* convincing. *Today* and the

*Star*, both nominally uncommitted at this stage, were also highly critical of a 'punitive tax' upon the middle and higher earners, with little real gain for the lower income bracket. In Scotland, however, the *Herald* thought that a 50 percent top tax rate 'seems quite reasonable'.

Taxation/public spending dominated national newspaper editorials during the campaign and came second only to opinion polls in front-page lead stories (Tables 9.8 and 9.9). For the Conservative press, tax was a key issue, at least partly substituting for the role played by defence in the elections of the 1980s. But the quantitative nature of the debate soon took its toll of general reporters; they began to dream of a post-election world in which there would be 'No More Arithmetic'.

Conservative papers were not all true to type in their coverage of the manifestos. *The Times* did not take a clear stand for the Conservative programme and proposed a 'voters' charter' to ensure that parties delivered their manifesto pledges. The *Daily Mail* began in tart fashion: 'You want to collect citizen's charters? John Major is your man.' It continued in more familiar Labour-bashing style, but was markedly less rhapsodic for the Conservatives than in Mrs Thatcher's day. The charter for hedgerows notwithstanding, the *Telegraph* also thought the manifesto lacked 'an electric charge'.

Of the less committed papers, the *Independent* felt that Margaret Thatcher's legacy had defined the manifestos and that neither party had really broken with the past. Labour had come a long way since 1987 but its broad economic philosophy was still suspicious of the market and would thus inhibit efficiency. The *Financial Times* also doubted the depth of Labour's conversion to the market; it 'talks the talk, but will it walk the walk?'. However, the *FT* was less than overjoyed with Major's vision, which was 'none other than the nanny state wearing a smart blue pinafore'.

The Liberal Democrat manifesto received its most prominent and favourable treatment in a tortuous editorial in the *Guardian*. Under the headline 'THE LITTLE BOOKLETS', it asked, 'How on earth do you judge a manifesto?' And in the end it decided it couldn't. The Liberal Democrats' manifesto offered the best read with its fizz of ideas; the Conservatives had sidled into the centre ground while Labour's programme for recovery seemed the best.

Manifesto coverage also coincided with the first open grumblings at the Conservative campaign. *Today's* commentator David Seymour wrote that 'Patten's puppies' were allowing Labour to get away with political murder. Along with other papers, the *Telegraph* also warned that Labour was winning the presentation battle: 'Thus far Labour appears fluent and confident. The Conservatives' leaders must relax, shake off tiredness, dress

*Table 9.9   Front-page lead stories about the election in daily newspapers, by topic*

| Topic | Number of stories | % of stories 1992 | (1987) |
|---|---|---|---|
| Opinion polls | 35 | 18 | (20) |
| Taxation/public spending | 31 | 16 | (7) |
| Party strategies and prospects | 28 | 15 | (9) |
| Party election broadcasts | 18 | 9 | (–) |
| PR/hung parliament | 8 | 4 | (–) |
| Exhortation to vote | 7 | 4 | (4) |
| Fitness to govern | 6 | 3 | (–) |
| Challenge of Liberal Democrats | 6 | 3 | (–) |
| Budget/shadow budget | 6 | 3 | (–) |
| Health | 5 | 3 | (6) |
| Mortgages | 4 | 2 | (–) |
| Devolution | 4 | 2 | (–) |
| Trade unions | 3 | 2 | (2) |
| Tone of campaign | 3 | 2 | (–) |
| City opinion | 3 | 2 | (–) |
| Defence | – | – | (19) |
| 'Scandal' stories | – | – | (10) |
| Other | 24 | 12 | (22) |
| Total | 191 | 100 | |

*Note*: 'Jennifer Bennett' stories coded under PEBs.

better and start looking match fit.' In the *Sunday Telegraph*, Paul Johnson, rarely an advocate of caution, wrote that 'John Major must shake the nation into an awareness of the impending calamity, the stark fact that the middle classes are about to be raped'.

As the twists and turns of the increasingly beleaguered Conservative campaign team filled the news columns, so editorials in the loyal press made free with advice. This was often contradictory. The *Express* and *The Times*, for instance, urged a more positive strategy while the *Daily Telegraph* complained that the campaign was not aggressively negative enough. The *Sunday Telegraph* and the *Sunday Times* also urged a far more aggressive campaign with a higher profile for the 'dogs of war', such as Michael Heseltine and Kenneth Clarke. Over the course of the campaign, the Conservative press seemed at least as panicky as the Conservative Party.

An exasperated Sir David English, editor of the *Daily Mail*, declared in his paper's leader that the Conservatives deserved to lose unless they pulled up their socks. His displeasure became a news story in its own right with his reported snub to John Major when he failed to greet the Prime Minister at the *Daily Mail* Ideal Home Exhibition. By the end, some Conservative broadsheets, in particular the *Sunday Times*, appeared to adopt an air of resignation, believing that an outright Conservative win had become the least likely outcome.

Fears of a scandal and smear-laden campaign gained currency in the early months of the year, fuelled by the revelations of Paddy Ashdown's affair with his former secretary. Such anxieties are regular features of recent elections and as usual proved to be greatly exaggerated. Rumours abounded but no story worthy of the label 'scandal' appeared on the front pages. By contrast, in 1987 10 percent of front-page election leads had dwelt upon political 'affairs' (Table 9.9). There were a few attempted smears: the *Sun*, for example, tried feebly to sling mud at Kinnock for falling out with the best man at his wedding. The *Star* revealed, on the basis of a *Sunday Express* story several years earlier, that the wife of shadow Social Services Secretary, Michael Meacher, ran a private (non-profit) nursing agency. It was paltry stuff.

Personal attacks on the political leaders, however, are standard tabloid election fare. The Conservative papers seized their opportunity following Labour's controversial party election broadcast, loosely based on the case of little Jennifer Bennett, who had waited nine months for an ear operation. In planning this broadcast, Labour had clearly failed to learn the lesson of 1949 about the dangers of mixing fact with fiction. In that year, the party had put out a leaflet showing a beaming child flourishing on a diet of free orange juice and NHS medical care. Tracked down by the ace reporters of the time, the boy turned out to be the Duke of Kent.

In 1992, the extraordinary 'war of Jennifer's ear' dominated political press coverage for three days. The fuss started slowly, however; the day after the broadcast was aired, only two tabloids, *Today* and the *Daily Express*, found it worthy of front-page news. On the inside pages, the *Mail*'s television critic described the broadcast as 'lethal and effective'. The *Express*, however, put in contact with Jennifer's surgeon by the Conservative Party, splashed an 'exclusive' to claim that the 'sick' broadcast was a fraud.

Thereafter the story exploded with accusation and counter-accusation from Labour and Conservatives while the media launched a 'whodunnit' hunt for the mole who had leaked Jennifer's name to the *Express* and *Independent*. All the nationals, bar the *Star*, gave this multi-page treatment, with background analysis, commentary and leader opinion. If newspaper coverage of the campaign could ever be separated from the campaign itself, the distinction was obliterated as pictures of print journalists squaring up to each other appeared in TV news – for 43 seconds on ITN.

But there was a marked contrast between broadsheet and tabloid coverage. The broadsheets, regardless of party preference, attempted to disentangle the merits of each party's claim to truth and innocence. The partisan tabloids, however, made no attempt at balance; facts which might have compromised their conclusions were simply disregarded. THE BIG LIE was the *Express*'s front-page verdict on Labour. On its front page, the *Sun* asked: 'If Kinnock will tell lies about a sick little girl, will he ever tell the truth about anything?' Its editorial emphasised the point: ARE LIARS FIT TO GOVERN? The *Mail's* leader column also attacked Kinnock's 'less than scrupulous ambition'. These attacks on Kinnock's credibility were maintained for two days and were to re-emerge in a fresh assault in the final days before polling. The *Mirror*, completely alone on this issue, counter-blasted with claims of dirty tricks by the Conservatives and their press supporters: 'What a bunch of fraudsters, toadies, hypocrites and liars they have turned out to be.' *Today's* scrupulous coverage of the affair stood apart. Its headline over a page-two summary captured the long-term 'significance' of the case: WHODUNNIT . . . . AND WHO REALLY CARES?

The broadsheet dailies also agreed that coverage of the case ignored the real issues confronting the NHS. The press's own contribution to the farce, with its massive interest in every tiny detail, was rarely acknowledged. Peter Riddell, in *The Times*, was an exception. The saga, he said, had lost all touch with voters' reality and was 'a classic illustration of the media's post-Watergate delight in seeking out alleged conspiracies and blowing them out of all proportion to their significance'. The fuss was really an indication of how tightly the parties had controlled the campaign agenda until that point. Confronting an uncontrolled, if hardly significant, story, the press reacted with all the suppressed energy of animals that had escaped from a zoo. It was an unedifying sight.

The Jennifer's ear saga was the major example in the campaign of the press dictating the agenda to the parties and television. The *Express* 'big lie' story, although apparently handed to them via the Conservatives, allowed government ministers to attack Labour's credibility which in turn put the story on television. The *Express* did not miss its opportunity to tell television how it should be done; according to its opinion column, newspaper reporters, unlike their tame TV counterparts, did not sit back and swallow Labour's broadcast without checking its veracity. Apart from opinion polls, carefully monitored by the broadsheets and selectively interpreted by the tabloids, research by the quality press on the economic consequences of the parties' spending plans provided the other major example of a significant press input into the campaign agenda.

The willingness of the press to analyse other media (including other papers) was a feature of the campaign. All the broadsheet dailies carried regular media watch columns, leading Christopher Dunkley (*Financial Times*) to comment that 'before long somebody will surely begin to do a regular survey of media monitoring, whereupon the wheels within wheels will become so complicated that our heads will start to spin'. The *Guardian's* media watch service[2] was by far the most extensive; some other commentators used their space to write more about the campaign itself than about media coverage of it.

The Jennifer Bennett controversy was the prime single occasion when the campaign veered out of control of the parties' 'spin doctors'. Journalists complained consistently in campaign trail reports that they were treated as extras at photo-opportunities and that they were denied adequate access to the party leaders, especially to Neil Kinnock. A note of disdain, a quality hitherto associated with American media treatment of presidential campaigns, was clearly discernible, especially in the specialist columns. After the election, David Seymour, executive editor of *Today*, wrote about his paper's particular problem: 'Our reporters who were following the party leaders had to struggle to find intelligent stories that were suitable for a mass market . . . . Other newspapers could find something to write about the TV appearances of the leader to whom they were antagonistic but trying to find a genuinely non-partisan political line was usually impossible.'[3]

In this context, Labour's Sheffield rally (April 1) was in a class of its own. In the *Guardian*, Andrew Rawnsley called it a party to celebrate winning the election; 'the fact that seven campaigning days stand between Neil Kinnock and Number 10 was treated as an incidental detail by the crowd of 10,000'. However there was little direct criticism of the Sheffield rally in the mass circulation newspapers. Indeed the *Mail* was forced onto the defensive with an accurate cliché that 'the opera isn't over until the Fat Lady's sung'. If Sheffield was a turning point, its impact came through TV images rather than press reporting.

The last week of the campaign saw the customary intensification of activity. Both parties launched a last-minute flurry of advertising and the papers published their final leaders (see above), with the Conservative tabloids focusing on the dire consequences of anything other than a Conservative victory. Old themes were discussed with renewed vigour.

Table 9.10   *Political advertising in national daily and Sunday newspapers*[1]

|  | 1987 Number of pages | 1992 Number of pages | 1992 Number of insertions |
|---|---|---|---|
| *Parties* | | | |
| Labour | 102 | 65 | 89 |
| Conservative | 217 | 48 | 47 |
| Natural Law | – | 41.8 | 32 |
| Liberal Democrat | 17 | 6.5 | 11 |
| Democratic Left | – | 0.2 | 6 |
| Green | 0.1 | – | – |
| *Pressure groups* | | | |
| NALGO | – | 73 | 73 |
| Institute of Directors | – | 18 | 23 |
| Inland Revenue Staff Federation | – | 10 | 10 |
| International Fund for Animal Welfare | – | 10 | 10 |
| Campaign to Save Assisted Places[2] | 3.4 | 4 | 4 |
| National Union of Teachers | – | 4 | 5 |
| League Against Cruel Sports | – | 3 | 3 |
| NHS Support Federation | – | 3 | 3 |
| Charter '88 | – | 1 | 2 |
| OXFAM | – | 0.3 | 2 |
| Mencap | – | 0.2 | 1 |
| Group of 16 student unions | – | 0.2 | 1 |
| London University Student Union | – | 0.1 | 1 |
| Other | 16 | – | – |
| Total | 355.5 | 288.3 | 323 |

*Notes*:

1. Electoral Registration advertisements excluded.
2. ISIS Association for Independent Schools in 1987.

Neil Kinnock came in for biting criticism: DARE WE REALLY TRUST THIS MAN? asked the *Express*. 'A man who could be drawn into a punch-up in a curry house', said the *Sun*. Other papers returned to the question of LABOUR'S TAX MUDDLE (*Daily Mail*), while several questioned Labour's economic competence: 'interest rates will rise within days of Kinnock entering Number Ten' (*Daily Mail*, again).

But some new points also emerged in this final week. Rather late in the day, the popular press discovered the theme of indecisive government following a hung parliament or the introduction of proportional representation: NAZI RIOTS WILL HIT BRITAIN, was a page-two headline in the *Sun* over a story that PR aids Fascists. In addition, the *Express* made particular play with Home Secretary Kenneth Baker's criticism of Labour's opposition to controls on asylum-seekers: BAKER'S MIGRANT FLOOD WARNING was its front-page splash on April 7.

Yet this profusion of knocking copy was rooted in a degree of anxiety about the outcome not seen in the press since 1974. WAKE UP BRITAIN commanded the *Express*, followed two days later by the equally nervy DON'T THROW IT ALL AWAY. No wonder then that on election day itself the Conservative press seized on the last-minute swing with enthusiasm born of desperation: TORIES CLOSING IN LAST POLLS (*Daily Mail*); MAJOR GETS POLL PERK (*Daily Star*); and TORY SURGE (*Daily Express*) (see p. 131). For the Conservative press, as for the Conservative Party, relief from the siege that was the 1992 campaign came not a moment too soon.

**Press advertising**

To the surprise of everyone except party treasurers, press advertising played a low-key role in this campaign. In fact, 1992 saw a shift in the terrain of paid advertising from press to posters. One commentator even described Conservative newspaper advertisements as 'posters in print'. In total, there were only 288 pages of paid political advertising in the national daily and Sunday newspapers in 1992, well down on the record figure of 355 pages in 1987 (Table 9.10). Even more surprising, the customary party balance in favour of the Conservatives was reversed: Labour's 65 pages (rate-card cost, £1.9m) were well ahead of the Conservatives' 48 (actual cost, £1.1m). The Conservatives concentrated their advertising in sympathetic papers while Labour spread its net wider, using Conservative as well as Labour papers. Labour also inserted many small advertisements requesting money for its election appeal. It asked for £15 from *Daily Mirror* readers but £30 from *Guardian* readers.

The balance tilts further to Labour when pressure group activity, accounting for almost half the total advertising, is taken into account. At 73 pages, NALGO was the largest single political advertiser in the press during the campaign, exceeding even the major parties. NALGO's public sector concerns – focused on health and education – were reinforced by material from the Inland Revenue Staff Federation and the National Union of Teachers.

The tone of press advertising was strongly negative, indeed more so than in earlier elections. Bombs, rockets and boxing gloves were favourite metaphors. This adversarial style was amplified by the recession which allowed the opposition to say how bad things were but restricted the governing party to the claim that things would be even worse under the opposition. Thus the modest burst of advertising in the final week saw a convergence on economic themes but a divergence of electoral implications. The Conservatives said VOTE FOR RECOVERY – NOT THE START OF A NEW RECESSION while Labour's advice was VOTE TODAY TO REBUILD THE ECONOMY.

Those advertisements that made any impact came at the start of the campaign. As the election was announced, Labour ran a full-page advertisement in seven daily newspapers, saying GEORGINA NORRIS DIED BECAUSE THE NHS IS SHORT OF MONEY. MEANWHILE, THE TORIES ARE CUTTING TAXES TO KEEP THEIR ELECTION HOPES ALIVE. Health Secretary William Waldegrave denounced Labour for 'cynical manipulation'. This led to a front-page lead story in the *Daily Mail* under the headline, LABOUR'S FIRST DIRTY TRICK. This proved to be an opening skirmish of what eventually became, in the context of another case, the war of Jennifer's ear. For the Conservatives, the most effective advertisement was believed to be LABOUR'S TAX BOMB SHELL, which used the image of a flying bomb to dramatise the impact of Labour's expenditure proposals (though some considered the key message to be YOU CAN'T TRUST LABOUR). Even if none of these advertisements affected voters directly, they did encapsulate the main campaign themes of each party.

Liberal Democrat advertising was even more modest than that of the two main parties. Its slogan was MY VOTE. Lest the meaning of these words prove elusive, the party and its agency were at pains to point out that the phrase represented a 'breakthrough' in multi-layered branding devices. The two simple words apparently encapsulated the messages that you will not be alone if you vote Liberal Democrat and that your vote will not be wasted, even though the voting system is unfair.

## Conclusion

So, was it THE *SUN* WOT WON IT? Clearly, the *Sun* occupied a unique position in the daily press. It was still read by 22 percent of the adult population (Table 9.1) and it had a high proportion of both Labour and uncommitted voters (Table 9.4). In contrast to the staunchly Conservative readers of the *Express* and the *Mail*, many *Sun* readers had little interest in politics and were electorally volatile.[4] So the *Sun* at least had the potential to crystallise and convert, and not just to reinforce. If the press mattered at all, the *Sun* mattered most.

But how much difference did newspapers make to their readers' votes? After the election, politicians of all colours claimed that the press mattered enough to alter the outcome. In his resignation speech, Neil Kinnock quoted Lord McAlpine, former treasurer of the Conservative Party: 'The heroes of this campaign were Sir David English, Sir Nicholas Lloyd, Kelvin MacKenzie and the other editors of the grander Tory press. Never in the past nine elections have they come out so strongly in favour of the Conservatives. Never has their attack on the Labour Party been so comprehensive .... This was how the election was won.' Joe Haines of the *Mirror* wrote that 'if Kinnock had been able to persuade four newspaper proprietors who don't even have a vote to support him, he would have been in No 10 today'.

These assertions were largely rejected by the editors and even the *Sun* had uncharacteristic second thoughts about its claim to have 'won it'. But the notion of a 'press effect' did not go unsupported. In the *Sunday Times*, Brian MacArthur argued that the late swing among *Sun* readers made the decisive difference in the decisive marginals, such as Basildon, which Labour had failed to win.[5]

A case can certainly be made that newspapers altered the outcome of the election. First, the Conservative press enjoyed 70 percent of the total circulation of national dailies, compared to Labour's 27 percent (counting the *Star* as Conservative and the *FT* as Labour). Though no larger than the bias at recent elections, this imbalance must have helped the Conservatives to some degree. Second, the assault on Labour by the Conservative press in the final week did coincide with a late swing to the Conservatives – about three percent among *Sun* readers and a surprising nine percent among *Express* readers.[6] Finally, academic studies of earlier elections do suggest it would be wrong to dismiss the impact of the press. Newspapers can influence the attitudes and votes of their readers. These effects are largest among uncommitted electors, of whom there were an exceptional number in 1992.[7]

But there is a stronger case against allowing a decisive role for the press in 1992. First, and contrary to Lord McAlpine, the Conservative papers were at least as partisan in 1983 and 1987 as in 1992. The Conservative tabloids were relatively muted for most of the 1992 campaign. Even the final blitz by the Tory press in 1992 was not self-evidently stronger than its performance in 1987 (remember defence?) or 1983 (remember Michael Foot?) So why, if the press is so crucial, was there not a comparable late swing against Labour in those earlier elections?

Second, the late swing in 1992 was not confined to the readers of Conservative papers. The swing to the Conservatives among *Mirror* readers was around the national average, despite the fact that the *Mirror*'s pro-Labour propaganda was just as extensive, and a sight more serious, than the *Sun*'s advocacy of the Conservative cause. In other words, the late swing was a national, not a newspaper, phenomenon.

Third, academic evidence of press impact is based on studies of the entire period from one election to the next, or at least on the year or so before the election – the 'long campaign'. These studies do not justify an expectation of a press effect during the final 'short campaign'.

Indeed, the main danger of focusing on the role of the Conservative press in the last few days of the 1992 campaign is that it will distract attention from the more significant impact of newspapers over the long term. Between the second half of 1991 and 9 April 1992, the pro-Conservative swing was nine percent among *Sun* readers and six percent among *Star* readers, compared to just one percent among *Mirror* readers.[8] If it was THE *SUN* WOT WON IT, it surely needed more than a week in which to do the job.

NOTES

The authors thank Professor James G. Kellas for contributing the section on Scotland and Paul Gliddon for preparing the tables in this chapter.

1.  Useful work on the press published since 1987 includes: C. Seymour-Ure, *The British Press and Broadcasting since 1945* (Oxford: Basil Blackwell, 1991); W. Miller, *Media and Voters* (Oxford: Clarendon Press, 1991); R. Snoddy, *The Good, the Bad and The Unacceptable* (London: Faber and Faber, 1992); P. Chippindale and C. Horrie, *Disaster! The Rise and Fall of the* News on Sunday (London: Sphere, 1988) and *Stick It Up Your Punter: The Rise and Fall of The* Sun (London: Heinemann, 1990); R. Franklin and D. Murphy, *What News? The Market, Politics and the Local Press* (London: Routledge, 1991); C. Wintour, *The Rise and Fall of Fleet Street* (London: Hutchinson, 1989); R. Fowler, *Language in the News: Discourse and Ideology* (London: Routledge, 1991); and D. Sanders, D. Marsh and H. Ward, 'The Political Impact of Press Coverage of the UK Economy, 1979–87', *British Journal of Political Science*, forthcoming.
2.  See M. Billig *et al.*, 'The Election Campaign: Two Shows for the Price of One', *British Journalism Review*, 3:2 Summer 1992.
3.  'The Potholes on the Campaign Trail', International Press Institute (London, 1992), p. 19.

4.   W. Miller, *Media and Voters* (Oxford: Clarendon Press, 1991), p. 192.
5.   B. MacArthur, 'Perhaps it was The Sun "wot won it" for John Major', *Sunday Times*, 12 April 1992.
6.   MORI, *British Public Opinion*, Volume 1 (London, 1992), p. xlix.
7.   W. Miller, *Media and Voters*; also M. Harrop, 'Press Coverage of Post-war Elections' in *Political Communications: The General Election Campaign of 1983*, ed. I. Crewe and M. Harrop (Cambridge: Cambridge University Press, 1986), pp. 137–149.
8.   W. Miller, 'I Am What I Read', *New Statesman and Society*, 24 April 1992, pp. 17–18.

# 10 MPs and Candidates

## Byron Criddle

A record number of 2946 candidates (compared to 2325 in 1987) fought the election.[1] The Labour and Conservative parties stood in all 634 mainland constituencies, and the Conservatives ventured into 11 of the 17 Northern Ireland seats. The Liberal Democrats contested all the mainland seats except the two (Greenwich and Woolwich) in which SDP MPs were seeking re-election. The overall number of candidates was boosted by the large number of Greens (253 + 3 joint Plaid Cymru/Green) and by 309 people standing for the highly eccentric and politically marginal 'Natural Law Party'. The SNP fought all 72 Scottish seats, and Plaid Cymru all 38 Welsh seats.

The new intake of MPs numbered 140:[2] 69 Labour, 63 Conservative, 5 Liberal Democrat, 2 Plaid Cymru and 1 Social Democratic and Labour Party. Of the 140, fourteen were former MPs: 9 Conservative, 3 Labour and 1 Liberal Democrat. Of these 14 'retreads' the most patient had been the Liberal Democrat, Paul Tyler, who had waited nearly eighteen years since his defeat at Bodmin in 1974 until his victory at North Cornwall (comprising part of his old Bodmin seat) in 1992, a political resurrection that was a record in the post-war period.[3] Labour's Bryan Davies (Oldham Central & Royton) had endured 13 years since his defeat at Enfield North in 1979, though he had spent the intervening years at Westminster as secretary of the PLP. John Horam, elected for the Conservatives at Orpington, was politically the most variegated of the returning MPs, having been a Labour MP between 1970 and 1981 and an SDP MP from 1981 to 1983. Nine other former MPs (3 Conservative, 1 Labour and 5 Liberal Democrat) sought, unsuccessfully, to return to the House.[4]

Seventy-nine MPs had retired at the dissolution: 56 Conservative, 19 Labour, 1 Liberal Democrat, 1 Plaid Cymru, David Owen and the Speaker. A number of the Conservatives were retiring early.[5] Keith Raffan (Delyn), born 1947 and an MP since 1983, declared that 'nine years is enough in parliament; some of my colleagues stay on too long'. Michael Latham, born 1942, vacated his blue-chip Rutland and Melton seat, observing that 85 percent of the work carried out by back-bench MPs was useless; that he did not think it 'tremendously helpful the way we bawl and shout at each other every Tuesday and Thursday'; and that he found himself 'increasingly thinking that there is a lot to be said for the other point of view'. He proposed to take holy orders, but opted initially for the directorship of the Council for Christians and Jews. John Moore, an ex-Cabinet minister, called it a day at 55.

More famously the Conservative retirements included Margaret Thatcher and a raft of her former cabinet ministers. On the Labour side Michael Foot, Denis Healey and Merlyn Rees led into retirement a largely undistinguished phalanx of old – and not so old – soldiers: Robert Clay (Sunderland North) a hard left, public school and Cambridge-educated former bus driver, was throwing in the towel at the age of 45.

For Labour, Michael Foot's retirement marked the end of an era. The last survivor of the 1945 parliament, he was also the last MP whose career originated in the Baldwin years with his unsuccessful candidacy at Monmouth in 1935 and his victory at Plymouth Devonport in 1945 over Mr Leslie Hore-Belisha. His exit also marked the end of a 70-year long Lib-Lab Foot dynasty, beginning with his father Isaac's election at Bodmin in 1922, continuing with his brother Dingle's election at Dundee in 1931 and then his own long (1945–55 and 1960–92) parliamentary career.

From Mr Foot's time (1980–83) as Labour leader, the party had inherited the system of mandatory reselection of MPs by the activist-based General Committee of each CLP (and selection of parliamentary candidates on the same basis). Fourteen Labour MPs were sacked under such a system between 1981 and 1986 and others driven into early retirement or, in the days of the SDP, out of the party. The system was unpopular with Labour MPs and seen by the leadership as affording too much influence to left-wing activists. Accordingly Neil Kinnock had sought, as early as 1984, to introduce selection not by the activist GC but by the whole local membership – 'one member one vote' (OMOV). The move was, however, blocked at the time by the unions who sought to protect the role they had in candidate selection through branch affiliation to the GCs. The leadership dropped its pursuit of OMOV until the 1987 conference when three options were debated: the status quo, OMOV and an electoral college comprising a mix of OMOV and union participation. This latter carried the day simply because it was the only option acceptable to the unions. The system involved an electoral college for candidate selection and reselection, in which at least 60 percent of the votes were allocated to local party members and a maximum of 40 percent to affiliated organisations, primarily unions. The precise share of the vote accorded to affiliated bodies was to be determined by the composition of the GC at the start of the selection process; voting was to be by single transferable vote, thus obviating the need for exhaustive ballots and denying the opportunity for voters to align themselves for or against particular candidates in subsequent ballots. Controversially – in the event – no regulations were laid down to determine how union branch delegates should decide to cast their votes (no requirement, for example, to ballot their members). All shortlists were to involve the mandatory shortlisting of women candidates. Postal voting was permitted in particular circumstances, such as sickness or absence on holiday.

This system was applied to all selections and mandatory reselections from January 1989 on. Of the 229-strong PLP elected in 1987, 205 MPs went through this process. Of these, 59, or approximately one in three, faced contested reselections. A number of the contests, however, had a certain token quality derived from the requirement to shortlist women despite their weak nominations. Thus at Aberdeen North, the Wrekin, Leicester West and Blackburn, the MPs respectively polled 96 percent, 89 percent, 84 percent and 83 per cent of the vote against a woman challenger. Twenty-three of the 59 contests were straight fights between the MP and a woman challenger, in 15 of which the challenger polled less than 20 percent of the vote. Twenty-nine MPs secured reselection with more than 70 percent of the vote and relatively few – fourteen – polled less than 60 percent, amongst whom four actually lost.

Labour officials anticipated fewer deselections than in the previous parliaments, on account of the widened franchise, the quieter mood in the party in the run-up to a crucial election, and the prospect in the mid-1990s of a boundary revision which would afford a less contentious means of replacing incumbent MPs. Initially seven MPs were deselected, though two of the deselections were later reversed – those of Frank Field (Birkenhead) and Gerry Bermingham (St Helens South). Of the five other MPs, two were voted out by their local parties: Syd Bidwell (Southall) and John Hughes (Coventry NE). One, Ron Brown (Edinburgh Leith), was barred from contesting a second selection following an earlier contest which he had won. The last two, Terry Fields (Liverpool Broadgreen) and Dave Nellist (Coventry SE), were expelled from the Labour Party by the NEC despite having been reselected by their local parties. Thus, strictly speaking, only two of the deselections (those of Mr Bidwell and Mr Hughes) were of a traditional kind.

Gerry Bermingham, MP for St Helens South since 1983, had, despite dual Tribune and Campaign Group memberships, never enjoyed good relations with his hard left and Militant-influenced local party, one member of whom – Brian Green, deputy leader of St Helens council – outpolled him by 55 percent to 40 per cent in the reselection ballot in October 1989. He challenged the validity of votes cast by unions and other affiliated bodies; the CLP threatened legal action against the NEC if the deselection vote was challenged, but the local party was duly suspended and Mr Green expelled (for reasons unconnected with the conduct of the selection ballot). A re-run vote in November 1991 saw Mr Bermingham reselected with 65 percent of the vote.

In December 1989, John Hughes (Coventry NE) was deselected in favour of Bob Ainsworth, deputy leader of Coventry City Council. Though beaten into third place, Mr Hughes appealed to the NEC alleging postal vote irregularities and threatening legal action if the party did not act on his complaints. An obscure back-bencher who had entered parliament surprisingly at the age of 62 in 1987, and who identified with the Campaign group, his deselection was endorsed by the NEC. The DPP did not act on Mr Hughes' complaint and he duly fought the 1992 election as Independent Labour, polling 4,008 votes (8.5 percent) and making no dent in Mr Ainsworth's large Labour majority. At Southall in April 1991, Syd Bidwell, MP since 1966 and 74 years old, was deselected, polling a humiliatingly low 9 percent of the vote and running a bad third behind two Asian candidates, Piara Khabra (45 percent) and Valerie Vaz, sister of the MP for Leicester East (28 percent). With the distribution of second preferences the votes divided 55 percent for Mr Khabra and 45 percent for Ms Vaz. Syd Bidwell's demise had been brewing for years, as the former railwayman sought to retain a seat in which even on the very outdated (1981) census figures 44 percent of the electorate were from ethnic minorities. He had survived in 1987 thanks to divisions within the Indian community, but in 1991 he was overwhelmed by the retired Sikh school teacher and president of the local Indian Workers Association, and one-time member of the SDP, Piara Khabra who at 67 was almost as old as Mr Bidwell. Confirming the intra-Asian factionalism in the CLP, Valerie Vaz, as well as Mr Bidwell, appealed to the NEC citing alleged irregularities such as canvassing by Mr Khabra and vote-rigging of various kinds. But eventually, in December 1991, Mr Khabra's selection narrowly won NEC endorsement, and he was duly returned as MP in April notwithstanding a rebel candidacy of Mr Bidwell which polled 4,665 votes (9.4 percent). Had Ms Vaz succeeded him, he would, he claimed, have stepped back for her.

Far more protracted was the attempt to drop Frank Field by the Birkenhead CLP. As in the St Helens case, the local party had strong elements within it identified with hard-left and entryist groups such as Militant and Socialist Organiser, in the Merseyside fashion. Frank Field had encountered local difficulties almost from the time of his first election for the seat in 1979 and at the reselection vote in December 1989 he lost by 46 percent to 51 percent for Paul Davies, a local TGWU official, despite having entered the contest vowing to resign and fight a by-election if deselected. A critic of the new selection process, Mr Field was an advocate of full OMOV in place of what he deemed a corrupt system. He appealed to the NEC, presenting a 150-page dossier alleging voting irregularities, bogus TGWU branch affiliation to the General Committee, Militant infiltration, and intimidating behaviour of Mr Davies; he repeated his intention of provoking a by-election unless the NEC acted on his allegations. But although Mr Field had limited support from the central machine, he, like Gerry Bermingham in St Helens, benefited from the fact that Labour's combative north-west regional organiser, Peter Kilfoyle, was conducting a round-up of Militant Tendency on Merseyside and was himself to inherit Liverpool Walton from Eric Heffer and fight a by-election in 1991 against the Militant-backed candidate whom he had defeated for the Walton nomination. By the time Frank Field's reselection was re-run in June 1991 – eighteen months after the original vote – the number of affiliated union branches (the basis of Paul Davies' 51 percent) had fallen. Despite an appeal from Mr Davies, the NEC endorsed Frank Field and suspended the workings of the Birkenhead CLP.

The deselections of the hard-left Ron Brown, Dave Nellist and Terry Fields were rather different. Ron Brown, MP for Leith since 1979, had been reselected by his party in October 1989, with 54 percent of the vote. He had nevertheless enjoyed a chequered career that involved (in the 1987 Parliament alone) suspension from the House for dropping the Mace, loss thereafter of the whip for three months, and of his AEU sponsorship, an allegedly poor voting record, and finally a conviction and £1,000 fine for criminal damage at the flat of his former secretary and mistress. This last event brought calls from Leith CLP branches for his resignation and a vote of no confidence. With NEC approval the Leith party reopened the selection process, but with Mr Brown barred from the contest, a process not previously invoked against a sitting MP. At a new selection ballot in September 1990, Malcolm Chisholm, a teacher whom Mr Brown had beaten in the original reselection, was chosen. A poll-tax non-payer, Mr Chisholm comfortably retained the seat despite Mr Brown's 'Independent Labour' candidacy (4,142 votes, 10.3 percent) and replaced Mr Brown in the Campaign Group, confirming that for the Leith CLP the Brown affair was less political than personal.

The two Militant-linked MPs, Terry Fields (Liverpool Broadgreen) and Dave Nellist (Coventry SE), had both been comfortably endorsed by their CLPs; Mr Nellist with 70 percent of the vote in November 1989, and Mr

Fields with 73 percent in February 1990. But they fell victim to the party leadership's decision to purge Militant from the PLP. In July 1991 Terry Fields was imprisoned for six months for refusing to pay the poll-tax, the event closely following the Liverpool Walton by-election in which Militant ran a candidate against Labour and Mr Fields was conspicuous by his absence from the Labour campaign. In September 1991 both Mr Fields and Mr Nellist were suspended from holding any office in the party and summoned before the NEC to deny their Militant links. Their refusal to dissociate themselves led to their expulsion from the party in December 1991. Dave Nellist and Terry Fields were deselected from on high, an example of the moderate leadership cancelling the hard left gains of the early eighties.

A number of other Labour reselections were protracted: Peter Shore was under pressure from both left-wing and Bengali challengers in Bethnal Green and Stepney, but emerged with 57 percent of the vote in July 1991. Clare Short (Birmingham Ladywood) also faced a two-pronged assault from the left and from an EETPU-backed Asian candidate, but survived with 53 percent of the vote in February 1992. An extremely prolonged dispute was that over the succession to Denis Howell in Birmingham Small Heath, a seat targeted by Asians in view of its large ethnic minority (39 percent on 1981 figures) population. It ended with Mr Howell's protégé, Roger Godsiff, a union official, triumphing over a Kashmiri city councillor, Mohammed Afzal.

Labour's selection system was widely criticised in the party. The union element was unreformed and open to manipulation by local branch secretaries who could prepare the ground, often for union officials, a number of whom appeared in Labour's new intake in 1992. The impact of the union element was however by no means injurious to the party leadership. The overwhelming pattern was of union votes supporting the incumbent MP. There was, however, the belief that the OMOV principle served to localise selections, with the wider membership more likely to choose local worthies, such as council leaders – of whom a good number featured in the 1992 intake – rather than nationally-known figures. Criticism was raised too of the cost of holding 'affirmative ballots' in cases where no challenge was made to sitting MPs. This hinted at the removal of *mandatory* reselection, and indeed the leadership had secured at the 1991 conference a vote in favour of the proposal for 'trigger' ballots – giving GCs the right to decide whether or not they wished to start a reselection process at all. The leadership had also pressed for full OMOV, with the removal or democratization of the union element, but the whole matter was to be the subject of a party investigation in 1992–93.[6]

Conservative selection processes continued on accustomed lines under the Central Office eye of Sir Tom Arnold, Vice Chairman responsible for candidates since 1985. The parliamentary selection board system at which would-be candidates are screened during residential weekends, and by which the party sets much store, was exposed more to media coverage than hitherto.[7] Central Office sought also to dispel the impression that Conservative association executive councils routinely submitted only one candidate for the approval of the association's general meeting, stressing that unless a candidate had obtained an overall majority on the first ballot in the executive council, the general meeting should be presented with a choice, a recommendation to be tested at Cheltenham.[8] Some little local difficulties arose over the future of four back-benchers. Only one of them – Sir Trevor Skeet (North Bedfordshire) – survived to fight the election under the Conservative Party's colours. Attempts were made to remove Sir Trevor (born 1918) on grounds of age. One of the few survivors of the 1959 Conservative intake, he had represented Bedford/N.Bedfordshire since 1970. In May 1989 some 60 of his executive committee voted not to recommend his readoption, but at a ballot in October 1989 he prevailed by 311 votes to 164, after threatening to provoke a by-election if rejected. He dismissed his local opponents as 'people who have hotted up like bad apples in a cask'; they in turn painted him as 'opinionated and arrogant'. He declared his victory as one which would help restore the age balance in the House, youth being 'over-represented'.

John Browne had a history of trouble with his Winchester constituency association, surviving a deselection attempt before the 1987 election. In 1990 he was censured by the Commons Select Committee on Members' Interests for non-disclosure of interests he had in a series of foreign payments, the largest of which being a £52,000 sum from the Saudi Arabian government. Following a Commons debate on the matter he was suspended from the House for a month. The Winchester association executive voted to open a reselection process, but a few days in advance of a general meeting to endorse this recommendation, Mr Browne announced his decision not to contest the seat again. In February 1992 he claimed he had been leant on to withdraw and said he would now oppose the new candidate, the former Aberdeen South MP, Gerry Malone, which he duly did, polling 3,095 votes (4.7 percent).

In January 1990, the Monmouth association executive committee voted not to recommend the readoption of Sir John Stradling-Thomas, former minister and deputy chief whip and MP for the seat since 1970. He was accused of neglect of parliamentary duties and awkward relations with some local party officers. Dogged by poor health Sir John had been banned for drink driving in 1987. A ballot was arranged for April 1990, within a few days of which Sir John announced he would not seek reselection. He died, aged 65, in April 1991.

Far more political than these three cases was the deselection of Sir Anthony Meyer at Clwyd NW in January 1990. His fall from grace had been predicted for many years. He had had to create a great fuss in order to secure selection for the redistributed seat in 1983; he had survived a deselection attempt during the 1983–87 parliament and in 1989 he committed the ultimate crime of *lèse majesté* by forcing Mrs Thatcher into a leadership contest, in which he laid down his political life as a 'stalking horse' for the more fateful challenge of Michael Heseltine in 1990. Within two months of his challenge to Margaret Thatcher the Clwyd NW association dispatched him with a vote of 206 to 107, following a suicidal speech in which he attacked Mrs Thatcher for opposing British membership of the European Monetary System, for imposing 'the unworkable poll-tax', and for there being 'virtually no circumstances when she is open to argument in Cabinet'. He toyed with the idea of seeking the nomination again despite his defeat, but following tabloid press speculation about his private life in September 1990, and the resignation of Margaret Thatcher as Prime Minister, he withdrew.

Following the subsequent challenge to and resignation of Mrs Thatcher in November 1990, a number of MPs were threatened in their constituencies, but all survived – mostly comfortably.[9] On the eve of the election, in March 1992, Alan Amos (Hexham) resigned his seat following an alleged act of indecency. The messiest Conservative dispute, however, followed the selection at Cheltenham of the 38-year-old Solihull-based black barrister, John Taylor, in December 1990. This was the first time a candidate from the ethnic minorities had been selected for a Conservative-held seat. From 254 original applicants, shortlisted down to 22 and then to 5, Mr Taylor's name was the only one put to the general meeting of the association, where the vote split 111 to 82 in his favour. It was alleged by one of his opponents that he had been 'bulldozed onto the constituency by head office, who are determined to have a black man in the Commons'. The nub was race: 'We simply can't have a black man representing Cheltenham: there are only about 100 black people in the town.' A local party stalwart, Mr Bill Galbraith, obtained considerable publicity for the observation for which he was expelled from the party: 'I don't think we should give in to a bloody nigger, even if Central Office have foisted him on us.' Local association officers denied Central Office involvement, but Mr Taylor's opponents secured a public meeting to reconsider the selection in February 1991 – at which Mr Taylor secured 406 votes for and 164 against. Plans to run a local white candidate against Mr Taylor were aired but then masked by a facade of unity, which did not however serve to retain the seat for the Conservatives. At the election Cheltenham fell to the Liberal Democrats by 1,668 votes, on a swing of 5.2 percent.[10]

Liberal Democrat selection procedures were comparable to those of the precursor (Alliance) parties. The search for sufficient candidates to cover 632 constituencies proved difficult. Archie Kirkwood MP appealed at the party's September 1989 conference for people to come forward, only 50 having been selected at that point. Procedure for access to the party's candidates list was not onerous, and a senior party spokesman's observation that of the candidates fielded in the election, the top third were good, the middle third adequate and the bottom third weak, was indicative of the extent to which resources were stretched.

The three main parties fielded 341 women candidates, compared to 243 in 1987. The Conservatives had selected 59 (46 in 1987) of whom 16 were sitting MPs; Labour had chosen 138 (93 in 1987), of whom 24 were sitting MPs, and the Liberal Democrats fielded 144 (105 in 1987) of whom one was a sitting MP.[11] A record total of sixty women MPs were elected: 37 Labour, 20 Conservatives, 2 Liberal Democrat and 1 SNP. In 1987, 41 women had been returned (more than double the figure of 19 in 1979). Twenty-one of the 60 MPs were new to the House: 14 Labour, 6 Conservative and 1 Liberal Democrat; two others had entered the House at by-elections in the 1987–92 parliament. The increase in the number of women candidates was of the order of 30 percent and of women elected 50 percent; for this large increase all the parties were responsible in different ways. Labour had established a special 'W' (women's) list of candidates and introduced mandatory shortlisting; this undoubtedly helped secure for women a quarter of the candidacies in the 100 key marginal seats the party needed to win. The large Liberal Democrat total of women candidates also owed something to the party's policy of mandatory shortlisting. The Conservatives, with no such mechanism to advance women candidates, did however, place new women candidates in six safe seats – for the price of only one departing woman (Mrs Thatcher). There remained, however, much criticism inside the Conservative Party of the obstacles to selection. According to a thwarted former candidate, Harriet Crawley, 'women are judged sight unseen from their CVs', and for Emma Nicholson MP, 'Central Office needs to send out a message to the constituencies saying "We want more women in parliament" . . . I have begged it, but it never comes'. Such complaints drew irascible responses from Central Office which saw the matter as one of local association autonomy. Others too have pointed to the consequences of the single member constituency system which restricts the influence of national party machines in candidate selection. Labour's developing interest in quotas – with the proposal to secure 50 percent of the seats in the PLP for women by the end of the century – seemed certain to run up against the tradition of local autonomy in candidate selection.[12]

The number of black and Asian MPs rose slightly from four (1987, all Labour) to six (five Labour; one Conservative). There had been an increase during the 1987–92 parliament with the victory for Labour of Ashok Kumar in the 1991 Langbaurgh by-election, but the seat was recaptured by the Conservatives in 1992. The two new MPs were the Indian Piara Khabra, who held Southall for Labour, and Nirj Deva, a 43-year-old businessman of Sri Lankan origin who retained the neighbouring seat of Brentford and Isleworth for the Conservatives, becoming the first Asian to sit on the Conservative benches since Sir Mancherjee Bhownagri represented Bethnal Green NE between 1895 and 1905. The loss of Cheltenham by John Taylor denied the Conservatives their first-ever Afro-Caribbean MP. The virtual stalemate in the number of MPs from the ethnic minorities was reflected in the selection of such candidates by the three parties: 23, compared to 28 in 1987. Labour fielded only nine (as against 14 in 1987): before winning Langbaurgh in 1991, Ashok Kumar was the only new Labour black or Asian candidate selected for a winnable marginal seat. The Conservatives fielded 8 candidates, two more than in 1987. The Liberal Democrats chose 6, two fewer than the Alliance parties in 1987. The list would have been longer had not three black/Asian candidates (one from each party) resigned before the election. The Liberal Democrat Verona Marfo explained her retreat from Hackney North and Stoke Newington by citing 'a high level of racism in the party'.

The failure to advance in the area of black candidates was probably a matter both of supply and demand. The supply – the number of would-be candidates on party lists – was not large: the Conservatives claimed about 30, and Labour's 'B' list contained 32 Asian names in 1991, and the 'A' list, of sponsored candidates, six. Equally, the demand for such candidates was slight, given the prejudices about the alleged unsuitability of ethnic minority candidates in seats other than those with significant black and Asian electorates. As in the case of John Taylor at Cheltenham, Ashok Kumar had been advised when seeking the nomination in Langbaurgh (a seat with only 250 Asian voters) to 'go and get a seat in Leicester'. On this argument, the difficulty was the shortage of seats with large ethnic minority electorates. The 1981 census identified 21 seats with more than 23 percent of such voters, all Labour-held in 1987, but only in four cases by black or Asian MPs. In one other in 1991 an aged white

*Table 10.1   Age of candidates (as at 1 January 1992)*

| Age on 1 Jan. 1992 | Conservative[1] | | Labour | | Liberal Democrat | |
|---|---|---|---|---|---|---|
| | elected | defeated | elected | defeated | elected | defeated |
| 20–29 | – | 40 | – | 23 | 1 | 63 |
| 30–39 | 47 | 114 | 34 | 131 | 3 | 165 |
| 40–49 | 129 | 93 | 115 | 153 | 9 | 215 |
| 50–59 | 112 | 43 | 82 | 44 | 7 | 128 |
| 60–69 | 46 | 8 | 40 | 12 | – | 41 |
| 70–79 | 2 | – | – | – | – | – |
| Total | 336 | 298 | 271 | 363 | 20 | 612 |
| *Median Age* | | | | | | |
| 1992 | 48 | 39 | 49 | 42 | 45 | 43 |
| 1987 | 48 | 36 | 51 | 38 | – | – |

*Note*:

1. The eleven Conservative candidates in Northern Ireland are excluded from this and all subsequent tables.

incumbent was replaced by an Asian candidate (Southall), but the rest were occupied by white incumbents who were undeselectable either by virtue of their front-bench status (Roy Hattersley), or NEC prominence (Clare Short), or their sex (Joan Ruddock, Kate Hoey and, again, Clare Short). The hard-won gains made by women were unlikely to be readily surrendered in the cause of increased black and Asian representation. The messy contest at Small Heath confirmed the uphill struggle for Asian aspirants, though it was conceivable that a membership-only ballot in that seat could well have gone in the Asian's favour. It was possible that the achievement of four black/Asian MPs in 1987 had taken some steam out of the issue. A Walworth Road source suggested that the failure to increase black or female representation significantly in safe Labour seats in 1992 was attributable to the widened franchise; that particularly in safe, largely old industrial seats, the wider membership was less likely to share fully the relatively progressive opinions of party activists on such matters. Whatever the explanation, the NEC, in imposing a shortlist on Nottingham East (where selection had been postponed by a dispute between rival Asian factions) in February 1992, included the London-based Valerie Vaz in a bid to find a favoured female Asian candidate a berth; but the local party chose a white male local councillor.

Twenty Jewish MPs were elected in 1992, eleven Conservative, eight Labour and one Liberal Democrat. In 1987 22 Jewish MPs had been

Table 10.2   *Parliamentary experience of MPs*

| First entered Parliament | Conservative | Labour | Liberal Democrat |
|---|---|---|---|
| 1950–59 | 10 | 2 | – |
| 1960–69 | 21 | 21 | 3 |
| 1970–74 | 74 | 47 | 2 |
| 1975–79 | 58 | 26 | 1 |
| 1980–83 | 66 | 35 | 7 |
| 1984–87 | 51 | 63 | 3 |
| 1988–92 | 56 | 77 | 4 |
| Total | 336 | 271 | 20 |

returned. The 1992 total included two newcomers, one Labour, one Conservative. The political balance in the Conservatives' favour served to confirm the end of the political alignment of the Jewish community with the Left.[13]

The oldest MP returned in 1992 was Sir Edward Heath (born 1916); he and his colleague, Sir Trevor Skeet (born 1918) were the only MPs over the age of seventy (Table 10.1). On the Labour side, six MPs were all born in 1923: Andrew Faulds, Mildred Gordon, Eddie Loyden, Stan Orme, Jo Richardson and Robert Sheldon. Almost as old as these budding septuagenarians was Labour's newcomer, Piara Khabra (born 1924); late also to the House came Eric Clarke (born 1933) and Glenda Jackson (1936). At the other end of the age range, ten MPs – all but two new to the House – had been born in the 1960s: six Conservatives, two Labour and two Liberal Democrats. The Conservatives were Harold Elletson (Blackpool North, born 1960), Michael Bates (Langbaurgh, born May 1961), Matthew Banks (Southport, born June 1961), David Faber (Westbury, born July 1961), Liam Fox (Woodspring, born September 1961) and William Hague (Richmond, born March 1961) who had won a by-election in 1989. Labour's sixties babies were Gregory Pope (Hyndburn, born 1960) and Angela Eagle (Wallasey, born February 1961). The two Liberal Democrat MPs were Nick Harvey (North Devon, born August 1961) and Matthew Taylor (Truro, born January 1963) – the only MP under the age of thirty. It was testimony to his exceptional youthfulness at the time of his original election to the House (at a by-election in March 1987) that Mr Taylor remained, two general elections later, the baby of the House.

As well as being the oldest MP, Sir Edward Heath was the longest continuous serving member (since 1950) and therefore became Father of the House; he was the fourth former prime minister of the century to have held that distinction.[14] Tony Benn, first elected at a November 1950 by-election, was the sole Labour survivor from the period of the post-war Labour governments.[15] In addition to Sir Edward and Mr Benn, only ten other MPs remained from the 1950s: nine Conservatives and one Labour member, John Morris (elected in 1959).[16] Only fifty-seven MPs remained from the pre-1970 parliaments and had thus been forged as politicians in the hey-day of the post-war consensus (Table 10.2). The large new intakes of 1992 served with those of the eighties to widen the gulf between the post 1945 and post-1970 political generations.

The educational backgrounds of MPs reflected established trends in the Conservative case, with a significantly lower proportion of new MPs elected in 1992 drawn from public school backgrounds: 55 percent compared with 65 per cent of re-elected MPs. In 1987 68 percent of all Conservative MPs had been public school-educated; the 1992 figure was 62 percent – a more marked drop than in previous years; and of unelected Conservative candidates only 35 per cent (41 percent in 1987) had attended public school (Table 10.3). The number of Conservative Etonians was the lowest ever: 34 (10 percent), compared with 43 in 1987. The new intake of 63 MPs contained only three Etonians, in place of twelve among the retiring MPs.[17] The proportion of public school and Oxbridge-educated Conservative MPs was also in decline: down to 32 percent from 38 percent in 1987 and from 50 percent in the sixties and seventies. Labour's public school component remained remarkably steady, with 40 MPs (14 percent), of whom ten in the new intake (also 14 percent). In 1987 the same percentage of the PLP had attended public schools. Liberal Democrat candidates were less 'elitist' than the Alliance parties' candidates in 1987: fewer were from public schools (20 percent instead of 33 percent) fewer from universities (58 percent compared to 71 percent).

Analysis of the occupational background of candidates is not without its difficulties. The practice here has always been to categorise candidates as far as possible by 'first or formative occupation', rather than by the job they happen to have at the time of the election. The classification of occupations has also remained largely unchanged in order to enable comparisons across a long series of elections; inevitably this leads to some categories becoming rather under-occupied and others over-crowded. The 'miscellaneous white-collar' category has, for example, inflated to accommodate Labour's union officials and growing numbers of voluntary sector employees; meanwhile among 'directors' and 'executives' are the expanding ranks of management consultants. The professionalisation of

*Table 10.3    Education of candidates*

| Type of education | Conservative elected | Conservative defeated | Labour elected | Labour defeated | Liberal Democrat elected | Liberal Democrat defeated |
|---|---|---|---|---|---|---|
| Elementary | – | – | 2 | – | – | – |
| Elementary + | – | – | 7 | – | – | 1 |
| Secondary | 19 | 40 | 34 | 60 | 2 | 79 |
| Secondary + poly/college | 28 | 53 | 61 | 93 | 2 | 152 |
| Secondary + university | 81 | 100 | 127 | 173 | 6 | 257 |
| Public School | 28 | 11 | – | 3 | – | 11 |
| Pub Sch + poly/college | 16 | 11 | 2 | 3 | 1 | 12 |
| Pub Sch + university | 164 | 83 | 38 | 31 | 9 | 100 |
| Total | 336 | 298 | 271 | 363 | 20 | 612 |
| Oxford | 83 | 24 | 28 | 23 | 4 | 40 |
| Cambridge | 68 | 23 | 16 | 9 | 2 | 31 |
| Other universities | 94 | 136 | 122 | 172 | 9 | 286 |
| All universities | 245 | 183 | 166 | 204 | 15 | 357 |
|  | (73%) | (61%) | (61%) | (56%) | (75%) | (58%) |
| Eton | 34 | 9 | 2 | – | – | 5 |
| Harrow | 7 | 2 | – | – | – | 3 |
| Winchester | 3 | – | 1 | – | – | – |
| Other public schools | 164 | 94 | 37 | 37 | 10 | 115 |
| All public schools | 208 | 105 | 40 | 37 | 10 | 123 |
|  | (62%) | (35%) | (14%) | (10%) | (50%) | (20%) |

politics has also been reflected in the rising numbers of MPs classified as 'politicians': in 1992, 20 Conservatives, and 24 Labour – and a total on the Conservative side alone of some sixty MPs who had had some experience at one time or another of work as political staffers.

Nevertheless, both major parties continued to rely most heavily for their parliamentary representatives on the traditional professions, if strongly rivalled in the Conservative case by business; in 1992, among unelected Conservative candidates, business had come to outrank the professions. Labour's distinctiveness lay in its still-large minority of manual worker MPs, but in 1992 this group, at 22 percent of the PLP, was at its lowest ever level, down from 29 percent in 1987, and with, as in 1987, even lower proportions (17 percent) of the 69-strong new intake drawn from manual occupations. Increasingly, Labour MPs were defined by white-collar public sector employment, whether in education, administration, politics or as officials in public sector unions; very small numbers of Labour candidates had any experience of either manual work or business.

The occupational profile of Liberal Democrat candidates shared characteristics of both Labour and the Conservatives: like Labour, the Liberal Democrats heavily relied on teachers, but were closer to the Conservatives in their share of candidates drawn from business. In these respects the Liberal Democrats were indistinguishable from the old Alliance parties.

Fewer trade unions sponsored successful Labour candidates in 1992 than in 1987, 15 as compared with 22, though the reduction was due to a number of union mergers since the previous election (Table 10.5). The NUR and NUS had emerged to form the RMT; ASTMS and TASS had formed the MSF; NGA and SOGAT had formed the GPMU; and APEX had been absorbed into the GMB. The process continued in May 1992, with the merger of the AEU and the EETPU to form the AEEU (the Amalgamated Engineering and Electrical Union). The TGWU easily led the field with 38 sponsored MPs, followed by the GMB with 17 and the NUM with 14. Apart from the EETPU, of whose ten sponsored candidates only three were elected, unions rarely supported candidates in unwinnable seats. With the expansion of the PLP away from its industrial heartland in 1992, the total of union-sponsored MPs, at 143, comprised a smaller percentage of the PLP than in 1987: 53 as compared with 56 percent. Twenty-two of the 143 union-sponsored MPs were women – a larger proportion (15 percent) than women comprised of the PLP as whole (14 percent), and a very large proportion of Labour women MPs.

The unions leading the field in sponsoring women MPs were the TGWU (7), GMB (4), MSF (3), NUPE (3), COHSE (2), and RMT, USDAW and ASLEF, one each. At Hampstead and Highgate, Glenda Jackson's ASLEF sponsorship owed less to her experience of the footplate than to the presence of the union's head office in the constituency. Of the Co-operative Party's 26 sponsored candidates, 14 were elected, none of whom were women.[18]

About one third of the 56 Conservative MPs who retired in 1992 were of the 'One Nation' tradition – men such as Sir Ian Gilmour, Sir Paul Dean, Peter Walker and Norman Miscampbell. All had started their parliamentary careers in the early 'sixties after being formed politically during the era of post-war Butskellism. These men were replaced in 1992 by a younger generation, many of whom did not come of age politically until the Thatcher years; indeed the youngest group of newcomers had been mere teenagers when Mrs Thatcher became party leader. The orthodoxies

*Table 10.4   Occupation of candidates*

| Occupation | Conservative | | Labour | | Liberal Democrat | |
|---|---|---|---|---|---|---|
| | *elected* | *defeated* | *elected* | *defeated* | *elected* | *defeated* |
| *Professions* | | | | | | |
| Barrister | 39 | 26 | 9 | 9 | 5 | 13 |
| Solicitor | 21 | 18 | 8 | 11 | 1 | 18 |
| Doctor/dentist | 4 | 6 | 2 | 5 | – | 13 |
| Architect/surveyor | 3 | 6 | – | 6 | – | 9 |
| Civil/chartered engineer | 3 | 4 | – | 9 | – | 23 |
| Accountant | 12 | 14 | 2 | 6 | – | 29 |
| Civil servant/local govt. | 10 | 5 | 16 | 21 | – | 20 |
| Armed services | 14 | 3 | – | – | 1 | 1 |
| Teachers: | | | | | | |
| University | 4 | 3 | 14 | 6 | 1 | 13 |
| Polytechnic/college | 2 | 4 | 24 | 33 | – | 46 |
| School | 16 | 16 | 38 | 73 | 3 | 103 |
| Other consultants | 2 | 2 | – | 1 | 1 | 3 |
| Scientific/research | 1 | – | 2 | 8 | – | 12 |
| Total | 131 | 107 | 115 | 188 | 12 | 303 |
| | (39%) | (36%) | (42%) | (52%) | (60%) | (50%) |
| *Business* | | | | | | |
| Company director | 37 | 30 | 1 | – | – | 20 |
| Company executive | 75 | 73 | 8 | 13 | 2 | 88 |
| Commerce/insurance | 9 | 15 | 1 | 5 | – | 22 |
| Management/clerical | 4 | 5 | 11 | 14 | – | 20 |
| General business | 3 | 8 | 1 | 12 | – | 22 |
| Total | 128 | 131 | 22 | 44 | 2 | 172 |
| | (38%) | (44%) | (8%) | (12%) | (10%) | (28%) |
| *Miscellaneous* | | | | | | |
| Miscellaneous white collar | 9 | 11 | 36 | 64 | 1 | 69 |
| Politician/pol. organiser | 20 | 17 | 24 | 17 | 2 | 10 |
| Publisher/journalist | 28 | 9 | 13 | 14 | 3 | 19 |
| Farmer | 10 | 15 | 2 | – | – | 8 |
| Housewife | 6 | 7 | – | 4 | – | 9 |
| Student | – | – | – | – | – | 6 |
| Total | 73 | 59 | 75 | 99 | 6 | 121 |
| | (22%) | (20%) | (28%) | (27%) | (30%) | (20%) |
| *Manual Workers* | | | | | | |
| Miner | 1 | – | 12 | 1 | – | – |
| Skilled Worker | 3 | 1 | 43 | 27 | – | 15 |
| Semi/Unskilled Worker | – | – | 4 | 4 | – | 1 |
| Total | 4 | 1 | 59 | 32 | 0 | 16 |
| | (1%) | (–) | (22%) | (9%) | (–) | (2%) |
| Grand Total | 336 | 298 | 271 | 363 | 20 | 612 |

Table 10.5    Sponsored Labour candidates 1992

|  | Total | Elected |
|---|---|---|
| Transport and General Workers Union (TGWU) | 44 | 38 |
| General Municipal and Boilermakers Union (GMBU) | 22 | 17 |
| National Union of Mineworkers (NUM) | 14 | 14 |
| Amalgamated Engineering Union (AEU) | 15 | 13 |
| Manufacturing Science and Finance Union (MSF) | 13 | 13 |
| National Union of Public Employees (NUPE) | 15 | 12 |
| National Union of Rail Maritime and Transport Workers (RMT) | 13 | 12 |
| Confederation of Health Service Employees (COHSE) | 6 | 6 |
| Graphical Paper and Media Union (GPMU) | 7 | 5 |
| Electrical Electronic Telecommunications and Plumbing Union (EETPU) | 10 | 3 |
| National Communications Unions (NCU) | 4 | 3 |
| Union of Shop Distributive and Allied Workers (USDAW) | 3 | 3 |
| Transport Salaried Staffs Association (TSSA) | 2 | 2 |
| Associated Society of Locomotive Engineers and Firemen (ASLEF) | 2 | 1 |
| National Association of Colliery Overmen Deputies and Shotfirers (NACODS) | 1 | 1 |
| Iron and Steel Trades Confederation (ISTC) | 1 | – |
| Union of Communication Workers (UCW) | 1 | – |
| Trade Union sponsored | 173 | 143 |
| Co-operative Party | 26 | 14 |
| All sponsored candidates | 199 | 157 |

into which they were schooled were inevitably different from those of the Macmillan years. In this sense, the new Conservative intake of 1992 implied a drift to the right as sixty-year-old One Nation Tories made way for thirty-year-old free marketeers.

In Labour's case the waters were more muddied, both by the large numbers flocking during the Kinnock years to the Tribune group merely as a badge of orthodoxy and in a quest for office, and by the uncertainty about alignments under a new leadership. The affiliation of over half the PLP to either Tribune or Campaign groups – as in 1987 – seemed unlikely in 1992. Interest, more than ideology, coloured the new PLP whose membership suggested deep roots in the public sector. Increasingly, however, on both sides, the House comprised career politicians for whom office counted as much as interest and where dogma became the servant of ambition.

Candidate selection remained the most notable example in politics of professionals (aspirants and party officials) confronting the amateurs (the local selectorate). The centre (Walworth Road and Smith Square) was bound to have a view as to the type of candidate likely to assist the party's electoral interests. The relationship between centre and periphery was never likely to be precisely divinable; the view of the centre as a 'marriage broker' – a Smith Square phrase – might appear to understate the influence of Central Office. In Labour's case, the centre's preoccupation with the party's national image clearly had an impact on candidate selection practices in the run-up to the 1992 election. In both cases, moreover, the centre clearly had to take account of the rising perceptions in the electorate of the low numbers of both women and black and Asian MPs. The idea of the centre operating as a hidden hand was neither new nor dated. For Labour, in addressing the matter of the role of the unions in candidate selection, the paradox was that they had traditionally acted as ballast for the leadership. But the centre – in another form – was to intervene before the next election: the Boundary Commission was about to shake over-ripe apples from the parliamentary tree.

NOTES

1. The total was 2948 if all three of Screaming Lord Sutch's candidacies at Huntingdon, Islwyn and Yeovil are counted.
2. In addition to the 140, 15 MPs (11 Labour, 3 Conservative and 1 Ulster Unionist) had entered the House at by-elections between 1987 and 1992; one of them (a Conservative) having sat in a previous parliament.
3. One other former MP had served in post-war parliaments with a wider gap in his service: Moss Turner-Samuels (Lab) was out of the House between 1924 and 1945; but Mr Tyler's absence was the longest of any MP whose career was entirely post-1945.
4. Of the 27 Conservative MPs who lost their seats at the 1987 election, seven found safe seats elsewhere; one returned at a by-election; one fought and lost a by-election; three remained to fight their old seats; one received a peerage. Of the remainder, most were either Scots who had scant prospect of alternative seats north of the border, or were disqualified by age or infirmity. Only two obvious casualties remained standing when the music stopped: Geoff Lawler and the ubiquitous Peter Bruinvels, narrowly defeated at several selection conferences.
5. Chris Hawkins (born 1937), Sir Peter Morrison (born 1944) and Mike Woodcock (born 1943) were also retiring early.
6. Only one MP, Calum Macdonald (Western Isles), had been reselected by an

electoral college consisting solely of individual party members. For an assault on the selection process by the candidate defeated by Peter Mandelson in the contest for Hartlepool, see Stephen Jones, 'The candidate's tale', *Tribune*, 26 January 1990.

7. 'Oh to be a Tory MP: Secrets of the Selection Board', *Sunday Times Magazine*, 28 October 1990.

8. See *Notes on Procedure for the adoption of Conservative Parliamentary Candidates* (revised edition 1990). Despite changes of emphasis here and there, these regulations remained remarkably unaltered since Lord Woolton's day.

9. In order of comfort: Charles Wardle, 85% of the vote; Peter Temple-Morris 74%; Tony Marlow 73%; Barry Porter 72%; Julian Critchley 69%; Michael Mates 65%; Ivor Stanbrook 61%; Cyril Townsend 59%; and Sir Peter Emery 58%.

10. Other disputes included that at the Western Isles where Central Office refused to endorse Mr Andrew Price, a Presbyterian fundamentalist who had declared that 'Catholics cannot be considered Christian'; at Carlisle, where Phil Pedley, a former national YC chairman who had helped expose alleged right-wing infiltration of the party, naming two MPs, was dropped allegedly on Central Office instructions: at Berwick, where Christine Smith was dropped as candidate and claimed that 'being from Yorkshire, a woman and an ordinary working person does not conform', and that 'John Major's classless society hasn't reached Northumberland yet'; and at Yeovil, where Fiona Burkeman, a sex therapist from Kingston on Thames, found nursing the seat (140 miles away) 'a real slog' and withdrew.

11. Of the SNP's 72 candidates, 14 were women (one of them having changed their sex); Plaid Cymru fielded 7 women (out of 38 candidates).

12. See J. Lovenduski and P. Norris, 'Selecting Women candidates', *European Journal of Political Research*, 1989, Vol. 17, p. 533–562; and D. Denver, 'Britain: Centralised parties with decentralised selections', in M. Gallagher and M. Marsh, *Candidate Selection in Comparative Perspective* (London: Sage, 1988), pp. 47–71.

13. *Jewish Chronicle*, 17 April 1992.

14. The others being David Lloyd George, Winston Churchill and James Callaghan.

15. Tony Benn was also one of 24 MPs whose fathers had been MPs (18 Conservative and six Labour). Two new MPs were in this number: the Conservatives Bernard Jenkin and Lady Olga Maitland. In addition three grandsons of MPs entered the House: the Conservatives Geoffrey Clifton-Brown and David Faber (Harold Macmillan's grandson), and the Labour MP Peter Mandelson, grandson of Herbert Morrison. The election of Labour's Gordon Prentice (Pendle) and Bridget Prentice (Lewisham East) added a third husband and wife pair to the Conservative Bottomleys and Wintertons.

16. Conservative MPs elected in the 1950s (* denotes interrupted service): Sir Edward Heath 1950; Sir Geoffrey Johnson Smith 1959*; Sir Richard Body 1955*; Sir Dudley Smith 1959*; Paul Channon 1959 (January); Sir Trevor Skeet 1959*; Julian Critchley 1959*; Sir Peter Tapsell 1959*; Sir Peter Emery 1959*; Sir Fergus Montgomery 1959*.

17. In this sense, the election of the old Etonian landowner Geoffrey Clifton-Brown at Cirencester & Tewkesbury, resurrecting a political dynasty comprising four MPs this century, including Mr Speaker Clifton Brown and his son-in-law Mr Speaker Hylton-Foster, was highly atypical.

18. As with the unions, the role of Co-operative affiliates was held to have been influential: in an outer London seat the candidate selected won by virtue of the Co-op affiliation keeping him afloat beyond the first count in which he obtained only four of the individual members' votes.

# 11 The Local Battle

There is a vast gap between the national campaign, the contest designed by the party strategists and seen by the television viewers, and the local campaign directly experienced by candidates, agents and constituency workers. In the answers to a postal questionnaire[1] candidates frequently testified to the total difference of focus between their activities and the obsessions of party headquarters.

As one senior Conservative said, 'As always, one is cocooned in one's own constituency'. Another, a Cabinet minister, remarked, 'I have never known a campaign where there was a bigger gap between our local efforts and the centre', while a third said 'the media circus was much more distantly related to the real election campaign than any in my experience'. A Labour veteran observed, 'The media reported how brilliant our campaign was and once again the voters passed by on the other side of the street. I do not think the Labour Party has yet grasped that it has still to inhabit the same world as ordinary voters.'

All parties are agreed on certain basic truths. Local electioneering is directed to securing as many votes as possible. Supporters have to be identified and, by securing postal ballots, by distributing leaflets, and by knocking-up on polling day, the recording of their allegiance at the ballot box has to be positively ensured. Waverers have to be approached in a fashion that is not counterproductive while opponents have to be left alone. In 1992, however, this optimum of campaigning was achieved in relatively few constituencies; the manpower and the skill was insufficient.

All parties admitted to falling membership and falling numbers of activists. Some senior politicians asked whether the age of mass parties was not finally over. Yet most winnable seats can still muster enough supporters for each of the main parties to mount a reasonable campaign.

The electoral registers which came into force on 15 February 1992, based on residence on 10 October 1991, contained 43,252,865 names. There were many complaints about the imperfections in the register. The actual number was only 0.2 percent up on 1987 although the adult population was reckoned to have increased by 1.2 percent. Some suggested that people had kept their names off the electoral register lest it be used as evidence to put them on the poll-tax register (although there was supposed to be a 'Chinese Wall' between the two registers). In practice, this does not seem to have been as serious a problem as many supposed. In some cases the fall in the numbers registered was simply due to new registration officers changing the local policy of carrying over from one year to the next the names of electors who had not returned their forms. Indeed the apparent increase in turnout in some inner-city areas (notably in Hackney) seems to have been largely due to the pruning of the register. Most of the constituencies where the poll-tax was seriously accused of cutting registration were in safe Labour areas, particularly in Scotland. It is certainly not possible to argue that Labour lost the election through the deliberate non-registration of its supporters.

However the condition of the register gave cause for concern. During the campaign in the six constituencies in Oxfordshire 700 cases emerged of qualified people being left off the register, and in other areas the number was greater. Clearly there were more complaints of registration errors than in previous contests.[2] People who had recently moved and been put on the poll-tax register were particularly indignant to find that they could not be on the electoral register.

In 1985 the franchise was extended to British citizens living overseas if they had left the country within the last five years; in 1987 11,100 were registered. In 1989 the time period was extended to 20 years and the 1992 electoral register included 30,000 overseas voters. However there were only 64 constituencies where the number exceeded 100 and only four where it exceeded 200 – Cambridge (261), Oxford West & Abingdon (204), Hampstead & Highgate (224) and Richmond & Barnes (232). In only two seats was the overseas vote greater than the majority (Bristol NW, 53 voters, Con majority 45; and Vale of Glamorgan 64 voters, Con majority 19). Since overseas voters were plainly not all Conservatives, and since many of them failed to record their votes, it may even be that no seat was decided by this facility, although £736,000 of public money had been spent advertising it in 1990[3] (and the Conservative Party had spent even more). Granada's *World in Action* on March 23 had a special item showing the total ignorance about British politics of a family who had lived for the last 18 years in South Africa and who were going to vote Conservative.

The Conservatives had about 300 full-time constituency agents at this election. The Labour Party had 100 professionals in the field and the Liberal Democrats 30 but many of these were campaign advisers rather than agents in the traditional mould. Often one regional party official would focus on a handful of seats and give close supervision to a local volunteer. But the majority of agents were amateurs, party workers who might have gone to a weekend school on election law or who just had long experience in local or parliamentary elections. Some of them were retired people or managers of great dedication and skill who could perform as well or better than any professional. Even with fewer high quality agents, stories of legal or administrative disaster were rare.

Few candidates could think of local issues which were important in the voting and it is difficult to find in the results evidence of the impact of the particular local scandals that were sometimes cited during the campaign as likely to have an influence. Some attributed Chris Patten's defeat to the exceptional impact of the uniform business rate in Bath but only one candidate elsewhere mentioned the arrival of poll-tax bills in late March.

An element in John Taylor's defeat in Cheltenham may have been his colour and the row over his selection. Local exploitation of racial issues may explain the exceptionally low swing in parts of the Yorkshire woollen area. The boom conditions in Aberdeen may account for the Conservatives' solitary gain from Labour. One Conservative incumbent blamed his defeat on defence closures in his constituency.

In the Appendix John Curtice and Michael Steed show that there is limited evidence of candidates influencing the outcome but incumbency did not prove so much of an advantage. Moreover the high television profile given to Mr Patten and Mr Cunningham as campaign managers certainly does not seem to have helped them in Bath or Copeland. During the campaign regional agents and others told us of specially good and energetic and of specially incompetent candidates, but their tips would not have helped anyone betting on exceptional swings.

Almost every candidate still issued an election address[4] and tried to get it delivered to every household or to every elector. But this form of communication has become less significant than fifty years ago when it was usual to distribute a personal credo, a statement of the candidate's record and policy stance, with an individual emphasis on those items of the party programme thought to have particular local or personal appeal. Nowadays more and more addresses are in standard format with centrally prepared text.

The availability of computers to be used for cheap desk-top publishing and for co-ordinating target mailings has meant a revolution in campaign propaganda in many constituencies. Both Liberal Democrats and Conservatives now regularly distribute a free newspaper to inform electors of the activities of their local councillors (*Focus* for the Liberal Democrats, *In Touch* for the Conservatives) and in many constituencies the 'Election Special' edition outweighed or even replaced the traditional election address. The Conservatives frequently, and other parties in some cases, also produced two or more different leaflets; with computer targetting it was possible to ensure that every household with more than one elector received two different leaflets by the Post Office free mailing. Consequently it would in many cases be arbitrary to define any one of these as '*the* election address' for the constituency, and the table which in past volumes in this series has analysed in detail the content of the election address would for 1992 be misleading. Nevertheless, it is possible to make some general observations.

Labour's addresses were mostly of a similar form – the familiar A4 leaflet folding in three to reveal a small window bill, monotone red-and-white in some unwinnable seats, but glossy red-and-yellow with colour photographs in most. A few made a point of conspicuously indicating that they were printed on recycled paper, an opportunity missed by the other parties. Content varied. All had a photograph of the candidate, and many of his or her family; a small number also showed Neil Kinnock (as Table 11.1 records). Photographs with voters, posed in recognisable locations in the constituency were popular (as they were with the Tories).

In their written material some Labour candidates chose to make a great many points briefly, but most preferred to concentrate on a small number of themes, devoting a headlined paragraph to each. The topics chosen varied, though emphasis on the National Health Service, education and economic management were almost universal; the relative importance accorded to different themes also varied considerably, no doubt reflecting the particular concerns of the candidate. Other topics regularly encountered, in descending order of frequency, were benefits and pensions, the environment, housing, low pay and the minimum wage, the poll-tax, crime, and women's rights or equal opportunities. Much rarer were mentions of defence, regional devolution and Europe. 'Socialism' was also rarely referred to, though a few candidates were plainly not frightened of mentioning it, as for example Vernon Coaker (Gedling) who put in bold type on the back of his address the words:

> Socialism is not just about managing the economy better – it is about a *better way* of managing it.

Conservative addresses varied much more both in form and substance. A far higher proportion used simple two-tone leaflets in blue and white, with around a third having only black-and-white photographs of the candidate; this applied not just to moribund organisations in hopeless seats but often to MPs expecting to be comfortably re-elected. It was plain that in some cases at least this was to allow the legally limited resources to be diverted elsewhere, for example to the production of glossy calling cards. The format of the addresses was also more varied, with many candidates opting for differently sized leaflets, varying in size from some which were folded to barely 6" by 3" (and could be sealed with a computer address label, being thus ready for the post without needing to be put into an envelope) to others consisting of four glossy A4 sides (and suitable only for hand delivery).

A very few constituencies still hold obstinately to traditional local party colours. Thus in Cheltenham and South Worcestershire the Conservative blue was offset in pink, and in Penrith and the Border the Conservative leaflet was in yellow and black, with no blue to be seen.

The themes most frequently addressed in Conservative leaflets reflected main campaign issues. Education, the NHS (in both cases defending the government's reforms), tax, law and order, the recession, and defence all recurred often, in approximately that order of frequency. Other less prevalent issues raised were inflation, the environment, housing, union power, the poll-tax and the Citizen's Charter. A few spoke of Britain's place in the world, attacked Socialism and argued that a vote for the Liberal Democrats was a vote for Labour; immigration and capital punishment appeared sporadically. Neil Kinnock was rarely attacked directly, but a few did it with flair, such as Greg Knight's flyer, picturing himself with John Major on one side and an unflattering photograph of Kinnock, 'the Alternative', on the other. Europe, the issue which had threatened to split the party, was not as conspicuously absent as might have been expected, but those addresses that did mention it underlined the party's difficulties – a few enthusiastically in favour, a few dogmatically against, but the majority desperately trying to have the best of both worlds by proclaiming that Britain's place was at the centre of Europe and that the Conservatives could be relied upon to make Europe work to Britain's advantage without any loss of independence.

The vast majority of Liberal Democrats emphasised the same five points: the economy, electoral reform, education, the environment and a 'caring society' (exemplified by commitment to the NHS and the social security benefits). In most cases they used one or both of two standard forms of text, though some candidates chose to express the same concerns in their own words, and about half amplified their case with local examples. In most seats where the Alliance had been second in 1987 they also emphasised the tactical position with barcharts (a more professional few with piecharts), and with frequent use of the phrase 'Everyone knows Labour can't win here'. One even versified it:

A vote for Labour,
Loony or Green,
Is, in the South Hams
A vote for Steen

(Anthony Steen was the sitting Conservative MP). The effect of this tactic cannot always have been beneficial. As one sardonic Tory MP wrote: 'The Liberal candidate even advertised the amount of my 1987 majority which, in view of the size of it seemed, to say the least, a rather peculiar thing to do.'

To these features were added local messages and information on the candidate. Almost universal was a reference to and a photograph of Paddy Ashdown, whose letter of endorsement of the candidate was frequently as prominent as the candidate's own appeal to the voters. In this locally written section of the address other issues were occasionally aired. Europe received surprisingly few mentions, though a smattering of candidates chose to highlight it. The poll-tax also received sporadic attention, though more often as an illustration of the evils of 'First-Past-the-Post' than in directly advocating Local Income Tax.

The Liberal Democrats almost invariably emphasised the local links of their candidates, especially if the opponents were not local. Andrew George, the Liberal Democrat in St. Ives, made the point that he was the only Cornishman standing by being photographed in a Cornwall rugby shirt.

The attitude to each party's leaders was the most striking contrast between the three parties. Both Major and Ashdown had been photographed with a considerable number of their candidates; but, failing this, Liberal Democrats were more determined to get a photograph of Ashdown alone. Kinnock, in stark contrast, was rarely seen at all.

Local variations were also occasionally evident in the self-descriptions that candidates chose to put on the ballot papers. A number of Liberal Democrats opted for variations on the theme 'Liberal Democrat (Leader Paddy Ashdown)'. More confusing were instances where independents ran against the official party nominees under similar labels. In Poole for example, the 'Official Conservative Party candidate for Poole' was opposed by a 'Poole Conservative'; in Grantham there was both a 'Liberal Democrat' and 'The Liberal Democrat Candidate'. Most complicated was Hove, where 'The Conservative Party Candidate' (the sitting MP, Tim Sainsbury) was opposed by Nigel Furness, who saved his deposit standing for the 'Official Hove Conservative Party'; here the confusion was compounded by the fact that the Labour candidate was labelled 'Hove and

*Table 11.1   Photographs of party leaders on election addresses (%)*

|  | Con | Lab | Lib Dem |
|---|---|---|---|
| Party leader with candidate | 41 | 6 | 47 |
| Party leader alone | 9 | 4 | 41 |
| Other front-bencher with candidate | 5 | 10 | 3 |
| None | 45 | 80 | 9 |
| TOTAL | 100 | 100 | 100 |

Portslade Labour Party'. In Mole Valley, Kenneth Baker ensured there was no such ambiguity, describing himself as 'Conservative Party Candidate and Home Secretary'.

In their own comments on how the national issues affected their campaign, candidates answering our questionnaire reported much hostile reaction to Labour's Sheffield rally and a strong but mixed response to the war of Jennifer's ear. Conservative and Labour alike noted the hostile doorstep response to Neil Kinnock though often a Labour candidate thought his personality was made a surrogate target for his party's unpopularity. A Conservative noted that this was the first of his many elections in which he had not encountered any personally hostile comments about his own party's leader. Several candidates thought that Paddy Ashdown had annoyed voters with too many bargaining demands. Some candidates observed that, to a quite new degree, they had party slogans played back to them on the doorstep, notably 'We don't want to pay £1250 more in tax'. One or two Conservatives said that Labour's attacks on the health issue boomeranged because their local NHS was so good. A disappointed Labour aspirant said, 'Unlike many colleagues, I think we lost on health. After Jennifer's ear I was taunted on the doorstep with "shroud-waving"'.

Candidates commented that they heard less from pressure groups than in previous years. But animal rights groups, particularly the anti fox-hunting campaign, the Keep Sunday Special group and, most of all, the anti-abortion lobby, made themselves felt locally. One Tory said that fox-hunting cost him a thousand votes; another complained that the local Catholics totally misrepresented his position – and his opponent's – on abortion. A Labour MP was angry that police time had to be wasted dealing with animal rights activists' threats against him.

"BRING OUT YOUR DEAD."

Nicholas Garland, *Daily Telegraph, 27 March 1992*

In 1992 new technology made a great impact on campaigning. Computers had been experimented with for many years but 1992 was the first election in which their use became almost universal, at least in marginal seats. Since the electoral register was now available on disk it was possible for an agent (or his software specialist) immediately to transfer onto it all the information from past registers, separating newcomers from old inhabitants and recording against each name the results of earlier canvassing, the record of voting in local elections, the willingness to buy raffle tickets, and often the telephone number. The information could be mechanically organised onto canvass cards and knocking-up lists for polling day. If age, sex and occupation were recorded as well as supposed partisanship it was possible to produce a variety of target lists of suitable recipients for particular kinds of direct mail which with the new desk-top publishing could be of very high quality presentation. In 1992, just before the election was announced, 1.5 million personal letters from John Major were sent to Conservative supporters in marginal seats; Labour dispatched over a million letters from Neil Kinnock in a similar operation. Many candidates paid tribute to the immense advantages of computerisation but sceptics remained. A Conservative defending a marginal observed, 'We used computers for the first time. But we hadn't the manpower to use them properly. I'd say they were a disadvantage. Certainly the Central Office recommended programme had serious deficiencies'. Not far off a Labour MP commented, 'We didn't use computers because it would have wasted too much time getting people trained and working the bugs out of the system'.

The management of many campaigns had changed. 'We're not in the old game of trying to knock on every door during the three-week campaign to get a 100 per cent marked-up register', said one organiser. 'We know we need 30,000 votes to win and we've pinpointed them long before; we've only got to make sure they actually vote.' Another commented that it was much easier to get people to canvass when they knew they were approaching people with some past evidence of support for the party. Agents remarked that in many areas the hours available for canvassing were shortening. More houses were empty for most of the day and more doors were firmly barred to callers after 7 p.m.

Telephone canvassing was heavily used in advance of the election. Conservatives in one highly organised safe seat near London helped a northern marginal with 8,000 long-distance phone calls. Some of the telephoning was persuasive and some was in search of financial contributions, but mostly it was directed to achieving a marked-up register. Agents noted that telephone canvassing also enabled the elderly or infirm to help with the job.

When it comes to telephoning the law on election expenses is ambiguous. Although there has been no serious challenge to a constituency election on the grounds of overspending since 1929, agents are still very cautious about transgressing the rules. If telephone canvassing were generally adopted it would certainly involve gross overexpenditure. Private citizens may spend up to £5 of their own money on the election, provided it is spontaneous; if it is co-ordinated, it must be included in the return of expenses. However this rule is impossible to police. As one agent said, 'Often a party worker is given a canvassing list which includes telephone numbers. It is not my concern if they ring their targets up rather than knocking on their doors.' One Conservative MP said firmly, 'Telephoning canvassing is illegal' but another said that most of his canvassing was by telephone. A Labour MP scheduled two hours of each day for random telephone canvassing. But one or two candidates reported complaints about the intrusiveness of telephone canvassing and thought it counter-productive. It was certainly used more by the Conservatives than by other parties.

Now that there is 85 percent telephone saturation in Britain it is clear that telephone canvassing has come to stay, although the fact that up to 20 percent of numbers are ex-directory limits its full effectiveness.

Even more than in previous elections there was a focus on target seats. Labour identified about 120 for special treatment, the Conservatives 70 and the Liberals 50. The exact number and identity of the seats was a closely guarded secret, primarily for internal party reasons – constituencies on the margin would resent their exclusion from a 'specially-winnable' category. The target seats were all eligible for financial aid if they needed it. They were given a special call on front-bench speakers. All the Conservative targets had a full-time agent and special supervision from the area office, as well as from a designated MP. Labour similarly ensured that every key seat had the support of a full-time organiser. Almost all Labour and Conservative key seats were fully computerised with extensive programmes of direct mail.

The Conservative headquarters posted daily notes to every candidate, in many cases faxing them – and marginals received extra attention; in the same vein Labour organised a daily briefing for constituency agents. Most candidates in all parties commented that the service from headquarters was good – and much better than in previous contests. But, as always, there were malcontents complaining of being deluged with too much paper which they had no time to read. However faxes and portable telephones were very much in evidence, particularly in constituencies covering a large area.

Most target seats were linked to one or more adjacent safe seats and workers were bussed in or gave help with telephone canvassing, but mutual aid of this sort was patchy. Activists can be reluctant to work away from their own locale and outsiders can be resented. This is one of the areas where military metaphors can mislead. Party headquarters, unlike army GHQs, cannot move their troops where they will: volunteers cannot be subject to discipline. But a few inspired partisans did sometimes compensate effectively for the lack of workers in a key seat and some marginals spoke gratefully of their neighbours' assistance. One Conservative MP in a safe seat boasted, 'We used a lot of good fluorescent posters to give the illusion of activity while we helped in the next door marginal'.

As Chapter 6 makes plain (p. 116) the 1992 election was exceptionally visible. There were ten thousand large posters on strategic hoardings across the country, in safe seats as much as in marginals, reminding motorists and ordinary passers-by that an election was going on. Constituency efforts were on a much smaller scale but the Liberal Democrats were notably vigorous in getting supporters to plant small placards in their front gardens. The display of window bills varied greatly in accordance with local custom. In some marginals there were hardly any to be seen. In others they were plentiful.

The obituary of the election meeting has been written at every contest for the last thirty years. As a veteran Conservative in a London suburb wrote, 'Alas. No meetings. It is not possible any more.' Another in a Derbyshire seat said, 'We had one meeting and got an audience of 10. In 1983 we had

15 meetings.' One Labour MP recorded his audiences '20, 3, 0, 5, 7, 1, 8, 7, 10, 0, 23'. But the meeting has not altogether disappeared. In urban areas it does now seem to be mostly confined to joint gatherings, organised by churches, teachers, environmentalists or other pressure groups; notably, in 1992, Charter 88's 'Democracy Day' meetings, some of which drew substantial numbers. Candidates, glad of any audience, usually agreed to go to them – although sometimes the presence of obnoxious fringe candidates led to a boycott. In one constituency all such meetings were cancelled because both the Conservative and Labour candidates refused to appear on a platform with a National Front candidate. But in rural areas village meetings persist – and draw an audience. The Perth & Kinross Conservatives had 40 well attended meetings. In Ross, Cromarty & Skye the Liberal Democrat number was cut from 60 to 40 but only because of Charles Kennedy's television commitments. Others lamented that, though they still held meetings, only the party faithful came – and they should have been out canvassing. The audiences at meetings were usually reported to be calm and many candidates paid tribute to the intelligent response they received – 'deferential', 'seminar-like'.

Very few big names proved big enough to draw an audience. Shirley Williams, who visited 70 constituencies, and Roy Jenkins, could still justify holding a meeting. Roy Hattersley and Douglas Hurd spoke in many places. But apart from the big party rallies there can have been few occasions when there was a four-figure gathering. In most areas it was only the candidate's adoption meeting that drew even a three-figure audience.

On the whole the front-benchers, when they visited a constituency, were used for media events – a walkabout in a shopping arcade, a newspaper interview, a visit to the local radio and, if possible, a TV appearance. Often senior figures merely went out canvassing for an hour or two with the candidate – a far cry from the round of public meetings that would have been arranged for much lesser spokesmen fifty years ago. The visits and public meetings of the party leaders preoccupied the parties' regional offices. There was some irritation when visits were cancelled (usually by Conservative Central Office) at short notice – and the security requirements that accompanied a prime-ministerial visit could cause much administrative frustration.

It was an orderly campaign. Although the Prime Minister was jostled a couple of times, there were few reports of rowdy meetings or vandalism, despite some defacing or removal of posters. The evidence of active interest was not high, but a majority of candidates reported greater enthusiasm than in 1987, although it was a surprise when polling-day revealed a general increase in turnout.

*Table 11.2   Public impact of the campaign*

Q.   During the past week have you . . . ? IF YES: Which party was that?

| | Con % | Lab % | Lib Dem % | Other % | Can't remember which party % | No/ Don't know % |
|---|---|---|---|---|---|---|
| (a) Seen any party political broadcasts on TV | 54 | 56 | 49 | 14 | 2 | 29 |
| (b) Heard any party political broadcasts on radio | 10 | 12 | 9 | 2 | 1 | 82 |
| (c) Seen any political advertisements on billboards | 43 | 36 | 13 | 3 | 2 | 45 |
| (d) Had any political leaflets put through your letterbox | 56 | 63 | 53 | 18 | 1 | 14 |
| (e) Been called on by a representative of any political party | 12 | 14 | 7 | 1 | 1 | 70 |
| (f) Attended a political meeting addressed by a candidate | * | 1 | 1 | * | * | 99 |
| (g) Helped a political party in its campaign | 1 | 1 | 1 | * | * | 94 |
| (h) Received letter signed by a party leader individually addressed to you | 7 | 5 | 3 | * | * | 87 |

* = less than 1 percent

Q.   And in the past week, have you discussed the election campaign with friends, relatives or workmates?

| | % |
|---|---|
| Yes | 78 |
| No | 22 |

The number of people actively engaged in the campaign was certainly down from previous years. 'I wrote 65 thank you letters but only 5 people really did any work', said one Conservative in a hopeless seat. At the other extreme though, there were some who wrote 1000 thank you letters and felt no shortage of manpower.

The extent of public involvement in the election is reflected in the findings of the *Sunday Times* panel survey conducted by MORI the day after the vote and reported in Table 11.2.

*Table 11.3   Time of voting*

| | All voters (%) | | Con (%) | | Lab (%) | | Lib Dem (%) | |
|---|---|---|---|---|---|---|---|---|
| | '87 | '92 | '87 | '92 | '87 | '92 | '87 | '92 |
| 7.00 a.m.–11.59 a.m. | 38 | 35 | 36 | 40 | 38 | 31 | 38 | 33 |
| 12 noon–4.59 p.m. | 25 | 27 | 25 | 24 | 26 | 29 | 25 | 21 |
| 5.00 p.m.–7.59 p.m. | 27 | 30 | 29 | 29 | 27 | 33 | 26 | 24 |
| 8.00 p.m.–10.00 p.m. | 9 | 8 | 6 | 6 | 7 | 6 | 9 | 11 |

*Source*: Gallup

In the past, Labour supporters voted later in the day than Conservatives; this made Labour more vulnerable to evening rainstorms and also left the party less time for knocking up. But in 1992 as in 1987 that difference had vanished as Table 11.3 shows.

During the campaign the weather was normal for the time of year. In London there was some rain on twelve of the thirty days between March 11 and April 9 but there were no reports of snow or storm interfering with party efforts. On polling day it was fine almost everywhere.

All the parties made special efforts to secure as many postal ballots as possible, but their success was limited. The number of valid postal votes actually fell. About 720,000 (2.1 percent) were cast, well down from the 793,000 (2.4 percent) cast in 1987; where an increase occurred it seemed to be due either to the election falling in the University vacation or to exceptional efforts in marginal seats.[5] In Cambridge the postal vote jumped from 2758 to 5085 and in Devonport from 1491 to 4325. In 51 of Labour's key targets the increase on 1987 averaged 50 per cent. The party was sure that some of its gains were due to its much greater efforts at recruiting postal voters.

But the closing date for postal votes was March 23, only 13 days after the announcement of the election and only 10 days after the Home Office advertised the facility on television and in the national press.[6] The parties and the Association of Electoral Administrators complained about the shortness of notice and about the complexity of the official forms.

The net effect of the postal vote is difficult to estimate. There seem to have been 56 seats where the postal votes cast exceeded the victor's majority. However most reports suggested a fairly even division of the vote. The Conservatives' own estimates of their share of the postal and proxy vote in 29 key marginals suggests that they secured little more than 50 percent. If the postal vote divided 60–40 in favour of the Conservatives it could be responsible for eight of their successes. At 55–45 it would account for five Conservative victories, against which must be offset some seats where Labour plainly seems to have secured a majority of the postal votes. Their victories in Warrington South and in Cambridge, where the largest postal vote was recorded, could be attributed to absent voters. Most of the smallest postal votes were in city centre seats such as Birmingham Small Heath (209), but in the vast majority of constituencies the figure ranged between 500 and 1500.

The use of proxy votes increased, particularly of course in the seats where postal votes were being most actively recruited. There were over 1500 in Cambridge and over 1000 in Darlington. There were 600 or 700 in most marginal seats. There were stories of abuse. After the election *Panorama* revealed odd facts about how Conservative local councillors had recruited some hundreds of proxy votes from among the elderly in St. Ives – but this does seem to have been an isolated case.

The expenditure of candidates as officially reported was fairly near to the maximum permitted, at least for major parties in marginal seats, and one or two admitted to creative accounting in order to keep within the limit. The way in which expenses incurred in advance, but applying to materials actually used during the campaign, are recorded in the accounts can be fudged. In some cases there were opinion polls in late February or early March designed for campaign use, publicly or privately. No candidate could afford to conduct a serious poll and stay within the permitted limit. Parties do not look too closely at their opponents' expenditure because they too may have slipped up. But this does not mean that there was gross overspending of the sort that had regularly occurred in by-elections.[7]

The fact that so many candidates spent to within a few pounds of the limits underlines the creative accounting which is universally acknowledged to occur in expense returns. What is an election expense? How should the computer or the office space paid for long before the dissolution be charged? When, for legal purposes, does the election begin? At the parliamentary level these questions have never been settled in contemporary terms. (There has been no serious petition over parliamentary election expenses since 1929.) Perhaps we should salute the Conservative agent in Monmouth who facing a ceiling of £7260.78 returned election expenses amounting to £7260.78.

The cost of the election to the Consolidated Fund was something over £42 million, quite apart from the annual cost of the electoral register (£40m in 1991–2). This was slightly offset by the £450,000 the Treasury

*Table 11.4   Total amount spent by candidates*

| Party | Average expenditure (£) | % of maximum | | % 1987 |
|-------|------------------------|--------------|--|--------|
| | | All Candidates | Victors | All Candidates |
| Conservative | 5840 | 80 | 91 | 78 |
| Labour | 5090 | 71 | 84 | 69 |
| Liberal Democrat | 3169 | 43 | 96 | 61 |
| SNP | 2861 | 40 | 99 | 43 |
| Plaid Cymru | 2698 | 38 | 90 | 40 |
| Green | 836 | 11 | – | 14 |
| Natural Law | 1858 | 26 | – | – |
| Ulster Unionists | 4166 | 86 | 60 | 55 |
| Democratic Unionists | 4299 | 58 | 76 | 63 |
| SDLP | 3504 | 47 | 91 | 54 |
| APNI | 1676 | 23 | – | 22 |
| Sinn Fein | 2171 | 29 | – | 42 |

gained from lost deposits,[8] of which over a third was incurred by the Natural Law Party. The Scottish National Party was the only party to lose no deposits: the Conservatives lost four – all in Northern Ireland – Labour one (at Eastbourne) and the Liberal Democrats 11 (of which 9 were in Scotland); Plaid Cymru lost 23. Among the 'other' candidates in Great Britain the unusually large number of 11 saved their deposits, but of these 8 were fighting constituencies for which they had been the MP.

Does the local campaign matter? There was less diversity in swing in 1987–92 than in previous recent elections and it was hard to pinpoint any constituencies where the quality of one side's efforts made a decisive difference. The fact that the swing to Labour was higher in marginal seats than elsewhere presents an awkward challenge: Conservative resources and organisation have been traditionally seen as being superior to Labour. Moreover the marginal seats mostly had incumbent Conservative MPs who, having won their seats in 1983 and 1987, were usually very assiduous in using all the resources available to an MP to enhance their visibility and their local appeal. If organisation reaps a reward the outcome in marginals should have been more favourable to the Conservatives. In fact the differential swing in marginals raises complex problems which are discussed in detail on p. 322ff. But it is hard to locate evidence of great benefits being reaped by the increasingly sophisticated and computerised local campaigning.

NOTES

1.  After the election we wrote to a large number of MPs and candidates, asking about their local campaign. It was not a rigorously designed sample and we have not reduced their responses to percentages, but this chapter draws heavily on their observations. We are most grateful to them for their help.
2.  See p. 142 for an estimate of the poll-tax effect. When the 1991 register was compiled the United Kingdom had an adult population of 44,361,354 (including perhaps 600,000 foreigners not entitled to vote). The electoral register contained only 42,361,354 names. This is a shortfall of 1,967,262 (4.4 percent). However, through legitimate double registration and through inadvertency many of the names on the register must have been duplicates. An OPCS study comparing the 1991 registration with that year's census should be published in 1993. It will show whether the error rate which was measured at 3–4 percent in 1950 and again in 1966 and at 6–7 percent in 1981 has still further increased.
3.  This included £450,000 on press advertising in Britain and £250,000 on press advertising abroad.
4.  The analysis of election addresses in this chapter owes a great deal to the work of Roger Mortimore.
5.  There were unsubstantiated stories from York and elsewhere of students voting by post and then personating absentees who didn't have postal votes.
6.  The cost to the Treasury of the Home Office advertisements was £508,000.
7.  This was acknowledged when the 1989 Representation of the People Act multiplied by four the amount that a candidate could spend in a by-election.
8.  £500 from each of the 897 candidates who failed to achieve 5 percent of the vote in one constituency, and £1,500 from Screaming Lord Sutch who failed to do so in three.

# 12 Retrospect: Mistakes and Triumphs

The 1992 campaign presents a challenge. The Conservatives' lead was so clear that the events of the final three weeks could not have altered the outcome. However, a mere one percent swing nationwide would have reduced the Conservatives to 312 seats, not enough for them to carry on as a government. Their victory was a near-run thing. The Conservatives, with a mistake or two, could have forfeited their triumph; the Opposition, acting differently, could have won. The campaign is worthy of scrutiny because it was, perhaps, decisive. It also deserves attention because of the intense interest it generated in the media. Even while it was going on it was analysed exhaustively so that, in a curiously circular way, the campaign itself became the issue.

There was much talk about 'a good campaign'. But what constitutes 'a good campaign'? The posters and the party broadcasts are fully under the parties' control but the way the media present the story to the mass electorate is not. The party leaders may aim to dictate the agenda but it is the media that decides what to cover, and it is their broadcast interviews and their press conference questions that shape what the campaign is seen to be about.

At the time the 1992 campaign perplexed many commentators. In the previous four elections the result had appeared a foregone conclusion; this time the polls showed that the two main parties were neck-and-neck; throughout the campaign a hung parliament seemed inevitable. The result therefore came as a surprise, a sharp refutation of most of the campaign commentaries. Was the Conservative campaign under-rated? Were the Labour and Liberal Democrats efforts overpraised? In retrospect it was tempting to look for potential turning-points – the shadow budget, the war of Jennifer's ear, the Sheffield rally, Neil Kinnock's PR commitment, John Major's defence of the Union. How far did any of these provoke the late swing (if there was one) that saved the government?

To an unprecedented extent in 1992 the media appeared to be the message. The politicians' day was shaped by the requirements of the broadcasters and the journalists – morning press conferences, photo-opportunities, walk-abouts and rallies. But the television coverage was

247

largely dictated by the parties' activities. The mutual interdependence of the campaigners and the media made them uneasy accomplices in what was presented to the viewer. However while television largely reflected what the parties were saying, the tabloids pursued their own partisan inclinations. Conservative strategists were angry at the way television – and to a lesser extent the press – focused on their campaign management and on opinion poll findings; Labour was infuriated, if not surprised, at the 'scare' stories run by the right-wing tabloids and at the over-reaction to the April 1 blip in the opinion polls.

It can, however, be a mistake to assume that attention given to a party's favourite issue necessarily works to its advantage. In the first week, coverage was dominated by the economy but this did not help the Conservatives because much of the economic news was in the form of gloomy official statistics on unemployment and trade and reports of closures. In the second week, the coverage of health was a mixed blessing for Labour because it was linked to the propriety of Labour's election broadcast on the issue. Because the parties tried as far as possible to stick to their pre-arranged themes there was often little direct debate. For Labour it was the social agenda and the recession, for Liberal Democrats education, and for Conservatives their own leadership and Labour's tax plans. All parties have come to depend on the journalists to carry their challenges and ask the tough questions of the other side at press conferences and interviews. Conservatives complained that Labour was let off lightly about its spending proposals and Labour alleged that Norman Lamont and William Waldegrave were being shielded from hostile questions; Labour eagerly spokesmen challenged their Conservative counterparts to debates. Both parties complained that no-one put hard policy questions to the Liberal Democrats.

But the media can also be important in deciding whether a campaign is successful or not. In the first week the Conservative efforts were widely damned by commentators for lacking direction, conviction or clear themes. By the end of that week opinion polls reported that voters also thought that the Tory campaign was markedly inferior to that of Labour and the Liberal Democrats. It is difficult to believe that voters and activists decided this spontaneously. It is more likely that the Labour lead in the opinion polls together with the commentators' criticisms, shaped public perceptions. Were voters echoing the media? After the election, Philip Gould, Labour's communications specialist, reflected, 'The polls were a verdict on the campaign, the election result a verdict on the parties.'

Ironically, in 1992, as in 1987, the campaign that the commentators and the opinion polls judged the least impressive was the one by the winning party. Post-mortems were being written on the Conservative campaign well before the end, but Chris Patten and John Major always made the point that an election campaign ran until election day. Conservatives talked in advance of intending to achieve maximum impact between nine and five days before polling day, in order to allow for the time-lag between the delivery of a message and its effect. Right up to the end of the campaign they insisted that their arguments about leadership and tax were at last getting through, and they contradicted the opinion polls by referring to the positive responses from the constituencies. But these dismissals of the polls convinced few in the media. Were voters echoing the media judgments on the parties' campaigns?

A danger is that such detailed analysis of the campaign, analogous to the ball-by-ball radio commentary of a cricket match, may result in an exaggeration of the effects of the bits and pieces of a campaign – a speech, a choice of press conference theme or speaker, an election broadcast or a 'gaffe' in an interview. The intense interest of the media in getting a 'story' has had its effect upon the politicians. It makes them try, as far as possible, to achieve a controlled campaign, one in which they set the agenda and eliminate 'accidents'. There were frequent allegations that on his tours and photo-opportunities Mr Kinnock was 'protected' from journalists' questions. At both the Labour and Conservative press conferences reporters were actively dissuaded or prevented from asking follow-up questions. Indeed press conferences resembled a game in which journalists tried to catch out the politicians who in turn tried to say as little as possible beyond getting the message of the day across. The party leaders pursued photo-opportunities relentlessly and addressed hand-picked and elaborately staged rallies. Important front-benchers who lacked televisual appeal were shunted to the sidelines.

All the surveys, even those conducted after the election, reported that Labour fought a better campaign than the Conservatives. In response to an NOP exit poll question about which party had fought the best campaign 30 percent replied Labour, 25 percent Liberal Democrat and only 18 percent Conservative. To a remarkable degree the party fought the campaign that it had planned. Front-bench speakers were disciplined, regularly employing well-rehearsed phrases for the media: 'A Labour government', 'On day one of a Labour government', 'Investing in public services', 'Make the election a referendum on the National Health Service' and 'Stop the privatisation of the National Health Service'. Mr Kinnock always ended his speech with 'It's Time For Change, It's Time For Labour'. Labour's

*Guardian*, 11 April 1992

agenda was focused on the social issues and on getting Britain out of the recession; its spokesmen stuck remorselessly to these themes. The row over Labour's NHS election broadcast, when Jennifer's name was released, was a set-back, largely because it alienated floating voters who thought that it showed Labour 'slanging' and negative but it did not reduce the party's lead in the polls.

There was also an emphasis upon the team, a response to the party's private surveys which showed that Labour's front bench was ranked higher than the Conservatives', and that Neil Kinnock ran behind John Major. Labour put up more front-benchers as spokesmen at their press conferences than the Conservatives and it was notable that they usually included a large representation of women.

Labour's communications and election settings also tried to assume the trappings of government. This was seen in the formal presentation of John Smith's shadow budget, in the frequent references to the measures which a future Labour government would take, and in the introduction of Mr Kinnock as the next Prime Minister and of other spokesmen as cabinet ministers for various departments. Labour was a government in waiting; it was now time for Labour. Many issues which had troubled Labour in the past did not appear important this time. Trade unions, defence, inflation and loony left-wing local councils hardly took off as election themes (except for their appearance in some tabloid newspapers) and for a time it appeared that the party had contained the tax issue. Mr Kinnock himself had a good campaign, except at the Sheffield rally where his exuberance caused offence. He regretted it immediately.

To the end, Labour leaders were sure that they had fought a good campaign and would win at least enough seats to deny the Conservatives a clear victory, although they might need another election to achieve a majority Labour government. 'The Tories have lost it, now we have to win it', said David Hill a week before polling day. There was also a sense of im nding victory among journalists accompanying the Labour leader. A fir.al report from Michael Cassell (*Financial Times*, April 9) stated that Mr Kinnock's team was exhausted but 'spurred on by the sweet smell of victory' and 'believe the ultimate prize is just hours away'. He quoted a Kinnock aide, 'This has been the easy bit. From Friday we start the real job'. At the same time there were rather down-beat accounts of the Major campaign from journalists accompanying the Prime Minister. Commentators were facing up to the prospect of a hung parliament, with Labour the largest party; they were discussing Mr Kinnock as Prime Minister.

There was therefore a great sense of shock in the Labour camp when the results came through. Newspaper headlines on election day, based on opinion polls, proclaimed that it was neck-and-neck as Labour's lead was being whittled away. None, however, suggested a Tory victory and the final polls showed an average 0.9 percent Labour lead. There were claims that there were a large number of floating voters. But the figure of 17 percent, reported by the MORI *Sunday Times* panel on the final weekend, was only slightly more than in 1987 (13 per cent) and 1983 (16 percent). And many of these were not expected to vote. But Labour's private polls carried warning signs throughout, particularly on the tax issue, and on the final Tuesday they showed that Labour's earlier lead had disappeared (although NOP's final larger and published poll showed a 3 percent Labour lead). 'We knew we had had it then', said one of Mr Kinnock's team. Nothing, however, prepared Mr Kinnock or his party for the large Conservative lead when the votes were counted.

Throughout the campaign the party's private polls had contained positive feedback on the Smith budget, and the party's election broadcasts. The themes of 'Time for a Change' and 'The recession has been caused by the government's incompetence' seemed well received. Yet the private and public polls reported that particularly after the NHS broadcast Labour was blamed more for 'slanging' than other parties and was more guilty of making promises the country could not afford; they also reported that many voters feared that a Labour government would lead to a rise in prices and mortgages. In the last week there were some indications that the

Conservative tax message was getting through. On the eve of the election some depression was caused by the private poll findings and by the party's qualitative research 'when we got underneath the numbers'.

But the public polls showed that health, education and unemployment remained by far the most important issues and that the Labour Party had a big lead on them. Tax as an issue remained near the bottom of the list of important issues. There was no public warning of what was to come. Labour, according to the questions asked by pollsters and the comments of the pundits, had won the battle of the agenda. Most of the Labour campaigners at the centre, drawing on their private research, were less sure.

Assessments of Labour's campaign were inevitably influenced by the shock of defeat. The favoured target for blame became John Smith's tax package. The claim that 8 out of 10 families would be better off under his budget had not been believed, for some 50 percent of voters feared that they would pay more tax under Labour. More damaging were Tory claims that Labour's manifesto promises would cost £38 billion. Earlier party policy documents had insisted that all public spending promises – apart from pensions and child benefit – depended on the availability of funds ('as resources allow'). This qualification was omitted from the manifesto and Conservatives costing the programme gleefully asked, 'Where is the money coming from?'. This was the basis for the claim of a '£1,250 tax bombshell'. After the election, some Labour front-benchers argued that the omission of this qualification was crucial. But this is far-fetched; the Tory costing had been launched the previous summer and the tax bombshell campaign had been launched in January, when the qualification still stood.

The Conservatives pursued from February onwards the so-called 'Double Whammy' – the extra taxes and higher prices – that a Labour government would bring. A third element, higher mortgages, was then added by Saatchi ('Five Years' Hard Labour') and Labour's private polls showed that this did register with voters. On tax the thrust of the Conservative message moved from the effect on take-home pay to the claim that lower taxes would speed recovery; vote your pocket and do the economy a favour. Conservative leaders seized on this last gloss, suggested by Jeremy Sinclair of Saatchi. They suspected that many voters were reluctant to state their pocket-book concerns as a reason for their choice of party and that Labour had not fully grasped this.

In their responses to our questionnaire, many Labour candidates were quick to condemn the proportional representation (PR) initiative in the last days of the campaign, on the grounds that it showed weakness, or distracted attention from the NHS or a counter-attack on tax, or simply because they opposed PR. Conservatives claimed that Labour betrayed its lack of confidence and was mistaken to introduce such an issue so late in the campaign. The party's manifesto statement that it would enhance the authority and extend the membership of the Plant committee was a signal of rethinking. Democracy Day, on April 2, seemed an obvious opportunity for Mr Kinnock to talk about leading a partnership government and inviting representatives from other parties to serve on the Plant committee. This would enable Labour to introduce a fresh theme, as well as appealing to Liberals and providing reassurance to those voters fearful of a Labour government. The party's research had persistently shown the public doubts about a Labour government. But because the two major parties were so closely matched in the opinion polls, the issue of electoral reform became caught up with hung parliaments and post-election deals. Clearly, there could only be a Lib-Lab deal, after John Major on April 5 reiterated his opposition to changing the electoral system or the union with Scotland. It was also to Labour's disadvantage that the media concentrated on hung parliaments rather than on health or the recession.

A more constructive line is that if the party was going to raise electoral reform then it should have broached the subject much earlier in the parliament, perhaps in the policy review or in Mr Kinnock's 1991 conference speech, or more positively in the manifesto. But in the pre-election discussions with senior colleagues, Mr Kinnock stated that he would not declare his own views, if he was asked. If he answered honestly then he and his deputy would be seen to be at odds. But he also risked being embarrassed – as he was on Granada TV on April 6 – if he refused to answer one way or the other. One unapologetic Labour adviser stated: 'If Labour had lost narrowly and not made moves towards some form of electoral reform, the campaign would probably have been open to criticism. Our research and the result showed that making a Labour government seem safe was a key campaign requirement.'

During the campaign there was much praise for Mr Kinnock's performance and the opinion polls showed that he narrowed the gap with John Major on some leadership questions and outscored him as a campaigner. Some commentators wrote, on the basis of these surveys, of the failure of John Major. But on the crucial question of rating the two men as Prime Minister, Mr Major continued to enjoy a substantial lead. Insofar as the campaign had a presidential element, the Conservatives clearly won.

Immediately after the event there were also the predictable charges that the campaign was too slick, and gave too much scope to 'spin doctors', media advisers and public relations experts. Party officials and shadow cabinet members, who felt excluded from decision-making, or disagreed with modern communications methods, attacked the Shadow Communications Agency, particularly Patricia Hewitt and Philip Gould. They complained that it had been too freewheeling, too secretive, had too much autonomy over opinion polling and election broadcasts and had made unwise decisions such as the proportional representation proposal. Six weeks after polling day a senior Labour politician asked us, 'Do you know who actually ran the Labour campaign? I don't.' An outspoken report from Labour Party headquarters reviewed the errors of the campaign, placed most of the blame on the agency, and declared:

> Decisions must be taken by politicians, advised by professional staff with politics in their bloodstream; who have experience the battle at close quarters; and whom the party can hold to account.

This was very much a cry from those who had felt excluded and ignored by the decision makers. Inevitably, in the heat of an election campaign, decisions had to be made quickly and this involved senior figures who were on the spot. Most of the key decisions were made by a handful of people at the centre, including Philip Gould and Patricia Hewitt as well as senior party officers and members of Neil Kinnock's private office. But some politicians were not completely at ease with the style of the campaign. Immediately after the 1987 election Roy Hattersley observed that the skilful presentation had exposed the poor quality of the party's policies. In 1992 he thought that the problem was that the slick presentation had distracted from what was now a good product and warned, 'We must not be so obsessed with the glitz and glamour that the medium becomes the message'. Another front-bencher reflected that, 'The whole business of one-liners, photo-opportunities and images does not help us, given the kind of party we are, and the kind of message we want to put over'.

Such criticisms fail to take account of the success which the communications strategy had achieved in bringing Labour to the apparent brink of victory; nor do they acknowledge the responsibility of senior politicians for decisions on strategy and policy. Indeed, some of the politicians who voiced criticisms of the campaign after the event had not grasped the opportunities to be more actively involved in campaign planning in the preceding months. Distrust of Labour and doubts about its taxation plans were major negatives for voters: they had been present throughout the parliament and were the responsibility of senior politicians. From the left, there was a predictable complaint that the Labour campaign was not socialist enough or class-oriented enough or union-oriented enough.

Another target was the biased coverage of the right-wing tabloid press. In his resignation statement on April 12 Neil Kinnock quoted Lord McAlpine's remarks in the *Sunday Telegraph* (April 11), praising the tabloids as the heroes of the campaign. Indeed, the *Sun* boasted 'ITS THE *SUN* WOT WON IT!'. (But Conservative campaigners dismissed this strange alliance of Kinnock and McAlpine as sour grapes, 'McAlpine thought we would lose and won't give us credit because we won without him'.) The tabloids were particularly abusive to Mr Kinnock in the final days of the campaign reinforcing the negative image of Labour. Subsequently, there were claims that the right-wing tabloids had influenced three percent of readers to switch to the Conservatives. But, as Martin Harrop shows in Chapter 9 (pp. 207–8), the case is far from proven.

A good political communication strategy is most effective if it reinforces predispositions, if it is negative and if it peaks at a time when voters are deciding. In this election the tabloid campaign may have appealed to long-standing doubts about Labour's tax plans under Labour or – as Conservative campaigners were careful to say – a Kinnock government, particularly among wavering voters. The tabloids were important in carrying the negative elements of the Conservative campaign, particularly in the crucial final week. Analysis has demonstrated that since 1979 the tabloids have given greater space to the party they oppose, e.g. Labour in the *Sun*, *Express* and *Mail* and Conservative in the *Mirror*. Martin Harrop (p. 189) shows that this pattern was evident again in 1992. What is surely crucial, however, is the existence of the doubts about Labour.

At the time, Mr Smith's shadow budget gained a good press and seemed to have seized the initiative. It also drew attention to Mr Smith, who was regarded by commentators – and by the public – as superior to Norman Lamont. Subsequently, Labour critics complained that the Smith budget had hurt the party by putting tax at the centre of the election. Chris Patten's blunt judgement on the episode was that 'Kinnock was right and Smith was wrong. Smith is a Scot and does not understand that £21,000 is not a king's ransom in the south-east'. In a letter to the *Guardian* (13 April 1992) the party's former chief press officer, Colin Byrne, criticised John Smith's rejection of phasing in the tax changes – 'brushing aside his leader's views and three years of policy review . . . cost the party dear'. Friends of John Smith dismissed the charge and regarded it as yet another example of Mr Byrne's attempts to undermine the shadow chancellor.

But in defence of the shadow chancellor it is not clear that he had much option but to present a budget and to frame it as he did (see above pp. 83–8). His view was that Labour should be clear about its spending and tax plans and avoid the disastrous disagreement between

Roy Hattersley and Neil Kinnock on Labour's proposals which occurred in 1987. John Smith proposed to raise sufficient revenue to fund the party's plans for pension and child benefits as well as the £1 billion health and £0.6 billion education commitments. In spite of criticisms of the budget from the *Independent* and the Tory tabloids, Labour strategists thought that the claim '8 out of 10 tax payers will gain' would transform a losing issue into perhaps a draw. Even Conservatives admitted that, if the claim had been believed, it would have damaged them.

For Labour, the similarities to 1987 were striking. Once again the party's campaign was praised by the media, morale among workers was high, largely because of the positive coverage, and Labour enjoyed a big lead on the social issues. Once again, Neil Kinnock led the Conservative Prime Minister when voters were asked which of the two party leaders had been the best campaigner, although he trailed on who would make 'the best Prime Minister'. In retrospect, Patricia Hewitt wondered if the favourable polls had convinced many voters 'leaning' to Labour that Labour could win, and if, as such people came nearer to the actual vote and considered the prospect of a Labour government, some couldn't bring themselves to trust the party. According to a senior shadow minister, 'At the time I did not accept it but I can now see that the poster "You can't trust Labour", got it exactly right.'

In retrospect, again, there were many critics of the Sheffield rally for its triumphalism. Conservatives quickly dubbed it 'the Nuremberg rally' and a Labour voter complained, 'It was like looking in at a party to which you had not been invited'. It was predictable that Dennis Skinner, as the left-wing maverick on the NEC, would later complain that Mr Kinnock's opening 'You're all ri', you're all ri'' had 'destroyed in ten seconds eight years practice by Mr Kinnock at being a statesman'. The rally, however, was originally designed to give Labour a boost in the final week, assuming that it was neck-and-neck with the Conservatives. It would show that Labour could attract thousands of people to a rally and generate a sense that Labour was on the move. In the event the purpose was not fulfilled because that day the polls reported a freakishly large Labour lead, and the politicians, notably Roy Hattersley, appeared over-confident.

Opinions differ about the health broadcast. Conservatives and some Labour officials considered that it was a great mistake and that Labour was never able to highlight health again. On the other hand Labour's campaign team point out that the party's large opinion poll leads came out four to five days after the furore faded. In many parts of the country health and waiting lists dominated local television news and local newspaper stories. The salience of health as an issue increased and appeared to stop the

Tory tax campaign gaining momentum. The people closely concerned with promoting it made no apologies. Indeed, one wrote at length on the matter:

> If Labour's campaign can be criticised it was because it was too smooth, too positive and not attacking or negative enough (partly because of an absence of Labour grenades and partly because of the highly interpretive media coverage). The health broadcast broke through the protective media cocoon, and burnt the issue into the electorate's consciousness. This was the only time Labour did this, and it was something that the Conservative campaign (rather than the tabloids) never achieved.

His one regret about the episode was that Labour had not carried on attacking the Conservatives' handling of the issue. The Labour campaign team retreated when accused of 'negative' campaigning, whereas the Conservatives carried on with their tax attack.

Some Labour strategists reflected that with another leader and different economic policies they could have won. This probably takes the 'if only' game too far. A different leader might not have managed to detach Labour from so many of the electorally damaging policies it had in 1983 and 1987, and to marginalise the left-wing. Perhaps only Kinnock could have made Labour electable but perhaps also he was the ultimate barrier to electoral victory. And the option of abandoning the commitments to increase pensions and child benefit – and thus avoid the higher tax rates for the well-off – would have divided the party. After the election, many Labour front-benchers and the strategists argued that the Labour lead in the polls had all along been false, that the change from Thatcher to Major provided an enormous boost for the Conservatives and that the tax and leadership problems were always going to make the party unelectable. 'We were misled for months by the polls into thinking that we had climbed the electoral mountain', said David Hill. If this assessment has any merit, then explanations for Labour's defeat have little to do with the conduct of the campaign.

The Liberal Democrat campaign played to an appreciative audience and, in contrast to the tensions of the dual leadership in 1983 and 1987, it was a happy one. As usual the party gained more coverage than in a non-election period and also profited from the perceived slanging of the two major parties. The Liberal Democrat campaign travelled light, with decisions essentially being made by Des Wilson, who was in charge of the campaign in Cowley Street, working closely with Paddy Ashdown. The party was single-minded in its concentration on the leader, on electoral reform and on education; it demonstrated the strength, as well as the weakness, of fighting a campaign on a limited front. It also showed what a third party could achieve in a leader-dominated campaign.

In the final days, as the debate moved onto electoral reform, hung parliaments and coalitions – largely through the initiative of the two major parties – so Liberal Democrats appeared to get squeezed. Opinion polls reported a growing disapproval of the idea of hung parliaments, and Liberal Democrat supporters anyway were fairly evenly divided between favouring a Lib-Lab coalition, a Lib-Con coalition, or an early election in the event of an indecisive outcome. Labour's expression of interest in PR clearly aligned it with the Liberal Democrats, and increased Ashdown's problem in appearing even-handed between the two major parties. John Major skilfully played on voters' fears of constitutional uncertainty and political instability and drove some 'soft' Liberals into the Conservative camp. In the words of Lord Holme:

> 'On polling day fear of Labour was much stronger than fear of the Tories. John Major was not a frightener.'

The Conservative campaign did not get a good press and there was an elegaic note among many of the end-of-campaign reports from journalists accompanying Mr Major. Consider these judgements made by shrewd observers before the result was known:

> It [the electorate] looks like decreeing that now is the time for a change.
>
> (Hugo Young, *Guardian*, April 9)

> Whatever the vote the Tory campaign will be remembered as a dismal one – confused in its message, ill-led and reactive.
>
> ('Bagehot', *Economist*, April 4)

Even from press sympathisers, doubts were expressed. At the end of the first week Lord Wyatt, in the *News of the World*, called for Chris Patten to be dismissed; Philip Stephens, in the *Financial Times*, stated, 'There comes a moment when one side begins to recognise that it is facing defeat. The Conservatives are perilously close to that point' (March 28); *The Times* complained of Mr Major's 'wooden phraseology' and flat campaign. Brendan Bruce on April 1 was asked on BBC television if the Conservatives had already lost, and replied, 'Probably'. He was one of a number of observers close to Mrs Thatcher who frequently criticised the way the party was handling affairs. Editors and commentators of Conservative supporting newspapers regularly complained to Mr Wakeham and to aides of the Prime Minister about the content and management of the campaign. The general refrain was 'The message is not getting through', or 'We are not getting a clear or consistent line from Central Office'. Five days before the vote the *Sunday Times* MORI panel found that Labour had dominated the agenda and had gained ground on the two expected Tory strengths of leadership and the economy. At the outset of the campaign Mr Major led Mr Kinnock by 26 points when voters were asked to express their satisfaction with how the leaders were performing; by the final weekend the leaders were equal. The Conservative campaign had also failed to persuade people that a Tory government would offer a higher standard of living.

The final reports of the NOP panel in the *Independent on Sunday*, and of the MORI panel in the *Sunday Times*, contained more gloomy reading. Under the headline VICTORY IS SLIPPING FROM THE GRASP OF THE TORIES, Peter Kellner, on the basis of the NOP data, wrote that Tory support was soft, that the party would do well to hold on to 38 percent of the vote, that any late swing was more likely to benefit the Liberal Democrats, that tax had failed as an issue, and that the Conservatives 'would have to overcome the lessons of history and the weight of evidence from our panel if they are to retain power with an overall majority'. The verdict of the polls and of their interpreters was clear (see Chapter 7).

After the election, Chris Patten and his team were scathing about the media coverage and unrepentant about the party's strategy. Conservative campaign managers were contemptuous of claims that Labour had 'won' the campaign. In what other market, they asked, do you win by finishing second? Chris Patten claimed that the party won because it tenaciously stuck to its three chosen issues:

- The leadership of John Major who the public were willing to trust – 'They will always give him the benefit of the doubt'.
- The economic fear of Labour; for all the resentment at the Conservative mis-management of the economy, a large number of voters were convinced that things would be even worse under Labour.
- Taxes, taxes, taxes.

Mr Patten also took some pride that the Conservatives had won an election on only one half of the expenditure incurred in 1987.

It is hard to compare campaign expenditures at the national level. The date at which the election is deemed to have started may not be the same and the parties differ in their categorisation of what should be included of capital, staff and other costs. The following are the parties' own estimates of what was spent during the actual campaign.

|  | 1987 | 1992 |
|---|---|---|
| Conservative | £9.0m | £10.1m |
| Labour | £4.2m | £ 7.1m |
| Alliance/Liberal Democrat | £1.9m | £ 2.1m |

The Liberal Democrats claimed to have raised almost as much money during the campaign as they spent. Larry Whitty reported that Labour had attracted £2m in contributions during the campaign, mostly in small amounts. The Conservatives certainly attracted some large contributions; their final burst of press advertising was reportedly fully met by last-minute contributions, but they ended the election further in the red.

For much of the campaign Mr Major seemed to be ill at ease with the routine of soundbites and photo-opportunities and complained that these media requirements were preventing the Conservative message from getting through. He sometimes asked: 'What do I have to do this for?' and his style and personality did not project themselves strongly on television. His 'Meet John Major' sessions were dismissed as tame by the journalists and they did not make good viewing. It took him time to find a style that suited him. But in the final week he managed to do so and the party's campaign was eventually what he wanted it to be. The soap box and the glad-handing with voters was his idea, as was the extra rally at Wembley. So, too, was his spirited defence of the constitutional status quo – which his office insisted on despite some Central Office reservations. Reports of rows and tensions between Downing Street and Central Office were much exaggerated. But some key people close to John Major had their doubts about Central Office as a campaigning body and were impressed by the volume of criticism in the first week. Personal relations between Patten and Major were good, and all concerned were determined to avoid another 'Wobbly Thursday'. The United Kingdom was something that he cared passionately about; he spoke eloquently on the subject at the press conferences on the final Saturday and Monday. Journalists (and some Conservatives) were amazed that he appeared to be wasting his time on Scotland when he should be fighting on bread and butter issues. Hugo Young in the *Guardian* on 7 April described it as an 'historic blunder' and 'an extraordinary way to end an election campaign'. After the election, Paddy Ashdown and senior Labour figures concluded that it had been a master stroke by John Major.

The political agenda, as reported in the opinion polls, was not good ground for the Conservatives. On the social issues, notably health and education, which appeared to be most salient to voters, Labour enjoyed a commanding lead (see Table 12.1). The issues on which the Conservatives were favoured – unions, Europe, and defence – were not ranked highly by voters and, according to the polls, the favoured Tory themes of tax and leadership never took off.

Central Office was unapologetic about accusations of negativism, although some hard-hitting messages, including a pamphlet on the far-left links of Labour candidates, were dropped. Mr Patten's aim was to exploit the voters' fear of a Labour government, sounding positive wherever possible, but getting across the negative arguments effectively and frequently. 'The vision thing can come after we have frightened the voters', said one of John Major's speechwriters. Originally, it had been planned that at each morning press conference senior Cabinet ministers would mount an attack on Labour, leaving John Major above the party battle, free to strike a positive stance. There would be a balance of positive and negative, of 'Mr Nasty' and 'Mr Nice'. But, because of the perceived weakness of Norman Lamont in carrying the economic message in the first week, this division of campaign roles failed to work successfully and Mr Major himself had to play Mr Nasty. The Conservative strategists were more reactive than Labour's, switching the themes of more than half of their press conferences at a day's notice. Chris Patten compared life at the centre to being 'on a roller coaster', and in 10 Downing Street another key figure recalled:

'It's like a battle. You live day by day, improvising all the time. I think that is healthy.'

More plaintively, however, some Conservatives asked what else a government with a record of thirteen years could do. The record was there and could be judged but since 1987 there was not a lot to show for it. On the other hand all that Labour could offer was promises. The government therefore had to try to debunk these by reminding voters of the performance of the last Labour government, exploiting the distrust of Labour, and emphasising the differences between Labour and Conservative. Ministers pointed enviously to the easy hand dealt to Labour: 'Elections are easy to fight in Opposition. You've nothing else to do.' Saatchi's strategists felt that the most effective refutation of the 'Time for Change' theme was the warning that Labour could not be trusted, that it would make things worse: 'We had to do our greatest demolition job.' The campaign was designed to be negative, built around the strategy of not trusting Labour, particularly not on taxation. Labour's manifesto was greeted by a poster stating 'Oh no, it's a tax demand'. The theme of 'Labour's Double Whammy' (more tax and higher prices) and 'Five Years Hard Labour' (more tax, higher prices and higher mortgages) appeared in broadcasts, posters and speeches. The penultimate election broadcast was a personal attack on the Labour leader, pointing out that he had changed his mind too often, that he lacked principles and that he could not be trusted.

Criticisms of the Conservative campaign tactics took insufficient account of the recession and, given the outcome, the alleged shortcomings of the campaign paled into insignificance. Maurice Saatchi, who had been closely involved in planning the three previous successful election campaigns, reflected on how the recession made this one the most difficult: 'We did not have the mechanism – economic success – which worked for us before.' Since 1959 a recurring theme of Conservative government campaigns has been 'Life's Better with the Conservatives. Don't Let Labour Ruin it'. In 1992 it had to be 'Don't Let Labour Make it Worse'. In the first week of the campaign the gloomy economic statistics about unemployment, business failures and reports from major companies formed a dismal launching pad for the Conservatives. They reminded voters of the recession, of how bad things were. A Conservative press conference on education was swamped by BBC and ITN presentations of figures showing a fall in factory output. Hugo Young, in the *Guardian* on April 2, found the Conservative campaign wanting but did not consider that this explained why they looked like losing the election: 'I think the moral of this election may be different; that 13 years in office make a winning campaign impossible to fight.'

Yet it cannot be denied that mistakes proliferated on the Conservative side. The party was slow to react to the John Smith budget and even more to cost Labour's manifesto. Indeed it was left to a newspaper, the *Sunday Times* (April 5), to demonstrate that most taxpayers would actually lose out in the first year of a John Smith budget. (Lamont's claim to this effect on March 17 was hardly reported.) Mr Waldegrave's press conference on the Jennifer Bennett affair, which suggested that Central Office had been involved in exploiting the issue, frustrated the tactic of leaving Labour dangling on a hook of their own making. Stories emanated from Central Office about poor morale and imminent resignations. The absence of Chris Patten in Bath for all but three afternoons in the campaign seemed to leave a vacuum in decision-making. Mr Wakeham, according to many, was unwilling to take decisions in Patten's absence or play a public role and he was unavailable to chair the Waldegrave press conference. In the war of Jennifer's ear the party chairman was not made aware that a fax from Jennifer's grandfather had been passed to Central Office ten days earlier. Nor was he informed about the telephone call in which a junior member of the press department put the Jennifer's consultant in touch with the *Daily Express*. The rumours of bad morale at headquarters contributed to the impression of a campaign that lacked direction and momentum. But the effects of these errors must not be exaggerated; the election outcome suggests that, however much they interested the journalists, they passed over the heads of most voters.

Indeed, many pre-campaign events were more important. Conservatives could feel that their assessment of the mood of voters and the impact of the tax and leadership issues were vindicated. Chris Patten and other Conservatives also pointed to the importance of their near term campaign, particularly the 'tax bombshell' effort in January. This enabled them, they claimed, to establish the campaign battleground. Some Labour strategists were inclined to agree, after the event, with the Conservative claim that important themes had to be planted well in advance. Several, when they looked back, claimed that the leadership had probably exhausted itself in removing negatives; it did not spend enough time setting out Labour's positive agenda. The distrust of Labour was there to be seen in the party's survey research, but some did not take it on board. David Hill's line was that voters were 'either ashamed, undecided, or unwilling to come clean about their concern over tax'. Indeed, chastened by the incorrect forecasts of the opinion polls, they concluded that they had probably been behind throughout the campaign and indeed from the beginning of January. They also complained that the recession was a doubled-edged weapon. For a significant number of voters fear of the recession merged with lingering distrust of Labour and worry over tax; the worse things were, the more they feared that Labour might make them still worse. The tabloids and Tory attacks were able to play on that longstanding fear of Labour. Chris Powell, in retrospect, wondered whether election campaigns really mattered, and asked, 'Were we doing a disservice to Labour? A good campaign may only take their minds off more fundamental problems and the need for radical changes'. Many of those most closely associated with the campaign felt that they never managed to overcome the popular distrust of the party which had been built up in the early 1980s.

Philip Gould reflected in May 1992 on what he had said soon after the 1987 election defeat: 'You can't win campaigns in four weeks, but only in four years.' He now added: 'After four years continual campaigning that excuse is no longer available.' Labour's campaign team were forced to look beyond the three weeks of the election campaign or even the five years of the parliament. Labour faced more fundamental and long-standing problems. The surveys, and particularly the qualitative research among wavering Conservative voters, showed that, however critical people were of the Conservatives, there was no enthusiasm for voting Labour. As one observer said:

'I always came away from the group discussions, even when we were ten points in the lead, feeling depressed. However anti-Conservative they might be, they were never going to vote Labour.'

Immediately after the election the Shadow Communications Agency commissioned an ambitious qualitative research programme. What came up was a combination of many factors – fear of change and of union power, mistrust of Labour and of Kinnock, and worries about taxation as well as aspirations and self-interest which could not be advanced through Labour. One analyst of the material observed that the problem was so widespread that: 'We were never going to win. The British public is aspirational, they want middle-class things. The Labour Party seems to have left the workers and the workers have left Labour.' Inevitably, debate about the point where Labour lost the fourth election merged into broader questions about changing demography, changing values, the role of any centre-left party in a late industrial, affluent society and the changing determinants of voting behaviour. These factors were all bound to shape the debate about the future of the Labour Party in the 1990s.

It is likely that commentators will have to re-think their criteria of good campaigning. In 1992 the key strategists in both the main parties agreed that the election commentators did not understand negative campaigning. Conservative ministers were regularly criticised at their press conferences for 'going on about taxation again' and spending more time attacking Labour proposals than presenting their own. Much qualitative research, both public and private, showed how unpopular Conservative election broadcasts were when they warned of the dangers of a Labour government, and how popular the positive messages of other parties were. It is doubtful, however, if these immediate readings of public reactions are useful guides to electoral behaviour. People do not like to appear supportive of appeals to fear. The real test of election communications is whether they influence voting behaviour. On this test Conservative campaigning in 1992 worked and Labour's 'positive' methods failed. According to the Labour General Secretary's post-election report to the party's National Executive

Committee in June fears of high taxation and 'the general unease about our economic competence or general distrust of the party and its leadership all took their toll'. This is surely testimony to the effectiveness of the Conservative campaign.

Complaints that there is too much election coverage on television or that there are too many opinion polls have become standard criticisms of modern British elections. But the 1992 election was peculiarly introverted. Perhaps because of the broad agreement between the parties on Britain's membership of the European Community and the removal of the military threat from the USSR, the outside world was hardly referred to. There was little discussion of Europe (although Britain was to assume the EC Presidency three months after the election), Britain's international role, the environment and the long-term health of the planet, or of the Third World. Joe Rogaly, in the *Financial Times*, complained that there had been no discussion of the 10–20 year demographic projections and the consequences for public expenditure. On April 4 the *Economist* lamented, 'Although this election ought to be a great moment, the politicians have not risen to the occasion'. Ironically, some of these complaining commentators were those most critical of John Major for raising in the last week the weighty issues of the United Kingdom and hung parliaments.

These criticisms are valid, although it is foolish to imagine that in the past there was some golden age of electioneering. One has only to think back to the scares in 1906 (Chinese slavery), 1924 (the Zinoviev letter), 1931 (the bankers' ramp), 1945 (Churchill's Gestapo speech) and 1951 (Labour's warmongering charge). But the media may share some blame for the way the 1992 campaign was fought. Was television too compliant in reporting the stage-managed unveiling of posters and the contrived photo-opportunities? Did journalists spend too much time talking to one another on radio and television to the exclusion of the politicians? In a 19-minute item on John Smith's 'shadow' budget on BBC, only 77 seconds were allowed to John Smith; the rest was given over to analysis and comment. Politicians might fairly complain that broadcasters' liking for animated pictures and for soundbites that last a mere 25 seconds do not conduce to the serious discussion of major issues. John Major had a step-by-step style of presenting his case and Mr Kinnock was fond of long sentences. In the *Independent* on March 24 Peter Jenkins complained that television, far from extending the democratic process, 'today stands in danger of subverting it'. Party leaders did not meet ordinary voters on their visits to shopping centres but were surrounded by a mob of 100 or so reporters and cameramen participating in a photo-opportunity. An article in the *Guardian* (March 25), mourned the death of the open public meeting with questions allowed from the floor and the way in which voters were relegated to walk-on extras who, 'may not inconveniently question. Their role is to be passive receivers, no longer active participants in a dialogue nobody controls. These are the politics of permanent condescension'. Did John Major sense this when he mounted his soapbox?

The journalists were at their most excited during the row over Labour's NHS broadcast. The health promises of the rival parties and their records on managing the NHS were lost in the dispute over the broadcast's truthfulness, over the behaviour of Jennifer's family and her consultant and over the source of the leak. The immense attention paid to national opinion polls was open to question. Indeed the effectiveness of the parties' campaigns was largely if not exclusively assessed through the ratings of the polls. On April 1, the day when three opinion polls showed substantial Labour leads and much of the media was writing about an imminent Tory collapse, John Wakeham remarked, 'We thought we were having a good campaign until 5.30 yesterday'. Conservatives had eagerly anticipated headline press coverage of their press conference on defence and they were mortified to see that story was overtaken by news of the opinion polls. The media's interest in the Scottish campaign was overwhelmingly concentrated on devolution and separatism, although these issues were well down the list of important concerns of Scottish voters.

According to the Loughborough University study of the media,[1] television coverage was dominated by discussion of poll findings and of campaign tactics and strategy. Topics such as Kinnock's leadership, the rise of the Liberal Democrats, the dissatisfaction with the Tory campaign, and the prospects of a hung parliament seemed to be raised in large part on the basis of survey evidence. Issues receiving less than one percent of mentions included Europe, foreign policy, the environment and social security. Subjects such as the polls, Scottish independence and 'the war of Jennifer's ear' were of interest to the London media much more than to the ordinary voters. John Major took a clear position in defiance of the opinion polls. He repudiated their voting predictions with his 'stone-cold' certainty of a clear victory. When confronted with survey evidence of the low importance attached to tax, the strong Scottish support for self-determination, and the popularity of PR, his reaction was to campaign even more strongly for his minority position. Candidates' responses to our questionnaires also reflect considerable resentment at how the media covered the national campaign. In a post-election discussion Chris Patten argued that the main culprits had been not so much the opinion polls, 'but the journalists who seemed unaware of anything else but the polls'.

Was the campaign decisive, or was the election won before it started? Most of those closely involved with the Labour effort came to feel that they had lost it all along. 'We had our problem with leadership and taxation at least a year ago, and they made us unelectable', said one. Another concluded, 'We were fighting the tide of history', and 'We were going up a down escalator'. Some Conservatives also said that they had been ahead throughout. The opinion polls were wrong: the country did not want Labour; constituency feedback made plain that the Tory vote was always solid. But others, particularly the non-politicians, argued that the Tory campaign was decisive. Of course, the Conservative overall majority was so narrow that Conservative campaign pluses and Labour minuses could have made the difference between an outright Conservative victory or being the largest party in a hung parliament. From Autumn 1991 until the last opinion polls, Labour's share of the vote had varied between 38 percent and 42 percent. To secure just over 35 percent on April 9 was an unexpected blow.

It is always tempting to concentrate on the three or four weeks of the election campaign. Yet the opinions and voting intentions of the great majority of electors have been shaped over the long term. It was apparent that many voters were torn between resentment at the government's record (especially the mishandling of the economy and the imposition of the poll-tax) and distrust of Labour. By polling day Conservatives were more successful in re-awakening and playing upon doubts about the Labour Party, particularly its economic competence. Key figures in the Labour and Conservative campaigns agreed that there was a disequilibrium of fear; in the end more voters proved fearful of Labour than of the government. There appears to have been something of a late swing – though how large it was seems arguable.

But what caused whatever late swing there was? Politicians and pollsters disagree on the issues that moved the voters. Labour and Conservatives reported that the major concerns at the end seem to have been the economy and taxation (the latter whipped up, complain Labour leaders, by the tabloids). According to the Harris exit poll, and the post-election surveys by MORI and by Gallup, Conservatives improved their position on economic management and taxation in the last few days. On the other hand, the post-election polls also show that it was the social issues, particularly health, unemployment and education, which voters claimed influenced them, and Labour still had clear leads on these.

A simple head-count of issues, therefore, does not deliver an answer to why the Conservatives won. Either the questions were not tapping the fundamental concerns of voters, or a significant number were not telling

*Table 12.1    The key issues*

|  | % |
|---|---|
| Health | 41 |
| Unemployment | 36 |
| Education | 23 |
| Prices | 11 |
| Tax | 10 |

(Q.   'Of all the urgent problems facing the country at the present time, when you decided which way to vote, which two issues did you personally consider most important?') *Source*: Gallup; survey conducted 10, 11 April 1992.

the whole truth. It is worth emphasising that *no* public survey, on the eve of election, had picked up a shift in the issues which could explain the imminent large-scale movement of voters to the Conservatives. In February 1974, by contrast, the polls did record a shift in the agenda which presaged a weakening of the Conservative vote (see Chapter 7).

By huge majorities voters told opinion pollsters that they preferred increased public spending on services to tax cuts and expressed readiness to accept more taxes to pay for the services. Did they mean it? Or did many take the view that favouring spending was the fashionable response? More telling, perhaps, were the voters' responses to the Gallup post-election survey, question: 'Would you be better off or worse off under Labour's tax and budget proposals?' 30 percent said they would be better off, 49 percent worse off, including 48 percent of C2 voters. By the end of the campaign Conservatives were effectively making the point that extra taxes on the higher paid would not help to get Britain out of recession. Labour's private polls reported before and during the election that around 70 percent of voters expected to pay more taxes under a Labour government. In spite of what the public polls were saying until election day, the 1992 election seems to reflect – however furtively and reluctantly – a classic pocket-book outcome in the classic mould. As Ben Chifley, the Australian Prime Minister, said in 1949, 'Voters are moved by the hip pocket nerve'.

NOTE

1.   See M. Billig *et al.*, 'The Election Campaign: Two Shows for the Price of One', *British Journalism Review*, 3:2 Summer 1992.

# 13   A Critical Election?

The 1992 election provided a remarkable victory for the Conservatives. To win by such a margin of votes over Labour (7.6 percent) if not of seats (21 overall and 64 over Labour) was totally unexpected. It was achieved in the trough of the longest depression since the 1930s and at the end of a campaign that had been much derided. It went against the trend elsewhere in Europe, where established government parties were meeting electoral rebuffs. The fourth successive election victory meant that by the end of the new parliament the Conservatives would have been in office continuously for 18 years – the longest period of one party rule since the Great Reform Act of 1832. One political commentator wrote, 'A four-term government is an affront against the two-party system'. At the next general election, nobody under the age of 40 would have voted in a general election that was not won by the Conservatives.

Newspaper reactions were predictable. The *Sun* proclaimed:

*Take a bow this morning, Sun readers.* It was you who decided the fate of Britain in the General Election. And in our view, decided wisely.

The *Daily Mirror* was more grudging:

It would be wrong to deny John Major the credit for this triumph. He based his appeal on the selfishness of the electorate and won enough of their votes to get back into Downing Street. We had hoped for something better . . . The voters may have proclaimed their idealism to the pollsters but they voted with their pockets inside the polling booth.

*Today* complained about the lack of an alternative to the Tories and blamed Mr Kinnock:

One man and one man alone is responsible for the result of the General Election. No, it is not John Major, it is Neil Kinnock. Mr Major did not win the election. Mr Kinnock lost it.

The *Independent* acknowledged the problem with the Labour leader but provided consolation:

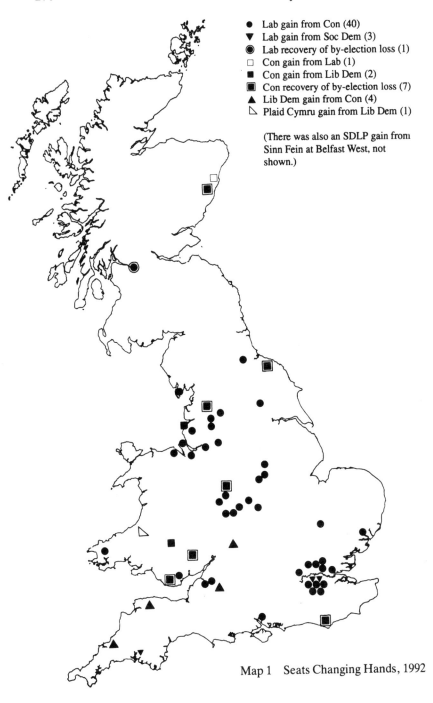

Map 1    Seats Changing Hands, 1992

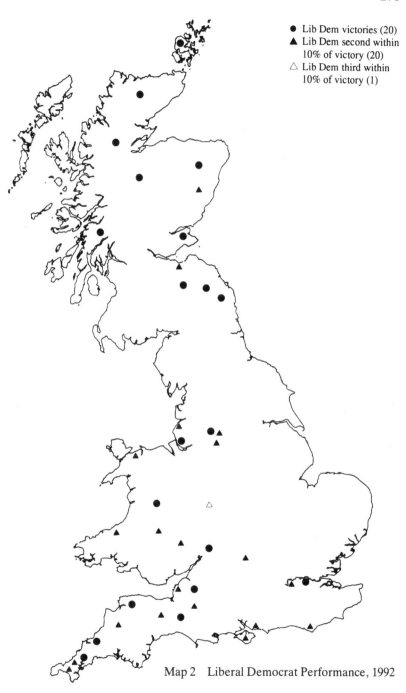

- ● Lib Dem victories (20)
- ▲ Lib Dem second within 10% of victory (20)
- △ Lib Dem third within 10% of victory (1)

Map 2   Liberal Democrat Performance, 1992

Swing

| | over − 3.6 |
| | − 2.8 to − 3.6 |
| | − 2.0 to − 2.8 |
| | − 1.2 to − 2.0 |
| | under − 1.2 |

Map 3    Regional Swing

Share of vote

0 – 19.9%
20 – 29.9%
30 – 39.9%
40 – 49.9%
over 50%

Map 4    Regional Conservative Strength

Mr Kinnock tried to do what every friendly critic outside his party told him needed to be done to make Labour electable. He gave old policies the boot, ruptured old alliances, brought in the image-makers, largely conceded the utility of the free market and (some would say) denied his party's socialist history and inspiration. His campaign made few mistakes.

The 1992 election was inevitably regarded as a personal success for John Major. In an extempore statement he said:

'I'm delighted I can now accept that the country has elected me in my own right to be Prime Minister.'

The result enabled him to separate himself more clearly from Margaret Thatcher and he achieved his natural ambition of winning his own mandate. However, it was not entirely obvious in what that mandate consisted. What, if anything, was Majorism? Mrs Thatcher claimed that the result was an endorsement of her record; having dismantled the poll-tax there were no other policies that John Major proposed to abandon. Others suggested that the election was an endorsement for post-Thatcherism.

On Friday April 10, the economic markets made clear their approval of the electorate's verdict, as the FTSE achieved its second-highest one-day rise and £30 billion was added to share values.

The earlier Conservative victories under Mrs Thatcher could be readily explained: 1979 followed the Winter of Discontent; 1983 followed the successful Falklands campaign and a divided Labour opposition; 1987 followed four years of steady economic growth and prosperity. The 1992 election, however, was won against the background of a disastrous recession and against a revived and seemingly electable Labour Party.

The outcome confirmed the asymmetric pattern of party fortunes in the twentieth century – lengthy spells of Conservative rule interrupted by brief spells of centre-left government. The pendulum between the right and the left in Britain has swung unevenly. In ninety years Labour has only twice enjoyed comfortable parliamentary majorities – from 1945 to 1950 and from 1966 to 1970. By the time of a mid-1990s election the Conservatives will have been in office for sixty-six years of the years since 1900. This lopsided party system resembles that which has prevailed for most of the post-war period in Sweden and in Japan, with rule by a dominant party, a 'natural' party of government.

Interpretations of the outcome fastened as much on the future of Labour as on the future of the government. If the electorate was torn between its reluctance to trust Labour and its unhappiness with the Conservative record, then the former seemed to be stronger. The result was more a rejection of Labour than a vote for the Conservatives; Mr Kinnock complained that it was the triumph of fear over hope. Some Labour optimists pointed to the scale of recovery – a gain of 3.6 percent of the votes, following a 3.2 percent advance in 1987; with an extra one percent swing nationally the party could have denied the Conservatives victory; only 33 more seats were needed for it to become the largest party. Some, however, argued that the recession had actually hurt Labour, reinforcing the voters' widespread worries about change. Economic adversity does not always operate to the advantage of the opposition or of the parties of the left. On the basis of surveys in the 1970s James Alt, in *The Politics of Economic Decline*, argued that affluence was necessary for voters to feel economically secure enough to support leftist policies of social reform and higher social spending. That hardly seems to have applied in 1987 or in the relatively prosperous 1950s when the voters rejected Labour. In the aftermath of 1992 there were Labour supporters who attacked the gullibility and selfishness of the still-affluent electorate.

It is necessary, however, to look beyond the entrails of the 1992 election. Labour was left with the continued challenge of recovering the 43 percent share of the vote it gained in 1970, a year when it lost; the party has never reached 40 percent of the vote in the six general elections since that time. Commentators were quick to argue that if Labour could not win in 1992, it was hard, given the present electoral system and the Conservative base in a seemingly solid 42 percent of the vote, to envisage it ever winning again. Labour's fourth successive defeat plunged the party into despair and left it poised to undergo yet another 'fundamental rethink' of party strategy and leadership.

As in 1987 Labour gained good marks for its campaign. Since 1987 it had dropped virtually all left-wing policies and embraced modern campaigning methods even more fully. With the exception of its promise of higher rates of taxation for the better-off, it had accepted most of Mrs Thatcher's achievements in the 1980s. Yet the election still appeared to have turned on fear of Labour and distrust of Mr Kinnock. If the party was now to renege on its commitment to redistribution then what would be distinctive about it? And looking abroad, it was difficult to point to any country where the centre-left had a distinctive message and was in the electoral ascendancy.

The party's deputy leader, Roy Hattersley, argued that the party should not compromise further but should campaign more vigorously for its policies emphasising the ground on which it differed from the Conservatives.

For the left Tony Benn insisted that the Kinnock project had failed and that a potential majority of voters for Socialism existed, if only Labour would campaign for it. There is nothing new in Labour speaking for the casualties of social and economic change rather than for its architects. What is new is that the 'haves' so greatly outnumber the 'have-nots', Labour's core constituency. In the nineteenth century, as the franchise was extended, the spectre of the 'tyranny of the majority' terrified the middle and upper classes. Today the majority is different and progressives wondered if 'the contented majority' is any longer prepared to support redistribution in favour of the less well-off.

The problems posed for parties of the centre-left by social and economic change are well-known. But Labour still failed to capture even half of the working-class vote. Much of the party's research after the election suggested that it was still out of touch with the ordinary voters' desires for greater opportunity and ownership, that it was seen as outdated, not forward-looking, a barrier to the aspirations of ordinary people. Tony Crosland, the spokesman for revisionism, had always claimed that Labour should promote equality *and* high living standards. He feared that although many voters approved of Labour's promotion of 'fair shares' the image of the party was still associated with the austerity of 1945 from which voters wished to escape. In 1964 Labour had been presented as the forward-looking party in contrast to the obsolete old-fashioned Tories. In 1992 the situation was reversed: Labour was regarded as backward-looking and the Conservatives represented opportunity. Now the surveys suggested that Labour was associated with 'holding back' and 'dragging down'. The party image was shaped by Labour's record in the 1970s and 1980s and – contrary to the findings of most opinion polls – the success of Mrs Thatcher in changing popular values may have contributed. Such considerations were more significant for the party's future than the attempts of some politicians and officials to blame the management of the campaign. 'We have to change even more or we will lose even worse next time', said one member of the Shadow Communications Agency. In *The Times* (18 June 1992) Jack Cunningham, Labour's campaign co-ordinator, concluded:

> Labour will have to make the economic, sociological – indeed cultural – changes necessary to regain contact with and the trust of many more voters. At every level of the party, reform is essential.

Having led Labour to two successive general election defeats, Neil Kinnock needed no persuasion to resign as leader. No other leader of a

Table 13.1 How Britain voted in 1992

| | AB | C1 | C2 | DE | Union Member | Council Tenant | Men | Women | 18–24 | 25–34 | 35–54 | 55+ | Total |
|---|---|---|---|---|---|---|---|---|---|---|---|---|---|
| All | 19 | 24 | 27 | 30 | 23 | 23 | 49 | 51 | 14 | 19 | 13 | 34 | 100 |
| | | | | | | | | | | | | | |
| Con | 56 | 52 | 39 | 31 | 31 | 24 | 41 | 44 | 35 | 40 | 43 | 46 | 43 |
| Lab | 19 | 25 | 40 | 49 | 46 | 55 | 37 | 34 | 39 | 38 | 34 | 34 | 35 |
| Lib Dem | 22 | 19 | 17 | 16 | 19 | 15 | 18 | 18 | 19 | 18 | 19 | 17 | 18 |
| | | | | | | | | | | | | | |
| Con–Lab Swing 1987–92 | 3 | 1 ½ | 2 ½ | 0 | 2 | 1 ½ | 3 ½ | ½ | ½ | 1 ½ | 3 ½ | 1 ½ | 1 ½ |

*Source:* MORI

party in Britain in the past 70 years has survived two such successive electoral rebuffs. There was widespread acknowledgement of Mr Kinnock's achievements in reforming the party but also a sense that he had done as much as he could. His achievements had been largely internal – reforming the Labour Party – and he never persuaded the wider electorate. Perhaps only a leader with his left-wing past could have so changed the party in the 1980s. The electorate, however, clearly had difficulty in envisaging him as suitable to be Prime Minister. But the party's problems went beyond Mr Kinnock. As Peter Jenkins wrote: 'Blaming Kinnock will not do. Labour lost because it was Labour' (*Independent*, 11 April 1992).

The challenge facing Labour after 1992 was not as steep as it was after 1987, but it was still formidable. By 1995 the work of the Boundary Commission will have taken account of the increase in the electorates in the counties and suburbs and their decline in the inner cities. Unless the recommendations of the Commission, due by 1994, are delayed by vexatious litigation, they are likely to be worth some 15 extra seats to the Conservatives. Labour will therefore still require a 5 percent swing to win an outright majority, more than it achieved in 1992, during a recession, and more than any party has achieved since 1945.

The election result was a disappointment to the Liberal Democrats. Some found encouragement in the sharp improvement to 18 percent of the vote from the 6 percent poll rating when Paddy Ashdown became leader, and from the 15 percent level with which it started the election. But this was still a marked reduction from the 22 percent in 1987 or the 26 percent of 1983, and was a letdown compared with the expectations which had grown during the campaign. Hopes for tactical voting and a better return in seats were not fulfilled. The 18 percent share of vote and the twenty seats were not very different from the level that the Liberal Party achieved in October 1974 (19 percent and 14 seats). The party continued to do well in the south-west, gaining over a third of the votes and it remained the main challenger to the Conservatives in many southern seats. But it made little progress elsewhere and significant support is now confined to a narrow regional base of Scotland and the West Country. Despite its long-awaited gains in Bath and Cheltenham, other expected victories in seats like Portsmouth South and Edinburgh West did not materialise. In a number of hopeful seats the recovery in the Labour vote stifled the Liberal Democratic advance.

Looking back on the 1992 campaign some Liberal Democrats felt that it was the prospect of a hung parliament or the possibility that Liberals might pave the way for a Labour government, the 'Trojan Horse' argument, that had stiffened Conservative support. If so, this reflected a 'no-win' situation. In 1983 'soft' Liberals had defected to the Conservatives because of fear of

Labour, in 1987 they had defected to Labour when a Conservative victory was assured, and in 1992 they defected to the Conservatives because of fear of Labour.

Mr Ashdown, however, could point to one undoubted achievement. In the 1980s there had clearly existed a substantial centre vote but no single centre party. Following the break-up of the Social Democrats and the transformation of the Liberal party, he had managed to retain a significant centre party vote for his new Liberal Democrats. They were assured of being a significant element in any regrouping of anti-Conservative forces.

The result was only a qualified endorsement of two-party politics. In elections between 1945 and 1970 the big parties shared 87 percent of all votes cast (Con 43 percent, Lab 44 percent). From 1970 to 1987 their share came to only 75 percent (Con 43 percent, Lab 32 percent). In 1992 the two party aggregate recovered slightly, to 78 percent, the largest figure since 1979. But it is significant that since 1970 neither Conservative nor Labour parties have managed to win office with more than 43 percent of the total vote. With the Liberals gaining between 18 and 25 percent of the vote, in five of the last six elections, hung parliaments still remained on the cards.

There were some interesting changes in the social bases of voting behaviour (as Table 13.1 shows). According to the NOP/ITN exit poll the only groups among which Labour enjoyed clear leads over the Conservatives were council tenants, the unskilled working class (DE) and Scots and northerners. The party sharply improved its vote share among the professional and managerial (AB) classes (up 9 percent) and among home-owners, largely at the cost of the Liberals. It also managed to increase its support among the skilled manuals (C2), with a gain of 4 percent from 1987. But in this key group it still trailed the Conservatives 39 to 40 percent. And the party suffered from the gender gap being its widest for any of the four elections since 1979. The Conservative lead over Labour among women was 8 percent higher than among men. In 1987 the comparable figure was only 4 percent.

The results are analysed in greater detail in the statistical appendix by John Curtice and Michael Steed. But a number of salient points do emerge.

1.     The country-wide variation in swing was a modest reversal of the long-term pattern that dates back to 1959 and which had been particularly marked in 1983 and 1987. This time the swing to Labour was higher in the southern half of Britain and was strongest in London and much of the Midlands. In contrast Scotland saw a swing to the Conservatives.

2.   This reversal of the long-term pattern clearly reflects the impact of the recent economic recession, which hit the southern half of the country more than the northern and western areas which had suffered worse in previous recessions. But the geography of party performance offered no apparent support for theories that Labour suffered for its tax proposals in areas of higher income or was hit specifically in 1992 by the Tory tabloid press.

3.   It is possible to discern, and map, a psephological version of 'Essex man and woman'. In contrast to the nationwide pattern, the variation within southern England outside London broadly repeated the geography of swing in recent elections; there was no obvious explanation for this in economic changes since 1987. The Conservatives continued to lose ground along the South Coast and more especially in the West Country, whilst maintaining their strength in most of the area East and North of London up to Lincolnshire. The Liberal Democrat performance was the converse of this pattern.

4.   Tactical voting proved to be more widespread and more important than in previous elections. In Conservative-held seats where the Alliance had been third or only narrowly second in 1987, Labour took more than the Conservatives from the falling Liberal Democrat vote. In turn, the Liberal Democrats benefited from new tactical voting in some seats, mostly south of the Thames, where Labour was a poor third. Due to this informal pact among anti-Conservative voters, Labour won at least six extra seats and, with 20 MPs, the Liberal Democrats won one more seat than they had at merger, despite a 4.8 percent fall from the 1987 Alliance vote. Altogether tactical voting on its own probably halved Mr Major's majority.

5.   The result was a considerable disappointment for the SNP who, despite increasing their share of the Scottish vote by 7 percent to 21 percent, still won only the three seats they had in 1987. In contrast Plaid Cymru won a fourth seat by increasing its support in Welsh-speaking areas while improving its share of the total Welsh vote by only 1.5 percent to 8.8 percent.

6.   The result was a disaster for Greens who utterly failed to repeat their European election performance; their average vote, 1.3 percent, was a shade lower even than in 1987 and worse than the performance of the splinter party formed by Liberals opposed to merger with the SDP.

7.   A few Independent candidates, especially deselected MPs, scored high votes; one, Dave Nellist, came closer to holding on to his seat than any rebel MP had since 1974, while the 19 percent vote for

Tommy Sheridan standing as Scottish Militant Labour in Glasgow Pollok is the highest share of the vote won by an Independent candidate who had not been an MP since 1945.

8. The number of ethnic minority MPs rose from five to six, including the first Conservative Asian MP in modern times, Nirj Deva. There was some continuing evidence that white voters are not fully prepared to vote for non-white candidates (though hardly enough to account for the defeat of the black Conservative candidate in Cheltenham), but Labour's four black MPs from 1987 all secured large increases in their majorities. This incumbency effect also benefited some controversial left-wing 1987 entrants to Parliament; more generally the results confirm the modest bonus that most new incumbents acquire during their first parliamentary term.

9. The Conservatives failed to win much support in Northern Ireland in their first attempt to win seats against Unionist opposition. The SDLP gained significantly in votes from rival Republican parties and, with the aid of tactical voting by Protestants, won a fourth seat, eliminating Provisional Sinn Fein representation.

10. Turnout at 77.7 percent was the highest since February 1974 and was 2.4 percent higher than in 1987. However, this increase was markedly uneven and turnout actually fell in the more urban seats in Scotland, Wales and the North of England. The concentration of turnout increase in the areas of Britain where Labour is weaker probably means Labour suffered more from apathy amongst its supporters. Turnout rose only 0.1 percent in Labour-held seats, but 3.5 percent in Tory-held ones.

11. This difference in turnout change, together with the regional variation in swing and the impact of tactical voting, dramatically affected the way the electoral system worked in 1992. Uniform application of the overall changes would have produced 20 Labour gains from the Conservatives and would have given Mr. Major an overall majority of 71. Instead he lost 39 seats net to Labour and despite winning a voting lead higher than anyone other than Mrs Thatcher had achieved since 1945, a majority in seats of just 21.

12. Labour by contrast could have won the election outright with no more than half a point lead in votes – and this bias is unlikely to be reversed by the next review of constituency boundaries.

It is worth expanding on the last two points. Before the April 9 election it was calculated that a 4 percent swing from the 1987 outcome would cost the government its clear majority. A 6 percent swing would put Conservative and Labour dead level in a hung parliament. An 8 percent swing would give Labour a clear majority.

The actual swing recorded on April 9 was 2.1 percent from Conservative to Labour. It left the Conservatives with 336 seats, 10 more than the 326 needed for a clear majority. But, if the swing had been 2.6 percent, only half percent more than it was, the Conservatives would have lost a further 12 seats and fallen below the magic 326. A further half percent swing, up to 3.1 percent, and they would have been down to 311 seats and dependent upon other parties to stay in office. A 4.2 percent swing (not the predicted 6 percent) would in fact have brought the parties level in seats. A 6.1 percent swing (not the predicted 8 percent), with the additional 4 percent swing spread evenly, would have given Labour a clear majority.

The outcome was a near-run thing. The 2.1 percent swing that Labour achieved should, if uniform across the country, have left the Conservatives with 356 not 336 seats. What happened to upset the traditional relationship between seats and votes, the regularity of which, in past elections has made it so easy to predict the final outcome from the early declarations? The way the system worked out on April 9 in fact reduced the humiliation of the forecasters. Although Labour secured fewer votes than the polls predicted, they won more seats than predictions based on uniform swing would have suggested.

Why did Labour fare better than would have been predicted if the 2.1 percent swing figure had been known in advance? It did so because it won 12 of the 18 seats that would fall on a 2.1 percent swing and it compensated for its 6 failures by gaining 17 of the 24 seats vulnerable to a swing of between 2 percent and 4 percent as well as a further eleven seats beyond that point. Of these 28 uncovenanted gains eight were in Greater London and seven were in the Midlands, where the swing in any case was higher than average. Conservatives piled up extra votes in their safest seats and less so in the marginals, while Labour gained votes in their crucial target seats. The party's key seats strategy clearly paid dividends, particularly in London. The four narrowest victories with majorities under 100 all went to the Conservatives but in the end it was Labour that was lucky. As the electoral outcome now suggests, while a uniform swing of 3.8 percent would bring the parties level at 39.0 percent apiece, this would result in Labour having 320 seats to the Conservatives 282. The Conservatives would no doubt be howling at the injustice of the electoral system.

What course did the election chart for Britain in the 1990s? At first sight it seemed to confirm the rejection of socialism, as in many other countries, and to show that the centre-left had no clear and electorally attractive political message. The *Sunday Times* headlined its post-election editorial 'SOCIALISM R.I.P.'. It was notable that constitutional issues came to the forefront in the last week of the election campaign. With the Labour Party open-minded about electoral reform, the main opposition parties were sympathetic to proportional representation and self-determination for Scotland, while the Conservatives resolutely set their face in favour of the constitutional and electoral *status quo*. The constitution and tax represented the clearest divide between government and opposition parties.

A longer perspective shows that few general elections are turning points. But some are: the election of a Labour government in 1945 was clearly a vote for the rebuilding of Britain and accepted as such by the defeated Tories; Harold Wilson's victories in 1964 and 1966 reflected a general desire for economic modernisation and social reform; the Conservative success in 1979, following the winter of discontent, was seen as a vote for a break with the failed policies of the 1970s. Nineteen ninety-two must be seen more as a vote to give John Major his chance than as an endorsement of Mrs Thatcher's record. But it appears more clearly still as a rejection of what was offered by Labour and raised again questions about the party's future as a party of government.

A critical election is one which breaks the existing mould of party politics. Labour's election victory in 1945, or the Conservatives' in 1979, have been regarded by some as critical elections. Such an election durably alters the balance between the main parties. Over four general elections, the Conservatives have averaged only 42 percent of the vote. That could be a base or could be a ceiling but in three-party politics it has proved enough to be decisive. It is the party's substantial lead over Labour in the four elections, 7.6 percent, 14.8 percent, 11.5 percent and 7.6 percent that is significant. Nineteen ninety-two echoed the earlier elections and confirmed the Conservative dominance over Labour and the imbalance in the British party system.

# Appendix 1  The Voting Statistics

Table A1.1  Votes and seats 1945–92 (seats in italics)

| | Electorate and turnout | Total votes cast | Conservative[1] | Labour | Liberals | Welsh & Scottish Nationalists | Communist | Others (mainly N. Ireland) |
|---|---|---|---|---|---|---|---|---|
| 1945[3] | 73.3% | 100%–640 | 39.8%–213 | 48.3%–393 | 9.1%–12 | 0.2% | 0.4%–2 | 2.1%–20 |
| | 32 836 419 | 24 082 612 | 9 577 667 | 11 632 191 | 2 197 191 | 46 612 | 102 760 | 525 491 |
| 1950 | 84.0% | 100%–625 | 43.5%–299 | 46.1%–315 | 9.1%–9 | 0.1% | 0.3% | 0.9%–2 |
| | 34 269 770 | 28 772 671 | 12 502 567 | 13 266 592 | 2 621 548 | 27 288 | 91 746 | 262 930 |
| 1951 | 82.5% | 100%–625 | 48.0%–321 | 48.8%–295 | 2.5%–6 | 0.1% | 0.1% | 0.5%–3 |
| | 34 645 573 | 28 595 668 | 13 717 538 | 13 948 605 | 730 556 | 18 219 | 21 640 | 159 110 |
| 1955 | 76.8% | 100%–630 | 49.7%–345 | 46.4%–277 | 2.7%–6 | 0.2% | 0.1% | 0.8%–2 |
| | 34 858 263 | 26 760 493 | 13 311 936 | 12 404 970 | 722 405 | 57 231 | 33 144 | 230 807 |
| 1959 | 78.7% | 100%–630 | 49.4%–365 | 43.8%–258 | 5.9%–6 | 0.4% | 0.1% | 0.5%–1 |
| | 35 397 080 | 27 859 241 | 13 749 830 | 12 215 538 | 1 638 571 | 99 309 | 30 897 | 145 090 |
| 1964 | 77.1% | 100%–630 | 43.4%–304 | 44.1%–317 | 11.2%–9 | 0.5% | 0.2% | 0.6% |
| | 35 892 572 | 27 655 374 | 12 001 396 | 12 205 814 | 3 092 878 | 133 551 | 45 932 | 169 431 |
| 1966 | 75.8% | 100%–630 | 41.9%–253 | 47.9%–363 | 8.5%–12 | 0.7% | 0.2% | 0.7%–2 |
| | 35 964 684 | 27 263 606 | 11 418 433 | 13 064 951 | 2 327 533 | 189 545 | 62 112 | 201 032 |
| 1970 | 72.0% | 100%–630 | 46.4%–330 | 43.0%–288 | 7.5%–6 | 1.3%–1 | 0.1% | 1.7%–5 |
| | 39 342 013 | 28 344 798 | 13 145 123 | 12 178 295 | 2 117 033 | 381 818 | 37 970 | 486 557 |
| Feb '74 | 78.1% | 100%–635 | 37.8%–297 | 37.1%–301 | 19.3%–14 | 2.6%–9 | 0.1% | 3.1%–14 |
| | 39 770 724 | 31 340 162 | 11 872 180 | 11 646 391 | 6 058 744 | 804 554 | 32 743 | 958 293 |
| Oct '74 | 72.8% | 100%–635 | 35.8%–277 | 39.2%–319 | 18.3%–13 | 3.5%–14 | 0.1% | 3.1%–12 |
| | 40 072 971 | 29 189 178 | 10 464 817 | 11 457 079 | 6 346 754 | 1 005 938 | 17 426 | 897 164 |

| | Electorate and turnout | Total votes cast | Conservative | Labour | Liberals, etc.[2] | Welsh & Scottish Nationalists | Communist | Others (mainly N. Ireland) |
|---|---|---|---|---|---|---|---|---|
| 1979 | 76.0% | 100%–635 | 43.9%–339 | 37.0%–269 | 13.8%–11 | 2.0%–4 | 0.1% | 3.2%–12 |
| | 41 093 264 | 31 221 361 | 13 697 923 | 11 532 218 | 4 313 804 | 636 890 | 16 858 | 1 043 755 |
| 1983 | 72.7% | 100%–650 | 42.4%–397 | 27.6%–209 | 25.4%–23 | 1.5%–4 | 0.04% | 3.1%–17 |
| | 42 197 344 | 30 671 136 | 13 012 315 | 8 456 934 | 7 780 949 | 457 676 | 11 606 | 951 656 |
| 1987 | 75.3% | 100%–650 | 42.3%–376 | 30.8%–229 | 22.6%–22 | 1.7%–6 | 0.02% | 2.6%–17 |
| | 43 181 321 | 32 536 137 | 13 763 066 | 10 029 778 | 7 341 290 | 543 559 | 6 078 | 852 368 |
| 1992 | 77.7% | 100%–651 | 41.9%–336 | 34.4%–271 | 17.8%–20 | 2.3%–7 | – | 3.5%–17 |
| | 43 249 721 | 33 612 693 | 14 092 891 | 11 559 735 | 5 999 384 | 783 991 | – | 1 176 692[4] |

*Notes:*
1. Includes Ulster Unionists 1945–70.
2. Liberals 1945–79; Liberal–SDP Alliance 1983–7; Liberal Democrats 1992.
3. The 1945 figures exclude University seats and are adjusted for double voting in the 15 two-member seats.
4. Other votes in 1992 included 738,338 for Northern Ireland parties, 170,368 for the Green Party, 62,807 for the Natural Law Party, and 64,744 for the Liberal Party.

*Appendix 1: The Voting Statistics*

Table A1.2   Regional results, 1992

### UNITED KINGDOM

| | Seats won in 1992 (% change since 1987) | | | | Share of votes cast 1992 (percent change since 1987) | | | | | |
|---|---|---|---|---|---|---|---|---|---|---|
| | Conservative | Labour | Lib Dem | Nat & Other | Turnout | Conservative | Labour | Lib Dem | Nationalist | Other |
| England | 319 (−39) | 195 (+40) | 10 | – | 78.1 2.7 | 45.5 −0.8 | 33.9 4.4 | 19.2 −4.6 | – | 1.4 −2.6 |
| South | 192 (−17) | 42 (+17) | 7 (+1) | – | 78.5 3.6 | 50.4 −1.4 | 24.9 4.1 | 22.9 −3.9 | – | 1.8 −2.8 |
| Midlands | 74 (−12) | 46 (+12) | 0 | – | 79.4 3.1 | 46.6 −1.2 | 36.3 6.3 | 15.9 −5.8 | – | 1.2 −3.7 |
| North | 53 (−10) | 107 (+11) | 3 (−1) | – | 76.5 1.1 | 36.9 0.3 | 46.0 3.9 | 16.1 −5.0 | – | 1.1 −1.8 |
| Wales | 6 (−2) | 27 (+3) | 1 (−2) | 4 (+1) | 79.7 0.7 | 28.6 −1.0 | 49.5 4.4 | 12.4 −5.5 | 8.8 1.6 | 0.7 −2.7 |
| Scotland | 11 (+1) | 49 (−1) | 9 | 3 | 75.4 0.3 | 25.7 1.6 | 39.0 −3.4 | 13.1 −6.1 | 21.5 7.4 | 0.8 2.5 |
| Great Britain | 336 (−40) | 271 (+42) | 20 (−2) | 7 (+1) | 77.9 2.4 | 42.8 −0.5 | 35.2 3.7 | 18.3 −5.4 | 2.4 0.7 | 1.3 −2.1 |
| Northern Ireland | 0 | 0 | 0 | 17 (+1) | 69.8 2.8 | 5.7 5.7 | – | – | – | 94.3 – |
| United Kingdom | 336 (−40) | 271 (+42) | 20 (−2) | 24 (+1) | 77.7 2.4 | 41.9 −0.4 | 34.4 3.6 | 17.9 −4.7 | 2.3 0.7 | 3.5 −2.0 |

### REGIONS

| | Seats won in 1992 (% change since 1987) | | | | Share of votes cast 1992 (percent change since 1987) | | | | | |
|---|---|---|---|---|---|---|---|---|---|---|
| | Conservative | Labour | Lib Dem | Nat & Other | Turnout | Conservative | Labour | Lib Dem | Nationalist | Other |
| South East | 154 (−11) | 38 (+14) | 1 (−2) | – | 77.8 3.8 | 51.2 −1.0 | 26.6 4.3 | 20.4 −4.5 | – | 1.8 −2.7 |
| Greater London | 48 (−10) | 35 (+12) | 1 (−2) | – | 73.8 3.1 | 45.3 −1.2 | 37.0 5.6 | 15.2 −6.1 | – | 2.5 −3.4 |
| Inner London | 8 (−5) | 20 (+7) | – | – | 69.3 2.3 | 36.2 −0.8 | 46.0 5.1 | 13.2 −7.8 | – | 4.6 −2.9 |
| Outer London | 40 (−5) | 15 (+5) | 0 | – | 76.1 3.5 | 49.5 −1.5 | 32.9 5.9 | 16.1 −5.3 | – | 1.5 −3.7 |
| Rest of S.E. | 106 (−1) | 3 (+2) | 0 | – | 80.2 4.0 | 54.5 −1.1 | 20.8 4.0 | 23.4 −3.8 | – | 1.4 −2.5 |
| Outer Met. Area | 56 (−1) | 1 (+1) | 0 | – | 80.9 4.7 | 55.5 −0.3 | 22.0 4.2 | 21.2 −4.7 | – | 1.3 −2.2 |
| Outer S.E. | 50 | 2 (+1) | 0 | – | 79.5 3.4 | 53.4 −1.9 | 19.4 3.7 | 25.7 −2.8 | – | 1.4 −2.8 |
| South West | 38 (−6) | 4 (+3) | 6 (+3) | – | 81.1 2.8 | 47.6 −3.0 | 19.2 3.3 | 31.4 −1.6 | – | 1.8 −3.2 |
| Devon & Cornwall | 12 (−2) | 1 (+1) | 3 (+1) | – | 81.3 2.5 | 46.0 −2.8 | 17.5 4.6 | 33.9 −3.7 | – | 2.5 −3.7 |
| Rest of S.W. | 26 (−4) | 3 (+2) | 3 (+2) | – | 81.0 2.9 | 48.3 −3.2 | 20.1 2.8 | 30.2 −0.6 | – | 1.4 −3.0 |
| East Anglia | 17 (−2) | 3 (+2) | 0 | – | 80.0 2.9 | 51.0 −1.1 | 28.0 6.3 | 19.5 −6.2 | – | 1.5 −3.7 |
| East Midlands | 28 (−3) | 14 (+3) | 0 | – | 80.6 3.1 | 46.6 −2.0 | 37.4 7.4 | 15.2 −5.7 | – | 0.7 −4.7 |
| West Midlands | 29 (−7) | 29 (+7) | 0 | – | 78.2 3.2 | 44.8 −0.8 | 38.8 5.5 | 15.0 −5.8 | – | 1.5 −3.1 |
| W. Mids. Met. Co. | 10 (−4) | 21 (+4) | 0 | – | 75.5 2.9 | 42.1 −0.5 | 44.0 4.2 | 12.0 −5.2 | – | 1.9 −2.4 |
| Rest of W.Midlands | 19 (−3) | 8 (+3) | 0 | – | 80.8 3.4 | 47.2 −1.1 | 34.0 6.9 | 17.7 −6.5 | – | 1.0 −4.0 |
| Yorks & Humberside | 20 (−1) | 34 (+1) | 0 | – | 75.4 0.9 | 37.9 0.5 | 44.4 3.7 | 16.8 −4.8 | – | 0.9 −1.6 |
| S. Yorks. Met. Co. | 1 | 14 | 0 | – | 72.1 −0.5 | 25.6 0.9 | 57.9 1.8 | 15.8 −3.2 | – | 0.6 −0.5 |
| W. Yorks. Met. Co. | 9 | 14 | 0 | – | 76.2 0.7 | 38.2 0.3 | 45.6 4.5 | 15.0 −5.7 | – | 1.2 −2.1 |

| Region | Con seats (change) | Lab seats (change) | Lib Dem seats (change) | Nat & Other seats | Turnout (share, change) | Con (share, change) | Lab (share, change) | Lib Dem (share, change) | Nationalist (share, change) | Other (share, change) |
|---|---|---|---|---|---|---|---|---|---|---|
| Rest of Yorks & Humb | 10 (−1) | 6 (+1) | 0 | — | 77.2, 2.3 | 46.9, −0.1 | 32.5, 4.9 | 20.0, −5.1 | — | 0.6, −2.5 |
| North West | 27 (−7) | 44 (+8) | 2 (−1) | — | 77.3, 1.1 | 37.8, −0.2 | 44.9, 3.7 | 15.8, −4.8 | — | 1.5, −2.0 |
| Gtr. Manchr. Met. Co. | 9 (−1) | 20 (+1) | 1 | — | 75.9, 0.6 | 35.5, −0.5 | 47.3, 3.3 | 15.7, −4.2 | — | 1.6, −1.9 |
| Merseyside Met. Co. | 4 | 12 (+1) | 1 (−1) | — | 74.1, −1.0 | 29.0, 0.1 | 51.4, 4.0 | 16.9, −6.5 | — | 2.7, −2.0 |
| Rest of N.W. | 14 (−6) | 12 (+6) | 0 | — | 80.6, 2.8 | 44.9, −0.8 | 39.0, 4.6 | 15.2, −4.4 | — | 0.9, −2.7 |
| Northern | 6 (−2) | 29 (+2) | 0 | — | 76.5, 1.2 | 33.4, 1.0 | 50.6, 4.2 | 15.5, −5.5 | — | 0.5, −1.6 |
| Tyne & Wear Met.Co. | 1 | 12 | 1 | — | 72.6, 0.1 | 28.8, 1.2 | 57.1, 3.5 | 13.7, −4.9 | — | 0.4, −1.1 |
| Rest of Northern | 5 (−2) | 17 (+2) | 1 | — | 78.7, 1.8 | 35.8, 0.8 | 47.2, 4.9 | 16.5, −5.9 | — | 0.5, −2.0 |
| Wales | 6 (−2) | 27 (+3) | 1 (−2) | 4 (+1) | 79.7, 0.7 | 28.6, −1.0 | 49.5, 4.4 | 12.4, −5.5 | 8.8, 1.6 | 0.7, −2.7 |
| Industrial Wales | 3 (−1) | 21 (+1) | 0 | 0 | 78.9, 0.7 | 25.5, −0.9 | 59.0, 4.6 | 10.0, −5.5 | 5.0, 1.3 | 0.7, −2.8 |
| Rural Wales | 3 (−1) | 6 (+2) | 1 (−2) | 4 (+1) | 80.9, 0.8 | 33.8, −1.2 | 33.6, 4.5 | 16.6, −5.6 | 15.3, 1.8 | 0.7, −2.8 |
| Scotland | 11 (+1) | 49 (−1) | 9 | 3 | 75.4, 0.3 | 25.7, 1.6 | 39.0, −3.4 | 13.1, −6.1 | 21.5, 7.4 | 0.8, 2.5 |
| Central Clydeside | 1 | 23 | 0 | 0 | 74.4, −0.5 | 18.9, 2.3 | 51.7, −4.5 | 8.5, −7.2 | 19.9, 8.5 | 1.1, 3.4 |
| Rest of Ind. Belt | 4 | 22 | 0 | 0 | 77.1, 0.7 | 25.3, 0.6 | 44.1, −2.9 | 10.0, −6.6 | 19.8, 8.3 | 0.8, 1.7 |
| Highlands | 0 | 1 | 5 | 0 | 72.6, 0.4 | 22.2, −0.1 | 21.0, 0.1 | 33.8, −7.0 | 22.0, 8.4 | 1.1, −0.1 |
| Rest of Scotland | 6 (+1) | 3 (−1) | 4 | 3 | 74.7, 0.7 | 35.8, 2.1 | 19.4, −2.1 | 18.4, −4.4 | 26.1, 4.1 | 0.4, 2.1 |

*Notes:* Changes in numbers of seats won by the parties do not sum to zero as an extra seat (at Milton Keynes) was contested in 1992. Liberal Democrat performance is compared to that of the SDP–Liberal Alliance in 1987.

The English Regions are the eight *Standard Regions* as defined by the Office of Population Censuses and Surveys.

The *Outer Metropolitan Area* comprises those seats wholly or mostly in the Outer Metropolitan Area as defined by the Office of Population Censuses and Surveys (OPCS). It includes: the whole of Surrey and Hertfordshire; the whole of Berkshire except Newbury; and the constituencies of Crawley; Horsham; Mid-Sussex (West Sussex); Aldershot (Hampshire); Dartford; Gillingham; Gravesham; Mid-Kent; Maidstone; Medway; Sevenoaks; Tonbridge & Malling; Tunbridge Wells (Kent); Beaconsfield; Chesham & Amersham; Wycombe (Buckinghamshire); Luton South; Luton North; Bedfordshire South-West (Bedfordshire); Basildon; Billericay; Brentwood & Ongar; Castle Point; Chelmsford; Epping Forest; Harlow; Rochford; Southend East; Southend West; Thurrock (Essex).

*Industrial Wales* includes Gwent, the whole of Glamorgan, and the Llanelli constituency in Dyfed.

The *Central Clydeside Conurbation* includes those seats wholly or mostly in the Central Clydeside Conurbation as defined by the Registrar-General (Scotland). It comprises the whole of the Strathclyde region except the following constituencies: Argyll & Bute; Ayr; Carrick, Cumnock & Doon Valley; Clydesdale; Cunninghame North; Cunninghame South; Dumbarton; Greenock & Port Glasgow; Kilmarnock & Loudoun.

The *Scottish Industrial Belt* comprises the regions of Central, Fife (except Fife North-East), Lothian and Strathclyde (except Argyll & Bute).

The *Highlands* comprises the following constituencies: Argyll & Bute; Caithness & Sutherland; Inverness, Nairn & Lochaber; Orkney & Shetland; Ross, Cromarty & Skye; the Western Isles.

*Appendix 1: The Voting Statistics*

### Table A1.3  Constituency results in Great Britain, 1992

This table lists the votes in each constituency in percentage terms.

The constituencies are listed alphabetically within counties (except that in Greater London the constituencies are listed alphabetically within each borough).

The figure in the 'Other' column is the total percentage received by all 'Other' candidates. (When there was more than one such candidate the number is indicated in brackets. When one of the 'other' candidates was the sitting MP for the constituency the figure is marked with a ¶).

† denotes a seat won by different parties in 1987 and 1992
‡ denotes a seat that changed hands at a by-election between 1987 and 1992
§ denotes a joint Green/Plaid Cymru candidate. Change in vote is compared with total of PC and Green vote in 1987. (These candidates are treated as 'others' in the regional and national statistics).

The 'Liberal Democrat change' column compares the 1992 Liberal Democrat vote with that received in 1987 by the Liberal-SDP Alliance candidate.

Italics indicate that figures are not directly comparable with the 1987 election. In Buckingham, Milton Keynes North-East and Milton-Keynes South-West there were major boundary changes between elections; the basis of comparison is a calculation of the probable results had the present constituencies existed in 1987, and is only approximate. In Orkney and Shetland there was no Scottish National Party candidate in 1987, but the vote for the Orkney and Shetland Movement, who ran with SNP backing, is treated as Nationalist.

Swing is given in the Conventional (or 'Butler') form – the average of the Conservative % gain and the Labour % loss (measuring % of the total poll) – but only in those seats where those parties occupied the top two places in 1987 and 1992. This is the practice followed by all Nuffield studies since 1955.

### Distribution of Economic Indicators by Constituency

On the left of these tables there are listed for the 634 constituencies in Great Britain (but not for the 17 in Northern Ireland) the following information:-

*% owner occupied 1981:* (1981 census; figures from the 1991 census were unfortunately not available at the time of going to press).

*% unemployed:* Registered unemployed as a proportion of the electorate, November 1991. (*Source: Employment Gazette,* January 1992)

*Poll Tax:* Community Charge paid by the average-sized household (in £) for the year 1991–2, based on information supplied by CIPFA on average Community Charge within local authority areas. (This figure is not included for constituencies in Scotland, and precise figures were not available for a small number of other constituencies, for which an approximation is given in brackets).

*Household income:* Average annualised household weekly income 1990–1 (in £00s). (*Source:* National Shopping Survey)

*% electorate change:* Change in size of constituency electorate June 1987 – April 1992, as a percentage of the June 1987 electorate.

The following information from the 1981 census was published in previous volumes in this series:
In *The British General Election of 1983*: % council tenants and % employers and managers.
In *The British General Election of 1987*: % car owners, % working class, % degree holders.

The following table is designed to show the approximate rank ordering of all constituencies in terms of these characteristics as well as the range between the highest and lowest figures for each characteristic.

| Ranking order of decile (%) | Rank order in number | Owner occupied (%) | Unemployment (%) | Annual household income (£00s) | Change in electorate 1987–92 (%) | Rank order in number | Poll Tax (household) 1991–2 |
|---|---|---|---|---|---|---|---|
| 0 | 1 | 2.4 | 3.3 | 152 | −18.3 | 1 | 0 |
| 10 | 63 | 30.2 | 5.5 | 201 | −5.4 | 56 | 322 |
| 20 | 126 | 41.9 | 6.4 | 212 | −3.2 | 112 | 385 |
| 30 | 190 | 49.6 | 7.3 | 223 | −1.9 | 169 | 414 |
| 40 | 253 | 55.4 | 8.1 | 234 | −0.8 | 225 | 440 |
| 50 | 316 | 58.9 | 9.0 | 244 | 0.3 | 281 | 467 |
| 60 | 380 | 61.7 | 9.9 | 252 | 1.1 | 337 | 484 |
| 70 | 444 | 64.6 | 11.0 | 264 | 2.2 | 393 | 502 |
| 80 | 507 | 67.9 | 12.5 | 281 | 3.2 | 450 | 531 |
| 90 | 571 | 72.4 | 14.9 | 306 | 4.5 | 506 | 568 |
| 100 | 634 | 84.3 | 24.2 | 358 | 13.7 | 562 | 735 |

*Table A1.3  Constituency results, Great Britain, 1992*

| ENGLAND | % Owner occupied 1981 | Unemployed % | Poll Tax (household) | Household income | Electorate change % | % voting | % change in voting | % Con | Con change 1987–92 | % Labour | Lab change 1987–92 | % Lib Dem | Lib Dem chg. 1987–92 | % Other | Swing |
|---|---|---|---|---|---|---|---|---|---|---|---|---|---|---|---|
| Avon, Bath† | 57.9 | 9.4 | 415 | 245 | −2.4 | 82.5 | 3.1 | 41.8 | −3.6 | 7.8 | −2.8 | 48.9 | 6.3 | 1.5(4) | – |
| Bristol East† | 61.5 | 11.7 | 677 | 240 | −2.0 | 80.4 | 1.7 | 39.2 | −4.4 | 44.6 | 9.1 | 15.7 | −4.7 | 0.5 | −6.8 |
| North-West | 50.8 | 9.6 | 652 | 247 | −0.2 | 82.3 | 3.0 | 42.3 | −4.3 | 42.3 | 7.7 | 14.2 | −4.6 | 1.2 | −6.0 |
| South | 47.2 | 12.5 | 677 | 225 | −6.4 | 77.9 | 3.9 | 32.4 | −5.7 | 50.1 | 9.3 | 15.7 | −3.8 | 1.8(2) | −7.5 |
| West | 56.6 | 14.8 | 677 | 250 | −2.5 | 74.4 | −0.6 | 42.2 | −3.3 | 24.8 | 3.9 | 30.7 | −0.7 | 2.3(5) | – |
| Kingswood† | 68.5 | 8.2 | 594 | 245 | −1.8 | 83.8 | 3.7 | 40.6 | −4.3 | 44.5 | 7.1 | 14.9 | −2.8 | – | −5.7 |
| Northavon | 73.2 | 7.0 | 569 | 295 | 6.4 | 84.2 | 4.0 | 50.3 | −4.1 | 14.6 | 0.7 | 33.4 | 1.7 | 1.7(2) | – |
| Wansdyke | 71.6 | 6.1 | 544 | 272 | 2.6 | 84.3 | 3.0 | 48.2 | −3.3 | 27.7 | 4.5 | 22.8 | −2.4 | 1.2 | – |
| Weston-super-Mare | 66.6 | 9.4 | 578 | 242 | 3.3 | 79.7 | 4.1 | 47.7 | −1.7 | 11.0 | −0.4 | 39.3 | 3.7 | 2.0 | – |
| Woodspring | 73.8 | 6.0 | 574 | 296 | 1.6 | 83.2 | 4.1 | 54.5 | −2.1 | 15.4 | 1.0 | 27.4 | 0.4 | 2.7(3) | – |
| Bedfordshire, Mid | 60.9 | 5.7 | 507 | 313 | 4.1 | 82.4 | 3.7 | 58.2 | −0.8 | 21.8 | 3.8 | 17.3 | −5.7 | 2.7(2) | – |
| North | 64.3 | 7.6 | 495 | 259 | 0.3 | 80.1 | 2.9 | 50.7 | −1.9 | 31.0 | 7.8 | 16.9 | −6.6 | 1.4(2) | −3.1 |
| South-West | 65.0 | 6.6 | 546 | 319 | 0.4 | 82.4 | 3.7 | 57.1 | −1.0 | 24.7 | 6.5 | 16.7 | −5.5 | 1.4(2) | −4.1 |
| Luton North | 67.8 | 8.0 | 492 | 296 | 3.6 | 81.8 | 4.2 | 53.7 | −0.2 | 32.9 | 6.1 | 12.0 | −7.4 | 1.4(2) | – |
| South | 66.0 | 11.2 | 485 | 277 | 3.1 | 79.1 | 3.9 | 44.8 | −1.4 | 43.5 | 6.8 | 10.4 | −6.7 | 1.3(2) | – |
| Berkshire, East | 51.8 | 5.5 | 399 | 325 | 2.9 | 81.4 | 7.6 | 59.7 | −0.6 | 19.7 | 5.3 | 20.7 | −4.7 | – | – |
| Newbury | 59.4 | 5.7 | 546 | 306 | 6.7 | 82.8 | 4.8 | 55.9 | −4.2 | 6.0 | −2.2 | 37.3 | 5.6 | 0.8 | −3.2 |
| Reading East | 60.9 | 7.1 | 611 | 304 | −3.5 | 75.0 | 1.8 | 53.8 | 0.0 | 27.0 | 5.5 | 17.6 | −5.6 | 1.6 | – |
| West | 66.1 | 5.9 | 607 | 306 | −3.5 | 78.0 | 5.7 | 52.9 | −2.4 | 27.8 | 6.6 | 18.1 | −4.3 | 1.2 | – |
| Slough | 56.6 | 8.2 | 369 | 282 | 0.6 | 78.2 | 2.3 | 44.6 | −2.3 | 43.7 | 4.1 | 7.0 | −6.4 | 4.7(5) | – |
| Windsor & Maidenhead | 65.6 | 4.3 | 268 | 336 | −2.5 | 81.7 | 6.3 | 55.5 | −1.3 | 7.9 | −3.3 | 35.1 | 8.1 | 1.5(4) | – |
| Wokingham | 81.9 | 4.6 | 536 | 358 | 1.7 | 81.8 | 5.9 | 61.4 | 0.0 | 12.5 | 3.8 | 25.1 | −4.8 | 1.0(2) | – |
| Buckinghamshire, Aylesbury | 61.6 | 5.9 | 448 | 318 | 2.8 | 80.4 | 5.9 | 57.4 | −0.1 | 13.4 | −0.5 | 27.7 | −0.9 | 1.5(2) | – |
| Beaconsfield | 69.4 | 3.8 | 461 | 351 | −1.2 | 79.1 | 4.5 | 64.0 | −2.0 | 13.5 | 3.2 | 19.3 | −4.4 | 3.2(3) | – |
| Buckingham | n.a. | n.a. | 408 | n.a. | 5.3 | 84.2 | 5.9 | 62.5 | 1.1 | 16.2 | 4.3 | 20.6 | −6.2 | 0.7 | – |

| | | | | | Constituency | | | | | | | | | | |
|---|---|---|---|---|---|---|---|---|---|---|---|---|---|---|---|
| 73.6 | 3.7 | 489 | 337 | -2.6 | Chesham & Amersham | 81.9 | 4.6 | 63.3 | 1.2 | 10.4 | 1.0 | 24.5 | -2.6 | 1.8(2) | — |
| n.a. | n.a. | 638 | n.a. | 12.7 | Milton Keynes North-East | 81.0 | 4.0 | 51.6 | 3.1 | 23.7 | 7.7 | 23.0 | -10.6 | 1.7(3) | — |
| n.a. | n.a. | 638 | n.a. | 13.7 | South-West | 77.0 | -0.0 | 46.6 | -1.4 | 37.4 | 7.6 | 14.5 | -7.6 | 1.4(2) | -0.9 |
| 62.7 | 6.0 | 543 | 318 | 0.9 | Wycombe | 78.0 | 5.2 | 53.1 | -0.7 | 21.6 | 2.9 | 23.0 | -4.5 | 2.3(3) | — |
| 45.0 | 6.9 | 603 | 251 | -0.5 | *Cambridgeshire,* Cambridge† | 73.2 | -4.8 | 38.5 | -1.4 | 39.7 | 11.4 | 19.9 | -10.7 | 1.9(3) | — |
| 61.5 | 7.8 | 446 | 237 | 7.7 | Cambridgeshire North-East | 79.4 | 2.0 | 54.0 | 7.1 | 13.8 | 5.3 | 30.3 | -14.2 | 1.9(2) | — |
| 58.8 | 4.1 | 413 | 290 | 7.4 | South-East | 80.6 | 4.1 | 57.9 | -0.8 | 20.0 | 6.3 | 20.3 | -7.2 | 1.7(2) | — |
| 60.6 | 4.9 | 427 | 299 | 3.4 | South-West | 81.1 | 3.4 | 56.8 | -0.9 | 13.7 | 0.4 | 28.1 | -0.8 | 1.3(2) | — |
| 63.1 | 5.4 | 399 | 291 | 7.8 | Huntingdon | 79.2 | 5.2 | 66.2 | 2.6 | 16.9 | 3.0 | 12.8 | -8.4 | 4.2(7) | — |
| 47.7 | 10.5 | 496 | 232 | 4.0 | Peterborough | 75.1 | 1.6 | 48.3 | -1.1 | 40.2 | 6.5 | 7.9 | -8.2 | 3.6(4) | -3.6 |
| 61.2 | 8.6 | 576 | 244 | -3.8 | *Cheshire,* City of Chester | 83.8 | 4.0 | 44.1 | -0.8 | 42.0 | 6.4 | 12.9 | -6.6 | 1.0(2) | — |
| 73.2 | 6.1 | 570 | 264 | 3.4 | Congleton | 84.5 | 4.0 | 49.0 | 0.7 | 20.0 | 2.2 | 30.3 | -3.5 | 0.7 | -1.3 |
| 62.7 | 8.5 | 579 | 256 | 2.8 | Crewe & Nantwich | 81.9 | 2.6 | 41.3 | -0.8 | 45.7 | 1.7 | 11.9 | -2.0 | 1.1 | — |
| 63.5 | 7.0 | 558 | 263 | 1.6 | Eddisbury | 82.6 | 4.5 | 51.0 | -0.1 | 30.5 | 7.0 | 17.0 | -6.6 | 1.4(2) | -3.3 |
| 59.2 | 8.1 | 599 | 233 | 0.3 | Ellesmere Port & Neston† | 84.1 | 3.1 | 42.8 | -1.6 | 46.1 | 4.9 | 9.9 | -4.2 | 1.2(2) | -2.9 |
| 48.4 | 11.9 | 586 | 212 | -1.2 | Halton | 78.3 | 0.0 | 28.7 | -1.6 | 59.7 | 4.2 | 10.4 | -3.9 | 1.3(2) | — |
| 70.0 | 4.8 | 514 | 306 | 0.6 | Macclesfield | 82.3 | 4.9 | 57.9 | 1.5 | 21.7 | 2.1 | 20.0 | -4.0 | 0.4 | -3.3 |
| 64.1 | 5.6 | 530 | 295 | -1.1 | Tatton | 80.8 | 4.1 | 55.1 | 0.5 | 27.5 | 6.2 | 16.7 | -6.9 | 0.7 | -3.2 |
| 53.3 | 9.8 | 557 | 244 | 3.9 | Warrington North | 77.4 | 2.2 | 33.6 | -0.6 | 54.3 | 6.1 | 11.5 | -6.2 | 0.7 | -1.2 |
| 62.5 | 8.3 | 563 | 265 | 4.6 | South† | 82.0 | 4.5 | 43.3 | 1.4 | 43.6 | 7.8 | 12.5 | -9.7 | 0.5 | -0.5 |
| 50.6 | 13.9 | 531 | 209 | -1.0 | *Cleveland,* Hartlepool | 76.1 | 3.1 | 34.9 | 1.0 | 51.9 | 3.4 | 13.3 | -0.8 | — | -1.9 |
| 62.5 | 10.9 | 610 | 248 | 0.5 | Langbaurgh‡ | 83.1 | 4.3 | 45.4 | 3.7 | 43.1 | 4.7 | 11.5 | -8.4 | — | -3.9 |
| 49.0 | 17.4 | 568 | 174 | -3.2 | Middlesbrough | 69.8 | -1.1 | 25.7 | 0.7 | 64.1 | 4.4 | 10.2 | -5.1 | — | -1.5 |
| 53.2 | 14.3 | 637 | 207 | -1.4 | Redcar | 77.7 | 1.7 | 32.1 | 0.8 | 56.0 | 8.6 | 11.9 | -9.5 | 1.0 | — |
| 49.3 | 13.4 | 505 | 223 | -1.4 | Stockton North | 76.8 | 1.5 | 32.7 | 0.2 | 52.3 | 3.2 | 14.0 | -4.4 | — | — |
| 70.8 | 10.7 | 559 | 248 | 0.9 | South | 82.8 | 3.7 | 45.2 | 10.2 | 39.8 | 8.6 | 15.0 | -18.8 | — | — |
| 62.2 | 13.6 | 419 | 217 | 5.5 | *Cornwall,* North† | 81.5 | 1.7 | 44.3 | -7.4 | 6.6 | 0.1 | 47.4 | 5.5 | 1.7(3) | — |
| 67.0 | 9.6 | 432 | 224 | 4.0 | South-East | 82.1 | 2.6 | 51.0 | -0.6 | 9.2 | 0.6 | 38.1 | -1.6 | 1.7(3) | — |
| 69.4 | 13.0 | 461 | 199 | 2.7 | Falmouth & Camborne | 81.1 | 2.3 | 36.9 | -7.0 | 29.2 | 8.3 | 31.2 | -3.4 | 2.8(4) | — |
| 63.6 | 13.9 | 413 | 207 | 5.9 | St. Ives | 80.3 | 3.1 | 42.9 | -5.4 | 16.0 | -1.8 | 40.1 | 6.2 | 1.0 | — |
| 68.2 | 10.9 | 451 | 222 | 3.7 | Truro | 82.4 | 2.5 | 38.3 | -2.6 | 9.8 | -0.3 | 50.5 | 1.5 | 1.4(3) | — |
| 71.1 | 9.5 | 509 | 237 | -2.2 | *Cumbria,* Barrow & Furness† | 82.1 | 3.1 | 41.3 | -5.1 | 47.7 | 8.5 | 10.9 | -3.3 | — | -6.8 |
| 49.1 | 8.1 | 548 | 223 | 0.2 | Carlisle | 79.4 | 0.6 | 39.7 | -0.4 | 46.8 | 4.5 | 13.1 | -4.5 | 0.4 | -2.5 |

| ENGLAND | % voting | % change in voting | % Con | Con change 1987–92 | % Labour | Lab change 1987–92 | % Lib Dem | Lib Dem chg. 1987–92 | % Other | Swing | % Owner occupied 1981 | Unemployed % | Poll Tax (household) | Household income | Electorate change % |
|---|---|---|---|---|---|---|---|---|---|---|---|---|---|---|---|
| Copeland | 83.5 | 2.2 | 43.4 | 0.4 | 48.7 | 1.5 | 7.6 | -1.5 | 0.3 | -0.5 | 45.0 | 8.6 | 453 | 248 | 0.4 |
| Penrith & the Border | 79.7 | 2.2 | 57.5 | -2.7 | 15.1 | 4.0 | 26.1 | -2.6 | 1.3(2) | — | 58.2 | 5.3 | 464 | 247 | 3.9 |
| Westmorland & Lonsdale | 77.8 | 2.9 | 56.9 | -0.7 | 15.1 | 1.8 | 27.5 | -1.7 | 0.5 | — | 62.3 | 4.4 | 518 | 247 | 2.3 |
| Workington | 81.5 | 0.9 | 34.7 | -2.4 | 56.9 | 4.5 | 6.4 | -4.1 | 2.0(2) | -3.5 | 52.2 | 9.4 | 391 | 230 | 1.2 |
| *Derbyshire*, Amber Valley | 84.7 | 3.5 | 46.1 | -5.3 | 44.9 | 10.6 | 8.9 | -5.3 | — | -7.9 | 67.8 | 7.7 | 477 | 244 | 2.4 |
| Bolsover | 78.9 | 1.6 | 25.3 | -3.0 | 64.5 | 8.3 | 10.2 | -5.3 | — | -5.7 | 49.6 | 9.8 | 409 | 210 | 1.6 |
| Chesterfield | 77.1 | 0.4 | 16.9 | -8.0 | 47.3 | 1.8 | 35.8 | 6.2 | 1.2(3) | — | 49.6 | 9.9 | 476 | 223 | 3.2 |
| Derby North | 80.7 | 4.9 | 48.4 | -0.4 | 40.9 | 3.6 | 9.6 | -3.8 | — | -2.0 | 55.7 | 8.6 | 483 | 222 | 2.0 |
| South | 75.5 | 5.6 | 37.9 | -2.6 | 51.7 | 8.1 | 10.4 | -5.4 | 0.4 | -5.3 | 57.6 | 10.5 | 483 | 214 | -3.6 |
| Derbyshire North-East | 83.6 | 4.3 | 38.2 | 0.5 | 48.8 | 4.4 | 13.0 | -4.9 | — | -2.0 | 56.5 | 8.7 | 529 | 228 | 0.9 |
| South | 85.5 | 4.2 | 48.7 | -0.4 | 42.1 | 8.8 | 8.9 | -8.8 | — | -4.6 | 67.0 | n.a. | 563 | 259 | 2.9 |
| West | 85.0 | 1.9 | 54.3 | 1.2 | 22.4 | 10.7 | 23.3 | -11.9 | — | — | 65.7 | 5.3 | (508) | 270 | 0.6 |
| Erewash | 83.0 | 5.6 | 47.7 | -0.9 | 38.6 | 6.5 | 12.8 | -6.6 | 1.0 | -3.7 | 64.7 | 12.9 | 509 | 220 | -1.2 |
| High Peak | 84.6 | 4.1 | 46.0 | 0.3 | 37.9 | 9.1 | 14.8 | -10.8 | 1.3 | -4.4 | 64.3 | 6.5 | (479) | 268 | 1.2 |
| *Devon*, North† | 84.4 | 2.7 | 45.7 | -5.2 | 5.9 | -0.4 | 47.1 | 4.3 | 1.3(2) | — | 66.1 | 10.4 | 467 | 223 | 2.3 |
| West & Torridge | 81.5 | 2.8 | 47.3 | -3.0 | 9.6 | 1.1 | 41.5 | 2.3 | 1.7(2) | — | 67.3 | 8.9 | 419 | 226 | 3.2 |
| Exeter | 80.9 | 0.3 | 41.1 | -3.3 | 36.2 | 13.7 | 19.4 | -12.3 | 3.2(3) | — | 59.9 | 8.6 | 448 | 226 | 2.0 |
| Honiton | 80.7 | 4.3 | 52.4 | -6.7 | 12.7 | 4.3 | 26.6 | -4.5 | 8.2(4) | — | 71.2 | 7.6 | 443 | 234 | 2.5 |
| Plymouth Devonport† | 77.8 | 1.0 | 34.2 | 5.0 | 48.7 | 20.3 | 12.3 | -30.0 | 4.7(2) | — | 40.6 | 11.1 | 462 | 203 | 2.0 |
| Drake | 75.6 | -1.0 | 43.7 | 2.4 | 38.6 | 14.5 | 15.1 | -18.2 | 2.6(3) | — | 52.9 | 15.6 | 462 | 203 | 0.9 |
| Sutton | 81.2 | 2.2 | 49.5 | 3.7 | 27.6 | 11.2 | 22.5 | -15.4 | 0.5 | — | 71.1 | 8.8 | 462 | 231 | 5.2 |
| South Hams | 81.1 | 2.4 | 53.4 | -2.0 | 12.0 | 3.8 | 33.0 | -1.1 | 1.6(2) | — | 66.7 | 9.3 | 441 | 222 | 5.4 |
| Teignbridge | 82.4 | 2.2 | 50.0 | -3.2 | 13.0 | 1.9 | 35.9 | 0.7 | 1.1(2) | — | 67.5 | 8.9 | 516 | 224 | 5.5 |
| Tiverton | 83.0 | 3.3 | 51.5 | -3.4 | 10.1 | 3.8 | 32.7 | -5.3 | 5.6(3) | — | 59.3 | 6.7 | 494 | 237 | 4.1 |
| Torbay | 80.6 | 4.3 | 49.9 | -4.1 | 9.6 | 1.2 | 39.8 | 2.2 | 0.7(2) | — | 72.5 | 13.5 | 458 | 207 | 1.0 |
| *Dorset*, Bournemouth East | 72.8 | 2.3 | 56.4 | -1.9 | 13.8 | 2.7 | 29.3 | -1.4 | 0.6 | — | 65.6 | 13.3 | 405 | 235 | -0.2 |
| West | 75.7 | 2.4 | 52.6 | -2.5 | 16.6 | 3.8 | 30.3 | -1.7 | 0.4 | — | 63.1 | 11.2 | 395 | 226 | 0.4 |

| | | | | | Constituency | | | | | | | | |
|---|---|---|---|---|---|---|---|---|---|---|---|---|---|
| 78.4 | 7.4 | 432 | 244 | 0.7 | Christchurch | 80.7 | 4.5 | 63.5 | 2.6 | 23.6 | -0.9 | 0.7(2) | — |
| 65.4 | 6.2 | 418 | 248 | 5.3 | Dorset North | 81.8 | 2.7 | 54.6 | 0.3 | 38.5 | 2.1 | — | — |
| 61.3 | 9.4 | 430 | 222 | 4.0 | South | 76.9 | 1.4 | 50.3 | 3.8 | 27.1 | -0.3 | 1.5(2) | — |
| 57.1 | 6.5 | 396 | 243 | 4.5 | West | 81.2 | 2.9 | 50.8 | 0.8 | 36.2 | 4.5 | 3.1(2) | — |
| 70.9 | 9.0 | 375 | 267 | 3.3 | Poole | 79.4 | 1.9 | 53.2 | 1.1 | 32.8 | 0.2 | — | -2.5 |
| 44.6 | 9.5 | 383 | 218 | 0.7 | *Durham,* Bishop Auckland | 76.5 | 2.4 | 31.8 | 2.0 | 18.2 | 1.0 | — | -5.0 |
| 64.2 | 10.8 | 498 | 238 | 0.2 | Darlington† | 83.6 | 2.8 | 43.0 | 6.5 | 8.3 | -3.5 | 0.6 | — |
| 47.3 | 8.7 | 517 | 241 | 2.5 | Durham, City of | 74.6 | -3.6 | 23.7 | 8.3 | 21.5 | -11.7 | 1.6 | — |
| 50.3 | 9.9 | 493 | 213 | 2.2 | Durham North | 76.1 | 0.1 | 24.8 | 3.7 | 15.3 | -7.3 | — | -3.9 |
| 50.5 | 11.9 | 445 | 218 | -0.3 | North-West | 75.6 | 2.0 | 27.6 | 7.0 | 14.6 | -6.2 | — | -2.1 |
| 30.2 | 9.2 | 389 | 193 | 0.3 | Easington | 72.5 | -0.9 | 16.7 | 4.6 | 10.6 | -5.0 | — | -1.7 |
| 45.9 | 8.1 | 425 | 219 | 0.3 | Sedgefield | 77.1 | 0.9 | 28.9 | 4.5 | 10.6 | -5.5 | 1.5(2) | — |
| 73.1 | 7.2 | 435 | 244 | 0.8 | *East Sussex,* Bexhill & Battle | 79.1 | 1.7 | 60.3 | 1.7 | 28.9 | 3.0 | 0.5 | — |
| 51.6 | 12.7 | 414 | 229 | -4.4 | Brighton Kemptown | 76.1 | 1.7 | 48.1 | 8.3 | 10.2 | -3.4 | 2.4(2) | -6.8 |
| 61.4 | 12.4 | 414 | 264 | -2.2 | Pavilion | 76.8 | 3.1 | 46.6 | 8.6 | 12.7 | -6.8 | 1.1(2) | -6.4 |
| 68.6 | 9.1 | 492 | 230 | 2.6 | Eastbourne† | 81.0 | 5.4 | 51.6 | -4.2 | 42.7 | 13.0 | 1.5(2) | — |
| 59.8 | 12.3 | 455 | 219 | -1.3 | Hastings & Rye | 74.9 | 3.1 | 47.6 | 2.7 | 35.2 | -0.8 | 7.2(3) | — |
| 57.8 | 11.3 | 331 | 256 | -7.1 | Hove | 74.3 | 6.5 | 49.0 | 6.2 | 19.4 | -2.4 | 1.3(2) | -1.4 |
| 69.9 | 7.2 | 455 | 264 | 1.0 | Lewes | 81.8 | 4.8 | 54.6 | 0.7 | 34.5 | 1.9 | 2.0(2) | -1.3 |
| 72.6 | 5.1 | 471 | 290 | 2.2 | Wealden | 80.8 | 5.9 | 61.7 | 0.9 | 27.1 | -0.4 | — | — |
| 35.1 | 11.1 | 675 | 259 | -0.6 | *Essex,* Basildon | 79.6 | 6.3 | 44.9 | 3.9 | 12.9 | -5.3 | 1.3 | — |
| 75.6 | 6.3 | 627 | 303 | 1.1 | Billericay | 82.3 | 5.1 | 56.5 | 1.5 | 22.5 | -3.1 | 1.0 | — |
| 55.3 | 7.6 | 426 | 279 | 2.5 | Braintree | 83.4 | 4.4 | 52.3 | 6.4 | 20.7 | -5.8 | 1.2 | — |
| 67.9 | 5.1 | 432 | 322 | -2.5 | Brentwood & Ongar | 84.7 | 5.7 | 57.6 | -2.3 | 30.5 | 5.5 | 1.1 | — |
| 84.3 | 7.7 | 388 | 292 | -0.4 | Castle Point | 80.4 | 5.4 | 55.6 | 5.0 | 19.2 | -1.9 | 0.9(2) | — |
| 65.3 | 6.3 | 447 | 300 | 1.1 | Chelmsford | 84.6 | 2.5 | 55.3 | 7.3 | 29.4 | -11.1 | 1.5 | — |
| 70.4 | 7.5 | 410 | 277 | 4.9 | Colchester North | 79.1 | 3.1 | 51.5 | 3.1 | 27.4 | -3.2 | 1.0 | — |
| 67.6 | 8.0 | 410 | 264 | 2.4 | South & Maldon | 79.2 | 3.9 | 54.8 | 6.2 | 23.0 | -7.6 | — | — |
| 63.1 | 6.5 | 474 | 304 | -0.3 | Epping Forest | 80.6 | 4.2 | 59.5 | 4.1 | 17.0 | -2.3 | — | -2.8 |
| 31.1 | 7.6 | 567 | 271 | -2.4 | Harlow | 83.2 | 4.8 | 46.6 | 4.9 | 11.9 | -4.3 | 0.4 | — |
| 78.3 | 12.4 | 374 | 218 | 4.0 | Harwich | 77.7 | 4.2 | 51.9 | 5.8 | 24.4 | -6.1 | 2.1 | — |
| 82.1 | 6.6 | 431 | 283 | 1.1 | Rochford | 83.0 | 4.9 | 61.1 | 4.2 | 20.3 | -7.0 | 0.4 | — |
| 62.5 | 6.1 | 421 | 305 | 2.3 | Saffron Walden | 83.2 | 4.2 | 56.6 | 2.8 | 28.6 | -0.3 | — | — |

| ENGLAND | % Owner occupied 1981 | Unemployed % | Poll Tax (household) | Household income | Electorate change % | % voting | % change in voting | % Con | Con change 1987-92 | % Labour | Lab change 1987-92 | % Lib Dem | Lib Dem chg. 1987-92 | % Other | Swing |
|---|---|---|---|---|---|---|---|---|---|---|---|---|---|---|---|
| Southend East | 60.2 | 12.7 | 369 | 249 | -4.0 | 73.8 | 4.5 | 58.8 | 0.8 | 27.4 | 9.6 | 12.2 | -12.0 | 1.6 | — |
| West | 75.2 | 8.7 | 369 | 275 | -6.2 | 77.8 | 2.5 | 54.7 | 0.3 | 12.3 | 4.7 | 30.9 | -7.2 | 2.1(3) | — |
| Thurrock† | 42.8 | 9.5 | 533 | 256 | 2.3 | 78.2 | 6.7 | 43.7 | 1.2 | 45.9 | 4.8 | 9.5 | -7.0 | 0.9(2) | — |
| *Gloucestershire*, Cheltenham† | 64.3 | 7.4 | 577 | 268 | 0.7 | 80.3 | 1.4 | 44.7 | -5.4 | 6.4 | -1.2 | 47.3 | 5.0 | 1.6(3) | — |
| Cirencester & Tewkesbury | 56.7 | 5.6 | 443 | 257 | 5.0 | 82.1 | 4.1 | 55.6 | 0.2 | 10.0 | 1.9 | 33.4 | -2.6 | 1.0(2) | -5.3 |
| Gloucester | 68.8 | 8.5 | 543 | 235 | 4.8 | 80.2 | 2.2 | 46.2 | -3.5 | 36.8 | 7.2 | 17.0 | -3.7 | — | -5.5 |
| Gloucestershire West | 65.9 | 6.7 | 508 | 249 | 2.6 | 83.7 | 2.5 | 43.7 | -2.6 | 36.3 | 8.5 | 20.0 | -6.0 | 0.1(2) | — |
| Stroud | 64.6 | 7.3 | 560 | 268 | 1.6 | 84.5 | 3.9 | 46.2 | -4.0 | 26.9 | 8.4 | 24.0 | -7.3 | 2.9 | — |
| *Greater London* | | | | | | | | | | | | | | | |
| Barking & Dagenham, Barking | 23.6 | 12.6 | 296 | 242 | -2.3 | 70.0 | 3.1 | 33.9 | -0.6 | 51.6 | 7.3 | 14.5 | -6.7 | — | -3.9 |
| Dagenham | 38.1 | 10.1 | 296 | 247 | -3.4 | 70.7 | 3.4 | 36.3 | -2.2 | 52.3 | 7.8 | 11.4 | -5.6 | — | -5.0 |
| Barnet, Chipping Barnet | 72.6 | 6.7 | 466 | 342 | -6.1 | 78.6 | 8.6 | 57.0 | -0.9 | 25.9 | 6.9 | 16.1 | -6.9 | 1.0(2) | — |
| Finchley | 61.7 | 8.5 | 466 | 302 | -8.4 | 77.6 | 8.2 | 51.2 | -2.7 | 35.7 | 4.0 | 11.1 | -2.8 | 2.0(3) | -3.3 |
| Hendon North | 54.5 | 8.4 | 466 | 317 | -6.5 | 75.1 | 9.3 | 53.2 | -2.4 | 34.8 | 9.3 | 10.7 | -8.2 | 1.4(2) | -5.9 |
| South | 59.1 | 8.1 | 466 | 326 | -11.3 | 72.4 | 8.6 | 58.8 | 3.2 | 24.4 | 3.5 | 16.0 | -7.6 | 0.8 | — |
| Bexley, Bexleyheath | 81.5 | 7.3 | 389 | 278 | -3.0 | 82.2 | 4.4 | 54.0 | 0.3 | 24.3 | 6.5 | 21.3 | -7.2 | 0.4 | — |
| Erith & Crayford | 57.1 | 11.2 | 389 | 272 | -0.1 | 79.7 | 4.3 | 46.5 | 1.3 | 41.5 | 12.0 | 12.0 | -13.3 | — | -5.3 |
| Old Bexley & Sidcup | 80.7 | 5.8 | 389 | 289 | -2.7 | 81.9 | 4.8 | 60.3 | -1.8 | 21.6 | 4.3 | 15.9 | -4.7 | 2.2(2) | — |
| Brent, Brent East | 41.1 | 16.1 | 600 | 286 | -12.6 | 69.2 | 4.7 | 36.4 | -2.1 | 53.1 | 10.5 | 8.8 | -5.7 | 1.7(2) | -6.3 |
| North | 72.5 | 9.6 | 600 | 313 | -6.6 | 70.6 | -0.4 | 56.4 | -3.5 | 32.0 | 7.2 | 10.0 | -5.4 | 1.6(2) | -5.4 |
| South | 49.4 | 15.7 | 600 | 271 | -10.7 | 64.1 | -0.8 | 30.5 | -1.9 | 57.5 | 5.6 | 10.2 | -5.5 | 1.8(2) | -3.8 |
| Bromley, Beckenham | 62.8 | 8.8 | 354 | 320 | -1.1 | 77.9 | 4.3 | 56.9 | 0.6 | 23.8 | 6.0 | 17.4 | -8.5 | 1.9(2) | — |
| Chislehurst | 63.0 | 6.6 | 354 | 292 | -3.2 | 78.9 | 3.4 | 58.4 | 0.7 | 22.4 | 3.0 | 15.8 | -7.3 | 3.5(2) | — |
| Orpington | 77.1 | 5.8 | 354 | 331 | -3.8 | 83.7 | 5.1 | 57.2 | -1.1 | 11.5 | 0.8 | 30.2 | -0.8 | 1.1 | — |
| Ravensbourne | 76.3 | 5.3 | 354 | 335 | -3.6 | 81.2 | 5.5 | 63.4 | 0.5 | 13.3 | 2.0 | 21.0 | -4.3 | 2.2(3) | — |
| Camden, Hampstead & Highgate† | 32.3 | 10.4 | 474 | 319 | -8.1 | 73.0 | 1.5 | 41.8 | -0.7 | 45.1 | 7.6 | 11.2 | -8.1 | 1.9(5) | -4.1 |
| Holborn & St. Pancras | 14.5 | 15.0 | 474 | 277 | -8.7 | 62.7 | -1.6 | 28.2 | -2.9 | 55.0 | 4.4 | 13.5 | -4.1 | 3.2(4) | -3.6 |

|  |  |  |  |  |  |  |  |  |  |  |  |  |  |  |  |
|---|---|---|---|---|---|---|---|---|---|---|---|---|---|---|---|
| 50.9 | 9.1 | 342 | 310 | 0.7 | Croydon, Central | 71.7 | 1.2 | 55.4 | -1.2 | 31.3 | 6.9 | 13.3 | -5.7 | – | -4.1 |
| 63.3 | 9.9 | 342 | 300 | 2.0 | North-East | 72.0 | 2.3 | 51.4 | -3.6 | 35.3 | 8.7 | 13.3 | -5.1 | – | -6.2 |
| 63.6 | 10.7 | 342 | 278 | -0.2 | North-West† | 70.8 | 1.6 | 43.5 | -3.5 | 47.3 | 10.3 | 9.2 | -6.8 | – | -6.9 |
| 80.0 | 5.4 | 342 | 358 | -0.5 | South | 77.6 | 3.9 | 63.7 | -0.4 | 12.8 | 3.1 | 23.0 | -1.3 | 0.5 | – |
| 48.3 | 9.7 | 477 | 318 | -12.6 | Ealing, Acton | 76.0 | 5.0 | 50.6 | -2.8 | 34.9 | 7.1 | 12.3 | -6.5 | 2.2(2) | -5.0 |
| 58.9 | 8.8 | 477 | 287 | -11.3 | North | 78.8 | 3.8 | 49.7 | -6.3 | 37.8 | 10.0 | 10.5 | -4.7 | 2.0(3) | -8.1 |
| 64.7 | 10.4 | 477 | 287 | -12.4 | Southall | 75.5 | 5.7 | 33.6 | -1.9 | 47.4 | -3.3 | 7.7 | -5.7 | 11.3(2)¶ | 0.7 |
| 61.7 | 10.8 | 492 | 269 | -4.6 | Enfield, Edmonton | 75.7 | 3.1 | 46.3 | -4.9 | 45.0 | 9.0 | 8.3 | -4.5 | 0.4 | -7.0 |
| 61.6 | 9.9 | 492 | 282 | -3.0 | North | 77.9 | 3.4 | 52.9 | -2.6 | 34.9 | 6.5 | 11.1 | -3.7 | 1.1 | -4.6 |
| 75.7 | 8.2 | 492 | 296 | -3.4 | Southgate | 76.3 | 3.7 | 57.9 | -0.9 | 26.2 | 7.4 | 14.4 | -6.5 | 1.4 | – |
| 46.2 | 10.5 | 420 | 264 | -3.8 | Greenwich, Eltham | 78.7 | 1.8 | 46.0 | -1.5 | 41.9 | 9.9 | 11.7 | -8.8 | 0.4 | -5.7 |
| 30.6 | 13.2 | 420 | 264 | -6.0 | Greenwich† | 74.6 | 1.2 | 19.5 | -3.8 | 41.0 | 6.2 | – | – | 39.5(5)¶ | – |
| 38.4 | 15.7 | 420 | 258 | -3.6 | Woolwich† | 70.9 | 0.2 | 16.6 | -4.6 | 44.2 | 7.2 | – | – | 39.2(2)¶ | – |
|  |  |  |  |  | Hackney |  |  |  |  |  |  |  |  |  |  |
| 22.3 | 20.9 | 537 | 252 | -18.2 | North & Stoke Newington | 63.5 | 5.4 | 26.9 | -2.0 | 57.8 | 9.1 | 11.5 | -7.7 | 3.7(2) | -5.6 |
| 10.9 | 22.2 | 537 | 253 | -18.3 | South & Shoreditch | 63.8 | 8.4 | 29.0 | 0.3 | 53.4 | 5.5 | 15.0 | -7.5 | 2.7(2) | -2.6 |
| 33.6 | 11.5 | 387 | 302 | -3.2 | Hammersmith, Fulham | 76.2 | -0.9 | 53.4 | 1.6 | 37.0 | 0.3 | 8.3 | -2.1 | 1.3(2) | 0.7 |
| 26.2 | 15.2 | 387 | 273 | -2.2 | Hammersmith | 71.9 | -0.8 | 37.0 | -1.1 | 51.0 | 6.0 | 10.0 | -5.0 | 2.0(3) | -3.6 |
|  |  |  |  |  | Haringey |  |  |  |  |  |  |  |  |  |  |
| 45.7 | 15.3 | 726 | 313 | -8.8 | Hornsey & Wood Green† | 75.9 | 2.5 | 39.2 | -3.8 | 48.5 | 8.5 | 10.0 | -5.2 | 2.4(3) | -6.2 |
| 41.2 | 22.0 | 726 | 248 | -10.2 | Tottenham | 65.6 | -0.5 | 29.8 | -5.6 | 56.5 | 12.9 | 11.4 | -6.4 | 2.3(2) | -9.2 |
| 73.5 | 8.0 | 483 | 318 | -7.9 | Harrow, East | 77.8 | 4.4 | 52.9 | -1.3 | 33.8 | 10.2 | 10.9 | -11.3 | 2.4(3) | -5.8 |
| 76.1 | 6.2 | 483 | 343 | -6.0 | West | 78.7 | 4.2 | 55.2 | 0.0 | 22.5 | 5.0 | 20.2 | -7.1 | 2.1(2) | – |
| 76.1 | 7.3 | 436 | 281 | -3.0 | Havering, Hornchurch | 79.8 | 4.5 | 53.5 | 2.3 | 34.5 | 6.1 | 11.1 | -9.3 | 0.9 | -1.9 |
| 73.4 | 7.9 | 436 | 300 | -3.0 | Romford | 78.0 | 5.1 | 56.6 | 0.6 | 29.5 | 6.6 | 12.7 | -7.5 | 1.3 | -3.0 |
| 67.4 | 7.3 | 436 | 293 | -3.7 | Upminster | 80.5 | 5.2 | 55.8 | 0.0 | 29.0 | 6.9 | 15.2 | -6.9 | – | – |
| 57.0 | 8.4 | 439 | 285 | -6.5 | Hillingdon, Hayes & Harlington | 79.7 | 5.2 | 44.9 | -4.3 | 44.8 | 9.3 | 10.3 | -5.0 | – | -6.8 |
| 71.9 | 5.4 | 439 | 329 | -3.9 | Ruislip-Northwood | 81.9 | 4.2 | 63.3 | 0.7 | 18.7 | 5.2 | 17.4 | -6.4 | 0.5 | – |
| 55.4 | 7.1 | 439 | 316 | -2.2 | Uxbridge | 78.9 | 2.4 | 56.4 | 0.0 | 29.4 | 6.0 | 12.1 | -6.8 | 2.1(3) | -3.0 |
| 53.6 | 9.2 | 528 | 305 | -1.0 | Hounslow, Brentford & Isleworth | 81.7 | 5.1 | 45.8 | -1.9 | 42.0 | 8.7 | 10.5 | -7.0 | 1.7 | -5.3 |
| 52.7 | 9.4 | 528 | 284 | 0.3 | Feltham & Heston† | 73.9 | 0.2 | 42.8 | -3.7 | 46.1 | 8.7 | 11.2 | -5.0 | – | -6.2 |
| 21.6 | 18.5 | 467 | 270 | -4.5 | Islington, North | 67.3 | 0.8 | 23.7 | -1.6 | 57.4 | 7.5 | 15.1 | -6.7 | 3.8 | -4.6 |
| 12.1 | 16.0 | 467 | 261 | -4.1 | South & Finsbury | 72.5 | 1.4 | 24.7 | 4.1 | 51.1 | 11.0 | 23.3 | -14.8 | 0.9(3) | – |

| ENGLAND | % Owner occupied 1981 | Unemployed % | Poll Tax (household) | Household income | Electorate change % | % voting | % change in voting | % Con | Con change 1987–92 | % Labour | Lab change 1987–92 | % Lib Dem | Lib Dem chg. 1987–92 | % Other | Swing |
|---|---|---|---|---|---|---|---|---|---|---|---|---|---|---|---|
| Kensington & Chelsea, Chelsea | 34.5 | 7.3 | 267 | 312 | -14.5 | 63.3 | 5.7 | 65.1 | 0.5 | 17.5 | 2.0 | 15.3 | -2.7 | 2.1(2) | – |
| Kensington | 28.8 | 11.6 | 267 | 280 | -12.6 | 73.3 | 8.6 | 50.3 | 2.8 | 38.8 | 5.6 | 9.0 | -8.3 | 1.9(3) | -1.4 |
| Kingston-upon-Thames, Kingston | 67.4 | 7.4 | 440 | 315 | -6.9 | 78.4 | -0.1 | 51.6 | -4.6 | 19.3 | 6.2 | 26.3 | -3.9 | 2.8(4) | – |
| Surbiton | 70.5 | 6.2 | 440 | 317 | -6.6 | 82.4 | 4.2 | 54.4 | -1.4 | 18.3 | 3.9 | 26.9 | -1.6 | 0.5 | – |
| Lambeth, Norwood | 29.0 | 18.8 | 540 | 280 | -7.3 | 65.9 | -1.1 | 32.3 | -3.7 | 53.2 | 4.7 | 11.8 | -2.9 | 2.7(2) | -4.2 |
| Streatham† | 38.3 | 14.8 | 540 | 301 | -6.1 | 70.8 | 1.3 | 41.3 | -3.7 | 47.0 | 7.8 | 9.6 | -6.2 | 2.1(4) | -5.7 |
| Vauxhall | 13.7 | 18.8 | 540 | 249 | -6.1 | 62.4 | -1.6 | 27.8 | -1.2 | 54.7 | 4.6 | 14.6 | -3.7 | 2.9(3) | -2.9 |
| Lewisham, Deptford | 28.8 | 19.2 | 250 | 245 | -2.0 | 65.1 | 0.1 | 27.9 | -3.8 | 60.9 | 11.3 | 11.3 | -6.0 | – | -7.5 |
| East† | 38.5 | 12.2 | 250 | 268 | -3.3 | 74.8 | 0.9 | 42.8 | -2.3 | 45.4 | 11.2 | 11.3 | -9.4 | 0.5 | -6.7 |
| West† | 43.5 | 14.2 | 250 | 287 | -5.7 | 73.1 | 0.9 | 42.8 | -3.4 | 47.0 | 9.1 | 9.9 | -6.0 | 0.3 | -6.2 |
| Merton, Mitcham & Morden | 55.5 | 10.9 | 464 | 287 | 1.0 | 80.3 | 4.6 | 46.5 | -1.7 | 43.1 | 7.9 | 9.2 | -7.5 | 1.3 | -4.8 |
| Wimbledon | 67.6 | 7.4 | 464 | 337 | -2.3 | 80.2 | 4.2 | 53.0 | 2.1 | 23.3 | 1.7 | 21.3 | -6.2 | 2.4(3) | – |
| Newham, North-East | 57.5 | 16.3 | 546 | 248 | -2.0 | 60.3 | -3.8 | 30.5 | -0.2 | 58.3 | 6.4 | 11.2 | -6.2 | – | -3.3 |
| North-West | 39.0 | 17.9 | 546 | 260 | -2.3 | 56.0 | -3.4 | 25.9 | 0.5 | 61.1 | 5.7 | 9.4 | -8.0 | 3.6(3) | -2.6 |
| South | 25.4 | 17.8 | 546 | 243 | 1.8 | 60.2 | 1.1 | 38.5 | 4.3 | 46.6 | 3.1 | 14.9 | -7.4 | – | 0.6 |
| Redbridge, Ilford North | 71.5 | 7.5 | 490 | 289 | -2.9 | 78.0 | 5.4 | 54.0 | -1.0 | 34.2 | 6.8 | 11.9 | -5.8 | 0.6 | -3.9 |
| South† | 72.8 | 10.9 | 490 | 295 | -4.8 | 76.8 | 5.0 | 44.4 | -4.0 | 45.3 | 7.8 | 9.6 | -4.5 | 1.9(2) | -5.9 |
| Wanstead & Woodford | 74.6 | 6.7 | 490 | 313 | -3.6 | 78.3 | 5.9 | 60.0 | -1.3 | 21.3 | 4.7 | 16.8 | -5.3 | 1.3(4) | – |
| Richmond, Richmond & Barnes | 55.3 | 7.2 | 464 | 326 | -3.0 | 85.0 | 1.8 | 50.7 | 3.0 | 5.8 | -1.3 | 42.2 | -1.7 | 0.6(3) | – |
| Twickenham | 68.9 | 6.2 | 464 | 334 | -2.5 | 84.3 | 2.8 | 50.4 | -1.4 | 9.2 | 0.9 | 39.7 | 1.3 | – | -3.0 |
| Southwark, Dulwich† | 38.0 | 13.6 | 262 | 283 | -2.2 | 67.9 | -1.4 | 41.8 | -0.6 | 47.3 | 5.3 | 10.9 | -3.6 | 0.9(2) | -4.7 |
| Peckham | 8.0 | 19.3 | 262 | 243 | -1.7 | 53.9 | -1.7 | 23.5 | -2.2 | 61.8 | 7.2 | 13.8 | -4.0 | 2.3(4) | – |
| Southwark & Bermondsey | 2.5 | 21.2 | 262 | 239 | 8.7 | 62.6 | -2.3 | 10.1 | -2.5 | 30.8 | -8.9 | 56.9 | 9.4 | 1.7(2) | – |
| Sutton, Carshalton & Wallington | 58.6 | 7.3 | 471 | 301 | -5.7 | 80.9 | 5.9 | 49.7 | -4.2 | 17.7 | -0.5 | 30.9 | 4.7 | 1.1(2) | – |
| Sutton & Cheam | 78.1 | 6.7 | 471 | 319 | -4.5 | 82.4 | 5.8 | 55.2 | -5.6 | 9.9 | -0.7 | 33.8 | 5.1 | | – |
| Tower Hamlets | | | | | | | | | | | | | | | |
| Bethnal Green & Stepney | 3.6 | 21.0 | 256 | 251 | -0.2 | 65.5 | 7.9 | 17.9 | -1.4 | 55.8 | 7.6 | 22.3 | -9.5 | 4.0(2) | – |

| | | | | | | | | | | | | | | | |
|---|---|---|---|---|---|---|---|---|---|---|---|---|---|---|---|
| -4.2 | 240 | 256 | 20.3 | 5.6 | Bow & Poplar | 65.8 | 8.5 | 18.4 | -1.6 | 49.5 | 3.1 | 27.0 | -5.7 | 5.0(3) | — |
| -2.5 | 298 | 524 | 9.0 | 69.4 | Waltham Forest, Chingford | 78.4 | 1.7 | 59.2 | -3.0 | 24.8 | 9.6 | 13.1 | -7.9 | 2.8(3) | — |
| -0.7 | 270 | 524 | 15.8 | 49.6 | Leyton | 67.4 | -2.1 | 39.0 | -6.1 | 52.6 | 11.4 | 21.2 | -8.5 | 3.2(3) | — |
| 0.9 | 264 | 524 | 15.2 | 45.1 | Walthamstow† | 72.3 | 0.0 | 37.2 | -1.8 | 45.7 | 11.0 | 14.5 | -10.7 | 2.6(3) | -6.4 |
| 1.8 | 288 | 0 | 14.1 | 28.9 | Wandsworth, Battersea | 76.7 | 6.0 | 50.5 | 6.2 | 41.2 | -1.2 | 7.0 | -4.9 | 1.3(2) | 3.7 |
| -1.9 | 289 | 0 | 9.0 | 34.6 | Putney | 77.9 | 2.0 | 52.2 | 1.7 | 36.6 | 0.5 | 9.6 | -2.8 | 1.6(2) | 0.6 |
| 0.3 | 295 | 0 | 13.0 | 43.0 | Tooting | 74.8 | 3.6 | 40.1 | -1.1 | 48.2 | 3.9 | 7.4 | -5.8 | 4.3(4) | -2.5 |
| | | | | | Westminster & London, Cities of | | | | | | | | | | |
| -5.1 | 321 | 254 | 7.8 | 21.1 | City of London & Westminster S | 63.7 | 5.5 | 60.3 | 2.5 | 21.8 | 1.4 | 15.5 | -6.3 | 2.3(4) | — |
| -0.8 | 313 | 57 | 12.0 | 19.7 | Westminster North | 75.8 | 4.7 | 49.0 | 1.6 | 40.6 | 1.1 | 7.5 | -4.6 | 2.9(3) | 0.3 |
| | | | | | *Greater Manchester* | | | | | | | | | | |
| -2.0 | 291 | 363 | 8.0 | 72.6 | Altrincham & Sale | 80.2 | 3.5 | 54.7 | 1.2 | 23.1 | 2.6 | 21.8 | -4.2 | 0.4 | — |
| 0.5 | 215 | 487 | 10.0 | 60.1 | Ashton-under-Lyne | 73.9 | -0.1 | 31.4 | 1.1 | 56.6 | 4.8 | 9.2 | -8.7 | 2.8(2) | -1.9 |
| -1.2 | 247 | 475 | 9.5 | 62.8 | Bolton North-East | 82.3 | 3.6 | 44.9 | 0.5 | 44.5 | 1.8 | 10.3 | -2.7 | 0.4 | -0.7 |
| -0.5 | 195 | 475 | 10.7 | 61.7 | South-East | 75.5 | 0.7 | 28.7 | -2.5 | 54.3 | 0.0 | 10.6 | -3.9 | 6.4(2) | -1.3 |
| 2.2 | 241 | 475 | 8.2 | 73.2 | West | 83.5 | 3.5 | 44.4 | 0.1 | 42.6 | 6.5 | 12.6 | -6.9 | 0.4 | -3.2 |
| 2.3 | 255 | 543 | 6.3 | 74.5 | Bury North | 84.8 | 2.2 | 49.7 | -0.5 | 41.6 | 3.8 | 8.5 | -3.6 | 0.3 | -2.1 |
| 1.2 | 248 | 543 | 7.7 | 67.8 | South | 82.1 | 2.4 | 46.0 | 0.0 | 44.6 | 3.7 | 8.9 | -4.1 | 0.4 | -1.9 |
| -3.2 | 301 | 566 | 4.6 | 83.1 | Cheadle | 84.4 | 3.4 | 58.2 | 3.2 | 11.5 | 2.4 | 30.0 | -5.9 | 0.3 | — |
| -4.4 | 275 | 363 | 9.7 | 65.2 | Davyhulme | 80.5 | 3.2 | 48.0 | 1.4 | 39.2 | 8.8 | 11.5 | -11.5 | 1.3 | -3.7 |
| -1.5 | 216 | 522 | 10.3 | 57.8 | Denton & Reddish | 76.8 | 1.3 | 32.2 | -1.6 | 55.2 | 5.6 | 9.4 | -7.1 | 3.1(2) | -3.6 |
| -3.1 | 213 | 504 | 11.3 | 48.5 | Eccles | 74.1 | -0.4 | 29.4 | -2.0 | 56.9 | 6.1 | 12.1 | -5.8 | 1.6(2) | -4.0 |
| -2.2 | 267 | 566 | 6.0 | 72.3 | Hazel Grove | 85.0 | 3.3 | 44.8 | -0.7 | 11.7 | -0.1 | 43.1 | 1.1 | 0.4 | — |
| -3.9 | 224 | 456 | 10.2 | 50.5 | Heywood & Middleton | 74.9 | 1.1 | 33.4 | -0.9 | 52.3 | 2.4 | 12.3 | -3.6 | 2.1(2) | -1.6 |
| 1.3 | 222 | 497 | 9.0 | 60.9 | Leigh | 75.0 | 0.9 | 25.5 | -0.8 | 61.3 | 2.7 | 12.6 | -2.5 | 0.6 | -1.7 |
| -0.8 | 264 | 480 | 6.9 | 68.4 | Littleborough & Saddleworth | 81.6 | 4.2 | 44.2 | 1.2 | 19.9 | -6.1 | 35.9 | 4.9 | | — |
| 0.9 | 239 | 497 | 8.1 | 66.1 | Makerfield | 76.1 | 0.3 | 27.1 | -0.2 | 60.4 | 4.1 | 9.4 | -7.1 | 3.1(2) | -2.2 |
| -6.1 | 197 | 436 | 12.7 | 44.0 | Manchester, Blackley | 69.3 | -3.6 | 27.8 | -1.0 | 60.2 | 7.7 | 11.3 | -7.5 | 0.8 | -4.4 |
| -10.3 | 167 | 436 | 19.7 | 19.4 | Central | 56.9 | -7.0 | 16.5 | -2.3 | 72.7 | 4.5 | 9.8 | -3.2 | 1.0(2) | -3.4 |
| -2.9 | 179 | 436 | 15.7 | 47.5 | Gorton | 60.8 | -9.6 | 19.5 | -3.8 | 62.3 | 7.9 | 14.0 | -7.7 | 4.2(5) | -5.9 |
| -2.3 | 230 | 436 | 12.1 | 46.0 | Withington | 71.3 | -5.9 | 31.3 | -5.0 | 52.7 | 9.7 | 14.2 | -5.6 | 1.9(2) | -7.3 |
| -8.1 | 183 | 436 | 12.5 | 20.5 | Wythenshawe | 69.7 | -2.5 | 28.4 | -0.2 | 60.5 | 3.7 | 9.7 | -4.3 | 1.3(2) | -2.0 |
| -6.0 | 213 | 493 | 11.6 | 55.9 | Oldham Central & Royton | 74.2 | 4.9 | 32.2 | -2.1 | 51.1 | 2.9 | 15.9 | -1.7 | 0.9 | -2.5 |

## ENGLAND

| | Swing | % Other | Lib Dem chg. 1987-92 | % Lib Dem | Lab change 1987-92 | % Labour | Con change 1987-92 | % Con | % change in voting | % voting | Electorate change % | Household income | Poll Tax (household) | Unemployed % | % Owner occupied 1981 |
|---|---|---|---|---|---|---|---|---|---|---|---|---|---|---|---|
| West | -2.9 | 1.3 | -2.3 | 13.5 | 3.4 | 52.8 | -2.5 | 32.4 | 3.8 | 75.6 | -5.4 | 209 | 493 | 9.9 | 63.3 |
| Rochdale | – | 1.6(2) | -0.6 | 42.8 | 1.4 | 39.4 | -2.4 | 16.2 | 1.9 | 76.5 | 1.2 | 226 | 435 | 10.6 | 56.4 |
| Salford East | -0.9 | 1.8(2) | -2.0 | 11.3 | 1.2 | 60.0 | -0.5 | 26.8 | -1.7 | 64.4 | -9.4 | 176 | 504 | 16.3 | 30.2 |
| Stalybridge & Hyde | -3.2 | 3.5(3) | -5.0 | 9.5 | 3.9 | 52.3 | -2.5 | 34.7 | -0.7 | 73.5 | 0.3 | 238 | 487 | 9.9 | 53.9 |
| Stockport† | -4.5 | 1.0(2) | -8.4 | 13.7 | 8.8 | 44.1 | -0.2 | 41.2 | 4.2 | 82.3 | -3.3 | 261 | 566 | 7.9 | 70.1 |
| Stretford | -3.5 | 0.7 | -2.4 | 9.9 | 4.4 | 59.5 | -2.6 | 29.8 | -3.1 | 68.8 | -5.4 | 205 | 388 | 18.4 | 52.1 |
| Wigan | -1.2 | 2.4(2) | -3.0 | 11.0 | 1.5 | 63.0 | -0.9 | 23.6 | -0.4 | 76.2 | 0.9 | 208 | 497 | 10.4 | 55.3 |
| Worsley | -2.4 | 1.5(2) | -5.3 | 11.6 | 4.3 | 52.4 | -0.5 | 34.6 | 0.6 | 77.7 | -1.4 | 235 | 502 | 10.9 | 54.0 |
| *Hampshire*, Aldershot | – | 1.6 | -1.6 | 27.6 | 1.5 | 13.3 | -1.5 | 57.5 | 4.7 | 78.7 | 1.8 | 325 | 498 | 5.1 | 61.8 |
| Basingstoke | – | 1.0 | -5.7 | 20.6 | 6.1 | 23.8 | -1.4 | 54.6 | 5.8 | 82.8 | 6.3 | 291 | 490 | 6.4 | 53.3 |
| Eastleigh | – | – | -4.0 | 28.0 | 4.0 | 20.7 | 0.0 | 51.3 | 3.6 | 82.9 | 4.8 | 260 | 385 | 6.6 | 70.3 |
| Fareham | – | 1.2 | -5.3 | 24.6 | 4.1 | 13.2 | -0.1 | 61.0 | 3.6 | 81.9 | 5.4 | 277 | 434 | 5.6 | 75.0 |
| Gosport | – | 0.6 | -3.9 | 27.6 | 3.7 | 13.6 | -0.4 | 58.1 | 2.0 | 76.8 | 2.2 | 251 | 432 | 6.7 | 63.0 |
| Hampshire East | – | 1.7(2) | -4.1 | 24.8 | 2.6 | 9.2 | -0.3 | 64.2 | 3.0 | 80.4 | 6.7 | 308 | 464 | 4.9 | 67.4 |
| North-West | – | 1.4 | -5.2 | 27.9 | 3.5 | 12.6 | 0.4 | 58.1 | 2.9 | 80.8 | 4.5 | 296 | 388 | 5.0 | 51.1 |
| Havant | – | 1.4 | -3.1 | 25.0 | 4.6 | 18.7 | -2.2 | 55.0 | 4.4 | 79.0 | -2.8 | 245 | 438 | 8.8 | 57.1 |
| New Forest | – | 0.6 | 2.0 | 28.9 | -0.3 | 8.2 | -2.3 | 62.4 | 4.2 | 80.8 | 0.4 | 239 | 376 | 6.6 | 71.6 |
| Portsmouth North | – | 1.0 | -8.3 | 16.5 | 10.0 | 29.9 | -2.7 | 52.6 | 2.3 | 77.1 | -1.1 | 239 | 352 | 8.2 | 62.0 |
| South | – | 0.8(2) | -0.9 | 42.0 | 1.7 | 14.6 | -0.8 | 42.5 | -2.2 | 69.1 | 1.8 | 222 | 332 | 11.5 | 56.1 |
| Romsey & Waterside | – | 0.8 | 0.1 | 32.1 | 1.1 | 12.6 | -2.0 | 54.4 | 4.1 | 83.2 | 4.4 | 261 | 381 | 6.1 | 70.1 |
| Southampton Itchen† | -6.6 | – | -10.6 | 13.0 | 11.9 | 44.0 | -1.3 | 43.0 | 1.1 | 76.9 | -0.8 | 225 | 493 | 10.5 | 55.7 |
| Test | -5.6 | 1.1(2) | -8.1 | 13.1 | 9.1 | 42.4 | -2.2 | 43.4 | 1.0 | 77.4 | -1.3 | 236 | 493 | 9.1 | 53.2 |
| Winchester | -1.6 | 4.7¶ | -2.4 | 37.8 | 0.9 | 7.4 | -2.3 | 50.1 | 3.1 | 83.5 | 3.5 | 279 | 427 | 4.6 | 58.3 |
| *Hereford & Worcester* | | | | | | | | | | | | | | | |
| Bromsgrove | -4.0 | 1.5 | -8.2 | 13.8 | 7.4 | 30.7 | -0.7 | 54.1 | 6.1 | 82.5 | 2.3 | 259 | 444 | 6.5 | 66.0 |
| Hereford | – | 1.1 | -3.6 | 41.2 | 2.9 | 10.6 | -0.3 | 47.2 | 3.2 | 81.3 | 3.9 | 242 | 388 | 7.9 | 57.1 |
| Leominster | – | 3.7(2) | -4.1 | 27.8 | 3.7 | 11.9 | -1.2 | 56.6 | 4.2 | 81.7 | 1.9 | 249 | 417 | 6.0 | 62.6 |

| Constituency | | | | | | | | | | | | | | | |
|---|---|---|---|---|---|---|---|---|---|---|---|---|---|---|---|
| Worcester | 64.0 | 8.1 | 468 | 233 | 7.6 | 80.9 | 4.2 | 46.3 | -1.8 | 36.2 | 7.8 | 15.9 | -7.5 | 1.6(2) | -4.8 |
| Worcestershire, Mid | 51.7 | 8.1 | 488 | 246 | 4.6 | 81.1 | 4.4 | 49.7 | -1.9 | 35.3 | 7.8 | 14.3 | -6.7 | 0.8 | -4.9 |
| South | 60.1 | 6.1 | 447 | 271 | 4.2 | 80.0 | 4.4 | 54.1 | -1.2 | 15.1 | 4.2 | 29.0 | -2.9 | 1.8 | — |
| Wyre Forest | 67.2 | 7.7 | 488 | 252 | 3.9 | 82.4 | 4.8 | 47.8 | 0.7 | 30.8 | 11.9 | 21.4 | -12.6 | — | — |
| *Hertfordshire,* Broxbourne | 68.8 | 7.2 | 450 | 316 | 2.1 | 80.0 | 4.7 | 62.6 | -0.6 | 21.0 | 4.1 | 16.0 | -3.9 | 0.3 | — |
| Hertford & Stortford | 63.1 | 5.8 | 439 | 332 | 1.5 | 81.0 | 3.3 | 57.5 | 0.0 | 16.3 | 3.5 | 25.0 | -3.4 | 1.3 | — |
| Hertfordshire North | 51.9 | 7.6 | 420 | 299 | 1.7 | 84.4 | 3.3 | 57.0 | 0.1 | 24.3 | 5.9 | 25.4 | -6.4 | 0.5 | — |
| South-West | 63.7 | 5.1 | 490 | 349 | -6.1 | 83.8 | 6.1 | 57.0 | 1.2 | 19.4 | 4.1 | 23.1 | -5.8 | 0.5 | — |
| West | 48.1 | 6.3 | 413 | 297 | -0.7 | 82.4 | 1.4 | 51.5 | 1.8 | 30.0 | 6.0 | 16.2 | -10.2 | 2.3(3) | — |
| Hertsmere | 59.7 | 5.9 | 446 | 327 | -4.7 | 80.9 | 5.5 | 56.8 | 0.2 | 23.7 | 4.1 | 18.9 | -4.9 | 0.7 | — |
| St. Albans | 68.6 | 5.5 | 462 | 348 | -1.5 | 83.5 | 3.2 | 52.8 | 0.3 | 19.4 | 7.9 | 26.3 | -8.2 | 1.4(2) | — |
| Stevenage | 39.0 | 8.6 | 537 | 269 | 1.0 | 83.0 | 2.5 | 45.7 | 3.6 | 37.3 | 11.9 | 16.6 | -15.9 | 0.4 | — |
| Watford | 64.0 | 7.3 | 527 | 313 | -1.7 | 82.3 | 4.4 | 48.8 | 0.1 | 32.7 | 4.5 | 17.2 | -5.9 | 1.2(2) | -2.2 |
| Welwyn & Hatfield | 40.1 | 6.7 | 593 | 290 | -1.9 | 84.3 | 3.4 | 48.4 | 2.7 | 34.5 | 8.1 | 16.7 | -10.6 | 0.4 | — |
| *Humberside,* Beverley | 72.3 | 6.2 | 567 | 266 | 2.6 | 79.9 | 3.6 | 53.3 | 1.1 | 18.6 | 2.1 | 27.8 | -3.5 | 0.3 | — |
| Boothferry | 64.8 | 7.5 | 456 | 258 | 7.4 | 79.7 | 4.0 | 54.8 | -0.9 | 27.5 | 5.6 | 17.7 | -4.7 | — | — |
| Bridlington | 68.4 | 10.7 | 519 | 224 | 5.9 | 77.9 | 4.3 | 50.8 | -4.0 | 23.1 | 5.0 | 26.1 | 0.6 | — | — |
| Brigg & Cleethorpes | 69.9 | 9.7 | 549 | 242 | 2.9 | 78.1 | 1.8 | 49.2 | 0.6 | 35.0 | 12.2 | 14.6 | -14.0 | 1.2 | -6.8 |
| Glanford & Scunthorpe | 58.9 | 9.4 | 507 | 223 | 0.9 | 78.8 | 0.7 | 38.3 | -4.3 | 52.9 | 9.3 | 7.1 | -6.5 | 1.7 | 1.1 |
| Great Grimsby | 64.2 | 12.9 | 542 | 201 | -1.6 | 75.3 | 0.0 | 36.2 | 7.8 | 51.0 | 5.5 | 12.8 | -13.3 | — | -4.4 |
| Hull East | 33.9 | 14.5 | 407 | 180 | 0.5 | 69.3 | -1.3 | 23.8 | -2.2 | 62.9 | 6.6 | 12.6 | -5.0 | 0.7 | -4.9 |
| North | 38.9 | 14.2 | 407 | 199 | -2.6 | 66.0 | -3.6 | 22.8 | -4.6 | 56.5 | 5.3 | 20.2 | -1.3 | 0.5 | -3.5 |
| West | 41.6 | 17.0 | 407 | 182 | 0.9 | 65.7 | -1.9 | 28.6 | -1.7 | 57.3 | 5.4 | 13.2 | -4.5 | 0.8 | — |
| *Isle of Wight* | 71.4 | 12.0 | 416 | 197 | 1.2 | 79.8 | 0.2 | 47.9 | -3.2 | 6.0 | 0.1 | 45.6 | 2.7 | 0.4 | — |
| *Kent,* Ashford | 59.3 | 7.5 | 343 | 253 | 2.5 | 79.2 | 3.5 | 54.6 | -1.9 | 20.0 | 5.3 | 24.1 | -3.3 | 1.4 | — |
| Canterbury | 64.0 | 8.0 | 365 | 243 | -1.0 | 78.1 | 4.2 | 50.8 | -3.0 | 15.2 | -1.7 | 32.4 | 5.0 | 1.6(2) | -4.4 |
| Dartford | 64.1 | 6.7 | 402 | 299 | -0.4 | 83.1 | 4.1 | 51.9 | -1.6 | 34.7 | 7.2 | 12.6 | -5.6 | 0.8(2) | -5.2 |
| Dover | 58.6 | 9.2 | 359 | 248 | -0.1 | 83.5 | 3.7 | 44.1 | -1.9 | 42.6 | 8.5 | 10.8 | -9.1 | 2.5(4) | — |
| Faversham | 64.8 | 10.1 | 362 | 274 | 3.7 | 79.7 | 2.8 | 50.1 | -1.0 | 25.1 | 4.3 | 24.3 | -3.8 | 0.4 | — |
| Folkestone & Hythe | 65.3 | 9.5 | 383 | 235 | 2.3 | 79.6 | 1.3 | 52.3 | -3.0 | 12.1 | 4.7 | 35.3 | -1.9 | 0.2 | — |
| Gillingham | 75.2 | 8.7 | 327 | 278 | 0.2 | 80.3 | 5.0 | 52.3 | -0.7 | 23.5 | 6.4 | 23.4 | -6.5 | 0.8(2) | — |
| Gravesham | 62.7 | 9.2 | 288 | 269 | -2.8 | 83.5 | 4.2 | 49.7 | -0.4 | 40.4 | 5.5 | 8.9 | -6.2 | 1.1(3) | -3.0 |
| Kent, Mid | 68.4 | 8.4 | 231 | 288 | 2.8 | 79.7 | 7.8 | 56.7 | 1.6 | 23.6 | 5.5 | 19.3 | -7.4 | 0.4 | — |

**ENGLAND**

| Constituency | % Owner occupied 1991 | Unemployed % | Poll Tax (household) | Household income | Electorate change % | % voting | % change in voting | % Con | Con change 1987–92 | % Labour | Lab change 1987–92 | % Lib Dem | Lib Dem chg. 1987–92 | % Other | Swing |
|---|---|---|---|---|---|---|---|---|---|---|---|---|---|---|---|
| Maidstone | 63.0 | 6.7 | 427 | 279 | −0.2 | 80.1 | 4.1 | 54.2 | 1.7 | 18.0 | 5.5 | 26.3 | −7.5 | 1.5(2) | − |
| Medway | 62.0 | 10.0 | 97 | 266 | −3.7 | 80.2 | 7.2 | 52.3 | 1.3 | 34.6 | 4.8 | 9.6 | −8.5 | 3.5(2) | −1.7 |
| Sevenoaks | 62.4 | 5.0 | 370 | 301 | −2.9 | 81.4 | 4.9 | 57.5 | −1.4 | 16.4 | 3.2 | 24.4 | −3.5 | 1.7(2) | − |
| Thanet North | 69.6 | 12.8 | 340 | 208 | 1.7 | 76.0 | 3.8 | 57.2 | −0.8 | 23.5 | 6.8 | 17.7 | −5.6 | 1.6 | − |
| South | 68.5 | 10.2 | 331 | 222 | −0.5 | 78.2 | 4.5 | 51.7 | −2.6 | 28.1 | 7.2 | 18.3 | −6.4 | 1.8 | − |
| Tonbridge & Malling | 64.9 | 6.1 | 408 | 306 | 0.6 | 82.7 | 4.9 | 57.2 | 0.3 | 18.1 | 5.0 | 23.5 | −6.0 | 1.3(2) | − |
| Tunbridge Wells | 59.7 | 5.4 | 404 | 290 | 0.7 | 78.1 | 3.9 | 56.9 | −1.5 | 13.8 | 2.3 | 28.4 | −1.6 | 0.8(2) | − |
| *Lancashire,* Blackburn | 61.2 | 10.7 | 485 | 204 | −2.1 | 75.1 | 0.1 | 37.5 | −2.6 | 48.4 | −1.5 | 11.5 | 1.5 | 2.6(3) | −0.6 |
| Blackpool North | 70.5 | 11.7 | 570 | 208 | −1.4 | 77.6 | 4.4 | 47.7 | −0.3 | 41.0 | 10.0 | 10.6 | −10.3 | 0.7(2) | −5.1 |
| South | 76.4 | 11.5 | 570 | 217 | −1.3 | 77.4 | 3.9 | 45.2 | −2.8 | 41.4 | 9.4 | 12.9 | −7.0 | 0.4 | −6.1 |
| Burnley | 69.6 | 8.0 | 363 | 211 | 4.5 | 74.4 | −4.4 | 30.6 | −3.2 | 53.0 | 4.6 | 16.4 | −1.4 | − | −3.9 |
| Chorley | 75.9 | 7.0 | 554 | 257 | 2.8 | 82.8 | 5.9 | 47.2 | −0.8 | 40.7 | 6.0 | 11.5 | −4.6 | 0.6 | −3.4 |
| Fylde | 72.0 | 4.8 | 513 | 274 | −2.4 | 78.5 | 1.5 | 61.4 | 0.7 | 18.8 | 4.5 | 19.3 | −4.9 | 0.5 | − |
| Hyndburn† | 77.8 | 7.5 | 426 | 224 | −3.3 | 84.0 | 3.5 | 42.9 | −1.5 | 46.9 | 7.1 | 9.9 | −5.3 | 0.3 | −4.3 |
| Lancashire West† | 57.9 | 10.1 | 514 | 247 | 1.8 | 82.6 | 2.9 | 43.9 | 0.2 | 47.1 | 5.6 | 7.6 | −7.2 | 1.4(2) | −2.7 |
| Lancaster | 67.4 | 7.3 | 514 | 235 | 2.6 | 78.8 | −0.4 | 45.6 | −1.1 | 39.2 | 6.8 | 14.1 | −5.8 | 1.1(2) | −3.9 |
| Morecambe & Lunesdale | 77.4 | 11.2 | 521 | 223 | 1.3 | 78.4 | 2.2 | 50.9 | −1.7 | 24.9 | 2.4 | 21.7 | −3.2 | 2.5(2) | − |
| Pendle† | 75.5 | 7.1 | 373 | 212 | 0.8 | 82.9 | 1.1 | 40.3 | −0.1 | 44.2 | 8.9 | 15.0 | −9.3 | 0.5 | −4.5 |
| Preston | 54.3 | 13.4 | 577 | 200 | 2.4 | 71.7 | 2.7 | 27.8 | −0.7 | 54.3 | 1.8 | 17.2 | −1.8 | 0.7 | −1.3 |
| Ribble Valley‡ | 79.7 | 3.9 | 551 | 252 | 3.9 | 85.7 | 6.7 | 52.4 | −8.5 | 6.5 | −11.2 | 40.6 | 19.2 | 0.5(2) | − |
| Rossendale & Darwen† | 68.8 | 7.1 | 466 | 233 | 2.5 | 83.1 | 2.8 | 43.7 | −2.9 | 43.9 | 5.6 | 11.3 | −3.8 | 1.1(2) | −4.2 |
| South Ribble | 76.7 | 6.3 | 563 | 261 | 4.7 | 83.0 | 0.4 | 47.5 | 0.3 | 38.3 | 5.2 | 13.8 | −6.0 | 0.4 | −2.5 |
| Wyre | 80.6 | 7.0 |  | 237 | 1.1 | 79.5 | 4.2 | 54.6 | 1.6 | 33.0 | 11.8 | 11.9 | −12.1 | 0.5 | − |
| *Leicestershire,* Blaby | 78.1 | 5.3 | 472 | 272 | 6.1 | 83.4 | 2.5 | 57.9 | −2.6 | 20.7 | 6.2 | 20.2 | −4.8 | 1.1(2) | − |
| Bosworth | 74.2 | 5.6 | 474 | 266 | 4.0 | 84.1 | 2.8 | 54.2 | −0.2 | 26.0 | 8.8 | 18.7 | −8.6 | 1.1 | − |
| Harborough | 76.9 | 4.8 | 555 | 270 | 2.4 | 82.1 | 2.8 | 54.6 | −4.9 | 11.9 | −1.0 | 33.0 | 5.3 | 0.5 | − |
| Leicester East | 54.6 | 10.1 | 564 | 189 | −4.4 | 78.7 | 0.1 | 33.7 | −8.8 | 56.3 | 10.2 | 8.1 | −3.3 | 1.9(2) | −9.5 |

| Constituency | | | | | | | | | | | | | | | |
|---|---|---|---|---|---|---|---|---|---|---|---|---|---|---|---|
| South | 52.0 | 11.7 | 564 | 202 | -2.9 | 75.2 | -1.8 | 34.6 | -6.2 | 52.3 | 8.2 | 11.7 | -2.1 | 1.3(2) | -7.2 |
| West | 43.4 | 13.1 | 564 | 192 | -3.4 | 73.7 | 0.2 | 38.5 | -3.5 | 46.8 | 2.3 | 13.3 | -0.2 | 1.4(2) | -2.9 |
| Leicestershire North-West | 66.2 | 6.7 | 517 | 259 | 2.6 | 86.1 | 3.3 | 45.5 | -2.1 | 43.9 | 9.7 | 10.2 | -7.0 | 0.4 | -5.9 |
| Loughborough | 69.6 | 6.3 | 476 | 264 | 2.4 | 78.5 | -0.7 | 50.7 | -4.0 | 32.4 | 7.9 | 15.1 | -4.6 | 1.8(2) | -5.9 |
| Rutland & Melton | 65.9 | 4.8 | 490 | 267 | 4.0 | 80.8 | 4.0 | 59.0 | -3.0 | 20.0 | 5.5 | 19.4 | -4.1 | 1.7(2) | — |
| *Lincolnshire* | | | | | | | | | | | | | | | |
| Gainsborough & Horncastle | 61.4 | 6.8 | 397 | 225 | 3.3 | 80.9 | 3.9 | 54.0 | 0.6 | 19.9 | 8.5 | 26.1 | -9.1 | — | — |
| Grantham | 57.7 | 5.8 | 398 | 235 | 5.1 | 79.3 | 4.3 | 56.2 | -0.9 | 26.6 | 6.1 | 14.9 | -6.4 | 2.3 | — |
| Holland-with-Boston | 59.0 | 6.8 | 415 | 206 | 3.6 | 77.9 | 5.7 | 55.1 | -2.8 | 29.0 | 8.4 | 15.9 | -4.8 | 1.0 | — |
| Lincoln | 57.2 | 10.6 | 418 | 211 | 2.4 | 79.2 | 3.5 | 46.1 | -0.4 | 42.8 | 9.2 | 10.1 | -9.3 | 1.6 | -4.8 |
| Lindsey East | 64.4 | 12.0 | 405 | 198 | 8.1 | 78.1 | 2.9 | 51.1 | -1.1 | 15.2 | 4.0 | 32.1 | -4.6 | — | — |
| Stamford & Spalding | 60.7 | 5.5 | 411 | 234 | 6.5 | 81.2 | 3.4 | 59.0 | 2.5 | 21.5 | 8.9 | 19.6 | -11.4 | 1.6(2) | -3.1 |
| *Merseyside,* Birkenhead | 50.3 | 17.9 | 590 | 201 | -4.5 | 73.0 | 0.6 | 25.1 | -1.2 | 63.6 | 4.9 | 9.7 | -5.3 | 2.9(2) | -5.9 |
| Bootle | 40.4 | 16.8 | 544 | 180 | -3.4 | 72.5 | -0.4 | 16.0 | -4.1 | 74.6 | 7.7 | 6.6 | -6.5 | 2.6(3) | -3.2 |
| Crosby | 81.4 | 7.9 | 544 | 275 | -1.6 | 82.5 | 2.8 | 47.4 | 1.3 | 25.7 | 7.7 | 24.3 | -11.6 | 3.8(2) | -2.9 |
| Knowsley North | 22.6 | 19.7 | 525 | 169 | -7.9 | 72.8 | -1.4 | 14.4 | 1.9 | 77.5 | 7.6 | 4.3 | -11.9 | 0.5 | -2.2 |
| South | 38.5 | 16.3 | 525 | 204 | -5.1 | 74.7 | 0.6 | 21.3 | -0.3 | 68.6 | 4.1 | 9.6 | -4.3 | 17.5(3)¶ | — |
| Liverpool Broadgreen | 52.4 | 18.4 | 585 | 187 | -4.8 | 69.6 | -6.3 | 12.9 | -2.6 | 43.2 | -5.4 | 26.4 | -9.6 | 2.7(2) | -0.3 |
| Garston | 38.6 | 15.1 | 585 | 211 | -6.1 | 70.6 | -5.1 | 26.9 | 3.0 | 57.1 | 3.6 | 13.3 | -9.1 | 0.3 | — |
| Mossley Hill | 58.2 | 17.2 | 585 | 216 | -0.9 | 68.5 | -6.6 | 10.3 | -7.2 | 41.6 | 2.7 | 47.9 | 4.2 | 3.4(2) | -2.5 |
| Riverside | 19.5 | 23.1 | 585 | 163 | -7.0 | 54.6 | -10.7 | 11.5 | -2.3 | 75.9 | 2.7 | 9.2 | -2.0 | 3.1(3) | — |
| Walton | 45.6 | 19.1 | 585 | 185 | -4.1 | 67.4 | -6.2 | 12.5 | -1.9 | 72.4 | 8.0 | 12.0 | -9.2 | 3.0(2) | -2.7 |
| West Derby | 28.3 | 18.3 | 585 | 178 | -6.3 | 69.8 | -3.6 | 16.6 | -2.5 | 68.2 | 2.9 | 12.2 | -3.3 | 0.5 | -1.5 |
| St. Helens North | 55.8 | 9.7 | 484 | 244 | 0.6 | 77.4 | 1.1 | 28.5 | 1.2 | 57.9 | 4.3 | 13.1 | -6.0 | 0.6 | -4.3 |
| South | 60.0 | 11.5 | 484 | 229 | -2.8 | 73.8 | 2.5 | 24.5 | -2.3 | 61.0 | 6.4 | 13.9 | -4.8 | 1.3(2) | — |
| Southport† | 74.2 | 9.2 | 544 | 240 | 0.0 | 77.6 | 1.3 | 47.0 | 2.5 | 10.2 | 3.8 | 41.5 | -6.4 | 1.4(2) | -3.8 |
| Wallasey† | 62.7 | 14.0 | 590 | 210 | -2.3 | 82.5 | 2.7 | 41.9 | -0.5 | 49.0 | 7.0 | 7.7 | -7.9 | 1.5(2) | -3.0 |
| Wirral South | 72.2 | 8.0 | 590 | 263 | -1.8 | 82.4 | 2.9 | 50.8 | 0.6 | 34.6 | 6.6 | 13.1 | -8.7 | 1.7(2) | -2.0 |
| West | 70.6 | 9.1 | 590 | 242 | -1.8 | 81.6 | 3.6 | 52.7 | 0.8 | 31.0 | 4.7 | 14.6 | -5.6 | 0.5 | -5.3 |
| *Norfolk,* Great Yarmouth | 61.6 | 13.0 | 467 | 213 | 3.8 | 77.9 | 3.5 | 47.9 | -3.8 | 38.0 | 6.8 | 13.6 | -3.5 | 0.3 | — |
| Norfolk, Mid | 68.6 | 5.8 | 457 | 253 | 8.7 | 81.6 | 3.5 | 54.3 | -2.4 | 25.4 | 7.6 | 19.9 | -5.6 | 1.2(2) | — |
| North | 59.3 | 7.5 | 348 | 227 | 5.7 | 81.0 | 3.5 | 48.2 | -5.1 | 23.2 | 3.3 | 27.4 | 2.4 | 0.5 | — |
| North-West | 59.8 | 8.4 | 391 | 212 | 5.0 | 80.7 | 1.8 | 52.1 | 1.6 | 33.6 | 16.1 | 13.8 | -18.2 | — | — |

| % Owner occupied 1981 | Unemployed % | Poll Tax (household) | Household income | Electorate change % | ENGLAND | % voting | % change in voting | % Con | Con change 1987-92 | % Labour | Lab change 1987-92 | % Lib Dem | Lib Dem chg. 1987-92 | % Other | Swing |
|---|---|---|---|---|---|---|---|---|---|---|---|---|---|---|---|
| | | | | | ENGLAND | | | | | | | | | | |
| 67.9 | 5.2 | 444 | 261 | 4.2 | South | 84.0 | 3.1 | 52.6 | -0.9 | 18.1 | 5.4 | 27.0 | -6.9 | 2.3(4) | – |
| 59.7 | 7.2 | 436 | 233 | 4.6 | South-West | 79.3 | 3.3 | 54.6 | -3.0 | 27.1 | 6.1 | 18.2 | -3.2 | 1.0(2) | -7.6 |
| 58.4 | 6.7 | 485 | 222 | 0.9 | Norwich North | 81.8 | 2.6 | 43.3 | -2.6 | 42.8 | 12.6 | 12.9 | -11.0 | 1.8(2) | -5.7 |
| 37.2 | 10.3 | 516 | 223 | -1.3 | South | 80.6 | 0.0 | 36.6 | -0.6 | 48.7 | 10.8 | 12.9 | -12.0 | 1.4 | -1.4 |
| 41.5 | 8.6 | 450 | 245 | 3.4 | Northamptonshire, Corby | 82.9 | 3.3 | 44.5 | 0.2 | 43.9 | 3.0 | 10.2 | -4.6 | 0.7 | – |
| 60.8 | 5.5 | 458 | 279 | 3.7 | Daventry | 82.7 | 4.6 | 58.4 | 0.5 | 24.3 | 3.8 | 16.5 | -5.0 | – | – |
| 68.2 | 6.8 | 443 | 237 | 2.9 | Kettering | 82.6 | 3.8 | 52.0 | 0.9 | 32.1 | 12.4 | 16.0 | -13.3 | – | -5.4 |
| 60.0 | 7.9 | 440 | 235 | -0.2 | Northampton North | 78.5 | 3.9 | 45.8 | -2.2 | 38.6 | 8.5 | 15.2 | -5.5 | 0.4 | -2.8 |
| 62.9 | 8.4 | 440 | 252 | 9.7 | South | 79.9 | 4.7 | 55.3 | -0.4 | 29.8 | 5.3 | 14.9 | -3.7 | – | -3.0 |
| 62.7 | 7.3 | 295 | 257 | 4.9 | Wellingborough | 81.9 | 3.8 | 53.4 | 0.6 | 33.9 | 6.7 | 12.7 | -7.3 | – | – |
| | | | | | Northumberland | | | | | | | | | | |
| 37.3 | 9.3 | 465 | 225 | 1.0 | Berwick-upon-Tweed | 79.1 | 1.8 | 32.8 | 3.3 | 22.9 | 5.4 | 44.4 | -7.7 | 1.0 | – |
| 49.3 | 9.8 | 542 | 200 | 3.1 | Blyth Valley | 80.8 | 2.6 | 15.6 | -1.3 | 49.9 | 7.4 | 33.5 | -7.1 | 1.6 | – |
| 56.5 | 5.6 | 578 | 254 | 2.6 | Hexham | 85.8 | 5.8 | 50.3 | 0.7 | 27.3 | 9.3 | 20.8 | -10.9 | 1.4 | – |
| 42.7 | 10.2 | 485 | 211 | 1.3 | Wansbeck | 79.3 | 1.3 | 23.6 | 4.2 | 59.7 | 2.2 | 15.3 | -7.8 | 1.3 | – |
| 71.1 | 4.4 | 467 | 282 | 0.7 | North Yorkshire, Harrogate | 78.0 | 3.9 | 53.9 | -1.7 | 12.2 | 2.0 | 32.7 | -1.7 | 0.9 | – |
| 56.9 | 4.7 | 390 | 262 | 4.5 | Richmond (Yorks) | 78.4 | 6.3 | 61.9 | 0.6 | 11.6 | -0.2 | 25.7 | -1.3 | – | – |
| 65.8 | 4.2 | 391 | 231 | 2.4 | Ryedale | 81.7 | 2.5 | 56.1 | 2.7 | 13.8 | 5.7 | 30.1 | -8.4 | 1.5 | – |
| 64.1 | 9.8 | 342 | 205 | 8.1 | Scarborough | 77.2 | 4.0 | 49.8 | -0.9 | 29.9 | 6.2 | 18.9 | -6.8 | – | -4.7 |
| 68.0 | 5.6 | 398 | 264 | 4.6 | Selby | 80.2 | 2.5 | 50.2 | -1.4 | 34.8 | 8.1 | 14.9 | -6.7 | – | – |
| 65.3 | 4.1 | 387 | 259 | -0.1 | Skipton & Ripon | 81.3 | 3.5 | 58.4 | -0.6 | 14.6 | 3.4 | 27.0 | -1.4 | 1.0(2) | -5.1 |
| 58.3 | 7.5 | 339 | 222 | 2.2 | York† | 81.0 | 2.6 | 39.3 | -2.4 | 49.1 | 7.7 | 10.6 | -5.3 | – | -7.1 |
| 58.4 | 9.4 | 207 | 207 | 0.8 | Nottinghamshire, Ashfield | 80.5 | 3.2 | 32.6 | -1.0 | 54.9 | 13.2 | 12.5 | -12.2 | – | -3.9 |
| 49.5 | 9.5 | 225 | 225 | 1.9 | Bassetlaw | 79.4 | 1.9 | 35.0 | -2.5 | 53.4 | 5.3 | 11.6 | -2.8 | 0.5 | -6.5 |
| 69.9 | 6.5 | 566 | 247 | 0.8 | Broxtowe | 83.4 | 4.2 | 51.0 | -2.6 | 34.8 | 10.5 | 13.8 | -8.3 | 0.3 | -5.9 |
| 72.4 | 6.8 | 502 | 242 | 0.3 | Gedling | 82.3 | 3.1 | 53.1 | -1.3 | 34.5 | 10.5 | 12.1 | -9.5 | – | -10.6 |
| 57.0 | 9.8 | 496 | 207 | | Mansfield | 82.2 | 3.8 | 33.1 | -4.3 | 54.4 | 16.9 | 12.6 | -9.6 | – | – |

| Constituency | | | | | | | | | | | | | | | |
|---|---|---|---|---|---|---|---|---|---|---|---|---|---|---|---|
| Newark | 58.3 | 8.5 | 527 | 227 | 2.3 | 82.2 | 4.6 | 50.4 | -3.1 | 35.8 | 8.1 | 13.0 | -5.8 | 0.8 | -5.6 |
| Nottingham East† | 41.7 | 18.9 | 509 | 204 | -0.5 | 70.1 | 1.3 | 36.4 | -6.5 | 52.6 | 10.6 | 7.8 | -6.9 | 3.3(3) | -8.6 |
| North | 29.1 | 12.5 | 509 | 186 | -0.2 | 75.0 | 2.4 | 35.1 | -6.5 | 55.7 | 10.8 | 8.6 | -3.1 | 0.5 | -8.7 |
| South† | 42.4 | 11.9 | 509 | 208 | 0.0 | 74.2 | 0.7 | 41.8 | -2.9 | 47.7 | 7.2 | 10.0 | -4.8 | 0.5 | -5.7 |
| Rushcliffe | 70.8 | 6.3 | 504 | 280 | 4.7 | 83.0 | 3.1 | 54.4 | -4.4 | 23.2 | 6.6 | 20.0 | -3.0 | 2.4(3) | -5.5 |
| Sherwood† | 58.9 | 8.0 | 491 | 241 | 2.1 | 85.5 | 3.6 | 42.9 | -3.0 | 47.5 | 9.3 | 9.6 | -6.3 | 0.4 | -6.2 |
| *Oxfordshire*, Banbury | 54.6 | 6.3 | 484 | 275 | 3.5 | 81.5 | 5.4 | 55.0 | -1.2 | 26.5 | 6.1 | 18.1 | -5.3 | 1.4(2) | – |
| Henley | 65.6 | 4.2 | 560 | 300 | -1.1 | 79.8 | 4.9 | 59.7 | -1.4 | 14.9 | 2.3 | 24.1 | -2.2 | 2.3(3) | – |
| Oxford East | 54.4 | 8.0 | 735 | 242 | 1.5 | 74.6 | -4.4 | 34.4 | -6.0 | 50.4 | 7.4 | 13.0 | -2.6 | 1.9(4) | -6.7 |
| West & Abingdon | 58.5 | 5.6 | 621 | 270 | 4.5 | 76.7 | -1.7 | 45.4 | -1.0 | 13.8 | -1.1 | 39.0 | 1.6 | 1.5 | – |
| Wantage | 58.9 | 4.3 | 538 | 292 | 2.8 | 82.7 | 4.8 | 54.1 | 0.2 | 19.4 | 3.8 | 25.0 | -5.5 | 1.5(3) | – |
| Witney | 60.4 | 4.7 | 469 | 280 | 4.2 | 81.9 | 4.6 | 56.4 | -1.1 | 21.3 | 4.6 | 20.8 | -4.9 | 1.4 | – |
| *Shropshire*, Ludlow | 58.0 | 5.8 | 440 | 246 | 4.2 | 80.9 | 3.8 | 51.5 | -2.4 | 21.0 | 5.9 | 26.1 | -4.8 | 1.2 | – |
| Shrewsbury & Atcham | 62.5 | 6.2 | 497 | 233 | -0.1 | 82.5 | 5.4 | 45.8 | -2.0 | 26.0 | 6.2 | 27.0 | -4.2 | – | – |
| Shropshire North | 58.2 | 5.7 | 502 | 233 | 7.2 | 77.7 | 2.2 | 50.5 | -1.7 | 24.2 | 3.8 | 25.3 | -2.2 | – | – |
| Wrekin, The | 40.8 | 10.2 | 571 | 235 | 10.2 | 77.1 | -1.2 | 38.8 | -1.8 | 48.3 | 5.5 | 11.5 | -5.2 | 1.4 | -3.6 |
| *Somerset*, Bridgwater | 59.9 | 9.1 | 499 | 229 | 6.2 | 79.5 | 1.3 | 46.8 | -4.8 | 21.7 | 3.5 | 29.7 | -0.6 | 1.8(3) | – |
| Somerton & Frome | 62.4 | 6.8 | 520 | 247 | 3.8 | 82.8 | 3.3 | 47.5 | -6.2 | 10.4 | 0.4 | 40.2 | 3.9 | 1.9(2) | – |
| Taunton | 58.7 | 6.7 | 467 | 231 | 5.1 | 82.3 | 3.0 | 46.0 | -5.3 | 12.7 | -2.2 | 40.8 | 7.1 | 0.4 | – |
| Wells | 66.5 | 7.6 | 511 | 250 | 3.9 | 82.7 | 3.1 | 49.6 | -4.0 | 10.6 | 1.9 | 38.0 | 0.5 | 1.8 | – |
| Yeovil | 60.3 | 7.1 | 519 | 240 | 3.8 | 82.0 | 2.3 | 36.9 | -4.3 | 9.6 | 2.3 | 51.7 | 0.3 | 1.7(3) | – |
| *South Yorkshire* | | | | | | | | | | | | | | | |
| Barnsley Central | 47.2 | 12.2 | 338 | 198 | -0.9 | 70.5 | 0.5 | 19.7 | 1.6 | 69.3 | 2.5 | 11.1 | -4.1 | – | -0.5 |
| East | 42.6 | 12.0 | 338 | 197 | 0.8 | 72.9 | 0.2 | 14.2 | 0.2 | 77.2 | 2.7 | 8.6 | -2.9 | – | -1.3 |
| West & Penistone | 50.2 | 10.1 | 338 | 208 | 3.8 | 75.7 | 0.1 | 28.0 | 1.4 | 58.3 | 0.9 | 11.7 | -4.3 | 2.0 | 0.2 |
| Doncaster Central | 52.6 | 13.7 | 373 | 218 | -1.2 | 74.2 | 0.6 | 33.5 | -1.7 | 54.3 | 3.2 | 11.8 | -1.8 | 0.4 | -2.5 |
| North | 49.6 | 14.2 | 373 | 207 | 2.4 | 73.9 | 0.8 | 25.9 | 1.5 | 61.8 | 0.0 | 12.3 | -1.6 | – | 0.7 |
| Don Valley | 56.3 | 11.0 | 373 | 223 | 2.5 | 76.3 | 2.5 | 31.7 | -0.5 | 55.0 | 1.9 | 11.9 | -2.7 | 1.4 | -1.2 |
| Rotherham | 40.7 | 13.2 | 437 | 199 | -1.0 | 71.7 | 2.4 | 23.7 | 1.7 | 63.9 | 4.3 | 12.3 | -5.9 | – | -1.3 |
| Rother Valley | 55.2 | 9.8 | 437 | 231 | 2.8 | 75.0 | -0.6 | 26.9 | 1.9 | 60.5 | 4.1 | 12.7 | -5.8 | – | -1.1 |
| Sheffield Attercliffe | 43.4 | 11.0 | 369 | 205 | 3.2 | 71.8 | -1.1 | 26.3 | 3.7 | 57.5 | -0.3 | 14.7 | -4.9 | 1.5 | 2.0 |
| Brightside | 25.2 | 14.3 | 369 | 178 | -1.8 | 66.3 | -2.5 | 16.8 | 1.1 | 70.4 | 0.5 | 12.5 | -1.9 | 0.4 | 0.3 |
| Central | 24.1 | 18.3 | 369 | 156 | -3.4 | 56.1 | -6.3 | 16.5 | -0.6 | 68.7 | 0.9 | 11.6 | -2.3 | 3.2(3) | -0.8 |

| % Owner occupied 1981 | Unemployed % | Poll Tax (household) | Household income | Electorate change % | ENGLAND | % voting | % change in voting | % Con | Con change 1987-92 | % Labour | Lab change 1987-92 | % Lib Dem | Lib Dem chg. 1987-92 | % Other | Swing |
|---|---|---|---|---|---|---|---|---|---|---|---|---|---|---|---|
| 72.7 | 7.4 | 369 | 255 | 3.3 | Hallam | 70.8 | -3.9 | 45.5 | -0.8 | 20.1 | -0.2 | 33.1 | 0.6 | 1.2(3) | — |
| 40.4 | 12.1 | 369 | 193 | -4.0 | Heeley | 70.9 | -1.1 | 25.9 | -0.3 | 55.7 | 2.3 | 18.4 | -1.9 | — | -1.3 |
| 60.4 | 8.4 | 369 | 234 | 1.4 | Hillsborough | 77.2 | -0.8 | 19.5 | 2.0 | 46.2 | 2.1 | 34.3 | -4.2 | — | — |
| 41.7 | 11.7 | 437 | 224 | 1.6 | Wentworth | 74.0 | 1.5 | 21.8 | 0.0 | 68.5 | 3.4 | 9.6 | -3.4 | — | -1.7 |
| 65.5 | 8.6 | 454 | 239 | 2.8 | *Staffordshire, Burton* | 82.4 | 3.9 | 49.7 | -1.0 | 40.0 | 6.4 | 10.3 | -5.5 | 0.8 | -3.7 |
| 61.4 | 8.9 | 519 | 237 | 6.6 | Cannock & Burntwood† | 84.2 | 4.4 | 43.6 | -0.9 | 46.0 | 6.5 | 9.6 | -6.3 | 0.6 | -3.7 |
| 58.3 | 7.7 | 516 | 227 | 0.8 | Newcastle-under-Lyme | 80.3 | -0.4 | 29.6 | 1.7 | 47.9 | 7.4 | 21.9 | -9.0 | 0.6(2) | — |
| 65.1 | 6.5 | 464 | 277 | 3.1 | Stafford | 82.9 | 3.5 | 49.9 | -1.5 | 32.3 | 11.1 | 17.3 | -10.2 | 0.4 | — |
| 64.0 | 7.1 | 485 | 256 | 3.0 | Staffordshire, Mid‡ | 85.7 | 6.3 | 49.6 | -1.0 | 39.7 | 15.0 | 10.3 | -12.9 | 3.8(2) | -8.0 |
| 77.5 | 5.3 | 475 | 258 | 1.0 | Moorlands | 83.7 | 3.3 | 46.6 | -6.3 | 34.8 | 6.0 | 14.9 | -3.5 | — | -6.2 |
| 67.5 | 7.5 | 424 | 281 | 4.4 | South | 81.5 | 3.4 | 59.7 | -1.2 | 26.1 | 7.1 | 14.2 | -5.9 | 1.6 | — |
| 58.1 | 10.2 | 491 | 248 | 6.1 | South-East | 82.0 | 1.6 | 50.7 | 3.5 | 38.2 | 12.1 | 9.6 | -17.1 | 0.4 | — |
| 52.9 | 9.7 | 502 | 196 | -0.7 | Stoke-on-Trent Central | 68.1 | -0.6 | 27.9 | -3.1 | 58.0 | 5.5 | 13.6 | -2.8 | 0.7 | -4.3 |
| 60.2 | 7.9 | 502 | 202 | -1.4 | North | 73.4 | 0.5 | 29.2 | -2.1 | 56.7 | 9.6 | 13.3 | -8.2 | 0.5 | -5.9 |
| 58.1 | 7.6 | 502 | 211 | 0.7 | South | 74.2 | 0.5 | 36.8 | -1.0 | 49.7 | 2.2 | 13.0 | -1.7 | 0.9 | -1.6 |
| 51.3 | 5.1 | 414 | 253 | 3.9 | *Suffolk, Bury St. Edmunds* | 78.7 | 4.6 | 53.5 | -5.8 | 23.6 | 6.2 | 22.0 | 0.5 | 1.4(2) | — |
| 56.3 | 7.9 | 598 | 239 | -0.7 | Ipswich† | 80.3 | 3.2 | 43.3 | -1.1 | 43.8 | 1.1 | 11.4 | -1.2 | 1.5(2) | -1.1 |
| 63.2 | 5.4 | 501 | 253 | 4.5 | Suffolk Central | 80.3 | 4.0 | 49.6 | -4.1 | 23.5 | 3.9 | 25.4 | -1.3 | 1.8(2) | — |
| 60.9 | 5.3 | 419 | 259 | 4.8 | Coastal | 81.6 | 3.7 | 53.6 | -2.1 | 20.9 | 8.1 | 23.8 | -6.0 | 0.6 | — |
| 58.4 | 6.3 | 464 | 261 | 3.5 | South | 81.7 | 4.1 | 50.2 | -3.3 | 24.0 | 5.3 | 25.3 | -2.6 | 0.4 | — |
| 67.7 | 8.8 | 459 | 214 | 2.8 | Waveney | 81.8 | 3.4 | 48.2 | -0.2 | 38.4 | 8.4 | 13.0 | -8.6 | 0.8 | -4.3 |
| 65.8 | 5.2 | 537 | 327 | -1.1 | *Surrey, Chertsey & Walton* | 80.3 | 4.8 | 60.2 | 0.7 | 19.0 | 5.7 | 20.0 | -7.2 | 0.6 | — |
| 75.2 | 4.6 | 596 | 331 | -3.6 | Epsom & Ewell | 80.1 | 4.8 | 60.2 | -2.0 | 15.7 | 1.2 | 23.5 | 0.3 | — | — |
| 74.0 | 4.2 | 617 | 348 | -5.3 | Esher | 80.8 | 3.9 | 65.4 | -0.1 | 12.0 | 3.2 | 22.6 | -3.1 | 0.4 | — |
| 61.7 | 5.2 | 478 | 309 | -0.7 | Guildford | 78.5 | 3.2 | 55.3 | -0.2 | 11.2 | 0.6 | 33.2 | -0.8 | 0.8 | — |
| 65.4 | 4.2 | 487 | 320 | -1.1 | Mole Valley | 82.0 | 5.0 | 59.3 | -1.5 | 9.6 | 0.3 | 30.2 | 0.3 | 0.9 | — |
| 66.3 | 5.1 | 523 | 314 | -0.1 | Reigate | 78.5 | 6.0 | 57.1 | -2.2 | 16.2 | 1.9 | 25.8 | 1.4 | — | — |
| 60. | 5.0 | 191 | 224 | 5.0 | Spelthorne | 80.4 | 6.3 | 58.5 | -1.5 | 22.9 | 5.9 | 16.5 | -6.4 | 2.0(3) | — |

| | | | | | Constituency | | | | | | | | | | |
|---|---|---|---|---|---|---|---|---|---|---|---|---|---|---|---|
| -2.8 | 330 | 519 | 4.3 | 69.2 | Surrey East | 82.5 | 5.4 | 62.3 | -1.1 | 10.6 | 0.2 | 25.4 | 1.4 | 1.7 | — |
| 0.7 | 354 | 472 | 5.0 | 68.6 | North-West | 78.2 | 5.7 | 63.9 | -0.1 | 13.5 | 2.3 | 20.5 | -4.4 | 2.2 | — |
| -1.0 | 310 | 495 | 5.1 | 65.5 | South-West | 82.8 | 4.4 | 58.5 | -0.9 | 6.4 | 0.8 | 33.5 | -0.9 | 1.6(3) | — |
| -2.0 | 339 | 483 | 4.9 | 68.7 | Woking | 79.2 | 4.1 | 58.9 | 0.9 | 12.6 | 2.1 | 28.0 | -3.4 | 0.5 | — |
| -0.4 | 223 | 380 | 8.8 | 53.1 | *Tyne & Wear,* Blaydon | 77.7 | 2.0 | 26.7 | 2.5 | 52.7 | 2.3 | 20.7 | -4.8 | — | — |
| -5.3 | 194 | 380 | 10.7 | 30.6 | Gateshead East | 73.6 | 1.8 | 24.4 | 0.5 | 63.5 | 4.3 | 12.1 | -4.8 | — | -1.9 |
| 1.8 | 209 | 385 | 11.0 | 35.6 | Houghton & Washington | 70.6 | -0.6 | 24.9 | 2.1 | 62.0 | 2.9 | 13.1 | -5.1 | — | -0.4 |
| -0.4 | 191 | 395 | 13.3 | 28.2 | Jarrow | 74.4 | 0.1 | 23.7 | 0.5 | 62.1 | -1.3 | 14.2 | 0.8 | — | 0.9 |
| -5.8 | 213 | 530 | 13.1 | 44.1 | Newcastle-upon-Tyne Central | 71.3 | -1.2 | 37.0 | -1.8 | 49.4 | 5.2 | 13.6 | -2.2 | — | -3.5 |
| -3.7 | 177 | 530 | 14.7 | 33.2 | East | 70.7 | 0.1 | 25.9 | -0.8 | 60.2 | 3.8 | 12.1 | -4.0 | — | -2.3 |
| -4.3 | 222 | 530 | 9.7 | 45.7 | North | 76.8 | 0.9 | 31.8 | 7.2 | 49.4 | 6.7 | 18.8 | -13.9 | 1.8 | — |
| -2.2 | 193 | 395 | 16.1 | 34.8 | South Shields | 70.1 | -0.7 | 27.4 | 1.7 | 59.8 | 1.9 | 12.8 | -2.6 | 1.7 | -0.1 |
| -3.7 | 176 | 385 | 14.4 | 38.7 | Sunderland North | 68.9 | -1.7 | 26.9 | -1.4 | 60.7 | 5.0 | 10.7 | -5.2 | 1.2 | -3.2 |
| -3.1 | 198 | 454 | 12.8 | 39.8 | South | 69.9 | -1.3 | 29.4 | -1.0 | 57.9 | 3.9 | 11.5 | -3.1 | — | -2.5 |
| -8.7 | 171 | 497 | 20.9 | 25.9 | Tyne Bridge | 62.6 | -0.5 | 21.4 | 0.8 | 67.2 | 4.1 | 11.4 | -4.9 | 0.9 | -1.7 |
| 0.7 | 242 | 497 | 10.1 | 55.1 | Tynemouth | 80.4 | 2.3 | 46.0 | 2.8 | 45.0 | 6.2 | 8.1 | -9.9 | — | -1.7 |
| 1.6 | 201 | 658 | 11.0 | 35.2 | Wallsend | 74.1 | -0.9 | 24.2 | 1.0 | 57.9 | 1.0 | 17.9 | -2.1 | — | 0.0 |
| 3.8 | 229 | 543 | 8.7 | 65.8 | *Warwickshire,* Nuneaton† | 83.7 | 3.4 | 43.0 | -1.9 | 45.8 | 11.2 | 11.2 | -8.0 | 0.3 | -6.5 |
| 1.5 | 266 | 537 | 7.1 | 69.7 | Rugby & Kenilworth | 83.7 | 4.1 | 52.4 | 0.8 | 32.0 | 7.1 | 15.3 | -8.2 | 2.1(3) | -3.1 |
| 1.9 | 268 | 557 | 5.7 | 59.4 | Stratford-on-Avon | 82.0 | 5.6 | 59.2 | -2.7 | 13.1 | 2.9 | 25.5 | -2.3 | 2.1(3) | — |
| -2.1 | 260 | 652 | 7.3 | 61.8 | Warwick & Leamington | 81.5 | 5.5 | 48.3 | -1.4 | 33.0 | 9.4 | 16.6 | -7.9 | — | — |
| 1.1 | 248 | | 8.3 | 62.0 | Warwickshire North† | 83.8 | 3.9 | 43.6 | -1.4 | 46.1 | 6.0 | 10.3 | -4.6 | — | -3.7 |
| | | | | | *West Midlands* | | | | | | | | | | |
| 2.1 | 247 | 537 | 8.5 | 61.8 | Aldridge-Brownhills | 82.6 | 2.8 | 54.3 | 1.0 | 33.3 | 4.9 | 12.4 | -5.9 | — | -2.0 |
| -2.5 | 259 | 472 | 12.7 | 51.9 | Birmingham Edgbaston | 71.3 | 2.7 | 49.0 | -0.8 | 37.6 | 10.8 | 11.7 | -9.3 | 1.7 | -5.8 |
| -3.3 | 213 | 472 | 15.6 | 48.3 | Erdington | 70.2 | 1.6 | 37.6 | -1.7 | 50.5 | 4.6 | 12.0 | -2.9 | — | -3.1 |
| -1.7 | 242 | 472 | 11.2 | 59.0 | Hall Green | 78.2 | 3.5 | 46.1 | 1.2 | 38.3 | 10.1 | 15.6 | -11.4 | — | -4.4 |
| -2.8 | 193 | 472 | 15.7 | 43.3 | Hodge Hill | 70.8 | 2.0 | 36.3 | -0.6 | 53.6 | 4.9 | 9.2 | -5.2 | 0.9 | -2.8 |
| -3.1 | 213 | 472 | 21.5 | 48.8 | Ladywood | 65.9 | 1.1 | 25.6 | -5.8 | 66.3 | 8.6 | 8.2 | -1.1 | — | -7.2 |
| -3.8 | 227 | 472 | 12.7 | 43.5 | Northfield† | 76.1 | 3.5 | 44.4 | -0.8 | 45.5 | 6.3 | 10.1 | -5.5 | — | -3.5 |
| -2.2 | 207 | 472 | 15.2 | 59.4 | Perry Barr | 71.6 | 2.0 | 36.6 | -0.3 | 53.2 | 2.8 | 10.2 | -2.5 | — | -1.6 |
| -0.1 | 243 | 472 | 12.8 | 55.4 | Selly Oak† | 76.6 | 3.5 | 42.3 | -1.9 | 46.0 | 6.7 | 10.3 | -5.1 | 1.4(3) | -4.3 |
| -2.7 | 188 | 472 | 24.2 | 38.0 | Small Heath | 62.8 | 2.3 | 25.0 | 3.9 | 65.3 | -1.0 | 7.2 | -3.2 | 2.4 | 2.4 |
| -2.7 | 208 | 472 | 20.5 | 42.3 | Sparkbrook | 66.8 | 3.3 | 24.8 | -0.9 | 64.1 | 3.2 | 8.8 | -2.5 | 2.4 | -2.1 |

| ENGLAND | % Owner occupied 1981 | Unemployed % | Poll Tax (household) | Household income | Electorate change % | % voting | % change in voting | % Con | Con change 1987-92 | % Labour | Lab change 1987-92 | % Lib Dem | Lib Dem chg. 1987-92 | % Other | Swing |
|---|---|---|---|---|---|---|---|---|---|---|---|---|---|---|---|
| Yardley† | 59.0 | 11.3 | 472 | 244 | -3.9 | 78.0 | 4.1 | 34.5 | -8.1 | 34.9 | -1.8 | 30.2 | 9.5 | 0.4 | -3.2 |
| Coventry North-East | 61.7 | 14.9 | 523 | 209 | -4.0 | 73.2 | 2.7 | 27.9 | -1.5 | 52.5 | -1.8 | 11.2 | -4.6 | 8.5¶ | 0.2 |
| North-West | 70.3 | 12.6 | 523 | 216 | -4.6 | 77.6 | 2.9 | 35.4 | 0.6 | 51.7 | 2.7 | 12.9 | -3.4 | – | -1.0 |
| South-East | 59.2 | 15.2 | 523 | 215 | -5.9 | 74.9 | 1.9 | 29.0 | -0.9 | 32.6 | -14.8 | 9.1 | -12.3 | 29.4(2¶) | – |
| South-West | 73.6 | 9.5 | 523 | 264 | -3.2 | 80.1 | 1.5 | 45.7 | 2.4 | 42.8 | 5.8 | 9.2 | -10.5 | 2.3(2) | -1.7 |
| Dudley East | 45.6 | 12.0 | 521 | 206 | 0.2 | 75.0 | 2.7 | 36.5 | -3.0 | 52.8 | 6.9 | 9.6 | -5.1 | 1.2 | -4.9 |
| West | 63.6 | 8.3 | 521 | 247 | 5.9 | 82.1 | 3.0 | 48.8 | -1.0 | 40.7 | 6.7 | 10.5 | -5.7 | – | -3.8 |
| Halesowen & Stourbridge | 66.6 | 7.7 | 521 | 263 | -0.5 | 82.3 | 2.9 | 50.6 | 0.5 | 35.6 | 7.8 | 12.4 | -9.6 | 1.4 | -3.7 |
| Meriden | 55.1 | 10.5 | 484 | 266 | -1.9 | 78.9 | 5.0 | 55.1 | 0.0 | 30.9 | 4.8 | 14.0 | -4.8 | – | -2.4 |
| Solihull | 79.0 | 6.1 | 484 | 304 | -1.0 | 81.6 | 6.5 | 60.8 | -0.2 | 16.7 | 1.7 | 21.0 | -3.0 | 1.5 | – |
| Sutton Coldfield | 78.8 | 7.1 | 472 | 307 | -1.3 | 79.5 | 5.0 | 65.2 | 1.2 | 15.0 | 3.6 | 19.3 | -5.4 | 0.6 | – |
| Walsall North | 35.3 | 12.5 | 537 | 209 | 1.9 | 75.0 | 1.2 | 39.4 | 0.4 | 46.7 | 4.2 | 12.7 | -5.7 | 1.2 | -1.9 |
| South | 50.9 | 12.7 | 537 | 217 | -1.7 | 76.3 | 0.8 | 41.9 | -0.8 | 48.2 | 3.3 | 8.3 | -4.1 | 1.7(2) | -2.1 |
| Warley East | 48.3 | 13.9 | 570 | 181 | -7.2 | 71.7 | 2.3 | 32.6 | -3.2 | 53.6 | 3.4 | 12.3 | -1.7 | 1.5 | -3.3 |
| West | 43.9 | 12.1 | 570 | 205 | -0.6 | 73.9 | 3.9 | 37.7 | 1.8 | 50.6 | 1.4 | 11.7 | -3.3 | – | 0.2 |
| West Bromwich East | 48.4 | 11.9 | 570 | 211 | -2.2 | 75.7 | 2.6 | 39.7 | -0.7 | 46.2 | 3.6 | 13.1 | -4.0 | 1.1 | -2.1 |
| West | 32.2 | 15.0 | 570 | 182 | -2.2 | 70.4 | 3.4 | 35.5 | -1.6 | 54.8 | 4.3 | 9.7 | -2.7 | – | -3.0 |
| Wolverhampton North-East† | 37.9 | 13.4 | 507 | 194 | -1.2 | 78.0 | 3.7 | 41.2 | -0.9 | 49.3 | 7.6 | 7.3 | -8.9 | 2.2 | -4.2 |
| South-East | 34.4 | 14.9 | 507 | 181 | 0.8 | 72.9 | 0.4 | 31.7 | -1.4 | 56.7 | 7.8 | 9.5 | -8.5 | 2.1 | -4.6 |
| South-West | 59.6 | 12.2 | 507 | 241 | -1.9 | 78.3 | 2.8 | 49.3 | -1.4 | 39.9 | 9.1 | 8.5 | -10.1 | 2.3 | -5.3 |
| West Sussex, Arundel | 71.3 | 9.0 | 394 | 240 | 2.4 | 77.1 | 5.9 | 58.0 | -3.4 | 13.6 | 2.6 | 25.5 | -2.2 | 2.9(2) | – |
| Chichester | 59.7 | 5.6 | 309 | 244 | 1.2 | 77.9 | 3.4 | 59.3 | -2.5 | 11.3 | 3.4 | 26.6 | -1.7 | 2.8(3) | – |
| Crawley | 44.5 | 6.1 | 450 | 280 | 2.1 | 79.2 | -2.8 | 48.7 | -0.8 | 36.2 | 7.2 | 13.8 | -7.7 | 1.2 | -4.0 |
| Horsham | 65.5 | 5.5 | 374 | 313 | 3.2 | 81.3 | 8.8 | 61.7 | -2.0 | 9.9 | 1.2 | 25.1 | -0.3 | 3.4(3) | – |
| Shoreham | 76.3 | 6.8 | 445 | 246 | -1.9 | 81.2 | 3.6 | 56.5 | -4.4 | 10.6 | 1.4 | 31.8 | 1.8 | 1.1(2) | – |
| Sussex, Mid | 74.5 | 4.3 | 404 | 319 | 0.9 | 82.9 | 5.7 | 59.0 | -2.1 | 10.4 | 3.0 | 28.4 | -3.1 | 2.2(4) | – |
| Worthing | 76.3 | 8.2 | 356 | 257 | 0.7 | 77.4 | 4.6 | 57.0 | -4.7 | 11.1 | 1.5 | 29.4 | 0.7 | 2.5(2) | – |
| *West Yorkshire, Batley & Spen* | 63.8 | 8.5 | 423 | 230 | 2.8 | 79.6 | 0.7 | 45.4 | 2.0 | 43.1 | 2.0 | 10.5 | -3.8 | 1.0 | 0.0 |

| | | | | | | | | | | | | | | | |
|---|---|---|---|---|---|---|---|---|---|---|---|---|---|---|---|
| 62.2 | 13.7 | 387 | 203 | -1.1 | Bradford North | 73.4 | 0.7 | 32.2 | -7.3 | 47.8 | 5.0 | 18.7 | 1.0 | 1.3(2) | -6.2 |
| 64.8 | 9.6 | 387 | 204 | 0.5 | South | 75.6 | 2.0 | 38.4 | -2.4 | 47.6 | 6.2 | 13.7 | -4.1 | 0.3 | -4.3 |
| 61.2 | 15.0 | 387 | 204 | -1.1 | West | 69.9 | -0.3 | 33.8 | -2.9 | 53.2 | 1.3 | 10.5 | -0.9 | 2.5(2) | -2.1 |
| 69.0 | 7.5 | 322 | 244 | 1.4 | Calder Valley | 82.1 | 1.0 | 45.4 | 1.9 | 37.4 | 4.1 | 16.1 | -7.0 | 1.0 | -1.1 |
| 74.2 | 7.1 | 423 | 246 | 2.6 | Colne Valley | 82.0 | 1.9 | 42.0 | 5.6 | 29.8 | 0.7 | 27.0 | -6.4 | 1.2(4) | – |
| 60.1 | 7.9 | 423 | 266 | 2.8 | Dewsbury | 80.2 | 1.4 | 42.7 | 1.1 | 43.8 | 1.4 | 11.2 | -4.7 | 2.2(3) | -0.1 |
| 61.3 | 5.8 | 481 | 275 | 2.2 | Elmet | 82.5 | 3.3 | 47.5 | 0.6 | 41.9 | 4.8 | 10.5 | -5.5 | – | -2.1 |
| 66.9 | 10.2 | 322 | 225 | 0.0 | Halifax | 78.7 | 1.0 | 42.7 | 1.4 | 43.5 | 0.1 | 12.7 | -2.6 | 1.1 | 0.6 |
| 46.5 | 10.9 | 388 | 216 | 1.3 | Hemsworth | 75.9 | 0.2 | 18.6 | 1.4 | 70.8 | 3.8 | 10.5 | -5.2 | – | -1.2 |
| 57.5 | 10.3 | 423 | 216 | 1.8 | Huddersfield | 72.3 | -3.2 | 33.9 | 2.5 | 48.7 | 2.9 | 15.9 | -5.6 | 1.5(2) | -0.2 |
| 74.7 | 8.0 | 387 | 250 | 1.0 | Keighley | 82.6 | 3.2 | 47.4 | 1.7 | 40.8 | 5.8 | 10.6 | -8.7 | 1.2 | -2.1 |
| 32.9 | 16.9 | 481 | 196 | 5.2 | Leeds Central | 61.3 | -3.5 | 22.7 | -2.8 | 62.2 | 6.6 | 15.0 | -2.9 | – | -4.7 |
| 44.2 | 13.2 | 481 | 203 | 0.9 | East | 70.0 | -0.2 | 28.3 | 1.8 | 57.7 | 9.0 | 14.0 | -10.8 | – | -3.6 |
| 64.6 | 8.1 | 481 | 260 | -0.4 | North-East | 76.9 | 1.6 | 45.4 | -0.2 | 36.8 | 11.6 | 16.7 | -11.6 | 1.1 | – |
| 60.5 | 7.1 | 481 | 225 | 1.7 | North-West | 72.8 | -2.8 | 43.0 | -0.5 | 27.3 | 5.5 | 27.8 | -5.6 | 1.9(2) | – |
| 44.1 | 8.7 | 481 | 214 | 3.9 | South & Morley | 72.6 | 1.0 | 36.1 | 1.9 | 52.2 | 2.6 | 11.1 | -5.3 | 0.7 | -0.3 |
| 47.4 | 10.0 | 481 | 219 | 1.1 | West | 71.1 | -2.2 | 26.2 | 3.0 | 55.1 | 11.9 | 8.9 | -24.7 | 9.8(3) | – |
| 58.5 | 7.6 | 411 | 252 | 4.2 | Normanton | 76.4 | 1.6 | 33.9 | -0.1 | 51.8 | 2.3 | 14.3 | -2.1 | – | -1.2 |
| 43.8 | 10.7 | 388 | 232 | 0.4 | Pontefract & Castleford | 74.3 | 0.8 | 20.9 | -0.3 | 69.9 | 3.0 | 9.2 | -2.1 | – | -1.6 |
| 70.1 | 5.0 | 481 | 260 | -1.2 | Pudsey | 81.0 | 3.0 | 43.7 | -1.8 | 29.1 | 8.6 | 26.4 | -7.6 | 0.8 | – |
| 70.3 | 6.3 | 387 | 257 | 0.2 | Shipley | 82.1 | 2.9 | 50.4 | 0.9 | 28.5 | 5.2 | 20.0 | -6.3 | 1.2 | – |
| 50.5 | 10.5 | 388 | 228 | 0.3 | Wakefield | 76.3 | 0.7 | 38.3 | -3.0 | 50.6 | 4.0 | 11.1 | -1.0 | – | -3.5 |
| 57.3 | 5.4 | 463 | 271 | 4.3 | *Wiltshire*, Devizes | 81.7 | 4.5 | 53.3 | -1.4 | 17.8 | 0.5 | 26.4 | -1.5 | 2.4(2) | – |
| 51.3 | 5.9 | 432 | 259 | -0.4 | Salisbury | 79.9 | 4.3 | 52.0 | -2.9 | 9.0 | -0.4 | 37.2 | 2.2 | 1.7(4) | – |
| 58.1 | 9.6 | 491 | 259 | 4.6 | Swindon | 81.5 | 3.7 | 43.3 | -0.6 | 39.4 | 2.8 | 16.0 | -3.6 | 1.3(3) | -1.7 |
| 65.5 | 6.6 | 476 | 259 | 3.2 | Westbury | 83.0 | 4.7 | 50.4 | -1.1 | 13.3 | 1.3 | 33.0 | -3.3 | 3.2(2) | – |
| 59.5 | 6.1 | 483 | 291 | 6.4 | *Wiltshire* North | 81.7 | 2.4 | 55.6 | 0.5 | 9.9 | 3.1 | 32.3 | -5.8 | 2.2(3) | – |

| WALES | % Owner occupied 1981 | Unemployed % | Poll Tax (household) | Household income | Electorate % change | % voting | % change in voting | % Con | Con. change 1987-92 | % Labour | Lab. change 1987-92 | % Lib Dem | Lib. Dem. chg. 1987-92 | % Plaid Cymru | PC change 1987-92 | % Other | Swing |
|---|---|---|---|---|---|---|---|---|---|---|---|---|---|---|---|---|---|
| Clwyd, Alyn & Deeside | 66.9 | 7.5 | 271 | 251 | 3.6 | 80.1 | -0.3 | 35.8 | 0.9 | 52.0 | 3.5 | 9.7 | -5.7 | 1.1 | 0.1 | 1.3(2) | -1.3 |
| Clwyd North-West | 68.5 | 11.5 | 284 | 207 | 1.9 | 78.6 | 3.5 | 46.2 | -2.3 | 34.8 | 10.0 | 15.1 | -7.6 | 3.6 | -0.4 | 0.3 | -6.1 |
| South-West | 52.8 | 8.0 | 271 | 219 | 4.3 | 81.5 | 0.5 | 33.5 | 0.2 | 43.5 | 8.1 | 12.2 | -10.7 | 9.8 | 1.3 | 1.0(2) | -3.9 |
| Delyn† | 71.1 | 7.5 | (360) | 256 | 4.2 | 83.4 | 0.8 | 41.3 | -0.1 | 45.0 | 5.9 | 13.8 | -5.8 | 2.5 | 0.0 | — | -3.0 |
| Wrexham | 50.4 | 9.1 | 294 | 251 | 2.2 | 80.7 | -0.2 | 35.2 | -0.4 | 48.3 | 4.4 | 9.4 | -5.7 | 2.8 | 1.7 | — | -2.4 |
| Dyfed, Carmarthen | 65.0 | 8.5 | 176 | 206 | 5.5 | 82.7 | -0.2 | 22.4 | -5.0 | 36.6 | 1.3 | 25.1 | -3.9 | 31.5 | 8.5 | — | — |
| Ceredigion & Pembroke N† | 64.6 | 9.0 | 160 | 203 | 4.8 | 77.4 | 0.9 | 24.8 | -2.0 | 18.8 | 0.3 | 12.7 | -11.6 | 31.3 | 15.0 | — | — |
| Llanelli | 60.8 | 9.6 | 206 | 197 | 2.0 | 77.8 | -0.3 | 16.9 | -0.3 | 54.9 | -4.2 | 10.9 | -0.8 | 15.6 | 5.4 | — | 2.0 |
| Pembroke† | 55.7 | 12.8 | 162 | 211 | 4.0 | 82.9 | 2.0 | 42.0 | 1.1 | 43.3 | 12.3 | 6.4 | -15.2 | 2.7 | 0.7 | 1.1(2) | -5.6 |
| Gwent, Blaenau Gwent | 55.5 | 10.6 | 221 | 181 | -0.7 | 78.1 | 0.9 | 9.8 | -1.7 | 79.0 | 3.1 | 5.7 | -2.5 | 4.8 | 1.1 | — | -2.4 |
| Islwyn | 53.1 | 8.5 | 227 | 208 | 1.3 | 81.4 | 1.0 | 14.9 | 0.2 | 74.3 | 3.0 | 10.9 | -3.6 | 3.9 | -0.9 | 1.3 | -1.4 |
| Monmouth‡ | 61.4 | 7.0 | 216 | 255 | 1.5 | 86.1 | 5.5 | 47.3 | -0.3 | 41.0 | 13.3 | 11.9 | -13.1 | 0.8§ | 0.0 | — | -6.8 |
| Newport East | 62.9 | 11.6 | 250 | 234 | -1.5 | 81.2 | 1.1 | 31.4 | -0.8 | 55.0 | 5.9 | 9.5 | -5.7 | 1.7 | 0.6 | — | -3.4 |
| West | 58.1 | 11.2 | 250 | 248 | -1.1 | 82.8 | 1.1 | 36.0 | -4.1 | 53.1 | 5.4 | 13.1 | -3.6 | 1.4§ | 0.6 | — | -5.6 |
| Torfaen | 39.5 | 12.0 | 220 | 218 | 2.0 | 77.5 | 1.9 | 20.3 | -2.0 | 64.1 | -0.3 | 5.8 | -6.9 | 2.6§ | 0.3 | — | — |
| Gwynedd, Caernarfon | 62.8 | 13.4 | 188 | 205 | 1.8 | 78.2 | 1.9 | 19.2 | -5.0 | 15.5 | 3.5 | 31.4 | -0.1 | 59.0 | 2.0 | — | — |
| Conwy | 60.4 | 11.2 | 196 | 219 | 2.5 | 78.9 | -0.7 | 33.7 | -1.8 | 25.8 | 1.9 | 8.9 | 0.1 | 7.4 | -0.5 | 0.5 | — |
| Meirionnydd nant Conwy | 60.6 | 11.3 | 220 | 207 | 0.6 | 81.5 | -1.0 | 26.5 | 1.3 | 18.8 | 6.6 | 4.4 | -5.9 | 44.0 | 4.0 | 1.8(2) | — |
| Ynys Môn | 59.0 | 12.9 | 240 | 204 | 1.5 | 80.6 | 0.2 | 34.6 | -2.3 | 23.5 | 3.7 | 10.3 | -2.3 | 37.1 | -6.1 | 1.8 | — |
| Mid Glamorgan, Bridgend | 66.3 | 10.3 | 224 | 238 | 2.4 | 80.5 | 0.7 | 35.7 | -1.3 | 51.3 | 5.2 | 8.5 | -1.9 | 2.8 | 0.5 | 0.4 | -3.0 |
| Caerphilly | 58.6 | 11.2 | 235 | 214 | 0.6 | 77.2 | 0.7 | 18.1 | 0.7 | 63.7 | 0.2 | 7.0 | -5.6 | 9.7 | 1.6 | — | -3.2 |
| Cynon Valley | 65.7 | 12.9 | 201 | 193 | 0.2 | 76.5 | -0.2 | 12.9 | -0.8 | 69.1 | -3.8 | 11.3 | -5.2 | 11.0 | 4.3 | — | — |
| Merthyr Tydfil & Rhymney | 52.8 | 12.5 | 192 | 193 | 0.3 | 75.8 | 0.6 | 11.1 | 0.1 | 71.6 | 2.4 | 6.8 | 3.2 | 6.1 | 1.4 | — | — |
| Ogmore | 60.3 | 11.6 | 208 | 225 | 1.1 | 80.6 | 2.7 | 15.1 | 0.8 | 71.7 | 4.5 | 8.5 | -2.8 | 6.3 | 2.0 | — | -1.1 |
| Pontypridd | 64.9 | 9.2 | 224 | 240 | 1.0 | 79.3 | -1.4 | 20.3 | 0.2 | 60.8 | 1.2 | 5.3 | -10.3 | 9.1 | 3.8 | 1.3 | -1.8 |
| Rhondda | 76.1 | 12.2 | 198 | 179 | -1.6 | 76.6 |  | 7.8 |  | 74.5 |  |  | -3.0 | 11.8 | 2.9 | 0.5 | — |

| | | | | | | | | | | | | | | | | | |
|---|---|---|---|---|---|---|---|---|---|---|---|---|---|---|---|---|---|
| Powys, Brecon & Radnor† | 57.7 | 6.7 | 189 | 203 | 4.3 | 85.9 | 1.5 | 36.1 | 1.4 | 26.3 | -2.9 | 35.8 | 1.0 | 0.9 | -0.3 | 0.9 | — |
| Montgomery | 52.1 | 6.7 | 161 | 231 | 4.0 | 79.9 | 0.5 | 32.7 | -5.8 | 12.4 | 2.0 | 48.5 | 1.9 | 4.8 | 0.3 | 1.5 | — |
| *South Glamorgan* | | | | | | | | | | | | | | | | | |
| Cardiff Central† | 65.4 | 12.1 | 248 | 214 | 9.1 | 74.4 | -3.5 | 33.9 | -3.2 | 42.0 | 9.7 | 21.4 | -8.0 | 1.7 | 0.4 | 1.0(2) | -6.5 |
| North | 74.5 | 7.6 | 248 | 267 | 3.8 | 84.1 | 3.1 | 45.1 | -0.1 | 38.9 | 12.2 | 13.6 | -12.9 | 1.9 | 0.4 | 0.4(2) | -6.2 |
| South & Penarth | 54.4 | 12.0 | 237 | 232 | 4.7 | 77.2 | 0.9 | 33.6 | -2.9 | 55.5 | 8.8 | 7.8 | -7.6 | 1.6 | 0.3 | 1.4 | -5.9 |
| West | 52.8 | 12.7 | 248 | 209 | 2.7 | 77.5 | -0.3 | 32.9 | -3.6 | 53.2 | 7.7 | 10.9 | -5.4 | 2.6 | 0.9 | 0.4 | -5.6 |
| Vale of Glamorgan† | 63.3 | 9.6 | 208 | 246 | 2.1 | 81.9 | 2.6 | 44.3 | -2.4 | 44.3 | 9.6 | 9.2 | -7.4 | 2.1 | 0.3 | — | -6.0 |
| *West Glamorgan*, Aberavon | 53.5 | 8.9 | (217) | 207 | -1.4 | 77.7 | 0.0 | 13.9 | -0.5 | 67.1 | 0.3 | 12.5 | -3.6 | 4.8 | 2.0 | 1.8 | — |
| Gower | 71.9 | 8.3 | 222 | 247 | -2.8 | 81.9 | 1.2 | 35.1 | 0.6 | 50.1 | 3.5 | 9.9 | -6.2 | 3.5 | 0.7 | 1.4(3) | -1.5 |
| Neath | 63.2 | 9.6 | 217 | 220 | 2.1 | 80.6 | 1.7 | 15.2 | -0.9 | 68.0 | 4.6 | 5.4 | -8.6 | 11.3 | 4.9 | — | -2.8 |
| Swansea East | 58.1 | 10.9 | 247 | 213 | 3.5 | 75.6 | 0.1 | 17.2 | -1.7 | 69.7 | 6.0 | 9.5 | -5.3 | 3.6 | 0.9 | — | -3.8 |
| West | 57.4 | 13.1 | 247 | 214 | -0.1 | 73.3 | -2.7 | 31.4 | -1.6 | 53.0 | 4.5 | 10.5 | -4.9 | 3.8 | 1.8 | 1.3 | -3.0 |

| SCOTLAND | % Owner occupied 1981 | Unemployed % | Household income | Electorate change % | % voting | % change in voting | % Con. | Con. change 1987-92 | % Labour | Lab. change 1987-92 | % Lib. Dem | Lib. Dem. chg. 1987-92 | % SNP | SNP change 1987-92 | % Other | Swing |
|---|---|---|---|---|---|---|---|---|---|---|---|---|---|---|---|---|
| *Borders,* Roxburgh & Berwickshire | 32.7 | 6.6 | 212 | 0.9 | 77.6 | 0.4 | 34.3 | -2.9 | 8.6 | -0.2 | 46.9 | -2.3 | 10.2 | 5.4 | – | – |
| Tweeddale, Ettrick & Lauderdale | 40.7 | 6.7 | 251 | 4.2 | 78.1 | 0.9 | 31.7 | 2.1 | 10.8 | -0.6 | 39.9 | -10.0 | 17.0 | 7.9 | 0.6 | – |
| *Central,* Clackmannan | 27.4 | 9.3 | 224 | -0.2 | 78.5 | 1.4 | 17.3 | 2.4 | 49.2 | -4.6 | 6.7 | -3.8 | 26.9 | 5.9 | – | – |
| Falkirk East | 25.8 | 9.0 | 214 | -1.2 | 76.9 | 1.9 | 20.7 | 2.2 | 46.1 | -8.1 | 6.9 | -4.8 | 26.2 | 10.8 | – | – |
| West | 24.0 | 9.5 | 239 | -0.2 | 76.8 | 0.1 | 19.6 | 2.2 | 49.8 | -2.8 | 6.3 | -6.3 | 24.3 | 6.9 | – | -0.3 |
| Stirling | 43.3 | 9.0 | 245 | 0.4 | 82.3 | 2.9 | 40.0 | 1.7 | 38.5 | 2.3 | 7.0 | -7.9 | 13.7 | 3.0 | 0.9(2) | -1.8 |
| *Dumfries & Galloway,* Dumfries | 42.1 | 9.8 | 223 | 3.0 | 80.0 | 4.4 | 43.1 | 1.3 | 30.0 | 4.8 | 11.8 | -6.2 | 14.3 | 0.0 | 0.9(2) | – |
| Galloway & Upper Nithsdale | 40.2 | 8.2 | 201 | 2.0 | 81.7 | 4.9 | 42.0 | 1.6 | 13.0 | 0.1 | 8.6 | -6.0 | 36.4 | 5.0 | – | 2.0 |
| *Fife,* Dunfermline East | 19.2 | 9.2 | 226 | -2.0 | 75.6 | -1.0 | 16.5 | 1.7 | 62.4 | -2.3 | 6.0 | -4.6 | 15.1 | 5.2 | – | 2.4 |
| West | 38.2 | 10.5 | 247 | -0.2 | 76.4 | -0.5 | 22.8 | -0.3 | 42.0 | -5.0 | 15.7 | -5.4 | 19.4 | 10.7 | – | – |
| Fife Central | 24.0 | 14.2 | 206 | 0.2 | 74.3 | -1.9 | 17.6 | 1.0 | 50.4 | -3.0 | 6.9 | -8.3 | 25.1 | 10.3 | – | – |
| North-East | 48.7 | 6.7 | 229 | 2.8 | 77.8 | 1.6 | 38.5 | -2.7 | 5.5 | -1.9 | 46.4 | 1.6 | 8.6 | 2.0 | 0.9(2) | 3.3 |
| Kirkcaldy | 30.8 | 9.7 | 225 | -2.8 | 74.8 | -1.8 | 21.8 | 0.5 | 46.0 | -3.5 | 9.6 | -7.8 | 22.5 | 10.8 | – | – |
| *Grampian,* Aberdeen North | 15.3 | 9.1 | 225 | -4.7 | 66.5 | -3.3 | 17.1 | 2.7 | 47.0 | -7.6 | 11.9 | -5.9 | 24.0 | 10.8 | – | – |
| South† | 52.7 | 3.9 | 297 | -6.5 | 69.8 | 2.6 | 38.5 | 3.6 | 34.8 | -2.9 | 11.6 | -9.3 | 15.1 | 8.6 | – | – |
| Banff & Buchan | 41.1 | 5.5 | 242 | 4.4 | 71.2 | 0.4 | 38.6 | -0.1 | 8.2 | 0.8 | 5.6 | -4.0 | 47.5 | 3.3 | – | – |
| Gordon | 50.4 | 4.3 | 264 | 9.0 | 73.9 | 0.2 | 37.0 | 5.1 | 11.3 | -0.2 | 37.4 | -12.0 | 14.3 | 7.1 | – | – |
| Kincardine & Deeside‡ | 45.3 | 3.3 | 278 | 4.8 | 78.8 | 3.6 | 43.7 | 3.1 | 9.1 | -6.8 | 35.1 | -1.2 | 11.3 | 4.9 | 0.7 | 0.7 |
| Moray | 41.3 | 7.2 | 231 | 1.7 | 72.5 | -0.2 | 38.1 | 3.1 | 11.9 | 0.6 | 5.7 | -4.7 | 44.3 | 1.1 | – | – |
| *Highlands,* Caithness & Sutherland | 37.6 | 11.1 | 209 | -1.2 | 71.9 | -1.6 | 21.0 | 4.3 | 15.7 | 0.7 | 45.1 | -8.5 | 18.2 | 7.9 | 1.5 | 0.0 |
| Inverness, Nairn & Lochaber | 39.1 | 11.4 | 231 | 4.1 | 73.3 | 2.4 | 22.6 | -0.4 | 25.1 | -0.2 | 26.0 | -10.8 | 24.7 | 9.9 | 1.6 | 2.1 |
| Ross, Cromarty & Skye | 44.9 | 11.0 | 217 | 6.0 | 73.9 | 1.2 | 23.0 | 3.3 | 15.3 | -3.8 | 41.6 | -7.8 | 18.6 | 6.8 | – | – |
| *Lothian,* East Lothian | 30.4 | 8.1 | 244 | 2.6 | 82.4 | 3.7 | 28.2 | -0.1 | 46.5 | -1.6 | 11.2 | -4.3 | 14.2 | 6.9 | – | 0.7 |
| Edinburgh Central | 62.5 | 10.5 | 287 | -5.1 | 69.3 | 0.3 | 33.4 | -1.3 | 38.8 | -1.4 | 11.5 | -6.4 | 14.1 | 7.9 | 2.2(2) | 0.0 |
| East | 47.7 | 9.5 | 228 | -6.6 | 73.9 | -0.2 | 24.4 | -0.3 | 45.7 | -4.6 | 10.2 | -5.3 | 18.4 | 9.0 | 1.3 | 2.1 |
| Leith | 46.1 | 20.5 | 248 | -6.4 | 71.3 | 0.5 | 21.1 | -1.8 | 34.2 | -15.1 | 12.3 | -6.0 | 21.8 | 12.4 | 10.5(2)¶ | – |
| Pentlands | 51.5 | 8.8 | 297 | -4.4 | 80.2 | 2.5 | 40.7 | 2.4 | 31.1 | 1.1 | 12.6 | -12.0 | 15.4 | 8.2 | 0.2 | 0.7 |

| | | | | | | | | | | | | | | | | |
|---|---|---|---|---|---|---|---|---|---|---|---|---|---|---|---|---|
| South | 53.4 | 5.8 | 259 | -3.9 | 72.7 | -3.1 | 32.1 | -1.7 | 41.5 | 3.8 | 13.4 | -9.2 | 12.8 | 7.8 | 0.2 | -2.8 |
| West | 58.4 | 5.4 | 289 | -5.2 | 82.7 | 3.3 | 37.0 | -0.3 | 18.0 | -4.2 | 35.2 | 0.4 | 8.4 | 2.8 | 1.3(3) | – |
| Linlithgow | 23.8 | 7.6 | 243 | 2.6 | 78.7 | 1.1 | 17.5 | 2.7 | 45.0 | -2.4 | 7.2 | -5.5 | 30.3 | 5.4 | – | – |
| Livingston | 22.6 | 11.4 | 250 | 8.0 | 74.6 | 0.5 | 19.4 | 0.6 | 44.4 | -1.2 | 8.6 | -10.5 | 26.6 | 10.0 | 1.0 | – |
| Midlothian | 27.5 | 7.6 | 234 | -0.5 | 77.9 | 0.7 | 20.1 | 1.9 | 43.9 | -4.4 | 13.1 | -8.9 | 21.9 | 11.3 | 1.0 | – |
| *Orkney & Shetland* | 50.2 | 4.8 | 236 | 1.4 | 65.5 | -3.1 | 22.0 | -1.2 | 19.8 | 1.1 | 46.4 | 4.8 | 11.2 | -3.3 | 0.6 | – |
| *Strathclyde, Argyll & Bute* | 40.9 | 10.5 | 223 | -1.7 | 76.2 | 0.7 | 27.7 | -5.8 | 13.6 | 1.5 | 34.9 | -2.4 | 23.8 | 6.7 | – | – |
| Ayr | 50.6 | 9.8 | 257 | -1.5 | 83.1 | 3.2 | 40.8 | 1.3 | 40.6 | 1.5 | 7.5 | -7.3 | 10.9 | 4.3 | 0.2 | -0.1 |
| Carrick, Cumnock & Doon Valley | 21.7 | 12.7 | 187 | -1.8 | 77.0 | 1.2 | 20.0 | -0.8 | 59.1 | -1.0 | 4.7 | -4.9 | 16.2 | 6.6 | – | 0.1 |
| Clydebank & Milngavie | 26.3 | 9.0 | 225 | -5.8 | 78.0 | -1.0 | 18.1 | 2.3 | 53.3 | -3.6 | 8.7 | -6.2 | 19.6 | 7.1 | 0.3 | – |
| Clydesdale | 36.2 | 9.3 | 235 | 0.4 | 77.6 | -0.6 | 23.4 | -0.1 | 44.6 | -0.7 | 8.2 | -8.2 | 23.1 | 8.3 | 0.7 | 0.3 |
| Cumbernauld & Kilsyth | 27.8 | 9.1 | 238 | 2.3 | 79.1 | 0.6 | 11.3 | 2.2 | 54.0 | -6.0 | 5.8 | -5.6 | 29.0 | 9.4 | – | – |
| Cunninghame, North | 45.2 | 13.5 | 241 | 0.0 | 78.2 | -0.1 | 34.1 | 0.1 | 41.0 | -3.4 | 6.7 | -5.4 | 18.2 | 8.7 | – | 1.8 |
| South | 20.7 | 12.2 | 232 | -1.7 | 75.9 | 0.9 | 16.3 | 0.0 | 52.9 | -7.9 | 6.2 | -5.7 | 24.2 | 13.2 | 0.3 | – |
| Dumbarton | 35.0 | 10.8 | 264 | -2.6 | 77.1 | -0.8 | 29.7 | -1.9 | 43.6 | 0.6 | 7.8 | -5.4 | 18.4 | 6.3 | 0.4 | -1.3 |
| East Kilbride | 30.2 | 8.1 | 259 | 1.6 | 80.0 | 0.8 | 19.1 | 4.4 | 46.9 | -2.1 | 10.5 | -13.3 | 23.5 | 11.0 | – | – |
| Eastwood | 70.7 | 6.4 | 312 | 2.9 | 81.0 | 1.6 | 46.8 | 7.3 | 24.1 | -0.9 | 16.5 | -10.8 | 12.4 | 4.1 | 0.3 | – |
| Glasgow Cathcart | 43.6 | 10.6 | 220 | -9.4 | 75.4 | -1.0 | 24.5 | 2.2 | 48.3 | -3.8 | 7.8 | -7.4 | 18.1 | 7.8 | 1.3 | 3.0 |
| Central | 27.6 | 15.7 | 189 | -5.9 | 63.1 | -2.5 | 13.9 | 0.9 | 57.2 | -7.3 | 6.3 | -4.2 | 20.8 | 10.9 | 1.8(2) | – |
| Garscadden | 7.9 | 14.6 | 157 | -13.9 | 71.1 | -0.3 | 11.5 | 0.8 | 64.4 | -3.3 | 4.9 | -4.5 | 19.0 | 6.7 | 0.2 | – |
| Govan‡ | 23.2 | 14.8 | 182 | -9.5 | 76.0 | 2.7 | 9.9 | -2.0 | 48.9 | -15.9 | 3.5 | -8.8 | 37.1 | 26.7 | 0.5 | – |
| Hillhead | 48.6 | 11.7 | 268 | -1.1 | 68.8 | -3.6 | 17.1 | 2.6 | 38.5 | -4.4 | 26.2 | -8.9 | 16.5 | 10.0 | 1.8(3) | – |
| Maryhill | 16.6 | 16.8 | 195 | -7.5 | 65.2 | -2.3 | 10.3 | 0.9 | 61.6 | -4.8 | 7.0 | -4.6 | 19.1 | 8.1 | 1.9(2) | – |
| Pollok | 27.2 | 11.0 | 226 | -10.2 | 70.7 | -0.9 | 15.8 | 1.5 | 43.4 | -19.7 | 5.9 | -6.2 | 15.6 | 6.1 | 19.3 | – |
| Provan | 2.6 | 16.5 | 152 | -16.4 | 65.3 | -3.8 | 7.8 | 0.1 | 66.5 | -6.4 | 4.0 | -3.3 | 21.7 | 9.6 | – | – |
| Rutherglen | 27.5 | 13.4 | 216 | -8.0 | 75.2 | -2.0 | 16.9 | 5.4 | 55.4 | -0.6 | 11.3 | -13.1 | 16.3 | 8.2 | 0.2 | – |
| Shettleston | 26.3 | 14.3 | 205 | -3.2 | 68.9 | -1.5 | 15.0 | 1.8 | 60.6 | -3.0 | 5.3 | -5.2 | 19.1 | 6.4 | – | – |

*Appendix 1: The Voting Statistics*

| SCOTLAND | % Owner occupied 1981 | Unemployed % | Household income | Electorate change % | % voting | % change in voting | % Con. | Con. change 1987-92 | % Labour | Lab. change 1987-92 | % Lib. Dem | Lib. Dem. chg. 1987-92 | % SNP | SNP change 1987-92 | % Other | Swing |
|---|---|---|---|---|---|---|---|---|---|---|---|---|---|---|---|---|
| Springburn | 17.8 | 17.1 | 178 | -11.1 | 65.7 | -1.8 | 8.7 | 0.5 | 67.7 | -6.0 | 4.1 | -3.8 | 19.5 | 9.3 | — | — |
| Greenock & Port Glasgow | 18.0 | 20.5 | 199 | -9.9 | 73.7 | -1.7 | 11.7 | 2.0 | 58.0 | -5.9 | 11.4 | -6.5 | 19.0 | 10.4 | — | — |
| Hamilton | 28.4 | 10.4 | 242 | -1.1 | 76.2 | -0.8 | 17.6 | 3.2 | 55.2 | -4.5 | 7.5 | -5.7 | 19.7 | 7.0 | — | — |
| Kilmarnock & Loudoun | 29.9 | 11.4 | 233 | -1.0 | 80.0 | 2.0 | 19.0 | -0.6 | 44.8 | -3.7 | 5.5 | -8.2 | 30.7 | 12.5 | — | — |
| Monklands East | 18.0 | 13.9 | 223 | -2.5 | 75.1 | 0.3 | 16.0 | -0.8 | 61.3 | 0.3 | 4.6 | -4.6 | 18.0 | 5.1 | — | — |
| West | 27.3 | 5.7 | 215 | -3.2 | 77.5 | 0.1 | 15.9 | 0.2 | 61.3 | -1.0 | 6.2 | -5.0 | 16.6 | 5.7 | — | — |
| Motherwell North | 14.9 | 10.6 | 215 | -0.6 | 76.7 | -0.6 | 11.4 | 0.3 | 63.4 | -3.6 | 4.9 | -3.1 | 20.3 | 6.4 | 0.4 | — |
| South | 17.4 | 11.4 | 210 | -4.0 | 76.2 | 0.6 | 16.0 | 1.5 | 57.1 | -1.2 | 6.2 | -5.2 | 20.4 | 5.0 | 1.4(2) | — |
| Paisley North | 31.5 | 11.0 | 203 | -6.2 | 73.4 | -0.1 | 16.4 | 0.6 | 50.7 | -4.8 | 8.2 | -7.6 | 23.3 | 10.4 | 0.3 | — |
| South | 23.8 | 7.8 | 225 | -6.3 | 75.0 | -0.3 | 15.9 | 1.2 | 50.7 | -5.5 | 9.1 | -6.0 | 24.1 | 10.1 | 0.3 | — |
| Renfrew West & Inverclyde | 45.1 | 6.0 | 269 | 3.4 | 80.3 | -0.2 | 32.9 | 3.1 | 36.6 | -2.1 | 10.0 | -11.4 | 20.2 | 5.4 | 0.2 | — |
| Strathkelvin & Bearsden | 66.9 | 9.7 | 315 | -2.5 | 82.3 | 0.1 | 36.0 | 2.6 | 42.3 | 4.1 | 9.1 | -12.3 | 12.5 | -1.9 | 1.0 | 2.6 |
| *Tayside, Angus East* | 40.7 | 5.8 | 229 | 3.5 | 74.2 | -1.2 | 38.5 | -0.5 | 12.8 | 2.0 | 7.2 | -0.5 | 40.5 | -6.8 | 0.9(2) | -0.8 |
| Dundee East | 24.1 | 16.1 | 217 | -3.0 | 72.3 | -3.6 | 17.7 | 4.9 | 44.0 | 1.7 | 4.0 | -0.6 | 33.3 | 8.3 | 1.4(2) | — |
| West | 21.9 | 11.2 | 203 | -3.2 | 69.8 | -5.6 | 18.5 | 0.5 | 49.0 | -4.4 | 7.5 | -5.2 | 23.6 | 8.4 | — | — |
| Perth & Kinross | 42.8 | 7.5 | 234 | 3.1 | 76.9 | 2.4 | 40.2 | 0.5 | 12.5 | -3.4 | 11.4 | -5.5 | 36.0 | 4.5 | — | — |
| Tayside North | 40.3 | 6.1 | 241 | 3.7 | 77.6 | 2.9 | 46.7 | 1.3 | 7.1 | -1.7 | 8.7 | -4.2 | 37.5 | 8.7 | — | — |
| *Western Isles* | 64.3 | 14.4 | 247 | -3.1 | 70.4 | 0.2 | 8.5 | 0.4 | 47.8 | 5.1 | 3.4 | -17.3 | 37.2 | | 3.1 | — |

Table A1.4  Northern Ireland constituency results, 1992

| | % voting | % Change in voting | Unionist parties | | | | % APNI | APNI change 1987–92 | % Con | Republican parties | | | | | | | % Other |
|---|---|---|---|---|---|---|---|---|---|---|---|---|---|---|---|---|---|
| | | | % UUP | % DUP | % Other U | Unionist ch 1987–92 | | | | % SDLP | SDLP ch 1987–92 | % SF | SF change 1987–92 | % WP | WP change 1987–92 | Repn ch 1987–92 | |
| Antrim East | 62.5 | 7.2 | 43.2 | 24.3 | — | −4.0 | 23.3 | −2.4 | 8.6 | — | — | 4.2 | −2.2 | — | — | −2.8 | 0.6 |
| Antrim North | 65.8 | 3.0 | 18.1 | 50.9 | — | 0.2 | 7.6 | −4.9 | 5.0 | 14.3 | 1.8 | 2.9 | −1.5 | — | — | −0.3 | — |
| Antrim South | 62.1 | 3.1 | 70.9 | — | — | 1.2 | 12.4 | −3.6 | — | 12.8 | 2.9 | 1.9 | −0.1 | — | — | 1.4 | 1.0 |
| Belfast East | 67.7 | 7.5 | — | 51.5 | 6.3 | −4.1 | 29.8 | −2.4 | 9.3 | — | — | — | — | 0.9 | −3.1 | −3.2 | 0.4 |
| Belfast North | 65.2 | 3.0 | 48.0 | — | — | −6.4 | 6.3 | −1.5 | 5.9 | 21.2 | 5.5 | 13.1 | −0.7 | 1.2 | −7.2 | −2.4 | 4.4(2) |
| Belfast South | 64.5 | 4.2 | 48.6 | — | — | −9.2 | 15.0 | −6.2 | 10.0 | 18.7 | 5.6 | 3.3 | 0.2 | 1.1 | −3.6 | 2.2 | 3.2(2) |
| Belfast West† | 73.2 | 4.1 | 11.9 | — | — | −6.7 | — | — | — | 43.6 | 7.8 | 42.1 | 0.9 | 1.9 | −2.6 | 6.2 | 0.5 |
| Down North | 65.5 | 2.7 | — | 9.8 | 42.9 | −27.8 | 14.7 | −4.7 | 32.0 | — | — | — | — | — | — | — | 0.6 |
| Down South | 80.9 | 1.6 | 40.9 | — | — | −4.8 | 2.5 | 0.6 | 2.4 | 51.2 | 4.2 | 3.0 | −1.2 | — | — | 1.8 | — |
| Fermanagh & S.Tyrone | 78.5 | −1.7 | 48.8 | — | — | −0.7 | 1.7 | 0.0 | — | 23.2 | 4.1 | 22.9 | −3.5 | — | — | −2.6 | 3.3(2) |
| Foyle | 69.6 | 0.6 | — | 26.4 | — | −2.1 | 2.7 | 0.1 | — | 51.5 | 2.7 | 17.6 | −0.3 | — | — | 1.3 | 0.8 |
| Lagan Valley | 67.4 | 3.3 | 60.8 | — | — | −9.2 | 12.7 | −1.1 | 9.0 | 9.4 | 2.5 | 6.8 | 0.4 | 1.0 | −1.1 | 1.2 | — |
| Londonderry East | 69.8 | 1.1 | 57.6 | — | — | −2.9 | 6.9 | 0.2 | 3.0 | 22.5 | 3.3 | 10.1 | −1.1 | 1.2 | −1.7 | 0.2 | — |
| Newry & Armagh | 77.9 | −1.3 | 36.1 | — | — | −1.8 | 1.8 | 0.6 | — | 49.6 | 1.5 | 12.5 | 0.6 | — | — | 1.2 | — |
| Strangford | 65.0 | 7.4 | 43.6 | 23.7 | — | −8.7 | 16.9 | −3.4 | 15.1 | — | — | — | — | — | — | −3.7 | 0.7 |
| Ulster Mid | 79.3 | 1.9 | — | 42.3 | — | −1.8 | 2.8 | −0.8 | — | 31.0 | 4.8 | 18.7 | −5.2 | 0.5 | −1.7 | −2.0 | — |
| Upper Bann | 67.4 | 1.8 | 59.0 | — | — | −2.5 | 5.6 | −0.3 | 3.4 | 23.4 | 2.9 | 6.1 | −1.3 | 2.5 | −2.3 | −0.6 | 4.7(3) |
| Northern Ireland | 69.8 | 2.7 | 34.5 | 13.1 | 2.7 | −4.4 | 8.7 | −1.2 | 5.7 | 23.5 | 2.4 | 10.0 | −1.4 | 0.6 | −2.1 | −1.1 | 1.2 |

*Notes:*

UUP: (Official) Ulster Unionist Party   APNI: Alliance Party of Northern Ireland   SF: Sinn Féin
DUP: Democratic Unionist Party   SDLP: Social Democratic & Labour Party   WP: Workers' Party
Other U: Other Unionist, viz. Independent Unionist (Belfast East), Ulster Popular Unionist (Down North)

'Unionist Change' is the change in the total vote for Official Unionists, Democratic Unionists and other Unionists.
'Republican Change' is the change in the total vote for the SDLP, Sinn Féin and the Workers' Party.

*Table A1.5    Outstanding results, 1992*

### 12 Closest Results

| %   | Votes |                                  |
|-----|-------|----------------------------------|
| 0.0 | (19)  | Vale of Glamorgan (Con)          |
| 0.1 | (45)  | Bristol NW (Con)                 |
| 0.1 | (53)  | Hayes & Harlington (Con)         |
| 0.2 | (85)  | Ayr (Con)                        |
| 0.2 | (120) | Rossendale & Darwen (Lab)        |
| 0.3 | (130) | Brecon & Radnor (Con)            |
| 0.3 | (191) | Warrington South (Lab)           |
| 0.3 | (162) | Birmingham Yardley (Lab)         |
| 0.4 | (185) | Bolton North-East (Con)          |
| 0.5 | (242) | Portsmouth South (Con)           |
| 0.5 | (265) | Ipswich (Lab)                    |
| 0.5 | (274) | Gordon (Lib Dem)                 |

### 12 Highest Turnouts

| %    |                      |
|------|----------------------|
| 86.1 | Leicestershire NW    |
| 86.1 | Monmouth             |
| 85.9 | Brecon & Radnor      |
| 85.8 | Hexham               |
| 85.7 | Ribble Valley        |
| 85.7 | Mid Staffordshire    |
| 85.5 | Derbyshire South     |
| 85.5 | Sherwood             |
| 85.0 | Richmond & Barnes    |
| 85.0 | Derbyshire West      |
| 85.0 | Hazel Grove          |
| 84.8 | Bury North           |

### 12 Liberal Democrat Nearest Misses

| %   |                        |
|-----|------------------------|
| 0.3 | Brecon & Radnor        |
| 0.5 | Portsmouth South       |
| 1.7 | Hazel Grove            |
| 1.8 | Edinburgh West         |
| 2.3 | Isle of Wight          |
| 2.4 | Conwy                  |
| 2.9 | St. Ives               |
| 5.2 | Taunton                |
| 5.5 | Southport              |
| 5.7 | Falmouth & Camborne    |
| 5.8 | Devon West & Torridge  |
| 6.0 | Hereford               |

### 12 Lowest Turnouts

| %    |                          |
|------|--------------------------|
| 53.9 | Peckham                  |
| 54.6 | Liverpool Riverside      |
| 56.0 | Newham North-West        |
| 56.1 | Sheffield Central        |
| 56.9 | Manchester Central       |
| 60.2 | Newham South             |
| 60.3 | Newham North-East        |
| 60.8 | Manchester Gorton        |
| 61.3 | Leeds Central            |
| 62.4 | Vauxhall                 |
| 62.5 | Antrim East              |
| 62.6 | Southwark & Bermondsey   |

### 10 Greatest Increases in Turnout

| %   |                              |
|-----|------------------------------|
| 9.3 | Hendon North                 |
| 8.8 | Horsham                      |
| 8.6 | Kensington                   |
| 8.6 | Hendon South                 |
| 8.6 | Chipping Barnet              |
| 8.5 | Bow & Poplar                 |
| 8.4 | Hackney South & Shoreditch   |
| 8.2 | Finchley                     |
| 7.9 | Bethnal Green & Stepney      |
| 7.8 | Mid Kent                     |

### 10 Greatest Falls in Turnout

| %     |                           |
|-------|---------------------------|
| −10.7 | Liverpool Riverside       |
| −9.6  | Manchester Gorton         |
| −7.0  | Manchester Central        |
| −6.6  | Liverpool Mossley Hill    |
| −6.3  | Sheffield Central         |
| −6.3  | Liverpool Broadgreen      |
| −6.2  | Liverpool Walton          |
| −5.9  | Manchester Withington     |
| −5.6  | Dundee West               |
| −5.1  | Liverpool Garston         |

*10 Greatest Increases in Conservative Share of Vote*

| % | |
|---|---|
| 10.2 | Stockton South |
| 7.8 | Great Grimsby |
| 7.3 | Eastwood |
| 7.2 | Newcastle-upon-Tyne N |
| 7.1 | Cambridgeshire NE |
| 6.2 | Battersea |
| 5.6 | Colne Valley |
| 5.4 | Glasgow Rutherglen |
| 5.1 | Gordon |
| 5.0 | Plymouth Devonport |

*10 Greatest Falls in Conservative Share of Vote*

| % | |
|---|---|
| −9.9 | Hove |
| −8.8 | Leicester East |
| −8.5 | Ribble Valley |
| −8.3 | Eastbourne |
| −8.1 | Birmingham Yardley |
| −8.0 | Chesterfield |
| −7.4 | Cornwall North |
| −7.3 | Bradford North |
| −7.2 | Liverpool Mossley Hill |
| −7.1 | Taunton |

*10 Greatest Increases in Labour Share of Vote*

| % | |
|---|---|
| 20.3 | Plymouth Devonport |
| 16.9 | Mansfield |
| 16.1 | Norfolk North-West |
| 15.0 | Mid Staffordshire |
| 14.5 | Plymouth Drake |
| 13.3 | Monmouth |
| 13.2 | Ashfield |
| 13.2 | Exeter |
| 12.9 | Tottenham |
| 12.6 | Norwich North |

*10 Greatest Falls in Labour Share of Vote*

| % | |
|---|---|
| −19.7 | Glasgow Pollok |
| −15.9 | Glasgow Govan |
| −15.1 | Edinburgh Leith |
| −14.8 | Coventry SE |
| −11.2 | Ribble Valley |
| −8.9 | Southwark & Bermondsey |
| −8.1 | Falkirk East |
| −7.9 | Cunninghame South |
| −7.6 | Aberdeen North |
| −7.3 | Glasgow Central |

*10 Greatest Increases in Liberal Democrat Share of Vote (compared to Alliance vote, 1987)*

| % | |
|---|---|
| 19.2 | Ribble Valley |
| 13.0 | Eastbourne |
| 9.5 | Birmingham Yardley |
| 9.4 | Southwark & Bermondsey |
| 8.3 | Taunton |
| 8.1 | Windsor & Maidenhead |
| 6.3 | Bath |
| 6.2 | Chesterfield |
| 5.6 | Newbury |
| 5.5 | Cornwall North |

*10 Greatest Falls in Liberal Democrat % Share of Vote*

| % | |
|---|---|
| −29.9 | Plymouth Devonport |
| −24.7 | Leeds West |
| −18.8 | Stockton South |
| −18.2 | Plymouth Drake |
| −18.2 | Norfolk North-West |
| −17.3 | Western Isles |
| −17.1 | Staffordshire SE |
| −15.9 | Stevenage |
| −15.4 | Plymouth Sutton |
| −15.2 | Pembroke |

*10 Greatest Increases in Nationalist Share of Vote*

| % | |
|---|---|
| 26.7 | Glasgow Govan (SNP) |
| 15.0 | Ceredigion & Pembroke N (PC) |
| 13.2 | Cunninghame South (SNP) |
| 12.5 | Kilmarnock & Loudoun (SNP) |
| 12.4 | Edinburgh Leith (SNP) |
| 11.3 | Midlothian (SNP) |
| 11.0 | East Kilbride (SNP) |
| 10.9 | Glasgow Central (SNP) |
| 10.8 | Kirkcaldy (SNP) |
| 10.8 | Falkirk East (SNP) |

*10 Highest Nationalist Votes*

| % | |
|---|---|
| 59.0 | Caernarfon |
| 47.5 | Banff & Buchan |
| 44.3 | Moray |
| 44.0 | Meirionnydd nant Conwy |
| 40.5 | Angus East |
| 37.5 | Tayside North |
| 37.2 | Western Isles |
| 37.1 | Ynys Môn |
| 37.1 | Glasgow Govan |
| 36.4 | Galloway & Upper Nithsdale |

*10 Highest Increases in Electorate 1987–92 (as % of June 1987)*

| % | |
|---|---|
| 13.7 | Milton Keynes SW |
| 12.7 | Milton Keynes NE |
| 10.1 | The Wrekin |
| 9.7 | Northampton South |
| 9.1 | Cardiff Central |
| 9.0 | Gordon |
| 8.7 | Mid Norfolk |
| 8.7 | Southwark & Bermondsey |
| 8.6 | Crawley |
| 8.3 | South Ribble |

*10 Highest Falls in Electorate 1987–92 (as % of June 1987)*

| % | |
|---|---|
| −18.3 | Hackney South & Shoreditch |
| −18.1 | Hackney North & Stoke Newington |
| −16.4 | Glasgow Provan |
| −14.5 | Chelsea |
| −13.9 | Glasgow Garscadden |
| −12.6 | Ealing Acton |
| −12.6 | Brent East |
| −12.6 | Kensington |
| −12.4 | Ealing Southall |
| −11.3 | Ealing North |

*15 Highest Other Votes*

| % | | | |
|---|---|---|---|
| 38.6 | John Cartwright* | Woolwich | Soc Dem |
| 37.2 | Rosie Barnes* | Greenwich | Soc Dem |
| 28.9 | Dave Nellist* | Coventry SE | Ind Lab |
| 19.3 | Tommy Sheridan | Glasgow Pollok | Sc Mil Lab |
| 14.2 | Terry Fields* | Liverpool Broadgreen | Soc Lab |
| 10.3 | Ron Brown* | Edinburgh Leith | Ind Lab |
| 9.4 | Sydney Bidwell* | Ealing Southall | True Lab |
| 8.5 | John Hughes* | Coventry NE | Ind Lab |
| 8.3 | Michael Meadowcroft | Leeds W | Lib |
| 5.8 | William Hardman | Bolton SE | Ind Lab |
| 5.3 | Nigel Furness | Hove | Hove Con |
| 4.7 | John Browne* | Winchester | Ind Con |
| 4.2 | Harold Luscombe | Plymouth Devonport | Soc Dem |
| 3.9 | Seamus Lynch | Belfast N | Noise Ab |
| 3.8 | David Morrish | Tiverton | Lib |

* indicates a sitting MP for the constituency

*Mean and Highest Votes for 'Other' Parties*

| Mean % | | Highest % | |
|---|---|---|---|
| 1.6 | Liberal | 8.3 | Leeds W |
| 1.3 | Green | 3.8 | Islington N |
| 1.2 | British National Party | 3.6 | Bethnal Gn & Stepney |
| 0.5 | Anti-Federalist | 3.4 | Staffordshire Moorlands |
| 0.8 | Loony Green Giant | 2.3 | Honiton |
| 0.6 | Official Loony | 1.6 | Workington |
| 0.4 | Natural Law Party | 1.5 | Warley E |
| 0.8 | National Front | 1.2 | Dudley E |
| 0.6 | Islamic Party of GB | 1.0 | Bradford W |

*A1.6 By-elections 1987–1992*

| By-election | | Turnout (%) | Con (%) | Lab (%) | LD/SDP (%) | Nat (%) | Other (%) | |
|---|---|---|---|---|---|---|---|---|
| Kensington | 1987 | 64.7 | 47.5 | 33.3 | 17.2† | – | (3) | 2.0 |
| | 14.7.88 | 51.6 | 41.6 | 38.2 | 10.8, 5.0 | – | (11) | 4.4 |
| | 1992 | 73.3 | 50.3 | 38.8 | 9.0 | – | (3) | 1.9 |
| Glasgow Govan | 1987 | 73.4 | 11.9 | 64.8 | 12.3† | 10.4 | (1) | 0.6 |
| *SNP gain* | 10.11.88 | 60.4 | 7.3 | 37.0 | 4.1 | 48.8 | (4) | 2.8 |
| *Lab. recovery* | 1992 | 76.0 | 9.9 | 48.9 | 3.5 | 37.1 | (1) | 0.5 |
| Epping Forest | 1987 | 76.3 | 60.9 | 18.4 | 19.4† | – | (1) | 1.3 |
| | 15.12.88 | 49.1 | 39.5 | 18.7 | 26.0, 12.2 | – | (5) | 3.6 |
| | 1992 | 80.6 | 59.5 | 22.4 | 17.0 | – | (1) | 1.0 |
| Pontypridd | 1987 | 76.8 | 19.5 | 56.3 | 18.9† | 5.3 | – | – |
| | 23.2.89 | 62.2 | 13.5 | 53.4 | 3.9, 3.1 | 25.3 | (2) | 0.8 |
| | 1992 | 79.3 | 20.3 | 60.8 | 8.5 | 9.1 | (1) | 1.3 |
| Richmond (Yorks) | 1987 | 72.1 | 61.2 | 11.8 | 27.0 | – | – | – |
| | 23.2.89 | 64.4 | 37.2 | 4.9 | 22.1, 32.2 | – | (5) | 3.6 |
| | 1992 | 78.4 | 61.9 | 11.6 | 25.7 | – | (1) | 0.9 |
| Vale of Glamorgan | 1987 | 79.3 | 46.8 | 34.7 | 16.7† | 1.8 | – | – |
| *Lab. gain* | 4.4.89 | 70.7 | 36.3 | 48.9 | 4.2, 2.3 | 3.5 | (6) | 4.9 |
| *Con. recovery* | 1992 | 81.9 | 44.3 | 44.3 | 9.2 | 2.1 | – | – |

| | | | | | | | |
|---|---|---|---|---|---|---|---|
| Glasgow Central | 1987 | 65.6 | 13.0 | 64.5 | 10.5 | 10.0 | (2) 2.0 |
| | 15.6.89 | 52.8 | 7.6 | 54.6 | 1.5, 1.0 | 30.2 | (4) 5.0 |
| | 1992 | 63.1 | 13.9 | 57.2 | 6.3 | 20.8 | (2) 1.8 |
| Vauxhall | 1987 | 64.0 | 29.0 | 50.2 | 18.2† | — | (3) 2.6 |
| | 15.6.89 | 44.4 | 18.8 | 52.8 | 17.5 | — | (11) 10.8 |
| | 1992 | 62.4 | 27.8 | 54.7 | 14.6 | — | (3) 2.9 |
| [The Green Party candidate took 6.1% at the by-election] | | | | | | | |
| Mid-Staffordshire | 1987 | 79.4 | 50.6 | 24.7 | 23.2 | — | (1) 1.5 |
| *Lab. gain* | 22.3.90 | 77.5 | 32.3 | 49.1 | 11.2, 2.5 | — | (10) 5.1 |
| *Con. recovery* | 1992 | 85.7 | 49.6 | 39.7 | 10.3 | — | (1) 0.4 |
| Bootle | 1987 | 72.9 | 20.1 | 66.9 | 13.0† | — | — |
| | 24.5.90 | 50.6 | 9.1 | 75.4 | 9.0, 0.4 | — | (4) 6.2 |
| | 8.11.90 | 39.7 | 9.2 | 78.4 | 7.9 | — | (4) 4.6 |
| | 1992 | 72.5 | 16.0 | 74.6 | 6.6 | — | (2) 2.9 |
| Knowsley South | 1987 | 74.1 | 21.6 | 64.5 | 13.9† | — | — |
| | 27.9.90 | 33.4 | 15.2 | 68.8 | 8.5 | — | (4) 7.5 |
| | 1992 | 74.7 | 21.3 | 68.6 | 9.6 | — | (1) 0.5 |
| Eastbourne | 1987 | 75.6 | 59.9 | 8.8 | 29.7 | — | (1) 1.6 |
| *Lib. Dem. gain* | 18.10.90 | 60.7 | 40.9 | 5.0 | 50.8 | — | (5) 3.2 |
| *Con. recovery* | 1992 | 81.0 | 51.6 | 4.6 | 42.7 | — | (2) 1.1 |
| Bradford North | 1987 | 72.7 | 39.5 | 42.8 | 17.7† | — | — |
| | 8.11.90 | 53.5 | 16.8 | 51.7 | 25.3 | — | (7) 6.1 |
| | 1992 | 73.4 | 32.2 | 47.8 | 18.7 | — | (2) 1.3 |

| By-election | | Turnout (%) | Con (%) | Lab (%) | LD/SDP (%) | Nat (%) | Other (%) | |
|---|---|---|---|---|---|---|---|---|
| Paisley North | 1987 | 73.5 | 15.8 | 55.5 | 15.8† | 12.9 | — | — |
| | 29.11.90 | 53.7 | 14.8 | 44.0 | 8.3 | 29.4 | (1) | 3.6 |
| | 1992 | 73.4 | 16.4 | 50.7 | 8.2 | 23.3 | (2) | 1.4 |
| Paisley South | 1987 | 75.3 | 14.7 | 56.2 | 15.1 | 14.0 | — | — |
| | 29.11.90 | 55.5 | 13.4 | 46.1 | 9.8 | 27.5 | (1) | 3.1 |
| | 1992 | 75.0 | 15.9 | 50.7 | 9.1 | 24.1 | (1) | 0.3 |
| Ribble Valley | 1987 | 79.1 | 60.9 | 17.7 | 21.4† | — | — | — |
| *Lib. Dem. gain* | 7.3.91 | 71.2 | 38.5 | 9.4 | 48.5 | — | (6) | 3.5 |
| *Con. recovery* | 1992 | 85.7 | 52.4 | 6.5 | 40.6 | — | (2) | 0.5 |
| Neath | 1987 | 78.8 | 16.1 | 63.4 | 14.1† | 6.4 | — | — |
| | 4.4.91 | 63.7 | 8.6 | 51.8 | 5.8, 5.3 | 23.4 | (3) | 5.2 |
| | 1992 | 80.6 | 15.2 | 68.0 | 5.4 | 11.3 | — | — |
| Monmouth | 1987 | 80.8 | 47.5 | 27.7 | 24.0† | 0.8 | — | — |
| *Lab. gain* | 16.5.91 | 75.8 | 34.0 | 39.3 | 24.8 | 0.6§ | (3) | 1.4 |
| *Con. recovery* | 1992 | 86.1 | 47.3 | 41.0 | 10.9 | 0.8§ | — | — |
| Liverpool Walton | 1987 | 73.6 | 14.4 | 64.4 | 21.2 | — | — | — |
| *Lab. gain* | 4.7.91 | 56.7 | 2.9 | 53.1 | 36.0 | — | (3) | 8.1 |
| | 1992 | 67.4 | 12.5 | 72.4 | 12.0 | — | (3) | 3.1 |

[The 'Real Labour' candidate took 6.5% at the by-election]

| | | Turnout | | | | | | | Oth |
|---|---|---|---|---|---|---|---|---|---|
| Hemsworth | 1987 | 75.7 | 17.2 | 67.0 | 15.8 | – | – | – | – |
| | 7.11.91 | 42.8 | 10.5 | 66.3 | 20.1 | – | – | – | (2) 3.2 |
| | 1992 | 75.9 | 18.6 | 70.8 | 10.5 | – | – | – | – |
| Kincardine & Deeside | 1987 | 75.2 | 40.7 | 15.9 | 36.3 | – | – | 6.5 | (1) 0.6 |
| Lib. Dem. gain | 7.11.91 | 67.0 | 30.6 | 7.7 | 49.0 | – | – | 11.1 | (1) 1.6 |
| Con. recovery | 1992 | 78.8 | 43.7 | 9.1 | 35.1 | – | – | 11.3 | (1) 0.7 |
| Langbaurgh | 1987 | 78.8 | 41.7 | 38.4 | 19.9 | – | – | – | – |
| Lab. gain | 7.11.91 | 65.4 | 39.1 | 42.9 | 16.1 | – | – | – | (4) 2.0 |
| Con. recovery | 1992 | 83.1 | 45.4 | 43.1 | 11.5 | – | – | – | – |

### Northern Ireland By-election 1987–92

| By-election | | Turnout | UUP | APNI | Con | SDLP | SF | WP | Oth |
|---|---|---|---|---|---|---|---|---|---|
| Upper Bann | 1987 | 65.6 | 61.5 | 5.9 | – | 20.5 | 7.4 | 4.7 | – |
| | 17.5.90 | 53.4 | 58.0 | 2.7 | 3.0 | 18.9 | 5.7 | 3.1 | (5) 8.6 |
| | 1992 | 67.4 | 59.0 | 5.6 | 3.4 | 23.4 | 6.1 | 2.5 | – |

*Notes:*

The 1987 vote in the 'LD/SDP' column is that polled by the Alliance candidate: those marked with a † were SDP candidates, the others Liberals. Where two votes are given in the 'LD/SDP' column at a by-election, the first is that of the Liberal Democrat, the second that of the SDP candidate.

§ indicates a joint Plaid Cymru–Green candidate.

# Appendix 2: The Results Analysed

## John Curtice and Michael Steed

The 1992 election was a disaster for the Labour Party. They were as much as 7.6% of the vote (in Great Britain[1]) behind the Conservatives, making it the fourth election in a row at which Labour were 7% or more behind the Conservatives. The last four results stand in stark contrast to those of the 1950–74 period. Then the most by which Labour trailed the Conservatives was by 4.2% in 1959. Only once did any election see a lead larger than 5% for the winning party – in 1966 when Labour led by 7.5%.

Yet so far as seats in the House of Commons are concerned, the outcome was relatively close. The Conservatives won just 336 seats, sufficient to give them an overall majority of 21. This is a smaller majority than that secured by the Conservatives in 1955, 1959 or 1970 – or indeed by Labour in 1966. The only post-war Conservative government to have enjoyed a smaller majority was Winston Churchill's in 1951. But then the Conservatives won 1.6% less of the vote in Great Britain than did Labour.

The election result therefore presents a major paradox. How could a result that was so substantial in terms of votes appear so close in terms of seats?

### The National Picture

Across the country as a whole there was a 3.0% swing from Conservative to Labour. This was slightly higher than the 2.8% swing in 1987 but still left Labour with a lower share of the total vote than in 1979. It was however the third election in a row at which Conservative support fell – with the consequence that it was the fourth election in a row at which a majority Conservative government was elected with a lower share of the popular vote than any such government since 1922.

Support for Britain's main third party alternative also fell for the second election in row. But its support was still four points higher than in 1979 and only half a point lower than in October 1974. With support for the Nationalists in both Scotland and Wales rising and a considerable increase in the number of minor party candidates, the combined Conservative and Labour share of the vote rose by just 3 points from 75% to 78%. This is still lower than at any election between 1929 and February 1974 and suggests that any conclusion that the election heralds a return to two-party politics is premature.

Table A2.1  Measures of change since 1987

| | Overall | Mean | Median | Standard Deviation |
|---|---|---|---|---|
| Change in Conservative vote | −0.5 | −0.9 | −0.8 | 2.5 |
| Change in Labour vote | +3.7 | +4.1 | +4.3 | 4.4 |
| Change in Lib Dem vote | −4.8 | −4.9 | −5.1 | 4.3 |
| Total-vote swing | −2.1 | −2.5 | −2.6 | 2.7 |
| Two-party swing | −3.0 | −3.4 | −3.6 | 4.1 |
| Change in turnout | +2.4 | +2.2 | +2.6 | 2.7 |

The following seats have been excluded from the calculation of the mean, median and standard deviation (excepting change in turnout): Greenwich and Woolwich (no Lib Dem candidate); Bolton SE, Coventry NE, Coventry SE, Ealing Southall, Edinburgh Leith, Liverpool Broadgreen (Independent Labour vote above 5%); Hove (Independent Conservative vote above 5%). Their exclusion has little or no material impact on the figures that would otherwise be quoted here. They are also excluded from all other analyses in this appendix unless otherwise stated.

Total-vote swing is the average of the change in the Conservative share of the vote and the change in the Labour share of the vote. Two-party swing is the change in the Conservative share of the votes cast for Conservative and Labour only (i.e. the two-party vote). In both cases a plus sign indicates a swing to Conservative, a minus sign a swing to Labour. All references to swing in this appendix are to two-party swing unless otherwise indicated. The change in the Liberal Democrat vote is the difference between the Liberal Democrat vote in 1992 and the SDP/Liberal Alliance vote in 1987.

Indeed, in many respects what is striking about the 1992 result (as indeed it was of the 1987 result) is not how different the outcome was to its immediate predecessor but rather how similar. The Pedersen Index,[2] a measure of the total amount of electoral volatility between any pair of elections is, at 4.9, only slightly higher than in 1987 (3.2) and lower than at all but two of the seven elections between 1964 and 1983. The notion that the British electorate has become more volatile does not receive any support from this result.

Of course, the movement since 1987 was not the same everywhere. Indeed, variation in the movement between one constituency and another was again a marked feature of the election result. The standard deviation in the swing is identical to 1987 and 1979 and lower only than 1983.[3] The result did nothing to rehabilitate the claim commonly made before 1979 that the swing at British elections is 'uniform'. True, the variation in the Conservative performance was lower than in 1983 or 1987, but the variation in Labour's was even higher, higher even than the traditionally variable Liberal Democrat performance.[4] Here is a first hint that perhaps we should be looking at the inter-relationship between Labour and Liberal Democrat performance, a hint which is strengthened by the fact that there was a positive correlation between the Liberal Democrat performance and swing – meaning that Labour generally did better where the Liberal Democrats did worse.

Table A2.1 has other important messages. The mean of the individual constituency swings to Labour was markedly higher than the overall swing calculated on the basis of the total votes cast across the whole country. Such a difference arises when a party succeeds in concentrating more of its vote in seats with a smaller electorate and/or lower turnout. And we can see that the median swing was yet higher still – indicating that there were more atypically good Conservative performances than there were Labour ones. We shall return to consider the significance of these differences in our discussion of the electoral system. For now we should note that all of the tables in this appendix are based on mean change rather than overall change and consequently the national benchmark against which the behaviour of any sub-group of constituencies might be compared is more favourable to Labour than indicated by the overall national swing.

## Regional Variation

The most striking geographical pattern in the results was, as it was in all the three previous elections, a North/South variation in swing. But in marked contrast to those elections, and to the long-term pattern since 1959, it was the Conservatives who were the more successful in the north and Labour in the south. As Table A1.2 indicates there was actually a 2.5% (overall) total-vote swing to the Conservatives in Scotland. Conservative support also broadly held steady or even rose slightly in the three northernmost regions of England, while in the South of England and the Midlands the picture was one of consistent albeit small decline.

The size of the difference in the behaviour of the two halves of the country was considerable. True, it was rather less than in 1987 or 1983 – but it was just as substantial as in 1979. Across the whole of the South of England and the Midlands the swing was −4.8%; in the North of England and Scotland it was −1.2%.[5] The difference between these two figures of 3.6 compares with equivalent figures of 5.0 and 4.9 in 1987 and 1983 – but with a figure of 3.5 in 1979. And if we compare Scotland with the South of England then the gap is almost as wide as in 1983. Once again the nation clearly failed to deliver a unanimous verdict.

The rebuff to the Liberal Democrats was, however, clearly a nationwide one. Their vote was lower than the Alliance's 1987 vote in every part of Britain (see Table A1.2). But their vote did fall rather less in the South West and in parts of the South East.[6] This relative success appears to have harmed both Labour and the Conservatives. But most importantly the coincident variation in Conservative performance in the South represents, in contrast to the nationwide story, a continuation of the pattern of party performance in 1987 rather than a reversal.

Thus the most important question we have to answer is why did the

North/South pattern of previous elections reverse itself? And secondly, we need to examine the variation in party performance in the South of England. In this section we examine each point in turn.

Much of the commentary on the political polarisation between north and south which was evident up to 1987 has suggested that one important reason for the divide was the contrast in the economic experiences of the two halves of Britain.[7] Broadly speaking the southern half of the country has consistently experienced lower levels of unemployment than the northern half – and the gap widened over the twenty year period prior to 1987. Equally, house prices have been more buoyant in the south than in the north. So southern voters would appear to have had greater reason to put their faith in the operation of the market economy and to vote for the party, that is the Conservatives, most inclined to uphold its virtues.

However the period between 1987 and 1992 saw a very different economic geography take hold. First of all the economic boom of the mid-1980s began to make itself felt more strongly in the northern half of the country in the period immediately after the 1987 election. Then, as the recession began to bite and unemployment began to rise in the spring of 1990, it did so more harshly in London and the South East.

Thus by the beginning of 1992, the level of unemployment was higher in the South of England than it was at the time of the 1987 general election. In the average constituency there, the registered unemployed as a proportion of the electorate had risen by 0.8 percentage points.[8] In contrast in the Midlands unemployment was 0.9 percentage points lower, in the North of England 1.8 percentage points lower (with the northern standard region showing a particularly marked drop of 2.3 points) while in Scotland unemployment was as much as 2.4 points lower.

This was not all. The recession also had a regionally differentiated impact upon the housing market. House prices fell sooner and more heavily in the south-eastern corner of the country than elsewhere. In many parts of the North of England and Scotland house prices did not stop rising until well into 1991. Overall, house prices in the average South of England constituency were just 22% higher in 1991 than in 1987, compared with 58% in the Midlands, 56% in Scotland and as much as 79% in the North of England.

At first glance the regional variation in the election result would appear to confirm that recent economic experiences do influence voters and that this relationship was responsible for the reversal of the North/South divide. But we cannot tell to what extent the variation in economic circumstances was responsible and how it compares with previous elections. In short, was the reversal of the North/South divide as large as might have been expected?

One reason why it might not have been is that there may have been countervailing forces at work. Certainly if either or both of two widely espoused explanations for Labour's defeat are valid then such countervailing forces should have been present. One such suggestion was that voters were

*Table A2.2    Regional variation in incomes and newspaper readership*

|  | Annual Household Income 1991–92 (£) | Number of Conservative Tabloid Readers per Labour Tabloid Reader |
|---|---|---|
| London | 28,988 | 2.8 |
| South of England (ex. London) | 27,106 | 2.9 |
| Midlands | 23,625 | 2.6 |
| North of England | 22,480 | 2.0 |
| Wales | 22,015 | 1.7 |
| Scotland | 23,241 | 0.8 |
| GREAT BRITAIN | 24,752 | 2.3 |

*Source*: Data kindly supplied by Richard Webber, CCN Marketing, Nottingham and derived from the National Shopper Survey.

reluctant to vote Labour because of the party's proposals for higher taxation on the better-paid. The other is that Labour lost support because of the strong attacks upon the party and especially its leader in the Tory tabloid press in the last days of the campaign.

If they were present these factors should have counterbalanced the impact of short-term economic forces because household incomes and readership of the Tory tabloid press are both higher in the south than in the north.[9] This can be seen in Table A2.2 which shows the average annual household income in constituencies in each of the main areas of Great Britain together with the ratio of Tory tabloid newspaper-buying households to Labour-buying households. So, if higher earners or Tory tabloid readers swung against Labour then this should have helped the Conservatives more in the south than in the north. Indeed, the potential impact of Labour's tax proposals upon those living in London and the South East was a prominent feature of the Tory campaign.

Identifying the impact if any of these contradictory pressures requires the use of a multivariate statistical technique. One such technique is regression analysis which produces an equation which summarises the association between a single dependent variable (such as change in share of the vote) and a set of two or more independent or explanatory variables (such as house prices, unemployment, Tory tabloid readership and income levels).[10] In particular, it enables us to estimate the independent impact of, say, unemployment, controlling for the influence of other variables such as income levels or newspaper readership.

We have estimated such an equation for each of the change in Conservative, Labour and Liberal Democrat support. In each case the same set of variables were available for inclusion in the equation. Apart from measures of the current level and recent trend in unemployment, the trend in house prices, Tory newspaper readership and household income, we also included certain

*Table A2.3.    Regression equations of party performance*

---

CONCH8792 = −6.74 − 0.72 UNCH8792 − 0.67 TLPRESS + 0.02 HINC −
0.08 AGRIC + 0.07 ALL87SH − 1.75 SW − 0.89 EM
($R^2$ = 27%)

LABCH8792 = 6.19 − 0.72 TLPRESS − 8.18 SCOTLAND + 3.38 EM +
2.60 EA + 1.73 GL
($R^2$ = 36%)

SLDCH8792 = −2.54 + 1.10 TLPRESS − 0.02 HINC + 0.21 AGRIC +
0.25 EDUC + 3.86 SW + 1.93 SE.
($R^2$ = 12%)

*where*

| | |
|---|---|
| CONCH8792 | = Change in Conservative share of the vote since 1987 |
| LABCH8792 | = Change in Labour share of the vote since 1987 |
| SLDCH8792 | = Change in Liberal Democrat share of vote since 1987 |
| UNCH8792 | = Change in proportion of electorate registered as un-employed Jan. 1992–June 1987 |
| HINC | = Household income 1990/91 annualised (in £000s) |
| TLPRESS | = Ratio of households buying a Tory tabloid newspaper to households buying a Labour one |
| AGRIC | = Percentage of residents aged 18+ employed in agriculture (1981 census) |
| EDUC | = Percentage of residents aged 18+ with degree or equivalent qualification (1981 census) |
| ALL87SH | = Alliance share of the vote 1987 |
| GL | = Constituency located in Greater London |
| SE | = Constituency located in South East |
| SW | = Constituency located in South West |
| EA | = Constituency located in East Anglia |
| EM | = Constituency located in East Midlands |
| SCOTLAND | = Constituency located in Scotland |

---

Equations only include variables whose association is statistically significant at the 5% level of probability.

measures of the social and geographical character of each constituency such as the percentage employed in agriculture, the percentage with a degree and standard region.[11] In addition we also included measures of party performance at the 1987 general election.

There are three things to look for in these equations. Firstly, to what extent do our measures of the local impact of the recession form part of each equation – and how do these equations compare in this respect with similar equations for previous elections? Secondly, do either the level of household income or of Tory tabloid readership enter the equations – and if so, do they do so in a way which corroborates the claims that have been made about their influence upon the election outcome? And thirdly, do any of the variables for the individual regions enter the equation – if they do this indicates the presence of regional variation which cannot be accounted for by the geography of the recession or of incomes or newspaper readership.

The equations, which are presented in detail in Table A2.3, provide some important findings on all three counts. The government's performance in a constituency was indeed influenced by the trend (although not the level) in unemployment in a constituency.[12] According to the equations each one point rise in unemployment cost the Conservatives 0.7% of the vote. This is a little lower than the estimate of 1% derived from a similar analysis of the 1987 equation by Spencer et al, but clearly indicates that the government again suffered where the recession had been at its worst.[13]

However, two things are missing from these equations. Firstly the local state of the housing market had no impact upon either Conservative or Labour performance – in stark contrast to 1987. Secondly, neither the level nor the trend in unemployment was associated with the performance of either of the opposition parties. In short, while the result clearly did reflect the geography of the recession it failed to do so by the extent to which it might have done. Herein may lie a clue as to one of the reasons for Labour's defeat, viz. its inability to reap full political benefit from the recession.

But what of taxation and newspaper readership? Is there evidence of their influence? At first glance the equations do seem to suggest that there is. Controlling for the everything else in the equations, the Conservatives did slightly better where household incomes were above average. And Labour did worse where Tory tabloid newspaper readers were more numerous.

But a closer look reveals that everything is not quite as would be expected. There is no sign that Labour did worse where household incomes are higher; rather the Conservatives appear to have made their gains at the expense of the Liberal Democrats whose proposals for higher taxation were not so clearly directed at the better-off.

Equally, while the equations say that Labour may have done worse where there were more Tory tabloid readers, they also say that the Conservatives did worse – just as one would anticipate given the strength of the Conservative performance in Scotland and the low proportion of Tory tabloid readers there. Rather, it is apparently the Liberal Democrats who benefited from the local presence of readers of the *Express*, *Mail* and *Sun*! In practice this variable is at least in part probably picking up the success of the Liberal Democrats in squeezing Labour tactically in some constituencies (see further below) where Labour was third, seats where typically Labour tabloid readership is low.[14]

Finally the variance explained by all three equations is low, and especially so in the case of the Liberal Democrats. Many other things evidently influenced the outcome other than the recession, the tabloids and taxation. Further, all three equations indicate a systematic regional variation that cannot be accounted for by any of these potential influences. They clearly

*Table A2.4    The south-eastern triangle*

| | Change in % vote since 1987 | | | Change in % vote 1983–92 |
|---|---|---|---|---|
| | *Con* | *Lab* | *Lib Dem* | *Con* |
| East Anglia | −1.9 | +6.6 | −5.3 | −1.5 |
| North Metropolitan | +0.5 | +5.1 | −6.2 | +3.0 |
| S.E. Midlands | +0.0 | +6.2 | −7.1 | +1.8 |
| Thames Valley | −1.3 | +2.8 | −2.8 | +0.1 |
| South Metropolitan | −0.6 | +3.5 | −3.8 | +0.6 |
| South Coast | −2.7 | +3.7 | −1.9 | −3.1 |
| West Country | −3.9 | +3.1 | −0.3 | −4.9 |

*East Anglia*: Norfolk, Suffolk, OSE Essex.
*North Metropolitan*: Hertfordshire, OMA Essex.
*South East Midlands*: Bedfordshire, Cambridgeshire, Lincolnshire, Northampton-shire, OSE Buckinghamshire.
*Thames Valley*: Berkshire, OMA Buckinghamshire, Oxfordshire, Wiltshire, North Hampshire.
*South Metropolitan*: Surrey, OMA Kent, OMA West Sussex.
*South Coast*: OSE Kent, East Sussex, OSE West Sussex, South Hampshire, Isle of Wight, Greater Bournemouth.
*West Country*: Gloucestershire, Avon, Somerset, rest of Dorset, Devon (excl. Plymouth), Cornwall.

where: *OSE Essex* is that portion of Essex in the Outer South East sub-region as defined at Table A1.2; *OMA Essex* is that portion of Essex in the Outer Metropolitan area, etc.
*North Hampshire* consists of Aldershot, Basingstoke, Hampshire North-West, Hampshire East, and Winchester.
*South Hampshire* consists of the rest of Hampshire.
*Greater Bournemouth* consists of Bournemouth East and West, Christchurch and Poole.

confirm the strength of the Liberal Democrats' performance in the South West; and they also indicate that Labour's particular successes in London, the East Midlands and East Anglia, also identifiable in Table A1.2, were also greater than might have been expected.

Indeed, the limitations of an explanation addressed purely in terms of the geography of the recession are no less apparent when we look at the variation within the South of England, identified earlier as the second important pattern within Table A1.2. Here, the government's performance fails to correlate with local unemployment levels. Rather if anything it replicates the pattern of the Lawson boom of the mid-1980s. Further, rather than a reversal of the geography of party performance at the last election the differences between the different parts of the South of England have been magnified.

That variation is in fact not wholly captured by the boundaries used in Table A1.2. On the one hand, the story extends beyond the South of England and embraces the five easternmost counties of the Midlands. On the other, the variation within what we might call the south-eastern triangle of England (excluding London) crosses the sub-regional boundaries of Table A1.2.

Towards the apex of the triangle, in Cambridgeshire and Hertfordshire, Conservative support rose against the tide, by +0.8% and +0.9% respectively. Although geographically contiguous, these counties are in different standard regions. At the far end, Conservative support fell heavily in Cornwall (−4.6%) together with Somerset (−4.9%) and towards the third corner in East Sussex (−5.1%). This is remarkably similar to what happened in 1987. Then Cambridgeshire and Hertfordshire were in the middle of an L-shaped group of five counties (along with Bedfordshire, Essex and Northamptonshire) which produced the best Conservative performances outside London. Meanwhile the worst Conservative performances last time in the south were in Devon and Cornwall – followed by Somerset. And East Sussex produced the most disappointing results for the Conservatives in the South East.

Indeed, across all the constituencies in the south-eastern triangle[15] there is a positive correlation (+0.32) between the change in the Conservative share of the vote between 1987 and 1992 and the same statistic for 1983–1987. Liberal Democrat performance in 1992 and Alliance performance in 1987 are similarly correlated (+0.28), while the equivalent Labour figure is +0.10. In contrast, across Great Britain as a whole the equivalent Conservative (−0.23) and Labour (−0.24) correlations are clearly negative while the Liberal Democrat performance exhibits no correlation at all.[16]

The precise geographical pattern is described in Table A2.4.[17] In general it shows that the Conservative performance was better to the north and east of London than to the south or west. Equally it was better closer to London than further away. Both patterns are identical to what happened in 1987. But that better performance is not at the expense of Labour but of the former Alliance vote. The one exception was East Anglia. Here the Conservative performance was on average rather poor, although the Liberal Democrats were not the beneficiaries.

The table thus makes clear why our earlier equations indicated that the Liberal Democrats did better in the South West at the expense of the Conservatives – although it also makes clear that the precise area of their better performance excludes Wiltshire and part of Dorset. Further, as in 1987, the area of bad Conservative performances also extends along the South Coast all the way to Kent. With the exception of Plymouth there was indeed not a single constituency anywhere on or near the English or Bristol Channels where Conservative support rose. To the north of the Thames estuary, by contrast, it rose in 16 of the 21 seats in the North Metropolitan area of South Essex and Hertfordshire.

This Conservative success to the north and east of London appears to give credence to the popular notion of 'Essex Man (and Woman)'. He (or she) is, though, as likely to live in Hemel Hempstead as in Basildon. And they are remarkable for their aversion to voting Liberal Democrat rather than Labour.[18] And quite what it is that makes them distinctive is by no means clear.

It certainly is not simply short-term economic gain. There is no correlation at all in our south-eastern triangle between Conservative performance and the trend in unemployment between 1987 and 1992. More likely is that they have a longer memory of the benefits of Thatcherism. Perhaps here it was strong enough to shift cultural values. The North Metropolitan and South East Midlands areas experienced some of the sharpest drops in unemployment between 1983 and 1987. Conservative performance in the south-eastern triangle in 1992 also correlates positively with levels of household income and the percentage of the housing stock represented by sold council houses.[19] But how long these memories will last must remain a moot but crucial point for understanding the future of Britain's party system.[20]

The one other part of Great Britain where the pattern of party performance was consistent with 1987 was Wales. The Conservatives have now lost the gains they made in the Principality in the 1970s when the party appeared to be overturning its historic weakness there. Whereas in 1983 the party secured 14 seats, its highest since 1874, it now holds just six, the lowest number at an election which the Conservatives have won since 1955. Perhaps more significantly for the future, three of these have majorities of 2.1% or less, while the safest seat only has a majority of 11.4%. Before the 1992 election there was much excitement about the possibility that the Conservatives might lose all or nearly all their Scottish MPs. But in fact it is the gloomy prospects for the Tories in Wales which calls for attention.

One other variation is worthy of brief note. In 1987 there was some evidence that voters could be influenced by the behaviour of their local council.[21] This was also evident again. Of the five comparable constituencies in London where Table A1.3 shows a (total-vote) swing to the Conservatives, two are two of the three seats in Wandsworth and one is in Westminster. These councils have been presented by the Conservative Party as flagship councils for the way in which local government should be run, sym-bolised by a very low or non-existent poll-tax – though they have also pursued policies designed to encourage 'gentrification' of their populations.[22] Their policies appear to have made an impact upon their local electorate.

Equally there are signs of the impact of unpopular Labour councils. In 1987 high rate rises imposed by Labour authorities in Waltham Forest and Ealing were followed by the worst and the third-worst Labour performances in London respectively. This time Labour recovered some of that lost ground. The average rise in their vote in Waltham Forest (+10.7%) was their equal best performance in any London borough, while in the two comparable seats in Ealing their vote also rose well above average (+8.6%). Outside London the constituencies in two metropolitan districts where Labour has recently suffered heavy losses in local elections, Kirklees (average swing, +0.8%) and Calderdale (−0.5%), saw above average Conservative performances.

*Table A2.5    The influence of tactical situation*

| | Change in % vote for | | | | No. of |
| | Con | Lab | Lib Dem | Swing | Seats |
|---|---|---|---|---|---|
| *London* | | | | | |
| Con/Lab margs. | −1.4 | +7.0 | −6.1 | −5.2 | 21 |
| All seats | −1.3 | +5.9 | −5.5 | −4.6 | 81 |
| *South of England (exc. London)* | | | | | |
| Con/Lab margs. | −1.6 | +6.6 | −6.1 | −5.1 | 13 |
| All seats | −1.7 | +3.9 | −3.3 | −4.1 | 156 |
| *Midlands* | | | | | |
| Con/Lab margs. | −1.7 | +6.8 | −5.9 | −5.2 | 20 |
| All seats | −1.5 | +6.7 | −5.8 | −5.8 | 118 |
| *North of England* | | | | | |
| Con/Lab margs. | −0.5 | +6.0 | −6.0 | −4.0 | 25 |
| All seats | −0.2 | +4.4 | −5.0 | −2.7 | 161 |

Table confined to constituencies in England. Con/Lab marginals are defined as those seats where the Conservatives were first in 1987, Labour second and the Conservative lead over Labour was less than 16%. There were relatively few Con/Lab marginals in Scotland or Wales.

## Tactical Voting

One of the most striking features of the results was that the swing to Labour was distinctly higher in Conservative/Labour marginals than in the country as a whole. If we take those seats where the Conservatives were first in 1987 and no more than 16% ahead of a second-placed Labour candidate,[23] the average swing was −4.7% compared with the nationwide swing of −2.5%.

In part this reflected the geographical distribution of Conservative/Labour marginals. These were particularly numerous in London, the Midlands and the North West of England – and in the first two of these Labour did particularly well, even by the standards of the southern half of Britain. This geographical concentration of marginal seats is a notable feature of British elections and increases the possibility that regional variation could significantly advantage one party rather than the other, and this is what duly happened.

But this is not the whole explanation. As Table A2.5 shows, with the single exception of the Midlands the swing to Labour was higher in Conservative/Labour marginals even when compared to the regional average. Meanwhile the Liberal Democrat share of the vote fell by more than average – especially in the South of England. We appear to have clear *prima facie* evidence that Labour candidates benefited from a squeeze on erstwhile Liberal Democrat supporters.

But the pattern of this apparent tactical voting is not one that immediately makes rational sense. For it was not concentrated in those seats where it would

Table A2.6    The pattern of voting in Con/Lab seats

| Alliance % vote 1987 | Change in % vote for | | | Swing | No. of Seats |
|---|---|---|---|---|---|
| | Con | Lab | Lib Dem | | |
| Less than 15% | −1.2 | +4.6 | −4.4 | −3.4 | 28 |
| 15 to 19% | −1.7 | +7.0 | −5.9 | −5.5 | 51 |
| 19 to 23% | −0.9 | +7.9 | −7.7 | −6.1 | 44 |
| Over 23% | −0.3 | +8.9 | −10.0 | −6.5 | 16 |

Table excludes the four seats won by Labour in by-elections between 1987 and 1992 together with Birmingham Yardley (see text).

have most effect. Amongst those seats where Labour started off within 8% of the Conservatives the swing was −3.9%, whereas in those where they were between 8 and 16% behind the swing was −5.5%. Indeed, the swing was highest of all (−6.3%) in those seats where Labour were more than 16% behind the Conservatives and which were thus not apparently marginal at all.

However we need to bear in mind that the pool of potential new tactical voters may well be greater in some constituencies than in others. In particular tactical voting may have occurred in some constituencies already. In a number of those seats where Labour started off in second place it was the Alliance which secured second place in 1983 as it ran Labour close for second place across the country as a whole.[24] While Labour then recovered second place in 1987, a substantial and largely unsqueezed third-placed Alliance vote sometimes remained. In contrast in others of these Conservative/Labour seats the Alliance never achieved second place and was susceptible to being squeezed in 1987. This proves to be the key to understanding what happened as Table A2.6 clearly demonstrates.

The size of the drop in the Liberal Democrat vote in Conservative/Labour seats was related to the size of the former Alliance vote rather than the distance between first and second place. This represents a rare instance of a proportionate relationship between change in party support and previous vote. Further, there is a clear relationship between the size of the fall in the Liberal Democrat vote and the size of the swing to Labour. The reason why the swing was lower in the most marginal constituencies was that here the previous Alliance vote was generally at its lowest – in some cases because it had already been squeezed tactically in 1987.[25]

Virtually no Liberal Democrat with a substantial vote in a Conservative/Labour seat avoided the squeeze. In the very rare cases where it was partly or wholly avoided, the local Liberal Democrat was in an unusually better position to convince the local electorate of the credibility of his cause. There was just one such seat where the Liberal Democrat vote rose. This was Birmingham Yardley where, despite the fact that Labour started off just 6% behind the

Conservatives, the Liberal Democrat vote rose by as much as 9.5%. Indeed this was the highest increase for a Liberal Democrat candidate anywhere where the seat had not been won in a by-election. This seat has seen very strong Liberal Democrat performances in local government elections in recent years; in May 1991, for example, the Liberal Democrats took as much as 56.6% of the vote in the constituency.[26] Although some of its local election voters reverted to the Conservatives or Labour in the parliamentary election, the party's local campaigning evidently repaid considerable dividends.

Meanwhile there were two seats, Gloucester and Swindon, where although the old Alliance vote had been more than 19% in 1987, the fall in support was less than the 4.4% which was the norm for those seats with an ex-Alliance vote of less than 15%. In addition the squeeze on the Liberal Democrat vote was also less marked given the size of the previous Alliance vote in Bristol East, Gloucestershire West and Kingswood. It is likely that the credibility of the Liberal Democrats in these South West seats was enhanced by the substantial strength of the party in nearby constituencies.

The Liberal Democrats made much of the number of second places with which they rather than Labour started the campaign; indeed they presented a list of them all in their final election broadcast. If indeed second places did matter then the election result was a bitter blow to the party; its total of such places fell from 261 to 154 (and from 223 to 145 in Conservative-held constituencies). In fact the result also revealed that being in second place alone was a poor guide to the potential for new tactical switching.

In 1987 the Alliance nationally had been 8.4% behind Labour. During the election campaign most polls put the Liberal Democrats more than 20% behind although in the end the gap was only 16.9%. This implies that in a seat where the Alliance had been less than about 10% ahead of Labour in 1987 it was the Labour candidate who was better placed in reality to challenge the sitting Conservative in 1992. The results suggest that this was how the voters saw things too.

In the 81 seats[27] where Labour was third in 1987, but less than 10% behind the Alliance, the squeeze on the Liberal Democrats and the swing to Labour were almost as large and as consistent as amongst Conservative/Labour seats. On average, the Liberal Democrat vote fell by 6.1% and the swing was −5.2%. In the seats in this category, where the former Alliance vote had been greater than 27.5%, the Liberal Democrat vote fell by as much as −9.5%.

In just two of these constituencies did the Liberal Democrats manage to turn the squeeze onto Labour – in Carshalton & Wallington and in Littleborough & Saddleworth. As in Birmingham Yardley the party's credibility in each of them had been enhanced by good recent local government election results.[28]

Even when the Liberal Democrats started off more than 10% ahead of Labour they did not always do well. True, in many places they did. Indeed these seats provide 41 of the 63 instances where the Liberal Democrat

Table A2.7.  *Tactical voting in the south*

| Alliance lead over Lab 1987 | Change in % vote for | | | Swing | No. of seats |
|---|---|---|---|---|---|
| | Con | Lab | Lib Dem | | |
| Less than 10% | −0.8 | +5.2 | −5.6 | −5.1 | 29 |
| 10–18% | −1.9 | +3.0 | −2.0 | −3.8 | 38 |
| 18–25% | −2.2 | +1.7 | −0.7 | −2.6 | 32 |
| Over 25% | −2.6 | +1.0 | +0.6 | −1.9 | 22 |

Table based on those seats in the South of England – excepting that portion in the East Anglia, North Metropolitan and South East Midlands areas as defined at Table A2.4 – where the Conservatives were first and the Alliance were second in 1987. Plymouth Drake and Sutton (loss of Owenite vote) and Eastbourne (by-election victory) have also been excluded.

vote rose.[29] But they also provide some examples of some of the most disappointing Liberal Democrat results of the election.

A key distinguishing feature between these two groups of seats was geographical location. Sixteen of the 41 increases in Liberal Democrat support were in the West Country (as defined at p. 329). Another 18 were in one of the three other areas in the south-eastern triangle where the Liberal Democrats generally did relatively well – South Coast, South Metropolitan and Thames Valley. Conversely a majority of the Liberal Democrats who failed to capitalise on a strong starting position were in the remaining north-eastern corner of the triangle.[30]

But, as Table A2.7 shows, within the rest of the South of England (including London) there was a clear relationship between the strength of the local Liberal Democrat position, how well the Liberal Democrats performed and how well Labour did. The further the Liberal Democrats started off ahead from Labour, the better they did and the worse Labour did. The Conservatives also suffered somewhat when the Liberal Democrats did well. But there are here at least signs that some Labour voters reciprocated the behaviour of Liberal Democrat voters in Conservative/Labour seats.

But elsewhere there was little sign of at all of tactical squeezing. As we have already noted the Liberal Democrats did particularly badly in the three northernmost areas of the south-eastern triangle; indeed here the largest falls in Liberal Democrat support were in those constituencies in which the party started off furthest ahead of Labour. This was true both whether the old Alliance vote had been inherited from the Liberal Party (such as Gainsborough & Horncastle, Chelmsford and St. Albans) or had emerged with the advent of the SDP (Kettering, Norfolk NW). There are just two seats located in these three areas or in the Midlands where there is evidence of a squeeze on Labour – Brentwood & Ongar and Harborough – where again the Liberal Democrats did well in the 1991 local elections.

*Table A2.8    The concentration of the non-Conservative vote*

| Second Party 1992 | % vote 1983 | | | % vote 1992 | | |
|---|---|---|---|---|---|---|
| | Con | Lab | Alln. | Con | Lab | Lib Dem |
| Labour | 50.4 | 23.6 | 25.2 | 50.7 | 33.1 | 14.6 |
| Lib Dem | 56.1 | 11.6 | 31.5 | 54.0 | 14.9 | 29.5 |

Table based on the 331 seats won by Conservatives in 1983 and 1992. Buckingham and the two Milton Keynes seats are excluded.

And in the north of England and Scotland, where on the evidence of the 1987 election more tactical switching from Labour to the Liberal Democrats had already taken place,[31] there are only occasional signs. In Hazel Grove and Edinburgh West the previous tactical squeeze on Labour appears to have been held; elsewhere such as Ryedale and Crosby the fading of the memory of the local by-election victory saw voters return to the Labour fold.

Of course tactical voting need not necessarily be confined to Labour and Liberal Democrat voters in Conservative-held seats. Indeed in a handful of Scottish marginals the SNP vote does seem to have been squeezed tactically to the benefit of Labour or the Liberal Democrats (see p. 342). But otherwise there is little evidence of new tactical voting in Scotland. The SNP failed to squeeze any further support in the three seats where it was second to the Conservatives. Nor were third-placed Conservative voters generally prepared to vote tactically in favour of the Liberal Democrat, except in Tony Benn's Chesterfield (where the Liberal Democrat candidate had been unusually active) and in Liverpool Mossley Hill where a −7.2% fall in the Conservative vote helped to save David Alton his seat. Notably neither of the two Independent Social Democrat MPs, John Cartwright in Woolwich and Rosie Barnes in Greenwich, were able to squeeze the local Conservative vote sufficiently to save their parliamentary careers from the advancing Labour tide.

But just how important was tactical voting between Labour and the Liberal Democrats in determining the distribution of seats? Strikingly, it may have cost the Conservatives as many as ten seats and halved John Major's majority. There are six seats where Labour's victory was very probably the result of tactical switching by former Alliance voters, and two more where this might have been crucial.[32] These are all seats where the rise in Labour support was above the average for its sub-region, where the fall in the Liberal Democrat vote was above the average, and where any below-average Conservative performance was not sufficient to account for the Conservatives' difficulties. This means that nearly one in five of all Labour's gains were the result of tactical voting. Meanwhile of the four seats gained by the Liberal Democrats, two were clearly reliant upon tactical voting while it was all but clearly decisive in one other.[33] But if we take into consideration the tactical vote which has evolved in these seats over a longer period of time then all four can be regarded as tactical gains. At no previous general election has tactical voting had such a large impact.

Further, tactical voting could well prove to be yet more significant at future elections. For, as a consequence of the tactical switching which has occurred at both the last two elections, there has been some concentration of the non-Conservative vote in the hands of one of the opposition parties. This can be seen in Table A2.8 which shows the average share of the vote won by each of the main parties in Conservative seats according to who was second in 1992. The Labour vote in those seats where it is now second is nearly ten points higher than it was in 1983 – while at the same time its share of the national vote has risen only by seven points. Meanwhile, the Liberal Democrat vote has fallen by just two points in those seats where it stands second to the Conservatives, far less than the eight percent loss of support it has suffered nationally. Indeed with the Conservative vote having drifted down as well the Liberal Democrats are on average no further behind the Conservatives in these seats than they were nine years ago. This increased concentration of the non-Conservative vote clearly poses a potential challenge to the party's continued ability to win elections on little more than 40% of the national vote.

The 1992 election provides some important lessons for students of tactical voting. Firstly, the likely incidence of new tactical voting depends on what tactical voting may have happened in the constituency already. Previous tactical voters may switch back to the first-preference party in the wake of the failure of their second-choice party to make adequate progress. And secondly, voters' perceptions of whether it is worthwhile voting tactically may well not simply be influenced by the situation in their own constituency at the last election but by the results of recent local elections or the strength and credibility of a party more generally in an area.

But just one additional thought. Perhaps the pattern we have just examined was not simply the product of tactical voting. Maybe the increasing Liberal Democrat strength in the South West and the far South of England, and their loss of support in some of their isolated pockets of support elsewhere, is part of a growing identification of the Liberal Democrats with one particular part of the country. If so it would add yet another chapter to the denationalisation of United Kingdom politics. The most dramatic incident in that story was the divorce of the Northern Irish party system from British politics in the early 1970s. At the same time the Scottish and Welsh nationalists became a permanent presence at Westminster. And in the thirty-year period between 1955 and 1987 Conservative support became concentrated in the south and Labour in the north. The resulting variegated pattern of political competition in the United Kingdom now looks very different from the uniformity of the 1950s.

## Candidates

A record number of six non-white MPs (five Labour and one Conservative) was elected, compared with four Labour in 1987. This was despite the fact that fewer such candidates (25) were nominated by the three main parties than in 1987 (28). But whether the mainly white electorate is prepared to accept non-white MPs as readily as white ones remains in some doubt.

The most obvious reason for doubt was the defeat of John Taylor, the first candidate of Afro-Caribbean descent to be nominated by the Conservatives for a seat held by them. His selection was accompanied by well-publicised dissent from a few local Tories (see p. 111) and his defeat seemed to follow the precedent of the Clapham result in 1970 when the first black candidate to be nominated to defend a Labour seat, Dr David Pitt, was repudiated by enough of his party's supporters to ensure his defeat.[34]

Against this has to be set three other pieces of evidence. Nirj Deva succeeded in defending the marginal seat of Brentford & Isleworth to become the first Asian Tory MP in modern times. Voters in the four seats won by non-white Labour MPs for the first time in 1987 gave each of them a substantial increase in their majority. And, although he clearly lost support to the deselected former MP for the constituency who stood against him (albeit less than in three other such examples), Piara Khabra succeeded in becoming the fifth ethnic minority Labour MP by defending Ealing Southall.

To make a more systematic assessment of the views of the electorate we need to examine the 37 cases where either a party nominated a coloured candidate in 1987 but a white one in 1992 or vice-versa. Given the small number of seats involved, the variety of their racial mixtures (to say nothing of the varied ethnic background of the candidates concerned), and the presence in two of them of deselected Labour MPs, any assessment can only be made with caution. But it does appear that there is still a small but measurable resistance to an ethnic minority MP amongst some voters.

Thus in five seats[35] where Conservative voters had a white candidate in 1987 but not in 1992 the party's share of the vote fell by −2.6%, while in the four seats where the change was to a white candidate in 1992, the drop was only −0.8%, a difference of 1.8%. This finding is confirmed if we compare each of these nine cases with the average movement in the appropriate sub-region in Table A1.2. The same calculations for Labour suggest a similar level of resistance, but a bigger one amongst Liberal Democrats, perhaps reflecting the looser attachment of many of this party's supporters rather than a higher level of racialism amongst its loyal supporters. Overall in a typical predominantly-white constituency a party is likely to poll between 2% and 3% less if it puts up a black or a brown candidate. But in an inner-city constituency with a substantial ethnic minority population there may well be no net effect at all.

This suggests a need to look more closely at the Cheltenham result before concluding that John Taylor lost because of his colour. Despite the fact that the contest was known to be a close-run thing and received high national media attention, the rise in turnout was 1.5% less than in the rest of the sub-region and the actual level of turnout of 80.3% was 2.2% lower than in the similarly high-profile contest in nearby Bath. The drop in the Tory vote (–5.4%) was also 2% higher than elsewhere in the sub-region. So a few Conservative voters may well have stayed at home. If indeed, 2% of the electorate had voted Tory rather than staying at home, the Liberal Democrat majority would have been just 72.

In any case it is by no means clear that colour was the source of John Taylor's difficulties. His selection was criticised not so much for his race but because he was an outsider to the town while his predecessor, Sir Charles Irving, had been very much a local man. Claims that people prefer to vote for a local candidate are a familiar part of election rhetoric, but evidence is usually lacking. However Cheltenham, a rare case of a constituency that is also a clearly-defined local community, is unusual in having a well-documented tradition of voting for local candidates. At a by-election in 1937 a local Independent Conservative candidate who was a master at Cheltenham College defeated his party's official nominee and went on to hold his seat against Conservative opposition at the 1945 general election. Furthermore in October 1974 when Charles Irving was first elected, the local swing clearly indicated that his local reputation was a distinct bonus to his party.[36] Thus the real lesson from Cheltenham may not be that John Taylor's race alone cost him the seat, but that it did help call attention to something that was certainly important, his lack of local roots.

John Taylor's real misfortune may well prove to be that he did not have the chance to prove himself to Cheltenham's voters. In 1987 both Bernie Grant in Tottenham and Diane Abbott in Hackney North found that a similar combination – of being both black and left-wing – cost them votes. But standing at this election as incumbent MPs their vote rose by 12.9% and 9.1% respectively, suggesting that they largely recouped the votes they had lost five years earlier. The same was true of three other left-wing candidates whose vote clearly suffered in 1987 – Ken Livingstone in Brent East (+10.5%), Dawn Primarolo in Bristol South (+9.3%) and Alan Meale in Mansfield (+16.9%, the second highest increase in the Labour vote anywhere). Familiarity appears to be the best antidote to notoriety.

Indeed, no clearer evidence of the ability of individual left-wing MPs to establish a personal following was provided than by the vote cast for Dave Nellist in Coventry SE who came within 3.2 percentage points of retaining his seat after being deselected as a Labour candidate because of his alleged association with Militant. Indeed, around a quarter of his 28.9% vote appears to have come from people who would otherwise have voted Liberal Democrat. Substantial totals were also won by two other deselected left-wingers, Terry Fields in Liverpool Broadgreen (14.2%) and Ron Brown in Edinburgh Leith (10.3%). In contrast the one deselected Conservative MP to attempt to retain his seat, John Browne in Winchester, lost his deposit.

These performances by left-wing candidates were more than matched by the two remaining Independent SDP MPs, John Cartwright in Woolwich and Rosie Barnes in Greenwich, who both only narrowly failed in their attempt to defend their seats. Unchallenged by Liberal Democrat candidates, their vote was down just −2.5% and −1.1% respectively on the 1987 vote they won as SDP/Alliance candidates, suggesting that their refusal to join the new party did them no personal electoral harm.

The advantages of incumbency were also more generally if less dramatically revealed in two other situations. One was those constituencies where the incumbent MP was defending the seat for the first time, having first wrested it in 1987 from the then incumbent MP. The second was those constituencies where the incumbent MP was retiring. As in 1979 and 1987 these results revealed the ability of individual MPs to establish a small but potentially important personal vote, especially in marginal constituencies.[37]

The largest group of new incumbent MPs were those 20 Labour MPs who had ousted incumbent Conservative MPs in 1987 and who were defending their seats for the first time in 1992.[38] The average increase in their vote (+4.6%) was 1.7% higher than in those seats which Labour held before 1987 and where the incumbent MP was standing again. Meanwhile the Conservative vote fell on average by 1% more. MPs of course vary in the assiduity with which they promote the interests of their constituency, even in marginal seats, so not all new incumbent MPs will necessarily benefit. But if we compare the result in each of the twenty constituencies with their sub-regional average we find that the Labour vote rose by more than average in 13 cases while the Conservative vote fell by more than average in 14.[39]

The largest group of retiring MPs, fifty-seven, were Conservatives. Here there is no reason why the Labour candidate should have established a personal vote but any personal vote built up by Conservative candidate will not be passed on to his or her successor. Amongst all retiring Conservative MPs there is little systematic evidence to suggest that their successors lost out once we take into consideration the geographical location of the seats concerned – their vote fell on average by just 0.2% more than the sub-regional average.[40] However if we look at those seats which were marginals – and where there is the greatest incentive to establish a personal vote – the evidence is slightly stronger. The Conservative vote fell by more than the sub-regional average in 9 out of 14 seats where the 1987 Conservative majority was less than 16%,[41] with an average deficit of −0.6%.

However amongst the smaller group of 20 retiring Labour MPs (and where the incumbent did not stand against the new Labour candidate), the evidence is clear. Here the new Labour candidate underperformed compared with the sub-regional average in 16 cases, costing them an average of 1.9% of the vote.

Overall, these findings confirm our previous estimates that an MP can establish a personal vote of between 750 and 1000 votes. But in contrast to 1979 and 1987, personal voting had virtually no impact upon the outcome in terms of seats – simply because the party with most to gain from personal votes was Labour in whose favour the tide was flowing in England and Wales anyway. Personal voting might just have succeeded in saving Renfrew West & Inverclyde for Labour and might have saved Battersea for the Conservatives – but in both cases there are other plausible explanations for the outcome.[42] Two Conservative losses – Cambridge and Cheltenham – could be blamed on the retirement of the local MP, but in neither case is the evidence conclusive.

Speculation before the election that incumbency might help a number of Conservative MPs to defend their seats forgot that these MPs had nearly all first won their seats in 1983 and had already had a chance to develop a personal vote in 1987. By 1992 the personal vote was part of the majority they were defending rather than a new instrument that could ensure their political survival.

The incumbency effect only matters in terms of seats at an election if the electoral tide is flowing (modestly) against the party which made significant gains at the previous election. So in 1996 or 1997 it will only matter if there is a swing from Labour to Conservative. Then – and depending on the extent of any boundary changes – there will be 39 newly-elected Labour MPs who will have to defend majorities of less than 10%. Thus if there is a swing from Conservative to Labour at the next election of less than 5%, personal votes for new incumbents could well make a difference to the outcome in seats. Otherwise it will be irrelevant.

If in general being the local MP helps to gather votes, one result clearly stands out. Tommy Sheridan, leader of the Anti-Poll Tax Committee and serving a jail sentence at the time of the election, won 19.3% standing under the Scottish Militant Labour banner. This is the highest vote won in a post-war British general election by any independent or minor party candidate who was not previously an MP. The nearest precedent is the 14.5% won by Jimmy Reid, leader of the sit-in at the Upper Clyde shipyard in Glasgow in 1972, standing as a Communist in Central Dunbartonshire in February 1974. These unusually high votes for two unconventional working-class popular leaders from Clydeside suggests that the image of 'Red Clydeside' still has some substance to it.

## Nationalists

The result was a pleasant surprise for Plaid Cymru but a bitter disappointment for the Scottish National Party (SNP). The former secured an average increase in its vote of just 1.8% in the 35 seats it fought[43] leaving its share of the total Welsh vote still 2% short of its level in both 1974 elections. Yet it secured a record fourth representative at Westminster. In contrast, the latter's vote increased by an average of 7.4% in the 70 comparable Scottish seats,[44] leaving its share of the total Scottish vote just 0.4% short of the level it achieved in February 1974, the first election at which it secured a substantial presence at

Westminster. Yet it only held on to the three seats it won 1987, with Jim Sillars losing the Glasgow Govan seat he had won at a by-election despite securing twice as large an increase on his party's 1987 vote as any other candidate.

The key to Plaid Cymru's success lay in securing a yet stronger concentration of its vote in Welsh-speaking West and North Wales. All five of the seats where its vote rose by 5% or more are amongst the top ten Welsh speaking constituencies. Its largest increase resulted in the capture of Ceredigion & Pembroke North, the most unexpected result of the election and the first time a seat has changed hands between a nationalist party and the Liberal Democrats or their predecessors. The second largest increase, in Carmarthen, left Plaid Cymru just 5% behind the winning Labour candidate and well poised to add a fifth seat to its collection. Overall, Plaid Cymru's share of the vote now stands at an average of 40.6% in the five seats with the most Welsh speakers. Its highest share of the vote anywhere else is just 15.6%.

Equally the key to the SNP's failure was its continued and indeed increased inability to concentrate its vote. There were just 15 constituencies where its share of the vote rose by 5% or less. Its worst result was in Dundee East (−6.8%) where it was best placed to win a seat from Labour but where the personal vote previously secured by the former SNP MP, Gordon Wilson, evidently failed to transfer to his successor. Two more of the low increases were in Galloway & Upper Nithsdale and in Perth & Kinross, two of the three seats where the party had hopes of making a gain from the Conservatives. And three others were the seats which the party was defending against a Conservative challenge – including a fall of 1.9% in Angus East. In all of these poor results the party was unable to squeeze any additional tactical support from the third and fourth placed Labour and Liberal Democrat candidates; its previous success locally meant that winning over new voters was far more difficult that it was elsewhere in Scotland.

The SNP's aim in recent years has been to become the principal challenger to Labour in working class seats in the West of Scotland. There were some signs of success in this. There was a negative correlation between the party's performance and the proportion of employers and managers in the constituency as measured by the 1981 census (−0.37), although a number of its weak performances in middle-class Scotland would appear to be the consequence of a tactical squeeze rather than a reflection of a shift in the social profile of the party's vote.[45] But even so the party is left with not a single seat where it is less than 10% behind a Labour incumbent.

## Minor Parties

The election saw a record number of 930 candidates stand under a minor party or independent label. The largest number, 309,[46] stood under the banner of the newly-formed Natural Law Party whose campaign was designed to advertise the merits of transcendental meditation. Their message was uniformly ignored.

They won an average of just 0.4% of the vote, securing over 1% in only five constituencies. Even candidates standing under either the Official Loony or Loony Green Giant labels were more successful than this.

More serious challenges to the orthodox party system came from the Greens and the Liberal Party, a group of dissident Liberals who refused to accept the merger with the SDP. But the result was a serious disappointment for the Greens after their success in securing 15% of the vote in the 1989 European Elections. Their average share of the vote in the 253 seats they fought was, at 1.3%, slightly lower than in 1987. Equally in those 93 seats they fought in 1987 and 1992 their vote was on average fractionally down (−0.0%). Yet in the local elections held just four weeks later their candidates were still able to secure an average of 4% of the vote; evidently while the party can secure votes in second-order elections it is still not seen as a credible force in Westminster elections.

But if their share of the vote was unchanged there were changes in its distribution. In 1987 the party did best in the South West of England. This time its best performances were in the cities. Perhaps there are signs here that support for the Greens is beginning to come more from those who are actually most severely affected by environmental pollution rather than those who have so far avoided its worst excesses.

Most successful of all the minor parties (average share of the vote 1.7%) were in fact the Liberals. Michael Meadowcroft, their leader, was the only minor party candidate to save his deposit, in the Leeds West seat which he had held as a Liberal/Alliance MP between 1983 and 1987. But the party's strategy of concentrating its candidatures in the Liberal Democrats' best prospects backfired. They did badly (with the single exception of Tiverton) in the South West (mean vote 1.0%) despite its traditional Liberal vote, but well in Merseyside (2.4%) where Liberal strength is relatively new or non-existent. Nowhere did their intervention deny the Liberal Democrats a seat.

## Northern Ireland

Despite the intervention of Conservative candidates in eleven constituencies, the election in Northern Ireland was once again dominated by parties indigenous to the province. Northern Irish elections are primarily a battle for supremacy within the Unionist and Republican camps. Indeed, the election left the balance of Unionist and Republican representation unchanged, but the outcome of the battle within the Republican camp at this election may well have important implications for the balance of representation in future.

For the election saw a clear shift within the Republican camp in favour of the Social Democratic and Labour Party (SDLP). Its share of the vote rose in every seat it fought to 23.5% of the overall vote, while Sinn Fein's support fell to 10.0% and the small Workers Party was crushed, losing three-quarters of its 1987 vote.

Paradoxically, though, the SDLP's success in capturing Belfast West was achieved in the seat where it most failed to dent Sinn Fein support. Its victory was due to what was perhaps the most striking case of tactical voting at the election. Some three thousand voters switched from supporting the Unionists in 1987 to Dr Joe Hendron in 1992 in order to defeat the abstentionist Sinn Fein MP, Gerry Adams. But this figure understates the full extent of tactical voting in the constituency. In 1979 (after allowing for the 1983 boundary changes) there were well over ten thousand Unionist voters (nearly 30% of the vote) in the constituency. In 1983 over half of them voted for Gerry Fitt, the former SDLP leader standing as an Independent. Following Fitt's defeat in 1983, some of his voters returned temporarily to their Unionist home in 1987, but others switched tactically to Dr Hendron. Taking this vote into consideration, it is likely that over half of the Protestant or naturally Unionist vote in the constituency voted SDLP in 1992. So far as the Catholic community in the constituency is concerned, Sinn Fein is clearly still the more popular party.

But in the longer run the more significant development for Northern Irish politics may well be the SDLP's increased popularity amongst Catholics in the remainder of the province. When the province's representation at Westminster was increased from 12 to 17 in 1983 (thanks to Unionist pressure on the minority Callaghan government in the late 1970s), the new constituencies which were created included no less than six which have a natural Republican majority. But in the wake of the post-Hunger Strike surge of Sinn Fein the SDLP won only one of them in 1983. As it locally squeezed the Sinn Fein vote it won a second at the 1986 by-elections caused by the mass resignation of Unionist MPs, and a third in 1987. With its victory in Belfast West, the SDLP contingent has been increased to four. Its sights will now be set on securing the two remaining rural border seats which Unionist MPs hold on a minority vote, Fermanagh & South Tyrone and Mid Ulster. The SDLP are now ahead of Sinn Fein in both of them, and any further decline in Sinn Fein support would render them winnable by the SDLP. Ironically, it is possible that if there is again a minority government at Westminster, there might well be up to six SDLP MPs able to bargain in the interests of the Catholic community – an opportunity created for them by the pressure mounted by Unionists in the last hung parliament!

On the other side of Northern Ireland's communal divide, the electoral pact between the Ulster Unionists and the Democratic Unionists was not maintained in three constituencies, but in each case the sitting MP was comfortably returned. However, the total Unionist vote dropped to a record low of 50.3%. This but reflects the intervention of the Northern Ireland branch of the Conservative Party, who represented a more integrationist form of unionism and whose eleven candidates took 5.7% of the total vote, more than enough to account for the 4.4% fall in support for explicitly Unionist candidates. Easily the best Conservative performance (32.0%) was in highly middle class North

Down where a rebel Unionist advocating integration with British parties took 35.4% of the vote in 1987 and whose MP, James Kilfedder, is the only Unionist to sit on the government benches. The Conservatives probably also took some support from the non-sectarian Alliance Party whose vote dropped from 9.9% to 8.7%. But the party clearly faces a substantial task in establishing itself in the province.

## Turnout

The 1992 election was the first election since 1974 at which according to the opinion polls the result was in doubt. This could well have been responsible for the higher turnout which at 77.9% was 2.4% up on 1987 and the highest since February 1974. But the rise was far from uniform. Indeed the change in turnout varied as much as Conservative performance and by twice as much as it did in 1987 (see Table A2.1 above).

This variation was highly systematic. This is exemplified by the two columns in Table A1.5 which show the extreme changes in turnout. They consist of two very different kinds of constituency. All of the ten largest falls are in one of four northern cities – Liverpool, Manchester, Sheffield and Dundee. All of the ten biggest increases are in London or the Outer Metropolitan Area of the South East.

In short, there was a North/South pattern to the variation in turnout as well as in swing. Turnout rose more in the South of England and the Midlands than in the North of England, Scotland or indeed Wales. But this was not all. Turnout rose more in the South East except Inner London than in the South West. And it rose less in urban Britain than elsewhere, especially in the North of England and Scotland where there were widespread falls in turnout in inner-city constituencies. This pattern has a clear implication – that turnout rose more in Conservative seats than in Labour ones. Indeed this is the case. In those seats won by the Conservatives in 1987 it rose by 3.5% but by just 0.1% in Labour ones. Indeed it rose by most in the safest Conservative seats, with the consequence that turnout was higher in the safe Conservative seats than in marginals. Furthermore, turnout only rose by 0.9% in the 31 seats where the old Alliance secured over 40% of the vote in 1987. It was the middle-class Conservative communities of southern Britain who had shown the greatest support for Mrs Thatcher who were stimulated by the possibility of a change of government to vote. The working-class inner-city seats of the north who had shown Thatcherism the door in the 1980s reacted to the possibility of a transfer of power with apathy.

This is clearly shown in Table A2.9 which shows the change in turnout by geographical region, urban/rural type and who won the constituency in 1987. Even if when we have taken into account the sharp North/South and the milder (at least in the South) urban/rural variation there is typically still a 2% to 3% difference in the behaviour of a constituency according to its political complexion.

Table A2.9    *The pattern of turnout change*

| | Change in % turnout since 1987 in: | | | |
| | South Britain | | North Britain | |
| Seat won in '87 by: | Con | Lab | Con | Lab |
|---|---|---|---|---|
| Very Urban | +3.0 | +1.7 | +2.4 | −2.0 |
| Mainly Urban | +3.9 | +0.9 | +2.3 | −0.2 |
| Mixed | +4.0 | +2.0 | +3.0 | +0.5 |
| Rural | +3.6 | n.a. | +3.7 | +0.9 |

*South Britain*: South of England and Midlands.
*North Britain*: North of England, Scotland and Wales.
*Very Urban*: Electorate density (1982 electorate) greater than 24 electors per hectare.
*Mainly Urban*: Electorate density greater than 8 electors per hectare but less than 24 electors per hectare.
*Mixed*: Electorate density greater than 1.3 electors per hectare but less than 8 electors per hectare.
*Rural*: Electorate density less than 1.3 electors per hectare.

On this evidence, across the country as a whole more Conservative voters must have turned out and voted than Labour ones. But whether this was true in individual constituencies, which is what is crucial in terms of winning seats, is less clear. If it were the case then we would expect to find that the Conservatives did best where turnout rose most. But of course the Conservatives generally did worse in the southern half of the country where turnout rose most. True, within the southern half of Britain turnout did rise most in the Outer Metropolitan Area, in parts of which the Conservatives did best. Indeed within the south there is a mild (+0.17) correlation between Conservative performance and turnout change. But in the north there is none at all. So it may have been Labour as well as Conservative supporters in the south who were more excited by the prospect of a political change.

There is another important implication of the pattern of turnout change. There was much speculation both before and after the election as to whether some (mostly Labour) voters had taken their names off the electoral register in order to try and avoid paying the poll-tax. Full discussion of this proposition lies outside the scope of this appendix. Certainly there has been a widening of the gap between the number of persons on the electoral roll and the Registrar General's estimate of population since 1987.[47] But we would note that had there been significant poll-tax deregistration we might have expected an above-average rather than a below-average increase in turnout in Labour constituencies. For one would anticipate that those who left their names off the register would be those who in any case had a lower inclination to turn out and vote – resulting in a more motivated registered electorate.

Furthermore, there is in practice another reason why the numbers on the electoral roll should have dropped. Returning Officers have been encouraged to remove more quickly from the register the names of those who have died or moved. The potential impact that this can have on recorded turnout is no more clearly illustrated than in Hackney, which had the lowest level of turnout of any London borough in 1987. Its two constituencies between them 'lost' 20,000 voters between 1991 and 1992. That this resulted in a more accurate register is indicated by a rise in turnout in the borough of 6.9%, the third largest increase in London. Hackney North indeed appears in the list of the top ten largest increases in Table A1.5.[48]

There were two other clear influences on turnout. One was that the election took place during a university vacation rather than in term as in 1987. This meant that many university students were not in residence at their term-time address and had either to take the trouble to apply for a postal vote or else opt to vote in their home constituency if they were also registered there. The turnout in many university seats clearly suffered as a consequence with notable falls in Oxford East (−4.3%), City of Durham (−3.6%) and Cambridge (−4.8%) as well as those parts of larger cities with a substantial university population such as Sheffield Hallam (−3.8%), Cardiff Central (−3.5%) and Bristol West (−0.6%).

By-elections may themselves be notorious for producing low levels of turnout, but the result of a by-election can stimulate participation at a subsequent general election. There were nine by-elections in the last parliament in which the seat either changed hands or where the second-placed challenger moved to within 5% of the winner. Six of them were in the North of England, Scotland or Wales, while three were in London, the South of England or the Midlands. The average increase in turnout in the former group was +5.2% and in the latter, +6.8%, in both cases clearly above the relevant regional average.[49]

## The Electoral System

We return now to the major question we posed at the beginning of this appendix. Why did the Conservatives win only a majority of 21 seats given their comfortable lead over Labour in votes of 7.6%? The first half of this section of the appendix analyses precisely how the electoral system treated the two largest parties. Thereafter, we will widen the discussion to consider also how it treated minor parties. Together the two halves of this section raise some important doubts about popular notions of how the single member plurality system works.

Certainly, the 'uniform swing' model of the system would have led one to anticipate a very different outcome. If the overall total-vote swing of 2.1% had been replicated in every constituency, Labour would have won just 20 seats from the Conservatives, leaving John Major with a more than adequate majority of 59. In fact Labour won exactly twice as many, 40, and lost just one. Further, the Conservatives should also have made four net gains from the Liberal Democrats rather suffering two net losses. If we take this into account as well John Major's majority should have been as high as 71.

Equally, the outcome cannot be blamed on the decline in the long-term exaggerative quality of the electoral system which we have previously documented elsewhere.[50] In 1955 there were sufficient seats that were marginal between Conservative and Labour – 166 in total – that for each 1% swing in votes, 3% of the seats changed hands.[51] By 1983 this figure had more than halved to 80, rising only slightly to 87 in 1987. This decline was brought about by the long-term geographical polarisation in electoral support between the north and the south and between inner city and rural shire. Its consequence was that less than 1.5% of seats changed hands for a 1% switch of votes.

But as we have seen in 1992 there was something of a reversal of the North/South divide. And this had precisely the consequence that one would have anticipated on the underlying exaggerative quality of the electoral system. The number of marginal seats rose somewhat to 97.[52] Yet despite this the system failed for the first time ever to produce a winner's bonus. The Conservatives won 54.9% of the two-party vote and 55.4% of the seats won by Conservative or Labour – almost perfect proportionality! Something must have been operating to counterbalance the normal exaggerative quality of the electoral system.

To understand what happened we have to look at a separate feature of the electoral system, electoral bias. By electoral bias we do not mean that one party acquires a higher or lower share of the seats won than it did of the votes cast. Rather by electoral bias we mean that one of the two main parties gets a higher proportion of the seats for any given proportion of the votes than the other main party would get if it were to win the same proportion of the votes. In other words any exaggeration of votes into seats from which *both* main parties can benefit is not bias but simply the general exaggerative quality of the electoral system. Bias refers only to any exaggeration from which one party is able to benefit but not the other.

There are two main sources of electoral bias which can occur under the single-member plurality electoral system. First, one party may distribute its vote more efficiently than the other. The only votes that are cast effectively under the single member plurality electoral system are those that count towards winning a seat – that is the votes cast for the winning party of the constituency up to a majority of one. Any votes secured above that are wasted because they do not help elect an MP. The same is true of all votes cast for losing candidates.[53] Thus a party's vote is distributed more efficiently if it wins more seats than another by small majorities and fewer seats by large majorities.

The second potential source of bias arises from differences in the sizes of a constituency. Clearly a party will win more seats if its votes are concentrated more in smaller constituencies than in larger ones. Less obvious is that there is more than one way in which a constituency can be 'smaller' than another. One is indeed that it has fewer registered voters. But another way in which a constituency can be smaller is that fewer of its registered voters turn out to vote.[54]

We can measure the size and direction of these two sources of bias using two simple measures.[55] The impact of the differences in constituency size is captured by the difference between the mean share of the two-party vote won by the Conservatives and their overall share. Unlike the overall share, the mean share ignores differences in the sizes of constituencies and so the difference between the two measures neatly captures the influence of constituency size.

Meanwhile, any bias resulting from differences in the efficiency with which the parties' votes are distributed is identified by the difference between the share of the two-party vote won by the Conservatives in the median constituency and the mean share. Assuming no seats are won by third parties, the median seat is of course the crucial seat that has to be won to win an overall majority of one. Thus if the overall national vote is 50:50 and all seats are of the same size then the party which wins the election will be the one that secures more than 50% of the two-party vote in the median seat.[56] So the most crucial statistic for any party is not its overall vote or its mean vote, but its median vote. The difference between the median and the overall vote represents the total electoral bias in the system.

Table A2.10 presents these measures of bias for each of the last three elections. They tell a clear and dramatic story. In 1983 and 1987 the Conservatives clearly distributed their vote more efficiently. But in 1992 their advantage disappeared. But the reason why there is actually a bias towards Labour in the system is that it benefits from concentrating its vote in smaller-sized constituencies – and in 1992 this apparently persistent source of advantage to Labour increased yet further.

How did Labour's vote become more efficiently distributed? Two clear reasons have emerged in this appendix. The first is the concentration of high swings to Labour in much of the Midlands and in London where there were a disproportionate number of marginal constituencies. If the swing in each constituency had been the same as the overall swing in the sub-region of which it was a member then Labour would have made a net gain of 25 seats, five more than if the swing had been nationally uniform.

The second reason we have identified is the incidence of new tactical voting in Conservative-Labour marginals which we estimated helped Labour to win at least six additional seats beyond what could have been expected given the sub-regional variation in swing. Together these two factors meant that Labour spent less effort in piling up large majorities and won a few crucial extra votes in marginal seats.[57]

But on its own this redistribution of the Labour vote did no more than

*Table A2.10    Electoral bias at recent elections*

| | Con % of two-party vote | | |
|---|---|---|---|
| | Mean minus Overall | Median minus Mean | Median minus Overall |
| 1983 | −0.5 | +1.7 | +1.2 |
| 1987 | −0.8 | +1.4 | +0.6 |
| 1992 | −1.2 | −0.0 | −1.2 |

remove the bias which operated against it in 1983 and 1987. The overall equality in the efficiency of the distribution of the Conservative and Labour vote is indicated by the fact that the Conservatives won 29 constituencies from Labour with a majority of 4% or less, while Labour won 28 from the Conservatives.[58] The actual positive bias to Labour arose from the other source of bias, the concentration of its vote in smaller constituencies.

Both the reasons that we identified earlier as potential sources of this form of bias played a role. First of all, the electorates in Labour constituencies continued to decline while those in Conservative ones increased. This is a long-standing trend which has repeated itself at every post-war British election. It reflects the gradual and continuing shift of the population out of the (mainly Labour) conurbations into the (more Conservative) countryside. It is the reason why each boundary review necessarily takes seats away from Labour and gives them to the Conservatives.

Thus if we take those constituencies which Labour won in 1987 we find that on average the electorate declined by 1,088 voters between 1987 and 1992. In contrast in the average Conservative constituency the electorate rose by 657 voters. The gap in the size of the average Labour and the average Conservative constituency rose to just two short of 10,000 voters.[59]

But in addition, as we identified earlier (see p. 345), turnout also rose by far less in Labour constituencies than in Conservatives ones. On average, turnout in Labour constituencies was 73.5% compared with 80.2% in Conservative constituencies – a gap of 6.7%, twice that in 1987. If the turnout had been the same in every constituency, Labour's share of the two-party vote would have been 0.8% higher than it actually was. In short the turnout gap was worth two-thirds of the total electoral bias to Labour.[60]

The impact of the electoral bias to Labour in terms of seats can clearly be seen in Table A2.11. This table shows what the outcome would be if the current constituency boundaries were to be used at the next election and if the swing from Conservative to Labour were the same across the whole country. It assumes that support for the Liberal Democrats and other parties would remain unchanged.

*Table A2.11   The relationship between seats and votes*

| Swing to Lab | % Votes | | Seats | | | |
|---|---|---|---|---|---|---|
| | Con | Lab | Con | Lab | Lib Dem | Other |
| 0% | 42.8 | 35.2 | 336 | 271 | 20 | 24 |
| 0.5% | 42.3 | 35.7 | 325 | 280 | 22 | 24 |
| 1% | 41.8 | 36.2 | 316 | 290 | 21 | 24 |
| 2% | 40.8 | 37.2 | 303 | 301 | 23 | 24 |
| 2.3% | 40.5 | 37.5 | 301 | 302 | 24 | 24 |
| 3% | 39.8 | 38.2 | 294 | 307 | 26 | 24 |
| 3.8% | 39.0 | 39.0 | 282 | 320 | 25 | 24 |
| 4% | 38.8 | 39.2 | 279 | 323 | 25 | 24 |
| 4.1% | 38.7 | 39.3 | 275 | 327 | 25 | 24 |
| 5% | 37.8 | 40.2 | 257 | 344 | 25 | 25 |

Indeed, the picture is quite dramatic. The Conservatives' overall majority would disappear if there were just a 0.5% swing from Conservative to Labour. As some opposition politicians were keen to point out after the election, the Conservative majority rested on just 1,233 voters in eleven constituencies.

But the moral of that is not how unlucky Labour were, but how close the Conservatives came to being robbed of victory by the electoral system. For a 0.5% swing to Labour would still leave Labour over six-and-a-half percentage points behind the Conservatives. In other words the electoral system came close to robbing John Major of the election victory he would by conventional expectations of the system have deserved – even though he is the one party leader who remains unambiguously in favour of its continued use.

Labour by contrast would require just a half-point lead over the Conservatives to secure a bare overall majority of seats.[61] At an even division of the overall vote they would be 38 seats ahead of the Conservatives. And they would become the largest party while still 3% behind the Conservatives in votes.

However, almost certainly the next election will not be fought on the same electoral boundaries as in 1992. The Boundary Commission for England had already started work on a new boundary revision before the election was held. It was however uncertain whether the commission would report in time for new constituencies to be in place for a 1996 election. But one of the first measures placed before Parliament by the government after the election was a bill which would require all four boundary commissions to report by the end of 1994.

The political impact of the boundary review has been widely predicted to be the transfer of some 20 seats from Labour to the Conservatives. It will undoubtedly reduce the representation of declining counties which tend to have more Labour MPs, giving new seats to growing areas overwhelmingly

*Table A2.12    The impact of the Boundary Review?*

|  | Average electorate (and no. of seats) in seats won by | | Target Equal Electorate | Extra Con seats needed for equality |
|---|---|---|---|---|
|  | Con | Lab | | |
| England | 71,676 (319) | 64,094 (195) | 68,800 | +13 |
| Wales | 59,174 (6) | 59,627 (27) | 59,545 | 0 |
| Scotland | 60,408 (11) | 52,660 (49) | 54,080 | +1 |

dominated by the Conservatives. But the precise impact of this upon the parties' fortunes is impossible to predict; it will depend upon exactly how the seats are allocated between counties and the new boundaries are drawn.

But we can estimate what the impact ought to be if the redistribution were to be equitable. Table A2.12 shows just how many seats need to be switched between Conservative and Labour, separately within the three nations of Great Britain, to make the electorates of the seats represented by Conservative and Labour MPs as close to equal as possible. It suggests a more modest figure, fourteen,[62] as the likely benefit to the government.

If our estimate is anywhere near correct then it is clear that post-election speculation that the boundary redistribution will render it impossible for Labour to win the next election is wide of the mark. A fourteen-seat bonus to the Conservatives would not even remotely remove the electoral bias apparent in Table A2.11. If we were to re-estimate the calculations in Table A2.11 assuming that the Conservatives would win 14 extra seats throughout, the Conservatives would still be ten seats behind Labour at an even division of the national vote. And they would still require a 4.8% lead for an overall majority while Labour would require only a 2.1% lead.[63]

Of course this assumes that Labour maintains the relative efficiency of the distribution of its vote secured in 1992 while turnout remains depressed in Labour areas. Neither can be forecast with any certainty. The only virtually certain change is that by 1996 the new boundaries will already be five years out of date and the electorate in Labour constituencies already below the national average. Labour's problem at the next election will not be the electoral system but securing enough votes to be able to profit from its operation.

So the 1992 election result demonstrated that the single-member plurality system does not necessarily produce a winner's bonus by exaggerating the lead of the largest party over the second party. Rather, it revealed that the exaggerative quality of the system is now sufficiently weak that it can be overturned by electoral bias – and that the danger that the largest party in

*Table A2.13    Two perspectives on the UK result*

|  | All UK | | Excl. Lib Dem & SNP | |
| --- | --- | --- | --- | --- |
|  | *% Votes* | *% Seats* | *% Votes* | *% Seats* |
| Conservative | 41.9 | 51.6 | 52.2 | 53.5 |
| Labour | 34.2 | 41.6 | 42.6 | 43.2 |
| Lib Dem | 17.9 | 3.1 | – | – |
| SNP | 1.9 | 0.5 | – | – |
| Plaid Cymru | 0.3 | 0.6 | 0.4 | 0.6 |
| Unionists | 1.2 | 2.0 | 1.5 | 2.1 |
| SDLP | 0.6 | 0.6 | 0.7 | 0.6 |
| Others | 2.0 | 0.0 | 2.5 | 0.0 |

votes will not necessarily be the largest party in terms of seats, a danger already apparent in the results of the 1951 and February 1974 elections, has increased.

But this was not the only conventional expectation about the way in which the single member plurality electoral system operates which was overturned by the election result. The result also revealed that the system's ability to discriminate against third parties is also highly contingent upon the geographical distribution of their support and can vary over time. Indeed, the proportionality of the 1992 result was not confined to its relative treatment of Conservative and Labour. As Table A2.13 illustrates, the system also treated equitably, if not indeed more than equitably, three of the five other parties represented at Westminster – Plaid Cymru, the Ulster Unionists (here considered as one party) and the SDLP. The only parties against whom the system discriminated were the Liberal Democrats and the SNP. Indeed, as the table shows, if we exclude from the calculation of votes and seats won those votes and seats won by the Liberal Democrats and the SNP we could easily be forgiven for mistakenly believing that the election had been conducted under some form of proportional representation!

Plaid Cymru, the Ulster Unionists and the SDLP all prosper under the single member plurality system because although their vote is small it is geographically concentrated. Indeed, as we have indicated (see p. 342 and p. 344), both the Plaid Cymru and SDLP votes became even more effectively concentrated in 1992 and could well become yet more so in the foreseeable future. Both are parties which represent geographically-concentrated ethnic minorities. In achieving an increasing stranglehold on their respective cultural bases the electoral system has become a help rather than an hindrance to their cause, despite their small share of the overall national vote.[64]

But although both were discriminated against, the result also revealed a lack of stability in the relationship between seats and votes for both the Liberal Democrats and the SNP. Despite winning 0.5% less of the vote than in October

Table A2.14   *The changing distribution of Liberal Democrat and SNP support*

| | Standard Deviation of vote share | |
| | *Liberal / Alliance / Lib Dem* | *SNP* |
| --- | --- | --- |
| Feb. 1974 | 7.8 | 11.7 |
| Oct. 1974 | 8.3 | 9.4 |
| 1979 | 8.2 | 10.7 |
| 1983 | 7.3 | 9.8 |
| 1987 | 8.9 | 9.1 |
| 1992 | 10.2 | 8.3 |

1974 the Liberal Democrats won 20 seats compared with 13 on that earlier occasion.[65] In contrast, despite winning just 0.4% less of the Scottish vote than February 1974, the SNP won four seats fewer.

The two parties have experienced divergent trends in the extent to which their vote is geographically concentrated. As Table A2.14 shows, the standard deviation of the SNP vote was lower than at any time since its first major incursion into Westminster, indicating that its vote has become yet more evenly spread geographically. In contrast, with a standard deviation in double figures, the Liberal Democrat vote was less evenly spread in 1992 than that of any of its predecessor parties since the Liberal Party first resumed fighting on a nationwide basis in February 1974. If there is any further marked concentration in the Liberal Democrat vote then, as suggested earlier on p. 337, the implications for the future of British politics could be profound indeed.

## Conclusion

This appendix has underlined the fragility of the British two-party system. That system has been defended as an instrument which enables the electorate to choose between alternative governments and maintains the accountability of the governors to the governed. But its ability to achieve those objectives rested on two key foundations. One was an even balance of electoral support between Conservative and Labour. The other was an electoral system which kept small parties out and gave the winner a sufficient bonus to secure a safe overall majority.

Both are now clearly in question. Labour's defeat was not a narrow one but its fourth serious defeat in a row. Meanwhile the electoral system demonstrated that it could no longer be relied upon to give the winner a bonus, could conceivably have picked the wrong 'winner', and is an uncertain bulwark against the representation of small parties. The election of a fourth

Conservative government in a row might seem to suggest its key outcome was continuity. In fact it raises serious questions about the form that democracy should and will take in Britain in the twenty-first century.

## Acknowledgements

This appendix could not have been written without the extensive computing skill and assistance of Martin Range of the Social Studies Faculty Centre, University of Oxford. We are also indebted to the following for kindly making data in their possession available to us: Richard Webber, CCN Marketing, Nottingham; Peter Spencer, UK Research Dept., Lehman Bros.; Political Research Unit and the *Today* programme, BBC, London; CIPFA; the Dept. of the Environment.

## Notes

1.  All figures in this appendix refer to Great Britain only unless otherwise stated. The result in Northern Ireland is discussed separately on pp. 343–5.
2.  The Pedersen Index is calculated as the sum of the change in each party's share of the vote since the previous election (ignoring signs) and dividing by two. See further, M. Pedersen, 'The Dynamics of European Party Systems: Changing Patterns of Electoral Volatility', *European Journal of Political Research, VII* (1979), 1–27; I. Crewe, 'Introduction: Electoral Change in Western Democracies: A Framework for Analysis' and I. Crewe, 'Great Britain', in I. Crewe and D. Denver (eds), *Electoral Change in Western Democracies* (London: Croom Helm, 1985), pp. 9 and 102.
3.  Further the 1983 figure may be artificially inflated by inaccuracies in the calculation of the 1979 result on the basis of the parliamentary constituency boundaries introduced in 1983.
4.  A glance at Table A1.5 illustrates the difference in the degree of variation in the two parties' performances. There is a 40-point gap between the largest rise in Labour support and the largest fall, but only a 17-point gap between the equivalent Conservative figures.
5.  In this appendix the North of England refers to the Northern, North-West and Yorkshire & Humberside standard regions. The South of England includes London, the South East and the South West while the Midlands refers to the East and West Midlands together with East Anglia.
6.  The relatively high figure for Inner London (–7.8%) is inflated by the absence of Liberal Democrat candidates in Greenwich and Woolwich where the 1987 SDP/Alliance vote is included as part of the party's baseline.
7.  See, for example, R. Johnston *et al.*, *A Nation Dividing?* (London: Longman, 1988); J. Curtice, 'One Nation?', in R. Jowell *et al.*, *British Social Attitudes; the 5th Report* (Aldershot: Gower, 1988); A. Heath *et al.*, *Understanding Political Change* (London: Pergamon, 1991).
8.  Note that the calculation used here is different from the conventional

definition of the unemployment rate in which unemployment is expressed as a proportion of the working population. Estimates of the working population are not available for parliamentary constituencies and in any event the calculation used here is arguably more relevant in assessing the possible electoral impact of unemployment.

9. The concentration of Tory tabloid readers in the south means that they may have played a role in the increasing concentration of Conservative support in the South of England prior to 1987. Our concern here, however, is only with the relationship between newspaper readership and movement between 1987 and 1992.

10. The precise methodology we have used replicates that adopted in P. Spencer, R. Beange and J. Curtice, *The 1992 Election and the North-South Divide* (London: Lehman Bros., 1992).

11. These were dummy variables, one for each of the eleven standard regions as defined by OPCS, with London and the Rest of the South East coded separately.

12. Perhaps the clearest illustration of the relationship between unemployment and Conservative performance point is the 3.4% rise in the Conservative vote in Grampian region – the highest of any county or Scottish region. Over the last two years unemployment in the region has risen by just 0.3 percentage points, the lowest in mainland Britain. It was thus truly symbolic that the only Conservative gain from Labour of the election (Aberdeen South) should have come from this area.

13. See P. Spencer *et al.*, *op. cit.* Exploration of alternative models of the 1987 and 1992 results indicates that the precise estimate is highly sensitive to the specification of the regression model. The safest conclusion however appears to be that the impact of the inter-election trend in unemployment in the two elections is broadly similar.

14. We would not wish to claim that our regression models are fully specified. Readers will also note the relatively low proportion of the variance explained by these equations, especially so in the case of the Liberal Democrats, clearly indicating the importance of factors such as tactical voting discussed later in this appendix. Clearly any final analysis of the relationship between household incomes, newspaper readership and Labour's performance will also require examination of survey data. For a first such analysis see J. Curtice, 'Late Swings: Early Results', in M. Linton (ed.), *'Times' Guide to the House of Commons 1992* (London: Times Books, 1992).

15. Except the three constituencies in Plymouth, where the pattern is clearly broken by the collapse in Liberal Democrat support in the city in the wake of the demise of the SDP. David Owen, the former leader of the SDP who refused to join the Liberal Democrats, was an MP in the city, and there was a weak Liberal vote in the city prior to the formation of the SDP.

16. Further, in no other region of Britain does the internal variation in party performance display a positive correlation between 1987 and 1992.

17. The regions in this table have been constructed so as to identify groups of counties or obvious parts of counties where, firstly, the pattern of Conservative performance between 1987 and 1992 and, secondly, the pattern between 1983 and 1992, was internally heterogeneous and noticeably different from

other regions. In East Anglia however the internal variation is greater than in the remaining five regions.

18. Indeed, in the much publicised Conservative success in securing control of Basildon council from Labour in the local elections held four weeks after the general election it was in fact the Liberal Democrat vote which plummeted.

19. The correlation with household income was +0.37 and the correlation with the level of council house sales was +0.22. Again it is important to note that it is Liberal Democrat performance not Labour performance which was negatively correlated with both council house sales and with low rises in unemployment between 1983 and 1987. Data on the level of council house sales were derived from data available for local authorities kindly supplied by the Dept. of Environment. Sales, which are for the period 1979 to 1991, include disposals to housing associations as well as individuals. Data was missing for a handful of authorities. The proportion of the total housing stock represented by council house sales was calculated by multiplying the proportion of houses sold by the proportion of households living in council houses in the 1981 census.

20. The variation in Conservative performance in the south-eastern triangle will be a ripe topic for further research when data from the 1991 census for parliamentary constituencies become available. This will permit analysis of the association between party performance between 1983 and 1992 and social change during the 1980s. The absence of such census data has clearly limited some of the analysis that it has been possible to undertake in this appendix.

21. J. Curtice and M. Steed, 'Analysis', in *The British General Election of 1987*, pp. 342–3.

22. We should note that one of the two remaining constituencies is Newham South which had the highest swing to the Conservatives anywhere in 1987 and the second highest in London in 1992. This constituency has been much affected by the docklands development which has brought about an influx of middle-class people to the area.

23. Excluding the Vale of Glamorgan and Langbaurgh which Labour won in by-elections between 1987 and 1992.

24. Some indeed may have been induced to vote Alliance on that occasion because of the national strategic situation.

25. See J. Curtice and M. Steed, 'Analysis' in *The British General Election of 1987*, pp. 337–9.

26. C. Rallings and M. Thrasher, *Parliamentary Constituencies and the 1990/1 Local Elections* (Plymouth: Polytechnic South West, 1991).

27. Apart from Hove this figure also excludes Ribble Valley and Milton Keynes. In the former the by-election victory had completely altered the credibility of the local Liberal Democrat challenge and their vote was up +19.2% on 1987, by far their largest increase anywhere. The latter had been divided into two by the Boundary Commission.

28. In Littleborough the Liberal Democrats won 47.1% of the vote and were 25% ahead of Labour in the May 1991 local elections. In Carshalton the Liberal Democrats pulled 13.5% ahead of Labour in the 1990 London borough elections. (Rallings and Thrasher, *op. cit.*).

29. A further ten were in seats defended by Liberal Democrat MPs, including two of the three by-election victors.

30. This corner of eastern England accounts for nine out of the fifteen drops of above 7.5%. The one case where this happened in the rest of the triangle was in Plymouth Sutton.

31. See J. Curtice and M. Steed, 'Analysis' in *The British General Election of 1987*, pp. 336–7.

32. The six are Southampton Itchen, Stockport, Lewisham East, Nuneaton, Pembroke and Warrington South, where the 1987 Alliance vote averaged 22.3% in 1987 and the Liberal Democrat vote just 12.1% in 1992. The two unclear cases are Birmingham Northfield and Pendle. It is notable that in 1983 in both Southampton Itchen and Stockport the Alliance had had the advantage of being able to field the incumbent MP as their candidate.

33. The seats where new tactical voting was clearly decisive are Cheltenham (see also p. 338) and Devon North. Bath might just have been secured on the basis of the slightly below-average Conservative performance there alone.

34. See M. Steed, 'An Analysis of The Results', in *The British General Election of 1970*, p. 408 and M. Steed, 'The Results Analysed', *The British General Election of February 1974*, p. 335.

35. Bradford North has been excluded from this calculation because of the large personal vote for the former Conservative MP in 1987 and because the Conservative vote fell heavily (when represented by a white candidate) in a by-election in 1990. Exceptionally, however, Edinburgh Leith has been included.

36. See M. Steed, 'The Results Analysed', in *The British General Election of October 1974*, p. 344.

37. See J. Curtice and M. Steed, 'An Analysis of the Voting', *The British General Election of 1979*, pp. 408–10 and Curtice and Steed, 'Analysis', in *The British General Election of 1987*, pp. 333–35.

38. In only one of these cases (Strathkelvin & Bearsden) did the defeated Conservative MP attempt to reclaim his seat in 1992. Thus in this constituency any personal vote previously established by the former Conservative MP could have remained with him in 1992. Elsewhere, not only had the new Labour MP had the chance to establish a new personal vote over the last five years, but any personal vote for the previous Conservative MP would have been lost. The total of 20 excludes two seats won by Labour from the Conservatives in 1987, Norwich South where the Labour MP had been MP for the same constituency until the 1983 election, and Bradford North where the 1987 Labour victor died during the last parliament and the seat was defended by the 1990 by-election victor.

39. There were just five seats (Battersea, Ipswich, Thurrock, Wolverhampton NE and Walthamstow) which were defended by new incumbent Conservative MPs who had wrested the seats from Labour in 1987. However in one the seat had not been defended by the incumbent Labour MP in 1987 and in another the defeated Labour MP stood again. Having been won against the tide in 1987 the general validity of the evidence they provide is clearly open to question. But we may note that the Conservative vote rose by substantially above the sub-regional average in two of them (Battersea and Thurrock) while the Labour performance was well below the sub-regional average in Ipswich where Ken Weetch did not attempt to regain his seat and whose personal popularity had clearly been evident in previous election results. See

J. Curtice and M. Steed, 'Analysis of Voting' in *The British General Election of 1979*, p. 413 and Curtice and Steed, 'An Analysis of the Voting', in *The British General Election of 1983*, p. 334.

40. Taking into account the geographical location of the seats accounts for the discrepancy between our conclusion here and that of Ivor Crewe. See I. Crewe, 'Doubts cast on the two-party system', in A. Wood and R. Wood (eds), *'Times' Guide to the House of Commons 1992* (London: Times Books, 1992).

41. However we should bear in mind that two of these cases are Cheltenham and Brentford & Isleworth where there were ethnic minority candidates and a third is Winchester where the incumbent MP stood as an Independent Conservative. Milton Keynes has been excluded from the calculation because of its redrawn boundaries.

42. On Battersea, see p. 331. In Renfrew West Labour's vote had suffered from the defection to the SDP of Dr Dickson Mabon who fought the seat in both 1983 and 1987.

43. In three Welsh seats Plaid Cymru endorsed the Green candidate, whose votes are not included as Nationalist.

44. Apart from Edinburgh Leith, this figure also excludes Orkney & Shetland where the SNP stood down in favour of an Orkney & Shetland Movement candidate in 1987.

45. Its support rose by less than 5% in the Conservative marginals of Ayr, Stirling and Edinburgh West, as well as in the Liberal Democrat marginal of Fife North East. However, the party's failure to increase its share of the vote at all in the safest Conservative seat in Scotland, Dumfries, suggests that the correlation with class composition is not wholly artefactual.

46. This figure includes 9 candidates in Northern Ireland.

47. See 'In brief: 1991 Electoral Register', *Population Trends*, No. 64, Summer 1991, pp. 1–3.

48. The potential impact of changes in the manner in which the register is compiled was also demonstrated in London in 1987. See J. Curtice and M. Steed, 'Analysis', in *The British General Election of 1987*, pp. 346–7. Indeed, the variation in turnout change between London boroughs is again quite marked with large increases in (predominantly Tory) Kensington & Chelsea (+7.2%), Barnet (+8.7%), Sutton (+5.9%) and Westminster (+5.2%). But the largest rise was (despite the pattern of Table A2.9) in (predominantly Labour) Tower Hamlets, both of whose seats appear in the list of largest increases in Table A1.5.

49. For a similar finding in 1987 see J. Curtice and M. Steed, 'Analysis', in *The British General Election of 1987*, p. 345.

50. J. Curtice and M. Steed, 'Electoral Choice and the Production of Government: The Changing Operation of the Electoral System in the United Kingdom since 1955', *British Journal of Political Science, XII* (1982), 249–98; Curtice and Steed, 'Proportionality and Exaggeration in the British Electoral System', *Electoral Studies, V* (1986), 209–28; Curtice, 'The British Electoral System: Fixture without Foundation', in D. Kavanagh (ed.), *Electoral Politics* (Oxford: Oxford University Press, 1992).

51. This is the so-called 'cube law'. For further details see M. Kendall and A. Stuart, 'The Law of Cubic Proportions in Britain', *British Journal of*

*Sociology, I* (1950), 183–96. A marginal seat is defined as any seat (other than those won by third parties) where the Conservative share of the vote cast for Conservative and Labour combined would be between 45% and 55% should those two parties be equally popular nationally.

52. More generally the standard deviation of the two-party vote fell from 21.4 in 1987 to 20.2 in 1992. This figure is still however similar to the figure of 20.0 in 1983 and is well above the figure for any election prior to that date. Thus the extent of the depolarisation should not be overemphasised.

53. For further discussion of this point see R. Johnston, *Political, Electoral and Spatial Systems* (Oxford: Clarendon Press, 1979).

54. It should be noted that there can also be an interaction between the two main sources of bias. For example a party winning smaller constituencies may as a consequence win more seats with smaller (absolute) majorities. On the possible impact of votes won by third parties see note 60 below.

55. This follows the approach adopted by C. S. Soper and J. Rydon, 'Under-representation and Electoral Prediction', *Australian Journal of Politics and History, IV* (1958), 94–106. For a more elaborate approach which measures bias in terms of seats and which divides the first source of bias formally into its component parts (including the effective reduction in the size of constituencies which is brought about by third-party voting) see R. H. Brookes, 'The Analysis of Distorted Representation in Two-Party Single-Member Elections', *Political Science, XII* (1960), 158–67. For an example of the use of Brookes' technique in the analysis of British elections see R. Johnston, 'Spatial Structure, Plurality Systems and Electoral Bias', *Canadian Geographer, XX* (1976), 310–28. See also R. Mortimore, *The Constituency Structure and the Boundary Commission* (Univ. of Oxford, D. Phil. thesis, 1992), Chap. B.2.

56. It should then be borne in mind that this method of measuring bias is designed to measure the bias at an equal share of the two-party vote. The precise size of this bias can vary according to the actual distribution of the two-party vote. The extra swing required by one party compared with another party to win, say, 350 seats may be greater or less than it is to win 326 seats, depending on the precise character of the distribution of marginal seats. For a similar reason, the estimates used here cannot be simply compared with estimates based on seats. A party that would win half the seats less one on 50% of the vote may be as little as 0.1% behind in the median seat or as much as 1% behind. Under the method used here the bias would be much greater under the latter situation than the former, but identical under a method using seats as the basis for calculation.

It should also be remembered that this source of bias will reverse itself at some point. A party that wins lots of seats by small majorities if it wins 50% of the vote may well lose a lot if it loses with, say, 40% of the vote. This was apparent in the 1979 European election. See J. Curtice, 'An Analysis of the Results', in D. Butler and D. Marquand, *European Elections and British Politics* (London: Longman, 1980), p. 183.

57. While it is true that Labour have at most post-war elections had their vote less efficiently distributed than the Conservatives, this is not the first time that this has not been the case. The same methodology as used in Table A2.10 reveals that Labour actually positively benefited from this source of

electoral bias in February 1974 and in 1979. On the former occasion this was decisive in enabling Labour to win more seats than the Conservatives despite winning fewer votes.

58. See also I. Crewe, 'Doubts cast on the two-party system' in A. Wood and R. Wood (eds), *'Times' Guide to the House of Commons 1992* (London: Times Books, 1992).

59. Of course part of the difference between the size of Conservative and Labour constituencies is the consequence of the deliberate over-representation of Scotland and Wales.

60. This is not to argue that differences in the sizes of electorates only contributed one-third. There is a third potential source of bias which can also contribute to the difference between the mean and the overall Conservative share of the two-party vote. This is the distribution of the third-party vote. Votes cast for third parties have the same impact as abstentions on the difference between the mean and the overall share of the two-party vote. So if the third-party vote is concentrated in the constituencies of one of the main parties to a greater extent than the other this reduces the effective size of the constituencies won by that party. And of course the Liberal Democrat vote is higher in Conservative constituencies. The gap between Conservative and Labour constituencies in the size of their average two-party vote (5,891) is less than half the size of the gap of the average total vote (11,294). So this source of bias partly counterbalances the two sources of bias considered in the main text.

Indeed, it is clear that differences in the sizes of electorates are somewhat more important than turnout differences. The Labour share of the vote would have been as much as 1% higher if the electorate in each constituency had been the same size within each nation of Great Britain, but the differences between the nations had been retained. But given the existence of the counterbalance of the distribution of the third-party vote, the existence of the turnout difference is clearly crucial.

It is also worth noting that the advantage that Labour could have derived from differences in constituency size is rather less than it might otherwise have been because the swing to Labour since 1987 was on average higher in those seats with higher electorates and higher turnouts!

61. In other words if the final opinion polls had been correct in anticipating a one-point Labour lead the widespread expectation of a hung parliament might still not have been fulfilled!

62. This is three more than we estimated in 1987 undertaking a similar exercise on the basis of the 1987 results and electorates. The increase reflects the continuing decline in the size of Labour constituencies over the last five years. See J. Curtice and M. Steed, 'Analysis', in *The British General Election of 1987*, p. 357.

63. Note that the range of results that would produce some kind of hung parliament remains wide, covering a 3.5% range of results on this calculation compared with 4% in 1987. The slight decrease in the exaggerative quality of the electoral system has had only a marginal impact on the probability of no one party being able to win an overall majority.

64. Indeed it is worth noting that neither party would have secured representation under the Dutch national party list system, supposedly the system most

favourable to small parties in Western Europe. That system requires a party to win 0.67% of the national vote before it is granted any representation in the Tweede Kamer.

65. Undoubtedly the most fortunate MP to retain his seat in the election was Sir Russell Johnston in Inverness, Nairn & Lochaber who won just 26.0% of the vote. This broke the previous record set in Portsmouth Central in 1922 for the lowest share of the vote (26.9%) ever won by a victorious candidate in a British single-member constituency.

# Select Bibliography

The Bibliography details books and articles concerning British elections and parties published since 1987.

Adonis, A., 'Great Britain' in European Elections Issue of *Electoral Studies*, 1989.

Alderman, G., *Britain: A One Party State?* (Christopher Helm, 1989).

Alderman, R. K. and Carter, N., 'A Very Tory Coup – the ousting of Mrs Thatcher', *Parliamentary Affairs*, 1991.

Anderson, B., *John Major: the making of the Prime Minister* (Fourth Estate, 1991.

Aughey, A., *Under Siege: Ulster Unionism and the Anglo-Irish Agreement* (Hurst & Co., 1989).

Ball, A. R., *British Political Parties: The Emergence of a Modern Party System*, 2nd edition (Macmillan, 1987).

Barnes, G. P., 'The Use of Computers in Redistributing Constituencies', *Electoral Studies*, 1987.

Berrington, H., 'The British General Election of 1987: Have We Been Here Before?', *West European Politics*, 1988.

Blackburn, R., 'The Public Announcement of General Elections', *Electoral Studies*, 1990.

Blackwell, R. and Terry, M., 'Analysing the Political Fund Ballots: A Remarkable Victory or the Triumph of the Status Quo?', *Political Studies*, 1987.

Blais, A. and Carty, R. K., 'The Impact of Electoral Formulae on the Creation of Majority Governments', *Electoral Studies*, 1987.

Bochel, J. and Denver, D., *The Scottish Regional Elections of 1990* (University of Dundee, 1990).

Bogdanor, V., 'Electoral Reform and British Politics', *Electoral Studies*, 1987.

Brand, J., 'Faction as its own reward: Groups in the British Parliament 1945–86', *Parliamentary Affairs*, 1989.

Brand, J., 'Kavanagh and McKenzie on Power', *West European Politics*, 1989.

Bruce, S., *God Save Ulster: The Religion and Politics of Paisleyism* (Oxford University Press, 1989).

Butler, D., *British General Elections since 1945* (Basil Blackwell, 1989).

Butler, D., 'The Chataway Commission', *Electoral Studies*, 1992.

Butler, D. and Mortimore, R., 'A level playing-field for British Elections?', *Parliamentary Affairs*, 1992.

Butler, D. and Ranney, A. (eds), *Electioneering, A Comparative Study of Continuity and Change* (Clarendon Press, 1992).

Campbell, B., *The Iron Ladies: Why do women vote Tory?* (Virago, 1987).

Catt, H., 'Tactical Voting in Britain', *Parliamentary Affairs*, 1989.

Charlot, M., 'Les Élections Britanniques du 11 juin 1987. Tactiques et stratégies de campagne', *Revue Française de Science Politique*, 1988.

Clarke, H. and Whiteley, P., 'Perceptions of macro-economic performance, government support and Conservative Party strategy in Britain 1983–7', *European Journal of Political Research*, 1989.

Coates, D., *The Crisis of Labour: Industrial Relations and the State in Contemporary Britain* (Philip Allan, 1989).

Cole, M., 'The Role of the Deposit in British Parliamentary Elections', *Parliamentary Affairs*, 1992.

Cook, C., *A Short History of the Liberal Party 1900–88*, 3rd edition (Macmillan, 1989).

Cozens, P. and Swaddle, K., 'The British General Election of 1987', *Electoral Studies*, 1987.

Crewe, I., Day, N. and Fox A., *The British Electorate 1963–87: A compendium of data from the British Election Studies* (Cambridge University Press, 1991).

Crewe, I., Norris, P., Denver, D., and Broughton, D., *British Elections and Parties Yearbook 1991* (Harvester, 1992).

Crewe, I. and Searing, D., 'Ideological Change in the British Conservative Party', *American Political Science Review*, 1988.

Crewe, I. and Harrop, M. (eds), *Political Communications: The General Election Campaign of 1987* (Cambridge University Press, 1989).

Crick, B., 'The Fundamental Condition of Labour', *Political Quarterly*, 1987.

Curtice, J. and Payne, C., 'Local Elections as National Referendums in Great Britain', *Electoral Studies*, 1990.

Denver, D., 'The British General Election of 1987 – Some Preliminary Reflections', *Parliamentary Affairs*, 1987.

Denver, D. and Hands, G., *Issues and Controversies in British Electoral Behaviour* (Harvester, 1992).

Denver, D. and Hands, G., 'Issues, Principles or Ideology? How Young Voters Decide', *Electoral Studies*, 1990.

Dickson, A. D. R., 'Peculiarities of the Scottish National Culture and Political Action', *Political Quarterly*, 1988.

Eagles, M. and Erfle, S., 'Community Cohesion and Working Class Politics: Workplace-Residence Separation and Labour Support 1966–1983', *Political Geography Quarterly*, 1988.

Eagles, M. and Erfle, S., 'Community Cohesion and Voter Turnout in English Parliamentary Constituencies', *British Journal of Political Science*, 1989.

Evans, G., Heath, A. and Payne, C.,'Modelling Trends in the Class/Party Relationship 1964–87', *Electoral Studies*, 1991.

Ewing, K., *The Funding of Political Parties in Britain* (Cambridge University Press, 1987).

Farrell, D. M. and Wortmann, M., 'Party strategies in the electoral market: Political marketing in West Germany, Britain and Ireland', *European Journal of Political Research*, 1987.

Galbraith, J. W. and Rae, N. C., 'A Test of the Importance of Tactical Voting: Britain 1987', *British Journal of Political Science*, 1989.

Gamble, A., *The Free Economy and the Strong State: The Politics of Thatcherism* (Macmillan, 1988).

Gamble, A., 'The Politics of Thatcherism', *Parliamentary Affairs*, 1989.

Geekie, J. and Levy, R., 'Reselection, Activism and the Labour Party', *Political Quarterly*, 1988.

Girvin, B., 'Conservatism and Political Change in Britain and the United States',

*Parliamentary Affairs*, 1987.

Golding, P., Murdock, G. and Schlesinger, P. (eds), *Communicating Politics: Mass Communication and the Political Process* (Leicester University Press, 1987).

Grahl, J. and Teague, P., 'The British Labour Party and the European Community', *Political Quarterly*, 1987.

Greenwood, J., 'Promoting working-class candidature in the Conservative party: the limits of Central Office power', *Parliamentary Affairs*, 1988.

Halfacree, K., 'Residential Migration and the Electoral Register', *Parliamentary Affairs*, 1992.

Hansard Society Commission on Election Campaigns, *Agenda For Change* (The Hansard Society, 1991).

Hargreaves, R., 'Election '87: the TV Stopwatch Campaign', *Parliamentary Affairs*, 1988.

Harrison, M., 'Television Election News Analysis: Use and Abuse – A Reply', *Political Studies*, 1989.

Harrop, M. and Shaw, A., *Can Labour Win?* (Unwin Paperbacks (Fabian Series), 1989).

Heath, A., Jowell, R. and Curtice, J., 'Class Dealignment and the Explanation of Political Change: A reply to Dunleavy', *West European Politics*, 1988.

Heath, A. and McDonald, S-K., 'Social Change and the Future of the Left', *Political Quarterly*, 1987.

Heath, A. and McDonald, S-K., 'The Demise of Party Identification Theory?', *Electoral Studies*, 1988.

Heath, A. and Pierce, R., 'It was Party Identification All Along: Question Order Effects on Reports of Party Identification in Britain', *Electoral Studies*, 1992.

Hendrick, B. and Lanove, D. J., 'Attention, Asymmetry and Government Popularity in Britain', *Western Political Quarterly*, 1991.

House of Commons Home Affairs Committee, Third Report 1991–2, *Electoral Counting Methods*.

Hughes, C. and Wintour, P., *Labour Rebuilt: The New Model Party* (Fourth Estate, 1990).

Ingle, S., *The British Party System*, 2nd edition (Basil Blackwell, 1987).

Ingle, S., 'Change, Politics and the Party System', *Parliamentary Affairs*, 1989.

Jessop, B., Barnett, K., Bromley, S. and Ling, T., *Thatcherism* (Policy Press, 1989).

Johnston, R. J., *Money and Votes: Constituency Campaign Spending and Election Results* (Croom Helm, 1987).

Johnston, R. J., 'Review Essay: Can We Leave Electoral Reform to the Politicians?', *Political Geography Quarterly*, 1987.

Johnston, R. J. and Pattie, C. J., 'Are We really All Alliance Nowadays? Discriminating by Discriminant Analysis', *Electoral Studies*, 1988.

Johnston, R. J. and Pattie, C. J., 'A Nation Dividing: Economic well-being, voter response, and the changing electoral geography of Great Britain', *Parliamentary Affairs*, 1989.

Johnston, R. J. and Pattie, C. J., 'Class Dealignment and the regional polarisation of voting patterns in Great Britain, 1964–1987', *Political Geography Quarterly*, 1991.

Johnston, R. J. and Pattie, C. J., 'Tactical Voting in Britain in 1983 and 1987: An Alternative Approach', *British Journal of Political Science*, 1991.

Johnston, R. J., Pattie, C. J. and Allsopp, J. G., *A Nation Dividing: The Electoral Map of Great Britain 1979–87* (Longman, 1988).

Johnston, R. J., Pattie, C. J., and Johnston, L. C., 'The Impact of Constituency Spending on the Result of the 1987 British General Election', *Electoral Studies*, 1989.

Kavanagh, D., *Thatcherism and British Politics: The end of consensus*, 2nd edition (Oxford University Press, 1990).

Kavanagh, D., 'Thatcher's Third Term', *Parliamentary Affairs*, 1988.

Kavanagh, D. and Morris, C. P., *Consensus Politics from Attlee to Thatcher* (Basil Blackwell, 1989).

Kelly, R. N., *Conservative Party Conferences: The Hidden System* (Manchester University Press, n.d.).

Kimber, J., 'The Ideological Position and Electoral Appeal of Labour Party Candidates: An Analysis of Labour's performance at the 1983 General Election', *British Journal of Political Science*, 1987.

Leonard, R., *Elections in Britain Today* (Macmillan, 1991).

Levy, R., *Scottish Nationalism at the Crossroads* (Scottish Academic Press, 1990).

Levy, R., 'Third Party Decline in the UK: The SNP and SDP in Comparative Perspective', *West European Politics*, 1988.

Longley, L. D., 'The Politics of Electoral Reform in Great Britain and the United States', *Parliamentary Affairs*, 1988.

Lovenduski, J. and Norris, P., 'Selecting women candidates: obstacles to the feminisation of the House of Commons', *European Journal of Political Research*, 1989.

Lutz, J. M., 'Diffusion of Nationalist voting in Scotland and Wales: emulation, contagion and retrenchment', *Political Geography Quarterly*, 1990.

Lutz, J. M., 'Marginality, Major Third Parties and Turnout in England in the 1970s and 1980s: a Re-analysis and Extension', *Political Studies*, 1991.

McKie, D. (ed), *The Election: A Voter's Guide* (Guardian Books/Fourth Estate, 1992).

McLean, I. S., 'Ships that pass in the Night: Electoral Reform and Social Choice Theory', *Political Quarterly*, 1988.

Marquand, D., *The Unprincipled Society: New Demands and Old Politics* (Cape, 1988).

Marquand, D.,'Beyond Social Democracy', *Political Quarterly*, 1987.

Maynard, G., *The Economy under Thatcher* (Basil Blackwell, 1989).

Meadowcroft, M., 'The Future of the left: A Liberal view', *Political Quarterly*, 1987.

Messina, A., *Race and Party Competition in Britain* (Clarendon Press, 1989).

Miller, W. L., *Irrelevant Elections? The Quality of Local Democracy in Britain* (Clarendon Press, 1988).

Miller, W. L., Clarke, H. D., Harrop, M., LeDuc, L. and Whiteley, P., *How Voters Change: The 1987 British Election Campaign in Perspective* (Clarendon Press, 1990).

Miller, W. L., Sonntag, N. and Broughton, D., 'Television in the 1987 British Election Campaign: Its Content and Influence', *Political Studies*, 1989.

Mishler, W., Hoskin, M., and Fitzgerald, R., 'British Parties in the Balance: A Time Series Analysis of Long-Term Trends in Labour and Conservative support', *British Journal of Political Science*, 1989.

Mitchell, A., 'Beyond Socialism', *Political Quarterly*, 1987.

Mitchell, J., 'Recent Developments in the Scottish National Party', *Political Quarterly*, 1988.

MORI/Rowntree Trust, *State of the Nation poll 1991*.

Mughan, A., *Party and Participation in British Elections* (Frances Pinter, 1986).

Mughan, A., 'General Election Forecasting in Britain', *Electoral Studies*, 1987.

Mughan, A., 'Comparing Mid-Term Popularity Functions: A Cautionary Note', *Political Studies*, 1988.

Mughan, A., 'On the by-election vote of governments in Britain', *Legislative Studies Quarterly*, 1988.

Nelson, H. J., 'Unions in Politics: Public Opinion in the United Kingdom and Denmark', *European Journal of Political Research*, 1987.

Norris, P., *British By-Elections: The Volatile Electorate* (Clarendon Press, 1990).

Norris, P., 'Four Weeks of Sound and Fury: the 1987 British Election Campaign', *Parliamentary Affairs*, 1987.

Norris, P., 'The Rise (and Fall?) of Multi-Party By-Election Politics', *Parliamentary Affairs*, 1991.

Norris, P. and Feigart, F., 'Government and Third Party Performance in Mid-Term British By-elections: The Canadian, British and Australian Experience', *Electoral Studies*, 1989.

Norton, P., 'Choosing a Leader: Militant Tendency and the Parliamentary Labour Party 1989–90', *Parliamentary Affairs*, 1990.

Norton, P. and Wood, D., 'Constituency Service by Members of Parliament: Does it contribute to a personal vote?', *Parliamentary Affairs*, 1990.

Owens, J. R. and Wade, L. L., 'Economic Conditions and Constituency Voting in Great Britain', *Political Studies*, 1988.

Pimlott, B., 'Is there an Alternative to a Pact', *Political Quarterly*, 1987.

Pinto-Duschinsky, M., 'Trends in British Party Funding 1983–1987', *Parliamentary Affairs*, 1989.

Plant, R., 'Criteria for Electoral Systems: the Labour Party and Electoral Reform', *Parliamentary Affairs*, 1991.

Pulzer, P., 'The Paralysis of the Centre-Left: a Comparative Perspective', *Political Quarterly*, 1987.

Punnett, M., 'Selecting a leader and deputy leader of the Labour Party: the future of the electoral college', *Parliamentary Affairs*, 1990.

Punnett, R. M., 'The Alternative Vote Revisited', *Electoral Studies*, 1991.

Radice, G., 'The Case for Revisionism', *Political Quarterly*, 1987.

Rallings, C. and Thrasher, M., 'Local Elections in Britain: Comparing Myth with Reality', *Parliamentary Affairs*, 1988.

Rallings, C. and Thrasher, M., 'Turnout in English Local Elections – An Aggregate Analysis with Electoral and Contextual Data', *Electoral Studies*, 1990.

Rallings, C. and Thrasher, M., 'The Impact of the Community Charge on Electoral Behaviour: the 1990 Local Elections in England and Wales', *Parliamentary Affairs*, 1991.

Riddell, P., *The Thatcher Decade* (Basil Blackwell, 1989).

Rodgers, W., 'Realignment Postponed', *Political Quarterly*, 1987.

Rose, R. and McAllister, I., *The Loyalties of Voters: A Lifetime Learning Model* (Sage, 1990).

Rose, R. and McAllister, I., 'Reply to Johnston and Pattie', *Electoral Studies*, 1988.

Sanders, D., Ward, H. and Marsh D., 'Government Popularity and the Falklands War: A Reassessment', *British Journal of Political Science*, 1987.

Scarbrough, E., 'The British Electorate Twenty Years On: Electoral Change and Electoral Surveys', *British Journal of Political Science*, 1987.

Seaton, J. and Pimlott, B., *The Media in British Politics* (Gower, 1987).

Seldon, A. (ed.), *UK Political Parties since 1945* (Philip Allen, 1990).

Semetko, H., Blumler, J., Gurevitch, M. and Weaver, D., *The Formation of Campaign Agendas: A Comparative Analysis of Party and Media Roles in recent British and American elections* (Hillside, NJ: L. Erlbaum, 1991).

Seyd, P., *The Rise and Fall of the Labour Left* (Macmillan, 1987).

Shaw, E., *Discipline and Discord in the Labour Party* (Manchester University Press, 1988).

Shaw, E., 'The Labour Party and the Militant Tendency', *Parliamentary Affairs*, 1989.

Shepherd, R., *The Power Brokers: the Tory Party and its Leaders* (Hutchinson, 1991).

Steffen, J-P., 'Imprint of Militant Tendency on the Labour Party', *West European Politics*, 1987.

Studlar, D. T., McAllister, I. and Ascui, A., 'Electing Women to the British Commons: Breakout from the Beleaguered Beachhead', *Legislative Studies Quarterly*, 1988.

Studlar, D. T. and Welch, S., 'Understanding the Iron Law of Andrarchy. Effects of Candidate Gender on Voting in Scotland', *Comparative Political Studies*, 1987.

Studlar, D. T. and Welch, S., 'The Party System and the Representation of Women in English Metropolitan Boroughs', *Electoral Studies*, 1992.

Swaddle, K. and Heath, A., 'Official and Reported Turnout in the British General Election of 1987', *British Journal of Political Science*, 1989.

Taylor, A. J., *The Trade Unions and the Labour Party* (Croom Helm, 1987).

Taylor, R., 'Trade Unions and the Labour Party: Time for an Open Marriage', *Political Quarterly*, 1987.

Tivey, L. and Wright, A. (eds), *Party Politics in Britain* (Routledge, 1989).

Upton, G., 'The Impact of By-Elections on General Elections: England 1950–87', *British Journal of Political Science*, 1991.

Vallance, E., 'Two Cheers for Equality: Women Candidates in the 1987 General Election', *Parliamentary Affairs*, 1988.

Waller, R., *The Almanac of British Politics*, 4th edition (Routledge & Kegan Paul, 1991).

Watkins, A., *A Conservative Coup: the fall of Margaret Thatcher* (Duckworth, 1991).

Williams, A. L., *Labour's Decline and the Social Democrats' Fall* (Macmillan, 1989).

Wood, A. and Wood, R. (eds), *The Times Guide to the House of Commons April 1992* (Times Books, 1992).

Wood, D. M., 'The Conservative Member of Parliament as lobbyist for constituency economic interests', *Political Studies*, 1987.

Worcester, R., *British Public Opinion: A Guide to the History and Methodology of Public Opinion Polling* (Basil Blackwell, 1991).

Young, H., *One of Us* (Macmillan, 1989).

# Index